Pedaling Home

Pedaling Home

How the
Quest for Truth
Became
a Family Adventure

E. Epps Varela
& the Varela Family

AMIGOS

Published by AMIGOS

Copyright © 2015 by Emily Varela

All rights reserved. No part of this publication may be reproduced, distributed, or transmitted without the express consent of the author.

Published in the Unites States of America by **AMIGOS**, Gainesboro, TN
amigos@twlakes.net

Ordering Information:
amazon.com and other online sources

Quantity sales. Special discounts are available on quantity purchases. For details, contact the publisher at the address above.

Unless otherwise indicated, all Scripture quotations are from the King James Version of the Bible with Hebrew names restored.

Pedaling Home: How the Quest for Truth Became a Family Adventure / Emily Varela & the Varela Family – First Edition

Main category 1. Family 2. Biography

ISBN: 0996199403
ISBN-13: 978-0996199407

Cover Design by Well Trodden Road Productions (WTRP)

Printed and bound in the United States of America

Dedication

To our Father,
Abba YHWH,

and all who love enough to flee religion in order to know Him.

But this shall be the covenant that I will make with the house of Israel; After those days, saith YHWH, I will put my law in their inward parts, and write it in their hearts; and will be their Elohim, and they shall be my people.

Jeremiah 31:33

Table of Contents

Acknowledgments xi
Introduction xii
Notes to Reader xiii
Newspaper Article xiv
Book Helps xvi

Part 1 - In the Beginning

First Days

1 Preparations 2
2 Family 7
    In the Air; The Meeting; Marriage and Moving; Growing Family
3 Miracles 17
    Celebrating Feasts; The Accident; Phone Calls from *Abba*;
    David's Passport; *Abba* Makes Room; *Abba* Sends an Expert;
    Training
4 Amsterdam 30
    Abba Sends Bread and Water; *Abba* Explains Dorito Shirts;
    Anne Frank House
5 Sky Questions 37
    Welcome to Israel
6 HaAretz 47
    Benyamina by Train; Beach Questions; *S'dot Yam* Hospitality;
    Tzitziyot; *Shabbat* in the Schoolyard

Week 1

7 Caesarea 61
    Or Akiva; Delayed; At The Park
8 Zichron Ya'achov 72
    Tea with the Queen; Lush Green Grass; *Benyamina* by Bicycle;
    Orange Shirts and Yellow Jackets; Fox and Mosquitoes; *Bat
    Shlomo*; ~~Playground~~ Highway 70; Elyakim; No Overnight
    Parking
9 False Prophets 84
    Angels with Bicycle Racks; Scouting; Tying *Tzitziyot*
10 Mount Carmel 91
    Daliat El Carmel; Druze Hospitality
11 Osifia 99
    Or HaCarmel; The Musician; *Shabbat* on the Mountain

vii

Week 2

12 Gracious Host 106
    Fire!; Missionary Questions; Trouble in Tennessee
13 Down 116
    The Descent; Wipe Outs; *Yeshiva* Toys; Pedal Problems
14 *Haifa* 127
    Snagged Soldier; *Abba* Intervenes; Long Lost Brother; Sand
    Castles and Beach Ball
15 *Kiryat Chaim* 138
    Visitors; Beach Life; Pedal Repair; *Chabad*; Soldier Questions
16 *Kiryat Yam* 152
    Three Suppers; North by Bicycle; Change of Direction;
    Prospective Lodging; Tandem Friends; No Business on
    Shabbat
17 Mediterranean Rest 161
    Shabbat on the Beach; Beach Walker Questions; Angel Food

Week 3

18 Provision 167
    The Pastor; Better Prospective Lodging; Last Night Together;
    18 Yitzhak Sade; ~~Speaking~~ Russian; Eating Words
19 Lodging 178
    Eti Returns

Part 2 - The Scattering

20 *Levad* 186
    Nikolay to the Rescue; Sandwiched; The Community
21 Business 197
    Turbulence-Above and Below
22 Adjusting 203
    Elena; Bad News; Invitation; *Kiryat Motzkin*
23 Disappointment 210
    Dumpster Diving; Israeli Welcome Dinner; Pomegranate
    Parties; Company; *Shabbat* at the Lodging Place

Week 4

24 Sixth New Moon 219
    Preparing for *Rosh Chodesh*; Looking for the New Moon; Not
    Again...; Gone; The Dead Lady
25 *Abba*'s Hand 230
    Nashville; More Soaps; *Shuk*; Rabbi Questions Armando;
    Shabbat at the House; Driving Angels

Week 5

26 *Arnav* 240
    Voice on the Line; Scruffy; Worries; Emily's Story
27 *Chatul* 250
    B'hai Gardens; *Shabbat* in the Neighborhood

viii

Week 6

28 Mexican Surprise 257
   Vaccine Lesson; Ambulance Parking; *Moshe Rafael*; Little
   Man Without a Country; Sweet Solutions
29 Turmoil 271
   Playground Questions; Farm Help; Salt Water Tears
30 Akko 278
   Roll Call; Fish Boy; Bird Man

Week 7

31 Fishing 290
   Fishing Buddies; Endless Work; Comfort Food; Praying
   Mantis; Wall Between Us; Finally

Part 3 - The Regathering

32 *Echad* 302
   Discord; Synagogue; Next Door Questions; Harmony

Week 8

33 The Galilee 310
   Afula; Tiberius; The Singer; *Rosh Hashanah*; Fishing Lessons
34 Celebrations 320
   Free Fish; *Yom Teruah*; Cell Phone Couple; Galilee
   Experience; The Doctor; Long Walk; *Shabbat* at Home

Week 9

35 *Ain Arnav* 332
   Son of *El*; *Misrad Hap'nim*; All Choked Up; Science Museum;
   Silly Girls; Near Drowning
36 *Yom Kippur* 344
   Rabbinic *Yom Kippur*; Day of Atonement

Week 10

37 *Ain Chatul* 348
   Blue T-shirts; Gifting; South by Bus; *Mevaseret Zion*
38 Up to Zion 355
   Jerusalem; Religious Rules; Downtown; *Sukkah* in the Park;
   Rooftop *Sukkah*; Old City Markets
39 Old Jerusalem 370
   Temple Mount
40 Wedding 376
   Meeting the Ohioan; The Prophecy; The Tour Group;
   Prophecy Fulfilled; Physics Lesson; The Cowboy and the
   Sidekick
41 Cowboy Questions 386
42 *Shabbat* ~~Labor~~ 397
   Preparing for *Shabbat*; *Karaite* Clean and Unclean; Messianic
   Birth Pangs, Wrath and Salvation; Young Woman Questions

Week 11

43 Wall Labor.. 407
        Accounting Angels; Private Maternity Suite; Old City Tour;
        Scheduling Conflict; The Western Wall; Dinner Date;
        Youngsters in High Places; Contractor Manages Contractions
44 Stones.. 418
        Cow Sense in the City; David, Philistine, Sling, and Stone;
        Getting Away; Meeting Goes On
45 Birth.. 426
        Introductions; Living Words; Tennessean meets Launderer

Part 4 - The Last Days

46 8th Baby, 8th Day.. 440
        The Hospital; *Giliyah Batzion*; *Sukkah* to Home

Week 12

47 Documents.. 447
        Golan Heights; Doctor's Hospitality; *Misrad Hap'nim*, Tiberius;
        United States Consulate; Comfort ~~Inn~~ in *Be'er Sheva*; *Kibbutz
        Bet-El*
48 Foiled Robbery 457
        German Dinner; The Chase; Israeli Farewell Dinner; Meeting
        Neighbors

Final Days

49 Moving 464
        Packing; Separated Again; Jerusalem Bound; Nikolay Returns;
        Bad Taste
50 Home in Exile.. 471
        Reunion; Security; Back to the Farm

Afterword   478
From Mama Emily.. 479
Glossary 480
Appendix A, Special Hebrew Names and Titles 485
Appendix B, Names of Israel 486
Appendix C, Yearly Appointments of YHWH 487
Maps 488
Index 491

Acknowledgments

We give *Abba*, YHWH, Creator of the Universe all the glory and praise for any good that has or will come from this writing. And we give thanks to Him for allowing us the opportunity to:

> 1-Experience the things written of here, all of which have drawn us closer to Him;
> 2-Meet the people mentioned herein, all of whom have helped in some way to improve us;
> 3-Accomplish the actual writing;
> 4-Work with those He has provided to get the book in print.

We offer special thanks for and to:

> 1-Our parents, the grandparents of our children: Jesus and Margarita Varela and Byron and Albertine Epps. Besides the fact that without them none of us would be here, they each have brought us up to hunger for truth and to have a strong desire to walk in it.
> 2-Those who directly helped transform the manuscript into a book:
> -proofreaders Candy Norris, Tyrie Woodford, and Selina Mo;
> -cover creator, Derek Townsend, Well Trodden Road Productions
> 3-Those who indirectly helped:
> -With writing retreats: Employees and Volunteers at Great Smoky Mountain National Park, esp. at Elkmont and Sugarlands; Dave Epps & Diamond A Ranch; and Mom and Dad.
> - With assistance along the way: the Good Samaritan and the Gadsden, Alabama men's fishing group both of whom gave rides to the author when she ran out of gas (yes, twice).
> -With personal coaching: Becky Williamson (Wellcoaches) and Jonathan Roche (Boot Camp HUB)
> 4-Those who prayed for us from the time we began preparing for the trip (that many thought was ludicrous) throughout our time in Israel, and for the past six years that it has taken for us to get the book completed, with special thanks to Jessica Foley, Kati Trast, Debi Panicali-Schlosser, Faye Shaffer, Brian Ferrell, and Leslie Marie.
> 5-Mom Epps, Aunt Eva and others who have encouraged the author for decades to write a book.

Introduction

Thousands of years ago, a chain of events transpired which is culminating today in changed personal lives and major world events. Our lives have been affected, and we are honored and humbled to be involved in the fulfillment of Biblical prophecy on many levels.

Planning for our 2008 three month trip to Israel began in late 2006. In the earliest stages, we committed to writing a book about our experiences in the Land and what prompted us to go. The book would be for the purpose of sharing scriptural truths with others - truths that *Abba* had used to change and improve our lives as we read His written word and, guided by His spirit, implemented what was written within it.

At the time of planning, we had no idea how the trip would turn out or that we would be blessed with another child. We only imagined that the book would be in journal form, based on our experiences and lessons learned, and have references to the scriptures that influenced us in our lifestyle choices. We would wait to see what *Abba* would give us to journal. Even now, we are amazed at the true stories that make up our family's adventure.

Since 2007, the title of the book was to be *Pedaling Home* because we discovered early on that bicycles were the only mode of transportation we would be able to afford in Israel. Besides, it was a play on words with peddling (marketing) home. No matter where we reside, Israel (the land) is our home and Israel (the people) is our people. It is our desire that this writing will inspire other prodigals to return. Thus we are 'peddling home.'

But *Pedaling Home* is not just about Israel. It is about living life a notch above what we think we can. We pray the following pages will be inspiration and encouragement - whether to take the children for a walk around the block or to make a total life transformation. We are real, imperfect, growing people taking action and being surprised by the results. Come join us.

May *Abba* speak to the reader in a special way. Blessed be the name of the Mosh High, YHWH.

Notes to Reader

1 Capitalized Aliases are used to protect many identities, some for obvious reasons, but many because of potential political and religious persecution.

2 Original Hebrew names of YHWH or Yah (the LORD), Elohim (God), and Y'shua (Jesus) are used in place of their English counterparts. An explanation for this is contained within the text of the book beginning on page 386.

3 Glossary words are footnoted at first occurrence. Foreign words are italicized and can be found in the Glossary.

4 Biblical quotes are taken from the King James Bible (with important Hebrew names restored by this author) unless otherwise noted. KJV uses italics when adding English words that are not present in the original languages. Passages are often more true to the original when the italicized words are ignored.

5 In order to more accurately describe the perspective of all nine family members who were old enough to recall details, the writing has been done in the third person. Where there were disagreements concerning details, all views were compiled and written in such a way as to be acknowledged as accurate by everyone involved.

6 Truth in every detail has been preserved as well as possible. Conversations are written for ease of reading and, while it is impossible to have remembered and recorded them word for word, they are written as close to how we remember them as possible. While some wording may be somewhat different than occurred, the gist of the conversation and attitude has been preserved.

7 Enjoy. Be blessed.

JUST PRACTICE

Herald-Citizen Photo/Shawn Sidwell
The Varela family rides their bikes down Willow Avenue as they train for their three month trip to Israel, where they plan to bike instead of using automobiles. Riding are, from front to back, Emily, Moshe, Rebeka, Briana, Victor, Isabel;. Armando and David Varela. Not pictured is 1year-old Natanyah Varela, who is riding on the back of Emily's bike.

VARELAS: Family to bike Israel

AT A GLANCE:

With gas in the holy Land at $7 a gallon, family of nines decides on a cycling vacation.

Herald-Citizen Photo/Shawn Sidwell

Briana and Victor follow their family down Willow Avenue, practicing for the conditions that will await them for their family's trip to Israel. The family will bike across Israel and stay in tents to get an up-close look at the country.

xiv

Herald-Citizen

The Daily Newspaper of the Upper Cumberland
Cookeville, Tennessee, Sunday, June 15, 2008

Pedaling Varelas gearing up for cycling trip across Israel

Megan Trotter Herald-Citizen Staff

COOKEVILLE -- Those driving down Willow Avenue recently might have caught sight of a long line of children on bicycles, sandwiched between two adults. Those adults are David and Emily Varela, and all of the children are their own.

On June 6, they all rode their bikes from Highway 85 in Jackson County to Herbert Garrett Road, south of I-40 -- about 27 miles in total.

The family is practicing for their trip to Israel in August.

"We're going to be traveling by bicycle and camping," said Emily Varela.

But why decide to bike instead of drive?

"There are nine of us, so we'd have to rent a really big vehicle. And gas over there right now is $7 or $8 a gallon, and it's going up," Emily said.

The family also thought it would be more meaningful to see the Biblical land by being out in the country, instead of trapped inside a vehicle.

The Varelas don't want to just see Israel. They want to experience it. They plan to set up a tent to sleep in as they go, offering to do odd jobs for those who let them use their land. Mr. Varela owns a construction company, Amigo's Construction, making him fit to help with a variety of projects they might encounter.

And along the way, they've made plans to help anyone else they meet who needs it. "If we found anyone in need -- widows, orphans or anybody who needed help with something -- we would help them out."

The family originally planned the trip to only be eight days long, centering around celebrating the Jewish Feast of Tabernacles in October. But since the excursion is going to be so expensive, they decided to extend their stay to three months to get the most experience for their money.

"After all, who's to say when we'll ever be back," Emily said.

She also plans to have her eighth child while in Israel. After having all of her previous children at home, she does not worry about giving birth away from a hospital. "We'll have (the baby) in a tent or wherever we happen to be at the time," she said.

The family has been training for their tour for a while, learning the best way to manage their time and how to handle heavy traffic. During this latest practice, the Varelas estimated that they would need to stop every hour to hour and a half to rest and drink water. Because of the heat, they had to stop more frequently, but they saw that as a blessing in disguise.

"It's going to be hot over there (in Israel)," Emily said, "and we're going to be there in the hottest part of the year. So we were actually thankful for the heat because it was a good test." Busy streets have also put the family to the test. Especially on Willow Avenue where there is no shoulder and it is all uphill, the Varelas found they had to be extra careful. Even when they were given permission by the police department to ride on the sidewalks, the ride was tense.

"I think, when you're riding on the road, people treat you like a car, just a very slow-moving car, and so they go real slow and go around you. But since we were on the sidewalk, they were treating us like pedestrians. They weren't even paying attention to us, and a lot of people were just whizzing by," said Emily.

Traffic in Israel is likewise busy in the cities, and drivers don't always follow the rules of the road. The Varelas will try to avoid the worst of it, but periodically will have to travel through cities. The trial run helped them to learn what works and what doesn't when it comes to getting through heavy traffic safely.

"That's what we were doing, testing out in a safe environment how it was going to work," Emily said. "We hope never to have to ride 27 miles (in one day) there, but now we know that if we have to, we can."

Copyright 2008 Herald-Citizen, All Rights Reserved

Book Helps

Hebrew Names and Titles

God	-	*Elohim, Eloah,* or *El*
The LORD	-	*YHWH, Yehovah,* or *Yah*
Jesus	-	*Y'shua*

The Varela Family Photos

Names	Ages	Page
David & Emily		369
Armando	11	357
Briana	9-10	70
Victor	8	375
Isabel	6-7	337
Rebeka	5	463
Moshe	3-4	243
Natanyah	2	290
Giliyah	In utero-infant	431

Hebrew Days of the Week

Israel continues with the scriptural reckoning of days:
- beginning and ending at sundown; and
- numbered instead of named, except for the seventh day, *Shabbat* (Sabbath), from the word 'to rest' or 'to cease.'

#	Name	English	Begins	Ends
1	*Yom Rishon*	Day 1st	sundown Sat.	sundown Sun.
2	*Yom Sheni*	Day 2nd	sundown Sun.	sundown Mon.
3	*Yom Shlishi*	Day 3rd	sundown Mon.	sundown Tues.
4	*Yom Revi'i*	Day 4th	sundown Tues	sundown Wed.
5	*Yom Chamishi*	Day 5th	sundown Wed.	sundown Thurs.
6	*Yom Shishi*	Day Sixth	sundown Thurs.	sundown Fri.
7	*Shabbat*	Sabbath	sundown Fri.	sundown Sat.

Postcard

Front

The Varelas
David & Emily
Armando, Briana, Victor, Isabel, Rebeka, Moshe, Natanyah

Back

כי זאת הברית אשר אכרת את בית ישראל אחרי הימים ההם נאם יהוה נתתי את תורתי בקרבם ועל לבם אכתבנה והייתי להם לאלהים והמה יהיו לי לעם

But this shall be the covenant that I will make with the house of Israel; After those days, saith YHWH, I will put my law in their inward parts, and write it in their hearts; and will be their Elohim, and they shall be my people.
Jeremiah 31:33

דבר אלהם כה אמר אדני יהוה הנה אני לקח את עץ יוסף אשר ביד אפרים ושבטי ישראל חברו ונתתי אותם עליו את עץ יהודה ועשיתם לעץ אחד והיו אחד בידי

Say unto them, Thus saith YHWH Adonai; Behold, I will take the stick of Joseph, which is in the hand of Ephraim, and the tribes of Israel his fellows, and will put them with him, even with the stick of Judah, and make them one stick, and they shall be one in mine hand.
Ezekiel 37:19

Thank you for your kindness, The Varela family

Part 1

In the Beginning

And YHWH shall scatter thee among all people, from the one end of the earth even unto the other; and there thou shalt serve other gods, which neither thou nor thy fathers have known, even wood and stone.

Deuteronomy 28:64

1 - Preparations

Tuesday   8/5/2008

As the eastern star rose over middle Tennessee in the dark of early morning, Emily, wide awake and sweating, felt the baby in her womb began to move. She placed her hand on her abdomen as she offered morning prayers. Her husband, David, softly snored by her side. It was useless to stay in bed. The roosters were already crowing, and she had not slept for hours anyway. In spite of the muggy August air, there was an electric feeling, an undeniable excitement. She got up, quietly went to her office in the basement, being careful not to awaken the young Pennsylvania family that was sleeping in the small room on the other side of the bedroom door. She was glad it was cooler downstairs, making it more comfortable for them. A soft breeze made its way through the screen on the window near the ceiling, cooling as it hit her damp clothes.

She checked her emails for the last morning in the foreseeable future. Seeing nothing important, she checked once more the baggage requirements of the airline. Somehow, she had overlooked the fact that even empty water bottles could not be carried onto the plane. That was a major discovery, since their 19 one-liter bottles, most of them mountable to the bicycles with special carriers, were some of the most important objects they were taking. Glad to have found the information before it was too late, she went back upstairs to the living room to finish packing, hating that they would have to buy water during their long layover in Amsterdam.

Lined up on the couches were six open backpacks, four of them identical red and black except for the numbers one through four distinguishing their contents. Next to them was a stack of nine blue camping mats, custom cut to appropriate sizes and folded together accordion style, and two two-gallon buckets with resealable lids, originally containing goat kid milk replacer, but now one was left empty and the other filled with small rope for laundry line, clothespins, and soap. Beside the couch sat the bag which contained the family tent, the already worn label showing it slept eight. And in front of the couch were 11 boxes of various sizes, each within an inch of the maximum allowable free checked baggage requirements of the airline. Nine of the boxes were already sealed and labeled.

She stacked the laundry buckets, placing them in the open box that contained barely two-year-old Natanyah's bicycle carrier seat, then filled around them with the bottles and miscellaneous camping gear that had not fit in the already packed boxes. Over the previous days, David had brought large appliance boxes from town and worked on disassembling

Chapter 1   Preparations

the family's eight bicycles, while Emily built custom boxes and carefully packed the pieces, parts, and other belongings into them. They were unaware that they could have chosen El Al, the Israeli airline that counted a bicycle as a checked item, saving multiple hours of work.

Beautiful colors began to grace the sky as daylight approached. She continued working diligently, finishing final details before getting the others up to begin morning chores. David, Armando-11, and Briana-9, were awakened first so they could have some quiet time before the others got up. After a cup of coffee, David sent Armando to get the Pennsylvanian from the basement guest room while he went to the RV parked in the front yard to let the New Yorker know it was time to learn morning chores. As Briana helped Emily prepare a breakfast of fresh eggs, which they would eat with fruit and the fresh bread Briana had ground flour for and baked the day before, the men took care of the cattle, goats, dogs, and chickens. Briana would rather have been helping them, but knew her place that morning was in the house helping prepare food.

When breakfast was almost ready and chores finished, the other children were awakened. Victor-8, Isabel-6, Rebeka-barely 5, Moshe-3, and little Natanyah arose from their bunk beds and made their way to the long kitchen table, the little ones sitting on the bench Daddy had built. The families from New York and Pennsylvania joined them, as David and Emily gave instructions and went over final plans before leaving.

After breakfast and scripture reading, the New Yorkers went out, the Pennsylvanians went down, and everyone else pitched in to clean up, as David guided the little ones in their simple tasks and kept them away from the sensitive area in the living room. Having just one thing picked up and moved to another location at this stage could cause major trouble over the next few months. Emily went down and gave instructions to the Pennsylvanian Couple, who had been hired to help clean and finish packing the personal items the Varelas would leave, but which would not be useful to the New Yorkers as they stayed and took care of the farm. She instructed the couple to store the items in an empty downstairs room, then went back to final packing details, glad the New Yorkers and Pennsylvanians had children for hers to play with while she worked. One of the most challenging parts of her job had been keeping curious little helpers from displacing bicycle parts and needed supplies. For that reason, she had done much of her work in the evenings after little ones were in bed even though she felt better when getting to bed early.

In between making sure the children were being productive outside or playing with the visiting families' children, David busied himself pacing around the yard between the trees and high points that provided decent cell phone reception, talking to subcontractors on the two jobs he was leaving in progress. Work at the sites was nearing completion, but it had become obvious because of some previous delays that someone would have to be left in charge of finishing the final stages of the projects. David chose a Manager for the job, carefully lined out the order in which things

3

needed to be done, and readied the subcontractors necessary to do the work. He felt confident the jobs would both be completed successfully in less than two weeks.

Emily had been responsible for finding someone to stay at the farm while they were gone. She had found what she thought was the perfect family, but because of an emergency health issue, they had to back out, so she began looking for someone else. In the past, they had most often found farm-sitters online through the MOMYS[1] group that she belonged to, and they had been successful in their attempts to make the experience a blessing to both families. The Varelas got their farm and animals well-cared for, and the guest family got a time of free vacation on a farm, something many large families would not have been able to afford otherwise.

Since there was such short notice, it was more difficult finding the right family this time. Out of three possible candidates and after much prayer, they finally settled on a family from New York who was feeling led to relocate to Tennessee. For them, it would mean leaving New York a little earlier than they had planned, but they were willing to do so in order to have a free place to stay for them and their few livestock while the Varelas were away and they waited on final arrangements to be made at their new home farther west. Upon arriving the night before the Varela's departure, the parties signed a three month contract detailing the specifics of what was to be done so there would be no misunderstandings between them later. The New Yorkers were shown around the farm and given specific written instructions as to how to care for the animals, as well as maps of the property, and instructions on operating various equipment, such as the pump for the spring.

Things had gotten hectic at the last minute, since the jobs in town were not finished, and David was not able to come home to help Emily more with the packing and final details of cleaning and repairing things in preparation for the visiting family. David and Emily were thankful the farm-sitters had arrived in an RV where they could sleep for the night, since there was still much to be done in the house.

As everyone worked, a young man with whom they worshiped on a weekly basis came and volunteered his assistance with packing and cleaning up after the Varelas left. Emily made final arrangements with a friend who had designed an easy way for updates to be sent to the many people who had agreed to pray for them on their trip. She then quickly downloaded her remaining lessons of Pimsleur[2] Hebrew, onto an MP3 player to listen to on the plane. All of the packs and boxes were loaded into the back of

---

[1]MOMYS – Mothers of Many Young Siblings; an internet support group for Mothers who have had at least four children under the age of nine at any point in their lives.

[2]Pimsleur – An audio language program found at www.pimsleur.com.

Chapter 1   Preparations

the 14 passenger van that had been converted to an 11 passenger by removing the three rear seats to increase cargo space. As departure time approached, the children said 'goodbye' to their favorite pets, and David gathered everyone together on the front porch for prayer.

For the family, driving off the property was exciting, but sad too, as they anticipated missing many things about their home while they were gone. As they drove down the quarter-mile drive at the top of a cleared ridge, surrounded by trees on the steep inclines below, they discussed how they would miss their milk cow with all the fresh milk, yogurt, butter, and cheese to which they had become accustomed over the past several years. They had taken the cow, her yearling heifer, and their miniature pony that pulled a cart to some friends in a horse and buggy community to keep for them. They also discussed the possibility that because of world events they might never return. Things in the U.S. were not looking good, and they wondered if being called to Israel at 'such a time as this' might partially be to remove them from what they believed would soon befall America.

They drove to town, where David had some final business loose ends to wrap up. Then they met Emily's parents ('Mom' and 'Byron' to David) at their home. The elderly couple rode with the family to the airport to say their 'goodbyes' and bring the van back to keep at their home. The 80 minute drive to Nashville was spent discussing final details concerning how they could be contacted while in Israel and designing a plan so that Emily's parents could reach them in case of any emergency situation that might arise with their home, farm, or business. They felt confident they had done everything to ensure all would run smoothly while they were gone and were leaving things in the hands of their Creator.

At the airport all 19 boxes and packs were unloaded and hauled in carts to the ticket counter, where they were inspected and the family thoroughly questioned. They watched in dismay as every box, which had been so carefully packed and even labeled on the outside detailing its contents, was cut opened, rifled through, and the contents stuffed back in haphazardly. The couple had spent hours of the previous evenings disassembling the bicycles, and packing them in such a way as to fit everything in and have it all in good order when they arrived. Emily had begun with the 26" wheels, packing them carefully with clothing to keep the spokes from being damaged. She knew the first boxes would have to be 26" x 26", making 52" total, only 10" short of the maximum size for a free checked bag. So she made that box 10" tall and carefully fit as much as possible in before moving to the next one. They now wondered how many spokes and other parts and supplies they might have to replace when they got to Israel.

During trip planning, they discovered that bicycle, like most other things, were very expensive in Israel. Not only that, in order for them to train at home, they needed their panniers fitted to the bicycles they owned. To get decent bicycles in Israel in all of the various sizes needed for their family would be cost prohibitive, besides the fact that their equipment would likely

5

not fit, making it necessary to either buy more equipment or modify what they had. Instead of facing all those potential obstacles, the choice was made to go to the trouble of disassembling the bicycles they had already outfitted and were accustomed to using.

After the boxes had been desecrated, then taped securely with seemingly little regard to the placement of the valuable and fragile contents, they were set on the conveyer and sent out of sight with the stack of securely tied bed mats and three of the packs. The caravan of 11, including the grandparents moved toward the security line. Three of the packs would be carried onto the plane, so had been carefully organized in such a way that none of their important gear would be confiscated by airport security. The #1 pack contained all the original important documents, maps, and other paperwork they would need, as well as Granddaddy's laptop, which he had loaned them, and snacks for their trip. The number two pack contained copies of all the documents, as well as a set of clothing for each person. The other pack they took aboard contained the parts of their emergency supplies that were not prohibited to carry on the plane, as well as more snacks, and colored pencils and paper to keep the children occupied. At the security line, the family and Emily's nearly 80 years old parents said their farewells. It was a little after 3 PM, an hour and a half before the flight was scheduled to depart. The trip that had been in the works for three years was finally beginning.

2 - Family

In the Air

The family proceeded through security without much incident and waited to board their flight to Memphis. Most of the children had not flown before, so the airport was a new and exciting experience for them as they watched planes take off and land, workers load baggage while others refueled, and people of all sizes, shapes, and colors, dressed in various types of garb rush back and forth. Victor particularly liked all the different vehicles both inside and outside. And everyone delighted in the escalators and moving walkways.

They boarded a 50 passenger jet for their one hour flight to Memphis and enjoyed the clear skies, barely finishing their small airline snack before it was time to land. They family was the last to exit the plane in Memphis, partly because of the logistics of a large, young family, but also out of courtesy for other passengers who may have been in a hurry. The family had always tried to live in a manner that would not draw negative attention to themselves. For years they had been attention getters anyway, just because of the number of small children and the conservative way in which they dressed. Because of this they were often asked questions concerning their beliefs, which led into sharing the scriptures with their questioners. They were always aware that they were being watched and wanted to behave in a way that would glorify their Father in Heaven.

They thanked the flight attendants, who were enamored by the little ones, and walked off the plane into the Memphis airport. The first and last stops were always the restroom, so they went to the first one they saw. Upon leaving the restroom, they walked in a straight line to the last gate in the airport to catch their 7:20 PM flight to Amsterdam. Years before, they had developed a system of traveling that would be safe, effective, and bother the least amount of people. Emily, who was usually alone with the children, would lead and Armando the oldest, now 11, would follow at the rear. The rest of the children had a partner whose hand they could, or were required in certain situations, to hold. Since David was with them for this trip, they continued with the same order, except that he followed the crew, making sure no one wandered out of line. Whenever the walking areas got narrow or more people were coming towards them, Emily would glance back, and if the line had gotten a bit wide or dispersed, would command, "Straight line!"

Everyone would then assume their proper walking place behind her, usually next to the wall on the right side. David was the rear guard wearing the baby sling but holding Natanyah's hand so she could expend as much energy as possible. He was keenly aware of the surroundings and the people in them and was amused as, time after time, people counted the children, then looked at him in amazement. Often they would turn to someone else in excitement and dismay, saying something about "seven kids!"

Another family tradition they had started years before was wearing uniform dress every time they went to town. There were several reasons for this, the first being that, since they lived on a farm and got clothes very worn and dirty, having a special outfit to wear on their trips to town (about once per month), insured they would always have something clean and nice to wear, without having to make or buy new clothes so often. By making the town clothes uniform in color, everyone in the family knew which ones they were and knew not to wear them at home. They were also stored in a section by themselves in the laundry area where the family kept all their clothes. That way everyone knew they were off limits unless they were going to town. This also made laundry an easier task.

Wearing uniform clothes, which started out red T-shirts for all, jeans for the boys, and denim jumpers for the girls, also made the family more visible to each other, as well as to others. It made it very easy for Mama to spot the children right away, whether in a store, a group of people, or at a playground. It also caused people who saw the family to know they were together. There had been times when they would see strangers watching a child that was alone, then look over to see Mama and other siblings dressed the same way watching the same child, and realize the child was not really alone. In one instance, Victor, then six and unable to verbally communicate with people outside of the immediate family, wandered off in a large crowd of people in Williamsburg, Virginia, but others recognized his outfit as belonging with the family and brought him back safely. The Varela children were very good to watch out for one another and usually knew where each other were, but the addition of uniform dress made things much easier.

In addition, it was easy on Emily's eyes. Her thoughts were that if they were all dressed alike, there was some appearance of order. One of her most-oft quoted phrases to her children was, "Do everything decently and in order."[3] Order to her was equivalent to peace, and she learned that the Hebrew word *shalom*[4] also encompasses order. She felt that in the midst of chaos, if she (and others) could look at the family as a group or team (another term she used a lot at home), that would make up for some of the disorder that occurs naturally when a group with several small children travels together.

---

[3] 1 Cor. 14:40

[4] *Shalom* - Hebrew for 'peace,' but with a fuller meaning. Also, the common salutation used for 'hello' and 'good-bye' by Hebrew speakers.

Chapter 2   Family

Because of their uniform dress, it was easy for onlookers to know they were a family and easier for them to count the children. As it turned out, the 'uniforms' would provoke the most asked question on their entire trip, that being, "Why do you all wear the same color?" Therefore it was often what started conversations with others.

This particular day, they were wearing orange shirts that the family's horse-and-buggy friends had helped Emily to make especially for the trip. They were brand new and very bright. David called them the 'Dorito' shirts and said he felt like a big tortilla chip wearing his. The boys wore jeans and the girls wore pin-striped denim skirts that Emily had made a couple of years before. Since Briana had outgrown hers, it was passed down to Isabel; Isabel's to Rebeka; and Rebeka's to Natanyah. They did not have any more of the fabric other than some long triangular scraps that Emily had saved, but someone had recently given them a long straight denim skirt with a slit up the front. Emily ripped open all four seams and inserted the triangular pin-striped denim scraps, which fit perfectly. So Briana now had a fuller skirt with no slit that matched the others.

The flight from Nashville arrived at 5:35 PM, giving them nearly two hours, so they felt no need to rush to their gate. It was the last gate in the airport and they got there in what they thought was plenty of time, as it was still over an hour before their flight would leave. But when they arrived, there were already over 200 people in the waiting area. Upon reaching the counter, they learned that the airline for the flight they would be on did not make seat assignments until people checked in to board. They did not realize how that would affect them until 15 minutes later when the airline was still trying to get them seated together. They sat down on the floor in front of the counter as the attendant worked to rearrange empty seats on the computer screen. Finally, she looked up and said in a bewildered tone, "This is the best I can do," and handed them their boarding passes.

When they boarded the plane, David took the five youngest children, since he had not been home much for the preceding weeks. Armando was seated several rows in front of them, Briana on the opposite side of the plane, several rows behind David. Emily's seat was two rows behind Briana. It was not an ideal family situation for a flight that would be over eight hours long. The plane seated 298 people and was completely full. The parents were very thankful that it was a nighttime flight and were hoping they would all get plenty of rest.

Each seat had its own little movie screen with a selection of videos to choose from. The family was not accustomed to watching movies and the parents were very careful about what they allowed the children to watch, protecting their little minds from the influences of greed, immorality, materialism, bad character, and other maladies that were rampant on the screen. Knowing they would be watching *something*, even if it were not on their own screens, Emily, whose first language was English, looked through the list and approved three movies that looked the safest for the children and told David what they were, since he was sitting closer to them.

9

When Victor saw the choices of movies, nothing could contain his excitement. His shrill voice announced "Cars!" to everyone nearby. He could hardly wait for the plane to take off.

Shortly after take-off, Emily was able to make a deal with the young man sitting next to her, listening to his I-pod. Since Briana was in a seat with more leg room, he agreed to trade seats with her, so Mama and oldest daughter were able to sit together and have some one-on-one time. Emily had packed two pouches into one of the carry-on backpacks that contained pencils, crayons and paper, one for the boys and one for the girls to use on the plane and during other times on the trip when they might need something constructive to do. Briana found a crossword puzzle in the airline magazine in the seat pouch in front of her and went to where David, the children, and the backpacks were, to get a pencil. When she got there, David asked her to take Natanyah to the bathroom. The two-year-old had never flown before the short flight to Memphis and had never used an airplane lavatory. Always enjoying playing with the handles on toilets, she sat sideways on the seat and fiddled with the little stainless steel knob. It was entertaining until she accidentally pushed it hard enough to activate the powerful, pressurized system, which made a monstrous swooshing sound as the water rapidly swirled around and down the toilet as if attached to a giant vacuum. Terrified, Natanyah dove off, clinging to Briana's legs, screaming, "It's gonna suck me up!"

Briana calmed her down, reassuring her that it was just the way airline toilets flushed. She took Natanyah back to David and went to her own seat by Emily to work on the crossword puzzle before going to sleep. The children were used to going to bed around 8 PM, so most of them fell asleep shortly after takeoff. Emily occasionally got up to check on Armando, who was doing fine between the attention he was getting from the flight attendants and the ladies sitting on either side of him.

Emily tried to sleep so she would be ready to take care of her family when they landed, but sitting still, her feet and legs swelled, making her too uncomfortable to get much rest. She listened to her final Hebrew lessons, walking back and forth to the restroom as often as possible and drinking lots of water to try to combat the swelling. She knew part of it had to be from the airline food which, while very tasty, was much more processed than what they ate at home. Too tired to continue with her Hebrew lessons, but too uncomfortable to sleep, her mind began to think back over the events that had brought them to this place in their lives. She remembered thirteen years before, the first time she met David.

The Meeting

She had been a working cowpuncher in the Texas Panhandle, living on a 15,000 acre leased ranch. Most of her days were spent on a horse, taking care of thousands of cattle for others, as well as a couple hundred that she

Chapter 2   Family

co-owned. In the summer, she was less busy, so took on other jobs in the surrounding area of ranches and farms. On one particular day, she was driving toward New Mexico to do some custom work, when she picked up two Mexican hitchhikers who stood near the railroad tracks that led north to Colorado.

David had told the story many times from his perspective. He had been on that route several times, changing from the east bound grain cars to the north bound ones to get himself and his fellow Mexican companions from Mexico to Colorado where they worked in construction in and near the ski resorts. This particular day, something he could not shake impressed him to thumb for a ride. It didn't make sense. There were no cars in sight and he could hear the sound of the next train approaching. But, called by the unexplainable, powerful notion, he got up from his waiting place in the shade of the cottonwood trees and walked to the middle of the lonely highway, wondering why he would be impressed to ask for a ride when there was not a vehicle in sight. He looked toward town, then away, but when he turned to go back to the trees looked up again and saw a small dot approaching. The first vehicle that came by was a strange looking pickup, which slowed, its driver carefully observing the two travelers. After it passed and turned around, David and his friend ran and hid behind the cottonwoods, fearing it might be immigration, but when the truck passed them, then turned around again, driving nearer, they saw there was no threat and came out to catch their ride.

As with all strange men she picked up, Emily had them get in the back of her pick-up, which had a special stock rack built enabling her to carry a horse without pulling a trailer. This day, she was working without a horse, so had room for travelers. Having been in a position of needing a ride herself in country where it was many miles between towns, and having experienced walking for hours in the heat, she was more sympathetic to others in that position.

After driving off with her two new passengers, she began thinking of all she had to do that day and over the coming weeks and decided to ask them if they needed work. She had a quick job to do just off the highway before going to a big ranch closer to New Mexico, so turned onto a little dirt road. She would do the job quickly before taking them to the big ranch, where there was someone who spoke both English and Spanish and could present her proposal. The change of course bothered the occupants in the back, who began tapping on the window, knowing she was off their scheduled route and now taking them down a dirt road to who-knew-where. They had known of people to go missing permanently in similar situations. She gestured to them to wait, then pulled up to the pasture she had come to check, got out and asked the only word in Spanish she knew, "*Trabajo?*"[5]

---

[5]*Trabajo* - Spanish for 'work.'

They looked at each other, trying to figure out what she meant, but knew they did not have many options at the moment, and since she was gesturing that they would only be a few minutes, decided to help her. As they followed her through the pasture, David noticed the outline of the small gun she carried in her back pocket and pointed it out to his friend, who was already very nervous. David always enjoyed getting intense reactions out of people.

After feeding some animals, Emily took the men back to the pick-up, and feeling confident they were more concerned about her sanity than she was of theirs, allowed them to ride in the front until they got to the big ranch. Once there, a man translated her proposition to them and they agreed to work for her over the weekend, get some good food and rest, something they had not had for several days, then get back on the road to Colorado.

When lunch time approached, Emily got her water and the dried fruit she had brought along, never eating much when working in the heat. David reached in the small bag he was carrying and produced a can of beans and a package of saltine crackers that some kind people in town had given them when they had stopped and asked for water. Emily was impressed when he offered her some of their meager lunch, amazed that someone with nearly nothing between two people would offer to share with her. She in turn shared her dried fruit with them and they finished lunch together before working for the rest of the day in the heat. On the way back through town, she bought them each a set of clothes, since theirs were filthy, well-worn, and the only set they had, then took them to the ranch, where she had a small RV that was sometimes used by temporary laborers. They slept and ate there for the next two days before Emily asked them if they would like to stay and work on the ranch for a time. They agreed to stay for two weeks, but were eager to get on to Colorado where they had lots of friends and could make more money.

As things turned out, David's friend did leave in two weeks, but Emily had a need at the ranch while she would be gone to New Mexico for a weekend, so David agreed to stay and take care of things for her, leaving two weeks later. When the time came for him to go, the friend he was to meet never showed up, so she took David back to the ranch. By then, she had learned enough Spanish to give working instructions to him, and in the evenings they studied the Bible together. She had a Spanish-English dictionary and got David a Spanish Bible, where he followed along with her using her Southern Baptist Sunday School book as a guide.

After a few weeks, the Spanish-speaking Jehovah's Witnesses came to the ranch, leaving materials for David. That evening, he was excited to have his own book to use as a guide for their study. Upon seeing and recognizing it, Emily said in her best Spanish, "Oh no, you can't use that."

Chapter 2   Family

"*Porque no*?"[6] he asked.

She didn't know how to explain. In fact, she really did not know why herself, so she replied, "I don't know. You just can't use that."

Not going to be pushed around, and not really appreciating her rejection of the materials he was so excited about, he retorted, "Well, if we can't use mine, we can't use yours either."

She considered the bold statement briefly and decided it was reasonable, so she set aside her book, he set aside his, and they began studying only the Bible without the aid of any religion's viewpoints. Soon after, both of their lives began to change drastically. At the time, they had both been in turmoil in differing ways, both making decisions that had they continued, would have led to destruction. But through prayer and child-like study of the scriptures, their lives were changed.

Marriage and Moving

Within the year, the owner of the ranch decided to sell the property. Emily sold her share of the cows, horses, and most everything else she had and moved to Colorado where she and David were married. They moved into a huge trailer park full of mostly illegal Mexican workers. Learning she was pregnant threw her life into major transition. She knew she could not be the wife and mother she needed to be if she continued in the cowboy life she loved, which consumed all of her time and attention. Her horses and equipment sold, she began working for temp agencies, staying busy with whatever type of work they offered, mostly construction and office work, trading her active cowboy lifestyle for more sedentary, less exciting work. To stay fit, she chose to travel to work by bicycle if her job was within ten miles of home, so as to at least get *some* exercise and stay in decent physical shape. She had always felt better when active.

Although she was determined to deny her own desires in order to be a good wife and mother, coming directly from a ranch of over 23 sections[7] where the nearest neighbor was six miles away as the crow flies to a massive trailer park where she could have easily thrown a rock from her porch through her neighbor's kitchen window, was major culture shock and very difficult to get used to. As the baby grew in her womb, she wondered what kind of a life this would be for a child - no place to run, no animals (except the equally traumatized cat she had brought with her from the ranch after rescuing him from near death in town as a kitten), no place to grow food or play in the dirt. David was doing well working in construction at the ski resorts in the Vail area. He was in demand from the construction bosses because he understood more English than most of the other illegal

---

[6]*Porque no?* - Spanish for 'Why not?'
[7]Section of land is one square mile or 640 acres.

13

workers and was able to relay instructions. Once married, he got his permanent US residency, so was able to freely travel without fear of being deported.

Emily's thoughts, her pregnant state, and her husband's snoring kept her awake. Her mind went back to her grandmother's place in east Tennessee that had been deteriorating for years since her grandmother was going back and forth between her two daughters' homes, unable to live alone. She envisioned using the half-acre garden plot that had been so carefully built up to grow food for the family. She thought of the various types of fruit and nut trees that she had eaten from while visiting there as a child. And she knew she could take her high school and university animal science and production education, combined with years of experience taking care of hundreds of thousands of animals, and condense it into a couple of milk goats and a few chickens and produce healthy food for her little family, while living in a more peaceful environment. After David awoke in the morning, she asked him (in Spanish, since she was excited to learn his language and he had not yet learned hers), "How would you like to move to Tennessee?"

"Where's that?" he questioned.

She got out the atlas and showed him as she explained her idea. He responded, "I don't care where we live, as long as I can find work."

She immediately began making phone calls to check on the possibility of buying the house, having goats and chickens on the little place in town, and finding potential jobs for David. They knew once the baby came, her job would be raising it, but having the animals and yard full of food should satisfy her need to be outside and active. She was a good money manager and very frugal, and with David's strong work ethic, knew they would have no problem having their financial needs met.

A few months later, they bought the little house at 105 Main Street in Niota, Tennessee, built with stones picked up by Emily's mother and aunt as children when they went to visit their country relatives. David got a factory job and they invested the rest of the money Emily had from the sale of her cows and other property into a sad-looking apartment building in nearby Athens. Their plan was to hire people to fix their deteriorating home and rental building while David brought home regular income from his job. It was not long before that plan was changed, since David found himself paying person after person the hard earned money he made, and still having to redo the jobs he had paid them to do.

Not long after Armando was born, David left his factory job to work full time on the apartments, so they could be rented. In the meantime, the factory shut down, so when he got the apartments rented, he took a job at another factory job in nearby Sweetwater as he continued work on the house. When he and his colleagues at work discussed what they had done the evening before, David's contribution was always some form of

Chapter 2   Family

construction or home improvement. His fellow workers began asking him to do jobs for them, and soon he had more and better paying work to do *away* from work than he did *at* work. He left his job and went into business for himself, as he finished getting their home property ready for the goats and chickens. Being surrounded by Americans, he learned English and practiced speaking it to Emily at home.

Growing Family

When Armando was seventeen months old, Briana was born, and a year later, they were pregnant again. Emily was ready to have the goats and chickens to provide good quality food for her growing family. They finally finished fencing the place and built a movable hut, then purchased two milk goats. Two weeks later the battle with city government began, in spite of the fact that Emily had called and checked on applicable laws before even considering the move three years before. They later learned the trouble had been sparked by racial prejudice of a neighbor they thought they had a good relationship with. Though assured they would win in legal proceedings against the city and be able to keep their animals like others in the small town, they decided it would not be peaceful to live in a place under those conditions. Besides, it looked like they would soon outgrow the property, so they decided to move west to be closer to David's family in Mexico. But before leaving, they looked into property three hours west near Cookeville, where Emily's parents had recently returned shortly after their retirement. Emily and her two siblings had lived there longer than at any other home growing up and had graduated from high school there. On their first Internet search, they found the perfect place on 80 acres in Jackson County, mostly wooded and surrounded with hundreds of acres of timber at the end of a dead end road about 45 minutes north of Cookeville. They chose that for their new home instead of moving farther west.

Once settled in their new home, David continued doing home repairs and remodeling, while Emily took care of the three young children, a garden, a herd of goats, and bookkeeping for the business. The family continued to grow, adding a new child about every year and a half, until they had seven. David's business also continued to grow in Cookeville, keeping him away from home six days a week from morning till late at night. Emily had always felt more proficient at caring for barns and livestock than houses and children and was coping the best she could, but life alone on the farm was very difficult for her. Shortly after moving in, they found they had moved into the same situation they had left, living in an area where some were not particularly friendly to outsiders and less to their 'mixed-race' marriage. Emily faced instances of harassment when David was away, making her life even more difficult and causing her to long more for the presence of her man. Armando was growing up to be a good, responsible leader, but was still a child. Though even from an early age (as his name proclaimed) he was well-suited for an Army, his presence and ability to lead and protect was not the same as David's would have been.

15

As the children grew and David was not around much during waking hours, it became easier for him to communicate with them in English. So he practically gave up speaking Spanish altogether, even though Emily begged him to speak it at home for the sake of the children. He soon got his general contractor's license and began doing larger remodels and additions and building houses from the ground up, being experienced in all aspects of construction. The business was growing, which meant there was more bookkeeping for Emily to do. The family was growing, giving her more responsibilities with children and schooling. The plants and animals necessary to feed the growing family were increasing, adding more work for everyone and more supervision from her. And she was getting older and more tired with each pregnancy.

Besides the growth of family, business, and farming, the couple's spiritual growth, knowledge, and understanding increased. Emily attributed this as the reason she was able to endure the load she carried. As the couple and family continued to study their Bibles together, they began to follow more of the instructions that were written within it, seeing them described throughout scripture as 'wisdom', 'good', 'life,' and 'light,'[8] The more they walked according to those instructions, the more the scriptures came alive and the more understanding they received, not to mention the more blessings they began to experience in their lives in many ways. They began to celebrate the feasts instructed in the scriptures, which led them to where they were at that very moment - on a plane over the Atlantic, bound for Israel.

---

[8]Prov. 6:23 For the commandment *is* a lamp; and the law *is* light; and reproofs of instruction *are* the way of life:

Josh. 1:8 This book of the law shall not depart out of thy mouth; but thou shalt meditate therein day and night, that thou mayest observe to do according to all that is written therein: for then thou shalt make thy way prosperous, and then thou shalt have good success.

All of Psalms 119 and many others.

3 - Miracles

Celebrating Feasts

David first went to Israel in 2005 for Sukkot. The next year, the whole family celebrated the feast in one of their pastures, building a big sukkah out of branches and weeds. But as they continued studying and began to understand more about the tithes spoken of in scripture, they felt led for David to go to Jerusalem for the feast, even though it would be more difficult for Emily and the children to celebrate at home without him. They were not able to go to other gatherings because there was no one to care for the farm. And even if they had found someone, it would have been awkward for Emily to attend an event made up mostly of entire families while her man was gone. As they continued studying the scriptures and saw that in the seventh year the entire family was to go to Jerusalem, they excitedly began to prepare for their family trip to Israel.

They knew traveling to Israel would be very expensive because of the time David had spent there in 2005, but according to the scriptures, some of the tithes were set apart to be used to celebrate before YHWH in Jerusalem, so they began to set aside ten percent of their income every week to help fund their trip. Not wanting to use so much money on airfare to just stay a week, they decided to budget in order to stay there for the maximum amount of time they could. A tourist visa was for three months, so they planned for that. Since it would be too expensive to rent or buy a car and fill it with gas at over seven dollars per gallon, they decided the only way they could travel would be at a slower pace, more like how the people written of in the scriptures traveled. Cycling would be the perfect experience. They would see things the way the ancient peoples saw them, meet more people, stay active, be doing something fun and interesting for the children, and it would be free.

The other big expense would be lodging, but if they were cycling and meeting people, they could offer their experience in home repair and agricultural services to hosts in exchange for allowing them to camp at their place. They would base their route off of the contacts they would make before leaving and follow Yah's leading to whomever He wanted them to meet, help, and stay with, restricting their stay at any one place to three days. Their plan confirmed, David went back to Israel in 2007, this time traveling to Egypt as well, for the purpose of helping establish the route they would take on their bicycles. The adventures he had between the Israeli border and Cairo finalized his decision to keep the family in Israel, instead of going with their initial idea of traveling a route similar to the one the Israelites had traveled after leaving slavery in Egypt.

Pedaling Home   Part 1 – In the Beginning

Once back from his trip that fall, he reported what he had found and Emily went to work researching what they would need. As they prepared for their trip, Emily sent out an email to all those who had showed interest in what they were about to do, asking for names of contacts in Israel that they would be willing to share with the family. Since it had already been established that they would not be riding north from Egypt, they would use the contacts they received to establish the route they would ride.

Most of the few responses they got were very kind and helpful, but a few were negative, some extremely so. The couple had learned over the years that when Yah[9] gave them an assignment, there would be those on His side who supported them in it and those working against Him that would oppose anything He had given them to do. They were getting better at discerning which people were in which camp. They learned the difference between messages of warning and messages designed to put fear into them, but sometimes it was difficult to discern between the two. They prayed over each one, taking them all seriously. They noticed a trend beginning to happen: negativity creeping in. The most severe was from someone they did not even know, an American, living in Israel who had learned of them through one of their friends. He wrote telling them how expensive and dangerous things were in Israel. Something about the way he wrote was disturbing, but other than the fear factor, they could not put their finger on what it was. Wanting to take into consideration all of the counsel they received,[10] they sent the man a kind email, telling him they would pray over what he had written. A short time later, they received another email from him, highly discouraging them from coming to Israel, along with an attached news article telling how many pedestrians were killed by vehicles in Israel each year. Had they not known what they were to do, the letter would have put enough fear in them to keep them from going, but they knew that fear was not from YHWH,[11] recognized what was going on, and ignored further messages from the man.

In late winter, they learned they were expecting their eighth child to be born during the time they had planned to be in Israel. That was exciting and added a whole new dimension to their planned trip. As the weather warmed up, the family began training on their bicycles during good weather, riding daily to the community center, a little over a mile away, and weekly to another destination, sometimes five miles to the river down an extremely steep, curvy, long hill or into their little town of Gainesboro, eight miles away and down another long, steep hill. They were blessed to live in an area with such steep hills, getting experience they would appreciate

---

[9]*Yah*- abbreviated form of the name, *Yehovah*, Creator of the universe; appears at least 49 times in the Bible and is rendered 'the LORD' in most English versions, except in Ps. 68:4, where it is rendered, 'Jah.'

[10]Prov. 11:14 Where no counsel *is* the people fall: but in the multitude of counsellors *there is* safety.

[11]2Tim. 1:7 For Elohim hath not given us the spirit of fear; but of power, and of love, and of a sound mind.

Chapter 3   Miracles

once arriving in Israel. They learned that for children, going down can be as difficult as going up, since they have to brake the entire time and their little legs get tired. On their rides, they practiced safety rules, riding in a specified order, much like the one in which they walked while in town with Emily in the front and David guarding everyone from the rear, and trained in traffic and for endurance.

The Accident

All seemed to be going as planned and excitement was building, but as spring arrived, they began to be bombarded with more negative messages from various doubting people and were beginning to become discouraged. Life on the farm and in the construction business continued as usual, and the couple decided to extend the roof of David's shop, in order to cover an area behind the chicken house for animals that needed special attention. It was often they had small calves, goats, or sheep, that needed to be kept separate from the others, but they did not have a proper barn for such things. Armando helped David set up sheets of metal for the roof they had framed, and David continued teaching him construction skills. Today's lesson was in metal roofing. They climbed up onto the rafters and would pull a sheet up as they needed it, then screw it in securely before moving to the next.

About half-way through, David stepped on one of the sheets that still contained an oily substance from the fabricator, causing him to slide and lose his footing. He was falling sideways toward one of the sharp metal sheets that was standing on its end on the ground and sticking up about two feet above the roof, and to keep from decapitating himself, stuck out his left hand to break his fall. All the weight of his body came down on his hand as it hit the metal edge, slicing through the thick part of his thumb muscle and into the bone at the base of his thumb. He tried to stay calm, so as not to alarm Armando, as Armando asked, "Are you OK?" But as he asked, he saw the blood running down the sheet of metal.

David replied, "I'm OK, but I'm stuck on this metal."

Armando, realizing the severity of the situation, said, "No, you're not OK. I'm going to get Mama!"

He jumped from the roof, ran in the basement door and up the stairs to tell Emily.

David, clenching his teeth and using his right hand, took hold of his left and jerked it off of the metal. The tendon severed, his thumb flopped back and almost hit the back of his hand as blood sprayed everything nearby. He grabbed his thumb with his other hand and put it in place, trying to apply enough pressure on it to slow the blood loss. As he did, he heard the Father say, "I'm going to heal you."

Still having his senses and knowing he was getting weak, he climbed the ladder down from the roof.

Emily was working in the kitchen when she heard the unusual sound of intense running up the stairs and instantly knew something was wrong. Armando called, "Daddy's hurt! He cut himself!"

She knew from the tone of his voice that it was bad. She grabbed her pint container of cayenne pepper powder out of the kitchen cabinet as she prayed and rushed out the back door, and around the chicken house, following Armando. She saw David standing in a strange position, holding his hand. When he saw her coming with the cayenne, he screamed, "NO!!!"

He had never had her use it on him as a blood stopper, but knew how hot it was in the other medicines she made. She assured him it was the best thing and had him remove his right hand so she could apply it. When he did, blood sprayed heavily. She tried to ignore the severity of the situation and just take care of what needed to be done without thinking of all of the 'what ifs.' She applied the cayenne, then had him reapply pressure and told him to sit before he got weak enough to fall.

The cayenne, along with the pressure he was able to apply immediately stopped the bleeding, but there was no denying this was a major wound. The family had not been to a doctor in years and was learning, little by little, how to treat sickness and emergencies by relying on Yah's healing power and listening to Him concerning how to proceed. But this was big. Emily had to ask, "Do you want to go to the hospital?"

Dreading what she thought would be his response, she was surprised when he said, "No, the Father said He's going to heal me."

OK. With that out of the way, the next step was to call on people for prayer. Armando ran to get the phone and Emily began calling others whom she knew were praying people of faith, people who also attempted to walk according to the commandments of the Almighty. The people whose numbers she had in her phone assured her they would pray, some of them praying on the phone with them. She and Armando then walked beside David into the house where he could on the couch. Emily tried to clean the cayenne and dried blood off of his hand enough to get tape to stick, in order to hold the five inch gash back together. Regular medical tape would not hold, as the thick part of the wound had already swollen too big for the skin from one side to meet the skin of the other. While working with it, they saw the upper part of the white severed tendon hanging from his thumb, and could see the indention, a couple of inches below in his wrist, where the lower part had snapped back. Knowing she could not bring them together, Emily just focused on getting the wound closed.

She tried Band-Aids, but to no avail. The swelling was way too much. Then she tried butterfly bandages, but those were not strong enough

Chapter 3   Miracles

either. So she got super glue, glued one side of five different bandages and glued them to the upper part of the wound, then carefully closed it by putting glue on the other end of the bandages and pulling the wound closed tightly before gluing them down on the other side. It was not until years later she learned super glue was commonly used directly on open wounds by doctors. But because she did not know that, the wound was joined together without any unnatural substance.

After closing it, she applied several drops of oregano and lavender essential oils to kill bacteria and aid in healing. As she worked, both of them prayed for complete healing, David not forgetting the voice he had heard.

Doctoring finished, Emily called a few other people, including her mother, a nurse, as well as a nurse friend and a doctor friend. All of them told her they would need to get to a doctor and have surgery within a few days or the use of his hand would be lost. She then called another family they sometimes worshiped with and gave the phone to David who talked to him. The man also told David that he needed to get to the hospital. David, having heard the voice and trusting Yah, refused to listen to that counsel.

High on the list of questions that came up during the doctoring process was, "What about the trip?" David knew he could not ride a bicycle for a while, and training needed to continue. And they all knew that there was no way he could ride a loaded multi-speed bicycle with only one hand operational. It seemed this accident was just another weapon in the arsenal to try to sabotage their trip. But they knew that Yah had led them in their calling and planning and were leaving it in His hands.

The next day, several of the men came to pray with David. After praying, some of them again told him that he needed to go to a doctor. One even went as far as to say that Yah had told him so. David replied, "Well, He told me He was going to heal me, so I have to go with what he told me, not what you say He told you."

David was reminded of the lying spirit that went to a false prophet in scripture and resolved to listen to the voice he had heard personally.

Phone Calls from *Abba*[12]

Two days after the accident, David was still in bed recuperating from blood loss, which Emily was treating by giving him chlorophyll, the green substance from plants, which she had learned was chemically almost identical to human blood and easily converted by the body. The phone rang, was answered by Briana, and brought to Emily, who was at David's bedside. Emily asked, "Who is it?"

---

[12]*Abba* – Hebrew for 'Father' or 'Daddy;' often used to refer to YHWH.

21

Briana told her the name of a woman they had met when she had spoken at a little church near Nashville a couple of years before. They had hosted her to speak in their home later, as she traveled the world praying and interceding over people and places where Yah sent her. She was a woman of faith and a prayer warrior.

Emily was shocked. She had never received a call from the Intercessor before. Emily was amazed at the timing of the call, and knew it was no coincidence. "Hello."

Intercessor: How are you doing?

Emily: Fine, thank you, and you?

Intercessor: I'm fine. Does David play guitar?

Now this was getting a little too strange.

Emily: No, he's always wanted to learn, but hasn't been able to prioritize it high enough into his life for it to become a reality, yet.

Intercessor: Well, I'm here in east Tennessee with a couple who's about to migrate to Israel. They're giving away most everything they have, and they've got a guitar and an instructional video. I just thought of David.

Emily: Wow! You won't believe what's going on here! Two days ago David had a terrible injury to his left hand. He heard Abba[13] say He would heal him, and we're treating him at home. We know he will be healed, but your call is confirmation. We've been told by some that if we don't go to the doctor, he'll lose the use of his hand, but he can't play a guitar with no left hand. If Abba put it on your heart to call and give him a guitar, that's just confirmation of his healing!

Intercessor: Yes, he'll be healed. There's no doubt about that.

She gave the location and contact information for the Guitar Couple and they made arrangements to travel the three hours to pick it up in a few days, while David was still unable to work.

After getting off the phone, David and Emily rejoiced at how Yah encourages his people using other servants. The negative comments they had gotten from some were completely overridden by the confirmation He had given them though his Intercessor.

The next day, Emily received a phone call from her sister's husband, Bob. Bob had never called, so it was a bit strange to be hearing from him. In fact, their relationship with Bob was sometimes rather odd, with him

---

[13]Abba – Hebrew for 'Father' or 'Daddy;' often used to refer to YHWH.

Chapter 3   Miracles

seeming to question their walk and often getting into scriptural debates with David concerning whether or not Christians should be following the Old Testament instructions. They loved Bob and he loved them, but there often seemed to be a tenseness in their relationship. So hearing Bob's voice on the phone was unusual.

He asked, "Is David there?"

Emily answered, "No, could I take a message?"

"I have something to tell him. You can just tell him for me, I guess. I was at work today and was praying for him because Byron had told us about his accident. I was praying for his hand when God impressed upon me to stop praying for his hand and to pray for the work he was going to be doing in Israel. He showed me that you all were being sent on a special mission and that He had equipped you all to do the work that you were being sent to do. I know I could not do what he is sending you there for. I thought it was real important and just wanted to let you know."

Emily was brought to tears and nearly speechless as she responded, "Thank you, Bob. I'll give him the message. You have no idea what it means to us for you to call and tell us this."

She phoned David at work and told him what had happened. They both marveled at how Yah chose to go about encouraging them in the midst of so much discouragement. It was not that the words Bob spoke were so significant, or that the message was spectacular, though it was extremely encouraging. But this particular word coming from this particular person was the best encouragement Yah could have given them at this time. To have someone who had so adamantly disagreed with their position on the scriptures say what he had said, they recognized the word as coming directly from Yah Himself. It was the second witness in two days.

David's Passport

David had recently gotten U.S. Citizenship and had applied for his U.S passport. It was time to buy the airline tickets, but David's passport had not yet arrived. The people at the courthouse where he had applied had told him it could take six to eight weeks.

A few weeks after sending in the application, he got a letter saying that his passport could not be issued because the name on his driver's license was not the same as the one on his naturalization certificate. In Mexico, names consist of the given name, father's family name, a hyphen, and then the mother's family name. Because in English, the custom is to only use the given name and father's family name, David had applied for citizenship using that form of his name. Since he had previously gotten his driver's license using his Mexican Passport, which had since expired, the names did not match exactly for his U.S. passport application.

23

David called the passport office and asked what he needed to do about it. They lady on the line told him, "You'll have to get your driver's license changed to the name that you're trying to get on your passport."

David: How can I do that? We sent my Naturalization Certificate to you all with the application.

Lady: You can write us a letter explaining your situation and requesting to get the document back, then take it to get your driver's license, then send them in together.

David: OK. How long will it take to get the passport after I get all that to you?

Lady: Well, it has to come through this office first, then go through processing, then be made into the actual passport. You could have it in 4-6 weeks.

That was a big problem. The tickets needed to be bought right away. And in order to get the best price and to make sure they would all be on the same flights, they needed to buy them at the same time. There was nothing they could do. They would trust that Yah would work things out in His perfect timing. They knew that He was sending them to Israel, and they would wait for Him. Even so, it was not an easy wait. Emily knew that if they went much beyond their proposed departure date, the airlines would not allow her to fly because of the late stage of pregnancy.

Emily typed the letter that day, Tuesday, then put it in the mailbox in a Next Day Air envelope and she and David prayed. It was picked up by the mailman around 11 AM. Two days later, Thursday, there was a Next Day Air envelope in the mailbox. David and Emily were amazed at the speed at which their request had been acknowledged and at the speed of Next Day Air. How was it possible for them to send an envelope to arrive at the office the next morning, then for the office to get its letter in the mail in time to arrive at the Varela home the following one? It seemed like everything would have had to have gone just perfectly in order for that to happen. But they knew that Yah was quite capable of doing such things.

They opened the envelope as they walked back to the house and were shocked to find not only the Naturalization Certificate they had requested but also David's new passport with his English name on it! Amazed, they rejoiced all the way back to the house, then shared the miracle with the children. The process was supposed to take weeks from the time they sent the letter, yet it took only two days from the time they had made the phone call!

As planning for the trip continued in spite of David's hand injury nearly three weeks before, Emily saw a MOMYS post from another MOMYS who was cycling with her husband and four children in Europe, writing home school curriculum from wherever in the world they happened to be cycling.

Chapter 3   Miracles

Emily had never noticed the woman posting before and found it amazing that she would see it at this point in their lives. She wrote and told the woman of their plans and the other cycling mom was glad to help. She gave Emily information on good quality camping supplies, as well as recommending that she sign up on warmshowers.org, a bicycle hosting site where cyclists opened their homes to other cyclists. Emily immediately signed up and then sent an email to all the warmshowers.org members in Israel. A few wrote back welcoming them telling them they did not have room for a group that large. Of those that responded, the family made arrangements to meet four of them. As they placed their stickers marking willing hosts on their wall map of Israel, they immediately noticed a pattern and knew that was where Yah was sending them. Their route was to begin at *Kibbutz*[14] *S'dot Yam*,[15] then travel North, detouring through *Har haCarmel*,[16] then farther north, nearly to Lebanon before turning east to Tz'fat, and then south past Tiberius and the Sea of Galilee.

By that time, they would need to get off of the bicycles because Emily would be eight months along in the pregnancy. Then they would travel by bus to a few historically significant places, ending up in Jerusalem, where they would be for Sukkot, then down south to *Be'er Sheva* and *Ezuz* in the *Negev* Desert for a few days, until time to fly back to the States. Their route was now planned, but training had stopped while David's hand continued to recover. The family continued to pray over him and one day as he prayed for his hand, he was impressed by verses in scripture that talk about the importance and power of words.[17] He began commanding his hand to heal and for the tendon to reconnect. As he did, he started feeling strange sensations in his hand and after a few days was able to begin moving his thumb. Family and friends watched with amazement as he began moving his thumb in ways that he had been told would never be possible without surgery. Once he could bring the thumb to itself, Emily suggested he begin helping Armando milk the cow, as a physical therapy exercise. It was difficult at first, but strength and coordination in his hand increased day by day.

Abba Makes Room

Emily was very frugal and always combined trips when possible. She had a bulk food order ready to pick up an hour east of their home, so had scheduled the guitar pick up for the same day. Everyone got in the van,

---

[14]*Kibbutz* – Hebrew for 'gathering,' or 'clustering', a collective community traditionally based on agriculture.

[15]*S'dot Yam* – Sea Fields

[16]*Har HaCarmel* – Mountain of El's Vinyard

[17]Prov. 18:21 Death and life *are* in the power of the tongue: and they that love it shall eat the fruit thereof.

25

drove to the Mennonite community and picked up the large order of food: 50 pound bags of wheat, oats, rice, and beans, 25-30 pound bags of sunflower seeds and garbanzo beans, 30 pound boxes of raisins, 30 pound bucket of peanut butter, as well as several boxes and tubs of various spices, herbs, and dried onions and garlic. The family kept the last row of seats out of the van for times like these, in order to haul food and other supplies that they needed. Along with the drawers of regular and emergency supplies the family kept in the back of the van, once all of today's items were loaded, the back was completely full. There would barely be room for the guitar they were going to get.

They drove the additional two hours to the Guitar Couple's home and got to their side of town just as a light rain began to fall. As David drove at a leisurely pace down the curvy hill going toward their neighborhood, the van suddenly slid off the right side of the road. David did his best to steer it back onto the pavement, as it continued down the hill bumping up against the bank on the right side. At once, the van jumped up onto the road, then slid off the other side and continued bumping along the left bank. It was headed straight toward another car at the bottom of the hill which had slid off just before. The three ladies standing beside that car began running away when they saw the van heading towards them uncontrollably. But just at the last minute, it jumped back onto the road and continued on its path, as if nothing had happened. The couple praised Yah for keeping them all, including the other vehicle, safe.

Having been previously instructed to get ready to exit immediately after a crash, some of the younger children had unbuckled as soon as the van jumped off the road to the right bank. Some were scared and crying, so the parents, thankful that the children had listened to prior instruction, calmed them and re-instructed that they were not to leave their seat belts until *after* a crash was *over*.

They drove the two remaining blocks to the Guitar Couple's home, pulled into the driveway, Emily still trembling. They got out to assess the damage to their vehicle, David checking the driver's side and Emily the passenger's. They both reached the back of the van at the same time and were astonished, each having to check the other's sides, to find that there was not a scratch anywhere! They again praised Yah for putting his protecting angels around, not only their family, but their van, as well.

The Guitar Couple had come out onto their porch and introductions were made. The family explained what had just happened, and they all praised Yah for their safe arrival. The family was then invited into the home, where there were rooms full of things to be given away. The family had come to pick up a guitar, but was given *five* guitars with instructional training videos, a brass *menorah*[18] and candle lighting supplies, a segment of a several

---

[18]*Menorah* - seven-branch candlestick, representing Messiah. A large one was used in the tabernacle and temple.

Chapter 3   Miracles

hundred year old *torah*[19] scroll, and several other items. The man took David to his garage and showed him a room full of nice tools, telling him to pick whatever he wanted. David was astounded and humbled, but felt like since he had plenty of tools of his own, that there was someone else to be blessed with those things. Meanwhile, inside, the woman told Emily to look around and see if there was anything else they wanted. Emily had never been put in a position like that before and did not feel right to take more than the abundance of what they had already been given.

When David came back and refreshments were served, Emily asked, "Where are we going to put all of this? There's barely room for one guitar."

David agreed, so they went to the van to see if they could rearrange things in order to take all the Guitar Couple was sending with them. When David opened the back door to the van, the couple was once again shocked and amazed. The shaking that the van had gotten in the previous hour had rearranged the neatly stacked load in the van to make exactly enough room to fit in all that they were being given. The Guitar Couple rejoiced with the family at what an amazing *Elohim*[20] they all served. The children talked about how angels had stacked the bags and boxes just right.

On the way home, the family discussed the many miracles they had already witnessed as they prepared to go to Israel. They knew, without a shadow of a doubt, that *Abba* was sending them. Though they did not know exactly why, they were excited none-the-less, and were eager to continue on with whatever business he had for them to do.

Abba Sends an Expert

A few days later, Emily received an email from a cyclist named Tomasz who was cycling from Argentina to Canada. Later that day she got a call, "Hello. My name is Tomasz. I saw you on warmshowers. I will be in your area in a few days. Is it OK if I stay with you?"

Emily told him that would be fine, then informed the rest of the family that they were expecting their first cycling guest, a world cyclist! They were all very excited, but at the time did not realize how blessed they were. They had joined warmshowers.org only two weeks before and later learned that some people are members for several years before getting their first call. And the family was not situated in a highly trafficked bicycle area. It was another provision of their Father.

---

[19] *Torah*-Hebrew for 'instruction,' which is translated as 'law' in most versions of the scriptures. The term is also used as the name for the first five books of the Old Testament, commonly believed to have been written by *Moshe* (Moses).

[20] *Elohim* - the Hebrew word translated to English as 'God', 'god', 'gods.' It can also be translated 'mighty ones.' It is the plural form of the word '*eloah*' translated 'God' and 'god.'

Tomasz arrived on a Thursday afternoon prepared to stay outside, but the family gave him the guestroom and bathroom downstairs. He was very grateful and got along well with the children who excitedly showed him around the farm. They had him help them milk the cow, gather the eggs, and put the goats in for the night before they all came in for supper. At the meal, he was very grateful for the food set before him and shared about himself and his journeys on the bicycle. He was a young man from Poland who had cycled in various parts of the world. He knew how to travel light and was excited to hear of the family's upcoming adventure in Israel. He showed them his bicycle panniers and told them how to lighten their load in the summer by taking only bed sheets instead of a sleeping bag. The family thoroughly enjoyed his company and talked him into staying with them the next day, instead of leaving in the morning, as he had planned.

David was still recuperating from his accident and taking it easy with his hand, wanting it to fully recover soon so the family could get back to their practice rides. They had built a cellar to one side of the house, and David was to pour the concrete that Friday. When the truck arrived, Tomasz put trash bags over his shoes and joined David in pouring and finishing the concrete until time for evening chores. Since the family wanted to escort him out on their bicycles, something they would not do on *Shabbat*,[21] they encouraged him to stay for the next two nights. He was such a pleasant, helpful, and entertaining guest, and they all were delighted that he liked and appreciated the simple, wholesome foods they prepared.

On *Shabbat*, he asked lots of questions and they shared their understanding of the scriptures with him. He listened intently and shared appropriate things about himself and his travels. He gave them lots of advice, but three things that really stuck out:

1-Since it would be warm weather, take bed sheets sewn together, instead of sleeping bags.
2-A postcard with your picture on it is an appropriate gift and easy to carry on a bicycle.
3-Take a shower every chance you get because you never know when the next one will be.

Early the next morning, the nine of them rode with him a few miles across the ridge to where it dropped off toward the river, David able to rest his hand on the handlebar, but not yet ready to change gears with his left hand. No one really wanted to have to ride back up the long steep hill, so they stopped at the top, wished each other well, and the nine watched as their newest friend, another angel sent from above, rode down and around the curves out of site.

---

[21]Shabbat-Hebrew for 'Sabbath,' from the word, 'to sit' or 'to cease,' occurring from sundown Friday until sundown Saturday.

Chapter 3   Miracles

Training

Three weeks later, David's hand being nearly as good as new, they decided to make a training ride to the grandparents' house 27 miles away on the other side of Cookeville. Not knowing what they might face in Israel, and not having ridden in a big town, they thought it best to push themselves while they were still in safe, familiar territory. They did not think they would ever have to go that far in a day in Israel, but wanted to make sure they could do it, just in case, or to see what their limitations might be.

They started out early in the morning, but had trouble before even getting to the end of their road. Emily had a low tire and something had gone wrong with their pump, so they rode past the brick house to the shop of their Mechanic friend who had custom made pannier racks for some of the bicycles. He aired up her tire and they proceeded on their long journey. They stopped at suitable places approximately every hour along the way and sat down to have a snack. That kept the little ones looking forward to something and broke up the ride into small pieces. As the day wore on, it got extremely hot, which they saw as a blessing. That would help them adjust to the temperatures in Israel and help them better estimate how much water they would need to carry. They later learned that it was the hottest day of the year, and they praised Yah for arranging that just for them.

They perfected their traffic skills and everyone pushed themselves beyond their limits. They finally made it to the grandparents' house just before sundown and were offered a place to spend the night. David went home to care for the animals and came back the next day with a trailer to pick up everyone else. They had succeeded on their training mission and were ready to go on their journey.

The thoughts and recollections of what had brought them to this point of their journey occupied Emily's mind in the hours she was unable to sleep. She marveled at the places her Creator had brought her through on her life's journey so far, and wondered what He had in store for her and the family on this trip. Occasionally, she was able to doze off and sleep for up to half an hour since the shades were kept pulled down as the plane met the rising sun, but never for much longer because of the discomfort she experienced. Briana slept peacefully beside her. David and the children slept in their section of the plane, everyone waking up for breakfast after the shades were pulled up to reveal the light. Though it was only around 1 AM in Tennessee, the sun was shining brightly over the Atlantic Ocean beneath. They enjoyed their breakfast and, like they had with their leftover snacks from the first flight, saved what they did not eat for another meal as they began their descent.

4 – Amsterdam

Wednesday

They arrived in sunny Amsterdam at 11:10 AM, a seven hour difference from their home in Tennessee where it was just past 4 AM. They again waited until last to exit the plane. They did not eat, or even open, much of the food that had been served on the flight, so packed it in their packs and carried it out to eat for lunch. Though they had carefully budgeted for their trip, they were not sure how things would really turn out, nor were they accustomed to being wasteful, so it was second nature for them to take the food with them. As they left the plane, the flight crew cordially said their 'goodbyes' and commented on how well the children did on the flight. They generously gave each of the children a little winged badge and a bottle of water, and gave the parents a one liter bottle of water. The Varelas thanked them for their kindness and walked up the breezeway, discussing what a great blessing the gift of water had been. Since their special bottles were under the plane, they would have had to buy water for their long layover here. They knew the flight attendants probably had no idea they were acting on behalf of the Creator as they fulfilled the need that Emily had recognized the day before.

After stopping at the nearest restroom, they headed straight for the information counter to find out how to insure they could sit together as a family on the flight to Tel Aviv that would depart that evening. The airline personnel typed something into her computer screen and told the family it had been taken care of. As they walked through the airport, the children were excited to see more moving walkways. Emily was in the lead and enjoying the exercise after being cooped up in the plane. She walked on the outside of the moving walk and kept up with the little ones on the conveyer, reminding them to stay to the right side so that others in a bigger hurry could pass. Other travelers often stopped, stared at, and counted the children who were thoroughly enjoying their ride. At the end of each walkway, Emily waited for them to come off and for David and Natanyah in the rear to catch up before walking to the next walkway, where the children would excitedly get on again.

The family reached a special children's play area where they got out the left-over flight meals. They ate lunch while charging batteries for the cell phones and a PDA[22] bought especially for the trip which Emily carried in

---

[22]PDA – Personal Digital Assistant, a small hand-held device that functions much like a basic computer.

Chapter 4   Amsterdam

her fanny pack. She had installed on it a Hebrew-English dictionary, as well as the free Bible program, e-sword[23], which they used daily in their study of the scriptures. The program made available multiple translations of the scriptures, as well as concordances, maps, and other helpful information. Emily had downloaded the *King James Bible*, as well as translations in Hebrew, and Spanish, and *Strong's Concordance* for reference and understanding Hebrew and Greek. They had hoped to use the PDA to send email updates to those praying for them, but never could figure out how to do that, so Byron loaned them his laptop for that purpose.

Besides their two U.S. cell phones, they had two Israeli cell phones that had been loaned to them by a couple from the U.S. who lived part-time in Israel. The woman had been referred to Emily by an online friend from MOMYS. She and Emily's friend were on the same home schooling group. Emily's friend referred her to the Cell Phone Lady for information concerning various things in Israel and remarked once that she considered the woman to be the "Emily" of the home school group. By this, she meant there was a similarity between Emily and her concerning their passion and openness in sharing the scriptures. Emily emailed the woman shortly after the referral, and she and her husband immediately offered to let the Varelas use their cell phones while in Israel. It was an act of openness, trust, and generosity by which the Varelas were awed. They looked forward to meeting them in person while in Israel.

After lunch, they found a tour booth and inquired about things to do in Amsterdam during the several hours of daylight that remained before their final flight. Wanting to make the best use of time, as well as getting as much sunlight and exercise as possible to minimize the effects of jet-lag, they decided to investigate the Anne Frank, which had been mentioned on the flight. Briana, the reader of the family, remembered from a book that Anne was a survivor of some sort. The family proceeded to customs for their entry into Amsterdam.

They passed through and bought tickets for the downtown. Riding out of the airport, they were amazed at the beautiful scenery, but what struck them most was the number of bicycles they saw. There were literally thousands! Many more bicycles than cars. The train slowed as it passed a bicycle parking lot. They had never seen so many bicycles in one place before, and discussed how much better off the residents of Amsterdam would be when bad times hit than most people in the U.S. The Hollanders' mode of transportation did not need fuel and the riders were in much better physical shape to endure the hard times to come.

The family exited the train and proceeded in the general direction of the museum. After walking several blocks, they stopped in front of a sidewalk restaurant as they enjoyed the sights. A taxi approached, but not like any

---

[23]E-sword – free downloadable Bibles in numerous translations, as well as other study tools, maps, concordances, etc.from www.e-sword.net.

they had ever seen before. It was a *bicycle* taxi! Or more accurately, a *tricycle* taxi. The driver rode it like a bicycle, but there was a bench seat behind him which sat over two wheels. The passengers rode on the bench seat. The family watched as it went by and another approached.

Abba Sends Bread and Water

They turned to view the beautiful little restaurant behind them wondering how fancy it must be inside, and marveled at its uniqueness. A waitress came out and asked if the family would like to eat. It looked like it could be rather expensive and it had not been long since lunch, so they declined. She then asked if they wanted some water. David and Emily looked at one another and, not wanting to seem rude, nodded and said, "Yes...please."

Since the water the flight attendants had given them was gone, they would have to buy water somewhere anyway. As the waitress went back inside, Emily turned to David and asked, "I wonder how much the water's going to cost at this place?"

The woman returned shortly with a beautiful thick, dark, glass two-liter bottle of water. David asked her, "How much do I owe you?"

She cheerfully and sincerely responded, "Oh, *nothing*. It's *free!*"

The couple looked at each other in amazement, thanked the waitress and started passing the bottle around so the children could all get a drink. A moment later she returned with a big platter full of freshly-baked rolls and began handing them to the children. Again, David tried to pay, but was refused. So, standing between the restaurant and the street with the bicycles and tricycle taxis rolling by, they enjoyed the large, fresh rolls and water. Again, their Creator had provided their need for water, and even added bread. How blessed they felt to be His children!

A few minutes later, the woman came out again. David gave her the empty bottle and she asked they wanted more. David and Emily both told her 'no', but she insisted and went back in with the bottle, coming right back with another. They were not really thirsty enough to drink all of it, so they filled up the now empty big bottle that the flight attendants had given them. The glass bottle still was not empty, but they tried to give it back to the waitress anyway. She refused and said, "No, you take it with you. You'll need it later."

The parents again thanked her, looking at each other in amazement at the extension of such generosity. Little did they know that this was only the beginning of similar looks they would give each other, wondering why they were the recipients of such acts of kindness.

Chapter 4   Amsterdam

Abba Explains Dorito Shirts

They walked on, admiring the tall box-shaped row houses with steep roofs that sat side-by-side along the streets and the boats that floated down the canals in between. Every few blocks they would again ask where to find the Anne Frank Museum, and after several wrong turns that made more interesting sights available to them, they turned a corner to see a line of people that extended for over half the block. Recognizing the place, they found the end of the line behind dozens of youth wearing orange T-shirts, even brighter than their 'Dorito' shirts. As they neared, Emily, who had been studying Hebrew for several months, recognized the Hebrew letters on their shirts to say 'B'nai Akiva', translated 'Children (or Sons) of Akiva.'

As the line inched up little by little, Emily realized her Hebrew, with which she was beginning to feel quite comfortable, was not as good as she thought. An Israeli woman approached and began speaking with her in Hebrew, asking questions. "Who are you? Are you with a group?"

"No, we are a family," Emily tried to reply, but was surprised when she realized the words had come out in Spanish. Embarrassed, she repeated the phrase in Hebrew.

The woman asked, "Why are you dressed alike?"

She began to explain, but was having great difficulty and continued to accidentally intersperse Spanish with the Hebrew, "We always dress alike when we go out. It makes it easier for us to keep up with one another, for others to know we are together, and it makes laundry easier and ensures we always have nice clothes when we go out, since the ones we wear at the farm get stained and worn."

Wearing orange herself, she asked, "What is the significance of the color?"

Emily replied, still struggling to keep her words in Hebrew, "The orange doesn't mean anything special. It's just the fabric that was on sale when we were ready to make clothes."

The woman patiently listened to Emily as she struggled with Hebrew, not knowing she was the first live person Emily had spoken with in that language. She informed Emily, "In Israel, orange stands for the opposition to the Disengagement; blue stands for it."

The Varelas were unaware that three years previously in Israel, a ribbon war began to be waged as people openly voiced which side of the Palestinian issue they supported. Because Israel is such a tiny country, covering an area of just over 8,000 square miles (around the size of Massachusetts or New Hampshire) and is surrounded on all land sides by Muslim nations, all of which at one time or another have been her enemies, the country constantly maintains a strong defense for its citizenry. When a plan was adopted to separate the Israelis from what was determined by

33

the United Nations to be Palestinian Territory (over one quarter of Israel's land area), which included forcing many Israeli residents in several communities to leave their homes, the country was divided in opinion. The Palestinians, descendants of Biblical Philistines who have antagonized Israel since the time of Abraham around 2,000 BC, continued to be at war with her, even though in modern times they were receiving their utilities, water, fuel and other benefits from Israel.

Prime Minister Ariel Sharon adopted the plan to divide the land of Israel by separating Israelis and Palestinians, giving the Palestinians the Gaza Strip on the west and what is referred to as the 'West Bank'[24] of Judea and Samaria. He removed Israeli military presence from Gaza and ordered all Israelis out of there and from four other communities.[25] The Israeli families in those areas who refused to evacuate had their homes demolished and were forced to get out. Because of the intensity of the issue, people all over the country were divided in opinion. To voice opposition to the Disengagement, many began to wear and display orange ribbons. In response, supporters began to wear and display blue ribbons. The war of ribbons gained momentum, since Israelis are generally a peaceful people, able to stand for their beliefs without crossing the line into violence, and the color orange grew in significance as a symbol of opposition to the Disengagement.

Although the Varelas were only vaguely familiar with the events that had taken place in 2005, and knew nothing of the color war, they found themselves standing here with a group of 200 students wearing bright orange shirts for a reason, and now realized that Emily's choice of such an odd color off the dollar table at the fabric section of the store and the choice to use that color instead of another for this particular trip was actually inspired by their Creator. They were now orange for a reason, and the wearing of the orange would spark dozens of conversations with people who otherwise might have passed them by. They were awed at the incredible way their Creator worked through the tiniest of things to fulfill His purposes. They were humbled at the thought that He watched over them in such unique ways.

Anne Frank House

Armando and Briana were sent to the front of the line to check the cost of admission. They came back reporting that there was a sign on the door with that information which also said that no backpacks were allowed inside. Since David, Armando, and Briana all wore backpacks, someone was going to have to wait outside. It was nap time for Natanyah, and since she was Daddy's girl, David decided to wait with the backpacks and let her

---

[24]West Bank of the Jordan River.

[25]Communities spoken of here are often referred to as 'Settlements,' leaving the incorrect impression that the land does not belong to Israel.

have his ears for a nap. Massaging ears had been her comfort mechanism since infancy, and her parents and siblings obliged her endearing habit. Emily and the six other children made their way slowly in line to the ticket counter. After buying their tickets and entering, they headed straight to the restroom, as was their custom. Emily took the three girls, and Armando took Victor and Moshe. The girls took longer, initiating the family's use of their uniforms as a search and rescue tool.

After using the restroom, Armando helped make sure Victor and Moshe adequately washed their hands. As he washed his own hands, the two younger boys darted out of the restroom, ready to get on with the museum tour. Armando rushed out after them, following them into the first room of the museum, where they excitedly looked at photos and interesting articles.

Upon exiting the restroom and not seeing the boys waiting in the lobby, Emily's heart skipped a beat. She sent Briana to the front door to see if they had stepped back outside where David and Natanyah were watching ducks, paddle boats, and canoes on the canal across the street from the museum, and some men waiting in line who were juggling various objects. Briana brought the negative report back to Mama, who then glanced at the ticket-selling woman watching her. The woman gave a confident nod and pointed toward the inner entrance of the museum. Emily understood the body language and took Isabel and Rebeka by the hands as Briana followed into the next room, where they found the boys. After learning what happened, giving the little boys a good scolding, and regaining her composure, they settled down and watched a short film relating the history of Anne Frank.

They continued through the museum which was the actual house where Anne, as a young girl, and her family had been hidden during the Holocaust. They had lived in a small room in the upstairs of a print shop. The house was now filled with pictures, artifacts, and documentaries of the era, as well as some diaries of Anne Frank and others that touched her life. Emily read the exhibit cards to the little children, while Briana and Armando looked around on their own. She answered lots of questions for them, reminding them that Satan and his angels are now ruling this world, and atrocities like this will continue to occur until Messiah comes back to reign.

As they walked up the very narrow, steep, wooden flight of stairs to the attic where the family had lived, Emily whispered to get the children's attention, "Think about how quietly Anne and her family would've had to have been to protect themselves and their gracious hosts. If they had made noise at the wrong moment, they could have been found out, endangering the lives of everyone. Let's practice being real quiet. Walk quietly up the stairs. Don't let your feet be heard. Shhh. This is good practice. You'll never know when we may be in a situation that we'll need to be quiet to save our lives or the lives of someone else."

The children walked like quiet mice, much to the enjoyment of Mama, who always preferred quiet over noise and order over chaos. They completed the tour of the museum within a couple of hours and stopped at the bookstore. Briana was very interested in several of the books, but Emily explained to her, "Remember that anything we get now has to be packed on the bicycles. We don't have room for anything more than what we brought. We'll have to get a book another time. Maybe we can find one online or even in Israel after we get off the bicycles, toward the end of our time there."

Briana understood and determined to look for the books while in Israel or in the Amsterdam airport on the way back in three months. She was thinking of ways to get a book as they stepped out of the museum where they met David and Natanyah, who had finished her nap and were again watching birds and boats on the little canal, and waving at tourists to keep themselves entertained. The beautiful bottle the lady at the restaurant had given them filled with water was heavy, even when empty. They could not take it with them, but could not stand the thought of throwing it in the trash. It had to be worth something to someone, even if just for a deposit refund. So they left it sitting next to a trash barrel, praying it would be a blessing to someone.

Walking back to the train station, they took in all the new sites as the sun was going down. Emily carried Natanyah in the sling; David carried the #1 backpack that included important documents and Granddaddy's laptop; Armando carried the #2 pack that included copies of the important documents and the activity pouches with pencils, paper, and crayons; and Briana carried the black backpack, which included the leftover airline food and water. At the station, they presented their round trip tickets, took another rest stop, and then boarded the airport-bound train which appeared within a couple of minutes. On the ride back, they enjoyed their final views of Amsterdam's canal streets and row houses from the ground.

5 – Sky Questions

Once inside the airport, David and the children again enjoyed riding the walkways while Emily got her exercise just to the side of them. They checked in and took out more leftover airline food from Briana's pack to eat before boarding the plane. Just as they finished their meal, it was time to go, so they loaded up the packs and stepped onto the 737 which was to leave at 9:10 PM for Tel Aviv. They had been assured earlier that they were seated together, but once aboard, they discovered they had been assigned to the emergency exit rows, and since children were not allowed in those rows, they had to be split up again. It was not so bad this time, though, as they were fairly close to each other and only in two groups. The flight attendants on this full flight were particularly friendly and jovial, which made the experience much better than the flight the night before had been. Everyone got a little sleep and the younger children slept most of the way.

The young woman seated across the aisle from Emily, traveling with an older lady, greeted her. "*Shalom.*"*

"*Shalom,*" Emily responded.

"*Ma shlomech?*'[26]

"*Tov, todah. V'at?*'[27] Emily replied, glad to be able to practice Hebrew before arriving in the Land, and hoping it would come out in Hebrew this time, instead of half Spanish like it had at the museum.

The conversation continued, switching back and forth between Hebrew and English as the need arose for both ladies, "Do you live in Israel?" Emily questioned.

"Yes," the woman replied. "I'm going home with my mother", gesturing to the older lady beside her. "We've been visiting my sister in Amsterdam. Are these children all yours?" she asked.

Emily replied, "Yes."

"You have a beautiful family."

"Thank you. They are all blessings from Elohim."

---

[26]*Ma shlomech?* - Hebrew for 'How are you?' when speaking to a woman.
[27]*Tov todah. V'at?* - Hebrew for 'Fine, thank you, and you?' when answering a woman.

The woman agreed, "Yes, blessed be He!" then asked, "Why do you all wear orange shirts?"

"It's just easier for us to keep up with each other dressed alike, and easier for others to recognize that we're a group."

"That's a good idea. So the orange doesn't stand for anything?"

Emily replied, "No. It's just the fabric we happened to have on hand when we were making clothes for the trip."

"So you didn't know that orange is significant color in Israel?"

"No, we didn't know that until just a few hours ago. We met a woman at the Anne Frank Museum who was with a group of young people wearing orange T-shirts that said 'B'nai Akiva."

"Oh, yes. B'nai Akiva is very outspoken in their opposition to the disengagement."

Emily was digesting all the woman had said, and finding the circumstances intriguing. What were the chances that at a layover and at a museum they had not known existed, they would see a large group of people visiting from the country to which they were traveling? And from that meeting they would learn how widely known it was that the color of shirts the family happened to be wearing stood for opposition to the disengagement?

The family knew it was wrong for governments to give away the land that the Almighty had promised to the children of Israel. They were aware that prophecy spoke against those who would try such things. They had learned years ago that the Palestinians were descendants of the Philistines mentioned in the scriptures. They also knew that most Arab Muslims were descendants of Abraham through Ishmael.[28] Others were descendants of Esau (the twin brother of Jacob/Israel) who had his

---

[28]Ishmael-Abraham's son by Sarah's Egyptian handmaid, making him the half-brother of the promised son, Isaac.

Gen 16:11-12 And the angel of YHWH said unto her, Behold, thou *art* with child, and shalt bear a son, and shalt call his name Ishmael; because YHWH hath heard thy affliction. And he will be a wild man; his hand *will be* against every man, and every man's hand against him; and he shall dwell in the presence of all his brethren.

Gen 17:19-21 And Elohim said, Sarah thy wife shall bear thee a son indeed; and thou shalt call his name Isaac: and I will establish my covenant with him for an everlasting covenant, *and* with his seed after him. And as for Ishmael, I have heard thee: Behold, I have blessed him, and will make him fruitful, and will multiply him exceedingly; twelve princes shall he beget, and I will make him a great nation. But my covenant will I establish with Isaac, which Sarah shall bear unto thee at this set time in the next year.

Chapter 5   Sky Questions

blessing stolen by Jacob and hated him.[29] They did not blame the violence in the Middle East on Arabs or Muslims, but knew that Satan was using them in his game to rule the world and destroy the chosen people of YHWH. And they also knew the game was nearing its end and violence would increase until the time Messiah would return, setting His feet on the Mount of Olives in Jerusalem.[30]

The woman asked, "Are you Jewish?"

Emily smiled and said, "No."

"But your husband and sons wear *tzitziyot*?"[31]

The woman had not noticed that the girls wore tassels or fringes, too, since on this particular outfit, they had tied them in the hems of their skirts in colors matching the skirts, instead of at the waist in all white with only one strand of blue. David and the boys wore theirs in a more traditional Jewish way, except for the strand of blue, which is commanded by scripture, but left out by most modern day Jews.[32]

Emily picked up the fringes at the bottom of her skirt, and said, "Yes, it is commanded in the *torah*. We follow the *torah* the best we understand. We keep *Shabbat*, the feasts, and all of its instructions to the best of our knowledge and ability."

The woman asked again, with a surprised look on her face, "But you're not Jewish?"

"No. The *torah* is for all of the people of Elohim."

Emily pulled out one of the postcards that the family had printed to give

---

[29]Gen. 27:41 And Esau hated Jacob because of the blessing wherewith his father blessed him: and Esau said in his heart, The days of mourning for my father are at hand; then will I slay my brother Jacob.

[30]Zech. 14:4 And his feet shall stand in that day upon the mount of Olives, which *is* before Jerusalem on the east, and the mount of Olives shall cleave in the midst thereof toward the east and toward the west, *and there shall be* a very great valley; and half of the mountain shall remove toward the north, and half of it toward the south.

[31]*Tzitzit*, plural *tzitziyot* – tassles or fringes worn on the four corners of the garment, as instructed in Numbers 15:38-40 and Deut. 22:12.

[32]Num. 15:38-40 Speak unto the children of Israel, and bid them that they make them fringes in the borders of their garments throughout their generations, and that they put upon the fringe of the borders a ribband of blue: And it shall be unto you for a fringe, that ye may look upon it, and remember all the commandments of YHWH, and do them; and that ye seek not after your own heart and your own eyes, after which ye use to go a whoring: That ye may remember, and do all my commandments, and be holy unto your Elohim.

Pedaling Home   Part 1 – In the Beginning

people they met along the way and handed it to her. On the front was a recent family photo and on the back were the two verses written in Hebrew and English:

"But this shall be the covenant that I will make with the house of Israel; After those days, saith YHWH, I will put my law in their inward parts, and write it in their hearts; and will be their Elohim, and they shall be my people. Jeremiah 31:33"

"Say unto them, Thus saith the Master YHWH; Behold, I will take the stick of Joseph, which is in the hand of Ephraim, and the tribes of Israel his fellows, and will put them with him, even with the stick of Judah, and make them one stick, and they shall be one in mine hand. Ezekiel 37:19"

Emily continued, "The Jews are not all of Elohim's people, not all of the children of Israel. Jacob/Israel had 12 sons, and from those 12 sons there were 13 tribes, as both of Joseph's sons were blessed as Israel's own sons.[33] After King Solomon turned away from Elohim to the idols of his foreign wives, the kingdom was divided into two houses, the house of Judah, today's Jews, including the tribes of Judah, Benjamin, and most of Levi, and the house of Israel or Ephraim, the other ten tribes.[34] Ephraim was divorced by YHWH and sent away or scattered into the nations to the point they were unrecognizable as a nation because of their continued idolatry and adopting the worship practices of the pagan nations around them.[35] Almost all of the prophets tell of the latter days when Elohim will take back His people Ephraim/Israel, join them with their brother Judah, and bring them back to the Land.[36] That is what's happening today! The

---

[33] Gen 48:5 And now thy two sons, Ephraim and Manasseh, which were born unto thee in the land of Egypt before I came unto thee into Egypt, *are* mine; as Reuben and Simeon, they shall be mine.

[34] 1Ki 11:31 And he said to Jeroboam, Take thee ten pieces: for thus saith YHWH, the Elohim of Israel, Behold, I will rend the kingdom out of the hand of Solomon, and will give ten tribes to thee:

1Ki 12:20-21 And it came to pass, when all Israel heard that Jeroboam was come again, that they sent and called him unto the congregation, and made him king over all Israel: there was none that followed the house of David, but the tribe of Judah only. And when Rehoboam was come to Jerusalem, he assembled all the house of Judah, with the tribe of Benjamin, an hundred and fourscore thousand chosen men, which were warriors, to fight against the house of Israel, to bring the kingdom again to Rehoboam the son of Solomon.

[35] Jer 3:8 And I saw, when for all the causes whereby backsliding Israel committed adultery I had put her away and given her a bill of divorce; yet her treacherous sister Judah feared not, but went and played the harlot also.

[36] Ezek 37:19-22 Say unto them, Thus saith YHWH Elohim; Behold, I will take the stick of Joseph, which *is* in the hand of Ephraim, and the tribes of Israel his fellows, and will put them with him, *even* with the stick of Judah, and make them one stick, and they shall be one in mine hand. And the sticks whereon thou writest shall be in thine hand before their eyes. And say unto them, Thus saith

Chapter 5   Sky Questions

prophet Jeremiah tells us that Elohim will make a new covenant with the house of Israel, one in which He will write His laws on their hearts.[37] That is why we obey the *torah*. His laws are being written on our hearts."

The woman asked, "So you're not Christian?"

"We believe and live by the entire Bible, the *TaNaK*[38] and the *Brit Chadashah*.[39] But the *Brit Chadashah* never contradicts the *TaNaK*, like most of Christianity and Judaism teach that it does. The word 'Christian' means different things to different people. And many definitions of 'Christian' would not describe at all what we are or believe. It was people calling themselves 'Christian' who carried out the Inquisitions in the Dark Ages. And Hitler referred to himself as a 'Christian.' In the fourth Century AD, the religion of Christianity threw out the feasts of the Almighty that He gave to His people[40] and adopted the pagan festivals that most of them continue to keep. They replaced Sabbath with Sunday worship in honor of the Sun god whom the Roman Emperor at the time worshipped. They made it against Roman law to celebrate the feasts of the Creator, and instituted pagan sun worship festivals, renaming them and giving them Christian meanings. December 25 went from being the celebration of the birth of the sun god to the celebration of the birth of Y'shua,[41] whom they called 'Ieosus.' There is never an account in scripture of YHWH's people having an annual celebration of someone's birth, but it was a pagan tradition that went from being in honor of the sun god to Ieosus. The first Sunday after the first full moon after the spring equinox went from being the celebration of the fertility goddess to being the celebration of the resurrection of Ieosus, but even the name Easter continues to bear

---

YHWH Elohim; Behold, I will take the children of Israel from among the heathen, whither they be gone, and will gather them on every side, and bring them into their own land: And I will make them one nation in the land upon the mountains of Israel; and one king shall be king to them all: and they shall be no more two nations, neither shall they be divided into two kingdoms any more at all:

[37] Jer 31:33 But this *shall be* the covenant that I will make with the house of Israel; After those days, saith YHWH, I will put my law in their inward parts, and write it in their hearts; and will be their Elohim, and they shall be my people.

[38] *TaNaK* - the Hebrew word for the writings which Christianity uses as the 'Old Testament' It is comprised of the letters T, N, and K, which in Hebrew stand for *Torah* - meaning 'instructions' - the first five books of scripture; *Nevi'im* - translated 'prophets'; and *Ketuvim* - translated 'writings' - which include all the other books in the Old Testament.

[39] *Brit Chadashah* - Hebrew for 'Covenant New,' as in the sense of renewed like the new moon is a renewed moon each month. The Hebrew word for 'month' or 'new moon' is '*chodesh*' and is directly related to the word '*chadashah*.' The Brit Chadashah is what Christianity refers to as the New Testament.

[40] Lev. 23

[41] *Y'shua* – Hebrew for 'YHWH's salvation' or 'salvation of YHWH;' the original name of 'Jesus' of the Bible.

witness to the fact that it celebrates the fertility goddess Ishtar. For these reasons, we do not call ourselves 'Christian', though we do believe that Y'shua is the Messiah. Y'shua never went against the *torah*. His disciples never went against the *torah*. And the earliest of his followers, both Jew and non-Jew continued to practice the instructions of the Almighty given in the *torah*. The *Brit Chadashah* clearly reports all of this, but because of misunderstandings and false teachings brought on by tradition, most Christians are unaware of it. It wasn't until the fourth century that the religion of Christianity as we know it today, with its pagan practices, was instituted."

The woman continued, "So you're not Jewish, but you keep the *torah*, and you're not Christian, but you believe in Y'shua?" As Emily nodded, she continued, "Interesting. Very interesting. So why are you coming to Israel?"

"We're coming for Sukkot."

"But that's over two months from now!"

Emily replied, "Yes. It was so expensive to fly the whole family that we worked out a way we could stay for the entire time of the tourist visa, three months. And when we found out I was pregnant, we knew we would have to stick with our plan of arriving early because a few weeks from now until after the baby is born, I wouldn't be permitted to fly overseas."

The woman said, "Staying three months will be expensive. Things are expensive in Israel."

Emily replied, "Yes. We plan to tour the country on bicycles, camping out in various places along the way, anywhere we can find that's free."

"You *all* ride bicycles?"

Emily answered, "All but Natanyah, the two-year-old. She rides in a carrier on the back of my bicycle."

The woman was impressed that even the younger children would be riding bicycles. The topic of conversation turned to her and Emily learned that she was from a *kibbutz* in the south of Israel not far from Gaza. The rockets fired and other forms of violence perpetrated against Israelis by the Palestinians seemed as normal to that woman as hearing deer rifles in the woods during hunting season was to Emily. Emily thought it strange that a threat to one's life by people who harbored genuine hatred could be so easily dismissed. She would soon learn by speaking with many Israelis, that they are so accustomed to terrorist attacks and violence against them that it has become an accepted way of life. Most Israelis continue about their daily lives being grateful for what they have instead of complaining about what they cannot change.

During their conversation, the flight attendant came by serving a snack. The ladies excused each other so they could eat and they never resumed any involved topics, since just afterward, the descent into Tel Aviv began. It was just after 2 AM when the city lights came into view. The plane soon landed and the parents carefully woke the younger children as the older ones helped gather their belongings. Again they were the last to exit the plane and were sent off with blessings from their kind, smiling KLM crew.

Welcome to Israel

Yom Chamishi[42] (Fifth Day of the week, Thursday)

The breezeway in the airport was empty by the time the family got there. The children took full advantage of the opportunity to run back and forth freely without getting in anyone's way. After their usual restroom stop, they continued toward customs and baggage claim; Emily made out the signs in Hebrew as best she could, then looked at the English to check herself.

They reached the visa checkpoint where a female immigration officer sat high up in her enclosed booth with thick glass separating her from anyone in front of her. Her countenance held a forced hard and grouchy look, something the family had encountered at U.S. border crossings between Mexico and Canada, and that David had seen before in Israel as well. It almost seemed as if their official position of authority would not carry any weight if they were to accidentally crack a smile or say a friendly word. Of course, there were exceptions to this rule which they had seen over the years, but they were few and far between.

Since Emily was wearing all nine passports in a carrier which hung from her neck, David had her stand in front of the window to talk to the stoic woman. Being only five feet tall, she bent her head back as far as possible to try to make eye contact with the officer high above in the booth. Emily stood there in ignorance, waiting to answer questions, unaware that she was expected to first hand over the passports, which had been neatly arranged in order of birth. There was a moment of tense silence before the woman barked, "I need to see your passports!"

Emily quickly removed them and handed them to the officer, who had already figured out that the family had not yet earned the label 'world travelers.' The woman took a quick look at the passports and began asking questions.

Officer: How long do you plan to stay in Israel?

Emily: Three months.

---

[42] *Yom Chamishi* - Day Fifth, occurring from sundown Wednesday until sundown Thursday.

Officer: Three *months*?!?

Emily: Yes.

Officer: Why so long?

Emily: We're coming for Sukkot, but it's very expensive to fly the whole family, so we wanted to get the most for our money.

Officer: What about school for the children?

Emily: We home school.

Officer, snorting and rolling her eyes: Home school. Where will you be staying?

Emily: "We'll be riding bicycles and camping out in various places.

Officer, whose expression changed to quizzical, but still disgusted: Who do you know here?

Emily: No one, really. We've met a few people on the Internet.

Officer: So you're coming to Israel for three months and you don't know anyone and have no place to stay?

Emily, as confidently as she could: Well, we have connections we've made on the Internet and we have a tent.

Officer: And how do you intend to support yourselves while you're here? Things are expensive in Israel.

Emily: We've saved and budgeted and have enough for our stay.

The officer then abruptly changed the focus of the interview and started looking over the group of children. She took out a passport and said, "Armando."

Armando was supposed to know that he was to identify himself, but he was also unaware of the procedure. He stood there quietly thinking she was just reading the passports out loud. Emily, still in international ignorance, remained quiet, as well. David, who had traveled more than the rest of the family, remained silent and was just enjoying the show.

The officer barked, "Armando! Who is Armando?!?"

Armando responded and Emily quickly turned to the children and told them to raise their hand and say 'here' when she called their name. They were used to the 'here' routine, since they recently began calling role in the van

Chapter 5   Sky Questions

anytime they went somewhere, after accidentally driving off without Moshe a few weeks before.

Emily remembered the day well. She and the children had intended to take a quick 17 mile trip to the nearest mid-sized town. They jumped in the van in the pouring rain and sped off. Emily drove the quarter mile up the driveway, Armando opened the gate, and they pulled out before Rebeka noticed and announced that Moshe was not there. Armando reopened the gate and Emily began backing down the driveway. About half way to the house, they met Moshe in the downpour, scared and crying from having been left home alone. When questioned he said he had been in the bathroom when they had walked out, and had resumed his car playing in the living room in front of the window when he saw them drive away. He then got scared and ran out and up the drive, planning on catching up with them in town. That was the day the roll call began.

The children were doing well with their newly acquired roll calling skills, but no matter how tall the officer stood on her tiptoes or craned her neck down, she could not see them because of the security of her high booth. David moved all the children about 15 feet back for her ease of viewing. After they had each been identified, the passports were stamped and they were dismissed to baggage claim. Emily breathed a sigh of relief that none of the children had decided to play identity games, which may have raised suspicions and gotten them involved in an international investigation. David just smiled at the whole ordeal and helped herd the children down through the next empty section of the airport.

Before reaching baggage claim, they saw their large boxes going round and round on the conveyer. Most everyone else who had been on their flight was already gone. David knew the little luggage carts would not be big enough to handle more than two or three boxes, and there were 11 in addition to the three backpacks they were wearing, two more backpacks, and the tent. So he was relieved to spot a very large trolley cart in a small alleyway. He sent Armando to get it, but as Armando returned and was about half way up the alley with it, an attendant who had just come in from a smoke break came running toward him yelling something in Hebrew. Seeing Armando going towards David, the man summoned David to the other carts and pointed angrily at a sign written in Hebrew which said something about 100 shekels. David figured out that the cart must have also come with a now very upset attendant. The man continued to chew them out as he called his supervisor. The supervisor, several years older and appearing to have had much more experience, calmed the young man who was trying to get the attention of the nearby police. The supervisor told the attendant to calm down and follow the customers to the conveyers.

By the time they got there, Emily had all of the boxes and packs off of the belt and stacked neatly on the floor. She was keeping an eye on the children and reminding them to keep their fingers out of the belt as they tried to figure out how it worked. They loaded all of the boxes and packs on the large cart and walked right past customs who just nodded at the

Pedaling Home   Part 1 – In the Beginning

attendant. Emily breathed another sigh of relief, and offered a prayer of thanksgiving, as she had dreaded having their boxes torn open again and having to deal with whatever problems might occur from that at 4 AM.

They went on through to the train station, which sat just inside and below the airport. Since Emily could speak some Hebrew, she bought the tickets to Benyamina, where they were to meet their first contact, one they had found through warmshowers.org. Nikolay wrote saying that his apartment was too small for the family but that he, with the help of his mother had lined up a place for their first few nights at *Kibbutz S'dot Yam*, near Caesarea, on the shore of the Mediterranean Sea. That would give the family enough time to reassemble the bicycles and get over jet lag.

With tickets in hand, they began the work of getting all of their things to the area below where they would board the train. The task was complicated by the fact that the cart would not fit through the pylons going into the station area. So all of the boxes and packs had to be unloaded outside the area, pushed and carried several yards to the elevators, loaded in the elevators, unloaded down at the train area, and then grouped together in a place where they could be quickly loaded onto the train, since they would only have about two minutes to load once the train arrived. As Emily got the children geared up for the task of moving boxes and packs, David paid the attendant and gave him a good tip, causing his demeanor to change to one of delight. As he walked away smiling, everyone who was big enough to push a box did. And those were too small to push one by themselves, teamed up behind one box. By the time all was accomplished, it was around 30 minutes before the train was due to arrive, so they got out their airline leftovers and had breakfast.

Just in time for them to finish, get their hands and faces washed and go to the restroom, the train pulled into the station. Their planned strategy went smoothly, as the older children helped get the younger ones onto the split-level train and up the stairs while David and Emily quickly loaded the baggage. The children sat down as the parents continued throwing packs and boxes into the train. Seeing the family with several small children, a couple of Israelis jumped out and helped the parents. They all jumped in seconds before the doors closed and the train moved ahead, frightening six-year-old Isabel, who was unaware that her parents were on board. She was soon relieved to see them at the bottom of the steps. Since there would only be two minutes to unload everyone and everything at Benyamina in a little over an hour, the baggage was taken upstairs, enabling it to be rolled back down quickly just before arrival. While David carried the boxes and packs up, Emily stacked things as nicely as possible out of the way of the aisle in case the train began to fill with passengers from other stops. They had been told that Thursdays were sometimes busy with soldiers relieved of their duties to go home for the weekend.

6 - *HaAretz*[43]

Benyamina by Train

As it turned out, not many people boarded. The ride to Benyamina began at 5 AM and the first light of morning was seen soon after leaving the airport. Emily called Nikolay to let him know they were on their way. Shortly after, they received a call from the father of a family of 10 from Colorado, with children nearly the same ages as the Varela children, who had visited the Varela home a few months before. They had also just arrived in Israel that morning and were wondering if they could meet up and travel with the Varelas. David let him know that they were on their way to a *kibbutz* where they knew no one and would be staying in a tent. They had no way to bring another family along, nor did they have any idea where another family could stay. They visited shortly, as the train continued north. The younger children fell asleep and the others enjoyed the scenery from the train windows. When they passed through the town of *Netanyah*, Emily made the announcement so they could all see the town that shared the meaning of Natanyah's name, gift of Yah.

The sun was near to rising when the train reached Benyamina. David had asked a gentleman who spoke English which side of the train they would need to exit so they could have their things in place at the door. They rolled the boxes down the stairs and had them waiting on the west side when the train stopped. Briana took the little ones, as the kind gentleman helped David and Armando throw the boxes off during the quick two minute stop before the train would take off again. Emily counted to make sure they had everyone and everything; the doors shut, and the train quickly pulled out of the station.

The little family stood and looked around, trying to figure out the best way to proceed. The tracks were several feet below the sidewalk and separated the family from the station where they were to meet Nikolay. They were at least 50 yards from the elevator that would take them to an enclosed walkway bridge above the tracks. After reaching the elevator, they would have to cross over the tracks, ride another elevator down on the other side, and come back the distance to the station. It looked like quite a job, but they did not see any alternative, so off they went, carrying, rolling, and pushing boxes, while keeping children a safe distance from where the sidewalk dropped off onto the tracks.

---

[43] *HaAretz* – Hebrew for 'the Land,' specifically referring to the Promised Land.

As they worked, getting the boxes to point 'A' - the elevator to go up, Emily's phone rang. She answered to hear Nikolay, "Did you get off at Benyamina?" he asked in Russian accented English.

"Yes, Emily replied. We're here."

"I don't see you."

"Oh, we're here by the elevator across the tracks. We have a lot of things to move. It will take us a little while."

"OK. I would come to help you, but am not allowed to cross the gate without a ticket."

"It's no problem. We're getting things moved. It just takes a while. It's normal for us," she said, smiling.

But after waiting a little longer, then seeing the young family with the mountain of boxes, Nikolay got permission from the station attendant to jump the barrier and go to their aide. They had made it onto and up the first elevator to point 'B,' then off and across the tracks by way of the enclosed bridge to point 'C'- the second elevator; down to point 'D,' and were beginning their final trek to point 'E'- the station house. Nikolay quickly met the family and jumped in by helping to carry the heavier boxes.

They went through the station to the taxis waiting outside under palm trees. The drivers were happy to do their job in transporting adults, but their countenances changed when they saw how many children and boxes there were. Nikolay did his best to negotiate a decent price, but more importantly, to convince them to even *transport* the family and their things. The Varelas observed as the drivers' voices raised and the discussion got more interesting. Finally, Nikolay offered to stuff all of the boxes that could possibly fit into his small Suzuki Swift car. That only left the backpacks and a couple of boxes to put into each of two taxis.

Then began the quick, heated discussion concerning how many children were allowed to ride in each car. The drivers said no more than three in each back seat and none in the front. So, finally (which is just a few seconds later when speaking the language of taxi drivers), it was decided that Armando could ride in the front of one car, since he was nearing *bar mitzvah*[44] age.

Emily put Rebeka, Moshe, and Natanyah in the back seat of the first taxi and was trying to get them in seat belts, as the extremely impatient driver ordered her in Hebrew to hurry up and get in. His tone and body language would have been understood in any language. Armando got in the front

---

[44]*Bar mitzvah* - Hebrew for 'son of the commandment' and is a rite of passage for young men, usually at 13 years of age.

seat of the other taxi and Briana, Victor, and Isabel got in the back. David got in the front of Nikolay's car and then Nikolay stuffed the last box into his lap, till it fit much like an inflated air-bag would have. The taxi drivers drove like madmen the few miles to *S'dot Yam*, as their passengers held on to whatever was available. Emily was thinking that now would be a good time to be wearing their bicycle helmets. Victor, in the second taxi, was having the ride of his life. He could barely suppress the giant grin that kept trying to envelope his face as the taxi whizzed around curves and made sudden take-offs and stops. He had ridden a bumper car once as a small child, and decided this was the more fulfilling experience.

Emily tried to visit with her driver, who was not at all impressed by her elementary Hebrew. All she could make him out saying was something about the Polish man, apparently speaking about Nikolay, who was Latvian, not Polish. And by his tone and facial expression, she decided that he did not think much of their negotiator. So she gave up communicating and just listened, as he put his phone on 'speaker' and called another taxi driver. She held on tightly, while glancing back occasionally to remind Natanyah (who was used to being strapped in a car seat) to stay sitting. Natanyah really wanted to stand to see where they were going. The driver, too, kept glancing back, not accustomed to having small children in the back seat of his taxi without an adult.

David and Nikolay briefly discussed the trip so far and how difficult the taxi drivers had been. Nikolay then told David, "My mother has arranged a place for you to camp in *S'dot Yam* near the beach. She is waiting for you at the *kibbutz*."

David's view was limited to a small area on his right side, since he could not turn his head. The box was jammed between his legs and the top of the car; between his chest and the dash. He tried to express his appreciation to Nikolay for the arrangements he had made for them and for getting them a ride to their first destination. He listened as Nikolay pointed out sites of interest, including Caesarea, along the way.

The first taxi pulled up to the guard gate and a gray-haired gentleman stepped out and asked in Hebrew what business they had there. Emily tried to tell him that the family had been given permission to camp there for a few days, but communication was slow and the driver did not have enough patience to endure that. Finally, the gate man waved the driver into a parking lot just inside the gate that was secured partially by metal spikes in the road, mumbling something about the woman not being able to speak Hebrew. Emily got the children out of the taxi and watched them as the driver unloaded the boxes. The taxi with Armando in the front seat drove up and unloaded, and after a few minutes Nikolay and David, who were not in as big of a hurry, arrived. David paid the drivers, giving them a little extra for their aggravation, and they sped away. With Nikolay there, the gate man was able to understand what was going on and after calling the *Kibbutz* Chief, told Nikolay where to take the family.

Kibbutz S'dot Yam

About that time, Nikolay's mother, a fit woman in her late fifties, rode up on her bicycle from the nearby town of Or Akiva. She and Emily attempted communication while Nikolay drove David around the many pomegranate, olive, fig, and date palm trees to a grassy area, which the Varelas would later find out was between the Caesarea Museum and an art shop. After Nikolay pried the large box out from between the dash, windshield, and David's lap, the two men unloaded the other boxes. David stayed with those boxes while Nikolay went back to the *kibbutz* gate and picked up the rest of the family and their things. He was in a hurry to get to work in Haifa, so he left them with his mother and took off, leaving the family in a little chunk of paradise, from where they could see the Mediterranean beach only a hundred yards in the distance. They prayed prayers of thanksgiving for safety in travel for such a beautiful and secure place to stay, and for their gracious host, who had already gone above and beyond what they could have expected of him.

Nikolay's mother, Polia, and Emily were able to communicate some. Polia asked in Hebrew, "Would you like to take a tour of the *kibbutz*?"

Emily replied, "Thank you for the offer! We would love to, but right now we should probably get some things unpacked so we can get our camp set up. But would you point us in the direction of a market where we can get some food for lunch?"

Polia was delighted. "I'll show you where the store and cafeteria are!"

Jet lagged, some of the children were already tired and ready for a nap, so Emily stayed at the campsite while David, Armando, and Briana went with their escort to the market, watching as she pointed and gestured at interesting things along the way. Her first and second languages were Russian and Hebrew. David's were Spanish and English. Neither Polia nor David were especially talkative people, anyway, so there was nothing lacking in their communication. Armando and Briana talked with each other, admiring the beautiful pomegranate trees and discussing the thrill of the recent taxi ride.

At the market, they bought fresh whole wheat bread and pitas, hummus, and several types of fresh fruits and vegetables. Polia showed them the *kibbutz* restaurant above the market and brought them back around on a little road from where they could see more of the beach. When they returned, Emily had already begun unpacking and sorting the contents of the boxes as she kept the younger children occupied with left over snacks from the airlines. She had all of the boxes labeled, and was opening them beginning with the number one box and the one containing the tools. She had carefully laid things out in an efficient order so that David could easily begin putting the first bicycle together. She was surprised and very thankful to find minimal damage and loss to their things, in spite of the

Chapter 6   *HaAretz*

treatment they got at the airlines. There were no damaged spokes, and it appeared that everything of real importance was still there.

The family sat down on the lawn facing the beach to eat lunch. The children could hardly wait to go to the beach and get in the water. The parents assured them they could go later in the day, but that things needed to be done in order. First was lunch, then scripture time (which was usually done after breakfast), then getting their camp set up. After work was finished, it would be play time. During their meal, the tall, thin Kibbutz Chief rode up on his scooter. The family watched as a woman came out of the nearby shop and, with the same tone, volume, and facial expression of the taxi drivers, confronted him about something, while he responded calmly with a smile in his South African Hebrew. It seemed there had been some miscommunication and the people who ran the museum and shop were not happy with what may have appeared to them to be vagabonds setting up camp in their territory. The Kibbutz Chief told the family, "It would be good for you to move across the street to the school yard. There's a nice place there in the shade, and you'll be welcome to use the kitchen and bathrooms there, including showers. But you'll need to wait here until school is out in a little while."

The family was not sure if they had been kicked out of their first home already or just been asked to leave because people were concerned about bathroom facilities and wanted them to have a better place. They were prepared to deal with personal issues on their own, with their buckets, bathing supplies, and large tent, but were grateful for such a kind offer from the kibbutz. They visited with the Chief for a few more minutes before he left them to finish their early lunch.

After scripture time, David started putting together the first bicycle; Emily and the children set up the tent so there would be a shady place for them to take a nap. Since it was early August, it was getting hot already, even though it was only mid-morning. Natanyah, Moshe, and Rebeka were soon asleep in the tent and Emily began repacking everything that she had so nicely laid out so that it could be moved to their new home more easily once the school children were dismissed. They were disappointed that they had already seemingly caused problems for people in Israel, since it was their intent from the beginning to be a blessing wherever they went and never to be a burden. The Kibbutz Chief had assured them everything was all right and that it had been a misunderstanding within the kibbutz, but they were disappointed none the less and resolved to make up for it any way they could. The other children finished their lunch, ate nuts from the airlines that were still in their packs, and picked up figs from under the nearby centuries-old tree, as they watched the kibbutz preschool teachers walking toward the beach with their classes for a stroll. The babies rode in big cribs on wheels and the toddlers picked up trash as they walked, keeping the kibbutz very neat and clean.

David got his bicycle and Emily's assembled and was then ready to take a break. Emily got everything cleaned up and hidden behind the tent so that it would not be any more of an eyesore than it had to be. Then she and David got their bed mats out and took a nap outside in the shade of the tent, since the tent was full of children sleeping in various positions. It was extremely hot now, but outside they could feel the ocean breeze. They all slept hard for around two hours, then began to get up, still groggy from jet lag.

Briana emerged from the hot tent, still partially asleep and rubbing her eyes. "You told us you were going to take us to the beach!" she said in an aggravated tone.

David replied, "We're planning to. We just have to get the work done first."

"But you told us you were going to take us *yesterday*!" she returned, still waking up.

David and Emily realized she was so tired that she thought she'd been asleep all night. The jet lag was difficult for all of them, but affected each of them differently. The others woke up and came out, some sweating, and sat in the shade while the parents, Armando and Briana prepared to move things to the schoolyard. Emily was glad they had made the decision to refrain from using air conditioning at home that year to help prepare them for the hot conditions they would face here. Besides being more accustomed to the heat, everyone in the family had learned that it is, indeed, possible to sleep while you sweat. Emily had been horrified at the thought of being 7-9 months pregnant in Israel, riding bicycles and sleeping in a tent after having come from an air conditioned home, so she pleaded with David to have them refrain from turning it on when it warmed up that year. Instead, they kept the windows opened and enjoyed the fresh air, even as the temperatures got hot.

They decided to move the tent first, and instead of tearing it down, just picked it up and carried it through the trees and across the street, where they placed it under a big shade tree in the schoolyard. They came back to get other things when Yosef, a pleasant gentleman in his 60's, walked over to make sure everything was going well with the family. He saw them loading up things on the bicycles to move and insisted that they use a wheelbarrow.

David answered, "Thank you. But we're fine like this. We'll be finished in a few minutes."

Chapter 6   *HaAretz*

"No. I bring wheelbarrow!" he declared with a big smile.

He left and quickly returned with his wheelbarrow, a converted baby doll stroller. He insisted that they use it and left it there with them. They were tickled with their 'Israeli wheelbarrow.' It wasn't heavy duty enough to carry much of their bulky equipment, but made for great entertainment for Moshe and Victor, who used it to haul little things to their new site.

Emily unpacked everything again and sorted it into little piles and stacks under the canopy of the school. They had already been invited by several people to the beach, so thought now would be a good time to go. The shore was just on the other side of the shop from where they had first set up. It was the most beautiful any of them had ever seen. They had not been to many beaches, but had been in the Gulf of Mexico, and Emily had been to the coast of South Carolina. The beach here was very clean and the waves were great fun. Natanyah enjoyed standing at the edge of the water on the wet sand and running back as the water came closer, squealing about the water chasing her. She would then follow the water as it went back out to sea and run back in with the next wave. The children all enjoyed finding various types of pretty shells.

Beach Questions

Many people on the beach came and spoke to them, asking questions that would become typical of those asked the entire time the family was in the Land – things like whether the children were all theirs, why they dressed alike, where they were from, what they were doing in Israel, etc. They gave out several of their postcards and answered more questions.

A woman with a baby approached Emily and began talking to her. After typical greetings, she asked, "Are you Christian?"

Emily replied, "We believe Y'shua is the promised Messiah, but we don't practice the religion of Christianity."

The woman was excited to meet a family that believed in Y'shua as Messiah, as she did. "So are you Messianic Jews?"

"We're not Jewish that we know of."

The woman explained, "My husband is Jewish, but not a believer in Y'shua. He attends Sunday church with me, and I attend synagogue with him, but neither of us is willing to convert to the other's religion."

"That is so exciting!" exclaimed Emily. "If the gospel were presented from the perspective of a first-century believer, rather than from the perspective of the modern, or post fourth-century church, you would be much more unified, and it would not take long before your husband would see that Y'shua is, indeed, the Messiah. His first coming fulfilled the prophecies of what the Jews refer to as 'Messiah ben Yoseph', the suffering Servant, and his second coming will fulfill the prophecies of what the Jews refer to as 'Messiah ben David', the conquering King. There is nothing about Him that contradicts the *TaNaK*. For a Jewish person to accept a Messiah who approved of such pagan things as Christmas, Easter, and the forsaking of the seventh day Sabbath set up at Creation by the Almighty, would be going against the *torah*, the instructions of the Almighty, and be in direct violation of His words!"[45]

After more questions and discussion, the woman left, excited and encouraged by what she had heard, and left with hope for their future unity of belief, where each embraced the truth held by the other and discarded the extra baggage of religion that they both carried. And Emily was excited to have been used to share the information with her.

S'dot Yam Hospitality

An hour before the sun disappeared on the horizon of the Mediterranean, the Kibbutz Chief came to the beach looking for them. In his gentle, friendly manner he said, "Ah, I thought I would find you here. How do you like the beach?"

"It's beautiful," the parents replied.

"And how do you like the kibbutz?"

"It is wonderful! We are so grateful for you all giving us a place to stay here, not even knowing us! And the people here are so friendly!" Emily exclaimed.

"I am glad you like it here. I left a basket at your tent, just a few pieces of fruit for you to enjoy."

The couple was awed at the kindness of their host. "Thank you very much! That is so kind of you!" Emily said, as David nodded in agreement.

The Chief sincerely replied that it was nothing, then turned to go home. The family left, as well, so they could get the salt washed off, get supper,

---

[45]Deut 13:1-4 If there arise among you a prophet, or a dreamer of dreams, and giveth thee a sign or a wonder, And the sign or the wonder come to pass, whereof he spake unto thee, saying, Let us go after other gods, which thou hast not known, and let us serve them; Thou shalt not hearken unto the words of that prophet, or that dreamer of dreams: for YHWH your Elohim proveth you, to know whether ye love YHWH your God with all your heart and with all your soul. Ye shall walk after YHWH your Elohim, and fear him, and keep his commandments, and obey his voice, and ye shall serve him, and cleave unto him.

Chapter 6   *HaAretz*

and get to bed by nightfall. They slowly walked back to the tent, letting Natanyah set the pace, while the other children found treasures of pretty shells and rocks along the way. The older ones admired the many strange-looking birds they had never seen in the Americas. Just before arriving at the tent, Briana and Emily saw an anteater cross a playground area and head for some bushes by a nearby fence. Upon arriving at the tent they found, not the small basket of fruit they had envisioned, but a very large plastic grocery tote overflowing with fruits, vegetables, canned fish, olives, crackers, and cookies, much more than one meal's worth for the family. They were awed that the community not only allowed them to stay on the property, but had given them such a warm, generous welcome.

After washing, sitting down for pitas with hummus and fresh veggies (saving the fish and crackers for *Shabbat*), they laid out their bed mats and sheets and had their evening scripture reading. They had a special time of prayer of thanksgiving for all of the people they met that day and their needs, and the children fell into a deep sleep. The Kibbutz Chief had invited them to sleep and cook inside the schoolhouse, but they declined, knowing it was much easier and more relaxing with so many little ones, to stay in their own territory than to be responsible for the things of others.

Yom Shishi[46] (Sixth Day of the week, Friday)

Since creation, sunset had marked the beginning of a new day, and Israel continued with that reckoning of time. As darkness fell, David remembered the Kibbutz Chief saying that the family was welcome to use the hot and cold water machine in the school. Emily had brought along some teas, so they enjoyed a cup together before bedtime, something they rarely did at home. They talked over the events of the day and how they saw the Creator's hand in so many things already. After enjoying watching the waxing moon set over the sea they joined their little ones in the tent to get rested for the next day's activities.

After a peaceful night's sleep, David and Emily awoke to the quiet of early morning in the little kibbutz. David began putting more bicycles together under the covered area of the school porch, as Emily packed things into their appropriate bicycle panniers. The children awoke one by one and came over to help. After everyone was awake, they ate fruit and more pitas and hummus as they marveled at the number of stray cats in the area who were obviously wild, but well-fed and healthy, though one black one was missing a leg. They would soon get accustomed to seeing hundreds of cats, but rarely a stray dog.

They all changed into their other set of clothes so they could wash what they had worn on the trip. Because every ounce on the bicycles would count, they brought only three sets of everyday clothes and planned to

---

[46]*Yom Shishi* - Day Sixth, occurring from sundown Thursday until sundown Friday.

wear only two of them, each for two days before changing, to prevent having to wash every day. The extra set would be used when they were unable to wash for longer than two days, or in case one of their outfits became unusable due to wear. They also brought along clothes to wear only on *Shabbat*, a family tradition they had begun a few years before.

Today's clothes were Kelly green tunics for everyone with fringes on the four corners.[47] The boys wore jeans and the girls wore skirts checkered with green, blue, and yellow. The outfits had been their *Shabbat* clothes since *Yom Teruah*[48] in autumn of the previous year, so had been worn many times but only lightly, since on *Shabbat* they did not do the same rough activities they did during the rest of the week. These clothes had been chosen for the trip because they were very lightweight. Emily added suspenders to the girls' skirts to keep them from being pulled down while riding. They had been told weeks before that green was a color representing the religion of Islam. After learning the significance of the orange shirts, they wondered what the Almighty had in store for them wearing their green. They reasoned that even if the color suggested Islam, the obvious Jewish-styled tassels would identify them with Israel.

Tzitziyot

The family had begun wearing tassels, or *tzitziyot* several years before after a friend had taught them how to tie them in the manner of the Jews. The number of knots tied was to equal 613, the number of commandments the rabbis had numbered in the *torah*. Wearing tzitziyot had given the family many opportunities to share their testimony with people in the States. After a few years, they began tying them in different ways, since the scriptures did not specify how they were to be tied. And they had experimented with attaching them in different ways and in different places in order to more accurately obey the command, having found through the years that the closer they followed the Almighty's commands, the more they came to understand Him and His ways and the more blessings they saw in their lives.

On the few occasions they had been around Jewish people, unlike

---

[47]Num 15:38-40 Speak unto the children of Israel, and bid them that they make them fringes in the borders of their garments throughout their generations, and that they put upon the fringe of the borders a ribband of blue: And it shall be unto you for a fringe, that ye may look upon it, and remember all the commandments of YHWH, and do them; and that ye seek not after your own heart and your own eyes, after which ye use to go a whoring: That ye may remember, and do all my commandments, and be holy unto your **Elohim**.
Deut. 22:12 Thou shalt make thee fringes upon the four quarters of thy vesture, wherewith thou coverest *thyself.*
[48]*Yom Teruah* - Hebrew for 'day of noise or blasts', referring to the Feast of Trumpets.

Chapter 6   *HaAretz*

Christians who would ask what the fringes were, the Jews would recognize them and begin a conversation, assuming the family was Jewish. In either case, it gave them many chances to share the scriptures with others. With Christians, they shared the purpose of the wearing of the *tzitziyot* and were also able to share examples in both testaments,[49] which were not obvious to most people who did not wear them themselves, including the prophecy concerning the end times and the regathering of the two houses of Israel.[50]

The Jews would most often begin by pointing out the blue cord in the *tzitziyot*. Most Rabbinic Jews,[51] those who follow the traditions of the rabbis, which included most in the religion of Judaism, did not wear the blue cord. They were taught that the particular color commanded came from a Murex snail, which once thought to be extinct, had only recently been found to exist in the deep waters of the Mediterranean Sea. The Varelas had come to a different conclusion in their studies, finding that it was highly likely that the blue used was from the plant-based dye, indigo, which would have been much more widely available throughout history. They found that the *Karaite* Jews also wore a strand of blue in their *tzitziyot*. *Karaites*, like the Varelas, were 'scripturalists,' meaning that they rejected the traditions of the religion of Judaism and followed the scriptures alone, just as the Varelas rejected the traditions of Christianity to follow only the scriptures. Except for the fact that to be a *Karaite* Jew one could not accept Y'shua as the Messiah, the Varelas found that many of their beliefs and practices were the same, desiring to obey the scriptures as written, and rejecting the oral *torah*[52] which is based on tradition.

There was a third group of people who would be attracted to the family because of their wearing of the *tzitziyot*. Those were comrades or brethren

---

[49] Ruth 3:9 Ruth asks to be covered by the skirt of Boaz; 1 Sam. 15:27 Saul tears the robe of Samuel; 1 Sam 24:4-11 David cuts Saul's robe; Matt 9:20 Woman with issue of blood touches the hem of Y'shua's garment; Matt 14"36 Many people desired to only touch the hem of Y'shua's garment for healing. In all of these cases, the part of the garment spoken of is where the *tzitziyot* were to be worn. They are not only an identifying mark of YHWH's commandment-keeping people, but have traditionally been viewed as a symbol of power, as in the case of Saul and Y'shua.

[50] Zech 8:23 Thus saith the LORD of hosts; In those days *it shall come to pass*, that ten men shall take hold out of all languages of the nations, even shall take hold of the skirt of him that is a Jew, saying, We will go with you: for we have heard *that* Elohim *is* with you.

[51] Rabbinic Jews - those who follow the interpretations of the rabbis as opposed to the simple reading of scripture when there is a discrepancy, comprising most practicing Jews today.

[52] Oral *torah* - the body of regulations followed by Rabbinic Jews and included in the Talmud, a book containing writings from the third to sixth centuries A.D. It is said to have been passed down by Moshe (Moses), however, many of the rulings and traditions contained therein are opinions of rabbis from thousands of years later, some of which contradict the written scriptures.

Pedaling Home   Part 1 – In the Beginning

who, like the Varelas, followed the instructions in both testaments of the scriptures. Many times they had met others like-minded in belief because of their wearing of the fringes and had been presented opportunities that could only have come from their Father in heaven

Emily got out the two special buckets with tight-sealing lids. They had hired the Mechanic to make special racks for her bicycle, enabling her to carry them at the rear under Natanyah's seat. One contained the laundry supplies-soap, line, and clothespins, and the other was left empty for emergency use. Both buckets were brought for washing clothes, but the emergency bucket would also be used for other purposes, mainly an emergency toilet, after which it would be carefully scrubbed so as not to contaminate clothing being washed. Living on bicycles, everything possible had to be multifunctional, and all emergencies needed to be prepared for ahead of time. Armando helped David assemble bicycles as Briana, Isabel, and Rebeka helped Emily with laundry. Victor, Moshe, and Natanyah went back and forth between jobs, depending on which was more interesting to them at the moment. Since it was hot and laundry involved water, Emily got more help than she would have on a cooler day.

Nikolay rode in on his folding bicycle after having caught a ride on the train from Haifa to Benyamina that morning. He came to take David to the bicycle shop in nearby Or Akiva because Polia had learned the day before that the S'dot Yam shop was closed while its owner was on vacation. They needed to get some parts and have some repairs done because of things that had been damaged in transit. David took off with him, going at a much faster pace than when riding with the little family, as Nikolay was an avid cyclist and in very good shape. Nikolay pointed out interesting sites as they passed Caesarea, and soon after, David began having trouble with one of his wheels. He told Nikolay to go on, since he had gone the extra mile in so many ways, and confident that the map he had drawn for them would get them to the shop the day they would leave S'dot Yam. David thanked him again and Nikolay rode the 10 miles to Benyamina to catch the train back to Haifa. David repaired the wheel the best he could and hobbled back to the tent in S'dot Yam on his crippled bicycle.

School convened at the schoolhouse, but only lasted until noon, since it was preparation day. A temporary Spanish-speaker teacher from Argentina visited for quite some time with the couple. She was very interested in the family's purpose for being in Israel. The school children and the Varela children watched each other from a distance, but did not make contact; shyness and language barriers on both sides prevented it.

David got bicycles put together for Armando, Briana, and Isabel. He had some trouble with Victor's, which had suffered a little damage by handlers, though not enough to keep it from being ridden to the shop. The family went back to the market to buy more food for Shabbat, then got showers in the schoolhouse and settled down for a peaceful evening. The ground outside the tent was bare dirt and sand, so Emily took some of the boxes that had contained their supplies and broke them down into huge mats,

58

Chapter 6   *HaAretz*

laying them outside the tent door to keep as much sand out as possible. Polia came by bringing watermelon and other goodies. "Would you like for me to give you a tour of Caesarea?" she asked in Hebrew.

"That would be wonderful!" Emily replied.

"I will be back tomorrow. I care for a man with special needs on *Shabbat*. I can take you to Caesarea on first day."

"Great! We look forward to seeing you again. You've been so kind!"

David phoned another man they had met on warmshowers.org, and had spoken with via Skype before leaving the U.S., who said he would come sometime the next day, as well.

Shabbat in the Schoolyard

Shabbat (Sabbath)

As the sun set, the family welcomed in a peaceful *Shabbat*, void of the hustle and bustle that continues on after sunset on Friday in the U.S.. It was truly a blessed, restful, peaceful experience for them, as every *Shabbat* in the land for the next three months would prove to be. David walked down the road to a little synagogue that he learned of, but was not aware of what time things started or what would go on there, as he had never attended synagogue before. Since he did not see anyone, he came back and had a time of singing and worship with his little family. Afterward, he and Emily enjoyed another evening cup of tea.

Emily woke up *Shabbat* morning to see the three-legged black cat leaping off of the table where some of their food was stored in the Kibbutz Chief's grocery tote. Upon inspection, she found that the expert thief had somehow managed to extract a package of pitas from beneath all of the fruits and vegetables that were on top, and had finished it off, leaving the wrapper strewn in a nearby bush. She was a little disappointed that the loss would make them short of bread for supper, but figured the cat needed it and that either *Abba* would provide bread for the evening meal or that they would not be hurt from fasting from bread for a short time. They had plenty of fruits and vegetables and had saved the fish, as well as the sweets, which the family was accustomed to eating only on *Shabbat*.

After everyone was up, they carried out their weekly tradition of donning special clothes for *Shabbat*. This time was extra special, as they had brand new outfits to wear which Emily's mother had made just before the trip. She took great care in her efforts to please whomever she was serving, and they were all delighted with their beautiful new outfits. The shirts for everyone were a bold turquoise color made of very soft stretchable cotton fabric. The skirts were a purple, lilac, and turquoise batik with suspenders, and Emily's had a bib, as well. The boys wore new black denim Amish-style pants that their friends in the horse-and-buggy community had made for them. David had a new black pair of jeans. They said a special prayer of thanks for and blessings on the grandparents and friends before going on with their *Shabbat* activities.

The family sat down at a little table under the tree across from the one that shaded their tent and had a breakfast of fruit, pitas, and hummus. Then they had a time of study in the scriptures, and worship through singing and prayer. Afterward, it was time for lunch and then a nap for anyone who needed it. Usually it was just Natanyah and Emily, but this time, everyone took advantage of nap time. Afterward, the warmshowers.org contact and his friend, Sheila, came with maps of Israel and visited for a couple of hours. David asked, "How did you find us? We've moved from where the gate man knew we would be staying."

"We just walked around until we saw the big tent," he replied in slightly accented Hebrew.

As they talked, the Varelas gleaned more from them about the Jewish people and the land of Israel, glad to have a relaxing time visiting with more warm, generous Israelis. During their visit, Polia rode in on her bicycle bringing more food which included a loaf of bread! They now had bread for supper! David and Emily looked at each other, in awe once again, of how the Almighty provides for all needs, no matter how small. Emily and Polia agreed that the tour of Caesarea would be for the next day. After all of the guests left, the Varelas went to the beach to walk at the edge of the water and relax for the final hour of *Shabbat*. When they got there, they talked about how this area may have been close to where Jonah was vomited out by the big fish when he tried to run from YHWH and the instructions that he was given to warn the people of Nineveh of the judgment that was coming if they did not repent.[53] They discussed the importance of obedience to the Creator no matter what He says to do and no matter how bad the outcome might look, but that, unlike Jonah, a good attitude should always accompany obedience.

---

[53]Biblical book of Jonah

7 – Caesarea

Week 1	*Yom Rishon*[54](First Day)	8/9-10

Just after sundown, they went back to the tent and ate supper, praising *Abba* once again for providing the bread for their meal, and for all of the other food, most of which had been gifts from people they had met in the past two days. That day began their tradition of praying for and asking blessings on everyone who blessed them with something along their way. They would soon have quite a long list. David found the Kibbutz Chief and told him of a couple of problems they had with the bicycles, asking if it would be all right for the family to stay an extra night. He wanted to be sure that if permission was not granted, the family could leave early enough to get somewhere safely for the next night. But the Chief graciously extended the stay to include the next night, which was quite a relief for both David and Emily, as they preferred to get on the road as early as possible the morning that they would leave.

After putting the children to bed, they again made tea and sat up enjoying some quiet conversation. Not long after lying down, they realized this night would not be as peaceful. The house nearest the tent began blasting loud music, which lasted till around 2 AM. The couple, not able to sleep, took advantage of more chat time, thankful that the children's rest was not affected.

Early morning *Yom Rishon* was as quiet as *Shabbat* had been, but very soon began to fill with the business of children and adults going to school and work. Unlike *Yom Shishi*, which was a no-work and no-school day for many, *Yom Rishon* was life as usual again. The family talked about how much more sensible it was that the 'weekend' in Israel was actually the end of the week, the sixth and seventh days, instead of the last day of one week and the first of the next, as it is in most other places.

David put Rebeka's and Moshe's bicycles together and Emily finished packing and loading the panniers onto all of the bicycles. Meanwhile, Armando and Briana found big brooms and swept the long sidewalk from between the shop and museum and around behind the museum, between it and the schoolyard. It had been filled with litter from the trees overhead, and they hoped this small gesture would be appreciated by the shop and museum owners who had seemed less than jubilant about their arrival.

---

[54] *Yom Rishon* – Day first; occurs from sundown on Saturday to sundown Sunday.

They decided to eat lunch at the kibbutz restaurant to show support to the community for allowing them to stay. They strolled the five minute walk, then went up the stairs over the market to a huge high-ceiling room that could seat several hundred people. There was a very large buffet with all kinds of wholesome fruits, vegetables, breads, and a few meat and fish selections. The family started at one end of the covered buffet and filled their plates as birds flew from beam to beam overhead and perched wherever they chose. Emily thought how different that was than in the U.S., where the Department of Health would shut the place down for having a live bird, yet would have allowed on the buffet over-processed, low-nutrient, non-food items, many of which are poisonous to humans. Here they ate wholesome, nutritious food, in an atmosphere peaceful enough for birds to feel at home.

Several people came to their table, greeting and asking the usual questions. They gladly answered and gave them postcards with the picture and scriptures on them. When Emily went to pay, the female cashier spoke with her for quite some time. The bill was more than they had expected, but was a confirmation that they had made the correct decision while developing their budget not to eat out often. They stopped downstairs and bought more whole wheat pitas, hummus, fruits and vegetables for the evening meal and to take the next day as they rode out. On the way back, they met Polia, who was ready to take them to Caesarea. They walked together back to the tent, where Emily was sure to secure the bread from stray cats. Then they walked back towards Caesarea, as they passed ancient pillars and parts of columns that had survived for over 2,000 years.

They assumed there was a charge to enter Caesarea, but Polia assured them there was none. Since she was a local, they would go in through a hole in the fence and would not have to pay. David, who had much practice at sneaking into places because of events in his background before he and Emily were married, was as calm as a cat by the fireplace. But Emily was trying to figure out how the family of nine, in their matching orange shirts, was going to go unnoticed by the people taking tickets.

The family followed Polia around to the backside at the beach and carefully walked through a big hole in the fence. It did not seem to bother Polia that she was bringing a very conspicuous looking group through the hole, so Emily followed her lead while looking around, expecting to see armed guards approaching to throw them out for breaking in. It was not until over half-way through the tour that she and Polia were able to communicate well enough for Emily to understand that the locals were actually given permission to enter at will and bring guests in for free. At that point, she relaxed and allowed the children more freedom in their escapades as they ran and explored.

They saw various statues, ruins of buildings, the arena where chariot races had been held, bath houses, mosaics, and many other interesting sites in the ancient complex, built in the first century BC. David pointed out things

Chapter 7 Casearea

as Emily told the children, "*Shaul*[55] spent two years of his life imprisoned here. Remember how he was on the road to Damascus to persecute believers in Y'shua, when he was blinded by a great light and spoken to by Y'shua? That encounter led him to be a believer that Y'shua was the promised Messiah, savior of the world, and he immediately knew he had been wrong to persecute others who believed. He then started preaching just as boldly as he had been persecuting before sharing the good news of Yah's Salvation[56] wherever he went. Many Jewish religious leaders were very angry about his conversion and plotted to kill him. When their plan was found out, the Romans whisked him away, put him into protective custody, and then escorted him here with 200 soldiers and 70 horsemen! He was right here when he wrote some of the letters that are in the New Testament."

They looked around the stone remains where they stood, noting a bathing place, and other rooms. Emily continued, "During his lifetime, his letters were misunderstood by both Jews and non-Jews, and nearly 2,000 years later they're still being misunderstood. Peter tells in one of his writings[57] that *Shaul*'s (Paul's) letters were difficult to understand by those who did not have a good grasp on the *torah*. *Shaul* was an expert in *torah*, being zealous enough to become a student of Gamaliel, the top rabbi of the day, and even regarded today as one of the best. I've heard that to be accepted as one of his students, you had to have the entire *TaNak* memorized. He knew the scriptures inside and out, and his level of knowledge was way above the common people, and especially above the Gentiles who did not grow up in *torah* observant homes. So when he wrote his letters, they were often misunderstood by people thinking he was speaking against the 'law', the instructions of YHWH. But we know because of what Paul himself says in other letters, what Peter says about Paul, and what Y'shua himself says, that this is not true at all. Y'shua said that whoever broke one of the least of the commandments and taught others to do so would

---

[55] Shaul - Hebrew name of the famous apostle Paul, author of 13 books of the New Testament.

[56] Yah's Salvation - in Hebrew is 'Y'shua.'

[57] 2 Pet. 3:16-17 As also in all [Paul's]*his* epistles, speaking in them of these things; in which are some things hard to be understood, which they that are unlearned and unstable wrest, as *they do* also the other scriptures, unto their own destruction. Ye therefore, beloved, seeing ye know *these things* before, beware lest ye also, being led away with the error of the wicked, fall from your own stedfastness.

be called least in the kingdom.[58] Between that and what Peter says about those who twisted *Shaul*'s writings to their own destruction to the error of the lawless, we know that Paul was not contradicting the Old Testament scriptures at all."

They continued with their tour of the ruins for a couple of hours, reading the information signs posted in front of points of interest. The older children ran around exploring every nook and cranny of the place. Polia took a few pictures of the family, but they were never able to convince her to be in one. Emily's parents called but reception was not good and they were not successful in communication other than to let each other know that everything was all right. It was their first communication since the family arrived in Israel three days earlier.

Since the children wanted to play in the water once more before riding out early in the morning, Polia walked with the family by way of the *S'dot Yam* beach before going to her bicycle to ride the three miles home. Everyone thanked her once again for the kindness she had shown by arranging such a great place to stay, gifting food, and now giving a free tour of a major site in Israel. After she left, they thanked YHWH for her and asked His blessings on her and Nikolay. Their first contacts in Israel had proven to be a great blessing.

After their last frolic in the water, they walked to the tent, the children picking up more pretty shells along the way. They showered, not knowing when they would get another one, washed their orange clothes, and went to bed. David and Emily took advantage of one last night's cup of tea together, then retired themselves, thankful for the absence of loud music.

Yom Sheni[59] (Second Day of the week)

In the morning, they folded up the tent and packed everything carefully in the panniers. The orange clothes they had washed the night before were still wet, so they packed them in plastic bags, hoping to get them hung out before they could mildew. Packing went slowly, it seemed, and they wondered if it were just because they hated to leave the security of the beautiful place they were staying or for the unknown that lay ahead. The children hauled off what remained of the empty boxes they had finished unpacking the day before and the ones they had used as a porch on the dirt outside of the tent, to the trash area a few hundred yards away. Their bicycle tire pump was not working properly, and while dumping the boxes, Armando found one that worked well enough to air the tires sufficiently.

---

[58]Mat. 5:19 Whosoever therefore shall break one of these least commandments, and shall teach men so, he shall be called the least in the kingdom of heaven: but whosoever shall do and teach *them*, the same shall be called great in the kingdom of heaven.

[59]*Yom Sheni* - Day Second, occurring from sundown Sunday until sundown Monday.

Chapter 7   Casearea

They praised YHWH again for providing for all their needs in the most interesting of ways.

School was in session before they rode off, and the children came out to say goodbye. There was a talkative young American in the group and he retrieved all the necessary information and related it to his classmates. They were very excited to receive the postcards, and the Varela children were just as excited to give them away. Finally, one of the teachers put a limit on how many each child could have, afraid the family would run short of them. They said *adios*[60] to the Hispanic teacher who had been so kind to them and rode off, taking the long way back around the kibbutz to test their bicycles before getting on the bigger road. They noticed a few problems, so stopped at the gate to make some adjustments. They gave a postcard to the elderly gate man and called the Kibbutz Chief to let him know where they left the basket he had brought them, thanking him again for his and the kibbutz's wonderful hospitality.

Or Akiva

They rode out of the gate and began the three-mile trip east to Or Akiva, where they would stop at a bicycle shop to get some parts and have some adjustments made. Emily's bicycle was loaded too heavily, and she was having a bit of trouble, but thought she would get used to it. There was a wide, smoothly-bricked sidewalk on the north side of the road that they were able to use most of the way. When they rode under the number two road (a high-speed interstate-type highway), they were amiably greeted by road construction workers. "Welcome to Or Akiva," they shouted in English, taking off their hardhats. The family indeed felt welcomed, and Or Akiva would prove to be one of their most fondly-remembered towns.

When the sidewalk came to an end, the cyclists crossed to the south side of the road and traveled until finding a place to eat breakfast on a grassy spot next to a round-about. They had waited to eat until on the move, in order make better use of time, and so as not to drag out leaving any longer than need be. They ate their usual breakfast of fruit and hummus. Lunch would be vegetables and hummus, and supper, more vegetables, hummus, and fruit for dessert. Israel was blessed with lots of hummus, and Emily was taking advantage of its nutrition and ease of preparation. All that was necessary was something with which to spread it. They added variety to lunch hummus by chopping and adding onions, peppers, and other vegetables, or adding a can of corn, black olives or tuna. After their breakfast, the children sat quietly on the grass while Mama read from the book of *Second Chronicles*.

They were in the habit of reading through the scriptures from cover to cover and then starting over with a different translation. They had been

_____

[60]Adios - Spanish for 'good-bye.'

Pedaling Home   Part 1 – In the Beginning

reading from *The Scriptures*, which had the Old Testament in the same order as the *TaNaK* and had reached the final book before departing. David carried his Spanish/English Bible on his bicycle, but instead of bringing along another heavy paper Bible, Emily installed e-sword on her PDA and used it for morning scripture readings. She could easily carry it in her bicycle handlebar pouch which doubled as a fanny pack.

When they finished eating and reading, they sang their song thanking YHWH for the food. Two years before, they had hosted a family of nine in their home who had just returned from Israel. It was the Varela's custom to give thanks after mealtimes because of the instruction given in Deuteronomy 8:10.[61] The visiting family then shared a song, which was very similar to the prayer the Varelas offered. When the family left and the Varelas could not remember the song verbatim, they did the best they could and came up with:

> "Now that we have eaten and we are satisfied
> We give thanks to Yehovah for the blessings He provides"

As they sang it after every meal, another family of nine who once visited with them took the song home and added:

> "We thank you for our home now, for clothes, and food to eat
> You are Yehovah Yireh,[62] and we worship at your feet."

The song was easy enough for everyone to sing and a reminder to be thankful for all the good things YHWH gave them.

They strapped on their helmets, mounted their bicycles, and rode into Or Akiva, following Nikolay's perfect instructions as to how to get to the bicycle shop. They rode to the door of the tiny workplace, not much bigger than their bathroom at home. David showed the owner what they needed and he went to work replacing a brake cable for Victor and a gear cable for Armando. David was so impressed by his speed and knowledge of bicycles that he gave him several other bicycles to adjust. While they waited, some of the younger ones got hungry again. Next door was a small bakery, and just past that, a produce and meat market. Emily sent Armando and Briana to ask how much a watermelon cost, telling them how to ask in Hebrew.

They walked past the bakery as the two Israeli ladies working there watched, and approached the fruit market where a large Jewish man with a long beard and wearing a *kippah*[63] stood. The two children entered the

---

[61]Deut 8:10 When thou hast eaten and art full, then thou shalt bless YHWH thy **Elohim** for the good land which he hath given thee.

[62]Yehovah Yireh - usually pronounced in English 'Jehovah Jireh' and meaning 'YHWH provides.'

[63]*Kippah* – Hebrew for 'dome;' a small disc-like head covering worn by many

Chapter 7   Casearea

market as the large man followed.   Armando asked, pointing at a watermelon, "*Cama ze oleh?*"[64]

After hearing his response, the children came back and reported to Mama, who did not understand what they had said.   She sent Armando to get bread and went to inquire for herself.   Once there she chose to get two large cantaloupe instead, since they might not be able to finish a watermelon and the leftovers would be difficult to pack on the bicycles.   As she picked one up, the store owner sent a man rushing over to help. Instead of cantaloupe, he got a watermelon.   Emily tried to tell him she wanted the smaller melons, but he insisted, and then waved her out.   As she reached for the money, the store owner waved her on again, saying, "...*bishvil hayeladim.*"[65]   Emily was dumbfounded by their generosity and quickly wrote a thank-you note on one of the postcards.   They seemed delighted.

As she walked back past the bread shop, Armando was coming out with the bread and the fifty shekel bill she had given him, telling her the ladies would not let him pay.   She sent him back in with postcard thank-you notes, shocked again at the generosity they were experiencing.   Shortly afterward, the two ladies came rushing out with two boxes of fresh-baked cookies and candy, also saying, "*Bishvil hayeladim.*"

The family did not know what to do besides thank them, marveling at the incredible way their trip was starting.   They had never been recipients of this type of hospitality and generosity before.   The bicycle man quickly finished all of the adjustments David had asked for and had to leave on an errand, while the family continued eating what was left of their watermelon and answering questions of the small group of people who had surrounded them.   Among them were two *da'atim*[66] boys around Armando's age, who were curious about the family's tassels.   They wore white *tzitziyot* of their own and had *payot.*[67]

After watermelon came the need of *hasherutim,*[68] which Emily had been informed was next door at the beauty parlor.   They went two-by-two, starting with the older children, so as not to overwhelm the small shop with the whole family at once.   Emily then took Natanyah, who was enamored with a lady's bright blue hair.   Everyone in the shop seemed delighted with the children, and some of them came out asking questions.   When the family was reunited at the bicycles again, Emily answered all the children's

---

Jewish men.

[64]*Cama ze oleh?* - Hebrew for 'How much does it cost?'

[65]*Bishvil hayeladim* - Hebrew for 'for the children'

[66]*Da'atim* - Hebrew for 'those with knowledge', a term used to refer to religious or Orthodox Jews.

[67]*Payot* - Hebrew plural for 'sides', used to describe the long curls of hair extending from in front of the ears of some sects of religious Jewish males.

[68]*Hasherutim* - Hebrew for 'services', commonly and in this case, 'restroom.'

questions concerning the strong smell of chemicals, the fingernails, the colored hair, and other things the children had never experienced before.

Delayed

Emily went back to the fruit market and bought two cantaloupe to take with them. They put their helmets back on, buckled Natanyah in her seat, and mounted their bicycles, Emily now carrying the extra bread and cookies with which that they had been so generously gifted. Not long after starting back down the road, she realized that even the little extra weight of the bread was too much for her on a bicycle that was already packed too heavily. But before she had a chance to get off the road, her shaky bicycle tipped over right in front of the slow moving traffic on the busy narrow street. Thankfully, the traffic was too congested to be moving fast, and people were kind and understanding. A man who had driven past the rest of the family, but was stopped when Emily and Natanyah fell in front of him, jumped out of his car to come help her pick up the heavy bicycle and move it to the side. Natanyah was frightened from the fall, but not hurt. Emily was not hurt either, but terribly humiliated, embarrassed and sorry to have caused inconvenience to the driver and other traffic.

They moved to the sidewalk, which they had not been using in this part of town because there were so many curbs to have to go up and down at the cross streets, making the sidewalk route more dangerous for riding than the street. That was one thing they learned on their practice runs in the U.S. – it was often safer to ride on the street, than on rough, narrow, or sporadic sidewalks. Since Emily was leading, and now going slowly as she pushed her bicycle, several of the older ones and David had to get off and push, as well.

They arrived at the main corner, back at the road they had come in on from *S'dot Yam* and Caesarea, and stopped in the shade at some park benches to repack and lighten Emily's load. Some of their equipment had been misdirected when they ordered it, and by the time they got it, they did not have a chance to try it out before the trip. Emily's front panniers were some of those items. They were not actually made to be front panniers, but were called 'grocery' panniers and could carry quite a load. In Emily's efficient manner, she packed them for all they were worth, only to find that there is a good reason that front panniers are made to be very small and not able to hold much. So they repacked, putting the lightweight empty collapsible water jugs and emergency water filters in her front panniers and moving everything else to David's and Armando's bicycles. They were loaded heavily, as well, but were able to handle their loads more safely and did not have the additional responsibility of carrying another passenger, which made Emily's bicycle more top-heavy already.

While repacking was taking place, Natanyah and Rebeka fell asleep on the park benches. Moshe fell asleep where he got off his bicycle on the sidewalk. So they decided to all take a rest, since the children were still

Chapter 7   Cascarea

obviously suffering from jet-lag. While sitting there, they answered many questions by an older man who was waiting for a bus. When he got up to leave, he gave them his bottle of water. As they watched him walk toward the bus, they saw a woman across the intersection park her car and walk determinedly toward them. She introduced herself as Malka.[69] She was excited to see a family on bicycles, explaining that she was in charge of a local youth program and that the Israeli government was trying to encourage cycling in the country. "Where are you staying?" she asked in English.

Emily replied, "Someone we spoke to on the street a few minutes ago told us about a park on the east side of town. We thought we'd stay there for the night."

"I know the park," Malka said, nodding. "Could I bring some friends and visit you there this evening?"

David and Emily glanced at each other, wondering why anyone would want to visit strangers who planned to camp in the city park, and Emily replied, "Sure! We'd love to have company!"

Malka rushed off and David and Emily excitedly discussed their upcoming meeting, knowing there was a special reason they would not reach their intended night's destination because of bicycle issues. They prayed, not knowing how the upcoming encounter would be significant. From the beginning planning stages of the trip they had resolved to leave everything up to the Almighty and be flexible so as to make all the appointments that He might be arranging. They felt confident that was already happening and were excited about the prospects of what was to come this evening.

At The Park

When the children awoke from their naps, the family got back on the main street and rode east toward the big tree-lined park with beautiful, lush grass, picnic tables, grills, and a very large playground area, David turned to Emily and jokingly said, "Well, no hot tea tonight without the school's hot water machine. We'll have to break our new tradition."

Emily replied, smiling, "I guess we'll just have to be thankful and fondly remember our few special nights at *S'dot Yam*."

The park was next to a large mall where they hoped they could get more food for supper and breakfast, as well as some string to make tassels for the new *Shabbat* clothes Emily's mother had made for them. First, they set up camp, strategically placing the bicycles in the corner of one of the little decorative chest-high rock walls in a way that they would not be easily

---

[69]*Malka* - Hebrew for 'Queen.'

stolen, leaving a little hidden area for dressing and using the emergency bucket, since there were no restrooms nearby. As the parents set up, the older children played with and supervised the younger ones on the very large set of playground equipment. Briana found a lizard and set it on her tunic to watch it camouflage itself. All the children enjoyed moving it from place to place and watch it change colors, but it seemed most content on their green tunics.

Once the bicycles were arranged, Emily unpacked the damp orange clothes and hung them on the bicycles, hoping they would dry during the night. Afterward, she walked to the mall with Armando and Briana, while David watched the younger children play. They took along a sample of the skirt fabric in order to find matching string for the tassels. First, they went to the grocery store and bought more hummus, yogurt, fruit and vegetables for supper and breakfast. They had plenty of bread from the kind bakery ladies. After getting groceries, they saw a store that sold string and were able to find 100% cotton in turquoise, lilac, white, and blue. It was thicker than what they were accustomed to, as it was a crochet-type yarn, but would match the skirts perfectly, and the softness of the thread would complement them. The girls' tassels would use a strand of each color, while the boys', to go on their black pants, would only be white with one blue strand.

Briana

As David was watching the children, he got a call from Nikolay, who asked where they would be staying for the night. A few minutes after speaking with him, Polia showed up at the park on her bicycle bringing more treats for the family to eat. She watched the children until the three arrived back from the store, surprised and delighted to see her. Not having been able to communicate with David, she told Emily in Hebrew, "This isn't such a good place to sleep. I can show you a better place across the highway."

Emily dreaded the thought of moving, since they had things so nicely set up for the night already and sundown was approaching. She replied, "I think we'll be fine here. We've already got things set up and it's getting late."

But Polia insisted, "No, let me show you. It's a good, private place over there."

Since Emily was busy preparing supper, David went across the main road

Chapter 7   Casearea

with Polia to the sandy, abandoned area. When they returned, David and Emily agreed they would rather stay put. Polia seemed very concerned, so Emily phoned Nikolay and asked several questions concerning the safety of staying in the park. "What is the risk here? Will they try to hurt us or take the children?" she asked.

"Oh, no!" Nikolay replied. "No one would hurt the children! But they might steal your bicycles or other belongings."

That settled it for the couple. Being accustomed to life in Mexico, where children were sometimes abducted for ransom or killed and used in the drug or organ trade business, among other things, the thought of only losing possessions was of little concern to them. The family had known all along that theft was a possibility, but trusted their Creator and Provider. If He allowed things to be stolen, He would show the next step to take. And at the rate He was currently blessing them, they had no doubts He would provide whatever was needed. Besides, thieves who were not interested in hurting people would have a difficult time getting to their things because of the fortress like arrangement.

Emily finished fixing the pitas and offered some to Polia, but she declined, wanting to get home before it was too late. David watched and played with the children, who were thoroughly enjoying themselves on the playground with the Israeli children. Emily used that chance to get the bed mats, sheets, and pillows laid out, concluding that the weather was nice enough they did not need to bother setting up the tent. That would allow them to leave earlier in the morning. They had only made it three miles their first day and wanted to cover more territory the next.

8 – Zichron Ya'achov[70]

Tea With the Queen
Yom Shlishi[71] (Third Day)

Emily called everyone to eat at a nearby picnic table. Just after dark, having finished supper as they watched other families barbecuing and playing, they got a call from Malka. She was in the park with some others and was looking for them. David and Emily were delighted and puzzled at their seeming popularity and prayed that *Abba* would use them and have them speak only His words.

Malka approached with her husband and her brother-in-law and his wife, all with arms full. She was speaking English as she set her load down on the picnic table. "Well, it's not much, but I made some chocolate chip cake, and here are some cookies for the children. And here are paper plates and cups, and suckers..."

Then, to David and Emily's amazement, she set down six beautiful glass cups and a steaming pitcher and continued, "...and some hot tea for us."

They would get their special tea time again tonight, and with guests! They blessed YHWH for the food and their new friends and began answering myriads of questions. They were able to share truths from the scriptures, as their audience was captivated and continued asking more and more. After those questions were asked and answered, and while the children continued to play, the couple learned more about their guests. Malka's husband was an attorney and kindly offered his services to the family any time they might need them. David and Emily were thinking at the same time that they hoped they would not. The other man there was an electrician and he and David talked construction for a while, while Emily answered more of the ladies' questions concerning the scriptures, the family, and their life in the U.S.

It got quite late, and the fellowship was good, but the little ones had begun falling asleep in their parents' laps, so the guests dismissed themselves, knowing the family needed to get to bed in order to get an early start on the bicycles. They urged them to stay in Or Akiva and even invited the

---

[70]*Zichron Ya'achov* – Hebrew for 'Memory of Jacob' or 'Jacob's Memorial,' a city founded in 1882 by Baron Edmond James de Rothschild, who bought the lands of the settlement, supervised and supported it, and named it after his father, Jacob.

[71]*Yom Shlishi* - Day Third, occurring from sundown Monday until sundown Tuesday.

family to stay with them, but David and Emily felt like they should ride out in the morning. They exchanged contact information and bid each other shalom as the guests left for home and the family bedded down after packing away the leftover treats their new friends and Polia had left them.

There were still many people in the park but most did not notice them in their far corner fortress in a darker area, though the parents did observe a few groups nearer by who continued to glance their way at what must have resembled a gypsy camp, the bright Dorito shirts hanging on bicycles. Regardless, the children fell into their usual deep sleep, and the parents slept more lightly as they protected their little brood.

Lush Green Grass

Around midnight, Emily was awakened by the sound of light rain, which seemed strange to her, knowing that summer rains in Israel were rare. As she listened, she noticed the sound was rhythmic and that she was not getting wet. She then realized the sprinkler system at the other side of the park had come on. They had not seen any sprinkler outlets when they chose their place to sleep, but she now concluded that it had been silly of them to lay out their bed mats on lush green grass in a place that had not received rain for at least two months. They had thought they had done well to avoid the anthills that were in the nearby sand, when they moved onto the grass. She awoke David, who sleepily decided that the sprinklers on their side of the park probably would not go off tonight, as the ground seemed damp already, and they must have gone off the night before. But they devised a plan, just in case. They took their enamel bowls out of Armando's rear panniers and, judging from where they could see the sprinklers across the park, figured out where a few of the outlets near them were. They then turned bowls upside down on top of them, covered them with large rocks to hold them on, and went back to bed.

At 3 AM, they learned where the sprinklers on their side of the park were. They heard the water, but did not immediately get wet, as their plan with the bowls had turned out to be pretty ingenious. But very shortly, they discovered they had missed some outlets and a couple of the others had sprayed hard enough to knock off the rock covered bowls, one being right near the bed mats. They jumped up quickly to try to get them covered before the children got wet, but were not fast enough. Some of the outlets were too tall for the bowls to stay on, so they grabbed bicycles and laid them over the bowls to try to hold them down. The younger children started waking up, startled and crying, not understanding anything other than that they were getting wet. Children, awake and wet at 3 AM, do not respond the same as children, awake and wet at 3 PM. At 3 PM, they happily run through the sprinklers, enjoying the cool water. At 3 AM, they are in a semi-conscious state that does not reason, even with comforting words from parents. So the quiet of the night was shattered by the half-conscious but loud cries of several small children being soaked with untimely artificial, and artificially hard, rain.

David woke up Armando and Briana to help with the little ones while he continued working frantically to get the remaining sprinklers covered, and Emily tried to get their sheets out of the way of the water that was running toward the bed mats, while trying to ignoring the cries, knowing that nothing but the children being warm and dry was going to stop them. Armando and Briana tried their best to help Mamma and Daddy by comforting the little ones. Natanyah generally got comfort by massaging someone's ears, usually Mama's. Briana lay down by Natanyah and offered her surrogate ears, since both parents were busy. Armando comforted Victor and Moshe. The other two girls began to calm down on their own as the 'rain' stopped. By the time David finished, Emily had managed to rescue two of the bed sheets, enough to cover the children. She and David lay back down wet, but satisfied that the others were dry and would be able to go back to sleep.

The tired family arose at daybreak and began packing. Because of the sprinkler incident, the clothes that had been hanging on the bicycles and fences still were not dry, so were rolled up neatly again, though damp, and repacked.

Shortly after sunup, park workers performed their cleaning duties, eying the family curiously, as if wondering how they had stayed dry during the night. The family was stirring happily and packing, never letting on the events of the previous few hours. When the friendly workers got closer, one showed Armando where he could fill up the water bottles. With bottles filled, bed mats secured on the back of Emily's bicycle, and everything else securely packed, they mounted up, had prayer and rode out of the park.

Benyamina by Bicycle

It was early enough that traffic was not yet heavy as they crossed Highway #4, a four-lane similar to a U.S. expressway, and rode north. They went about a mile, then turned east towards Benyamina. At that point, they reached their first steep hill where everyone had to dismount and push because of the weight of their loads. When they reached the top, they were all ready for breakfast. They sat under the shade of some orange and grapefruit trees and ate fruit from their packs. They sampled some of the fruit that had fallen to the ground and stashed a few in their packs for later, blessing their Provider for His generous gift of fresh fruit. Then they had their time of reading from the scriptures, before riding down the hill into Benyamina.

Once there, they went to a gas station to fill their two pint-size stove fuel tanks. They did not plan to use the stove, but not knowing what situation might arise, wanted to be prepared. Using the featherweight stove would be much more practical in some situations than building a fire. At the gas station, Emily asked the way to Zichron Ya'achov, and they rode in the direction they had been shown. They turned too soon, missing the foot bridge that went over the train tracks and had to go back around the block

Chapter 8   *Zichron Ya'achov*

and to the next intersection. On their way, they rode past a construction crew who cheered with encouraging words, "*Kol hakavod!*"[72]

They found the footbridge that crossed over the train tracks near the station where Nikolay had met them almost a week earlier upon their arrival in Israel. After crossing the bridge, they rode north, leaving Benyamina behind. It was mid-morning and the August sun was very hot, but the wind generated from the movement of the bicycles kept most of their sweat drying and cooled them. Shortly after getting out of town, with no shade in sight, Armando veered off the road a bit and picked up a thorn in his back tire, immediately flattening it. The others took a water break while David and Armando put Slime (a green goo that repairs holes in tires) in the tire and got it inflated. Then David wrestled his heavy bicycle up off of the thorny, sandy ground and gave the 'OK' for Emily to proceed.

Traffic was busy on this two-lane highway with very little shoulder, but drivers were patient and most were polite. Because there were eight bicycles in a line, with all riders decked in their bright orange safety vests, each having a bright orange flag, the group was visible enough that traffic slowed significantly when nearing them, and often northbound traffic had to wait for southbound cars to drive by before there was room to pass. The family was impressed with the kindness of the drivers, especially since they had heard many reports before their trip began about how bad and rude Israeli drivers were. So far, they had not found this to be the case at all - at least not for the majority.

They rode through the valley filled with groves of fruit trees and grape vines. In the distance, they could see the area where the Israelites were at war with the Philistines when David fought Goliath. They assumed the empty fields they saw were because it was the sabbatical year, the year of the land rest.[73] Surprised that more land was not resting, they later learned that it was acceptable according to some rabbis for the Jews to sell their land to a non-Jew for the year, so that they would not be guilty of breaking the command. The new 'owners' would continue to harvest, so much of the land was not getting its rest. They knew that was a tragedy because scripture was very clear that refusal to allow the land to rest every seventh year is one of the reasons the Kingdom of Judah was exiled to Babylon in the 6th century BC.[74]

---

[72]*Kol hakavod* - Hebrew literally meaning 'all the respect', but used in modern Hebrew to say 'Great job!'

[73]Lev. 25:4-5 But in the seventh year shall be a sabbath of rest unto the land, a sabbath for the LORD: thou shalt neither sow thy field, nor prune thy vineyard. That which groweth of its own accord of thy harvest thou shalt not reap, neither gather the grapes of thy vine undressed: *for* it is a year of rest unto the land.

[74]2 Chr. 36:21 To fulfil the word of YHWH by the mouth of Jeremiah, until the land had enjoyed her sabbaths: *for* as long as she lay desolate she kept sabbath, to fulfil threescore and ten years.

They wondered what judgments would occur and when they would be meted out by the Most High for the current refusal on the part of some to allow the land her sabbaths, and they gave thanks for and prayed blessings on those who were allowing the land to rest this year. They concluded that those who were not obeying had no idea how grateful they should be for those who were resting the land, as instructed. The obedient ones may be all that stood between the disobedient ones and judgment on the land.

The heat index continued to rise and everyone was ready for a lunch break, but there was still no shade in sight, except what slightly bordered a couple of buildings in the distance at the foot of the long hill they would soon be climbing. David and Emily decided that would be the best place to stop, so encouraged the children to keep going to the now visible goal, where they could sit in the shade of the buildings. After arriving, they arranged the bicycles propped together in pairs, balancing each other so that they would not fall. Since the loads were heavy, it was much easier to take the time to prop them than to have to pick them up again when they were ready to move on.

They left them near the road and walked to the tiny bit of noon-time shade on the north side of the building. After lunch and a short nap on the concrete, they went inside to make sure they were where they thought they were, as there had been some confusion when they left Benyamina. The woman behind the desk could not show them where they were on the map, but confirmed they were on the road to Zichron Ya'achov and that it was just at the top of the hill, a little over a mile away. She then gave permission for them to use the small restroom. After the girls came out, and the boys went in, Briana took one of the little postcards with a thank you note that Emily had written to the woman. The woman responded by giving a two-liter bottle of cold water for them to take on their journey. Briana was surprised, but thanked the woman, and rushed out to show the rest of the family their latest blessing from above.

A mile is not really a great distance. At least it would not be for a young, tight cyclist in his slick cycling clothes, packing only his water bottle. But this was a group in their modest street clothes - jeans for the boys and long skirts for the girls - headed by a slightly overweight middle-aged six-month pregnant mother toting a two-year-old, then three, five, six, eight, nine, and eleven year old cyclists, protected from the rear by their father packing the family tent along with other necessary items needed for two months' life on the road. Everyone over five years old was packing as much as safely possible. So off they pushed up the mile-long incline to the top in the heat of the midday August sunshine, with still no shade in sight. Distance is relative.

As they pushed their heavy bicycles, they began looking for a place to camp when they came to a small, mostly dry creek that looked like it could be a river during the rainy season. They continued to the top where there was a gas station. Leaning their bicycles against some olive trees,

Chapter 8   *Zichron Ya'achov*

Natanyah in her seat, everyone dismounted to take a break after the long uphill push. David went inside to see if there was a place where they could camp nearby, and the English-speaking cashier pointed across the highway to a park entrance. As they sat and took a water break, a woman from France with her daughter and granddaughter drove in to get gas. Upon spotting the children, she became overcome with emotion and began asking all sorts of questions in Hebrew. She then gave the children five shekels each, saying, "Go get ice cream."

The children looked back at Mama for the OK, then thanked the kind woman and hurried into the store, as instructed. The woman waited outside and watched to make sure they were all served before driving off. The children, besides still sleeping Natanyah, thoroughly enjoyed their cool treat and tried to finish it before it melted, which was no small task, especially for little Moshe and Rebeka. It was not often they got ice cream and even less often that it would come on a stick. It was tricky to get it eaten before the hot sun melted it. Emily was glad it was the second day of wearing the green clothes. They would surely need washing now.

The gas station attendant offered to fill their bottles with cold water, and they gratefully accepted, then rode toward the park. Upon arriving at the entrance, Emily spoke with the guard, who told them they could not enter because there was a special event going on that night. She asked where they could camp and he pointed to some trees outside of the park area. They rode in that direction, then got off the road, pushing the bicycles through the trees behind a nice building that was under construction. They found an ideal place and began unpacking their things, beginning with bed mats and dirty laundry. David, Armando, and Briana walked to the building that was under construction, where David, who always thoroughly scoped out the area, had noticed a water spigot when they rode past, and filled up one of the collapsible five-gallon water jugs. When they returned, he hung the clothesline up between two trees, trying to avoid the thorn bushes, and Emily hung the orange clothes that were still damp from their time at the beach two nights before.

Orange Shirts and Yellow Jackets

The children began exploring. It intrigued Emily that given any surroundings, children, especially younger ones, were always inclined toward the area that would get them the dirtiest. This time was no exception, as Victor, Moshe, Rebeka, and Natanyah discovered a previous camper's fire pit, which consisted of a few rocks around some burnt logs. Emily did her best to discourage their playing in or near it, but the dirtier something is, the more of a magnetic draw it seems to have on small children. Not only that, but young children also have a special magnetism for dirt, seemingly not even having to come in contact with it for it to jump on and adhere to them. So, even though Emily finally blockaded the area with fallen trees, the children still somehow got soot on themselves.

After sponge baths, the children put on their orange clothes, and began helping Mama wash the green ones in one bucket and rinse them in the other. Laundry by hand was not a chore in temperatures over 90 degrees after having been riding (or pushing) a bicycle for most of the day. It was not only fun for the children, but for a nest of yellow jackets, which got excited at seeing something colorful. Everything around was dry and mostly brown besides the leaves of trees that had especially good root systems and the Doritos shirts. The buzzing insects joined in the laundry party, trying their best to pollinate the bright orange clothes. Moshe's ear somehow got in the way, and when he felt a tickle, he reached up to scratch himself. Not appreciating being bothered at, the yellow jacket that had stopped there to rest stung Moshe's ear. He let out a wail like a siren, which sent Briana rushing to the first aid kit in her front pannier. She hurried back, made a baking soda paste, and applied it to his ear, which had already swelled so badly that it stuck straight out from his head. Moshe calmed down as the soda soothed his swollen ear.

After laundry was finished, they ate supper and Emily lay down with the younger children, letting Natanyah get her ears. David, Armando, and Briana went back across the highway to the gas station about a quarter mile away and brought hot water so the parents could continue in their new tradition of nightly hot tea.

Fox and Mosquitoes
Yom Revi'i[75] (Fourth Day)

The children went right to sleep and the couple had a few minutes of time together before drifting off themselves. The peacefulness of the night was soon interrupted by a car driving toward where the family slept. The light sleeping parents awoke and watched to be sure that it did not come too close in their direction, thinking they might be run over by an unsuspecting driver. The area was surrounded by trees, but did have trails through it that a car could travel if the driver knew his way around. They got up quietly and moved bicycles to strategic places, so that if someone did come, they would have to run over bicycles first, stopping them from harming any of the family.

The car stopped a safe distance away and the passengers got out, seemingly not having noticed the family. Within a half hour, however, more vehicles arrived on the scene. A party then ensued about 100 yards from the family's camp site. After beginning to walk around in smaller groups, some of the partiers spotted the sleeping family. David was ready to protect, if necessary, but they seemed to mind their own business, so he was able to sleep lightly off and on until some left and the others bedded down around 2 AM.

---

[75] *Yom Revi'i* - Day Fourth, occurring from sundown Tuesday until sundown Wednesday.

Chapter 8   *Zichron Ya'achov*

Emily, being a light sleeper anyway, did not doze much either until they were gone. Not long after the crowd left and she fell asleep, she was again awakened by the soft sound of a small rock shifting. She glanced up to see a fox grab her gallon zip lock bag of teas, herbs, and supplements, and run into the woods with it. Instinctively, she yelled, "Hey!" but the fox paid no attention. She had never seen an Israeli fox, and this animal was not like the pretty red and grey foxes with pointed ears on the tops of their heads that lived in Tennessee. At the time, she wondered if it were just a feral dog. It was scraggly, with ears pointed out more to the sides and a wiry tail, more like that of a Schnauzer than the fluffy tail of the pretty little red foxes she was used to seeing. It was a small animal and quite brave to have come within a foot of her to steal the bag of tea. She went back to sleep, hoping to find that the bag was not what the fox had hoped, and that he had left it behind after discovering its contents. She heard mosquitoes buzzing around, so covered her head with the sheet and slept well until morning.

When she awoke early, she noticed spots on Natanyah's face and realized that the two-year-old had slept so soundly she did not cover herself when the mosquitoes began to bite her in the night. As the others awoke, she also noticed spots on Rebeka and Isabel. She rubbed some herbal healing salve on the spots, as it always helped to relieve itching and to promote healing of bites, scratches, and miscellaneous other issues. She also applied some to Moshe's somewhat smaller, but still swollen ear. She had purchased the salve before leaving home, but it had actually come from a friend in northern Israel who had a business making oils and salves.

While they packed things, all of the young troops went searching for the lost bag of teas and supplements, but they were never found. In the process, David and Armando spotted a tan-colored viper, but it slithered away before anyone else was able to see it. The family had prayer and rode off early, trying to get as far as possible before the heat set in.

The place they had camped was nearly at the top, so they were able to ride into Zichron Ya'achov without having to push much. Just at the edge of town, they began riding down the mountain into the area of shops and stores. Armando thought he saw a bicycle shop, but by the time he was able to get the word to Emily, they had passed it. They stopped and Emily fixed breakfast on the sidewalk while David and Briana rode back to see if they could get some extra inner tubes. The shops were not yet open, and Emily found an outlet outside a wall where she could plug in the cell phone to charge while they were gone. She then cut into the melons that they had bought in Or Akiva and served the little ones. Many of the locals greeted them as they passed by on their way to work and school. David and Briana returned, the bicycle shop still being closed, as well. They ate the melon the rest had saved for them, then the family continued their descent.

Bat Shlomo

They rode down the very long steep hill from Zichron Ya'achov and then turned east onto four-lane Highway 70, which was much like a U.S. interstate. The traffic was fast, but there was a very wide shoulder. When they reached the little moshav[76] Bat Shlomo,[77] a community of about 500, they turned north and rode over the overpass and to a little market just inside the town gate. Emily and Briana went to buy some fruit and olives for lunch. The others found a shady place on the grass near a rock retaining wall where they could sit to eat and began getting things out of the panniers to go with what Mama was buying.

While eating, they saw a couple of women enter the store. A short while later they noticed a very loud conversation going on inside and the large woman came out noticeably upset. Emily took the girls to an abandoned building off in the weeds for a rest stop. While they were gone, the upset woman approached David and the boys frantically motioning for help. She got across to them that her purse had fallen in the dumpster and she could not get it out. It contained a large amount of money and she was upset that the store owner would not help her. He had told her there was no way to get into the dumpster. It was made in such a way as to prevent entry by people. Only cats could get inside.

David tried to calm her down by explaining the best he could that they would help. The four followed her to the dumpster where David was able to lay it on its side. He pried the door open wide enough for Armando to fit through. Armando rummaged through mostly newspapers until finding the lady's purse. He retrieved it and gave it to the very grateful woman. "Thank you! Oh, thank you! I will buy you a cold Coke or ice cream!" she exclaimed.

Since the family did not drink sodas, Armando looked at Daddy, got the approving nod, and said, "I'll take an ice cream."

The woman was so excited that she literally ran into the store and bought ice cream for Armando, and his shadows, Victor and Moshe, who had seen all the excitement and run after them into the store.

The girls returned, and the boys shared their ice cream with their sisters, while David went back into the store to try to buy more minutes for the cell phones. The friendly store owner told him, "The closest place to recharge with minutes is up the road at Elyakim."[78]

---

[76]Moshav - farming community

[77]Bat Shlomo – Hebrew for 'Daughter of Solomon,' also named by Rothschild in honor of a relative.

[78]Elyakim, a village of about 700 established in 1949, and named after **Judah**'s King Elyakim, whose name was changed by King Nebuchadnetzer to Yehoiakim, in the fifth century BC, at the beginning of the Babylonian captivity.

Chapter 8   *Zichron Ya'achov*

~~Playground~~ Highway 70

"Thank you," David offered, then went out to the family where they mounted up and began riding east again. It was after noon and the traffic was much heavier and continued to worsen. The semi-trucks and other large vehicles traveling at interstate speeds within just a few feet of them was beginning to really wear on Emily's nerves. David was doing better, and was able to see all the children in front of him, but he, too, was ready to be out of the traffic. The day continued to get hotter and, again, there was no shade in sight.

As they were pushing the bicycles up a hill, a police officer pulled over and walked back to Emily, "This is not a safe place to ride," he informed her. "You will be better on another road."

Emily: Yes, we can see that now. Is there another road?

Officer, pointing to the nearby exit: Yes, there is a road here. You can get off here.

Emily, noticing that the road he pointed to ran perpendicular to the one on which they were traveling: We are going to Elyakim. Does that road go to Elyakim?

Officer: No, not to Elyakim, but it is better.

Emily: We are traveling. We need to get to Elyakim.

Officer: It is better to take the children to a playground.

Emily: I understand. But we are traveling and need to get to Elyakim. It is just up the road, right?

Seemingly frustrated by the language barrier and lack of cooperation of the American woman, the officer replied, "Yes, just up the road. When you get to Elyakim, get off of this road."

"Yes, thank you. We will," Emily replied smiling, never intending to frustrate him but not being able to understand how any of his suggestions solved their problems.

Elyakim

They soon reached the exit at Elyakim, exited, crossed the highway on a bridge, stopped at a very large, abandoned, and vandalized Burger King, and sat down for a snack. David scoped out the Burger King to see if it might be a good place to spend the night, when he discovered a lemon tree in the courtyard on the other side. He told the children about it and then rode across town to get the cell phones recharged with minutes, while

81

Emily prepared the food. When he got to the store, he was surprised at the greeting he got. "My Friend! My Friend! You made it to town!"

It was the friendly man from the Bat Shlomo store.

"Yes," replied David. "What are you doing here?"

"I have two stores," the man informed him. "I am surprised to see you here. You made it on the bicycles with all the family! Where is the family?'

"They're down at the Burger King waiting for me," David said.

Meanwhile, back at the vandalized Burger King, the children found the lemon tree and brought back several lemons they had picked up off the ground. Emily had them help her make lemonade using the sugar given to them in their basket of goodies by the *Kibbutz* Chief in *S'dot Yam*. At home, they rarely used sugar, and Emily had wondered what they would do with it. The lemons were the perfect solution and one that everyone was happy about.

David purchased the minutes for the cell phones, then rode back to the family, where they discussed what to do next. It was around 2 PM, the time that they would normally want to begin looking for a place to stay so as not to be out after dark. They decided to go on, as opposed to staying in the abandoned Burger King, since they had been told there was a place just before starting up the mountain where they could camp under the trees.

No Overnight Parking

They began their trek up Mount Carmel, looking for a place to camp. Armando drew their attention to some trees that looked like a possible camping area, but the parents did not think that was the right place. They were expecting more of a traditional camping area, like what is typical in primitive campgrounds in the U.S. So they rode on and began pushing upward. There was no other place to stay on the way up, as there were fences on both sides of the road. The terrain was very rough open forest and they saw quite a few cattle in the creek beds and on the sides of the hills. About 4 PM, when everyone was getting tired, Emily spotted what looked like the perfect place on the west side of the road. She had remembered, when researching for the trip online, reading some things about the Mount Carmel Bike Club. She thought this must be one of their areas.

There was a yellow road warning sign showing a cyclist, and just across from it, an area where the fence was much farther from the road. Within the area were plenty of scrubby trees and some homemade tables. They pulled off there and soon discovered, in places hidden from the road, that there were stashes of filled water bottles, chairs, and other items that

Chapter 8   *Zichron Ya'achov*

would be useful to cyclists. They decided this would be the perfect place to spend the night.

David strung up the clothesline so they could rehang the damp green clothes they had washed the night before, and Emily prepared food for the children. She then hung out the clothes, while David fed them and they explored a little. She decided this would be a good place to use her dad's laptop to write an update to send to those in the States who were praying for them. Up until now, there had been no opportunity for that. She unpacked the computer and got it turned on, when a car drove into the little area. An Arab man who spoke no English or Hebrew got out and proceeded to tell the family that they could not stay there. He motioned that it was his place and they could eat there but not spend the night.

By this time, the sun was clearly on its way down, and it would take them a fair amount of time to get the clothes off the line and repack everything. They knew there was no way they could beat sundown, if they had to leave. He gave David a ride up the mountain to show him where he could stay and then brought him back. Emily waited until they got back to pack things, thinking David's great negotiating skills would be able to convince him to let them stay just for the night. But when they pleaded with him, even offering to pay, he still would not relent. He did motion that there was a place they could stay at the bottom of the hill, to which they could have arrived much more quickly, but no one in the family wanted to go back down, only to have to come back up in the morning. David said the place they could stay at the top was not far, so they quickly packed and began pushing up Mount Carmel again.

83

9 – False Prophets

Angels with Bicycle Racks
Yom Chamishi (Fifth Day)

The sun was going down as they began and everyone was tired, but encouraging words kept the little ones going. After the sun set, a large police jeep-type vehicle with lights flashing came by and stopped in front of them. Emily walked up to talk to them, but did not want to be standing on the driver's side in the dangerous evening light. The passenger side of his vehicle was at the top of a steep rocky hill, with not enough room for her to get through with her bicycle. She left her bicycle with Briana so she could walk over and safely talk to them, and just as she got to the side of the vehicle, it pulled away. Frustrated, knowing that their vehicle was big enough to haul most of the family along with the bicycles, she walked back, mounted, and they started off again.

It got dark, and they did not know how much farther they had to go. They had no nighttime protective measures on their bicycles, other than regular reflectors, most of which were covered up by their gear, since they had never planned to be out after dark. It was a steep, curvy road, so most traffic did not go very fast, but it was still a nerve-racking continuance to what had started on busy Highway 70 a few hours before. The parents, each in their respective positions of the caravan, had both been praying that YHWH would send an angel to help them get where they were going. Within minutes, a car with bike racks for two on top pulled over. A Jewish family of six, including three young children, from Bat Shlomo, who had seen the Varelas eating their snack earlier in the day stopped to see if they needed help. David told them their situation and they immediately began picking up people and bicycles and hauling them up to the camping area, which was well-known to them.

They first loaded Emily's and Victor's bicycles on the car, filled the back of the car with panniers and bed mats, and Emily, Isabel, Rebeka, Moshe and Natanyah scrunched into their car with them. They explained that they were on their way back from practice for their oldest son's *bar mitzvah* that would be held on top of Mount Carmel on *Shabbat*. They drove the family about half a mile up the mountain and turned left onto a dirt trail. There they stopped for everyone to unload and get their things out, while the man got the bicycles off the roof. Emily had the children help her start taking the bicycles and other things up a small hill to where they would camp. There was no light, but the moon had come out by then, so they could see enough to pick out a spot that looked like it would be suitable for sleeping.

Chapter 9   False Prophets

The angel family went back down the mountain and loaded Armando's and Briana's bicycles on top, Rebeka and Moshe's bicycles in the back, and took Armando, Briana, and Victor, leaving David behind with his bicycle and Victor's. They returned once again to get David and the other bicycles. By the time David got to the camp, the younger children were already asleep on their mats. Emily had lined the bicycles up between trees, where they would be difficult to steal, since they were not sure what kind of area they were really in. Later, after she saw headlights coming down a dirt trail on the other side of them, she moved a couple of bicycles up onto the hill, so that they would, once again, offer a shield of protection from an unsuspecting, nighttime driver.

David tried to pay the family, at least for their gasoline, which cost close to $10 per gallon, but they refused. They would not even take a bottle of the healing salve that Emily tried to give them. Taking nothing but lots of thanks, they said goodbye and headed back down the mountain to Bat Shlomo. David and Emily lay down on their mats on either side of the children, sandwiched them between them for safety, praised YHWH for sending such wonderful, helpful people with bicycle racks at the time they were most needed, and fell off to sleep, exhausted.

Scouting

The tired family awoke after sunup to birds singing in the trees and decided to stay put and rest for a day, obviously at a campsite and confident they would not be asked to leave. After taking both collapsible five-gallon water jugs a few hundred feet to a restroom to get water for laundry, David, Armando, and Briana unloaded some things from their bicycles and rode north into town to check out the surroundings and get more food. On another one of Mount Carmel's ascents, Armando spotted a beautiful circular basket lying among some trees near the shoulder of the road.

"Daddy, look! Can I stop and get it for Mama?" asked Armando.

"Wait till we're on the way back," answered David.

Armando looked forward to giving it to Mama. He knew she always liked baskets and containers.

~ ~ ~

Emily hung the laundry lines in a triangle between three trees, hanging the sheets in a smaller triangle in one corner to make a private place to put the bucket, since the facilities were too far from the camp for little ones and pregnant women to have to go in case of emergency.

The little park was a mess, appearing that a group or groups of people had been there, had a big party, and then left all their trash scattered around. Emily got out her trash bags and told the children she would pay them two

85

Pedaling Home   Part 1 – In the Beginning

shekels for each bag of trash they filled up, beginning around their own camp. She started laundry, as she encouraged their clean-up efforts.

Before the next ascent, David stopped and greeted three Orthodox[79] Jewish cyclists who were assembling their bicycles after unloading them from their little van. One was armed with a pistol, which Armando noticed right away. David called, "Hello!"

"Hello, how are you?" came the reply in thickly Spanish-accented English.

"Habla Espanol?"[80] David asked the man who had responded.

"Si!"[81] the man replied with a relieved smile.

David continued in Spanish, "So you are Sephardic?"[82]

"Yes, and you, also?" he asked David.

"I'm not Jewish that I know of, maybe so. I'm from Mexico. Hey, could you tell me how far it is to town?"

"It's close, less than three miles," came the reply. "So, what are you doing in Israel?"

"We came to be in Jerusalem for Sukkot," David answered, "but have arrived early to spend more time in the Land."

"Very good! We, too, plan to be in Jerusalem. Maybe we'll see you there!"

David thanked them, then rode up the hill with Armando and Briana as the three men rode down. Since much of their load was left at the camp, going up was much easier. They soon arrived near the top of Mount Carmel, to a sign pointing up to the site where Elijah defeated the prophets of Baal and Asherah.[83] They rode to the top and took in the awesome view, able to see for miles in several directions. David pointed in the distance, to various areas mentioned in scripture, including the valley of Megiddo, explaining their scriptural significance.

They stood near a chain-link fence where a person collected admission fees near the entrance. Since the three needed to get on with their food buying, they chose to walk around the fence to see what could be seen from there, waiting for a future time to enter. They talked about how Elijah got all of the water he needed to drench his sacrifice the way he did,

---

[79]Orthodox - the branch of rabbinic Judaism whose adherents try to strictly adhere to the *torah* as taught by the sages.
[80]*Habla Espanol?* - Spanish for 'Do you speak Spanish?'
[81]*Si* - Spanish for 'yes.'
[82]Sephardic - Jews of Spanish descent
[83]1 Kings, Chapter 18

surmising there were springs nearby, judging by all the areas of green. They discussed Elijah running down the mountain when he became afraid of Queen Jezebel, and how it would have been easier for a person to run in that terrain than for a chariot pulled by horses. After seeing all they could from outside the fence, they rode back down to the main road and into the town of *Daliat El Karmel*, a bustling Druze[84] village of about 15,000. There they bought mixed nuts, hummus, pitas, bread, canned corn, a watermelon and some other fruit, a bottle of orange juice for Mama, and ice pops for the three of them to eat before starting back to camp.

Emily fed the children lunch and laid them all down for a nap, wondering what was delaying the others and thankful they had not all gone, giving her and the little ones a chance to rest and get more laundry done. The weather was beautiful. Though it was hot, their temporary home was surrounded by large trees which offered plenty of shade. And there was often a breeze, which kept them very comfortable.

~ ~ ~

On the way back down the mountain, the three stopped to pick up the basket, admiring the workmanship that had gone into making it. Armando carefully tied it to his rear pannier rack, and they continued on. About a half mile before returning to camp, they heard the dreaded 'psssss', as David's back tire went flat. They redistributed the food to get more weight off of David's bicycle, Armando and Briana rode on, and David walked, pushing his crippled bicycle. It was around 3 PM.

They returned, excited to tell Mama about their adventures without her. Armando gave her the beautiful basket, and she promptly set it on the table and placed some of the fruit in it. She felt blessed that he had thought of her and gone to the trouble of bringing back something she would like.

Armando and Briana got into the clean-up efforts so they could earn a few shekels as well while David disassembled his back tire to replace the ruined tube. As they worked, a pick-up truck containing a clean-up crew of three men got out. Armando, Briana, Victor, and Isabel carried close to

---

[84]Druze – An Arab people who are not Muslim, but whose religion broke from Islam in the eleventh century. They are considered friendly by the nation of Israel and faithfully serve in the Israeli Defense Forces (IDF). They have the reputation of being very friendly, hospital people.

twenty filled kitchen trash bags to the men to throw in their truck. The workers were impressed with the hardworking children and happy that most of their work had been done for them. They visited with the family for a time before driving off to their next job.

While the older children busied themselves earning shekels by picking up trash, the younger ones rode their bicycles around camp for quite some time. The parents thought it comical, especially in light of the fact that there were people who believed taking this trip would be too hard on the children. If only they could see them now, jumping on their bicycles at every opportunity. After getting tired of riding, they went exploring in the nearby trees and woods, something they often did at home on the Varela property, which was mostly timber.

Tying *Tzitziyot*

Emily had wanted to journal, but it seemed there was never much time for that by the time children were cared for and work finished. She got out the *tzitziyot* string she had found at the mall in Or Akiva three days before to use on the new *Shabbat* clothes that Grandmother had made them. The string was a crochet thread and much thicker than what they usually used, but was all she could find in 100% cotton. Because of the command against mixing fibers, that aspect was important to them.[85] They reasoned that since the stated purpose of wearing the tassels was to remember to do the commandments, it would not be appropriate to make the tassels themselves out of a mixed fiber. Emily had been able to find the commanded blue string,[86] as well as white, lilac, and turquoise to go with the *Shabbat* outfits for the girls.

David, Emily, Armando, Briana, and Isabel sat at the picnic table tying while the others played and rode bicycles nearby. Briana and Isabel helped Emily stich the strings into the band of the skirts, one set on each of the four corners, before beginning to tie them. When they were finished, the tassels were visible so as to be in obedience to the command and they complimented the pretty outfits that Emily's mom had made. David and Armando tied tassels for the boys with three white strings and the blue, using the traditional Jewish pattern of knots. They made loops in the end so they hang in the belt loops of their pants or on the boys' suspenders, standing out on the black pants instead of blending in like the girls' did.

While they tied, they blessed and gave thanks for Grandmother, who had so carefully and lovingly made their special clothes. When the younger

---

[85]Deut. 22:11 Thou shalt not wear a garment of divers sorts, *as* of woollen and linen together.

[86]Num 15:38 Speak unto the children of Israel, and bid them that they make them fringes in the borders of their garments throughout their generations, and that they put upon the fringe of the borders a ribband of blue:

Chapter 9   False Prophets

children took a break from playing, David, Armando and Briana shared details about the site of Elijah's altar that they had seen earlier in the day. The family discussed all the passages of scripture they could think of which mentioned Mount Carmel. High on the list were the events of Elijah and his encounter with the prophets of Baal and Asherah.[87] Because of their in-depth studies into the scriptures and the origins of modern Christian traditions, they were well aware that Baal was a name of the sun god, whose birthday had been celebrated for thousands of years on the date now known as December 25. Asherah was a name for the fertility goddess, also known in scripture as 'Ashteroth' and the 'queen of heaven' and whose high celebration occurred on the first day of the week after the first full moon after the spring equinox every year. Her name in another culture was Ishtar and was where the Christian name 'Easter' originated. And, in fact, the celebration of Easter was held on the same date and using many of the same traditions as those used in the worship of Asherah.

The modern celebrations of Christmas and Easter had their official origins at exactly the same time as the official institution of Sunday or the 'day of the Sun' as the Christian 'sabbath' and day of rest and worship. They were all three instituted by the fourth century Roman Emperor, Constantine, who just added Christian meanings onto the long-celebrated pagan festivals. They talked about how, had Elijah been in the same situation today, he could just as easily have been calling for the prophets of 'Christmas' and 'Easter', since their origins are from the false gods Baal and Asherah.

The Varelas were passionate about refraining from mingling the worship of YHWH with the worship of the pagans, something He is so against in His word.[88] And they were passionate about sharing with Christians the truth about where their traditions came from and what they really stood for, but found that most did not want to hear. Now they were sitting on Mount Carmel, a short distance from where Elijah uttered the challenge, "If YHWH be Elohim, follow Him, but if Baal, then follow Him!"[89] Their location brought on a discussion of what it really meant to follow YHWH alone.

---

[87] 1 Ki 18:19-22 Now therefore send, *and* gather to me all Israel unto mount Carmel, and the prophets of Baal four hundred and fifty, and the prophets of the groves [Strong's H842 - Ashera] four hundred, which eat at Jezebel's table. So Ahab sent unto all the children of Israel, and gathered the prophets together unto mount Carmel. And Elijah came unto all the people, and said, How long halt ye between two opinions? If YHWH *be* **Elohim**, follow him: but if Baal, *then* follow him. And the people answered him not a word. Then said Elijah unto the people, I, *even* I only, remain a prophet of YHWH; but Baal's prophets *are* four hundred and fifty men.

[88] Jer 10:2 Thus saith YHWH, Learn not the way of the heathen [Strongs 1471 'goyim' - Gentiles], and be not dismayed at the signs of heaven; for the heathen are dismayed at them. ['Signs of heaven' includes sun worship.]

[89] 1Ki 18:21 And Elijah came unto all the people, and said, How long halt ye between two opinions? if YHWH *be* Elohim, follow him: but if Baal, *then* follow him. And the people answered him not a word.

They discussed the tragedies of mistranslations in most English Bibles that the enemy used to cover up the truth on many issues, and how the word 'Asherah', the precursor to 'Easter,' occurred over 50 times in the Hebrew Old Testament, but is translated into English as 'grove' or 'the groves', causing most readers to remain clueless that it is really addressing worship of the fertility goddess that used some of the same traditions still being used in modern celebrations of Easter.[90]

They talked about the bravery of Gideon, who though considering himself a weak man, had the courage to destroy the altar to Ba'al and the Asherah of his father.[91] And they marveled at the noble response of his father once he found out what happened.[92] They discussed how tragic it was that most Christians truly believe they are honoring YHWH by partaking of these festivals that He calls 'abominations.'[93] And they renewed their pledge to continue sharing the message of truth with those who truly want to follow Him and walk in His ways. They finished the day with their evening reading of the *torah* and went to sleep in their comfortable new home.

It had been a relaxing solitary time to finish catching up on needed things before packing to head out early in the morning. As evening approached, they took down the dry clothes and laundry lines and neatly packed them along with the *Shabbat* clothes and other things they had used that day.

---

[90] 1Sam 7:3-4 And Samuel spake unto all the house of Israel, saying, If ye do return unto YHWH with all your hearts, *then* put away the strange gods and Ashtaroth from among you, and prepare your hearts unto YHWH, and serve him only: and he will deliver you out of the hand of the Philistines. Then the children of Israel did put away Baalim and Ashtaroth, and served YHWH only.

[91] Jdg 6:27-28 Then Gideon took ten men of his servants, and did as YHWH had said unto him: and *so* it was, because he feared his father's household, and the men of the city, that he could not do *it* by day, that he did *it* by night. And when the men of the city arose early in the morning, behold, the altar of Baal was cast down, and the grove [Hebrew, Asherah] was cut down that *was* by it, and the second bullock was offered upon the altar *that was* built.

[92] Jdg 6:28, 30-31 And when the men of the city arose early in the morning, behold, the altar of Baal was cast down, and the grove [Asherah] was cut down that *was* by it, and the second bullock was offered upon the altar *that was* built...Then the men of the city said unto Joash, Bring out thy son, that he may die: because he hath cast down the altar of Baal, and because he hath cut down the grove [Asherah] that *was* by it. And Joash said unto all that stood against him, Will ye plead for Baal? will ye save him? he that will plead for him, let him be put to death whilst *it is yet* morning: if he *be* a god, let him plead for himself, because *one* hath cast down his altar.

[93] Deut 17:2-4 Throughout scripture, the pagan worship practices that originated at the tower of Babel are condemned by YHWH as abominations. They are mentioned by various names, but translate into modern western culture as the practices of Christmas, Easter, and Sunday as the primary day of worship (as opposed to worship on His Sabbath as instituted in Gen. 2).

10 – Mount Carmel

Daliat El Carmel

Yom Shishi (Sixth Day)

Up at dawn, they finished loading their bicycles and headed north again up Mount Carmel. The early morning was cool and comfortable for their ride into Daliat el Carmel. They passed the site of Elijah's altercation with the prophets of Baal and Asherah but did not ride the extra six mile round trip to the actual site. It was preparation day, and they wanted to be sure and get to their destination in time to set up and clean up before *Shabbat*. Neither of their two Mount Carmel contacts was confirmed, so the first business of the day was to find a place to spend the next two nights.

One contact was an acquaintance of another they had made online. They had never spoken to him, but kept his name as a backup. The other was a ministry they had learned of online and had previously contacted. An email was sent back to the family telling them to call when they were in Israel and that they might have a place for the family to set up a tent. David had called them the previous week when they had expected to be on Mount Carmel much sooner, and they had given permission for the family to stay overnight. But now it was approaching *Shabbat*, so the couple was not sure if the invitation would still stand. They were hoping to find somewhere they could stay for two nights, then ride out on the morning of *Yom Rishon*.

One thing they learned from riding that would not have stood out so much by car was the fact that Mount Carmel is not just one ascent to the top, but is a series of very steep roller-coaster-type hills. The family spent the biggest portion of the day pushing the bicycles uphill, since the downhill parts went very quickly. While riding through town, they received many friendly waves and greetings, letting them know they were in friendly territory, something they would learn to appreciate even more before leaving Israel. Only one person seemed to be upset with them, a bus driver who gestured in disgust with his palm facing up. They could not figure out what he was upset about, as they had not interfered with traffic in any way, so just smiled and waved at him as he passed.

Steep is an understatement when referring to the hills at the top of Mount Carmel. Emily, in the lead, would walk up the wide stone sidewalk counting each step with her right foot until she reached 100 (200 total steps), then stop and let the others catch up and rest. That is what she

had done for all the uphill treks to this point, but on this particular part of the journey, the 100 count was getting them just over 100 feet at a time. As they approached the midway point of the current incline, David drew the children's attention to the stone retaining wall next to them and told them to watch the height of it to know when
they were at the top. He kept encouraging them by commenting on how the wall was getting shorter and that they were almost there. It seemed they were 'almost there' for an hour, probably due to the fact that at one point, the wall actually got taller again.

When they got to the top of the hill in Daliat el Carmel, they sat down to rest and eat some melon, and hummus on pita bread. David got out the contact numbers, prayed for YHWH's will to be done, and called the messianic congregation, *Or haCarmel*[94] they had previously contacted. He was told the person he needed to speak with was out of town, but that his wife was available. When he finally got in touch with a person in charge, he was told they were not sure whether the family could set their tent up that day or not and that they would call back. David then called the other contact, who was friendly, but not necessarily inviting either. He was a little taken aback, as it was not often that American cycling families called him wondering if they could set up a tent at his place. The family finished their meal in the hot sun on the sidewalk of the mountainous town, knowing that YHWH was in control of where they would stay that night and that He would use the situation for His glory, wherever it was.

They packed the leftover food - Armando tying the new fruit basket onto his rear pannier - mounted again and rode a short level distance before descending the steep hill that went through an area with busy shops crowding the road on both sides. The streets and sidewalks were a maze of cars, pedestrians and wares for sale. The family continued receiving friendly greetings as they rode slowly with their brakes on. Upon reaching the bottom of the hill and out of the business district, one of the girls needed to use the restroom, but there was no place in sight, as they were now in a residential part of town, with little houses sitting very close together. Just as they dismounted to push up the hill in Osifia, another Druze village at the top of the mountain, Emily noticed what appeared to be an abandoned shop or covered concrete parking lot. There were concrete walls all around to shield the view of passersby or people in the nearby homes and plenty of big weeds that appeared they could use

---

[94]*Or haCarmel* - Light of El's Vinyard.

Chapter 10   Mount Carmel

watering. Emily took all the girls inside the tall concrete walls and took
care of their needs very quickly.

Druze Hospitality

While she was gone, a man from the auto shop next door approached
David and the boys and began speaking to him in broken English, asking
questions about the family. When Emily first saw him on their way back,
she was afraid he might be upset with them for trespassing, but he was
very friendly and seemed to be aware of why all the pretty (though sweaty
and somewhat dirty) little girls had disappeared into an abandoned lot of
weeds with their mother.

"Come," he invited, "sit in the shade," gesturing toward his shop. A little
reluctantly, as they wanted to hurry on to where they might be staying, but
not wanting to turn down the kind man's invitation, they followed him to the
tiny strip of shade under the side roof. As they parked their bicycles, a
little elderly Hebrew-speaking man approached them and, having nothing
of importance to say, just began singing *Hava Nagila*.[95]

The family had often danced to the upbeat, cheerful song during worship
in their home and at various places, so Emily grabbed the girls' hands and
they danced in a circle while David, after being prompted by the cute little
man, helped him sing. The boys stood and watched, sweating from the
heat alone, while the girls danced with Mama. David, a little timid that they
were in such a public place and not wanting to make a spectacle of
themselves (any more than they already were), signaled Emily when it was
time to stop. She thought the dancing went fine with their surroundings -
friendly, happy people bustling from here to there on preparation day, but
none-the-less, was just content that her husband had even allowed such
an escapade, so squashed her urge to continue dancing. The children
were all relieved for various reasons.

They sat down in the small shaded area to the north of the building,
scrunching up against the wall, as it was midday and shade was sparse.
The shop owner who had been talking to David asked, "Where are you
going?"

David replied, "Or HaCarmel," even though he still did not know where
they would be staying for the night. "But we're not exactly sure where it
is."

"Oh," his smile grew, "I know the place. I will give you a ride, all of you!"

David and Emily exchanged glances, thinking how much work it would be
to load all of their loaded bicycles into whatever type of vehicle he had.

---

[95]*Hava Nagila*, - 'Let us Rejoice;' a well-known Hebrew song.

Pedaling Home   Part 1 – In the Beginning

David replied, "It's OK. We're traveling by bicycle and would rather ride. Thank you, though." Even though the previous hill had been very difficult, everyone enjoyed a sense of accomplishment by conquering it.

"But the hill is very steep," he kindly argued. "The children cannot make it up."

"It's OK," David countered. "We go slowly. They'll be fine."

"Let me drive you up, the man said. I will show you how big and steep the hill is. I will show you where you are wanting to go. Then you decide."

David had to agree to this offer, so as not to be rude to the kind man who was trying so hard to do something to help. But, before getting his car, the man hurriedly disappeared behind the shop.

He returned from his mother's house behind with two bags of frozen food, one was homemade Druze pitas and the other another type of Druze food that his mother had made. He gave it to Emily, "*Bishvil hayeladim!* Save it for later," he said with his kind smile."

She was glad he clarified, as she was not sure if they were expected to eat the frozen food there or not, since it would thaw quickly. She thanked him, thinking the words seemed so hollow for such an act of kindness. He turned and walked quickly to his car, summoning David to join him. As they drove up the steep, curvy hill, another man came confidently striding down the street and set on the pavement in front of Emily an ice-cold two liter bottle of soda and several plastic cups, gesturing toward them in a very friendly way, and said, "*Bishvil hayeladim.*"

Emily was dumbfounded. The kindness continued. Unbelievable. But now she was in a predicament. She had been so careful to guard her children from the poisons of American junk food and drink, and most of them had never tasted a soda, but she felt awful to decline the hospitality of this stranger who just showed up off the street, so she thanked him, immediately opened the lid, and began pouring it into the little cups for the children. The man, satisfied with his good deed, left in the direction from which he had come. Emily quickly became acquainted with Israeli plastic cups, which she immediately did not really like. They were nearly paper-thin and very flexible. She had to train the children how to carefully hold them to keep them from crushing them in their little hands and spilling the sticky soda all over themselves and the pavement in front of the shop.

The children made strange faces as they tasted the carbonation bubbling on their tongues. Some of them did not like it, but those who seemed especially fond of sugar guzzled down their cupful and wanted more. Emily drank some too, in an attempt to save the children from over consuming the poison substance, but had she had to give an honest review, she would have had to say that she really enjoyed it, as she had not had a soda in years, quitting completely because she was prone to

94

Chapter 10 — Mount Carmel

drink too many. She reasoned that the sweet, caffeinated (something else the children had never had) beverage would help boost them up the hill, when it was time to go.

The man drove David to Or HaCarmel, on the other side of town, about half a mile beyond the top of the hill. He asked all the usual questions in broken English, and David was able to share with him about what they were doing in Israel.

When they returned, the kind man brought a garden hose out from behind the building and offered for the family to wash their hands and faces, since now, not only were they covered with streaks of sweat mingled with dirt, many had traces of soda on faces, hands, and clothes. Everyone was happy to get a good washing and they all looked much more presentable afterward. After providing water for their clean-up, he invited them back to his mother's house. David and Emily were a little nervous about the time, as he had told her after his ride that it was really going to be a tough go to the top, it was preparation day and they would need to be set up and get cleaned up before sundown, and they still did not know for sure where they would be staying. But there was no kind way to resist these loving gestures from total strangers, so they consented. They even wondered if this is where YHWH would have them camp.

They walked around to the back where his elderly mother was sitting under the shade of her massive grape vines, coring out little squashes and carefully placing small grape leaves in neat stacks on the small table in front of her. Emily spoke to her in Hebrew, thanking her for the gifts of food and learned that she was planning to stuff the squash with the grape leaves to cook for supper. Or that's what she *thought* she had said, anyway, as her Hebrew was not yet fluent. After visiting with the woman for a few minutes and exhausting anything that could be discussed between people who did not speak much of each other's language, her speaking mostly Arabic, Emily took the children up the driveway, which was completely covered and shaded by a long archway full of bunches of plump, ripe grapes. On their way back to where the woman sat, they picked up the fallen grapes as prompted by her, and ate them. They thanked her for her hospitality, gave her a postcard with a note on it, said 'shalom,' and went back around the shop to the bicycles. They again thanked the man, giving him a postcard and declining, one more time, a ride to the top.

They began the steep ascent in the early afternoon, resting at Emily's every one hundred step count. They stopped under a date palm tree hanging over a concrete wall to rest, after making it around the first part of the S-curve, north and to the left with a spectacular view of the village across the narrow road and below them to the left. As they enjoyed the inspiring view of the places from which they had come, they were met by a cyclist from England heading down. He was dressed for his ride, packing only his water, and riding an expensive bicycle made just for the type of excursions he liked to take. He stopped at the front and spoke with Emily, as the older children picked up sweet, yummy dates and shared them with their younger siblings. The man asked many of the usual questions and then told them of a quieter, scenic route that they could reach by going back down to the curve, then veering off a block or so. Although they would have enjoyed seeing the whole Jezreel Valley, no one in the family wanted to go back down, even a few feet, and have to push back up again. They generously thanked the man for the kind visit and information and resumed pushing up the hill as he rode down.

After rounding the second part of the S-curve, above the cliff that dropped off on the other side of the street, they came into a busier part of town again that was bustling with activity. Just a few hundred feet before reaching the very top of the hill, and after climbing the steepest part, a young man approached them from a large house on the other side of the street, in the residential area next to where the hill dropped to the valley from where they had just come. He spoke good English with an Arab accent and asked, "Would you like to take a break and rest in the shade of my porch?"

The parents glanced at one another again and David nodded. They were beginning to become accustomed to the hospitality of the Druze people, and though they were still feeling a little pressed for time, they again left it in YHWH's hands and decided to take up the kind man on his offer.

He showed them where to park their bicycles on the sidewalk, and they secured them out of the way of others who might walk by. After removing their helmets, they followed him up the steps to the large shaded porch and walked among the many beautiful plants to a picnic table at the far side. "Have a seat," he instructed, pointing at the table, and they all sat down, wondering what would happen next.

He went inside and came out bringing "juice," a bowl of hard candy, and another of frozen cacti. He set things down on the table in front of them and encouraged them to eat and drink. He showed them how to eat the cactus, which was cool refreshment in the heat, and Emily encouraged the children to only take two pieces of candy and drink water after a cup of "juice." They had learned that in Israel, as in Mexico, "juice" was a term used loosely to refer to any drink besides soda that was sweet and colorful.

They learned the young man who had graciously invited them into the shade of his porch was an attorney, the second the Varelas had met on

Chapter 10   Mount Carmel

their trip so far. He had learned English at the university and spoke it well. He lived in the home with his mother, his sister, and her two year old son. The man was very inquisitive about the family, their life, and the reason for their trip, which gave them plenty of opportunity to share with him truths from the scripture. Being Druze, and living in Osifia, he was familiar with different religions, as there were also quite a few Catholics there. He was intrigued by what he learned from the family.

Their conversation went in several directions, all related to the scriptures until he finally asked about the spots on the faces of Rebeka, Natanyah, and to a lesser extent Isabel, which now were almost a glowing red against the lighter background of their facial skin.

"They need a doctor," he suggested. "I know a good doctor you can take them to."

Emily responded, "Oh, it's just mosquito bites. We got them when we camped at Zichron Ya'achov three nights ago. They'll be fine. We've been putting salve on them. They're healing up nicely. They just look horrible."

He was not the first to say something about them; most people had been certain they were chicken pox or mumps and sure they needed a doctor. Emily did not want to explain that the family avoided doctors unless they were in dire emergency. Throughout the years, they had come to trust their Father more and more and recognized that most illness could be avoided by staying away from things like sugar and processed food and living an active life outdoors. When illness did occur, they had learned how to use herbs and essential oils for healing, like those spoken of in scripture did. They prayed over the sick and followed *Abba's* leads for treatment. For injuries, they also prayed and treated with herbs and oils. Several of the children had never been to a doctor, and the parents preferred it that way. Through research and trust in their Creator, they knew man-made pharmaceuticals were toxic to the body and could never heal, whereas, herbs had been created for healing.

After visiting for a while, David indicated that it was time to move on. They thanked the man for his hospitality and began walking toward the bicycles when the man's sister stepped out of the house with a tray of Druze coffee and everything to go with it. They knew they did not have time to sit down again, but did not want to refuse this additional offer of hospitality either, so stood outside the door with them and David and Emily rather quickly sipped the shot glass-sized cup of thick, strong coffee. Emily was not a coffee drinker, but eager to experience more of the Druze culture, it never crossing her mind that the effects of this little brew would still be with her as she lay wide awake in their tent at 4 AM, over twelve hours later.

After finishing the coffee and saying, "Shalom," David loaded Natanyah in her seat, everyone strapped on their helmets, and they began pushing their bicycles up the final ascent of only a couple hundred yards. Once at the top, they got on and began riding through the last part of town, and

97

once again were greeted in a snobbish way by the thoroughly disgusted bus driver who had gestured to them earlier that morning on the other side of Daliat HaCarmel. They waved cheerfully, just as they did to all the other people who were greeting them through open windows with cheers of, "*Kol hakavod!*" some even slowing to snap pictures as they slowly drove by. The family soon came to the beautiful green, tree-lined, gated entrance to Or HaCarmel, which they soon learned was a ministry center that was involved in various projects to help the local community, as well as immigrants to Israel. They dismounted and waited for traffic to clear before crossing the road and pushing up the hill towards the main office, where they were met by several friendly faces asking all the usual questions.

11 – Osifia

Or HaCarmel

The children were escorted inside the foyer and immediately given cool water, bread, pitas, peanut butter, spreadable chocolate sauce, and two chocolate bars each, while Emily spoke with two inquisitive women outside. David was approached by a man, temporarily in charge, who decided after a few minutes that it would not only be fine for the family to set up their tent on the property for the night, but that they were welcome to use the washing machine and showers, as well. They were then given access to a phone port so they could get online and were also given permission to use the public computer there at the office if they were unsuccessful at connecting their own. They were awed by the hospitality they were receiving, not knowing an hour before if they would even have a place to sleep.

Many people came in and out while the children were eating their snack on the floor of the lobby. Several African women and their children were being housed and cared for there while their husbands were in prison for working in the country illegally. The families had escaped persecution and poverty in Sudan and Ethiopia but were unable legally to work. The past plight of the ladies and children, though, did not show through their beautiful, dark, almost black, cheerful, radiant faces. The little dark children were enamored with the Varela children and bicycles and were excited when Armando and Briana helped them to ride for a few minutes.

In the meantime, Emily was bustling around with only a few hours before *Shabbat* and so much to do. There was the tent to set up, laundry to wash and hang, food to be bought, showers to take, and computer work to do, as this was the first access they had had since arriving in Israel eight days before. Since much of their business was conducted online, it was important for them to check in regularly. They decided it would be best to first set up the tent, so they could have a place to put things as they unpacked. It was the first time since leaving *S'dot Yam* that they had used the tent, but since they were in such a public place, thought it would be much better for privacy and for the sake of keeping their camp looking neater out of respect for their hosts. If there was any mess, it would be able to be contained within the tent. They took their bicycles around behind the building where they were instructed to set up on the grassy lawn, glancing around for hidden sprinklers as they went. They hid the bicycles neatly in the trees and quickly set up the tent.

Emily then took advantage of the opportunity to use the washing machines for their sheets and other items that were more difficult to wash, while

David took the children about a block away to buy some fruit and hummus to eat on *Shabbat*. After getting the laundry in, she tried to get an Internet connection on her dad's computer, but was not successful, so went in to the public computer to check for important emails and pay a few bills. The first one she looked at was from an electrician who was working on the jobs in Tennessee. They had tried to get in touch with him and the contractor who was in charge of the job, but were mostly unsuccessful because of time differences and being on the bicycles in places with no service during appropriate hours, so she was glad there was some type of communication there from him.

Upon receiving the bill, she informed David, who had just returned from the store with the children, bringing food for *Shabbat*. As soon as he saw the amount, he knew there was a problem, but did not indicate to Emily the scope of it. He told her how much to pay and that he would need to talk to the electrician before sending the rest. She went back to the computer prepared to pay the electrician and the contractor through Pay-pal, the online bill-pay system she had used for years. She did everything just as she normally did, but before finishing checking the emails, got a message back from Pay-pal, saying there was a problem with her account. The large sum of money she tried to send to the electrician was put on hold as being suspect of fraudulent activity.

She did not have time for these glitches and, unaware that her sense of urgency was not just because it was getting close to *Shabbat*, but because her entire system was buzzing from the effects of the Druze coffee, she attempted in every known way to contact Pay-pal to resolve the problem. It would not be until after they would return home that she would learn that Pay-pal cannot be used outside of the country of the account holder, a small piece of information that they would *never* forget.

David got on the phone, trying to reach the contractors back home and was able to have some success, but was already learning that there was a problem, though at this point, he was not clear as to why it was happening. He took the children to the television room, where others were watching a video called "Flushed Away" of a rat that got flushed down the toilet. It was not something the family would have watched at home, but under the circumstances, the parents thought it would be all right for their children to watch with the others for a little while, as they took care of needed business. David stayed with them for a short time, but was unable to get a good cell signal, so when the other man that was in the room told him it would be better outside, David went out, in order to be able to finish up the needed business before *Shabbat*. Besides the man, there was another woman in the room with the children, so he felt it would be fine to step outside for a few minutes. The children, not being accustomed to television, were glued and would not be causing anyone any problems.

Emily, down the hall, not being aware that David had left the children, was soon approached by a woman telling her that their rules required an adult to be in the room with the children at all times. The two adults who had

Chapter 11   Osifia

been there when David left had now gone, leaving the seven Varela children alone in the room with ten others. Emily left the computer, a little distressed that she had not finished the business yet, and went to the television room, where she found all the children sitting calmly watching the movie. It annoyed her jittery, highly-caffeinated self to have to be supervising completely zombieized children as they watched an approved movie, but she understood the necessity of rules in an organization and did not want to treat with contempt their gracious hosts. She did keep her head out the door, though, and flagged David's attention the first chance she got, so that he could take her place when he got off the phone. He was a coffee drinker and, though not accustomed to Druze coffee, was not bouncing off the walls like she was.

She went back to the computer to finalize any business and then typed out a quick email update to the people that had been praying for them on their trip.

> Shalom!
>
> We arrived in Israel 8/7 around 3AM. We're doing great, but have very limited and sporadic inet access. This is the first access we've had since being here and we don't have time to write. We have LOTS of great stories already of how the Almighty has blessed us and allowed us to meet many people.
>
> Please keep us in your prayers. The adventure is wonderful and is providing our family with lots of great memories and time spent together, but sometimes can be very dangerous. Please also pray that we will be constantly in His will and becoming the people He wants us to be.
>
> We'll give a better update as soon as possible, but we have no idea when that will be. We are currently on top of Mount Carmel, where we will probably be for a couple more nights before heading N, but we won't be in the same spot each night.
>
> *Shabbat* shalom,
>
> The Varelas

After finishing, she got the clothes out of the washer and hung them up on the lines of the patio, among the hundreds of other clothes belonging to other guests and workers. When the movie was over, David and the children went back to the tent where they once again began helping the Sudanese children to ride the two smallest bicycles. After a few minutes, the young man called David into the kitchen and told him they would be welcome to drink coffee and tea. He even offered the family food that was leftover from lunch and use of the kitchen, so long as they followed the rules of the mission and cleaned up after themselves. He also showed them the showers and offices and where he could be located if they

101

needed something. David was impressed with his generosity and the hospitality of the place.

While he was inside, a man approached the children and pulled one of the Sudanese boys of about four years old off of a bicycle, leaving it to roll by itself down the hill, off the retaining wall, and crashing into a tree below. The children were puzzled by what happened but just shrugged it off as none of their business. Briana went down to get the bicycle and Armando watched as the man walked off and the now angry little boy picked up a flat rock about the size of a baseball and threw it through the window of a shed in the laundry hanging area. Armando went to find and tell David, afraid the Varela children would be blamed for the glass breakage. After telling David, who reported the problem to one of the adults working there, the children went back to helping their new friends ride the bicycles.

Emily returned from quickly hanging the laundry and gathered the *Shabbat* clothes, towels, and other showering necessities and the family headed to the nearby shower rooms. She gave David the boys' *Shabbat* clothes and she took the girls' into the ladies' room next door. They quickly showered, to the distress of only Natanyah, who had not yet learned the benefits of being doused with water on the head and face as a way of coming clean. They quickly dressed, leaving another set of dirty clothes to be laundered. Emily had timed the washer and knew there was enough time left to get them washed and hung before *Shabbat*, so quickly threw them in, taking advantage of the convenience. They then went to the tent, where she pulled out the Druze pitas and other food that the sweet family at the bottom of the hill had given them earlier in the day, in preparation for supper.

The Musician

While inside the lobby, they had learned that a large Jewish family headed by a Musician was also going to be staying at the facility that night. It turned out to be one of the contacts the Varelas had made arrangements to stay with while still in the U.S. The Varela family was scheduled to arrive at their place in the north in a couple of weeks. Just before getting ready to eat, they were able to meet the musician and his precious family. As they sat outside on the back steps near their tent eating the Druze pitas and blessing the woman who made them and her son in Osifia, the Musician's wife approached them, "Would you like to join our family for the *Shabbat* dinner?" she asked.

Emily was surprised and honored and replied, "Sure, we'd love to. We've already eaten some, but as you know, children are always hungry."

"We're setting up now. Come when you're ready," she returned.

Shabbat on the Mountain

Chapter 11   Osifia

Shabbat

David and Emily gathered all the children and went inside to sit with their visiting hosts. They had never been to a Jewish *Shabbat* meal. Their *Shabbat* meal at home was usually whatever was easy enough to prepare on a day that was filled with other preparation activities in a farm home full of young children. Typically, they rushed right up until *Shabbat* and Emily was exhausted and too tired to enjoy the meal, which was usually just bread, grape juice, and one big pot of soup. The situation in front of them was completely different and a blessing to be a part of. First, the Musician did the traditional blessings in Hebrew for the bread and wine, as his large family shared their giant whole wheat Arab flat bread, wine and juice with the Varelas. Then the families together partook of a huge feast, which included bountiful chicken, rice, and other delicious fixings, a welcome fare for a family who had been surviving mostly on hummus, fruits, vegetables, and nuts. The Varelas were truly blessed by the hospitality of their new friends, people who were much like them in many ways, as well as the special meal they were able to share with them. As the younger children began to doze off, both families knew their time of fellowship was over for the night. The family thanked their hosts and went the few yards to their tent outside.

Everyone except Emily, on her caffeine high, seemed to sleep well. She lay awake most of the night reflecting on their time already spent in Israel and praying for many of the people they had met, as well as for the spiritual needs that she saw in her own family. Until around midnight, she watched through the screen window of the tent the people in the house next door, which was so busy that it actually appeared to be a bar or restaurant. She could hear their voices and the clattering of dishes through their open windows as she enjoyed the other nighttime sounds of the insects in the trees overhead. She was finally able to dose off to sleep a little after 4 AM, about an hour before dawn, her usual time for waking.

The whole family slept later than usual. When they awoke, they thanked YHWH for *Shabbat*, the day that He blessed and set apart from the creation of the earth for all to rest,[96] to bask in His presence, and to gather with others for the purpose of worshipping Him.[97] In their thankfulness,

---

[96]Gen. 2:2-3 And on the seventh day Elohim ended his work which he had made; and he rested on the seventh day from all his work which he had made. And Elohim blessed the seventh day, and sanctified it: because that in it he had rested from all his work which Elohim created and made.

[97]Lev. 23:2-3 Speak unto the children of Israel, and say unto them, *Concerning* the feasts of YHWH, which ye shall proclaim *to be* holy convocations, *even* these *are* my feasts. Six days shall work be done: but the seventh day *is* the sabbath of rest, an holy convocation; ye shall do no work *therein:* it *is* the sabbath of YHWH in all your dwellings.

A 'holy convocation' is a 'set-apart gathering or rehearsal.' This command was

they prayed as they often did for the many people who did not receive the blessings on this day because of false teachings passed down through the centuries.

Already wearing their *Shabbat* clothes since showering the evening before, they straightened up the tent by stacking the bed mats and folding and stacking the sheets, which had been freshly washed the previous day. Then they got out the fruit, hummus, and the Druze pitas from Osifia. They had also been given some giant sunflower seeds in a mixture with peanuts covered in a sweet crunchy batter. They sat on the U-shaped steps going down to the lower level of the back of the building that was near the tent, and ate breakfast in the quiet of the *Shabbat* morning.

After breakfast and some quiet time, they went over to the worship center up the hill in preparation for *Shabbat* service. It was a big, circular building that would seat several hundred people in folding chairs. The family found a row toward the back that would seat all of them. They had brought along their Bibles, notebooks, and coloring pencils, and a sheet on which little ones could lie, since they did not know how long the service might last.

They very rarely attended large congregations, so each one was a fresh, new experience for them. At Or HaCarmel, they found the music louder and with more of a contemporary beat than to what they were accustomed. But the songs were in Hebrew, very beautiful, and most were very worshipful. A screen in the front had the words transliterated, so those who spoke no Hebrew could still follow along and sing.

The message by the speaker was concerning the need for YHWH's people to pray and the power potential of prayer. It was very inspirational and thought-provoking. The little children colored in their notebooks until they got tired. Victor and Moshe fell asleep in the chairs, and after Natanyah fell asleep in Emily's lap massaging her ears, Emily laid her down on the sheet so she could then hold Rebeka, who was trying to drift off as well.

When the service was over, the family exited to the porch where there was a beautiful view of the city of Osifia. While standing there, they were approached by an American man asking, "Are you the cycling family?"

A little surprised (as their bicycles were hidden with their tent behind the office buildings), David answered, "Yes, we are."

"I'm the man you called yesterday, asking about a place to stay. Some mutual friends gave you my number."

"Oh, yes!" David replied, "It's nice to meet you!"
"It's nice to meet you all, too. I wanted to tell you that you are welcome to

---

given to all of YHWH's people, not just the Jews who are only a small part of Israel.

Chapter 11   Osifia

come and stay at our place for a night or two. We have an apartment where you can stay."

"That's really kind of you," David replied. "We plan to stay here tonight, since we're already set up and don't want to tear down on *Shabbat*, but we could come tomorrow."

"That would be fine," said the man. "I'll come back tomorrow and lead you to our place."

David and Emily were delighted at the invitation to stay with and meet someone new. In planning for their trip, they had known that they would be led of YHWH and did not want to pass up any opportunity to be with anyone that He would choose.

After a lunch of spaghetti that had been offered to them by a nice lady at Or HaCarmel, food that would have been wasted as it was left over from a big meal they had prepared for the Sudanese and Ethiopian families, Emily lay down in the tent with Natanyah for a nap while the others rested and played with the African children under and around the trees.

Nikolay had called, asking for directions. He and his wife had decided that their traditional *Shabbat* ride this week would be up the long steep hill from Haifa to see the family again and offer any help with trip planning. The family was glad to finally meet his wife, who seemed like a sweet lady and a fine match for him. They visited for a while and told Nikolay of their plans to stay on the mountain a little longer. Nikolay told them of a good road to take when leaving so they could avoid the major city of Haifa and head north toward Akko. This would work well with the general direction they had felt led to go before leaving the U.S. based on the contacts they had made. Their next known contact, another warmshowers.org host, was a two-day ride away for the little family, and had offered to come transport them and their bicycles up from the bottom of the big hill upon which his community was built. He had five children though some were grown, and the Varelas looked forward to meeting the family there as their experience through email and phone had been very pleasant.

After Nikolay and his wife left, the family spent more time with the Musician father of the large family, who said he would come back the next day and talk about them visiting and helping on his place in a couple of weeks, once they got that far on the bicycles. He left to take his family back to where they were staying with extended family, and the Varelas ate more of the food they had received at the bottom of the hill, blessing those who gave it.

105

12 - Gracious Host

Fire!

Week 2   *Yom Rishon* (First Day)   8/17

Since they were waiting to hear from the Musician and their new Host would not be ready for them until noon, Emily put their *Shabbat* clothes in the wash first thing after getting up, then took down the clothes they had hung just before *Shabbat*. The family disassembled the tent and packed their belongings. For breakfast, they finished all the food that had been given to them at Osifia and Or HaCarmel. Knowing the clothes would not have time to dry before they needed to leave, Emily took them out of the washer, shook them out, then rolled them neatly and placed them in plastic bags to hang once at their new destination. Shortly after, their Host arrived along with his two older children on their bicycles, a nine-year-old boy and seven-year-old girl, to show them the way to their home. They left a message for the Musician with Or HaCarmel and followed the Host to his house. His children rode happily along with the Varela children, excited to be riding bicycles.

The family followed him back in the same direction from which they had come, but not going as far as the house of the attorney they had visited with two days before. As they rode slowly past the markets, they noticed smoke rising just ahead of them. When they came closer, they saw the fire in a shed beside a little market near the street. The owner and his helpers were scrambling, trying to remove boxes or anything else that would feed the flames. The shed was full of cases of sodas, water, and other merchandise that the man sold in his store. David, always ready and willing to help people, left Emily to hold his bicycle, while he ran to assist them. Emily, seeing that the men working there were opening and dumping bottles of drinking water in an attempt to extinguish the growing flames, quickly passed the bicycle off to Briana and emptied her laundry buckets that were under Natanyah's seat, giving them to Armando to take to the scene.

The old man gladly motioned for Armando to come, then led him around the store and down an alley which descended by steps for about fifty feet. He stopped and opened a door in the block wall, quickly tied a rope that had just arrived from another youngster about Armando's age onto one of the buckets, then dropped it through the door into a cistern under his house. He had larger buckets there, but was unable to use them because the cistern door was too small for them to fit through. He brought the two gallon bucket up over and over again, filling up two five gallon buckets and the other small bucket of the Varelas. He passed the three buckets off to

Chapter 12   Gracious Host

Armando and the other youngster, who then ran back up the alley and handed them off to David and the other men who were actively fighting the fire.

The Host and his children stood at the sidewalk with Emily and the other Varela children to make sure they were safe from traffic and any potential explosions resulting from the fire. Emily began to feel that they were in a predicament, since the Host was leading them to his house. She felt stuck in a situation of possibly being disrespectful of one person's time in order to be of help to someone else, but at the same time, very glad that David was one to always try to help those in need. The Host began to pace and act rather nervously, but the fire was beginning to be conquered, so Emily knew it probably would not be much longer before they would leave. Finally, the Host got David's attention and motioned him to come back. David felt satisfied that the people at the store could now handle the dying fire without his help, so brought the bucket that was not being used at the cistern and came back with Armando.

Emily asked for the other bucket, but was then told that it was being used. She did not know about the whole rope and cistern situation, so was a little confused as to why she could not have her special bucket back. She did not want to leave without it, as her bicycle had been custom fit for it and it was so useful on their trip. But the Host seemed to be in a hurry, so the shop people told David they would save it for him and he could come back later to get it. Emily stuffed all the laundry supplies back into the one bucket and loaded it on her bicycle, praying that she would soon get the other back. It seemed like such a silly thing to be so possessive of a bucket, but these were of a rather odd size, were perfect for what she needed, had sealable lids, and would be next to impossible to replace, even in the U.S., but much more so in Israel. She thought of how little they had brought on this trip, but how important those few things were to them and how much more difficult things would be made if they were without them. There was a freedom in traveling with only what they needed, but it did make those few things seem very necessary.

They finally left the scene and followed the Host to his home a couple of blocks away. He lived tightly with his wife and three children, the youngest being one year old, in the downstairs of his in-laws house. They had lived across the brick driveway in a small apartment with a living room, kitchen and bath downstairs and two bedrooms on the second level, but had left that apartment in order to use it for guests. "You can stay in this apartment," he offered.

"That's very nice of you," David replied, "but we're fine in our tent or even just outside on our mats."

The Host insisted that they slept inside, and the couple sensed that the in-laws might be opposed to having people sleeping outside at their place, so David told him, "Ok. We'll sleep inside, but we don't need to use the

107

upstairs. We can just put our mats out on the floor here, if it's OK for us to move the coffee table to make more room in the center."

"Oh, sure. That will be fine," he agreed, then continued, "You're welcome to take showers, but water in Osifia is only turned on during certain hours, and we don't always know when that will be. If the water is on, you are welcome to it."

Missionary Questions

The Host then gave the family a tour of their small home and introduced them to his wife's father, mother, and sister who lived upstairs. They were a Druze family and very friendly, especially his mother-in-law. They visited for a while at a table outside when a lady missionary from the U.S. came and began asking questions. The Varelas' simple lifestyle seemed as intriguing to woman as the description of her cozy lifestyle funded by donations was to Emily.

She asked Emily, "So why do you wear tassels?"

Emily: Because of the instruction to wear them to remember to keep the commandments.

Missionary, surprised: So you keep the Old Testament commandments?

Emily: Yes, we do our best to.

Missionary: So, you keep *all* of the commandments?

Emily: All that apply to us, yes.

Missionary, interested: What about circumcision?

Emily: Yes, that is one of the commandments, and it still applies to Yah's people today.

Missionary: So you circumcised your sons on the eighth day?

Emily: Actually, no. I was brought up in a Christian home and was taught that circumcision was no longer important. David was born at home and never circumcised. We had planned a home birth for Armando and saw no need to take him to a doctor to get circumcised. We tried to do things naturally, and I felt that the foreskin was put there for a reason and that, since it was no longer necessary to take it off, it should stay. And David's response to the idea was, 'They're not messing with *that*!

"Even then, we were trying to live our lives according to the scriptures, but believed some false teachings. My parents encouraged us to get Armando circumcised at birth for health reasons, and I remember telling them that if

Chapter 12   Gracious Host

we did decide to get him circumcised, we would do it on the eighth day, like scripture says to. But at the time, we still thought it was unnecessary.

"When Victor was born, we were of the same opinion, but shortly after that, we began to see the importance of keeping the scriptural seventh-day Sabbath. Within a couple of years, we began to see that the 'Jewish' feasts were actually the feasts of YHWH[98] and were meant for *all* of His people, not just the Jews, and had begun keeping them. I had also come to the understanding from my study of scripture by then that circumcision was still important, that the covenant of circumcision had never been abolished, but David was in disagreement about it.

"We had planned a trip to Mexico in the fall of 2004, when we found out we were pregnant with our sixth child. I asked David, 'What if it's a boy? Will we circumcise him?', and he agreed to study the scriptures on the subject. Because we wanted to have the baby at home, we moved our trip up a month so that we could be home a couple of weeks before the birth, but Moshe was born unexpectedly a month earlier than we had planned. Thankfully, he was full-term; we had just been off a month on our dates. After we saw that the baby was a boy, I asked David again what he was going to do, reminding him that he only had eight days to study it. He told me not to worry, that he would. But along with the unexpected birth of our sixth child came several obstacles for him.

"The seven of us had come to Mexico in a seven-passenger minivan. David had to find a junk yard with a bench seat that could replace the two bucket seats in the middle of our van, making it eight passenger. We also had to get another car seat, then decide which of our things we were willing to leave in Mexico, since we could not take everything back. He also had to try to get a birth certificate, which was not easy, since he was not born in the hospital. And all that on top of taking care of the five other children, checking in on me, and visiting his relatives that he rarely saw.

"We were nearing the time that we had to return to the farm, since we had only made arrangements to be gone for a month. The people staying at the farm would have to get back home and we would have bills coming due. Moshe's eighth day was the day we had to leave, and David had still not studied. I offered to drive so he could read his scriptures, but after being up so late with family the night before, he only studied for about an hour before I heard him beside me snoring.

"I woke him and reminded him that it was the eighth day and we needed to do something. He told me he had studied enough and that Paul's writings made it clear that it was no longer necessary. I was horrified. I knew from reading the scriptures that Y'shua's death and resurrection had

---

[98]Lev. 23:2 Speak unto the children of Israel, and say unto them, *Concerning* the feasts of YHWH, which ye shall proclaim *to be* holy convocations, *even* these *are* my feasts.

109

Pedaling Home   Part 1 – In the Beginning

not changed the commands of the *torah*. Instantly, my whole body felt like it was on fire. I had to do something! My husband was making a wrong choice and I had to make it right, just like Tzipporah did when Moses hadn't circumcised his son.[99] So I devised a plan. We would be driving across the border in a couple of hours. I'd just go to a pharmacy, buy a scalpel, and do it myself. I'd envisioned, from studying all the passages in scripture discussing circumcision, how it would be done. I felt sure I could safely do it. And a strange feeling replaced the fire in my body, a sort of numbness. Just afterward, I heard the voice, one of the most pronounced times I've heard it. It said, 'Don't do it. I know your heart. It's not your responsibility.'

"At that instant, I felt a warm peace come over me, starting at my head and flowing down over my body. I had never experienced that before, or since, but I knew it was YHWH and that I was to just let it go. But every time I changed that baby's diaper, I had to forgive David again because I knew he was wrong.

"Sixteen months later, I was doing our morning scripture reading, as usual, and we were reading in Exodus about the Passover, and it mentioned that no uncircumcised male should eat of it. About two weeks afterward, we were sitting at the table and, out of the blue, David said, 'I'm going to study circumcision again, and if I see that it's still for today, I'm going to take all the boys and go get us circumcised.

"I almost fell out of my chair. I had never once imagined that he would even consider being circumcised himself. I had known that if I were a man, I would have wanted to have it done, but I never had that expectation of him. So I was excited. And, sure enough, by the time he finished studying all the passages concerning circumcision (with a circumcised heart this time), he was convinced. At the time, we didn't know anyone else who had ever done this, so we searched and *Abba* found us a doctor who was willing to do it on most of our terms, in his office, without general anesthesia, starting with David, as he requested, being the head of the house.

"So, yes, now they are all circumcised, though none on the eighth day. Armando was nine years old and had been wanting to be circumcised for over a year. He has a very tender heart for Yah and knew it was the right thing to do."

The children played together on the tile patio while Emily shared the story with the women. David was in between the two groups, preferring to spend time with his children than to participate in a ladies' conversation, but was still interested in what they were saying. She patiently answered the woman's questions from the scriptures, explaining that the covenant of

---

[99]Exo. 4:24-26

Chapter 12   Gracious Host

circumcision was for all of Abraham's descendants forever and for those who were joined to them in the worship of YHWH.[100]

Missionary: But the New Testament is very clear that circumcision is not necessary for salvation.

Emily: That's true, but that's not the issue concerning whether or not to circumcise. The salvation issue was cleared up in Acts 15 and 21. We are not saved by our works. But once we are saved, we *want* to obey Him. Since we are redeemed and grafted back into Israel when we follow Yah and accept His Salvation, all of the blessings and instructions that He gave to Israel now apply to us. We can't claim the promises that come with obedience if we're not willing to obey.

Missionary: But what about Paul? He speaks against circumcision.

Emily: That's what some people *say* he says. In reality, he is being grossly misunderstood. Remember that Y'shua in Matt. 5:18 says that anyone who breaks one of the least of the commandments and teaches others to do so will be called least in the kingdom?

Missionary: Yes.

Emily: If Paul is really teaching us to break the commandments, he would be called 'least' in the kingdom. If he's going to be called 'least' in the kingdom, do we really want to listen to him and trust what he says? But before you think I'm against Paul, remember what Peter said in 2 Pet. 3:15-17, that people during his day who were unlearned and unstable (unlearned in *torah*, because that's what Paul was learned in), were twisting Paul's writings to their own destruction, to the error of the wicked, 'wicked' there being 'lawless' or 'without *torah*.' Then he goes on to warn his readers not to fall for the twisting of Paul's writings, lest they fall to their own destruction. In other words, Peter is defending the integrity of Paul's writings from being twisted by those who did not have a good understanding of *torah*. That's exactly what's happening today. We are being told by people who do not understand *torah* that Paul is telling us we don't need to follow it anymore. But when we read Paul from the perspective from which he wrote, that of a highly *torah*-educated observant

----

[100]Gen. 17:10-14 This *is* my covenant, which ye shall keep, between me and you and thy seed after thee; Every man child among you shall be circumcised. And ye shall circumcise the flesh of your foreskin; and it shall be a token of the covenant betwixt me and you. And he that is eight days old shall be circumcised among you, every man child in your generations, he that is born in the house, or bought with money of any stranger, which *is* not of thy seed. He that is born in thy house, and he that is bought with thy money, must needs be circumcised: and my covenant shall be in your flesh for an everlasting covenant. And the uncircumcised man child whose flesh of his foreskin is not circumcised, that soul shall be cut off from his people; he hath broken my covenant.

111

Jew, it's clear that he never says obedience to the *torah* is not important.
Missionary: But in Galatians he actually says not to become circumcised.

Emily: Galatians is the book most often used by people teaching others
not to keep the commandments, those people who Y'shua says will be
called 'least' in the kingdom. In fact, it was because of Galatians that one
Christian doctor turned us down and refused to do the circumcisions,
though he would have done it for medical reasons. The problem most
people have with Galatians is that they are not recognizing terminology
used in the first century. Once that's cleared up, the book aligns with the
rest of scripture, instead of contradicting it. The example you are speaking
of is cleared up when we look at other scriptures and realize that 'the
Circumcision' was actually a term used to describe religious Jews who
were followers of Y'shua, but continued with their man-made traditions,
one of which was the traditional circumcision of converts to Judaism. An
example of this is in Acts 15 and 21. These followers were described by
Luke as 'the Circumcision.[101] Understanding this makes Paul's writings in
Galatians easier to understand in the proper context. In Galatians 2:7 it's
very clear that the 'uncircumcision' refers to Gentiles, while the
'circumcision' refers to Jews.[102]

"Basically, in Galatians, what Paul is saying is that we can't work for, or be
justified by works, by keeping *torah*. We can only be justified through faith.
Just like Abraham was counted as righteous before he was circumcised.
He was counted righteous because of his faith. His faith is what caused
him to obey. Obedience is the fruit of faith. That's why James says, 'Faith
without works is dead.'[103]

"In other words, we are justified by faith, just like Abraham, who truly
trusted in Yah and His Salvation. But our faith is exhibited by our works,
our level of obedience to our Creator. If we are not following His
instructions because we have been taught that it's no longer necessary,
when He clearly states in His word that following these instructions bring
life and blessing and disobeying them brings death and curses, do we
really have faith? According to numerous places in scripture, we don't.
And that brings us back to circumcision. It's a sign of his people and is
directly related to the land of the promise.[104] Ezekiel even says that when
the millennial temple is built, the uncircumcised will not be able to enter

---

[101]Acts 11:2 And when Peter was come up to Jerusalem, they that were of the
circumcision contended with him,

[102]Gal. 2:7 But contrariwise, when they saw that the gospel of the uncircumcision
was committed unto me, as *the gospel* of the circumcision *was* unto Peter;

[103]Jas. 2:26 For as the body without the spirit is dead, so faith without works is
dead also.

[104]Gen. 17:7-8 And I will establish my covenant [circumcision] between me and
thee and thy seed after thee in their generations for an everlasting covenant, to
be an Elohim unto thee, and to thy seed after thee. And I will give unto thee,
and to thy seed after thee, the land wherein thou art a stranger

Chapter 12   Gracious Host

it.[105] I think that's one of the things that really struck David and had him make the decision he did concerning himself and the boys.

Missionary: Wow, that's an amazing testimony, but I'm still not convinced about Paul. I'd like to bring my husband over this evening to meet you all and talk about these things. He knows the scriptures well.

Emily: That would be great! We'd love to meet him and share with him what *Abba* has shown us.

The talk turned to lighter subjects, and soon the Missionary left to return home. Emily excused herself from the other two women. "I need to hang out a few things that we washed this morning," she said, intending to hang them on the bicycles.

The Host's generous wife offered, "You can hang them here on our lines."

Emily was again amazed at the hospitality they were experiencing, being offered to use rationed water as much as they wanted, and now being offered to use laundry lines that were limited, and on a day that the ladies were also doing laundry. She expressed her thanks to the woman and brought the damp clothes from the panniers to hang. She hoped they would be dry by the time water was turned on and the Host's laundry was ready to hang. One day's laundry for the family of nine used up a significant amount of space on the lines.

As she hung the clothes, her Hostess talked more about the water rationing situation, then stressed, "But when the water is on, take as many showers as you like. It gets very hot here, so sometimes we bathe the baby several times a day."

That was a foreign concept to Emily, who quickly realized that the woman only had three children, two of them much older, lived in the home with her parents, had close family nearby, had her children in public school, and did not run a business or operate a farm - a completely different life with a baby than Emily had ever known. She wondered what a life like that might be like, but doubted that, even in those circumstances, she would bathe a baby several times per day. She reasoned that must be one happy baby.

After an hour or so, David returned with Armando and Briana to the store to retrieve the laundry bucket. The shop owner had hidden it on a top shelf behind some boxes of sodas after all the excitement from the fire was over. He expressed his gratefulness for the use of it as he gave it back to David. They left there and stopped at a market on the way back, where they bought hummus and bread for supper and fruit for breakfast.

---

[105]Eze. 44:9 Thus saith Lord YHWH; No stranger, uncircumcised in heart, nor uncircumcised in flesh, shall enter into my sanctuary, of any stranger that *is* among the children of Israel.

Shortly after his return, the Missionary arrived with her husband. She had briefed him on the previous conversation with Emily, and after friendly introductions, he quickly got down to business and proceeded to inform David about circumcision: "It's not for non-Jewish believers of today."

David asked, "Could you show me where it says that in the scriptures?"

The man began looking, but was unable to find the passages he was thinking of. As often happened in situations like these, because of his seriousness of his family's walk with Yah and the hours of study they had amassed in an attempt to live according to His word, David was able to provide the man with verses that he needed to use against him in the argument. David knew them all well, as he had used them in the past to justify not circumcising his own sons. As he gave the man a verse and the man confirmed that was the one he needed, David showed, using the scriptures, how the verse did not mean what the man had been taught to believe that it had. This went on until the Missionary had no more argument against circumcision. David always marveled at how Yah's word is completely consistent throughout, when subjects are studied using scripture to interpret scripture, instead of using commentaries and opinions of men.

Trouble in Tennessee

The couple soon left and the Varelas ate and took quick showers. The girls all jumped in with Emily and then the boys in with David in order to conserve water and because with so many little ones, it just worked better that way. The Host returned and asked, "Would you like to walk with us to my mother-in-law's mother's home a couple of blocks away?"

David gladly consented, since they had mostly been sitting in one place, and the now squeaky clean family walked with the Host's family through the Druze village to a house across the small valley that could be seen from where they were staying, but that could more easily be accessed by walking around on the roads. Once there, a small crowd assembled as all of the relatives who lived nearby gathered to see and talk to the larger-than-average American cycling family. Many questions were asked and answered and sweet treats, ice cream and candy given to the children.

As sundown approached, the family said their farewells and headed back with their Host and his family to their home and the accommodations that they had provided for the Varelas. Since it was now late morning in the U.S., David tried to reach people concerning the jobs and the farm, but was not very successful, as it was the first day of the week and still considered the weekend there. That fact was becoming more burdensome to the family, even after being in Israel for only such a short time and living according to a more scripturally correct calendar. David was able to reach the New Yorkers at the farm, who reported that all was well, then added, "But we're having problems with the refrigerator and stove."

David: What kind of problems?

New Yorker: Well, the refrigerator's not cooling and the stove is not heating. But we're working on trying to fix them, and it's not a big problem because we're able to use the appliances in the RV.

David: OK, good. I'm glad you've got appliances in the RV, but I don't understand what can be wrong with ours. They're both fairly new and were working fine when we left. If you're not able to get them working, let me know and I'll send someone out to repair or replace them.

David was finally able to reach the Manager of the construction jobs for the first time since arriving in Israel, and found that the projects had all but stopped. The report was confusing, so he began trying to reach other people, but was still not able to get everything resolved. He was becoming more and more concerned that his return would be necessary in order to straighten things out. Emily was aware of what was going on through hearing his side of the phone conversations, both in English and Spanish, and was not liking what she was hearing, already imagining being left in Israel while he went back to the States.

13 - Down

Yom Sheni (Second Day)

Neither David nor Emily slept well. They both spent a lot of time in prayer concerning the situation back home and what it might mean for their trip. Their accommodations were very comfortable, though they found sleeping indoors to be stuffier than being out in the fresh air like they had been, even with the door open all night. After a breakfast of fruit, pitas and hummus, they talked to their Host, who was aware of some of the situation that had transpired on the phone the night before. He had offered up front for the family to spend two nights, which they decided to accept, but now offered for them to stay as long as they needed. The only problem with that offer was that the property was not really his, but his father-in-laws, and final approval would have to come from him.

The Varelas did not feel comfortable staying longer than the two nights, and Emily certainly did not feel good about being there if David were not. The Host's father-in-law was a nice man, but was not especially accepting of children and the messes they make. He faithfully hosed off his very large patio every day and had things in perfect order at all times. And in fact, before he returned from work, the ladies bustled around making sure everything was in order and would meet with his approval upon his arrival. Emily had seen the flash in his eyes when something did not quite meet with his approval and could not fathom the thought of the stress of them being there without David for an unknown amount of time.

Their Host's children went to school and the Varela children played on the large patio for much of the day. Emily visited with his wife and her mother and sister. David took some of the children and bicycles next door to the gas station to air some of tires that were low. They returned and readjusted packs, making things ready to leave in the morning.

In the afternoon, David began trying to reach people back in the U.S. which he had not been able to contact since they had arrived. He had to wait till 3 PM on the second day of the week to begin making phone calls, as that was only 8 AM central time on Monday in the U.S. As soon as he was able to begin reaching people, he knew the problems had become too complicated for him to resolve from thousands of miles away. He did not know the source at the time, but knew he was the only one who would be able to straighten things out. He and Emily prayed together that YHWH's will would be done and that the problems would resolve themselves. David talked to the Manager, as well as one of the owners of the restaurant they were remodeling and a couple of other subcontractors, but the situation had become quite confusing.

Chapter 13   Down

They both put the problems behind them temporarily in order to give thanks for Briana completing her tenth year. They had quit celebrating birthdays over the past few years because they knew its origins were in paganism. They did not see any harm in acknowledging the day, but did not recognize it as having any value either, as YHWH does not go by man's calendar. But in the interest of extended family, and not seeing a direct conflict with the word, they usually shared a special meal and had cake near the birth date of each child. They decided to eat pizza and cake, things they had not yet tried in the Promised Land and would be thought of as special by the whole family. David and Briana went to the market and got the food, then came back and invited their Host and his family to join them. Upon finding out it was Briana's birthday, his sister-in-law gave Briana a little porcelain figurine, some hair rubber bands, and Winnie-the-Pooh stickers. It was a sweet gesture from a new friend, and a memory Briana would treasure for a long time to come.

David got back on the phone and tried his best to work out more details, but did not have much success. He was able to get the job going again, but not in an efficient manner, as two of the contractors had left because of a management problem and another because of a misunderstanding. He left it in YHWH's hands. If *Abba* wanted him to return to the States, He would have to provide the right place for the family to stay.

Yom Shlishi (Third Day)

They went to bed, neither of them sleeping well again, but spending much more time in prayer. Emily even went upstairs and tried to sleep on one of the beds in an attempt to get some much needed rest, but to little avail.

The family awoke to another beautiful day that would soon turn very hot. They packed their belongings, including a few baby clothes their Hostess had given them. It was hard to say no to such generosity and they were clothes that a couple of the girls could use. But the family looked forward to a time soon when they would mail unneeded items back to the U.S. so their load would be lightened.

The Descent

They said their goodbyes, then headed from Osifia toward Haifa with their maps and the directions given them by Nikolay. A few miles out of town, they stopped for their mid-morning breakfast at a park just off the road. A crew was working there, so they did not use the picnic tables, but sat under some trees near the road and ate. The children ran around, some exploring, as David and Emily briefly discussed what was going on back home and how they needed to deal with the situation. They decided it might be good to call the Musician, since they had failed to reconnect with him and wondered if his place might be a good one for Emily and the children to stay in order for David to be gone for a couple of days. David decided to pray about that and possibly call him later in the day.

117

They left the park and started the steep descent down Mount Carmel toward Haifa. The view was incredible as they could see for miles and, through the haze, the Mediterranean Sea in front of them. They passed a big radio tower, but failed to remember it as the landmark described by Nikolay, telling them where to turn. They came to a road that they questioned might be the right one to avoid Haifa and ride north toward Akko, but could find no road signs. They discussed what to do, prayed, and believed they were to continue on straight down the hill toward Haifa.

They came to a busy tourist look-out and used that opportunity to do some adjustments on the bicycles and packs and use the restroom that was just at the entrance. They loaded up again, rode through the University of Haifa and turned right to follow the road at the edge of the city. It was at this point they realized for sure they had missed the road that Nikolay had told them about, but from looking at their map, they found an alternate way to continue north. They knew there was a reason they had missed the road and were confident that YHWH was in control of the whole situation. They saw no need to push their bicycles up the big hill again to get on the intended route. That would have made them too late to have reached the designated place to sleep under the trees for the night, anyway.

After leaving the university, they continued down the long, steep hill, this time on a four-lane road divided by a grass median with a curb on each side. There were roads coming from the left, but no through streets, as they were on the very edge of the city. At each intersection, there was a traffic light. The children had been instructed during their training in the U.S. of the importance of the color of the lights. Normally, it was possible for everyone to get through a light before it changed, but if a light ever turned yellow, the children had been taught to stop, even if the person in front of them had started through.

It was difficult to ride slowly, as the hill was so long and steep. The family rode with their brakes on almost the whole time, and Emily knew that it was hard on the legs of the little ones who had foot brakes. They had some experience on steep hills back home and found it to be more difficult for some of the children to ride down the hills than to ride up, because of the need to constantly be braking. Because of this, Emily went faster than she normally would have, in order to give the children more space behind her so they could let off their brakes some and speed up before having to brake again.

Wipe Outs

The order of riding was Emily with Natanyah in the front, Rebeka, Moshe, Briana, Victor, Armando, Isabel, and David in the rear. Upon passing the third intersection, the light turned yellow just before Isabel reached it. Not knowing it would have been safe to continue on at her speed, with no traffic present and being a 'T' intersection, she pushed harder on her brakes

Chapter 13   Down

which she was already riding, causing her bicycle to slide sideways in the small bit of gravel that was scattered in the road. David watched, helplessly, as her bicycle slid and entered the passing lane. He maneuvered his bicycle into that lane behind her to protect her from traffic coming down the hill, which came to a screeching halt behind him. He watched as she fell hitting her chin on the pavement, which broke the skin and caused blood to spew heavily.

~ ~ ~

At precisely the same instant, Moshe, who was four children in front of Isabel, turned his head to look at some big construction cranes that were working nearby and bumped into the indention of the curb at a bus stop, crashing his bicycle. He bumped his head on the sidewalk and skinned his left elbow, tearing a hole in his orange shirt. Briana, riding just behind Moshe, had to slam on her brakes to avoid hitting him and his bicycle and crashed into the curb, but did not fall, crediting her bicycle with having good shocks. Armando, coming fast behind her, was unable to veer to the left without entering the passing lane, and not knowing if traffic was behind him, intentionally swerved to the right, ramped the curb at the bus stop, became airborne, then landed safely on the sidewalk. His frequent ramping at home, using various pieces of leftover construction materials and metal pieces found around the farm, proved to be good practice for this critical event.

~ ~ ~

Isabel, up the hill screaming in pain, looked up from the pavement and thought the ambulance racing from the bottom of the hill was coming for her. She watched as it continued up on the other side of the median, and then turned to see David approaching. At that moment, the two young ladies in the car behind them jumped out and ran to aid David in caring for her. David gathered her up in his arms, moved her to the sidewalk, and went to move her bicycle out of the road, while the ladies opened their first aid kit and began doctoring. David worked on calming her, and then ran down the hill to check on Moshe.

~ ~ ~

Briana moved her bicycle and Moshe's off of the road and got out the first aid kit to help him, still not aware of Isabel's accident farther up the hill. After moving the bicycles and noticing that Isabel and David were not there yet, she looked up and saw Isabel, whose face was covered in blood. Armando, having seen Moshe's accident, continued his descent rapidly to inform Emily. As Briana opened the first aid kit, a kind gentleman stopped his car, a small square mini-van, to help. He picked up crying Moshe and laid him on a nearby bench, comforting him as Briana began getting out supplies. Then he took over with the doctoring, himself.

~ ~ ~

Emily, at the front, had looked back just before the incidents occurred, so was unaware that anything was wrong until a car came up behind her beeping. A man yelled out the window something in Hebrew about 'up the hill' and she could tell by his voice that something was badly wrong. She stopped and looked back, but because of the curve she had just gone around, could not see anyone besides Rebeka. She pulled up on the sidewalk under the solitary bunch of young trees, the only shade for quite some distance and decided to wait, knowing it would take her and Rebeka several minutes to push the bicycles back up to where the others were, and not wanting to walk up herself, leaving Natanyah and Rebeka there alone.

Just as she was thinking maybe she *should* go up, Armando came racing down, announcing, "Moshe crashed!"

"Is he all right?"

"I think so."

"You *think* so?!?" she questioned excitedly. "Go back up and let me know what I need to do."

They all knew he could run faster than she could seven months pregnant, and she still did not want to go herself, even leaving Armando there with the young girls.

Armando jogged up the hill, not able to run because of its steepness and the heat of the sun, and upon reaching Moshe, who was moaning in pain as the kind gentleman doctored him, saw that he was all right. He had noticed Briana going up the hill and yelled, "What's going on?"

She yelled back to him, reporting in a few words what she had been told by David during his short visit, "Isabel busted her head open!"

Armando jumped on Moshe's tiny bicycle and raced back down to inform Emily, "Isabel crashed and busted her head open!"

"Ok, stay here with the girls!" Emily told him as she began trotting and waddling as fast as she could up the steep hill, praying as she went, hoping for the best but imagining the worst.

After comforting Moshe for a few seconds and seeing that his injuries were not as serious as that of Isabel's, David left him with Victor and the gentleman and took nurse Briana to return to Isabel with the powdered cayenne that the family used for blood stopper, as he saw Emily coming up the hill.

When Emily reached the kind gentleman, he held the supplies ready for her to use as necessary, though he had already cleansed Moshe's wounds

Chapter 13   Down

with peroxide. The man then left, driving all the way down the hill to where he could turn around, then unbeknownst to them, passed them again on his way up to where Isabel was, and turned around again to head back down. David sent Briana back down to Moshe, so that Emily could come to where he and Isabel were. He had applied cayenne and held pressure on Isabel's chin until bleeding had completely stopped. Emily approached the scene and saw that Isabel's chin had a gaping wound, but it was not nearly as bad as Briana, Armando, and she had imagined. One of the two ladies there asked, "Do you want us to call an ambulance?"

Emily answered, "No, thank you. I think she'll be fine. Thank you so much for your help!"

Emily put two butterfly bandages on the wound and tried to console Isabel, who was very frightened and upset.

The young ladies saw that they were no longer needed and said goodbye, with sincere thanks from the parents. One thing they really appreciated about Israel was the fact that all young people at the age of 18 years are required to serve in the military for 2-3 years. As a result, a large percentage of Israelis are trained in first aid and in the use of weapons, making for a safer, more aware, more secure society.

While they comforted and doctored Isabel, the kind man who had stopped to help Moshe appeared beside them in his van and asked, "How can I help you?" Having seen that Armando, Rebeka, and Natanyah were a hundred yards or so down the hill, he asked, "Can I give her a ride down, so you all can be together with the other children?"

"Oh, that would be so helpful. Thank you," replied Emily.

David nodded in agreement and told her, "Why don't you ride with them. I'll bring the bicycles."

"I can take the bicycle in my car," offered the man.

"Thank you," said David, "That would be a lot of help!"

Emily and Isabel got in the back seat of the kind man's car, while David put Isabel's bicycle in through the rear door behind them. They rode to where Moshe was, as David and Briana coasted down on their bicycles. Emily put Isabel in her lap to make room for Moshe to sit with them, and they rode down the hill to the meeting place while David, Briana, and Victor, who had stayed near Moshe, rode the bicycles down. The van stopped at Armando and its crew unloaded. Emily got the kind gentleman's contact information and thanked him profusely for his willingness to help strangers. He was glad to do it and began to drive off, when Armando noticed that he still had Isabel's bicycle in his car. The man noticed at about the same time and backed up to return it. They all laughed a little, a great lightening up from the previously tense situations.

121

They rested for a short time to let Isabel and Moshe get their bearings, but the clump of a few young trees did not provide enough shade for the whole family. Isabel and Moshe were put in the shade, along with the other three younger children while the parents and two oldest children sat in the sun. Since noon was approaching, it only took a few minutes before the shade diminished so that even fewer of the children could enjoy it. They all took a good drink of water and, after seeing that the two injured were feeling well enough to travel, started slowly down the hill on the sidewalk; Isabel, still shaken up, walked beside her bicycle.

As they descended slowly at Isabel's pace, David wondered what else could possibly go wrong. He was thankful that the injuries sustained were not worse than they were, but was frustrated at the whole turn of that day's events so far. Not knowing what was in the future, but thinking he was about to have to leave his family there without him, 6,000 miles from home, had him uneasy. Besides that, he knew his wife was not at all happy about the prospect. Then they missed the turn, had no idea where they would spend the night, and now two of his children were injured. Trying to look beyond the situation and give thanks, he glanced down at his water bottles and was just thankful that at least they were secure and that he had installed good holsters for them before leaving home. Within seconds after thinking that thought, one of them that was empty inched up and fell out. He quickly got off and picked it up before it could roll down the hill and within less than a minute, one of Victor's also fell out. No one had lost a water bottle on the trip until now. Again he wondered what else was going to go wrong before the day was over.

Yeshiva[106] Toys

Just after reaching the bottom of the hill, they came to a small brick park with trees and benches. They lined their bicycles up neatly there and began preparing lunch. They noticed some Orthodox Jews peeking out from the nearby building at them, but continued with their meal preparations. In a few minutes, they were approached by a large young Orthodox man who spoke to them in Hebrew. He asked, "Are you all right?"

Emily responded, "Yes, thank you. A couple of the children had accidents on the way down the hill, but they'll be fine."

"It is hot. Would you like to take showers?" he offered.

Emily translated the offer to David. Remembering the advice of Tomasz, their world-cycling friend, they were tempted. They thought it odd to shower in the middle of the day, then get back on the bikes and sweat, but did not know what *Abba* had in store for them. Maybe they were to stay

---

[106] *Yeshiva* - religious school.

here? After agreeing on a plan, Emily told him, "That's really nice of you. Yes, we would take showers, but we need to feed the children first."
"If you want to shower, you would need to do it now because the building will be in use soon for classes," he replied.

They really wanted to use the showers, not because they were dirty, but because they were interested in learning more about the man and the place he was going to show them. However, food and hungry children came first, so they graciously declined his offer.

The kind young man went back to the building from which he had come and in a few minutes a woman came out with a black trash bag full of toys for the children to play with, saying they could have whatever they wanted to take with them. Her gestures and mannerisms were very kind toward the children, but extremely harsh with Emily, while she all but ignored David. She asked several times in Hebrew, "Why?" seeming to be highly disapproving of the children riding bicycles and not about to understand Emily's explanation. Emily and David thanked her none-the-less, and she turned and walked back down the brick walkway to the building from which she had emerged. The family noticed some young people sticking their heads out the doors and windows of what they concluded must have been some sort of *yeshiva*.

Now the children, including Isabel and Moshe, were distracted from the lunch they were so hungry for a few minutes before, as they dumped out the trash bag and rifled through its contents looking for the perfect toy. Emily took that opportunity to get out the laptop to see if she could find any clues as to where they might stay, contacts on their list that might be nearby, or any other helpful information. This was the first time they had been able to get online since arriving in Israel, besides the short time at Or HaCarmel where a password had been required. But before she could get any helpful information the battery died.

After being in the quaint park for a little over an hour and praying about what they were supposed to do, they decided they had better move on to find a place to stay the night. They had called one number they had in Haifa, the daughter of a contact they had made while in the U.S., but that person was unable to give them any ideas of where in Haifa they could put their mats for the night. They thought of calling Nikolay, but did not want to abuse his friendship and felt like he had already done so much for them. They did not want to burden him or give him the impression that they would be dependent on him for the duration of their trip. They had committed to coming to Israel to bless others, and after hearing many stories of people who went to Israel and ended up burdening others, were even more committed to the idea that they would not.

David was burdened, however, knowing that he was going to have to make the decision to leave his family in Israel while he returned to fix the problem that was happening with the business. His mind was reeling with thoughts of where his family would stay for the few days he would need to be gone.

He called the Musician, with whom they had planned to stay in a couple of weeks, and told him about the situation. The man said he knew someone who could pick up the family and their bicycles in a truck and take them to his place for a reasonable fee. When David got off the phone with him, he told Emily, and they discussed how that might be the best option, as that would be a safe place for the family when David was gone. But when David called back to tell him that, he felt like the man was backing out of the offer or that maybe he himself had misunderstood something in the original conversation. Since English was not the first language of either of them, David was not comfortable with their communication by phone.

So they moved on, off course because of a missed turn, at the edge of a big city with which they were unfamiliar, with two slightly battered and quite shaken up children, not knowing which way to go. They had been praying all day for YHWH's direction, but did not seem to be hearing from Him. Things began to get tense between David and Emily, with David's mind on the longer term problem of finding his family a place to stay and Emily struggling with the fact that he would be leaving them. Those issues along with what had happened in the past few hours were making things even more uncomfortable as they sweated in the hot sun, riding their bicycles slowly down the Haifa sidewalk.

Pedal Problems

About a mile from the little park, they stopped at a small gas station to use the restroom. Just after starting up again, the right pedal fell off of Emily's bicycle, stopping the caravan, so that Armando could get the tool kit off of his bicycle and do the necessary repairs. Emily's nearly eight month pregnant state, kept her straddling the bicycle instead of performing all the awkward maneuvers it took to dismount between Natanyah and the loaded front panniers. Armando quickly replaced the pedal, and they slowly rode on again

They came to the end of the road they had been on since before the accidents occurred and had to make a decision as to whether to turn right and go out of the city, possibly hooking up with the road they should have turned on as per Nikolay's instructions, or to turn left and go through the middle of the big city towards the Mediterranean Sea. They knew they could lay their mats out on the beach, but had been told that since Haifa was a port city, the only beaches were on the south side, miles out of the way of their planned route, or to the north in the smaller city of *Kiryat Chaim*.[107] They decided to stay on their route and go through the city toward *Kiryat Chaim*. All they knew to do was head towards the sea and keep praying.

Because of the injured youngsters in their caravan, they now traveled even

---

[107]*Kiryat Chaim* - Place of Life

Chapter 13   Down

more slowly than before. Haifa had wide, safe, easily usable sidewalks, with ramps at the curbs making crossing streets much easier and safer. The family preferred riding on the roads in most places because getting the fully-loaded bicycles pulled up onto some of the high curbs was a difficult feat and one which took lots of energy from everyone in the family at every intersection they had to cross. But because they were traveling much slower now anyway and because since they were at the edge of the city where there were not so many cross streets, they remained on the sidewalk.

A couple hundred feet after turning west, Emily's pedal fell off again. David, at the rear of the pack was not the least bit amused at the new turn of events, continuing to wonder what else could possibly go wrong that day, but being thankful they were all safe and well after the accidents.

Armando got the pedal back on, but when it fell off for the third time, called his dad to come and fix it. It was a major ordeal for David to have to get off of his bicycle, since it was so heavily loaded. When Armando dismounted, Briana could hold his bicycle up while he worked, but David's was too heavy. If he laid it down, it was problematic to get it back up as the load would begin to shift. No one except Armando and Emily were strong enough to hold it up while on their bicycles, and there was not always an easy place to do this without clogging up the entire width of the wide sidewalk. The best way to handle David's bicycle situation was to park it up against a big tree or building, but those were not always available at the needed times like this, so he was a little aggravated that he was having to dismount to solve the problem.

After repairing the pedal to his satisfaction, he gave the tools back to Armando to put in his pouch, wrestled his bicycle back to standing position and made sure the load was secure, before motioning to Emily to move ahead. She rode slowly, thankful the pedal was repaired and that it would present no more problems for them. And they rode a few hundred feet before it fell off again.

This time, she just had Armando pick it up and give it to her. She decided it would be easier to push the bicycle, since they were riding almost that slowly anyway. But David was not happy to see his wife pushing when he was riding, so called for another time out while they went through the whole ordeal of getting everyone off to the side of the sidewalk so he could pass them, then getting Armando to hold his bicycle up so he could once again replace the pedal. All his attempts of repairing the bicycle failed, as it was beyond repair with the simple tools they had.

They started west toward the sea again, Emily and David at each end pushing their bicycles, as the children rode slowly between them. The girls all wore pants under their skirts, and Emily had taught them to tuck the fronts of their skirts up into their waist bands while riding to keep them out of their bicycle chains. As they rode slowly west, Rebeka's skirt came loose, got caught in her chain, and began pulling as more and more of the

125

fabric got drawn in. She stopped and called for mechanical help, and Armando once again came to the rescue. While he was trying to get Rebeka's skirt out of her chain, David noticed a mechanic shop on the other side of the busy four-lane street. He propped his bicycle up against the nearby wall, waited for a break in the traffic, then ran across with the pedal to see if there was a welder there who could repair it. Emily and the children used this break as a time to cut into a cantaloupe to quench everyone's thirst and lose some of the weight off of her bicycle. In the meantime, Armando had to take Rebeka's chain off to get her skirt out. When he attempted to replace the chain, his right index finger, wet with sweat, slipped and got caught between the chain and the sprocket cutting his finger. He cried out in pain, but was attached to the bicycle because it was a pedal brake type and the sprocket could not turn backwards to release his finger. He had to work his badly bleeding finger out between the teeth of the sprocket and the chain.

David was unsuccessful in his attempts to find a welder or any other way to attach the pedal back onto Emily's bicycle. He trotted back across the street to find blood gushing out of another one of his children. As he comforted Armando while he continued to work to free his damaged finger, Briana once again got out the first aid kit and was ready to apply peroxide, iodine and then cayenne to stop the bleeding once his finger was out.

Emily, almost unable to believe the way things were happening told the others that she did not know what was going on or what Yah wanted them to do but that they had better pray. So there on the sidewalk at sundown, with the noise of buses and taxis rushing by, the family took a few minutes to pray asking again for protection and guidance from their Father in heaven. Feeling a little better (all except for Armando's finger) and realizing after the prayer that this day was a test for them, they resumed their positions and continued on slowly west toward the sea with little daylight left.

14 - Haifa

Snagged Soldier

Yom Revi'i (Fourth Day)

As the sun finished setting, they came to a major 'T' intersection that was several lanes wide in all directions. Having been instructed to turn north there and that that road would take them to the beach, they assembled at the first crosswalk and waited for the light to change before they all crossed together. This was a practice they had begun when Armando was only a year old and they would walk to the Post Office each day and to church each week from their home in the small eastern Tennessee town of Niota, where they had lived at that time. They taught him and then Briana, when she came along and was old enough to walk, that they would all stop at the curb, look both ways, then 'all cross together,' stressing safety in numbers.

After crossing the first intersection, there were still several more to go before getting all the way to the other side. The air was filled with the noise of cars, taxis, and buses as they started, stopped, and sped through the intersection, and the smell of diesel fuel was heavy. The buses tilted so when going around the curve, that they almost appeared they would tip over. Bus after bus went by, and after crossing the entire intersection and turning north they saw that there was a huge bus station located in front of them, just past the rental car businesses. There was so much bus traffic that special bus lanes had been built on the main north south road, Highway 4, which ran along the coast of the Mediterranean from Lebanon through the Gaza Strip to Egypt.

They were relieved to finally be traveling north, which meant they were parallel with the sea and their arrival at the beach was getting noticeably closer. David replaced Emily's pedal one more time, but the threads on the pedal were weakened and it would not even stay on when pushing the bicycle now. Before leaving to go to Israel, Emily and Armando had ridden 17 miles from their home to Standing Stone State Park to spend a couple of days together, a tradition that the family had begun several years before of taking one child at a time for a special adventure every 5 years. While there, Emily had slid on the gravel and wrecked, bending her pedal a little. She never thought of it as something serious and had not mentioned it to David. She had had no trouble with it until this particular day, which was turning out to be the longest one of their trip in many ways.

Everyone was tired, being accustomed to being ready for bed by this time. But there was nowhere to bed down, so they continued, Emily pushing her bicycle and the others riding slowly behind. As they approached a small amusement park with go-carts near a footbridge crossing the highway, they were met by three young ladies in military attire who were walking south. Emily asked them if they knew where the beach was and they responded that they did not, as they were not from Haifa. She thanked them and they all started walking again.

As the Israeli Defense Force troops chatted amongst themselves amid the roar of the traffic, the night lights and lights of traffic caused them to fail to see the flag on Emily's bicycle, which had shifted a little more to the left than usual, and was no longer standing straight up. Emily thought it felt like it was getting harder to push her bicycle, but attributed it to the tiredness she was feeling. After a few steps, she finally heard Armando over the traffic of cars, taxis, and buses, as his calls for Mama escalated to a yell, 'MAMA!!!' Startled, she turned toward her bicycle so she could look behind her while still holding it with both hands. She was surprised to see her flag leaned all the way over. She had to turn more, following it to whatever the flag was tangled in.

Meanwhile, Armando and David (the others being too tired to really care), did not know whether to laugh or to try to aid the female IDF member whose hair and badge was tangled in the flag. Emily gasped and apologized, but there was nothing she could do quickly, as she had to hold up her bicycle. Thankfully, IDF troops are trained in all types of disaster, and the three ladies were able to successfully get the hair freed from the flag with no visible damage resulting.

The parties walked off in their respective directions, giggling in embarrassment at what had just happened. The experience helped to ease the family's tension and tiredness for a few minutes. They finally approached a large intersection and knew that to get to the beach, they had to go left. They turned and continued, shortly coming to a railroad crossing. After waiting for the passenger train to go by, they proceeded carefully across the tracks toward the beach. Moshe, however, noticed some pretty rocks at the crossing and laid down his bicycle so he could pick them up. When he tried to pick his bicycle up again, he was unable because the pedal was stuck in the railroad track. Everyone else crossed the tracks successfully, but Armando had to lay his bicycle down to go help Moshe get his loose. They heard another train coming and the bars came down again as Armando tugged and worked quickly to get the bicycle loose. Moshe did not want to leave his bicycle, so Armando pushed him underneath the bar to safety and finally got the bicycle out just as the light of the train came around the bend a few hundred feet away. The family had had enough adventure for one day and just wanted a place to lie down.

It was time for a restroom break, and there were no facilities in sight. Emily, looking back frequently to David for guidance, led them down some dark streets in the industrial zone, looking for any place that might serve as a rest area. They finally found a place near a corner behind a little dumpster. Still not knowing how far they had to go or when they would come to a

Chapter 14   Haifa

place to use the restroom, they ducked behind the dumpster, two at a time, to relieve their bladders. They did not particularly like the idea of going on the pavement where there would be no benefit to nature, but since there was no other known option, they were just grateful for a place to go.

David spotted a restaurant nearby and went in to ask how much farther it was to the beach. The answer again was, "Not far." With renewed hope, they trekked on along the edge of the industrial zone, finally reaching a major intersection with what looked like a giant grocery or furniture store on the southwest corner. Since they needed to go north, were on the east side of the major road, everyone was so tired and they were not really sure what type of store it was, they decided to resist the urge to cross the street to buy a few food items. They needed bread and wanted to get some fruit, something that would mash easily to feed to Isabel, who because of her injury had not been able to eat since the accident.

Abba Intervenes

Just after turning north, they saw, on their side of the street, a little bakery. They moved their bicycles to the edge of the sidewalk, and David gave Emily his wallet so she could go in and get some bread for a very late supper and for the next day. Emily entered the little shop still filled with the aroma of fresh baked bread, even though it had been hours since any bread had been baked. She quickly but carefully walked through looking at all the types of bread in order to find the whole wheat products she was looking for. As she scoped out the items, most of which were rather scant this time of evening, she noticed a man behind her frantically filling up bags with bread. She reasoned that he must know exactly what he wanted and be in a hurry to go somewhere. She reached for a bag and put in several little loaves of whole wheat bread sprinkled with rolled oats. She approached the counter where the owner sat behind the register in a wheelchair. They were greeting one another when a smart looking woman stepped up and began asking Emily questions about where they were from and what they were doing. Out of the corner or her eye, standing near the front of the store, Emily saw the man who had been in such a hurry to get his bread and wondered why he had not yet paid and left.

After learning the family was from America and cycling, the woman called the man over and, taking the three bags of bread from him said, "This is for you."

Emily was puzzled, to say the least. She did not understand why anyone would show this type of kindness toward her. She told the woman, "Thank you very much. I need to pay you for this though," she said, holding up her bag.

"No, you take that, too. We want to give it all to you," she replied, kindly waving her out of the store.

129

Emily left holding back tears of gratitude and carried the bread to David, who was still straddling his bicycle. Moshe and Rebeka had leaned their bicycles up against an unused table and had lain down, Rebeka on a bench and Moshe on the sidewalk, already asleep. Emily related to David what had just happened and they praised Yah and blessed the kind owners and workers in the bread store. This had been the worst day since arriving in Israel, with them at times questioning if they should even be there. They were truly blessed by what they knew were gifts from Yah given through His servants.

Emily then took David's wallet past the closed market next door to the fruit market on the other side. She passed the green grapes on the way in, wanting to see what other fruits were available before deciding how much to get. The market was well-stocked with more choices of fruit than she expected to find that time of night. She chose some bananas and grapefruit; things she thought would be enjoyed by all and easily eaten by Isabel, and headed towards the front of the store, to get the grapes. In her tiredness, she noticed two people frantically filling bags with fruits and vegetables and marveled at how Israelis did not waste time shopping.

The cash register was towards the front of the store with the grapes on beyond toward the street. Emily felt a little strange walking past the cashier to get the grapes and hoped she did not think she was walking out with the groceries. As she reached for a bag to put the grapes in, separate from the heavier fruit, a man approached her, stopped, and extending his hand with his palm up, motioning toward a row of filled grocery bags on the floor said in broken English, "Thees is for you."

To say that she was shocked was an understatement and she again marveled at how Yah was blessing them through another group of kind people. She told the man, "Thank you! But I need to pay for these," holding up her bag in one hand and the grapes in the other.

But like the woman at the bread store, he said, "No, we want to give it all to you."

She thanked them again, blushing, put the grapes in a bag, then walked toward the bags of food on the floor, wondering what they would do with them. She could not even carry them out by herself, much less get them on the bicycles, which were already heavily packed. Two men and a woman working there helped carry the groceries out, the woman asking Emily, "Where are you staying?"

"At the beach, but we don't know where it is."

"Oh, it's not far, just up the road," one of the men replied.

David saw Emily coming out of the store with three people carrying groceries beside her and wondered what was going on. Had the long day

130

Chapter 14   Haifa

in the hot sun made her crazy? Where did she think she was going to put all that stuff?

Just then the Israelis saw the bicycles and realized the family had no place to carry the food. The bicycles were fully loaded, only leaving enough room for the few things Emily had purchased herself. Upon realizing that this was an impossible situation, the woman offered, "I'll drive these to the beach in my car."

Emily explained to David what was going on as they watched in awe the angels busying around them, offering ways they could best serve the family. They watched, still stunned, as the market workers loaded up all of the groceries, including the bread, into the car. Emily quickly wrote thank-you notes on two of the postcards, which Briana delivered to the man at the bread store and a man at the fruit market.

Emily asked, "How do we get to the beach?"

One of the men replied in Hebrew, "Oh, it's not far," he said pointing north. "Go up the road to the..." then spoke a word Emily didn't understand, but knew was of extreme importance to getting the directions correct. "Then turn left and it goes all the way to the beach."

"I don't understand the word. Where is it we turn?" she questioned.

A discussion arose among the three, but none of them could think of the way to say it in English. They turned back to her, each one of them making hand signals and gestures that went around. Emily and David decided they must be talking about round-about, an intersection with no lights, but where incoming traffic would yield to those already in the intersection. They seemed to be very efficient and the Varelas had ridden through many of them already. They thanked the people, then started on their way, everyone in their positions, expecting to see a round-about soon.

Natanyah was asleep in her seat on Emily's bicycle and little Moshe was becoming too tired to even push his. David and Emily felt bad for the children who, like them, were so very tired. It was already past 8 PM, their upper limit for bedtime since arriving in Israel. When Moshe could not go any farther, David put his little bicycle on his own handlebars and Emily put Moshe on her seat and instructed him to hold onto her as she pushed. The caravan was moving more and more slowly and the beach was still nowhere in sight.

They passed some empty lots and a large wooded area before reaching another large intersection. There, in the northeast corner was a giant round fountain. Now they were confused. They had understood their instructions to be leading to a round-about. But now they were at this thing which could have easily matched the description that the Israelis at the store had given them. After some thought and trying to find out from others at the intersection if there was a round-about anywhere nearby, they

131

decided this must be the place they were to turn west, toward the Mediterranean Sea.

Upon turning, they knew they were headed toward the beach, but wondered how they would ever meet up with the lady that had taken the food. They reasoned that even if they never saw her again, they were still blessed by the fact that people had shown such kindness, and particularly at a time when they had been feeling so down. They were awed by the hand of Yah in their lives.

The sidewalk to the beach was very wide and included bicycle lanes. The Varelas were not sure where they were supposed to be, since they were cyclists, but at this point were just pedestrians pushing a cumbersome load of bicycles. They stayed in a straight line, trying to be considerate of the many people who were out strolling or exercising in the warm night air. They were greeted jovially by many and were stopped briefly by a few for pictures and questions as they proceeded toward the beach. They distributed several postcards to those showing interest.

As they reached the beach, with the concession houses and pavilions, still wondering how they would ever find the woman with the groceries, they saw a figure walking rapidly toward them.

"Where have you been? I've been here almost an hour," she said.

It was only then that they realized it was the angel woman from the fruit market. They were all so tired they had not even remembered who it was they were to meet. She led them to a pavilion near the sea where she had unloaded all of the bags of groceries, as Emily answered, "Well, we move slowly anyway, and now everyone is very tired besides. I'm sorry you have been waiting."

"Oh, it's no problem," she insisted. "I just didn't know if you were going to come."

Then she said of the pavilion, "You can sleep here."

She pointed out the bathrooms, now closed for the night, and the outdoor showers. After giving them all the helpful information she could think of, she turned to go. They watched in awe as she walked the long distance back to her car, realizing that she had made the trip several times to get all of the food and water to the pavilion. As they watched, David said to the family, "You know, they're doing what scripture says to do. They're loving strangers.[108] They're being faithful to Yah and His instructions in the scriptures. They're doing what Y'shua reminded us to do. But they're

---

[108]Deut. 10:18-19 [YHWH] doth execute the judgment of the fatherless and widow, and loveth the stranger, in giving him food and raiment. Love ye therefore the stranger: for ye were strangers in the land of Egypt.

performing their kind acts without realizing that we're not just strangers, we're part of their long lost brother, Ephraim, returning from the pigsties where he had wasted his inheritance."[109]

Long Lost Brother

Bags of food

As she opened bags of fruit so the children could begin to eat, she added to what David had said, "Remember the parable of the prodigal son? It represents the younger son, Ephraim, taking his Father's inheritance and leaving to a far country. At the time of the division of Israel into the house of Judah and the house of Israel, Israel set up Samaria as their capital city and their King Jeroboam set up two golden calves, one at Dan and one at Beit El, to discourage the people from going back to Jerusalem to worship, as commanded in the *torah*.

"The parable tells that the younger son wasted his father's inheritance with riotous living. Then there came a famine in the land and he began to be in want, so he went to work for a citizen of that country, who sent him into his fields to feed swine. Ephraim, while having Yah's inheritance, the *torah*, the instructions for life, shirked them off following Jeroboam into idolatry. The Assyrian army later conquered Israel in 722 BC and carried them into exile, as prophesied in many of the prophets, who had tried to warn Israel for years to turn back to Yah and His *torah*. The house of Israel (Ephraim) was scattered to the winds, never to be heard from again as a nation until the last days when they would resurface and be joined to their brother Judah.

---

[109] Luke 15:11-32 is the well-known Prodigal Son parable, taught by Y'shua;s most often understood in Christianity as referring to a person who has drifted; but is first a parable referring to the two houses of Israel: Judah, the older brother and Ephraim, the younger, who turned away from his father, YHWH, wasting all he had in riotous living before deciding to return, humbly, as a servant. The events of the parable describe accurately the wandering away of Ephraim and his return, which has begun worldwide as His people see the error of their ways and return to Him and His covenant, and to their brother, Judah. Many within Christianity are a part of this phenomenon, without realizing it, as YHWH's covenant is being written on their hearts and they begin to shed their pagan ways and walk according to His desires for them, as set forth in scripture.

"In the parable, the younger son was so hungry that he wanted to feed himself with the swine's food, but no one would feed him. He finally came to his senses and realized that his Father's servants were eating better than he was, so he decided to return home, ask forgiveness and ask to live as a servant in his Father's house. The parable is lived out as Ephraim, now scattered throughout the earth and mingled with every nation, begins to wake up to the fact that he is starving from lack of substance, that almost everything he has been taught in the name of religion consists of manmade tradition and is worthless. He recognizes that Yah's word is full of meat and is the only thing that can satisfy him, so he repents, turning back to the ways of his Father and heads home.

"In the parable, when he is still a long way from home, his Father, who had been waiting for so long, runs to meet him. As the son asks forgiveness and expresses his desire to live as a servant, the Father calls for a celebration, 'My son was dead, and is alive again; he was lost, and is found!' This parable is what was spoken of in several of the prophets, when they tell of the return of Ephraim to the land to join Judah before the Messiah comes to reign over them. We are incredibly blessed to be part of this return, both spiritually and physically as Ephraim, scattered into every nation worldwide, is beginning to wake up and return to Yah and His ways! We love Him, His Word, His instructions, our brother Judah and His land, Israel, like thousands more of our brothers and sisters. And it's because of that love and the blessings we've seen in our life since we've repented, that we have such a strong desire to share these truths with others.

"The parable goes on to tell of the older brother's jealousy when the Father accepts the younger home. The older brother has been home all along, following his Father's instructions, not squandering the inheritance. But the Father reminds him that everything He has belongs to him and that he should be glad because, 'for this thy brother was dead, and is alive again; and was lost, and is found.'

David added, "Most Christians are familiar with the story of the prodigal son. But just like these Jewish people are caring for their long lost brother Ephraim without knowing it, many within Christianity don't know that they *are* that long lost brother to Judah!"

Now in Israel, among mostly Jewish people, they were experiencing nothing but kindness. They had come to bless their brothers who lived in the Promised Land, but found themselves being blessed over and over. Tonight's show of kindness to weary travelers was truly another example.

The family (with the exception of Natanyah, still asleep in her seat on Emily's bicycle) sat down by their bicycles on the brick patio near the pavilion to eat and take inventory of their newly gifted groceries. They blessed YHWH for people, food, safety, and the beautiful sea that lay before them. On the brick in front of them lay: apples, oranges, lemons, mango, grapes, grapefruit, pears, plums, peaches, bananas, tomatoes, potatoes, onions, cabbage, eggplant, cucumbers, carrots, a six-pack of two liter water bottles, bread of all shapes and sizes, and some cookies and candies. As they gave thanks for their food and those who had provided them, they watched the lights of giant ships at sea, knowing that some of them were guarding the country from its nearby enemies. They gave thanks again, this time for their secure surroundings.

Exhausted from the day's events, but so grateful at how things had turned out, they feasted lightly on what lay before them. Even with Isabel's stiff and painful jaw, she was able to eat a variety of the fruits now available to her. Emily laid out the bed mats while the older children made sure food and bicycles were arranged in an orderly way. David laid Natanyah down next to where Emily would sleep, and everyone bedded down for the night. Their accommodations were much more than what they had expected, mats on a brick floor in a semi-enclosed area made by the benches, and a roof over their heads. Briana slept on a bench, the rest on the bricked ground with David next to her, then the boys, the other girls, and Emily at the end nearer the shore. There were people sitting under the shelter at a picnic table talking, but the family was too tired to care. The rhythmic crashing of the waves and the warm sea breeze gave them peaceful sleep. The parents rested well, since their prayers for direction had been answered. They knew where they were to be for the next few days, since they now had too much food to travel.

Sand Castles and Beach Ball

The sight of the beautiful beach and sea greeted them in the morning. An occasional early riser walked or jogged by on the damp sand near the water's edge. A big yellow bulldozer drove up and down the beach, scraping and leveling it for the day's visitors. The family saw the exercise and outdoor shower area just a few yards from the pavilion to the south and the concession and bathroom facilities to the north and farther off the shoreline. After all were awakened and mats and sheets neatly stowed under a bench, they had a breakfast of fruit, cream cheese, and bread. When scripture reading was over, everyone was ready to explore and experience the beach.

As the morning wore on, the concessions opened and more and more people began to arrive, many for exercise, some just to enjoy the beach, some for swimming in the life-guarded area, and several just north of the pavilion to play beach ball, a game with oversized Ping-Pong paddles that was played by hitting the smooth, rubber ball back and forth. Several retired people played in the area between the pavilion and the life guarded swimming area. After tiring of what interested the younger ones, and noticing that the beach ball game going on looked like they should have four players, instead of only three, Armando asked, pointing, "Can I go play with them?"

The parents thought it was a great idea for him to be interacting with the older people if they would allow it. They watched as he approached the players, who were very friendly towards him, gave him an extra paddle and welcomed him to the game. He was correct in his assessment, and they were glad for the extra player. He played for  quite some time before their time at the beach that morning was over. They seemed to really enjoy playing with their new friend and he certainly enjoyed doing something more active than playing in the water with the younger children.

David and Emily were blessed to watch him fit right into the game and by the mutual kindness that flowed back and forth between the generations. After the games were over, a lady who had been playing in the group, but in another game approached the family, saying, "We really enjoyed Armando playing with us. We were short a player today and were glad to have him. He's a very talented player. You should get him into beach ball. He will be a champion," she declared.

They smiled and Emily replied, "Thank you for your kind words and for letting him play. It was really good for him to get to do something besides play with his younger siblings."

"We were glad to have him. I hope you'll still be here tomorrow!" she said.

David and Emily looked at each other knowingly, as they had way too much food to pack and knew they were stationed there for at least that long.

Around 11 AM, a lady came over from the nearby concession stand and introduced herself as Nesimi. She was so excited to see the children and hear the family's story and invited them over to the stand for ice cream. Emily took them while David was inspecting the bicycles and making adjustments. She bought them all a Popsicle and shared their story with everyone at the stand, employees and regulars of the beach. The children gave their postcards to all who showed interest and Emily wrote a thank you note on the back of the one to give to Nesimi.

The frozen treats had to be eaten quickly to keep from melting in the hot sun. The children sat down at a little table with a nice older gentleman who was asking more questions. Most everyone was enamored with the little brood of children, donned in their Dorito orange shirts and their light blue or beige swim pants.

Chapter 14   Haifa

When they finished their treats and their visit with the kind people at the concessions, Emily brought the children back to the pavilion where David had thoroughly inspected her pedal and decided it definitely needed to be welded. They prepared and ate more of the fresh foods they had been given. After lunch, Emily lay down under the pavilion with Natanyah and Moshe while David took the others to play in the waves and sand a few feet away.

Numerous people stopped, asking questions about the family and their reason for being in Israel, and most all seemed to soak up the information given. After Emily got up from getting the little ones to sleep, a security guard at the beach approached. He visited for quite some time with the parents and asked the usual questions, as well as more personal questions about their lives in the U.S. He was very friendly and intrigued with the family's story.

As evening approached, David made more phone calls to the U.S., but continued to be unable to get the jobs there moving again. The family went to the showers near the concessions to clean off the sand and salt before bedtime. The smell of urine got stronger as they approached to find that the doors were locked. They learned that the bathrooms closed when the concessions did, the strong smell due to people relieving themselves outside when they could not get in. The family went to the other side of the pavilion near the exercise station to use the outdoor showers, taking a sheet to hold up for privacy, since there were still people all around. After playing in the water in the hot Israel sun for a good part of the day, then getting good showers, the family lay down again for another peaceful night's sleep.

15 - *Kiryat Chaim*

Visitors

Yom Chamishi (Fifth Day)

The family slept well in their sheets sewn together to make thin sleeping bags, with the soothing sound of waves crashing into the shore and the warm breeze blowing over them. At around nine thirty, Emily awoke to the sound of feet treading lightly in the sand nearby. Approaching her were two ladies whose arms were laden with pillows and blankets. Thinking the two had come to spend the night, she was surprised when they walked right to her, extended the bedding and explained in Hebrew, "These are for your family."

Emily told them, "Thank you. That's very kind. But we have everything we need."

"No," they insisted, "keep this so you don't get cold."

Emily was overwhelmed at their kindness, "All right, we can use them tonight. Thank you. Where can we bring them tomorrow?"

The ladies shook their heads and firmly said, "No, no you keep it."

"We're traveling by bicycle and we can't take it with us. Where can we return it?" she asked again.

The ladies refused to give any information, just insisting the family keep the things. One of them took a pillow and placed under Briana's head on the bench, then stepped back and admired her work. Emily had them write down their names and phone numbers as a remembrance and they headed away from the sea in the direction from which they had come.

Though the wind was warm off the water of the Mediterranean, Emily wanted to be respectful of the kind, generous ladies, so she covered the children with the two big blankets, one of which was very warm, soft, and heavy and the other a little lighter, but still suitable for winter sleeping. She then took one of the fluffy pillows to David, who had discretely watched the whole ordeal, and kept one for herself, as the children were comfortable using their pillowcases that Grandmother had made them with their clothes folded inside for bulk. She lay back down, immediately noticing the difference in comfort of her head on the pillow in comparison to the hard thin pillowcase of the day's clothes that she had been resting her head on

Chapter 15   Kiryat Chaim

before. She thanked Yah for His provision of such luxury and blessed the messengers who brought them. She soon drifted back to sleep feeling a peace that came from Yah's bountiful provisions of food, water, and now bedding after yesterday's long, hard day of physical and spiritual turmoil.

Emily was awakened again around eleven o'clock to the sound of voices. Thinking someone must be sitting at the nearby picnic table, she rolled from her left side where she had been facing the sea onto her back so she could get a better look at the table that was behind her and on the other side of the bench that separated the little area where they slept from the picnic area. To her surprise, the voices were from two ladies who were standing just behind that bench and were leaning over marveling at all the children sleeping under their new blankets. Emily's movement caught their eye and as they looked at her she greeted them, "Shalom." They immediately began asking questions in Hebrew, but once Emily answered that the family was from the United States, the bolder of the two began speaking in a heavily accented English. After several questions, Emily got up to talk with them further. The bold lady, Eti, invited her to sit down with them at the picnic table nearby as she told them the family's story.

Eti sat in awe hearing the testimony of the family and of why they were in Israel and what they were doing. But she could not get over the children sleeping outside. "They need to be inside. It's not good to sleep outside," she said.

"Actually, even at home, where we have beds, we often sleep outside," Emily replied. "The air is fresher and it's cooler in the summer outside with the breeze. Really, it's OK. They like it."

"I can find you a place to stay," she insisted.

"Really," Emily insisted, "this is how we planned to spend our nights while here in Israel. It is possible, though, that we would need a place for a few days. It looks like my husband may need to go back to the U.S. to take care of some business. If that happens, we will need a place where we can be safe and lock up the bicycles while he is gone."

Eti, now overjoyed at the prospect of helping get the children indoors at night, got on the phone and began chattering away in Hebrew about a family that needed a place to stay.

Emily assumed, as late as it was, that she must have been talking to a dear friend, but in a moment, she covered the phone and said, "This is Chabad.[110] They will help you."

---

[110]*Chabad* - acronym for *Chocmah* (wisdom), *Binah* (understanding), and *Da'at* (knowledge), and as an organization is part of the Hasidic Jewish sector of Orthodox Judaism whose name comes from the word '*chesid*' for loving kindness and '*chasid*' for 'pious.' *Chabad* is a large worldwide Jewish

139

Emily, not knowing what Chabad was, listened to the conversation as Eti, in her quick, strong, and businesslike manner of speech, gave the man a synopsis of her interpretation of the family's situation, then handed the phone to Emily.

"What do you need?" asked the man on the other end of the line.

"Well, really nothing now," Emily answered. "But my husband may need to return to the U.S., and if so, the children and I will need a place to stay for a few days."

"Ok, I will call your friend back in the morning and tell her what to do," he said quickly, then hung up. Emily handed the phone back to Eti, not really knowing what was going on, but grateful for the kindness of her acts of concern, anyway. She asked, "Who was that?"

Eti replied, "A man I know who is a leader in Chabad."

"What is Chabad?"

Surprised, she exclaimed, "You don't know Chabad? Chabad is people who help people. They give food, and clothes, and a place to stay."

Emily was beginning to feel like a charity case. She didn't like the feeling, but knew that Yah was doing something in her life. She had been raised to be independent, not accepting help from others. Now, here to give, she was not being given the opportunity to give but was constantly on the receiving end. It was a difficult place for her to be, but she was thankful, all the same. She knew it was Yah pouring out His love on them, and maybe at the same time humbling them, teaching them to graciously accept help from others instead of always being on the giving end.

Her head was reeling with the events of the past two days and the kindness shown them by so many strangers, but Eti's questions kept coming. David heard the talking and raised his head off of his new pillow to see his wife at the table with the other ladies, said a prayer for her, then fell asleep again, dozing in and out as he kept a watchful eye.

Eti: Ok, so you're not Jewish?

Emily: Not that we know of.

Eti: But you wear the tassels. You keep *Shabbat*. You come to Israel for Sukkot. You are *Jewish*!

---

organization which is known for its hospitality and providing outreach to Jews through community centers, synagogues, schools and camps.

Chapter 15   Kiryat Chaim

Emily: But we're not born Jewish, that we know of. And we're not Jewish by religion.

Eti: So what are you?

Emily: We don't have a name for what we are. We believe we are from the house of Ephraim, the ten scattered tribes that will be reunited with Judah in the last days. We love *Abba* and we love His *torah*, but we are not Jewish by birth that we know of, or by religion. We believe the Jews are our brother Judah, who has held onto the *torah*, and as we return to the ways of our Creator, He brings us back to our brother, like Ezekiel says.[111] Do you know what I'm talking about?

Eti: I have heard something about that, but I don't know, really.

Emily gave her a postcard with the verses on the back and explained the one in Jeremiah.[112] "Jeremiah tells us that the Almighty will make a new covenant with Israel, putting His laws on our hearts. That's what has happened to us. We love to follow His instructions because we know they are good for us. He has put them on our hearts. Scripture says that all of this will happen before Messiah returns."

The woman with Eti was mostly silent, but every once in a while posed a questions of her own in Hebrew. Emily was glad to be able to share with them the prophecies from their own Jewish scriptures concerning the return of Ephraim in conjunction with the coming of their Messiah. They seemed amazed at the knowledge of the prophets and *torah* that this non-Jewish mother of seven possessed. In reality, the Jewish ladies present had only studied the *torah* as part of their schooling and knew very little of their own prophets or what their writings actually said. Emily did not consider herself a scholar, but studied out of a love for her Savior, wanting to understand more about living a life that would honor Him.

After sitting there for over a half hour, two other young ladies joined the group and many of the questions were asked and answered again. Emily was ecstatic to be able to share the things she was sharing from the scriptures, and even though her eyes were heavy and desiring sleep, her adrenaline was pumping at the thought of what all this meant and the scope of what she was doing.

---

[111] Ezek. 37:19 Say unto them, Thus saith Lord YHWH; Behold, I will take the stick of Joseph, which *is* in the hand of Ephraim, and the tribes of Israel his fellows, and will put them with him, *even* with the stick of Judah, and make them one stick, and they shall be one in mine hand.

[112] Jer. 31:33 But this *shall be* the covenant that I will make with the house of Israel; After those days, saith YHWH, I will put my law in their inward parts, and write it in their hearts; and will be their Elohim, and they shall be my people.

After another half hour, a group of young men carrying a small grill and several bags and bottles made their way to the other side of the pavilion to set up for their party. It was obvious they were enjoying their drinks, but not in an obnoxious sort of way. One of the two newer ladies saw the grill and got very excited, asking Emily, "Have you ever had...?"

Emily did not understand the word she used and told her, "I don't know."

"Oh, it is meat, beef, very good. You'll really like it," she said before getting up to go talk briefly to the young men, pointing back toward the direction of the other ladies and family.

The young men nodded their heads and the woman returned. She told Emily that the men would be bringing her some meat to try when they got it cooked. Emily, surprised, asked, "Oh, so you know them?"

Nonchalantly, she replied, "No, but we're all Jewish! It's OK!"

In a few minutes the four ladies decided quickly that it was time to go. Eti said, "I will come for you tomorrow. Wait here for me."

The lady who had spoken with the young men told Emily, "Wait right here. The meat will be ready very soon," and they all rushed off without another glance back. Emily sat there at the table digesting what had just transpired, while watching the grilling party out of the corner of her eye. She knew as a mother of little ones that her lack of sleep was not something that would be good for her family, and there was no way she was going to sit alone at a picnic table after midnight waiting for strange men to come and feed her. So as soon as the ladies were out of sight, she got up from the table, repositioned the blankets on a couple of the children and went to bed praying for the ladies she had just met and the events that would come from it. Her eyelids heavy from exhaustion and the warm breeze off the salt water, she quickly fell asleep.

She was awakened again around 1 AM by deeper voices. She was facing the other way this time, towards David who was on the other side of the children from her, so only had to open her eyes to see a group of men standing behind the bench that was to David's back. One young man was in front of the bench kneeling down at David's head holding a paper plate containing a stack of steaks around ten inches high along with some kosher wieners. A man behind him had a bag full of paper plates, plastic utensils and cups. Another had two two-liter Cokes and two Mountain Dews, and yet another held two-liter bottles of water.

David raised his head off his pillow at the sound of a man's voice, unaware of the discussion between them and the young lady or their grilling party. He was stunned to see a huge midnight snack being presented at his pillow by strangers. The man bearing meat was a little unsteady on his feet as he told David in his thick accent. "Dees is for you, from the bottom of my heart."

David looked across at Emily who was giving him a look that he knew meant this was somehow normal, so he sat up and took the plate of meat while the men laid all of their other bags and bottles down on the bench behind him, perpendicular to the one where Briana was sleeping. He thanked them several times as they left, disappearing towards the town of *Kiryat Chaim*. While David continued to awaken, Emily explained what had transpired over the past few hours. Armando and Briana woke up, either from their parents' conversation or from the smell of the first beef they had had since arriving in Israel.

They woke up the other children, and everyone shared in the feast. The family was again in awe of Yah's provisions of so much more than they could have ever imagined. They prayed blessings on all of the ladies and men that He had sent to them over the past couple of days. With tummies full of meat, they lay back down and slept soundly until nearly sunrise, when joggers, beach walkers, and exercisers at the nearby equipment began their daily routines. The bulldozers were already finishing up the morning's work

Beach Life

After a time of prayer and reflection on the past night's events, they prepared fruit, hummus, and bread for breakfast. They were careful to eat of their gifts in order of which foods would be the most perishable, so as not to waste what Yah, through His kind servants, had given them. All of the grapes and peaches were now gone, and the pears, mango, and plums would be finished off that morning. Things like potatoes, onions, cabbage, and apples would be saved for last, as they would keep the longest.

After breakfast, scripture time, folding their new blankets along with their sheets, and packing everything nicely under the bench that supported their bicycles, they took to the beach. Eti called to check on the family and let them know that she had made arrangements for them to go to Chabad. It was then they realized this woman was really serious. She had set up an appointment for them to be at Chabad around noon.

Since their showers were so public the night before, they had not taken time to shampoo and clean up really well. Knowing they would be leaving and remembering Tomasz's advice to 'always take a shower because you never know when you might get another,' they took the clean green clothes to the shower house to try once again. Inside, the smell was not so strong. Emily helped the girls shower in one building while David helped the boys in another. The family was not accustomed to showering in public, so part of the parents' challenge was in keeping the little ones' eyes off of the naked bodies of others showering there. After showers, the parents instructed the children to play very carefully and only in the dry sand since this was the first day of clean clothes, which always had to last for two days.

Armando's beach ball partners came, and the lady who had spoken with his parents the day before brought two paddles and ball for him to keep. He and Briana played with them while the younger children enjoyed the sand and David and Emily began packing things into the bicycle panniers. As they worked, putting each thing in its proper place, making sure the loads were balanced, a family came their way with two small children. They offered them the unopened two liter sodas they had been given them the night before, but the family refused them. They were struck with the cultural difference concerning diet that existed between Israel and the United States. They offered the sodas to several people, but could not even give them away.

Finally, along came the security guard again. He asked more questions and visited for a while, noticing that the family was packing. They offered him the sodas and he refused as well, until Emily told him, "We don't have room for them on our bicycles and we'll just have to throw them away if you don't take them."

He reluctantly took them, then visited for a few more minutes before continuing his rounds. They packed all the remaining food, trying to fit everything in without overloading the already heavy bicycles. The most perishable foods left went in the basket that Armando had found on Mount Carmel, which had its prominent place on top of his rear panniers. The new heavy, big, beautiful blanket went on top of Emily's front panniers. Armando's bicycle took the smaller blanket and the laundry in its special pannier, Briana's one of the pillows, and David's got the other two.

As they finished their packing, a group of IDF soldiers in training came running by wearing backpacks and carrying a stretcher filled with sand bags, in preparation for carrying wounded soldiers. They ran back and forth along the beach for several minutes being drilled by a commander before returning in the direction from which they had come. The family had been well aware of the military presence since arriving in Israel, as they often saw military planes flying overhead and some of the ships they saw in the sea were obviously naval. But watching the soldiers in training added another dimension to their experience.

Pedal Repair

The beach ball game ended, and Armando came back beaming about his new paddles and ball. The lady said they were professional paddles that she no longer used. She came over, very impressed with his skills and again encouraged David and Emily to get him into professional beach ball. The parents smiled again and did not bother to tell her that he had been gifted in all areas of athletics since he was very young, but that they felt there was a greater calling on his life than to pursue professional sports. They thanked her again for letting him play and for being so kind. He gave her a postcard and found a way to tie the paddles onto his rear panniers with the basket. Since the lady had come on a bicycle, David asked her,

Chapter 15   Kiryat Chaim

"Do you know where we could get a pedal?"

"Oh, yes," she answered, "I know the perfect place. Follow me."

David took the pedal, pushing Emily's crippled bicycle, and Armando and
Briana jumped on theirs, eager to accompany their new lady friend. The
four made their way slowly down the bicycle lane, went a few city blocks
east, past the giant round fountain landmark they had passed two nights
before, then weaved in and out of some smaller streets following their
friend to a bicycle shop. The smiling man there took a look at the bicycle
and in broken English said, "It does not need new pedal. Don't worry. I
fix."

He pulled out a tube of something David recognized as resembling a
heavy duty weld-type glue. He asked David, "Do you want new pedal?"

David replied, "No, that's good."

The kind man slathered a generous amount of the gooey black stuff on the
pedal bolt, screwed the pedal on, and told them not to use it for about two
hours. That was perfect timing for the family, as David knew that Emily
was lying down for nap time with the younger children, and it would be that
long before they could leave, anyway. The kind beach ball woman stayed
long enough to make sure the bicycle would be repaired, then waved,
"Shalom," and rode toward her home.

Emily had all five younger children lie down for nap time, since Isabel and
Moshe were still needing more rest than usual because of their injuries.
That just left Victor and Rebeka not particularly needing a nap, but they
had played hard all morning in the sun and sand and were very compliant
about lying down for a few minutes. After a half hour or so, Emily and
Rebeka got up and began getting lunch ready, while the others continued
sleeping.

The three Varelas made their way back to the beach with David still
pushing Emily's bicycle. Lunch was on the picnic table when they arrived
and they ate a little more quickly than usual, not knowing how long it would
take to get to Chabad, where they were supposed to meet someone about
possibly getting a place to stay while David was gone. After lunch, they
finished packing their bicycles, checked their load, said shalom to Nesimi
and the others at the beach concession, had prayer, got on their bicycles,
and slowly made their way inland toward town.

Chabad

The bicycles were packed way too heavily now with the extra food and
bedding, so they traveled very carefully to keep from falling. Eti had given
them directions to Chabad which was only a couple of miles away. They

145

were heading back in the direction of the bicycle shop from which the three had just come. They were able to stay mostly on streets that did not have the brunt of city traffic. They soon found the place Eti had told them to go at the back side of a religious neighborhood, and while getting off their bicycles and trying to prop them up were met by two men with long beards, dressed in the Orthodox clothing of black long-tailed suits and white shirts. The men looked them over and listened as Emily spoke to them in Hebrew, "Last night we spoke with a man who told us to come today."

"What do you want?" one asked, rather gruffly.

"We may need a place for the children and me to stay while he goes back to the U.S. for a few days," she replied, gesturing toward David.

They asked a few more questions, one of the men speaking a little English. Then they took David inside to get more information. Once inside the little building, which turned out to be a not-so-small synagogue, the man who spoke better English asked David, "What do you need?"

David replied, "We're traveling by bicycle, but I have a problem back home with the business. I need to return for a few days and need to find a place for my family to stay while I'm gone. I have money to pay for it," he clarified, not wanting them to think he was a charity case.

The man responded, "We do not take money from people. We are an organization that helps people, all over the world. We take donations of money, food, and clothing to help people."

David offered, "Then we have some things we would like to donate, some blankets and pillows, if you can use them."

The man seemed to ignore the statement, but said, "I think we can help you, provide a place for your family to stay for a few days, but I need to get approval."

While David was gone, Emily took the girls just inside the door to where she saw a restroom. Inside the inner doors she could see men in Orthodox attire praying with *tefillin*.[113] She quietly got the girls in and out of the building, not wanting to disturb the praying men.

The man with David made a phone call, spoke in Hebrew and then had David follow him out and around the building through a little alley to some small one story apartments. Emily was curious about what was going on as David walked by, but was given the look that meant not to ask

---

[113]*Tefillin* – a set of small boxes tied to the arm and head by many Jews during prayer, the rabbinic interpretation of Deut. 11:18 – Therefore shall ye lay up these my words in your heart and in your soul, and bind them for a sign upon your hand, that they may be as frontlets between your eyes.

questions. David followed the man to where two more men were waiting by a fence. As they approached the other men, also in Orthodox dress, he immediately knew that the large, heavy one was the boss. David quickly sensed greed as the man he had followed began talking with the boss in Hebrew and a small argument ensued. The big one in charge turned to David, "You have money?"

David: Yes.

Man: Are you Jewish?

David: No.

Man: Americans?

David: Yes.

Man: Why are you going back to America?

David: I have a problem in my business that I need to settle.

Man: What kind of business?

David: Construction. I'm a general contractor.

Man: What do you do?

David: I build houses, restore them, whatever needs to be done to them.

Man: For how long do you need a place?

David: A few days, not more than a week, I'm sure.

The two men began arguing again, and David knew enough Hebrew to know it concerned how much money to charge. Finally, the big man said, "Ok, 2,000 shekels per day."

David was shocked, knowing that was the equivalent of around $650.00 per day, much more than a hotel would cost. Having done business since childhood, and having a knack for knowing what kind of people he was dealing with, he was also a little perturbed by the ordeal. "2,000 shekels per day! There's no way I can pay that much!"

The man sternly replied, "Then there's no way I can give you a room."

The younger man was visibly upset with the greedy one and mentioned something about not being supposed to charge money. And another argument ensued.

While Emily and the children waited for David, an elderly man in the same type of dress as the two other men and having a nearly white beard came and began speaking with her in Hebrew. He was very kind and quite interested in her story. His eyes sparkled and were much brighter and more cheerful than those of the other men she had seen both outside and when she had snuck into the restroom. He did not exhibit the same religious spirit as that of the other men who looked the same in all other regards. When Emily told him they had been sent there for a place to stay for a few days, his face changed and he said, "I do not know if they will let you stay. You are not Jewish, yet you follow *torah*."

She thought maybe she was misunderstanding his Hebrew, so questioned him, but he went on to say the same thing in another way, mentioning something about *Shabbat*. She was puzzled as to why the fact that they kept *torah* would rule against their getting a place to stay, when obviously this was an area of religious Jews. She knew the family would abide by all the Jewish rules out of respect for them (as long as they were not contrary to scripture), just like they would respect any other host's rules.

David came out and informed the family that they would not be able to stay. They were both confused, as according to Eti and the man on the phone, there would be no problem with them being there. Emily asked David to give the blankets and pillows to the stern man inside, since they would be much too heavy for them to pack for long, especially with the extra food they now carried. She so hated to part with the beautiful blankets but thought the center there could put them to good use while being hospitable to others (even though for reasons unknown to them at the time, they were turned away). The man took them, never letting a smile or 'todah'[114] cross his lips.

The family rode west again, and when they were a couple of blocks away, Emily called Eti as instructed to let her know what had happened. She was furious and ordered, "Wait there! I am on my way."

A few minutes later, she sped up in her car. After getting more details, she said, "There is another place. Come. I show you a park where you can stay tonight."

She gave Emily a ride to the little park so they would know how to get there, then rushed back to whatever other business she needed to attend to. Emily led the family to the park about three blocks away where there was a nice playground. They leaned their bicycles against the trees at a far corner of the play area, and the little ones started playing while Emily got things out to prepare supper. They had not cooked a meal since their arrival in Israel, living off of fresh fruits, vegetables, hummus, and bread, but needed to use the potatoes and some of the other vegetables that had been given to them two nights before. So Emily and David got out the little

---

[114]*Todah* - Hebrew for 'thank you.'

Chapter 15   Kiryat Chaim

camp stove, the soup pot, potatoes, tomatoes, onions, cabbage, eggplant and carrots and began preparing a soup.

They had been watching their surroundings, and when the restroom was once again needed, Emily and the girls headed toward a synagogue near which they had seen a separate out building that looked like it could be a restroom. This area was like none other they had seen in Israel, so far. All of the men there wore *kippot* and had long beards and white *tzitziyot*, some of which were very long. They saw one man with blue in his *tzitziyot*, and he was one of the few who smiled at their greeting. Most had very hard faces and viewed the family with eyes of suspicion. Emily met some ladies on her return with the girls from the restroom, but they barely spoke an audible 'shalom' in answer to Emily's friendly one. The religious spirit was very visible and heavy.

Soldier Questions

After the girls returned from the restroom, David took the boys. When he walked around to the men's side of the building, he recognized the

neighborhood as the one in which they had Emily's bicycle repaired. The man at the bicycle shop across the street saw David and waved cheerfully. David was glad to see him again and returned his kind greeting. When he came back with the boys, Moshe began riding his bicycle around the playground while the others played on

the slides and other equipment. A man wearing street clothes with *tzitziyot* containing the blue thread, a military beret, carrying a green canvas bag, and having an M16 rifle slung over his shoulder approached. He was coming back from synagogue and stopped to talk to David because he saw his *tzitziyot* also contained the blue string. After greeting one another, he asked in English, "Are you Jewish?"

David responded, "No, not that we know of."

He seemed very surprised and asked, "Why do you wear *tzitziyot* if you are not Jewish? Only Jews are commanded to wear *tzitziyot*."

David replied, "The command in the *torah* is for all Israel, not just Jews."

The man argued, "The *torah* and *Shabbat* are only for Jewish people, which is why non-Jews are not allowed to keep *Shabbat*. In fact, if a non-Jew keeps *Shabbat* perfectly, they would have to be killed."

149

David, in his usual calm manner, replied, "I disagree with that."

Emily found it comical that her husband was in a religious Jewish park disagreeing with a man armed with an M16 rifle about whether or not the family should be killed for keeping *Shabbat* perfectly. David was prepared to show him in his own *torah*, but the man refused, preferring to believe his rabbi. But now the family understood why they would not be able to stay in the community over *Shabbat*. And they were thankful that the people there were gracious enough to evict them, as opposed to killing them.

The question was not whether or not they might keep *Shabbat* according to the scriptures, but whether or not they might keep *Shabbat* perfectly according to the oral *torah* of the Jews. If they keep *Shabbat* perfectly (according to Jewish rabbinic law), they must be killed, since according to rabbinic oral *torah*, *Shabbat* is only for Jews. They knew this went against the scriptures which say there is only one law for the native Israelite born and those who sojourn among them.[115] But the family had learned years ago that much of what is referred to as Jewish oral *torah* actually goes against the written *torah*. The prohibition of turning lights on and off on *Shabbat* and many other regulations have been added to the written *torah*, a practice specifically prohibited in scripture.[116]

Over the centuries, judgments for breaking the manmade laws had also been instituted. The family knew this was exactly the type of spirit and law that Y'shua came against in the first century AD. Having never once transgressed the written *torah* and always encouraging others to follow it, he only steered them away from keeping the 'traditions of men' that were contrary to the written word, otherwise known as portions of the oral *torah*.

The young man asked, "Where do you plan to sleep?"

David gestured to the spot on the edge of the park near the bicycles. The man told him, "If you were Jewish, the whole community would come together and give you a place to stay, so you would not have to sleep outside."

David replied, "We are fine outside. We came to Israel planning to camp."

Their conversation came to a friendly close, both firm in their position, and the family was relieved when the young man walked away without having used his machine gun.

---

[115]Exo. 12:49 One law shall be to him that is homeborn, and unto the stranger that sojourneth among you.

[116]Deut. 12:32 What thing soever I command you, observe to do it: thou shalt not add thereto, nor diminish from it.

Chapter 15   Kiryat Chaim

The children continued playing on the play set and riding their bicycles around while Emily and David prepared supper and talked.

"It is amazing what religion does to people," Emily said.

"Yes, the rabbis made laws, then made judgments for breaking them. It's hard to believe they would be so prejudiced as to kill a non-Jew for perfectly keeping their *Shabbat*. That is exactly the kind of spirit and law that Y'shua came against in the first century," David replied.

Emily agreed, "I know. He never once transgressed the written *torah* and always encouraged others to follow it. He would certainly have been against this law. He only steered people away from keeping the 'traditions of men' that were contrary to the written word, the additions of the oral *torah*. I guess we've experienced it firsthand now."

When the delicious soup was ready to eat and served in the family's bowls, they gathered, blessed YHWH for the food and began eating. A small crowd of young adults with little children began gathering at the other side of the park. Emily recognized some as the women she had seen walking around over the past couple of hours. An elderly man approached the family saying something in Hebrew that they could not understand. Finally, he reached into his pocket and brought out a few shekels, then extended his hand as if offering them to the family. They just looked at him in surprise, and Emily said in Hebrew, "Thank you, but we don't need anything."

They were humbled that a little old man would offer them his change. But after offering numerous food items as well as the sodas to people on the beach, they had learned how to turn things down, as well. It did seem a little uncomfortable to deny someone the opportunity to bless them, but they felt strongly that they should not take the man's money.

16 - *Kiryat Yam*

Three Suppers

Yom Shishi (Sixth Day)

As the sun went down, Emily laid out the beds in their safe sleeping order, the children sandwiched in between the parents. Shortly, a pizza delivery car drove up, making a delivery to the crowd of people at the other side of the park. Eti called and said she was on her way, then showed up a few minutes later. She took Emily to the nearby Akiva building, named after the same Rabbi Akiva that the family had learned of while in Amsterdam and who the first town they passed through was named after. Eti's request was met with the same answer there, and she, not being religious herself, was extremely annoyed by the fact that they would not give the family a place to stay. On the way back, she stopped at a little stand by the street and turned to Emily, "You like falafel?"[117]

Emily replied, "I don't know. I've never tried it."

"You've never tried *falafel*!?! You must try it. I buy for you."

Falafel is as common in Israel as hamburgers are in the United States. Emily had them put a little of everything on hers and, as soon as she bit into it, understood why Eti had said she had to try it. She gave an approving look and Eti asked, "You like?"

Emily nodded, as she chewed, and Eti said, "I buy two more so the family can try."

Emily swallowed and said, "No, it's OK. We've already eaten supper."

Eti argued, "It doesn't matter. I buy anyway. They can try."

She bought two more, and as they walked back to the park across the street, the pizza delivery car drove up again, and the driver walked toward the group with another pizza. One of the ladies that Emily had greeted earlier pointed toward David and the children and the driver took the pizza to them. David, not seeing where the driver came from told him, "I didn't order pizza."

---

[117]Falafel - pita cut in half and stuffed with fried balls of hummus, then topped with a special sauce and having the eater's choice of toppings added, including things like cabbage, peppers, onions, and various salads.

Chapter 16   Kiryat Yam

The driver replied, "Those people bought it for you," gesturing toward the little religious crowd at the other side of the park.

David thanked him and took the pizza. The delivery man met Emily and Eti as they approached the family with the falafel.

"Where'd you get that?" David and Emily asked each other at the same time.

They answered one another, marveling at their provision once again. Emily excitedly told Eti, "Yes, people have been so nice to us here. A little while ago an elderly man came and tried to give us his change."

Eti replied, "No, probably he was a beggar, wanting you to give to him."

Emily was very relieved that she had not taken his coins under the circumstances, and felt badly that they had misunderstood him. All they could do about it now was laugh at what must have gone through his mind when Emily told him they did not need anything.

The family ate a second supper of falafel and pizza as they praised Yah for the many provisions He had made for them thus far and prayed for the little old man and the others in the community. Emily then sent the children to the group with postcards which contained the prophetic scriptures and a thank you note for the pizza on the back. The recipients seemed to read the cards, then discretely threw them in the trash, almost as if they were not allowed to be in possession of them.

With full stomachs again, the family bedded down. The crowd left after about an hour and things quieted for the night. The family slept peacefully, only inches from an ant bed on the other side of the trees.

North by Bicycle

Another beautiful morning appeared out of the comfortable night. The Varelas ate breakfast, packed the bedding and remaining food, and then rode to another place near the park to which Eti had sent them. Once again, there was no room for a family who was not Jewish, so they traveled north toward Akko, following the original layout they had prayed over before leaving the U.S. The family still did not know where they would be staying when David went back to the States, but after the events of the past few days, was confident that Yah would put them just where He wanted them- just where they needed to be.

As they rode north through *Kiryat Chaim*, they saw an apartment building that had a 'for rent' sign hanging from the third floor. They called the number, but got only an answering machine, so continued riding north. They rode through traffic light after light under the tall date palm trees that lined the road. Shortly, they came to a long park that served as the median

153

Pedaling Home   Part 1 – In the Beginning

between the north- and south-bound lanes. Remembering that the sparkly-eyed elderly man in front of Chabad had mentioned they could stay there, they surveyed the place, but did not see how it would work for them to stay over *Shabbat*. Since it served as the median for the busy road, there would be traffic all night, much too close for comfort.

They continued slowly north to the outskirts of the city, not realizing they had passed from *Kiryat Chaim*, to *Kiryat Yam*.[118] They rode to the northern edge of *town* and saw a shade tree where they could have lunch and give the little ones a nap before proceeding the few miles to Akko (Acre). They veered off the main road, past some apartments and up a small hill to the shade of the lone tree where they could see the intersection below.

After they ate, Emily laid out the sheets and took a nap with Natanyah and Moshe. David took the others down to the intersection just southwest of them to buy hummus, since they did not know what they might encounter before arriving wherever they would be staying for the next two nights. They did not want to take a chance on going through *Shabbat* unprepared. While there, yelling caught the attention of the children who walked to the corner to investigate and saw that under the various tents just northwest of them was a *shuk*,[119] where all manner of foods and other wares were being sold. The venders were yelling out their prices for various goods. David knew that nap time would not be over for a while, so he took the children to see what was going on.

As they approached, the shouts got louder as the vendors tried to get rid of their goods before mid-afternoon. On preparation day, most markets were closed by 3 PM and people were headed home to prepare for *Shabbat*. The produce that was left with the vendors would spoil before the weekend was over, so the more the day wore on, the louder they yelled and the lower their prices went. The *shuk*, surrounded by big sand dunes and having only a trail through the sand for a road, was crowded as people bustled to get their wares home. Some impatient ones tried driving their cars through, always causing a jam and much aggravation to all involved. Besides the yelling of the vendors, there were the noises of car horns and aggravated people.

The first thing to greet them was the smell of fish, as they walked through the sand made wet from the water running off of the fish trucks. Past the fish was the smell of fresh bread, and then the sweet smell of various types of fruits. Armando caught a glimpse of some fishing tackle that greatly interested him. "Daddy, can I get this?" he asked.

David reminded, "We don't need to be carrying any extra weight. Maybe you'll have a chance to get something like that once we're off the bikes before Sukkot."

---

[118]*Kiryat Yam* - Hebrew for 'Place of the Sea.'
[119]*Shuk* - open air market.

Chapter 16   Kiryat Yam

Armando put the fishing tools down and looked forward to finding some like them in a couple of months.

They left the *shuk* and went back to the market on the way back to Emily and the younger children. Briana and Armando each purchased a sack of marbles, knowing they would have to pack them on their bicycles for an undetermined amount of time, but looking forward to having something else to do during their rest times.

Change of Direction

Just as nap time was over and David and the others were getting ready to return to the lone shade tree, Eti called Emily. "Where are you?" she asked.

"On the north end of *Kiryat Yam*, heading toward Akko," she replied, having just studied her map.

"You've gone that far already! You must not go to Akko! It is way too far for the children to ride!" she chided.

It was actually less than five miles and the family could have easily made it in a short time, but she left Emily no opportunity to say anything for a minute while she ranted. Finally, when she took a breath, Emily said, "We need to keep going north. We made some contacts there before leaving home, and we need to ride in that direction until we find a place to stay while David is gone."

After catching her breath, Eti continued, "Do not go to Akko! I have found an apartment for you to rent."

Emily dreaded the thought of riding back the way they had just come. And what if it was something else that did not work out? She asked Eti, "Where is it?"

"In Kiryat Yam, just a few blocks from where you are. I am coming right now. I will take you to the apartment."

"OK. I am on the hill by the apartments with the two little ones. David is at the market across the street," Emily told her.

"Ok, I find you. I take you to the apartment. See if you like," she said, then hung up, in a hurry as always.

Less than a minute later, she called back, "Where are you? I don't see you."
As Emily explained where they were, Eti saw David, then followed them

155

back to where Emily was. They left their bicycles with her, and David and Armando rode with her to look at the apartment.

They headed west toward the Mediterranean, drove a few short blocks before turning south, and stopped in front of building 18, one of many run-down three-story apartment buildings lined up like parallel Lego blocks, perpendicular with the sea, only one road separating them from the beach. After rapidly surveying the outside of the building from the car, Eti said to David, "This is where you can rent," then made a quick U-turn and headed back to the bicycles, giving David instructions of how to proceed.

Meanwhile back on the little hill, Briana took the younger children to explore the grassy area around them, where they found sweet dates fallen from the trees to eat while waiting. As they feasted, a woman and her daughter, looking to be about the age of Briana, came out of the nearby apartment complex bringing two big bottles of water to the family. Though they had water, they were grateful for the act of kindness on the part of the ladies. It was extremely hot by that time and any and all water was appreciated. They could save theirs for farther down the road. Emily visited with them for a few minutes, then asked if they could use their restroom. The ladies gladly obliged and took them up three flights of stairs to a small, cramped and cluttered living space. It appeared to the guests that these people were of the poorer class of Israelis, yet they were willing to give what they had. The mother even insisted that each of the children take a cookie on their way out. Emily thanked them and they walked back to the bicycles to get ready to ride.

Prospective Lodging

They arrived just as Eti drove up to deliver David and Armando. She rushed everyone along and said she would meet them back at the apartment in a little while with the owner. The family spent a short time in prayer thanking Yah for His provision and being awed at the proximity of their prospective temporary home to their current location, and the timing of it all. Then they rode back the short distance toward the sea and the apartments. Upon arriving, they met several occupants. There were children and young people unsupervised and into trouble, but everyone seemed to be friendly. A young couple with a baby began asking questions of the family and took a real interest in them. When Emily mentioned needing to charge her cell phone, they yelled up to someone in the second floor window, asking permission. When granted, Emily sent Armando and Briana up to charge the phone.

After going up the dingy steps to the second floor, the young cycling pair knocked on the apartment door and were invited into a room filled with smoke from a hookah pipe, a device containing water that is used to smoke tobacco and other herbs. The young people in the apartment, high school and junior high age, were enjoying whatever it was they were smoking in their pipe. They offered some to Armando and Briana, but they

Chapter 16   Kiryat Yam

kindly declined. The television was on and they tried to keep their eyes off
of what was being shown, trained at home to be very careful about what
they watch. There were so many strange sights, sounds, and smells in
the apartment that they were not really sure how to proceed. So they just
left the cell phone there and returned to their parents, who, after finding
out the environment upstairs, were very glad that they had.

While their phone was charging, the young couple let David use theirs. He
and Eti traded several calls, her being aggravated that the owner had not
shown up yet. On one call, she began, "I do not know why she is not here,
yet. But you wait. The apartment is on second floor. It is 1,500 shekel for
one month. You take. It is hard to find for one month only. This is good
price for one month."

David agreed to wait for the landlady. The young couple with whom they
had been visiting knew the apartment. The wife told them, "In that
apartment, there is not water and gas. They do not work."

Emily replied, "I'm not worried about the gas. I don't plan to cook much,
and I have a little camp stove. But water could be a problem. Are there
showers at the beach?"

"Oh, yes," she said, pointing toward the beach, "very close, just across the
street."

"Then I don't see a problem," Emily reiterated. "I can get water there for
washing clothes. He'll just be gone for a few days, then we can ride north
again. We just need a safe place to sleep and to lock up the bicycles for
when we go out. We won't be able to ride while he is gone because he
rides behind us to make sure everyone is OK."

"This is a good place," said the young wife. "Lots of nice people live here.
You'll like it."

The afternoon wore on and sundown was quickly approaching. The family
was accustomed to bathing on preparation day as part of their routine to
prepare themselves for *Shabbat*. It had just been the previous morning
since they had had a good shower, but the two August days in between
were extremely hot and their bodies were in need of another to feel the
clean that they liked to feel going into the day set apart as a special
appointment with Yah Himself.

Tandem Friends

Emily asked David, "Why don't I take the girls over to the beach to shower
and change clothes while you wait for the owner? Then when we get back,
if she's still not here, you guys can go get your showers."

David agreed that was a good plan, so she gathered up their clean

Shabbat clothes, their two towels, and shampoo which they also used for soap. They walked past the apartment building toward the sea, crossed the road, and then walked south toward the outdoor Amigos bar, situated just beyond the showers. There was a fence between them and the beach area which required going through the parking lot and then the bar itself in order to reach the showers. The music was blaring and Emily walked purposefully toward the little buildings that she recognized as bathrooms, only to get there and find they had already been locked for *Shabbat*. A little distraught, she turned the girls around and walked back through the bar to the outdoor showers where a woman who was watching pointed. Though they had used the outdoor shower at Kiryat Chaim, this one was not an option. It was right in front of the bar area, which already contained over a hundred people. They had not brought a sheet with them, and even if they had, it would have just drawn attention to the fact that they were showering in front of everyone. Besides that, the horrifying thought of the sheet being dropped raced through Emily's mind before she turned to get out of there as quickly as possible.

She was hot and sticky and had her heart set on being clean for *Shabbat*. That coupled with the fact that David was about to leave them for a few days was almost more than she could bear at the moment. She had wanted to walk back by way of the peaceful beach, but from where they stood, would have to walk back through the bar past the speakers blaring loud music in order to get to the northern beach area. So she chose the parking lot route, taking Natanyah and Rebeka by the hand and had Isabel and Briana follow her out   toward the large lot, now filling with cars.

As they walked quickly past the parked cars, Emily was taken aback by what she saw. Riding straight towards them on their tandem bicycle were Nikolay and his wife. The random chances of the family running into Nikolay at a bar in Kiryat Yam, when he expected them to be far north of Akko by now and the fact that Nikolay lived in the big city of Haifa and had plenty of choices as to where to bring his wife for a Friday evening, were astronomical. *No one* in their right mind could chalk this up to coincidence! The girls happily greeted Nikolay and his wife who were just as surprised to see them. Nikolay had not known anything of the wrong turn, the bicycle accidents, David's having to return, or any of the other events that had transpired in the last few days. They turned the bicycle around and rode slowly beside the girls as they walked back toward the apartment, and Emily explained what was going on. She welled up and broke into tears when she said, "I just wanted to have a shower before *Shabbat*." She felt ridiculous for being so emotional about a shower, but the whole situation had sent her over the edge. She did not consider that pregnancy hormones could have something to do with her current emotional state.

As the group continued down the sidewalk, Emily quietly prayed, thanking Yah for sending His angel in the form of Nikolay, who had already been much more of a host than they could have imagined to have received in Israel.

They passed one and then another of the giant Lego blocks as they made their way to the one the family was thinking of moving into. On the way, Nikolay asked, "How much will you have to pay for rent?"

Emily happily told him, "Fifteen hundred shekels."

"*Fifteen hundred shekels!*" The man she had come to know as calm, congenial and quiet flew into a small rage. "I can't believe someone would charge such exorbitant rent in this rundown little Harlem!"

Emily was startled at his reaction and was rather amazed to see that he could be so angry, yet handle the tandem bicycle with such ease, never changing his creeping pace on the pedals in order to stay beside the young walking girls. He was even more upset to find that the apartment did not have gas or water. Emily really had not thought of the rent being so bad, since they were in a bind and just needed a secure place to stay for a few days. It was much better than the 2,000 per day that Chabad wanted to charge them. It definitely was not the kind of place they would choose to live, but it was better than her sleeping out on the beach with the children and no husband. And they viewed even finding *this* place as a real blessing and opportunity from Yah.

No Business on *Shabbat*

They reached David and the boys, who were also surprised and excited to see Nikolay. They were still waiting for Eti and the owner of the apartment. They had learned the apartments there were individually owned, instead of one owner owning the entire building or group of buildings, as is common in the U.S. Time ticked away and the sun got lower in the sky. The family would not rent an apartment on *Shabbat*, and *Shabbat* was closing in fast. While they waited, Nikolay offered, "This is not good. No water. No gas. Too much money, especially for this area. I will help you find something nicer or less expensive, or both."

David agreed, "It's almost *Shabbat*. We need to get settled. We'll just go camp on the beach and try to find something Sunday. If you can find us something, we would be grateful, but we wouldn't want you looking on *Shabbat*. We can't tell you what to do, but we would not ask you to do that."

"I understand. Don't worry. I will get online and find you something," he told them, and they rode back to the bar.

A boy in his early teens who had been observing the family pointed out his family's apartment to them and told them, "You can come back tomorrow night and I'll call the owner again for you. And you can take showers at our place if you want."

It was such a kind offer, but by then, it was too late. They needed to get settled before *Shabbat*, not knowing exactly where on the beach they would stay or the difficulties they might face there. While the family had been speaking with Nikolay, the young couple disappeared with their baby, but now reappeared with sandwiches for everyone, as well as two-liter orange and grape sodas they had just purchased. It was obvious, again, that these were not people of means, yet they had sacrificed and given what they had to strangers.

The family said shalom to all their new friends, then pushed their bicycles west through the sand between the apartments. Emily, though grateful for the kindness of the people, was cringing at the thought of how much sugar the children had been getting since their arrival. The sandwiches were not a burden to take, but the sodas were. Before crossing the street, Emily had Briana leave them on a brick at the apartments to be a blessing to someone else. She felt badly for not taking the gift or returning it to its donors, but could not bring herself to pack it with them and then see her children consume more sugar and food colorings and did not know where the couple had gone. She found herself being defensive when the children wanted to bring it along and wished she had spoken with more kindness.

The family pushed the bicycles up the street until they found a play area where they could enter on hard packed sand, which was much easier to push through than the loose mounds that were blown up all around. They followed the sandy path toward the sea and parked on a flat area above the main part of the beach. To their left, they could see the Amigos Bar a half mile down the shoreline. And 100 yards or so to their right was a huge rock pier jutting into the sea, where people were fishing. It was a very quiet, seemingly private place compared to the area they had camped for two previous nights that week. Yet it was the same sea, the same water and salt, the same sand. It was like home, only more like home, since it was private and quiet.

They leaned their bicycles together in pairs to keep them from falling with the weight of the loaded panniers. There was no need to set up the tent, so they got the bed mats ready and laid things out before it got dark. After the ten minutes it took to do all of that, they went to the water and waded out deep enough to wash the sweat and accumulated dirt off of their bodies and clothing. The salt water bath did not leave them with the same clean feeling that fresh water would have, but it was the best they could do. They walked, dripping, to the play area they had passed, so the children could play as they all dried before they had supper and went to bed. They did not know the plan or where they would be staying or when, but because they would not travel on *Shabbat*, they knew they were where they were supposed to be for the next two nights. They blessed Yah and thanked Him for giving them more direction, then left the situation in His hands.

17 - Mediterranean Rest

Shabbat on the Beach

Shabbat

They watched the big orange sun slide below the Mediterranean Sea as the clothes dried on their salty bodies, the children sliding and seesawing as the parents watched. Returning the few hundred feet to their camp site, they ate the newly gifted sandwiches, as well as hummus and more of the fruits and vegetables they had received earlier in the week, then lay down in their sheets on the mats. Something was different here. It was more peaceful. There were no artificial lights, this part of the beach not having been developed yet like the one at Kiryat Chaim. There were no audible voices, the fishermen being too far away and the few beach walkers' conversations drowned by the sounds of the sea. It was perfect. The family did not have the squeaky clean bodies they had desired, but their surroundings, their lodging place, was perfect.

The children fell quickly asleep, but David and Emily lay awake on their mats on either side of their blessings and talked as the full moon rose higher in the sky. There was no need for any other light. The moon's glow cast a shadow from anything it touched. The pair discussed how blessed they were above billions of people in the world to be having this experience, to be able to sleep with nothing in between them and the sea, to be able to be lulled all night by its singing, and to have the light of the moon and stars overhead. They felt sorry for all of the tourists who were at that very moment bustling around on the streets, in bars, and in their hotels with hot running water and all their amenities. *This* was the good life. And most would never know it.

Beautiful colors formed and merged with one another as hints of the forthcoming sun began to appear over the land of Israel. Emily lay on her back watching and praying, the only one awake to enjoy the display, her view unencumbered by a pavilion like they had slept under at the beach a couple of miles farther south. There was no reason to get up. It was *Shabbat*, Yah's day of rest that He graciously provided for all man to desist from their labors and join in sweet fellowship. There was no work to do, no place to go, only quiet time with Him.

A few early risers could be seen walking or jogging on the beach, but there was no traffic. They had only spent two Sabbaths in Israel as a family, but already loved the fact that almost everything shut down for His day of rest. There were no sounds of trains or buses. And traffic and other activity in

Pedaling Home   Part 1 – In the Beginning

general was much less than during the week. It was so peaceful, like nothing they had ever experienced anywhere else.

The family got up slowly and ate their regular breakfast, then put on their *Shabbat* clothes. The sun got hot quickly and they talked about how it might have been wiser to have set up their tent the evening before. Not wanting to do it on *Shabbat*, they took a multicolored sheet they found blown into the sand dunes and tied it to the bicycles making a tent for shade from the scorching sun. They talked about how they were experiencing a small part of Abraham's life and how he must have been accustomed to the hot wind blowing and rhythmic response of the flapping of his tent. They discussed what measures he and his people might have taken to overcome some of the little issues, like bits of sand getting blown into their food. Did they get used to crunching down on sand, or did they just learn how to sit or lean to avoid those types of annoyances? Probably some of both, the family concluded. It was already extremely hot by mid-morning and the strong wind coming from the sea could no longer have been classified as a breeze. Most people may not have enjoyed the experience, but the Varelas used it as an opportunity for learning and another dimension of understanding the scriptures.

A lone female beach walker approached their bicycles. Most of the walkers had been down on the edge of the beach, where the sand was wet or damp and easier to walk on, but this young lady was on the hard part of the beach, several feet above the main sandy beach, where the first stage of a road was being built, and was coming straight toward them. Emily greeted her with 'shalom' and the young woman returned her greeting, stopping to inquire of the family. Emily was becoming fairly comfortable with Hebrew by then and was able to effectively communicate the answers to her questions. It was more difficult to understand her, though, as she had a speech impediment. She seemed like a rather shy person, yet she had walked directly to them and immediately began asking questions. Emily invited her to join them as they sat on one of their sheets in the shade of the three foot tall bicycle sheet tent.

Beach Walker Questions

After the usual questions like, "Where are you from?" "What are you doing in Israel?" "Are you Jewish?" "But you wear *tzitziyot*?" "And you follow *torah*?", her interest became more evident, so Emily began to share with her more about their lives and how they lived, not according to the rabbis and the traditions of Judaism or Christianity, but according to the scriptures, Yah's word alone. She shared the prophecies in Jeremiah, Ezekiel, Hosea, Deuteronomy, and other places that talk about how Ephraim (otherwise known as the ten lost tribes, the Northern Kingdom, or sometimes just Israel) would one day be joined again with his brother Judah (otherwise known as the Jews or the Southern Kingdom) and be brought back to the land of Israel to live in peace with Messiah their King. She showed her from the scriptures how the prophecies talk about lost

162

Chapter 17   Mediterranean Rest

Ephraim returning to *torah*, to the ways of Yah, and how he would be living according to a renewed covenant, one in which the *torah* was written on his heart. She explained how their family, as well as a growing number worldwide, were being drawn into a closer relationship with their Creator and learning to follow His desires for them by living in obedience to the instructions He gave them in His word. The woman sat and listened with great interest, asking more questions, for over an hour. David cut apples for the children's snacks and watched them enjoy finding shells as he listened to the conversation, picking out enough words to know that what Emily was saying could be life-changing for the woman. As he listened, he prayed quietly that Yah would open her eyes and ears to His words.

After exhausting all of her questions and having her ears filled with an abundance of scriptural truth, of which she had been previously unaware, she asked, "Do you need food or anything?"

Emily replied, smiling, "No, in fact, people here have been so kind to us." She went on to tell of the many times since they had been in the Land that people had given to them. She motioned to the food they still had and told her it was all gifts from different people that *Abba* had used to bless them. The woman stayed for a few more minutes, then excused herself and went back towards the north east of town, taking with her the family picture postcard which Emily had given her that contained the two important verses on the back.[120] Emily excitedly told David more about their conversation:

> She asked all the usual questions, but she kept going. She was really interested in the prophecies. I was able to tell her about Ahijah coming to Jeroboam with the prophecy of the ten tribes being separated,[121] then how the division occurred,[122] and about the idolatry of the Northern Kingdom.[123] She kept asking questions and I was able to tell her about Hosea and how he prophesied that in the last days YHWH would restore the house of Ephraim[124] to

---

[120]Jer. 31:33 But this *shall be* the covenant that I will make with the house of Israel; After those days, saith YHWH, I will put my law in their inward parts, and write it in their hearts; and will be their Elohim, and they shall be my people.
Ezek. 37:19 Say unto them, Thus saith YHWH Elohim; Behold, I will take the stick of Joseph, which *is* in the hand of Ephraim, and the tribes of Israel his fellows, and will put them with him, *even* with the stick of Judah, and make them one stick, and they shall be one in mine hand.
[121]1 Ki. 11:29-43
[122]1 Ki. 12:1-24
[123]1 Ki. 12:25-33
[124]In scripture the whole house of Israel refers to both the kingdoms of Judah (the Jews) and Israel or Ephraim (the 10 lost or scattered tribes). Sometimes 'house of Israel' is speaking about the whole house and sometimes it speaks only of the house of Ephraim, which is also referred to as 'Israel.'

Himself and take them as His people again[125] and that Jeremiah describes the new covenant being written on their hearts[126] and how Ezekiel prophecies that they will be reunited with their brother, Judah, in the last days.[127] She was able to understand that the House of Judah is the Jews and that the House of Israel/Ephraim is currently scattered but beginning to reappear. And she seemed to understand the role that Y'shua played in the restoration. She said she was going to go home and begin reading the *torah* and prophets. She was really intrigued. It's so exciting to be a part of watching the light come on in someone's eyes, and to be used to inspire them to dig into His word and come into a closer relationship with their Creator and Savior!

David said, "I could tell you were sharing a lot of scripture with her and that she was truly interested. That's why I took care of the children and fed them their snacks, so they wouldn't interrupt you. May Yah bless her and draw her closer to Him."

"*Amein*,"[128] replied Emily, as she got out the hummus, chopped up a few vegetables to add to it and spread it on bread for their lunch. They had already been drinking lots of water, as the heat and wind drove them to thirst, and had been eating fruit off and on since breakfast, but their stomachs were now ready for something more solid.

Angel Food

After everyone was satisfied, they sang and had a time of reading the scriptures, with more discussion and study than they had on the other days of the week. Then the older children went back to exploring in the sand, while Emily lay down with the younger ones under the sheet tent. She had not been down long when David said, "Someone's coming."

He got up and looked out, surprised to see the young woman coming back, this time bearing two grocery bags. She approached the family and told

---

[125]Hos., chapters 1-2, ending with Hos. 2:23 - And I will sow her unto me in the earth; and I will have mercy upon her that had not obtained mercy; and I will say to *them which were* not my people, Thou *art* my people; and they shall say, *Thou art* my Elohim.

[126]Jer. 31:33 But this *shall be* the covenant that I will make with the house of Israel; After those days, saith YHWH, I will put my law in their inward parts, and write it in their hearts; and will be their Elohim, and they shall be my people.

[127]Eze. 37:19 Say unto them, Thus saith the Lord YHWH; Behold, I will take the stick of Joseph, which *is* in the hand of Ephraim, and the tribes of Israel his fellows, and will put them with him, *even* with the stick of Judah, and make them one stick, and they shall be one in mine hand.

[128]*Amein* - Hebrew for 'so be it,' commonly anglicized as 'Amen.'

Chapter 17   Mediterranean Rest

them, "I brought you something to eat." As she took the food out of the bags, she continued, "It's not much. I only cook for myself. It's what I had left in my refrigerator for the last two days."

Emily was deeply touched to see that the woman had gone all the way home in order to get food to bring to them. She had said earlier that she lived a long way from the beach. And in spite of the fact that Emily had made it clear that the family had plenty and had even offered some of what they had to her, she walked all the way back to bring what she had made to the family. The woman did not stay around long this time, "I need to go now. It was nice to meet and talk to you."

Emily replied, "We don't know where we're going from here, but I hope we see you again sometime."

She agreed, and turned to go back home. After she left, Emily opened the containers and divided the food among everyone, so they could each try the different dishes. There was a delicious cucumber salad, an eggplant dish, some meatballs, green beans and other food. They again blessed Yah and prayed blessings on the woman, both physically and spiritually, that her eyes would be open even more to who He is and what it means to follow Him. She already had treated strangers with kindness, something commanded for His people, showing that His laws were on her heart. Emily forgot to have her write her name and contact information in the little pink notebook she carried. She hoped their paths would cross again another time.

After the younger children woke up from their nap, the family went down to the water's edge and walked along the beach, instructing the children not to get down and play in the sand and water like they did on the other days of the week. Part of the reason for wearing the clothes set-apart for *Shabbat* was to help the children to remember that this was a special day of resting in YHWH and not going their own way doing as they please, but focusing on Him and His desires for His people.[129] The family walked along the water's edge picking up and examining beautiful shells and getting their feet wet. Natanyah began a game of racing with the water, to which the other children soon joined in. She followed a wave out toward the sea and then ran back toward the beach as another was coming in, trying to keep it from catching her, all the while squealing with delight.

The winds were not as strong down at the water's edge as they had been

---

[129]Isa. 58:13-14 If thou turn away thy foot from the sabbath, *from* doing thy pleasure on my holy day; and call the sabbath a delight, the holy of YHWH, honourable; and shalt honour him, not doing thine own ways, nor finding thine own pleasure, nor speaking *thine own* words: Then shalt thou delight thyself in YHWH; and I will cause thee to ride upon the high places of the earth, and feed thee with the heritage of Jacob thy father: for the mouth of YHWH hath spoken *it.*

165

at their lodging place. They enjoyed the short walk, not getting too close to Amigos bar farther south, so as to maintain the attitude of the peacefulness of the day. As sundown approached, they strolled back to the bicycles to eat supper. There were plenty of leftovers from the sweet young lady, so they ate until they were full and packed the rest away in a food pannier, knowing that, without refrigeration, they would need to eat it soon before it spoiled. They again prayed for the lady as they ate and prayed for themselves and their difficult situation, asking Yah to give them clear direction as to where Emily and the children would stay.

18 - Provision

The Pastor

Week 3   *Yom Rishon* (First Day)   8/23-24

Just after sunset, Emily noticed a family leaving the beach area heading toward the playground by the street. It appeared to be a man and wife with seven children, about the ages of their own. They were dressed conservatively, the women wearing rather long dresses. She wondered if they might have more things in common, so turned to David and said, "Let's go talk to them! We haven't seen many big families here."

Because scripture described children as blessings,[130] often people they met who lived their lives according to both testaments recognized the blessings and had larger families David, never as eager to talk to strangers as his wife seemed to be, replied, "You go. I'll stay here with the children."

Emily didn't wait for him to change his mind. She got up, dusted off the sand, and then walked towards them as they strolled to the parking area near the playground. "Shalom," she greeted cheerfully.

One of the ladies, more reservedly replied, "Shalom."

After breaking the ice, she learned they were Russian Christians who lived in *Kiryat Tivon*, about twenty miles away, east of Haifa. They warmed up when they found out the Varelas, too, were believers in Y'shua as the Messiah, but there were still communication glitches, as Hebrew was their second language, as well. Some of the Varela children came over as Emily spoke with them, and one of the Russian children gave them two of the kites they had been flying. It was a precious gesture from a brand new friend, not knowing if they would ever meet again. The family had a ways to drive to get home, so they soon said their goodbyes and departed.

Emily went back to David and the bicycles and reported on the people she had just met, as the children tried out their new kites. They had been in prayer as to how to proceed, and decided that after dark David would return to the apartment complex and find the young man who had said he knew the owner of the apartment in question, so they could once again

---

[130]Psa. 127:3-5 Lo, children *are* an heritage of YHWH: *and* the fruit of the womb *is his* reward. As arrows *are* in the hand of a mighty man; so *are* children of the youth. Happy *is* the man that hath his quiver full of them: they shall not be ashamed, but they shall speak with the enemies in the gate.

attempt to rent it. About that time, they received a call from Nikolay who had been trying to find them a better place to stay. "Hello David, I think the apartment is the only thing to rent. I tried several places, but nobody wants to rent for less than three months. I am sorry I could not find anything."

"It's no problem. Thank you for trying," David replied before hanging up. Since the Varelas' visas expired in just a little over two months, and David only planned to be gone for a few days, it was not practical for them to rent something for that long. So they prayed again.

As darkness was falling, Emily saw another conservative-looking family leaving the beach. It was only the third large family they had seen since arriving in Israel (the first being the Musician's family on Mount Carmel). This time, it appeared to be a man and wife with six children accompanied by another woman. She again turned to David and said, "Let's go talk to them!"

Again, David replied, "You go. I'll stay and watch the children."

She approached, greeting them in Hebrew and introducing herself. They were a little more outgoing than the previous family and began asking questions right away. Emily learned that they, too, were Russian Christians and that this man was the pastor of the congregation that the other family attended. She was then even more eager to share from the scriptures the answers to the questions they were asking her, thinking that surely Christians in Israel would be more receptive to the message they had than those in the U.S. often were. So as they asked, she answered, knowing that, since he was a pastor, they should have a fairly good knowledge of the scriptures.

After a few minutes, the man sent for an interpreter. Emily was excited, thinking they were so interested in what she was telling them concerning the scriptures that they wanted to get the whole thing more clearly. While they were waiting for the interpreter, Emily went and told David what was going on. It was mostly the pastor, not the ladies, asking questions and she felt more comfortable for David to be talking with him. Since the interpreter was on the way, that would now be possible.

Within a few minutes, the Interpreter arrived, and they were surprised to learn that he was from Tennessee only a couple of hours from where they lived. The pastor asked him, "Find out what this family needs."

The Interpreter asked David and David replied, "We don't need anything. We came to Israel traveling by bicycle and prepared to camp."

Emily was disappointed, having thought the reason for the Interpreter was so they could share the scriptures. She left the group to take care of the unsupervised children at the bicycles who had been joined by some of the Russian children, and there were indications that foolishness might be

Chapter 18   Provision

brewing. David stayed and continued talking with the men, while the other ladies stood there on the sand and listened.

"You are not Jewish and you believe in Y'shua, so why do you wear tassels?" he asked.

David answered, "Y'shua was our example of how to live, and he wore them. Scripture tells us to wear them as a reminder to keep the commandments. Remember the woman with the issue of blood?"[131]

"Yes," the pastor replied.

"She knew the messianic prophecies. Zechariah tells us that the Messiah will come with healing in his wings.[132] 'Wings' there is 'kanaf', the corner where the tassels go. Since Messiah kept all the commandments, we know he kept that one. And when the woman touched the hem of his garment, the word there is also 'kanaf.' She knew if she took hold of the corner of his garment, she would be healed. The blue in the tassel reminds us of Messiah."

"But when he died, all of that changed. We don't have to wear them anymore," the pastor said through his Interpreter.

"We don't see it that way at all. In fact, we don't see any instance in all of the New Testament where Y'shua's followers actually broke a commandment or taught others to, though Paul was sometimes misunderstood and accused of it."

Better Prospective Lodging

The pastor asked more about the family and then once again asked what they needed. David replied, "We have everything we need, but it looks like I'm going to have to go back to the U.S. for a few days. We're looking for a place for my wife and children to stay while I'm gone. We found an apartment yesterday, but it was getting too close to *Shabbat* and the landlady had not come, so we're going to try to reach her again tomorrow."

The pastor immediately began to speak Russian to the single woman who was with them and then got on the phone to someone. After making a couple of phone calls, he told David through the Interpreter, "I have found you a place to stay. It's close to here. Would you like to go see it?"

---

[131]Matt. 9:20 And, behold, a woman, which was diseased with an issue of blood twelve years, came behind *him,* and touched the hem of his garment:

[132]Mal. 4:2 But unto you that fear my name shall the Sun of righteousness arise with healing in his wings; and ye shall go forth, and grow up as calves of the stall.

169

"Yes!" he replied. "Let me go tell my wife, so she'll know where I'm going."

David quickly walked to the bicycles where Emily was putting the children to bed and said, "They've found a house for you to stay in. I'm going to go look at it with them. They said it's close to here."

"Ok," she replied. Emily felt a little strange being left at the beach alone at night with all the children, but trusted Yah and gave thanks that He was providing them a place to stay.

David went in the Interpreter's car, and the Russian family followed in their minivan: one street past the beachfront street, turning right, taking the first left past some of the Lego apartments, and turning right again shortly after. They stopped at the third house on the little brick lane that was just barely wide enough for two cars to pass. This particular house had a tile porch covered with tin and a brick patio, which could be seen hiding under the overgrowth of tall weeds.

David had seen enough to know that this would be a fine place, much better than the apartment they were trying to get the afternoon before. He asked, "How much will it be?"

The pastor replied, "1,200 shekels per month."

David was delighted with the area and the price, both being much better than their known alternative, and was mentally converting shekels to dollars and processing all that had happened in the past half hour since they had prayed. His hesitation cause the pastor to think that the family was short on funds and he offered, "I can pay the rent for you."

After the Interpreter told David, he quickly assured him, "No, we have the money to pay. I was just thinking of how the Father has been working in our life. This is a much better place than where we were going to rent, and the price is good. Just before we met you, my wife and I had prayed, wondering what we were going to do. We had decided to go back to the apartment in the morning and try to contact the landlady again. But there is no water or gas in the apartment, and this looks like a much nicer neighborhood. Our Father is amazing, the way He loves and provides for us! Thank you for making yourselves useful to Him."

At that, the Pastor and Interpreter got excited, as well, "Yes, it's very exciting to see someone pray and to know Elohim has used us to answer their prayer!"

They all rejoiced standing outside the yard gate. Just then the owner, Tzipporah, a slim woman looking to be in her late fifties and her cousin, a man not much older than she, walked toward them as they stood outside the little wrought iron gate. Tzipporah explained in confident English, "Someone's things are still in the house, mostly in one room. The man will come to get them by the end of the week."

Chapter 18   Provision

"That's not a problem," David replied.

"We can meet you here mid-morning tomorrow," she said.

"I'll see you then," David agreed.

The landlords turned and walked back in the direction from which they had come as the Pastor and Interpreter asked David, "What else do you need? Beds? Stove? Refrigerator? Food?"

David was in awe, but told them again, "Thank you, but we have everything we need. And I only plan to be gone for a few days."

"We'd really like to help any way we can," insisted the Interpreter. "They'll need a refrigerator, won't they?"

David gave in, knowing they were really wanting to be helpful, "Ok, I guess they could use a refrigerator."

"We'll have one here tomorrow," said the Interpreter, as the Pastor took his family home, and he and David got back in his car to go back to Emily and the children.

David walked across the hard-packed sand toward the bicycles, with a joyful spring in his step. He came to Emily with the great report. "We've got a house for you! With a porch and a yard! 1,200 shekels for a month! And they're bringing you a refrigerator tomorrow."

"*HalleluYAH!*[133] Thank you, Father!" rejoiced Emily, adding, "But we don't need a refrigerator."

"I know, but they're really wanting to help. They were trying to give us beds, food, and a stove, but I turned it down because we don't need it."

"Good!" she said. "I don't want anything to do with a stove. I'm enjoying eating fresh, raw food, without all the preparation like I do at home. I don't want the burden of a stove and having to prepare cooked meals. I think it's good for all of us to be eating a simpler diet, and the food here is so fresh and good."

"Yah is so good!" David said. "You know, earlier in the day, we were thinking the reason we didn't get the apartment rented was so we would be at the beach to meet the young lady. But now we know it was also so that we would meet the Russian families and the Interpreter and get a much better and cheaper place for you all to stay while I'm gone."

---

[133]*Halleluyah* - Hebrew for 'praise be to YHWH.'

Emily replied, "I know. Yah has a something for us to do here. I'm excited to see what He's going to do in us and through us with the people around here. What if we hadn't guarded *Shabbat*? What if we had stayed and met the landlady after sundown? We would have been on the second floor of the dingy apartments with no water and gas and paying 1,500 shekels for the month. I am always amazed at the way Yah rewards His people for obedience! And, you know, having been given food from so many people, we've saved enough of our projected grocery budget to pay the rent!"

David rejoiced with her, "Praise Yah! He always provides!"

Last Night Together

They then spent some time in mourning, as this would be their last night together for a while and their last night sleeping out under the stars. Beginning tomorrow night, Emily and the children would once again be confined to a house with a roof, leaving the freedom of the open air they had come to enjoy so much. And David would begin his journey back to face the problems at work. This interruption in their plans was something neither of them looked forward to, but they both knew there was a reason for it and that YHWH would work all things out for good.[134]

They stayed awake late under the light of the waning but still very big moon, talking about what Yah had done so far in their lives over the short period of time they had been in Israel, as well as discussing what they might do over the course of the next few days and how it would affect the remainder of their time there. As difficult as it was to reach the point of sleep this last night together, once it was determined the time had come, Emily went back to her mat nearest the bicycles at the other end of the row of children, and they both fell into a comfortable, peaceful rest.

The beautiful morning light, the wind off the sea, and the sound of the waves crashing just yards away was appreciated even more this morning, as David and Emily again came to grips with the fact that they had reached a point of change. Breakfast of fruit, bread and hummus, and more leftovers from the kind lady was served, the scriptures read, and the spare set of clothes unpacked. Laundry had not been done since leaving their Host on top of Mount Carmel five days before.

Since they wore their clothes for two days before laundering and had their special outfits for *Shabbat*, they were able to make it until now without having to use the spare set. The men's shirts and ladies' dresses were some that their horse-and-buggy friends had helped Emily to make just before they left. They were made from the only fabric Emily had that was

---

[134]Rom. 8:28 And we know that all things work together for good to them that love Elohim, to them who are the called according to *his* purpose.

Chapter 18　　　　　　　　　　　　　　　　　　Provision

big enough to make everyone clothes. It was a coarse, stiff gray fabric, and while it looked nice and a bit on the dressy side, it was not the best outfit for hot summer days. Since they had not been able to shower before *Shabbat*, they went in shifts, men and ladies, down to the bar area and took showers in the indoor shower houses, now opened. Refreshed, and in clean clothes, they returned to the bicycles, a little over a quarter mile north on the beach. As they walked each way, what stood out on the east side of them were the rows of apartments that had almost become Emily's and the children's home for the next few days. While they would have been grateful for that, they once again gave thanks that Yah had provided them something better.

David got a call from the New Yorker at the farm, saying that all was well, but that he was unable to get the appliances working. He reported, "I can haul them off if you buy new ones."

David was perplexed, knowing that both appliances had been working well when they had left, and the stove was still under warranty. He told the man, "I'll be glad to have new ones sent out if I need to or you can go pick them up, but first let me get someone over there to check them out."

"We really need something done today," the man replied.

That increased David's concern, knowing that the family had brought their motor home with them and that it had a working stove and refrigerator. "Why would it be so urgent that the one in the house work," he wondered.

The time to meet the landlady had not yet arrived, so the family loaded everything on the bicycles and pushed them through the small sand dunes and over to the play area while they waited. The children enjoyed the three-story spiraling slide, climbing toys, seesaws and other equipment. Eti called to check on the family and Emily excitedly gave her the great news. She was happy for them and said she would come by later.

18 Yitzhak Sade

As their scheduled meeting time approached, the family rode the short distance to their new abode. They first rode east parallel with the rows of the Lego block apartment buildings, turned right to ride in front of one of them, then left down a narrow street with speed bumps and cars parallel parked on the north side. They passed four tiny blocks and turned right onto Yitzhak Sadeh,[135] and proceeded to house number 18, the third house on the right, directly across from a two-story synagogue.

The house was made of stucco and joined the houses on both sides of it, just like all of the surrounding houses. Extending from the front was a tin roof covering a tile porch with a stucco fence around it, three feet tall in the front and five feet tall on the sides between its porch and the neighbors on either side. The small front yard consisted of a brick patio on which stood two leaning 'T' posts which held a mess of tangled laundry lines. Emily was thrilled to see those, as there was plenty of room to hang all of the family's laundry, and there were even clothespins left hanging there from previous tenants.

At the front of the yard, which was sand covered with weeds several feet tall, was a three-foot concrete block fence, which ran the length of the entire road, separating everyone's house from the little brick lane. The lane itself was barely wide enough for two cars to pass and was designed so that cars could be parked on the right, leaving room on the left for people to pass the parked cars to get to their houses farther down the lane. At the south end of the lane were metal pylons, preventing through traffic. Emily was thrilled again to see what a safe street Yah had provided for them to be living on while David would be gone.

Another small house was just to the south of 18 Yitzhak Sade, and next to that was a much larger two-story house, bustling with activity. A huge black shade cloth extended from the house all the way to the fence on the opposite side of the street. The family parked their bicycles outside the fence at what would become their temporary home, walked back to the opposite side of the street, and sat in the edge of the shade provided by the neighbor's shade cloth, wondering why so many well-dressed people came in and out, mostly men. Emily began to wonder if maybe it were a house of ill repute. After a few minutes of waiting, a young man from the house approached their fence speaking with an attractive young woman. After she left, he smiled at the family and greeted them with, 'Shalom.'

Emily stood and walked toward him, knowing he had questions to ask her, and she had a few of her own. After explaining to him they were planning to rent the house two doors down, she asked, "What is this place?" assuming the house was some type of business.

He clearly stated something that was not in her Hebrew vocabulary, and his matter-of-fact way of stating it left no room for her to ask more questions. So after finishing the conversation, she had no more idea of what it was than she had before, only that there was a kind young man

---

[135]*Yitzach Sade* - a street named for the Russian man who immigrated to Israel and was one of the founders of the Israeli Defense Force at the time of the establishment of the State of Israel in the 1940's.

Chapter 18   Provision

welcoming people at the gate. She walked back to the family and relayed
her conversation to them.

~~Speaking~~ Russian

The battery in one of the cell phones was no longer working, so David
suggested Emily find out where the Post Office was in order to buy a new
one. He reasoned that since that was where minutes could be purchased,
they would also have batteries. Emily learned from the kind young man
where the nearest Post Office was, and David suggested she go buy a
battery while he waited for the landlords to take his payment and give him
the key. She took Armando and Briana, while David waited with the
younger children in the shade.

They walked south on the brick road, past the houses and past the metal
pylons, turning east on Weizman toward the shops. Emily stopped at one
of the first shops where a man was sitting outside and inquired as to where
to find the Post Office. He gave her directions and gestured farther east
and across the street. They walked past where he had told them, but
never saw what they thought looked like a Post Office. She stopped and
asked another shopkeeper who stood outside and he directed her back in
the direction from which she had come. They crossed the street and finally
found the small building squished in the corner of a little shopping center.
They entered and waited their turn in the line.

When the people in front of them left, Emily approached the man sitting on
the other side of the window with the little hole at the bottom and kindly
asked in her best Hebrew, "Do you sell phone batteries?"

He did not understand the question and did not have much patience with
her lack of proper vocabulary. She tried again, showing him the battery.
He waved his hand, as if to shoo her away, telling her that they did not sell
them there. She asked, "Do you know where I can get one?"

He became angry and asked, "Do you speak Russian?"

"No."

"French?"

"No."

She had studied it in high school for two years but knew less French than
she did Hebrew and was not about to admit knowing any at this point. The
fact that she did not speak any of his approved languages threw him into
such a rage that the woman sitting beside him at the counter motioned for
Emily to come to her window. Emily tried to hide the sigh of relief as she
moved over and a Russian woman stepped up to her spot in front of the
angry man's window.

175

This woman was very kind and wrote down an address in the nearby city of *Kiryat Motzkin* where Emily could buy a battery for the phone. She even gave some basic directions so that Emily would know the general direction to go to find them. Emily thanked her and started out of the Post Office with Armando and Briana, one at each side. She felt humiliated by the treatment she had gotten from the grouchy Russian man. She had noticed on the way that all of the street and store signs were in Russian as well as Hebrew, and it had not taken her long to realize that this section of Israel was mostly made of Russian immigrants.

The hot sun was beating down and sweat was rolling off of them as they walked back toward the house. Emily was fuming over the Post Office incident and the fact that they would have to park the bicycles while David went home to the business, something she still was not accepting with much grace. They walked past sign after sign written in Hebrew and Russian and heard people speaking Russian as they walked by shop after shop. Most of the faces were without smiles, and while some were helpful, there seemed to be a general lack of friendliness all around. Armando and Briana knew Emily was upset and Armando asked her, "What's wrong, Mama?"

At once, all of her pent up emotions came spewing out of her mouth. "I did not spend hours and hours of time before leaving home learning Hebrew so that I could come to Israel and be surrounded by RUSSIAN!!! I don't want to learn Russian! I want to learn HEBREW! And now here we are stuck in this snobby little Russian town!"

There. It was out. She had said it. And immediately she felt both a sense of relief and a sense of guilt. She knew deep down that Yah had put them in this particular place for a reason and she knew that it was the best place for them. She thought of her sister and husband back in Texas who were working on adopting a child from Russia and wondered if she were supposed to learn Russian. She longed to learn more Hebrew, but knew she should be content in whatever circumstances she found herself.[136] She was upset with the mean man at the Post Office, but did not stop to think that their dear Nikolay, the young man who had arranged their first lodging and had gone way above and beyond what could have been expected of a stranger met online, spoke Russian as his first language. And she was not taking into consideration all of the kind Russian people who had just helped them find their temporary home, given the children kites, and pointed her to the Post Office in the first place. Even though they were not particularly friendly, they certainly had been very helpful. They reached Yitzhak Sadeh and turned north toward their new little house where David and the other children still waited for the landlord. She had cooled off by the time she reached them and explained to David that she was not able to get a battery for the phone there.

---

[136] 1 Tim. 6:8 And having food and raiment let us be therewith content.

Chapter 18   Provision

Eating Words

As she spoke with him and told him about the Post Office incident and her inappropriate reaction, she noticed out of the corner of her eye, a small, jovial woman approaching them from the south end of the street carrying a tray of fruit and drinks. The woman approached the family who was still at the north edge of the shade cloth and gave Emily the tray on which sat grapes, bananas, carefully cut apples, oranges, peaches and pears, two bottles of flavored soda, and a stack of plastic cups, announcing that it was *bishvil hayeladim*. She was a sweet little Russian lady with a twinkle in her eye, who stood and visited with the family for a few minutes before waddling back to her house at the southwest corner of the street. That was all it took to bring Emily to complete repentance concerning her recent feelings and the statements that had come out of her mouth only minutes before. She offered a prayer of confession and asked forgiveness for speaking against, not only a whole town of people, but against the plans that Yah had for her and the children over the next while.

Before she had even finished praying, the young man at the entrance to the gate under the shade cloth came towards them carrying a box of crackers and a dairy spread, similar to cream cheese. They thanked him, again amazed at the hospitality they were experiencing in what Emily had just repented of speaking ill of. They ate their snacks as Emily answered more of the man's questions about themselves.

177

19 - Lodging

The owner of 18 Yitzchak Sadeh drove up the narrow brick road bordered by concrete and stucco fences on each side. David left Emily visiting with the neighbor and walked over to speak with Tzipporah, accompanied again by her male cousin, asked smilingly, "Is this your family?"

"Yes."

"You are a blessed man," she announced. "Look around the place and make sure it is suitable for them."

He already knew it was, but took a quick tour of the premises to appease her.

As they showed him through the house, they explained, "The furniture belongs to the previous renter, but he will be here within a couple of days to get them."

David was not especially comfortable knowing that another man would have access to the house his family would be staying in, but the couple assured him, "Don't worry. We will come with him. The family will be safe."

Finding everything acceptable, David told her, "Everything is fine. We'd like to rent it."

She affirmed, "The price is 1,200 shekels per month. You will be responsible for paying taxes and utilities. I understand you are only wanting to rent for one month?"

"Yes. Could we get something in writing?"

She seemed to think that was a strange request and seemed somewhat uncomfortable until he told her, "You can just write something yourself saying that we have the apartment for one month at 1,200 shekels."

"That's no problem. I will do that," she agreed.

Chapter 19   Lodging

Besides being in the construction business and being accustomed to having written contracts, the family had owned rental property in the States and knew what kind of trouble either party could get into by not having a written agreement. They did not know how things were in Israel, but did not want to learn something the hard way. Tzipporah, her cousin, and David walked two streets west to her home so that she could get a pen and paper to write out an agreement. David gave her the rent money which came from money they had budgeted for food for the previous two and a half weeks, but that had not been used because of all the donations of food they had received from others. They were amazed at how Yah had provided the rent money for them. They would not have to go over their budget in order to pay this unexpected expense!

The issue of paying taxes on a property they did not own was confusing. They learned that a house built on the land is owned, but the land itself belongs to Israel, so a tax is charged. Essentially, it is rent paid for the use of the land, the same as property tax in the States had come to be, though Americans typically did not view it in that light. And the tax in Israel was much higher than the property tax to which they were accustomed paying in the U.S.

After writing out the agreement, the three walked back to 18 Yitzchak Sade. David asked Tzipporah, "Would be all right to clean up the yard and do a few minor repairs."

"Do whatever you think you need to," she replied. "I'll bring a key for the back door later."

As they spoke, her cousin moved the remaining possessions of the former renter into the room with his other things. Emily was glad, not liking to be responsible for other people's things.

A distinguished couple and another well-dressed man drove past them in a very shiny, black, elegant-looking sedan and parked under the shade cloth. They got out and went inside the mystery house, Emily still curious as to what was going on. After a half hour or so, while she and the children remained sitting along the wall snacking on the various foods that had been given them by their new neighbors, the people came back out, got in their car, and began to back down the narrow street between the bicycles lined up against the west wall and the family on the east. As the car backed out, a hand protruded out the window as the driver gave a twenty shekel bill to Armando, then as the car continued to back down the lane, he said to Emily, "*Bishvil hayeladim.*"

She wished there were something she could say besides *todah*, and was again dumbfounded at the way they were being treated. Why were people being so kind to them? Why was it happening over and over again? What were they supposed to be learning from all of this?

After the exchange of money, key and contract, Tzipporah and her cousin greeted Emily and the children, then got in their car and backed down the lane. Everyone was excited about checking out their new home. The tall weeds brushed against them as they crossed the brick patio to the covered porch. The smell of cat urine got stronger with each step they took toward the house. They had seen a couple of cats scurrying away when they arrived and now decided that there must be a territorial dispute involving their home, as from the smell it was obviously being marked by more than one male.

Inside the little wall dividing the porch from the yard was a tile floor which was broken up in places near the wall of the house and was covered in sand. At the end of the porch sat a broken white dresser that Emily assumed belonged to the man who owned the rest of the furniture inside, which was now squished into one room.

Once inside the front door they saw that the entire floor throughout the house was tile. They walked into the small entry way which was between the south wall of the house and the south wall of the bathroom. The little hallway opened up into a bigger room with the door to the bath on the right.

Inside the bathroom was a sink and commode on the left with a window above the small space between the commode and the tub and shower on the right. The window was several panes in a wooden frame which hinged open toward the inside and had burglar bars on the outside to prevent entry when the window was open. The tub was very large, and Emily was already figuring that all four girls could fit in at the same time. The most unusual feature of the bathroom was the shelf above the tub and shower that contained a big water heater laying on its side. Theirs seemed to be the only house anywhere around that did not have a solar water heater on the roof. Emily said, "I don't like the looks of all that weight sitting on that little metal shelf above the heads of bathing people. But I guess it's probably been there for years and hasn't caved in, yet, so probably won't while we're here.

Briana countered, "I think it would be easier to cave in, since it's been here for a long time and is old."

Emily, reassuring herself and all the other future bathers said, "Well, this house was Yah's provision for us. I don't think he brought us here to be smashed by a hot water heater."

180

Chapter 19   Lodging

Making a right turn out of the bathroom brought them into the quaint kitchen area. The east and north walls were lined with cabinets painted brown, with the exception of the small window facing the street, again equipped with burglar bars. The sink and a small bit of counter space was on the north wall and to the left was a bar separating the kitchen from the dining area. Emily felt extremely blessed that it was similar to their home in the States in that it was open and she would be able to see everyone from the kitchen in the other rooms with much ease. Beyond the bar and dining area were two sliding doors with beautiful frosted windows which could be closed to separate the far room from the dining room. On the west wall was an air conditioning unit under a very large window and to the left at the end of the south wall was the back door, painted royal blue, which could not be opened from either side without the key. To the south of that room, west of the room they first entered was the second bedroom with a small window on the west, now full of the former tenant's belongings.

After taking a quick look through the house, the family took pictures to protect themselves as renters, and began cleanup efforts. The girls and Emily got to work sweeping and mopping the front room with the broom and mop they found there. The broom was what they were accustomed to, but the mop was something they had never seen before, an apparatus in which a large thick rag was secured. Emily immediately liked the mop and recognized what an improvement it was over the string and sponge mops typically used in the States. The towel was easily removed for thorough cleaning, and when it wore out, was easy to replace. Furthermore, if one was in a pinch, an old bath towel could easily have been substituted for the recommended cloth. She was quite impressed with the idea and quickly saw how well it worked on the tile floors.

David and the boys worked outside on the brick patio, which was missing several bricks. They dug out sand and inserted bricks from a pile to make a smooth walkway. David dug in the sand and secured the 'T' posts firmly, then placed bricks around them for added support. He untangled the laundry lines, retied the broken ones, then began sweeping and cleaning the front porch. Emily got the girls to work wiping out the kitchen cabinets, then came out and began helping the boys pull the tall weeds, being careful not to pull anything that looked like it was supposed to be there. They discovered several geraniums along the south wall once the big weeds were pulled. David went in and helped the girls clean the bathroom.

Eti Returns

Early in the afternoon, Eti came bringing lunch in nice, reusable plastic containers, as well as a huge trash bag full of toys that her daughter no longer used. Emily gratefully took the food, still learning the humility of accepting gifts from others. The children excitedly dumped the toys out on the floor of the front room and dug through to find treasures to show to each other and their parents. Emily had so enjoyed the fact that their life had been simple on the road, no junk in the way, no messes to clean up, just fresh air and the things they needed on their bicycles. A sense of dread came over her as she saw the pile of toys and imagined having to start normal life again, keeping and reminding others to keep things picked up, refereeing disagreements over possessions, having to go through the things herself to make sure there was nothing inappropriate in it, and then having to go through the painful ordeal of explaining to the children why they could not keep this or that toy. She turned her attention back to sweet Eti, who was speaking her deep, thickly accented English at her usual rapid pace, trying to make sure the family was cared for in a proper way. She told Emily, "Electricity in Israel is very expensive. This," touching what looked like a light switch on the wall, "is for the hot water. Only turn it on before you need hot water and remember to turn it off when you don't need. It cost very much."

She continued through, inspecting the house and declared, "You need stove, refrigerator, and beds."

"No, we're fine, really. We're not moving in, just staying for a few days until David returns. We're happy with just the things we have on the bicycles. Our plan while in Israel was to eat mostly fresh, raw food. I don't want to have to do the cooking, like I do at home. I'm having a nice break. We do have a camp stove, small pot, and skillet if we decide we want to cook.

"We have our bed mats for sleeping. And someone is planning to bring a refrigerator later. Thank you for offering, but, really, we're fine with what we have here."

Eti finished her walk around making sure things were acceptable and told Emily to call her if she had any problems. Then she was off to her next assignment, this time to pick up her nine-year-old daughter from school.

When she left, Emily went through the toys and removed anything that looked demonic or otherwise inappropriate for the children, putting them in a bag to go to the dumpster across the street at the north end of their lane. She was surprised at how little she had to discard in comparison to toys they had received in the States. She was also impressed at some of the things that Eti gave them. There were several notebooks and lots of pencils and markers. There were balloons, whistles, balls, stickers, baby dolls, cars, and a beaded jewelry making kit. And best of all, there was a soap making kit that looked like it had only been used once, containing the shavings to make molded soap.

Chapter 19   Lodging

After going through the toys, Emily had the children put the ones they would keep in one of the lower kitchen cabinets and then help her bring all the bicycles in and neatly line them up against the front room wall. They would not need them until David returned. They planned to put them in the spare bedroom as soon as the former tenant moved his things so that they would not be an eyesore in front of the entryway.

As they worked cleaning up the place, Nikolay called to check on them. David told them about the place he had rented and Nikolay asked, "When do you plan to leave?"

"As soon as I can get a plane ticket. The sooner I get things straightened up back there, the sooner I can be back. If I leave tonight, I should be able to return Thursday."

Nikolay gave him the number of his travel agent, who he said could get him tickets at a reasonable price on short notice. After the call with Nikolay was ended, David called the agent and made arrangements to fly out just after midnight arriving in the U.S. first thing Monday morning and leave the States Wednesday evening in order to return to Israel Thursday afternoon. He would be required to be at the airport three hours before flying in order to get through the security checkpoints, and would need to give himself about an hour and a half to get to the airport from the train station at *Kiryat Motzkin*. He called Nikolay back to let him know and Nikolay, being very knowledgeable about scheduling, told him what train he needed to catch and when he needed to be there. He would have to leave around eight o'clock in the evening.

The house was a bustle of activity. David continued helping get things cleaned up and repaired while Emily helped the children get their new toys put away so they could all help clean. Tzipporah returned with the back door key, only to find it was the wrong one. She said she would return when she found the right key. Mid-afternoon, an elderly lady came from under the shade cloth, bringing sodas. She introduced herself as Sarah, and visited with Emily for a few minutes.

Everyone worked together to get their temporary home in order. After David got the bathtub cleaned, Emily took both sets of dirty clothes and the *Shabbat* clothes out of the panniers and put them in to soak. They had not done laundry since leaving Mount Carmel and were on their last set of clothes. The family worked together to wash, ring out, rinse, ring out again, then hang the clothes on the newly repaired laundry line, complete with colored plastic clothespins. As they worked, a young lady of fourteen years appeared over the fence of the house to the south. She introduced herself as Olga and using a Hebrew-English dictionary, pointed to the word 'work,' asking if she could help the family in any way. Emily was not sure what she could put her to do, since they seemed to have everything under control. But she then offered to do laundry. By that time, most of the laundry was washed and being hung on the line, but Olga insisted on taking the clothes that the family was now wearing, when the others got

183

dry enough to put on. The family consented, though Emily felt rather awkward having someone else wash their dirty clothes.

After getting things to a satisfactory point, the family walked to the beach to have some play time before David left. Among the treasures the children found was a full sized broken surf board. They took it out into the water and used it to ride on like a raft. Several of the bigger children straddled it while Armando pushed it to a big wave, then turned it quickly and jumped on the back with them, riding as far as they could before falling off. For a more exciting ride, Armando took only one rider who put one foot above the foot straps as he pushed it backwards toward the wave, then jumped on behind and rode toward the more shallow water, where the wave picked up the board and stabbed it into the sand, throwing off its riders. While all this excitement took place, the smaller children built castles in the sand with David and Emily.

They returned to their little house to find a roll-away bed, an extra mattress, and a refrigerator waiting for them on the porch. They took their dry clothes off the line, took quick baths and put on the freshly cleaned clothes, then shook their sandy clothes off and gave them to Olga next door, who was waiting to do their laundry. They moved the refrigerator and beds inside, and David took a large scrap of plywood that was on the patio and laid it across some bricks and buckets he found lying around to make a short table on which to put their supper. They had done without one since they had arrived in Israel, but now that they were in a house, a table seemed in order.

They enjoyed their last meal together as the children played with their new toys. David then read to them from the scriptures and said it was time for him to go. The family walked down their little street to the metal pylons at the junction of Weizman. Nikolay had told David which number to watch for on the *sherut*[137] that could take him to the train station. He hugged all the children and kissed his wife as the *sherut* approached. It stopped in front of them, he stepped in, the doors closed behind them, and it drove toward the beach. They all waved and watched until it turned south and went out of sight for the ten minute trip to the train station at *Kiryat Motzkin*. They turned around, and with mixed emotions, walked back to their little house as darkness began to fall on the sea.

---

[137]*Sherut* - share taxi service, usually minivans that can carry 12-15 passengers, which run along bus routes, but can customize the route for the passenger.

Part 2

The Scattering

And YHWH shall scatter you among the nations, and ye shall be left few in number among the heathen, whither YHWH shall lead you.

Deut. 4:27

20 - *Levad*[138]

Yom Sheni (Second Day)

David, too, left with mixed emotions. He was torn between the agony of leaving his family alone in a foreign country and gratefulness to Yah for providing such a perfect place for them to stay. There was only one other passenger in the *sherut*, and he was occupied with whatever was playing on his earphones. The driver tried to have a conversation with David, but David did not understand anything he said, so the ride past Amigos Bar then east toward Kiryat Motzkin under the city lights and palm trees was quiet. When they arrived at the train station, the driver said, "Five shekels," and motioned to David where to go to enter the small station for the southbound train. David paid him, thanked him and walked purposely up the ramp toward security.

Minutes after buying his ticket the lights of the train appeared in the north. When it arrived and the doors slid open, David entered with the numerous other rushing people that were traveling south from Kiryat Motzkin. He walked up the stairs and got a seat by the window. The train departed as David continued to think about the family he had just left and the situations he would be facing once he got home. His thoughts were interrupted by another passenger who asked, "Where are you going?"

"To America," David replied, knowing that most Israeli's understood that to be the United States.

The man then asked, "Where are your bags?"

It had not occurred to David that it might appear strange to be making a several thousand mile trip with no luggage. He explained the situation to the man's satisfaction before that man's destination was reached and he left the train. After picking up more passengers at another stop, David received the same line of questioning from another man.

After nearly an hour and forty-five minutes, the train came to a stop under Ben Gurion Airport in Tel Aviv. The passengers disembarked and went up the stairs and elevators to the main floor. David, having no bags to carry, took the stairs. As he made the turn to go up the second flight, he was immediately spotted and questioned by security, asking, "Where are you going?"

David: To the U.S.

---

[138]*Levad* - Hebrew for 'alone.'

Chapter 20   *Levad*

Officer: Where is your ticket?

David: I don't have one.

Officer, appearing ruffled: How do you expect to fly with no ticket?

David: My ticket is supposed to be waiting for me at the counter. I paid for it by phone.

The suspicious officer called a comrade on his two-way radio who came to his aid, also questioning David. David tried to explain the situation again, being interrupted several times, and was finally escorted by the guards to the ticket counter.

After paying for the round trip ticket, which would have him returning four days later, David got in the security line and waited behind numerous people with lots of luggage. He felt eyes from all around watching him and began to think it may have been better for him to have brought along a bag of some sort, even though he did not need one. Because of the terrorism that the Israeli people live with daily, they are on much higher alert than most other people groups. A young, rather dark-skinned, bearded man without the well-known religious garb preparing to board an international flight in an Israeli airport was enough to get some people's attention. But the fact that he had no luggage upped the suspicions even more. He considered trying to help someone with their baggage to keep from looking so suspicious, but remembered that one of the questions asked at security is whether anyone else has handled your baggage, so decided he was better off leaving things as they were. When it was his turn to be questioned by security, it did not take long for them to whisk him away to a private room where they could search him more thoroughly.

Once inside the little room guarded by two officers, the other two officers continued their questioning.

Officer: Where are you going?

David: "To the U.S.

Officer: Where is your baggage?

David: I don't have any.

Officer: Why not?

David: I'm making a quick trip, coming back Thursday. I don't need anything.

Officer: What were you doing in Israel?

David: Visiting with my family.

Officer: Why are you leaving on a U.S. passport and returning in less than five days?

David: There's a problem with my business and I need to go straighten it out. I'm leaving my family here, so I want to return as soon as possible.

Officer: What is your business?

David: Construction. I'm a licensed general contractor.

Officer: You are too young to be a licensed general contractor.

Officer 2: If you were a contractor, you would have someone working on the problem and would not have to return to repair something yourself.

David: The problem is not that something needs to be repaired. I do have someone in charge of the business, but the situation involves management and can't be fixed without me there.

Officer: Do you have proof that you are a contractor?

David pulled out the laminated wallet-size copy of his General Contractor's License and handed it to them. They seemed shocked that he actually could prove he was a contractor, but the proof was all that was needed for them to end the questioning, search him with the hand held detection device and let him go.

Two of the guards escorted him toward his gate, one of them turning back at the half-way point to return to his station, the other escorting him all the way past the gate security checkpoint to keep him from having to endure the entire scenario again. Because Israel requires people to be at the airport three hours before an international flight departure time, David found himself sitting in the airport late at night with nothing to do. It was so much different traveling alone than traveling with his family. He noted that three hours passes much more quickly when the waiting periods are interrupted by having to check numerous bags, make trips to the restroom, dig through packs to get snacks, answer loads of questions from little inquiring minds, and pay attention to numerous comments, some very comical, made by little people concerning their surroundings. He sat there in quiet and peace, missing his little family.

Nikolay to the Rescue

Emily was getting their new home in order and preparing for the night. She had wanted to sleep outside on the back porch, but they did not yet have the key which would unlock the brown metal exterior door just beyond the royal blue interior one. They had not been in their backyard but had seen

Chapter 20   *Levad*

through the large window that it contained a pomegranate tree loaded with nearly ripe pomegranates, an olive tree, and a tiny date palm tree that someone had planted right in the middle of the path that led to the gate opening in the rock wall at the edge of the back yard. As she unpacked items from the panniers and some of the children helped her put things in their places, the others played back and forth through the open door from the front porch. As Emily laid the sheets on the bed mats, Briana walked in and said, "Someone's outside."

Before Emily had a chance to straighten up and walk out, a large young man appearing to be in his early teens walked into the house. Somewhat startled, she asked in Hebrew, "What are you doing?"

"I'm looking at the bicycles. How much do you want for them?" he asked.

"They're not for sale. We're traveling and we're going to need them in a few days."

He was insistent and Emily did not understand all he was saying, though she did gather that he lived in a house behind them to the northwest. Just as she was beginning to get a little nervous about the fact that he was not leaving, Nikolay walked in the front door. He saw Emily's perplexed look and she explained in English, "He just walked in here looking at the bicycles."

Nikolay quickly took charge of the situation, told the young man in no uncertain terms that the bicycles were not for sale, put his hand on the young man's shoulder and escorted him out the front door, making it clear in a nice but firm way that it was time for him to leave the premises.

Emily was relieved that Nikolay had once again come to the rescue. He explained, "I was north of Akko and heading back home. I just wanted to stop by and check on you to make sure everything is OK."

"Thank you. You got here just in time. I didn't know what to do about the young man."

"You are welcome. Would you like to see the B'hai Gardens in Haifa? There is no charge for admission."

"Oh, yes, David and I talked about it and thought it would be a good thing to do this Friday, if you're available. He should be back Thursday evening, and we'd like to start riding again Sunday, so Friday, while we're here nearby would be the best time. That will give David a relaxing Friday and *Shabbat* to get rested and over his jet lag before we ride out again."

Nikolay gave brief information about how they were to meet for the tour, then made sure everything was fine in their new place and told them, "Call if you need anything."

Emily thanked him again for watching out for them and was sure to close and lock the door as he left.

As the children put away the last of the toys, crayons, and books, the phone rang. Emily answered to hear the voice of a friend from Tennessee who now lived in Israel, "Emily, there are problems in Tennessee."

"What's wrong?" Emily asked.

"I've received a call from [the Pennsylvanian]. He said someone is getting ready to sue David. He needs to talk to David right away. He's on my computer on Skype right now. Would you like to talk to him?"

"David is on his way home. He was alerted that something is wrong back there. But I'd still like to talk to him, since you have him there."

The Pennsylvanian, who also had been doing some painting work for David, knew something of the problems. The friend put her cell phone to her computer so that he and Emily could talk. He informed her, "The electrician says he's going to sue David for non-payment."

"I don't know what's going on," she told him. "We've always had a good working relationship with him, and I tried to pay him some a few days ago, but Paypal wouldn't let it go through. David's been trying to reach him, but hasn't been able to. I don't know why he's resorting to something like that. He knows David always pays."

"Well, I'm glad David's coming back. Maybe he can get things worked out. Tell him to call me and I can pick him up at the airport," he offered.

Emily warned him, "Don't tell anyone he's coming. He wants to see what's going on before anyone knows he's there."

"Ok," he agreed, and her friend ended the Skype call and the cell call, wishing both parties, "Shalom."

She was confused about what the problem could be, but knew David could work it out. She said a prayer for everyone involved, then went back to the children in the other room.

The family, minus David, bedded down in the west room by the big window.

Chapter 20   *Levad*

Though it was open all the way, the air was much stuffier in the house than it had been a few blocks away at the beach. The few little streets of houses between them and the shore kept the sea breeze from being able to reach them as effectively. Emily looked forward to getting the key to the back door so they could lay their mats outside under the stars as they had most every night since they had been in Israel. She refrained from turning on the air conditioner, not wanting them to get accustomed to the cool air and then having to head out again on the bicycles in just a few days. They had not used their air conditioning at home that summer, even on the hottest of days, in preparation for their trip. She was not about to start now. So she lay down, prayed with her children, and thought about David in the airport, praying for him and what he would face in the U.S. as well as for whatever it was that she and the children were to do while they were in Kiryat Yam. It was difficult to get to sleep with the family divided, and sweating in the stuffy room with only an occasional breeze through the open windows did not make things any easier. She finally drifted off to sleep as David waited to board his flight to New York.

Sandwiched

David got a window seat on the right side of the big plane and continued thinking and praying about the family he had just left, as well as what he would face at home. Because flights from Israel to America go west with the sun, a twelve hour midnight flight such as the one David was on would reach New York just at sunrise, giving him a much longer than normal summertime night in which to get some rest. But he did not sleep well on the plane with the distractions of passengers getting up and down, flight attendants moving about, and the occasional messages from the cockpit.

Not long after seating himself by the window, a very heavy American man sat down in the seat next to him. The man could not fit in between the armrests of the seats on either side of him and his shoulder and arm pressed into David. Both the men were in discomfort, but the heavy man was obviously in distress and the twelve hour flight had not even begun. He asked David, "Would you mind changing seats?"

"I'd be glad to," David answered. By doing so, the man's extra weight was able to extend to the wall of the plane, giving him more room and thereby freeing David up just a bit.

David, now seated in the middle seat, looked up and greeted the Israeli man who was putting his bag in the overhead bin and was ticketed to sit in the aisle seat. Though he was less heavy than the man now to David's right, he still took up more than his allotted amount of space. The flight soon readied for take-off and, once in the air, the Israeli man to David's left fell asleep. David was looking forward to getting some rest, but his new companion got to sleep first and his head began to fall on David's shoulder. Sandwiched between him and the heavier American man now pressed up against his right arm, he was too cramped to be able to get much rest.

While the Israeli on his left slept, the American in the window seat informed him, "I've slept all day, and I'm ready to be awake all night!"

He enjoyed the snacks that the stewardess brought, but could not reach them from her hand, so David had to pass them to him. Shortly after consuming the snacks, he had to go to the restroom. This was a major ordeal that would happen several times before the plane landed. First, David had to awaken the sleeping Israeli, since the American could not maneuver himself in such a way as to do it. Then David had to get out so that the heavy man could exit the row. David and the sleepy Israeli would sit back down and wait for the American to return, since they would both have to exit again in order to give him access to his seat. Sometimes the line to the restroom was long, so it would be quite some time before he returned, yet the two sleepy men could get barely a wink it seemed before he was back and ready to sit again. And then the process started all over the next time snacks were served. David dozed off just in time to be awakened.

The Community

Emily got up and prayed, wondering how David's flight was going, knowing he was now somewhere over the Atlantic. She cut some fruit in preparation for when the little ones awoke and alternated between watching them sleep and watching the occasional passersby out both her front and back window. The streets were quiet, and she gave thanks for the peaceful atmosphere in which they found themselves. She marveled at how her Creator was so loving and how He considered everything about her when putting them in this perfect little place. The house was spacious enough to store the bicycles and give the family lots of area to lay their mats in one room. The neighborhood was quiet, and most of all, the synagogue across the street, going from her neighbor to the south all the way to the north intersection, kept her from having any neighbors directly in front of them. She had always enjoyed being more distant from people, and though Israel seemed so crowded, instead of being on the second floor of a dingy apartment building, neighbors all around, above and below, as they could have been, here she was with a front and back yard and no one in front of her.

Her mind went back to the apartment building, and she realized that it had

Chapter 20   *Levad*

been a test, like many they had faced over the years. A test of faith and obedience. Had they waited for the landlady and done the business of renting on *Shabbat*, they would have missed the blessing of the much better place here. She gave thanks to her Creator, who knew how she preferred to be in His open country. She thought of the 80,000 acre ranch in New Mexico where she worked for a time, and the even larger ranches where she had done day labor as a cow puncher. She remembered leaving the ranches and moving to the crowded trailer park, then stretching back out a bit when they moved to the little east Tennessee town. The half-acre property with a large established garden plot and numerous types of fruit and nut trees including cherry, peach, pear, apple, fig, pawpaw, muscadine, pecan, walnut, as well as raspberries and volunteer asparagus, was a welcomed transition back toward peacefulness from the busy Colorado trailer park.

When it was time to leave there, Yah (who they called 'God' at the time) showed them a sanctuary on a ridge at the end of a dead-end road, surrounded by timber, but with just enough cleared land for Emily to have some open spaces and run some livestock. Their nearest neighbor was a quarter mile away, but was out of sight because of the trees between them. Being on the ridge top also allowed for more breeze than was received by the typical Tennessee resident, something for which they were always grateful.

Before coming to Israel, Emily had never imagined the closeness in proximity of people and towns. She thought moving from the Texas panhandle to Colorado, then to Tennessee was restricting, since the western states' populations were so sparse in comparison. But Israel made Tennessee look spacious. So to be in a town with houses built against one another, Emily felt like her temporary dwelling, with the synagogue across the street instead of neighbors, had been custom made for her.

After the children awoke, ate, had scripture time, and cleaned up, Emily readied them to take a walk into the market area of their new little town. They went out the yard gate and turned south passing Olga's house, walked under the black shade cloth at the next house, continued past several more homes on both sides of the little brick lane and headed toward the metal pylons at the end of the street. When they reached the busier street, they turned left toward the shops. They walked half a small block before reaching the first one, a clothing store. The next shop was the little market where they had first asked directions to the Post Office. The man there sold snack items, as well as milk and various dairy products. A cooler full of ice cream and popsicles was out front under the canopy that extended to the edge of the sidewalk.

As they slowly walked by observing the little shops from the outside, they came to one full of freezers. Emily, only having learned to read Hebrew block letters, not yet Hebrew script, could not tell from the sign what was sold there, so they stepped inside. She opened one of the white chest-

193

type freezers to find it was full of chicken, sorted neatly according to cut. As she turned around to exit the store with her small brood behind her, the little shop owner in the white coat and colored *yarmulke*[139] finished with the customer he had been helping and rushed over toward them excitedly speaking blessings over *hayeladim*. He placed his hands on each one's head and spoke blessings which Emily did not fully understand. They all stood there rather shocked, knowing that what was being spoken over them was definitely a good thing, but amazed that it came in the middle of a little meat store they had just 'happened' into.

After blessing everyone, the little man in white asked in Hebrew, "What do you need?"

Emily replied, "We were just looking to see what you sold here."

He whisked them over to the cooler to the left of the door, opened it and gave her a package of chicken necks. Emily tried to explain, "Oh, no, I don't need anything right now. We were just looking," but he would not take 'no' for an answer.

"You take it *bishvil hayeladim*," he insisted.

She thanked him, and as they left the store, Emily quietly prayed blessing on the little man in white and thanked Yah for the refrigerator that they now had to keep things like this from spoiling.

They continued down the street looking in shop after shop familiarizing themselves with the wares that each one sold. They entered a shop filled with the aroma of spices which sold dried beans, grains, and various dried fruit and candy. The owner spoke some English and gave the children each a piece of cough drop candy as she got to know Emily. Emily answered her questions, telling her about their most recent development of David having to go back to the US for a few days. The tall, slender, dark woman was very kind and since she spoke English, Emily took the opportunity to ask her, "Do you know where I can get a battery for the cell phone?"

The woman kindly wrote the name of a place in Hebrew script and told her, "It's in Kiryat Motzkin."

The place she told of was the same one the kind woman at the Post Office had described. She gave Emily basic instructions as to how to get there, and they visited for a short time more before Emily took her little crew down the street to check out the other shops.

Farther down was a shop that sold most anything someone could need in

---

[139]*Yarmulke* - a type of head covering worn by many Jewish men, resembling a brimless cap.

Chapter 20   *Levad*

their home, including paper towels, cleaning supplies, cooking utensils, notebooks, other school supplies and toys. A very nice lady worked there who also spoke English and also asked Emily lots of questions. After leaving there, they passed a fruit market, a Russian Restaurant, a sidewalk café with a bus stop in front, a bakery, and another store that carried all kinds of household goods, as well as more personal care products and some groceries. The man who owned that store was a Jewish immigrant from Florida and spoke good English. He was also very friendly and interested in the family.

Emily and the children crossed the street to check out the stores on the south side. There was the tiny shopping center with the Post Office, a little cafe, a grocery store, and a couple of clothing stores. No one on that side of the street seemed to take much interest in the newcomers and none initiated any conversations with them. Emily was rather glad, as she was getting tired of visiting and the children were getting hungry. After waiting for buses and taxis to pass, the little group carefully crossed the busy street, Emily carrying the bag of chicken necks. Once across, a tall elderly man, appearing to be of little means, approached them and without saying anything, handing them a Styrofoam carry-out container with food inside. Emily thanked him and the group continued walking toward home, occasionally glancing back to see that the man was following them. Emily was not sure what to think of that and was a bit bothered by it, not knowing anything about the man, other than that he had given them something in a box.

They passed the metal pylons that blocked their little lane from traffic and were walking toward the black shade cloth, when the little elderly lady who had brought them fruit and drinks the day before came quickly waddling out of her house on the corner, calling out to them. They turned around and greeted her as she gave them a platter of cookies and an orange soda. She then motioned for Armando to follow her into her house. He looked at Mama, who gave them the OK, then shrugged his shoulders and followed her in. The strange man was now standing at the corner watching, but the elderly lady did not seem to be disturbed by it, so Emily relaxed. When Armando stepped inside the door, he watched as the woman reached for and took hold of a small *yarmulke*, then stood still as she carefully placed it on his head, smiling, and said, "This is for you to wear. Be sure to wear it."

She was delighted that he agreed, and he felt honored that she gave it to him. It was beautifully embroidered in a royal blue with designs in other colors. They stepped back outside, carrying a framed picture. Emily told her, "We're on our way home to eat lunch. We'll save the treats until afterward."

She smiled with understanding and said, pointing to the picture, "I am a widow now, but I had eight children myself. I understand. They need to eat lunch first."

195

They all looked at the picture with her, then thanked her for the treats and *yarmulke*, and continued their walk home. As they went, they greeted the neighbors they had not yet met and then the people under the shade cloth before turning into their gate. After unlocking the door, the children all rushed in and Emily took the chicken necks and put them in the freezer of their new refrigerator, which they had placed in the front room of the house beside the bicycles. She had not planned on doing any cooking, but now was gifted with the beginnings of a good soup broth which they could use to cook the remaining potatoes, onions, and tomatoes that had been given them by the kind people at Kiryat Chaim the week before.

Everyone was excited to see what was in the carry-out container from the strange, quiet man. Emily opened it, and they all looked in to see a neatly packed lunch. Had he given them *his* lunch? Or was it an extra? In any case, they felt honored to eat the food Yah had given through the seemingly poor man. Not knowing what it was, but trusting that because he was obviously Jewish and kind it was fine to eat, the eight mouths quickly consumed the delicious contents before preparing more of their typical lunch of vegetables, hummus and bread. As they ate, they prayed blessings on all the people who had enabled their feasting, including the Interpreter and the Russian Christian pastor who had been so kind and diligent in finding them a place to stay and then going above and beyond to bring them luxuries like the cot, two bed mats and the refrigerator. Emily smiled as she remembered the translator offering to bring her a stove and her pleading with him to please *not* do so. Eti had already left a hot plate and small pan, and that was more than enough to meet their needs for the short time they would be there.

After their typical lunch, the family ate the cookies from the kind widow lady. Emily lay down with Natanyah and Moshe saying a prayer for David somewhere over the Atlantic, while the older children quietly colored and played with the toys from Eti.

21 - Business

Turbulence - Above and Below

Monday

In the hour just before sunrise, as the flight crossed the Atlantic nearing New York, the pilot's voice came over the intercom, "Good morning, everyone. It looks like there's some turbulence ahead, so we're going to go ahead and turn the seat belt signs back on. Return to your seats and buckle up until we get through this."

The plane bumped through the rough spot and things calmed down a bit before the pilot spoke up again, "It looks like there's more turbulence ahead, so we'll leave those seat belt signs on. Make sure your seat belts are securely fastened. The flight attendants will be up serving breakfast."

David served as liaison between the flight attendant and the American, passing his two cups of water, a cup of juice, a cup of coffee, a cup of ice and his food to him. He wondered how the man was going to keep all of that on the little drop-down tray on the seat back in front of him, which only had two small cup holders. David asked, "How are you going to manage all that in the turbulence that's coming up?"

The Israeli on his left answered for him, "Things remain secure during turbulence. Everything will be fine."

David got water and coffee with his meal and ate after blessing Yah for the food. All three men finished eating and passed their trays back to the flight attendant, only keeping their remaining drinks. The American asked for another sandwich, unwrapped it and devoured a third of it in one bite. Just then, the second round of turbulence hit with a vengeance. The plane seemed to drop twenty feet as cups flew nearly two feet into the air and screams came from passengers all over the plane. David caught his own coffee cup with his right hand and covered it with his left as the remaining part of the American's sandwich jumped off of his tray and onto David, slapping him in the chest and smearing condiments on his shirt. While the American was holding onto his seat and his sandwich was attacking David, his own coffee cup flew up and spilled, dumping coffee all over himself from his head to his lap. To David's left, the Israeli was also being covered with his own drink.

After the turbulence subsided and the Israeli let go of his seat, he admitted, "I guess you were correct in wondering about things staying put during turbulence. Why didn't *your* coffee spill?"

David responded, "Because I grabbed it and covered it, so I wouldn't get drenched."

The Israeli commented, "We should have thought of that, too, but I was frozen to my seat in panic."

As they all three and the rest of the passengers cleaned themselves, he asked David, "Why didn't you get scared?"

David told him, "I was watching for what to do next. You can't do anything when you're panicking."

The Israeli agreed, having just experienced it firsthand.

All the ruckus, along with the sun coming up and their proximity to New York left the men unable to try to get any more sleep. Soon they landed, passed through customs, then on into the terminal where David would prepare for the flight to Nashville. Once inside, he purchased a phone card and called Emily to let her know he had arrived.

She told him, "[The Pennsylvanian] called just after you left. He said to call him and he'd pick you up at the airport."

When they hung up, David began trying to call the Pennsylvanian. No one answered and he left no message, not wanting people to know he was back, yet. Since he did not know the nature of what was really going on, but had some suspicions, he wanted to be able to enter a scene that was as undisturbed as possible. He thought it strange how he now had troubling activity going on at both the farm and the job.

The flight to Nashville was uneventful, and upon arriving at the airport, he again used the card to try to call the Pennsylvanian, but with no success. He approached a taxi, but learned it would cost $60 to get him home, they could not do it until 4 PM, and then he would have to get someone to give him a ride back to the airport Wednesday for his return flight to Israel. He tried to call Emily's father, but was unable to reach him, as well. David's pick-up and cell phone were at the farm, and he had no way to get them. There were problems at the house and at the job site, which he only had three days to solve. He was becoming frustrated.

Upon exiting the restroom, he saw a rental place and learned he could get a car for two days for about the same price as the one-way taxi. He jumped at that opportunity, filled out the necessary papers, paid for the car, and began driving east, praying as he went that he would handle appropriately what he was about to face.

He drove a little over an hour to Cookeville, the big town nearest the farm, where Byron and Mom lived, and where the Varela family business - Amigos Construction - did most of their work. He pulled into the empty parking lot of the soon-to-be breakfast house, the building he had been

Chapter 21   Business

converting from a store to a restaurant. No one was there working except Paco, a young Guatemalan cook, who was cleaning equipment in preparation for the opening of the restaurant. Upon inspection, David found that the jobs were not finished, yet he had people threatening to sue him for non-payment. The Electrician had told him on the phone in Israel that he was over half-way done and would be finished that day. That day had been over a week ago while the family was on top of Mount Carmel. The men who were to do the molding and paint had not finished, and they had been paid ahead of time. The tile people were almost done.

Paco loaned David his phone, and he called the Electrician. "What are you doing, man?" David asked.

Electrician: Just over here working on the job.

David: Which job?

Electrician: Here at the restaurant.

David: I don't think so.

Electrician: Why's that?

David: Because *I'm* at the restaurant and I don't see anyone here.

David could hear the Electrician's shock over the cell phone as his voice crackled, "I just left to get materials. I'll be back over there in a little while."

After hanging up, David called one of the restaurant owners and told him in Spanish. "I flew back into town and don't have much time. I'd like to meet with you this evening. Will 9 o'clock work for you?"

He confirmed that it would.

David was going to get things straightened out once and for all. Each one he called was shocked that he was in town. As he got off the phone with the last one, the Electrician drove into the parking lot, his face becoming pale as he saw that David really was there. When he got out of his van, David approached him, "What's going on?"

He replied, "I was waiting for materials so I could finish the job."

David was disgusted by the excuse, since just minutes before he had told him he was working at the site. "I left my family across the world. I'm in a hurry. I've called a meeting at 9 PM. Be there."

He agreed and left. After surveying the situation, David took Paco as a witness to what went on at the farm, and also hoped he could give him some details concerning what had been happening while he had been gone. They drove the rental car toward the farm so David could change

199

into his work clothes, get his pick-up truck, phone, and tools, check on the animals, and find out what was going on with the appliances.

They drove the curvy 25 miles and arrived just after 5 PM. The New Yorker met David in the front yard, his face turning bright red when he realized who it was. "I can't believe you're back. You didn't have to come back from Israel because of the appliances," he said in amazement.

David replied, "Come inside and show me what the problem is." He did not want to enter the house without the man, since it was now their house for the duration of three months. Just then he saw the wife walk very fast to their motor home, never to reappear.

David first checked the stove, thinking it may have come unplugged. But when he got to it, he saw that the lights on the digital clock were working. He tried each of the eyes and they all came on. He tried the oven and it also worked. He then opened the refrigerator, which was working perfectly, as evidenced by the thermometer reading. David told the man, "Everything's working fine."

The New Yorker seemed shocked and said, "My wife told me it wasn't working."

David replied, "But *you* told *me* it was not working."

The man apologized and David tried not to let his disapproval show as he told the man, he needed to get to work. He grabbed a few clothes, took his cell phone and quickly walked towards his shop, where he could get better reception, and then began calling the other Restaurant Owner and the subs[140] to invite them to the 9 PM meeting. They all were surprised to hear from him and especially that he was back in town, and, hearing the tone of his voice, each of them agreed to meet him. Once he got them all called, he and Paco took some basic tools from his shop and loaded them in the pick-up, then carefully looked over the farm and animals. He was relieved to find everything there in good order. He signaled Emily that he had made it home by calling and letting her phone ring once before hanging up. That way, if she woke up in the night wondering, she could glance at her phone and know that he had called and was all right. He had learned in earlier years of marriage that she greatly appreciated him staying in communication with her. He learned from experience that going for days without calling was not the best way to enhance their relationship.

He and Paco made the 45-minute drive and started right away installing the molding that had been abandoned. The other subcontractors and the two Owners all showed for the meeting. David was glad to have been working hard before they arrived, so that he had an outlet for his frustration with them. Jet lag was beginning to affect him and he was very tired, but

---

[140]Subs – short for 'subcontractors.'

Chapter 21   Business

the fast-paced work kept his blood pumping and kept him awake. When they all got inside, David had them stand in a circle, then asked them one by one in front of the Owners, if they had been paid. As he got to each one, the tile man, cabinet man, gas man, Electrician, paint man, molding man, Manager, they each admitted that they had been paid, some completely in advance, and some partially in advance, the balance to be due when their part of the job was completely finished. As he came to each one, he asked individually, "Do I owe you anything?"

The response came from the paint man, "No."

Molding man: No.

Electrician: No, not till the job is done.

David: Is the job done?

Electrician: No, not quite.

David continued around the circle with the tile man: Do I owe you anything?

"No."

Cabinet man: No

Gas man: No

Manager: No

David: Then who's threatening to sue me?

Everyone was silent. David waited a few seconds and then said, "Someone's lying. The job is not done. People are wanting money before they do the job. What's going on here? If someone's lying, be man enough to tell me here and now! If I owe you or if I treat you bad, tell me here in front of everyone. Don't make stuff up behind my back! Someone told the Owners the reason the job stopped is because you weren't getting paid. You all owe ME because I paid you ahead of time! I want you to get to work and get it done!"

As the men went to work and the hours ticked by, some of them came individually and apologized to David, then headed home for the night. As the truth came out, he learned that one of the men had told another that the Varelas might not return from Israel. Because of a recent situation in town where a large contractor took an extended trip and did not pay the subcontractors that were on the job while he was gone, some of the subs were nervous and decided to go to work on other jobs, now afraid that David was going to follow the example of the bigger construction company. David was saddened by the fact that they would buy into something like

201

that after knowing and working with him over a period of time, some of them several years. He was saddened that his witness for Yah was not strong enough to keep people from believing things like that about him.

Around 11 PM, David, Paco, and the painters who regularly met with the Varelas on *Shabbat*, finally quit working. David dropped Paco off at his house a city block from the restaurant and drove the five miles to Emily's parents' house. Upon arrival and after the customary greetings, he learned more bad news.

Byron: I hope I did all right giving that check to the Manager.

David, surprised: What?

Byron: He didn't tell you?

David: No.

Byron: He called me because he couldn't get hold of you and said the workers were going to quit working if he didn't pay them something. He said I needed to give him the check so he could take it back to the Owners and get a partial payment in cash to pay the workers so the job could continue.

David: Oh, no.

Byron: He didn't talk to you about that?

David: No.

Byron: Oh dear. I'm sorry.

David: It's OK. You were in a tough situation, not being able to reach me. The reason, though, that I gave you the check is because the Owners are weil-known for stiffing people on the final payment. That's why I got the payment up front and had them postdate it so that you could deposit it in my account after the job was finished.

Byron: I'm really sorry. I didn't realize that was the situation. I don't think the Manager did either. I sure hope you get your money.

David: Don't worry about it. Everything will work out. We really appreciate all you've done.

There was nothing he could do about it now, so decided to hope for the best. Mom and Byron fed him a good supper and gave him a comfortable place to stay for the night. He was exhausted from missing the last night's sleep, as well as from jet lag and stress.

22 - Adjusting

Yom Shlishi (Third Day)

Mid-morning, the landlady, Tzipporah came with her cousin and the man who owned the things in the south room. He was a pleasant middle-aged fellow with a European accent. It did not take long for them to remove all of his things as Emily kept the children with her and out of their way in the north room. The children watched as they hauled off pillows, chairs, pictures, dishes, and even inflatable swimming pools. Emily reminded Tzipporah about the key for the back door, and she agreed to bring it later that day.

After they left, the family cleaned the room that had just been vacated and moved the bicycles from the front room into it, lining them up neatly against the south wall. That left a large area in the front room with only the refrigerator, making it less cramped.

During nap time, Emily had the older children play quietly in the kitchen and front room while she got a little rest with Natanyah and Moshe. In her typical fashion, Natanyah comforted herself by massaging Emily's ear lobe until she drifted off to sleep. Each of the children had enjoyed a different comforting mechanism, and Emily was grateful for Natanyah's. She had learned years before that the ears were one of the areas that contained nerve endings from all over the body, making ear lobe massage a very beneficial practice. Natanyah had learned to play with Mama's ears when she was a nursing baby, and the practice continued after weaning whenever she was tired or needed comfort. Satisfied with her usual half hour of rest, Emily got up, leaving the little ones sleeping and let the others out to the front yard. As they were playing, she had them help her bring the white dresser in from the front porch. The former tenant no longer wanted it, and Emily thought it would be easier to get their things in and out of drawers than bicycle panniers.

The children wanted to go to the beach, and since it was the second day of wearing their green clothes and they would need to be changed anyway, Emily consented. After Moshe and Natanyah woke up, they walked the few short blocks and enjoyed the sand and sea for a couple of hours. The older children dug the surfboard out of the sand dune where they had left it and all but little Natanyah enjoyed piling on top of it and riding the small waves into shore. The smaller children went back and forth between playing in the sand, building castles and motes to finding and collecting beautiful shells. When it was time to go back, they buried their surfboard in the sand again, then walked home.

Elena

Once inside, Emily turned on the switch on the wall to start the hot water heating. As she put more things in the drawers while waiting for the water to get hot, the children played in the front yard. Suddenly, the smiling face of a dark-haired woman appeared over the tall part of the south side fence at the front porch, startling the children. Briana quickly went inside and told Mama, "There's a woman here."

Emily hurriedly left her project, walked through the front room and encountered the smiling face over the edge of the wall. She greeted the sparkly-eyed woman, who introduced, "*Shalom! Ani*[141] Elena." Their conversation continued in Hebrew, "I'm Olga's mother."

Emily expected that's who she was because of where she had shown up. "It's very nice to meet you, and so kind of you all to wash our clothes," Emily replied.

After answering the usual questions, Emily asked, "Where are you from?"

"Russia," she responded. "I immigrated here about 10 years ago with my husband and Olga."

Emily learned that she was a Christian Russian immigrant who spoke Hebrew as a second language. She was very patient with Emily's Hebrew and kindly corrected her when she misspoke. They visited for a while as the children took baths, Elena insisting that she and Olga do the family's laundry. Emily humbly consented, it being obvious that the offer was genuine.

Emily asked, "Is there a library nearby?"

"Oh, yes, it's not far. Olga needs to go tomorrow. I'll have her walk you there when she gets home from school."

She then asked, "What's the place next door?"

Elena: A house.

Emily: What kind of house? There are always people going in and out over there.

Elena: Oh, you don't know. The man just died, right before you came. That's why they have the black shade cloth. People are coming to visit. They're in their seven days of mourning.

That explained a lot. So Sarah had just been widowed. And in the midst

---

[141]*Ani* - Hebrew for 'I am.'

Chapter 22   Adjusting

of that, they got new neighbors and had treated them with such kindness, bringing food out to share with them, when others were coming to support them in their time of grief. Emily thanked Elena for explaining. She enjoyed her company, her kind spirit, and the way she was so patient and helpful with Emily's Hebrew. Before excusing herself, Elena reminded, "When baths are finished, don't forget to bring the dirty clothes over."

Emily agreed, then got the four girls in the big tub for baths, noting there was still room for more. After they got out, the boys got their baths while the girls gathered the dirty clothes and took them next door, then returned to playing in the front yard. Just after finishing her own bath, now hardly giving a thought to the water heater looming above the tub except that its power needed to be switched back off, Emily got a call from David.

Bad News
Tuesday

It was morning in Tennessee and he had just awoken, wanting to update her. They talked for over half an hour as he told her of the events that had taken place so far with the farm and business, and she told him about Elena and their experiences in Kiryat Yam. He was glad to learn they were doing well and continuing to meet nice people; she was glad he was there to get things back in order, but was sorry he was gone from them and aggravated with the chain of events that brought the whole situation about. He had to inform her, "I don't see any way I can get this mess straightened up enough to fly out tomorrow night."

He could hear the disappointment in her voice when she said, "I was afraid of that. But let's just hope for the best. Maybe things will work out."

He prayed she would handle things well if he did not return as scheduled. The job had gotten so far off track by the hold ups that he needed to make sure everything was moving full steam ahead before he left, to prevent having to return again at a later date. He knew Emily had suffered a lot in the past by him leaving her with all of the family responsibilities while he worked later than planned on jobs. He also recognized that he was needed there for them at this late stage of the pregnancy and found himself torn between needing to be in two places at once. He prayed for them all before starting the business of the day, calling the subs and getting the day's work lined up.

Knowing by then that he was going to have to postpone his trip back, he left his in-laws and had the Manager drive his company truck to the farm so he could pick up the rental car. Then he followed him to the airport in Nashville, where he dropped it off. Most of the ride there he spent on the phone, answering questions from the various subs. On the way back, he discussed details with the Manager in order to get the job moving as quickly as possible and to prevent similar problems from happening in the future.

205

Invitation

After the call ended, the family worked together to prepare a soup for supper, thanks to Eti for the hot plate, the little man in white for the chicken necks, and the people at Kiryat Chaim for the vegetables. They blessed Yah and all their generous friends before eating. As they finished, Tzipporah returned with the back door key, for which they were all grateful. They quickly unlocked the door to check out their newly opened territory. Just outside was a small tile porch that went the length of their south room to the edge of Elena's house, covered with sand and some miscellaneous construction materials. Just west of the porch was the loaded pomegranate tree and to the north the smaller olive and the date palm.

As they moved the doors and other materials off their porch in preparation for laying out their mats, a thin, shapely young woman, whose clothing accentuated her feminine features, approached from the house behind and introduced herself. She said, gesturing to the construction materials the children were moving. "These are our things, but you can put them in the empty yard next door," referring to the yard to the north. "Why don't you come to our place for supper?"

"That would be very nice," Emily answered. "When would you like for us to come?"

"Tomorrow evening around 6:00 would be good. Bring the whole family."

"My husband will not be here until Thursday."

"Ok, then wait till Thursday evening, 6:00."

"Ok, what can we bring?"

"Oh, no, no!" she said adamantly, "We have everything! You just come."

Emily was again amazed at the hospitality of the Israelis they had met so far. As their conversation ended, a group of children came walking down the street. They stopped and introduced themselves as part of a family that lived just a few houses south and across the little street. There were ten children, and from that time forward, would be kindly referred to by the Varelas as the Family of Ten. The children were glad to meet other children their age.

The Varela children helped Emily clean the yard and porch, then put down their mats and were once again outside under the stars, the way they had planned to be while in Israel. They were thankful to be in the fresh air where they could better feel the Mediterranean breeze. They sang their nighttime song, Psalms 23 set to a hymn-like tune, and said prayers. The neighbors they had just met in the house behind now had company out on their porch, so the little family drifted to sleep to the sounds of voices and laughter.

Chapter 22   Adjusting

~ ~ ~

David and the Manager returned from Nashville around noon, checked on the job, then David got Paco and drove to the farm to get a hammer drill and various other tools. Since he was back, he wanted to speed things along as much as possible and knew it would be faster for him to bring his own tools for some of the jobs rather than wait for subs to do them. Around 1:30, they returned to the restaurant and resumed working on installing an emergency exit from the kitchen. Once it was too dark to work well outside, they moved to various inside jobs, bringing supplies from the store and helping the Electrician.

Around 10 PM, Byron showed up at the job site and convinced David to quit working and join them at home for supper. David listened to his wisdom, took Paco home, ate super with his in-laws and went to bed at their home.

Kiryat Motzkin

Yom Revi'i (Fourth Day)

Emily awoke early, prayed, read the scriptures from the PDA and began preparing fruit to mix with yogurt for breakfast. The birds were awake, singing, and neighbors soon began to rustle about. Loud voices came from the house just across the back street and to the north, shattering the peaceful morning sounds. Emily soon learned it was the family of the young man who had walked into their house the first night they were there. They had a daughter a few years older than him, who was kind and spoke fairly good English, as well as an older son who was in the IDF. They seemed like a nice family, in spite of the noise.

The children awoke, ate, had scripture time, and cleaned up, then Emily decided to take them to Kiryat Motzkin to get the battery for the cell phone. As they walked through their little town and the now-familiar shops, they stopped by to see the Spice Lady. She gave each of the children a sucker and when she learned where they were going said, "That's so far! And you're going to walk?"

Emily could tell from her map that it was not much more than a mile. She replied, "We all need the exercise. The children are used to being on the farm, so will do fine on the walk. We're not in a hurry. We have all day.

"I will call you a taxi," she offered.

"No, really, we do need the exercise, but thank you for the kind offer," she said.

They made their way slowly east on *S'derot* Weisman for quite some time, then continued south. At beautiful Szold Garden, they stopped for a snack of fruit, then continued south and then east, crossing beautiful, palm-lined

S'derot Yerushalayim with its long park running between the north and southbound lanes of traffic. They turned south again, delightedly picking up and eating the sweet ripe dates that had fallen to the wide brick sidewalk.

Not knowing the area, Emily missed the turn on Tsahal and continued to a shopping center. Upon realizing she had missed the turn, they turned south there, thinking they could make it to Kiryat Motzkin that way, not knowing the track for the passenger train would prevent them. When they reached the fence by the tracks in an abandoned area, they entered what appeared to be a trash dump, where people had left furniture, rugs, and all sorts of things, some of which were still usable. The children spotted a beautiful rug, "Mama, look!" they cried. "Can we take it home?"

"It is beautiful," she confirmed, "but way too heavy to carry. And besides, we'll be leaving soon. Just leave it here for someone else."

Their disappointment did not deter them from looking to see what other treasures might be there. Briana found a pretty green apron and asked, "Can I have this, Mama? I can wash and mend it and it will work fine."

"Ok," Emily consented, "but you'll have to pack it, when we start up again on the bicycles."

She proudly took her pretty apron, folded it, and stuck it in the backpack with their lunch.

They followed the tracks back north to the bridge on Tsahal, but were not able to climb onto it because of a chain link fence. As they left the fence to go under the bridge so they could get onto it from the other side, Rebeka found a nest of kittens snuggled underneath. They all admired the tiny creatures and the children pleaded to take them home. Emily had to disappoint them again, and they walked back west on the north side of the bridge, through a park and up onto the sidewalk. They followed it over the tracks and to the round-about with a pool in the center surrounded by fountains of water spewing from the mouths of penguin statues. The shopping center was just beyond and on the north side of the street.

After passing through security, they went inside to find the battery. They took their time as they became somewhat familiar with the various shops. Once they found what they came for, they walked back to their home in Kiryat Yam, getting there in time for naps. As Emily unlocked the front door, a large black male cat darted out through the kitchen window, to escape being caught by the new occupants of his house.

In the afternoon, Olga came to take them to the library. They walked with her south a few blocks, where Olga helped Armando and Briana with the little ones in the children's library while Emily went to the Internet section upstairs to check emails. Olga kept the children busy and they were content, not having been to a library for several months. Emily quickly

Chapter 22   Adjusting

checked to see if there were any important messages, then typed a note to those around the world interested in their travels, letting them know that David had to return to the U.S. for a few days. The library was spacious and open, with a balcony near where she sat, so she was able to easily view what was going on below, though not directly into the children's section.

Downstairs, Briana found some books in English and was reading to herself, while Armando read to the children and Olga looked at picture books with them. She and the children took turns identifying the words in English and Hebrew for one another. When Emily finished upstairs, she descended and gathered her little brood. They walked the three large city blocks back north to the house, thanked Olga and had supper.

Wednesday

David continued with his work on the restaurant, mostly running to and fro getting supplies and materials and answering questions from the subs. When he was not busy with that, he jumped in to help the work go faster wherever he could, mostly installing the shiny white wallboard sheets on the kitchen walls. He also got a phone card so he could call his parents in Mexico who were unaware that he was back in the States. He had not planned to talk to them from Israel because of the expense, but felt the need to let them know what was happening in his life with the recent changes. Besides that, he was lonely without his wife and children and could use the encouragement of his wise parents.

23 - Disappointment

Yom Chamishi (Fifth Day)

Just after lying down to sleep, David called to tell Emily he definitely would have to stay longer and asked her to book a flight for Sunday night, arriving Monday night. He talked to her for about half an hour, trying to be available as much as he could, knowing she was having a hard time with the news. He let her know that he could not leave the job until things were straightened out, and she knew there was no way around it.

Emily then called Nikolay and told him, "David has run into more problems than he expected and won't be here until Monday. I guess we need to cancel our appointment with you for B'hai Gardens this week."

"I am sorry to hear that," he said. "But it's not problem for me. We can reschedule for another time. Just let me know once he is back."

She then called the airlines, but learned that there was no advantage to buying the tickets at that time. They told her they would apply his missed reservation to the next one and add an exchange fee. She spent a long time on the phone with them at her expense, and was tired, so decided to wait until Sunday to buy the tickets, and went to sleep disappointed that he would not be returning the next day.

~ ~ ~

David and some of the subs worked another late night, though not as late as some of the previous ones. He went back to Mom and Byron's to eat supper and bed down, thankful for their kindness and generosity, but being with Emily's parents by himself caused him to miss his own parents even more. Since this day's work got done earlier, he took the opportunity to phone Mexico and catch up with them.

Dumpster Diving

Emily awoke to dawn on the back porch fully aware that David should have been on his flight back, but knowing he was not. While disappointed and ready to be back on the bicycles, she was enjoying meeting the people in their little neighborhood and praying that the family would be a light to them, while at the same time, gleaning beneficial things in their own lives from the experience. Getting the back door unlocked seemed to open a whole new world of people. Starting with the ladies behind, then the loud family north of them. To the south, there was the Family of Ten, who nearly

Chapter 23   Disappointment

always had other children from the neighborhood with them. The Varela children were excited about all the new friends they were meeting. And Emily was glad for them to have others to play with. She noticed they were already picking up a fair amount of Hebrew and was thankful for that.

Since the family had not planned to be in one place for so long, a void was left in the children's schedule. While the Israeli children were in school, the older children began exploring the neighborhood and soon began to enjoy the art of scavenging at the dumpsters, otherwise known as 'dumpster diving.' Armando and Briana were the main adventurers and developed a system that would bring the least amount of shame to the family. They would look in all directions to make sure no one would see them, then Armando quickly helped Briana in before jumping in himself. If anyone came to dump trash while they were there, they just hunkered in the corner and stayed real quiet.

They faced various challenges and did not bother telling Mama, knowing her fragile hormonal state and the fact that she was already sad about the change in the family's plans. There was no use upsetting her further. It was very hot inside the metal dumpster, since all doors but one were usually shut. They were often filled with disgusting things like rotting coconuts or other produce, and sometimes even dead animals. But the biggest challenge was trying to avoid the feral cats who lived in or near them. As soon as a person climbed up to jump in, the action inside began; cats would dart and race from where they were in order to escape. Those that could not make it out in time would sometimes scream and lunge at the children, as they quickly jumped through the hole on top. The object of the childrens' new game was to spot what they wanted, then get in and out with it as quickly as possible, so as to avoid being seen or getting sick from the awful stench that was often inside.

Their first trip to the dumpster yielded them two riding toys for the younger children. After getting out quickly and discretely, they proudly wheeled the toys home by way of the back yard. As Victor saw them coming, his shrill voice screamed in delight, "Mando and Bana have someting! They're binging someting!"

All the other children raced to the fence and were excited to see the new toys. Mama had questions though, "Where did you get those?" she asked.

"Oh, just over there at the dumpsters," came the reply, leaving out all the details, of course. "Can we keep them, just till we have to leave?"

"I guess that will be fine," she said, finding no reason to have to disappoint them this time.

Thursday

David continued keeping the subs busy and efficiently working on the job. Since the painters were finished at the restaurant, he took them four miles

211

southeast to the spec[142] house to get started painting it. He had intended for both jobs to be done by now, but since he had the same subs lined up at both places, when one stopped, so did the other. The spec house was not as critical to finish as the restaurant job, but it was important, none-the-less. He wanted to get it finished and on the market, since its sale would help the family financially after having been gone to Israel for three months. But the restaurant job was under a contract which expired at the end of September. If it was not completed on time and the restaurant not able to open, Amigos Construction could be liable for breach of contract, as well as for loss of income for the restaurant.

Israeli Welcome Dinner

After their regular routine, then going to the beach after nap-time, they again took baths and changed into their green clothes, taking their orange ones to Olga to wash as Elena had insisted. Emily fixed the girls' hair, and they made their way through the small backyard, across the back alley to the house behind. They learned it was the home of a beautiful middle-aged mother, three daughters, and a granddaughter. The older daughter who had introduced herself previously was the main hostess, but was helped by both of her sisters and her mother. When the family walked through the gate in the stone fence, they were welcomed by a long table beautifully set for an informal banquet with paper plates, several types of Israeli salads, vegetables, fruit, boiled eggs, pudding and other desserts, and sodas to drink. Emily felt awkward in such a generous social setting without David. She was extremely grateful and humbled because of the time and energy that had obviously been put into the feast, but did not know if she was adequately expressing it to her hostesses.

The children were happy with all of the different types of food and ate their fill before getting up from the table and playing with the myriad of toys belonging to the young granddaughter, about Moshe's age. Emily visited with the ladies and answered their questions about the family as they listened with interest.

"Where do you come from?" asked the hostess.

"Tennessee," replied Emily.

"What is it like there?"

"Where we live, the temperature is much like here, though we get rain year round and it is often humid. We live on a beautiful place with lots of trees."

"What do you do there?"

---

[142]Spec – short for 'speculate;' when used with 'house,' refers to a house someone is building to sell, speculating on the housing market.

Chapter 23   Disappointment

"We are in the construction business, but we live on a farm. David builds houses, and we help when we can, but mostly we are at home taking care of the animals and garden."

"Where do the children go to school?"

"We home school them."

"You mean they don't go to school?"

"We teach them at home."

"Oh, you must be very smart."

Emily laughed, "Lots of people in America home school. We see it as our job to raise and train up our children. If we send them to school, we lose several hours a day with them and someone else is teaching them what the government determines they need to know, instead of what the scriptures say they need to know. Scripture says, 'children are a blessing,' and we believe if we are training them ourselves, we can better influence them to walk according to the scriptures and to be true blessings."

"So, you are Jewish."

"No."

"So why do you wear these?" picking up one of Emily's tassels.

"Scripture tells us to wear them. We try to walk according to the scriptures. We keep *Shabbat* and the feasts. We eat clean."

"So you are Jewish!"

"No, we follow the same scriptures, but we are not part of the Jewish religion. We follow only the written *torah*, not the oral *torah*."

"Ah," she said, as if deep in thought, trying to figure out what that meant.

Emily elaborated, "For example, we would not eat pork because scripture tells us not to eat it, but we would eat a cheese burger because scripture does not tell us not to mix meat with dairy."

"Ok," she said, seeming to have a better understanding. "So, you want to live in Israel?"

"We would love to live here, but they won't let us because we're not Jewish."

213

"But you *are* Jewish! You keep *torah*. You should live here!" she declared enthusiastically, as Emily smiled back at her. She continued, "My mother has a lot of friends. If you want, I take you to *Misrad Hap'nim* to get papers so you can live here. But here, the children will have to go to school, I think."

Emily did not know what to think about the offer, but told her, "I'd be glad to go with you, but need to wait for David to return so he can stay with the children."

"Ok, I will talk to my mother and get everything worked out. She has connections there."

Yom Shishi (Sixth Day)

It was getting near bedtime for both families. The younger girls needed their rest before school the next day and the ladies had to go to work, so Emily and the children thanked them for supper and for the generous amounts of leftovers the hostesses had gathered and insisted the family take. The eight walked the few meters back across the street to their house, put the food in the refrigerator, and bedded down on the back porch under the stars, as had become their custom. They thanked Yah for all the people they were meeting and the experiences He was allowing them to have in His special land. As the little ones drifted off, Emily answered a call from David. She told him about the offer made by the neighbor, and they both speculated about what it could mean, praying that Yah's will would be done and that they would walk according to His plan for them.

David was back and forth between the two jobs for the rest of the day bringing supplies, overseeing, answering questions, and helping the various subs. He bought some fruit and other healthy snacks to keep him and his crews going, as they all cooperated to get the jobs done. As they finished up, late into the night again, David decided to spend the night at the spec house instead of driving the four miles west to Byron's. He was worn out, and every minute of rest was crucial.

Pomegranate Parties

For breakfast, the family ate some of the leftover food from dinner at the neighbors, then picked three pomegranates off of the tree. Emily and the older children sat around their new tiny plastic dumpster table, peeling them into bowls, so as not to lose any seeds. When all the fruit was peeled, they gathered the younger ones to eat at their pomegranate party. For lunch, they feasted again on food from the evening before. Emily led the children in thanks for the hospitable ladies. The family then walked to the markets and bought special sweet breads for *Shabbat*. The little pastries came in various flavors - apple, fig, cream cheese, and chocolate. Normally, they did not purchase milk, knowing that the raw, unadulterated

Chapter 23   Disappointment

milk they raised was far superior, but bought it for a *Shabbat* treat. They also bought their now customary fare of fruit, yogurt, hummus, and vegetables.

Friday

David rolled over on the hard bed surrounded by the smell of fresh paint, only to remember he was sleeping on the newly carpeted floor of the spec house. After his regular morning prayer and scripture time, then calling Emily to check up on his family, he got to work calling subs, and arranging meetings and pick-ups for materials. While waiting for other jobs to get finished at the restaurant, he continued with the spec house, having his gravel man prepare the driveway, and dump and smooth the gravel to get it ready for the asphalt people. Driving back and forth to the restaurant and supply stores, he noticed a bumping under his pick-up, called the Mechanic near the farm that had made the bicycle panniers for them, and bought a rod, according to his advice. He wondered what more could be added to his already swamped schedule.

The spec house was far enough along to list, so David called the realtor to make arrangements, then drove to the farm to check on things again, having an unexplained concern about things there. Everything seemed fine, so he returned to Cookeville, accepting an invitation from Byron to eat supper with them. Before sundown, he bought food for *Shabbat*, as well as some grape juice to contribute to the *Shabbat* meal at one of his helpers' houses the next day.

Company

Late in the afternoon while the children were getting their baths, Eti came by to check on the family. She was sorry to learn that David was not back, but her kind words encouraged Emily in her disappointment. She gave the family several plastic containers of food that she had made as she prepared her own family's *Shabbat* meal. Emily was amazed again at how Yah was providing for their physical needs. They now had hot delicious meatballs, potatoes, and couscous that she had done nothing to prepare. What a blessing! She thanked Him again for the neighbors behind and for Eti.

Before supper, Olga came over and asked, "Do you have more clothes to wash?"

"No," Emily replied, not wanting her to do laundry for them on *Shabbat*. Olga spoke Hebrew well, but was just learning English in school and relied heavily on her Hebrew-English dictionary when trying to speak English with Emily. Knowing that, Emily normally chose to speak Hebrew with her, to try to improve herself. She had not noticed Olga's father since they had been there, so asked her, "Where's your father?"

215

Olga explained in Hebrew, but Emily did not understand. Seeing her confused look, she explained a different way. Emily said, "I'm sorry. I don't understand."

Finally, Olga flopped her hands from side to side and said, "*Hu met.*"[143]

Emily was sorry to not have been able to understand what she had said the first two times. They spoke more and Olga told her the story. "Three years after we moved here, when I was seven, he was killed in a car crash."

Emily was stunned. The help they were getting from their next door neighbors was coming from a widow and an orphan, the very ones that scripture commanded them to take care of. Again, she was amazed at how *Abba* was working in their lives. They had come to give and bless, but they were constantly receiving and being blessed, and often by those who deserved their help the most.

After Olga went home, the family ate their gifted meal on the plywood table with bucket legs, as they sat on chairs and toys the children had scavenged from the dumpster. Sarah's sons stopped by to see if Armando wanted to go to synagogue with them. Since the family was still sitting *shiva*[144] and would continue mourning their father for the next year, the young adult sons were home most of the time and would be attending synagogue more often than they usually did, in honor of their father.

Shabbat at the Lodging Place

Shabbat

The rest of the family enjoyed the quiet evening on the front porch, listening to the men's prayers and singing coming from the open windows of the synagogue across the street, once again giving thanks for the place they had been put for this time they were separated from their leader. Mama was enthralled with the beautiful singing and said to the children, "Isn't it beautiful to hear the men sing? They're singing to Yah, and they don't care if they can sing well or not. They're just singing to their Creator, their Savior, with joyful voices. They're singing loud and it's so beautiful."

The children could not really relate to what Mama was saying. She had grown up in churches where much of the singing was done by trained voices and was very beautiful. In congregational songs, usually the women out sang the men. But here, across the street from the little synagogue, the sounds she heard were so different. They were beautiful

---

[143]*Hu met.* - Hebrew for 'He died.'
[144]Sitting *shiva* - the Jewish traditional seven (*shiva*) days of mourning after the death of a loved one.

Chapter 23   Disappointment

in a different sort of way, not that they were out of tune or sounded badly, but they were just regular voices, raised together in joyful unison, praising their Savior. It was comforting to hear a congregation of devoted men.

Sabbath

David went to supper with Mom and Byron, and returned to the spec house for the night, praising Yah for commanding him a day of rest. With his stomach full of spaghetti and the exhaustion of working late every night, he promptly fell asleep on the floor again.

~ ~ ~

Emily woke up about the same time as usual, but stayed in the sheets on her mat next to Natanyah dozing in and out as the sky changed from black, to gray, to light blue. Natanyah shifted, her hand searching for Emily's ear, as Emily felt the baby moving in her womb. She placed her hand on her tummy to feel it kick and prayed for a while before Armando woke up, looking forward to going to synagogue.

They got out the breakfast foods as the others woke up, folded their sheets and mats, and came to the front porch to eat. The young men two doors down stopped by to get Armando, while the others changed into their *Shabbat* clothes. About an hour later, Sarah stopped to see if the family was ready to go with her. Emily followed the children out, then locked the door and walked the few steps to the synagogue across the street. Sarah led them up the stairs to the second floor where the women and children sat. She gave Emily a copy of the *TaNaK* and a prayer book. Emily sat next to Sarah, Natanyah on her left side, and gave instructions to the other girls to sit quietly beside, in front of, and behind them on the theater seats looking over the balcony to the service below.

Everything was new to all of them. Briana and Emily tried to follow along with the Hebrew readings, Emily getting help from Sarah when she lost her place. After a while, the children began to get restless, so she was not able to concentrate as well, and finally gave up. She loved to hear the music. Some of the women sang, but not with nearly as much gusto as the men. It impressed Emily how strongly the service was led by and participated in by the men. She admired the dedication and leadership they demonstrated.

After the service, which included a special reading because it was the week of the new moon, the women and children had wine, grape and orange flavored sodas, and bread and cookies upstairs, while the men had wine and bread on the main floor. Everyone then dismissed and walked back to their nearby homes. Emily thanked Sarah, Armando thanked her sons, and they went inside to eat the rest of the leftovers from the party and those that Eti had brought the day before. It was a peaceful *Shabbat*, though Emily was sad that David was still gone and wondered when he would return. The baby in her tummy was growing and it would not be many weeks before they planned to get off of the bicycles. She was ready to continue on their journey, though hoped they would not be on any more roads as frightful as Highway 70 had been.

Emily received a call from a Jewish American friend who now lived in Israel and had a business selling healing oils. The Oil Lady said she was coming with a surprise and to meet her at the beach. Emily told the children, who were so excited about a surprise that they rushed out the door without first using the restroom. She called them back in to do necessary business while, making sure there was nothing sitting out that would be disturbed by feral cats. They walked quickly to the beach and were, indeed, surprised to see the Oil Lady with several of her children, as well as the Guitar Couple. They had a sweet reunion and the adults visited for a while as the children played near the water and picked up shells.

Before they left, Emily took them to her home to show them the place Yah had blessed them with. They did not seem as impressed as she was. It was a dumpy little place by some people's standards. But she was excited none-the-less, knowing it was what Yah had given them and was much better than the apartment they had almost rented, for which they would have been grateful under their circumstances at the time.

Once their guests were gone, Emily called David's phone, then hung up, the signal for him to call her back, to avoid incurring extremely high charges. The call woke him earlier on *Shabbat* than he would have normally awakened, but he was glad to get the report from their first *Shabbat* in the synagogue.

While they talked, the twins and others from the Family of Ten came to play, excited to learn English while teaching the Varelas Hebrew. A boy Armando's age from the opposite direction near the dumpsters came with them and introduced himself as Aaron. His grandfather, Humberto, lived between the ladies behind and the Family of Ten. The children enjoyed the rest of the afternoon together learning hand-clapping games and playing in the backyard and the narrow brick alley behind the house.

~ ~ ~

After talking with Emily, David went back to sleep, then woke up early in the afternoon, took the juice and went to his helper's house to meet, worship, study, and pray with the others who were congregated. Several of the men there were the ones who had been helping David on the jobs. Most sympathized with him being so far away from his family and working so hard and such long hours in order to be reunited with them. No one seemed to mind that he slept sitting up in his chair, snoring off and on, during most of the meeting. After sundown, *Shabbat* being over, David shared the evening meal then prepared to go back to work. An energetic, enthusiastic young woman, who sometimes helped alongside her husband, suggested they all go help David. Several consented and he was very thankful to have the support of the little group. When the helpers left around 11 PM, David went to sleep on the floor again.

24 - Sixth New Moon

Preparing for *Rosh Chodesh*[145]

Week 4   *Yom Rishon* (First day)   8/31

Another beautiful Israel day greeted the family as they went about their regular activities. Knowing it was almost time for the new moon, Emily took the children to the markets and began inquiring of their new friends where they could buy a *shofar*.[146] Each month, the family looked in the western sky just after sunset and upon sighting the new moon, blew the *shofar*, as instructed in scripture, signaling that a new month had begun.[147] The next day, they gathered with others, usually at their home, where they feasted, oftentimes slaughtering a goat in the festive manner of Mexicans and other peoples around the world at the time of a joyous feast. This time, it looked like they would be alone for the celebration.

They were not able to find a *shofar* in the markets, but were told there was a store that sold religious articles a few blocks to the south in the bigger shops. Since they would not buy anything on new moon day, [148] they bought their special foods, and then came back, ate lunch, had nap time, and prepared to go to the bigger shopping areas. Olga came home as they were preparing to leave, "Where are you going?" she asked.

Emily: To the store to get a *shofar*.

Olga: Why do you want a *shofar*?

Emily: Because it's almost the new moon. Do you want to go with us?

Olga: I need to go to the library.

Emily: Well, the store they sent us to is in that direction. We can walk together, if you want.

---

[145]*Rosh Chodesh* – Hebrew for 'head of the month,' or 'new moon.'

[146]*Shofar* - ram's horn.

[147]Num. 10:10 Also in the day of your gladness, and in your solemn days, and in the beginnings of your months, ye shall blow with the trumpets over your burnt offerings, and over the sacrifices of your peace offerings; that they may be to you for a memorial before your Elohim: I am YHWH your Elohim.

[148]Amos 8:5 Saying, When will the new moon be gone, that we may sell corn? and the sabbath, that we may set forth wheat, making the ephah small, and the shekel great, and falsifying the balances by deceit?

Olga: Ok, let me put my things away and I'll be right out.

The children were excited; even though they could not understand much of what each other said, there was already a bond between them. She came right out and they walked south on their mission, talking as they walked along the sidewalks. Olga helped them find the store they were looking for, but the man in the shop said, "Sorry, no shofars here. You can find them in Jerusalem."

That did not help the family for this evening, so they thanked the man and left. They stopped in a little health food store on the corner to get some herbs for Isabel, who seemed to be getting sick. Emily found what she was looking for, then asked in Hebrew, "And do you have distilled water?"

The woman had an odd look on her face and said, "I don't understand."

Emily looked up 'distilled water' on her PDA and showed it to the woman, who then replied, "We don't have that here. You can get it at the hardware store."

Emily thought that sounded like a strange place to get distilled water, but decided to give it a try. In the meantime, Olga was outside the tiny shop with the children, who were being doted upon by one of the shop employees, a young Israeli woman. She got Emily's permission to give them a healthy sucker, then began asking questions. Emily spoke her best Hebrew and was answering them as quickly as the kind woman asked. She inquired about all of the usual things they had been questioned about since arriving in Israel, but when she learned that the family also believed the New Testament, her face began to change. Emily explained, "Y'shua never went against the teachings in the *torah*. In fact, all of His words, as well as those of the apostles and Paul established it."

The once sweet, kind, loving face turned brutally hard and she announced, "I worship *Elohim!*" then turned and went back into the store, never looking back.

Emily began, "So do we...," but it was useless. It seemed she had made up her mind that the family was not worth wasting her time with. Emily stood stunned, not having had that response before from a Jowish person and being sad that the woman did not understand. Emily was very familiar with the religious spirit that caused such behavior, as she had seen it many times in Christians, most notably seminary educated pastors when they found out the family lived by the commandments in the Old Testament. She and David had had numerous experiences of watching them turn from seemingly loving individuals to having an almost murderous glare in their eye once the subject came up. And, interestingly, every time it had been because the person had been questioning the couple, never because the couple had approached them. Emily quickly gathered the children who were happily licking their suckers and headed to the next block where she was told there was a hardware store.

Olga directed Emily to the store, then took the children to the pet store next door to keep them occupied. The children entered the crowded little shop and were greeted with the smell of various types of animal bedding. They enjoyed watching the puppies, raccoons, birds, frogs, and various kinds of fish, but noticed there were no kittens. They decided there were plenty of wild ones running around and hanging out in the dumpsters.

Inside the hardware store, Emily asked for the distilled water and was taken past rows of construction materials and supplies to the automotive part of the store. On the way, she passed the PVC hoses and remembered that the children often blew on pipes for new moon instead of shofars. Since they could not find a *shofar* in time, she decided to have them cut her a short length of thick, clear, hose. She then picked up a gallon of what the employee said was distilled water, with pictures of cars on it. Emily was not sure about using it for medicine, but they assured her that was what the PDA was telling her to get.

After buying the water and hose, she went out with the others. Olga left in a hurry for the library and the family agreed to meet up with her in a little while so they could all walk home together.

Sunday

David continued with the work at the spec house. He had paint, plumbing, and other miscellaneous jobs going on at both places and ran back and forth between sites delivering needed materials and answering questions to help the workers be the most efficient.

Late in the afternoon, the New Yorker called. "The house we've been waiting on west of here has come available."

David questioned, "Ok, but you're planning to be here till the beginning of November according to the contract you signed with us, right?"

The man had no reply and changed the subject to other things about the farm, which bothered David, but he had not said they were leaving. David concluded that the man was only informing him of the news. He got back to work, just trying to get things finished so he could get back to his family. He and several of his subs continued working at both places until nearly midnight again. Things were coming along and in good enough order that he felt he could leave Wednesday, but not tonight.

Looking for the New Moon

Yom Sheni (Second Day)

Emily and the children walked slowly toward the library as the sun set and found Olga waiting for them outside. They continued to the beach, then turned north toward home, looking up occasionally to try to see the tiny

Pedaling Home   Part 2 – The Scattering

sliver of the new moon. Natanyah and Moshe played in the wet sand at the edge of the beach and the older children raced the waves, playing a game of letting them get as close as possible without getting them wet. Emily visited with Olga while they walked, and answered her questions concerning the new moon.

"What is it you do? Why do you want a *shofar*?"

"Elohim instituted a calendar at creation that all of the people written of in scripture followed. His months begin with the visible sighting of the new moon, which occurs in the western sky just after sundown. When the new moon is sighted, shofars are blown to announce the beginning of the month, and it is a day of worship and refraining from business." Isaiah[149] and some of the other prophets[150] talk about it, as well as Paul in the New Testament."[151]

Olga replied, "I know the Jews do something on the new moon, but I don't know much about it."

"Yes, the Jewish religion recognizes the importance of the new moon, that it is a special day. The major difference for us is that they recognize the astronomical new moon and we recognize the sighted new moon."

"I don't understand."

"The astronomical new moon refers to the moment in time that the earth comes between the sun and the moon each month. That can occur at any time of the day or night, and no one can see it happen because of the way the heavenly bodies are set up. The only sign we can see to know the moon has become new is the first sliver, which always appears just after sundown in the western sky. Because of this, the Feast of Trumpets, the only scriptural feast that occurs on the first day of the month, or new moon day, is known as 'the feast that no one knows the day or hour.' In other words, we can't predict exactly when the Feast of Trumpets will occur, because we can't know it's here until we see the new moon. Y'shua mentions it in regard to His return.[152] We know He will return on a Feast of Trumpets because of other things scripture tells us, and this wording, that He actually uses twice, is another clue."

---

[149]Isa. 66:23 And it shall come to pass, *that* from one new moon to another, and from one sabbath to another, shall all flesh come to worship before me, saith YHWH.

[150]Eze. 46:3 Likewise the people of the land shall worship at the door of this gate before YHWH in the sabbaths and in the new moons.

[151]Col. 2:16 Let no man therefore judge you in meat, or in drink, or in respect of an holyday, or of the new moon, or of the sabbath *days:*

[152]Matt. 25:13 Watch therefore, for ye know neither the day nor the hour wherein the Son of man cometh.

Chapter 24   Sixth New Moon

"So why do the Jews have another calendar?"

"Because of Jewish persecution by the Romans and the scattering of the Jewish people after the destruction of the temple in 70 AD, religious leaders got together in the fourth century and instituted a calendar based on calculation instead of observation. Since few Jews were left in the land of Israel, they wanted to make sure that Jews everywhere would be able to continue keeping the feasts. The solution they came up with was to calculate a calendar that could be predicted with accuracy years into the future. They did this by beginning the months according to the astronomical new moon, instead of the sighting of the moon, since the new moon according to its sighting cannot be known in advance.

"They also determined a fixed system to establish when the year would begin, instead of going by the ripening of the barley, as had been done since the Israelites left slavery in Egypt nearly 2,000 years before. By doing this, Jews all over the world could know when to keep the festivals commanded in scripture of *Pesach*,[153] *Chag haMatzot*,[154] *Yom haBikkurim*,[155] *Shavuot*,[156] *Yom Teruah* (Feast of Trumpets, celebrated in Judaism as *Rosh Hashanah*),[157] *Yom Kippur*,[158] *Sukkot*,[159] and *Yom haShemini*[160] *(celebrated in Judaism as Shemini Atzeret)*.[161] Though the system served the people for 1,500 years and enabled Jews worldwide to be on the same page concerning the festivals, the man-made calendar is no longer necessary now that the Jews are back in the land with 21th century methods of communication. But sometimes it's hard to put aside something you're used to, even when it's obsolete.

"There is only one group of Jews that I know of that actually go by the sighting. They're called *Karaite* Jews, and are basically scripturalists, not following the oral *torah* of the rabbis, but going only by the written *torah*. I think our family is more closely aligned with them in our practices than with anyone else, except that as a religion, they also reject the New Testament and Y'shua."

"So who do you worship with? Are you the only ones who do this?"

---

[153]*Pesach* - Hebrew for 'Passover.'

[154]*Chag haMatzot* - Hebrew for 'Pilgrimage of Unleavened Bread', referring to the Feast of Unleavened Bread.

[155]*Yom haBikkkurim* – Hebrew for 'Day of Firstfruits.'

[156]*Shavuot* - Hebrew for 'Weeks,' referring to the Feast of Weeks, 'Pentecost' in Greek

[157]*Rosh Hashanah* - Hebrew for 'Head of the Year.'

[158]*Yom Kippur* - Hebrew for 'Day of Atonement'

[159]*Sukkot* - Hebrew for 'Tabernacles' or 'Booths', referring to the 'Feast of Tabernacles.'

[160]Yom haShemini – The Eighth Day.

[161]*Shemini Atzeret* - Hebrew for 'Eighth Day of Assembly,' a joyful celebration held the day after Sukkot.

"Oh, no! There are many more. Well, I guess 'many' is relative. Compared to a world population, there is only a tiny group, but thousands of people worldwide are beginning to be called back to the ways of the Creator, including the keeping of His calendar. Many within Christianity are beginning to see that the three major traditions they've been following for centuries originated in paganism and have nothing to do with our Creator and Savior. And, in fact, that He calls those festivals 'abominations' and has told His people not to worship Him in those ways.[162] They all originate in sun worship and can be traced back to the tower of Babel."

"And many within Judaism are beginning to see, as they study the *torah*, that their rabbis and the oral *torah*, have made changes to the word of YHWH in the scriptures, changes that He specifically forbade."[163]

Olga pondered what Emily told her, but was tired of the topic and ready to run and play with the children on the beach in the blackness of the early night. They had never sighted the moon, so would wait to hear if someone else sighted it. If not, new moon would not begin until the next evening.

Not Again...

They approached the long rock pier and turned toward the playground, the children playing for a few minutes there before they all returned home. Emily called David, "We didn't sight the moon. It was real clear out and we watched for a long time, so I don't think tomorrow will be new moon day. It should be fine for you to fly back tonight."

David replied, "I'm sorry, but there's no way I'm going to be able to leave tonight anyway. When everything stopped, it really messed up the flow and I don't have everything back on track, yet. I'll have to leave Wednesday instead, arriving Thursday, like I had planned to do last week."

Emily had seen it coming, but hearing it still wasn't easy, "I'm just ready to get back on the bikes. I need to stay active, and it's hard here with the children. It's a wonderful place, but there's nowhere for them to run, like at home. I feel like I have to be watching them all the time to make sure they're safe and not bothering people. They're doing great. I don't mean to sound like they're not. It's just hard for me. This isn't how we planned it. We're supposed to be together, riding, eating healthy, and having our first family time ever."

David: I know. I'm sorry. I just don't know what else I can do. If I try to

---

[162]Jer. 10:2 Thus saith YHWH, Learn not the way of the heathen, and be not dismayed at the signs of heaven; for the heathen are dismayed at them.

[163]Deut. 12:32 What thing soever I command you, observe to do it: thou shalt not add thereto, nor diminish from it.

Chapter 24   Sixth New Moon

come back and things aren't right here, I'll have to return. It's better just to fix everything while I'm here.

Emily: I know. We'll be fine.

David: I'll look for the new moon here tonight. If I don't see it, I'll work tomorrow and take off the next day. Everyone here is really trying to help me get back to you guys.

Emily was glad to hear that and thanked Yah for all the hired people in their little group who were faithfully helping David to get the jobs finished. Once the children were asleep, she lay on her mat, looking at the stars, praying, as the tears rolled down her face barely missing Natanyah's little fingers on her ear.

In the morning, Emily tried to make the colloidal silver with the water from the hardware store, but after the machine had run its three-hour cycle, the water was very dark grayish-black, instead of clear or golden, indicating she had used bad quality water. She tried the dark liquid and could taste the silver in it, so gave some to Isabel. Between that, the herbs, and prayer, Isabel got better quickly. But that evening when Elena popped her cheerful face over the porch wall, Emily showed her the jug of water and said, "I needed water to make medicine with and the health food store told me to go to the hardware store. This is what they had there, but it's not making the medicine right. Do you know where I can get better distilled water?"

Elena was horrified, "Oh, no! This is for cars! You need water from the pharmacy for medicine!"

"Where is that?" Emily asked.

"The closest one is in Kiryat Motzkin, at the mall."

Emily knew where that was, so put distilled water on her list of things to get when they went to meet David at the train station in three days.

When Emily gave David his wake-up call, he told her, "It looks like I'll be able to leave Wednesday, as scheduled, getting there Thursday evening."

"Great! I'll call Dad and see if he can get the tickets for me. I was on the phone for way too long with them last time and the toll free number call cost us two dollars per minute.

After getting off the phone, she called her dad, "Would you mind taking my information and calling the airlines to purchase David's flight back? The call costs a lot from here."

"I'll be glad to," he replied, being the one who taught her to be as thrifty as possible with phone usage.

225

As soon as she got off the phone with him, she had a renewed sense of energy, looking forward to being together as a complete family and on the bicycles again. She called Nikolay to reschedule their appointment at B'hai Gardens for preparation day, the day after David's newly scheduled return. That would give him a night of rest after returning to the Land, then a little walking tour before the good long rest of *Shabbat*.

Gone

Monday

The subs were busy working, so David took Paco and the parts for his truck and drove towards the farm for the Mechanic to replace his rod. Emily called again. "Dad called and is having trouble with the reservations. They told me before that you would have a credit from when you skipped your flight, but now are needing some numbers that you have. Can you call Dad and give them to him so he can make the reservations?"

"Sure. I'll call him right now. I'm on the way to the Mechanic's to have him fix my truck. I'll check things out at the farm while I'm there."

David called Byron and gave him the numbers so he could buy the plane tickets. He stopped at the Mechanic's shop, picked him up, then drove the additional mile to the farm gate where he and Paco got out and walked toward the house, leaving the Mechanic to drive the truck back for repair. Topping the hill, David saw there was no RV, no activity, and the other vehicle was gone. He was not sure when the people had left, but went around to check all the animals: cattle, goats, chickens, geese, dogs, and cats. Everything was fine, and he praised Yah for watching over them. He called Byron to let him know that there was no one to take care of the farm, so he would not be returning to Israel as scheduled. He dreaded giving Emily the news; she was having a hard enough time already dealing with the fact that her family was separated during the only time together to themselves that they had ever had. He prayed for the best way to tell her and for Yah to prepare her heart for what was coming.

David: I have bad news.

Emily, feeling her chest tighten: What's wrong?

David: The New Yorkers are gone.

Emily: What do you mean, 'gone'? You mean they *left*?

David: Yep.

Emily: When?

David: I don't know. Everything's fine here, but the chickens are almost out of water. It's a good thing I came when I did.

Chapter 24   Sixth New Moon

Emily's heart was sinking. She knew he could not leave the farm with no one to care for the animals. She was the planner/organizer of the family, so quickly came up with plan B. "Call the Oklahoma Lady. See if she's still interested in coming."

David: Ok, but you know this means I can't come back this week.

Emily: Yes, I know. It would take her two days to get there if she left today, assuming she has no other obligations and even still wants to come.

David: I'll call Byron and tell him to hold off on the tickets.

David called Byron back, but he had been on the ball and the tickets had already been purchased. He then called the Oklahoma Lady, "This is David in Tennessee. Are you still interested in coming to the farm?"

Oklahoman: Yes, but I thought you left already.

David: We did, but the people who were staying here disappeared. I'm back in the U.S. The rest of the family's in Israel. When can you get here?

Oklahoman: Well, it will take me a bit to get things together here. I'll get to work on it and let you know. I'd say I could be there within a couple of weeks.

David: Great! Call me if you have any questions.

The good news was she could come. The bad news was he would have to reschedule his flight again, since he would have to be there to show her around. He tried to focus on the good news as he called Emily back. She, like him, was relieved that the Oklahoman could come, but saddened that David's delay would be longer.

David and Paco had just finished getting the last of the tools they needed to take back to town when the Mechanic called to say he was finished with the pick-up. He then returned to get them, and they loaded the tools, dropped him off at his shop, and drove back to Cookeville.

David got the decking material for the spec house and delivered it to the workers there. Both jobs were coming together, communication had been restored, and things were back on track for the Manager to be able to take over and keep things moving until final inspections were done. The only hold up was that the restaurant Owners had hired a hood man to install the commercial hoods. Though it was not part of David's contract, the job could not progress to be ready for Final Inspection until the Hood Man finished his work. David had pressured the Owners, and when he got back to the site, he was glad to finally breathe a sigh of relief upon seeing that things had been moved around in preparation for installing the hoods.

227

The Dead Lady

Yom Shlishi (Third Day)   Sixth New Moon

After sundown, Emily and the children looked for and saw the sliver of the new moon. Armando blew blasts on the hose they had bought at the hardware store and they welcomed the sixth scriptural month from their mats on the tile back porch. Emily called David to let him know they had sighted the moon. He would call off his workers the next day.

For the special occasion, the family ate sweet breads for breakfast, like they did on *Shabbat*. They always had special treats on the day of the New Moon. After cleaning up, they busied themselves around the house and in the front yard. Unlike on *Shabbat*, the scriptures did not prohibit working around the house on the day of the new moon. But it was clear from the writings that it was not a day for business, though much easier to see in the Hebrew text than in the English translation.

Mid-morning, two men came through the yard gate carrying a box nearly large enough for a stove. As they carried it toward the open front door, the children who had been playing outside, ran in to tell Mama. She met them at the door and they explained in Hebrew, "We're cleaning out the house next door. The widow who lived there died recently and these are things she left. You're welcomed to whatever you can use here. What you don't want, you can just take to the dumpster. Or, if you'd like, we'll just take it to the dumpster now."

The children already had the box open and seven sets of inquisitive eyes persuaded Mama to say, "We'll go through it. Thank you very much for thinking of us."

"No problem. I hope you can find some useful things," said one of the men as they left.

The children excitedly began pulling clothing, towels, and dishes out of the box. Emily found a pair of boots, a pair of slippers, a linen skirt, and a coat she could use. The woman must have been about her size. They also found two sets of sheets, and Isabel found a large wooden-handled kitchen knife. She proudly put It In the drawer with tho paring knife they had bought the week before, then returned to see a plastic dish drainer, which she put on the kitchen counter next to the one that had been left by the previous renter. They were two-leveled drainers, unlike any they had seen before and were an efficient way of air-drying dishes. Isabel and Rebeka also found two purses they thought were wonderful and Briana found a pair of green Crocs sandals that fit her.

Included in the box were lots of clothes, mostly things that Emily did not need or want, but the children begged her not to send them to the dumpster. The children spent the rest of the day dressing up in various entertaining outfits. Not knowing the name of the deceased widow, nor anything about her other than what they could gather from the belongings they had been left, they affectionately referred to her as the Dead Lady.

After school let out, various new friends came over to play. The older children played ball in the alley behind, while Emily and the younger ones stayed in the back yard.

Tuesday   New Moon Day

David called the Restaurant Owner before 7 AM to make sure the Coke machine and sinks would be there, as scheduled, the next day. He would not have his subs working on the new moon. Emily's wake-up call came in while he was talking, so phoned her right back as soon as he finished. They talked for about an hour updating one another on the things that were going on in each other's lives.

For new moon, David went to the home of one of the men that was helping with paint and various other jobs. Some of the others were there with their families, several of which were planning to move to Mexico. David updated them on what was going on with Emily and the children in Israel, then spent most of his time answering questions about his home country, as they prepared for their move.

This was the first new moon David had ever celebrated without his family. It was strange seeing the other children playing together in the yard and woods without his. He missed them and felt awkward being a single man there with his family so far away. They spent time praying for one another and for David's family.

After sunset, he went back to work at the restaurant, and found out the Owner still did not have all of the restaurant equipment there that David needed to install. Since he was going to have to wait for the Oklahoman to arrive anyway, David wanted to see that this job was completely finished before he returned to Israel, so the family could finish their time overseas in complete peace. He pressed the Owner, who agreed, saying, "I'll get it tomorrow if you and Paco will go with me to pick it up."

David consented, then went back to help out at the spec house. He could do nothing else at the restaurant until the equipment arrived and the Hood Man finished. But now, the Hood Man had disappeared and neither David nor the Owner could reach him. David began to get nervous. He was pressured, knowing his eight month pregnant wife and young family were six thousand miles away, and losing patience with unnecessary holdups.

25 - *Abba*'s Hand

Yom Revi'i (Fourth Day)

After morning routine, Emily got out the soap making kit that Eti had brought when they had first arrived. It looked simple enough, but not wanting to waste anything or make a mess, she took the instructions to the ladies behind and had them translate them to her. After returning to the house, she and the children mixed the shredded colored soap with the required amount of water, then pressed them into the molds according to the instructions and marveled at their beautiful decorative soaps, some on little ropes, in the shapes of flowers, hearts, and shells. They soon ran out of shredded soap and decided they needed to go get more supplies.

"But what will we do with so many little soaps?" Emily asked.

Isabel quickly piped up, "We can give them to people!"

"That's a great idea!" Emily agreed, as the other children began calling out names and descriptions of all the special new friends they'd like to give home molded soaps to. "If we're going to give them as gifts, we should get some special little bags to put them in."

The new idea temporarily took Emily's mind off of the fact that her husband was not coming back as scheduled again. The children were used to not being around Daddy, so they did not miss him as much. But Emily was tired of the heavy load she pulled without him, both physically and emotionally. Getting him and the situation off her mind was good. She began making a list of all the things they should get, knowing they needed to go to Kiryat Motzkin for distilled water, anyway. Later, she called Nikolay to let him know that David was delayed again and that they would need to hold off on going to B'hai Gardens.

Nashville
Wednesday

David was with Paco and one of the restaurant Owners on the way to Nashville when he got and returned Emily's wake-up call. He explained the situation to her. "We needed to get some used restaurant equipment from a restaurant that the Owner closed over here. Once we get that, we've got to go to a specialty store to pick up the restroom stall dividers and doors. When the company delivered, they only brought what had been paid for. I got the Owners to pay for the rest so that I can pick them up and get them installed. They weren't going to deliver them for another week and they have to be in before I can get a final inspection. Since there's nothing I can do right now, I decided to get these things moving so things aren't so piled up when it gets closer to inspection time."

Emily was glad to hear that things were moving along and David was glad she seemed to understand. The Oklahoman called to tell David that she would be leaving in a little over a week and bringing the four youngest of her twelve children, the older ones old enough to be on their own. David was relieved that Yah had arranged for someone else to come on such short notice – one less thing on his mind as he rode back from Nashville, helped unload the equipment, and wrapped up the difficult situations in town.

He knew he could count on the framers who were working on the deck at the spec house, but really needed someone like that working on the restaurant hood. Since he could do nothing to help the jobs along, he went to the Farmer's Co-op, bought feed, and took it out to the farm to check on things again. After finding everything in good order, he returned to Cookeville, checked on the subs who were installing the equipment, then went to the supply store to get fixtures and other materials needed to do the final plumbing at the spec house, while the framers were finishing the deck. He then returned to the restaurant, where the Owner took him and Paco to Nashville again to get more equipment. David called and got directions before returning to Nashville, but when they arrived at the outlet store he was told that the items they needed were at the warehouse in another place. By the time they got there, the warehouse was closed, so the Owner took them to the nearby house of one of his relatives to spend the night.

More Soaps
Yom Chamishi (Fifth Day)

Emily was doing everything she could to keep her spirits up and not let the children know how upset she was becoming, but she could not hide it. Besides feeling like the only family time they had ever had together had been taken from them because of the job, something she felt was always competing for her husband's affection, she was beginning to wonder if she was going to have to deliver this baby by herself with the help of only the children. Armando and Briana were very capable, but she had always had David with her and did not want to go through this one without him.

The children had really enjoyed molding soaps, and Emily was glad they were doing a worthwhile project. They made the long walk to Kiryat Motzkin the same way they had gone when they bought the phone battery, without the detour by the dump, since they now knew how to get there. They arrived just after noon, so Emily treated them all to falafel in the middle of the mall. As they watched the Jewish men make their lunch, the one at the counter began asking the usual questions. The more Emily shared, the more he wanted to know. She shared with him the prophecies in Ezekiel, Hosea and others that talked about Ephraim coming back to the Father and His ways and returning to be reunited with Judah.[164] He was intrigued.

They continued the conversation through the family's first order and then another. Even though the children had snacked on oranges along the way, the long walk had them all hungry. It often amazed Emily how children always seemed to be able to eat, even if just a few minutes after they were full from the previous meal. When finished, they went to the pharmacy and got the horribly expensive distilled water, and several different colors and scents of soap. They found a craft shop in the mall where they bought string to use for soap on a rope, several dozen wedding rice bags and some scented potpourri to put in them to give as gifts. It was good to have her mind on serving others and off of her own situation. The children, too, were excited to be able to make and give gifts to their friends.

While there, they were approached by a woman who said she had a large amount of clothing in her car to donate. She asked Emily if the family would like to have them. Emily thanked her and said that they were traveling by bicycle and would not be able to use them, then looked the children over well, wondering if the woman thought they looked poor or if she just saw lots of children and assumed they needed clothes. Their orange shirts were already beginning to fade from being in the sun so much, and Moshe's had been mended on one elbow after his crash in Haifa. But all in all she thought they looked fine for people who were camping. And the thought of extra clothes made her wince, both from a management perspective and thinking of packing them on the bicycles once they started riding again. The available clothes were definitely meant for someone else.

Before leaving the mall, they stopped at the grocery where they bought some special foods for *Shabbat*, including pomegranate juice and high quality grape juice.

Thursday

David received his wake-up call from Emily, who was surprised again to find him in Nashville and was getting confused by the whole situation. He tried to explain things to her, but her mind was so consumed by her own life and issues there that she was not able to fully comprehend him. After ending their call, he called the Oklahoman to check her progress. He was beginning to feel desperate and was doing all he could to keep everyone moving. He was relieved to hear that she was still on schedule to leave Oklahoma the next week.

---

[164]Judah - in this context, referring to the House of **Judah**, the part of the House of Israel that is known as the 'Jews.'

Chapter 25   *Abba*'s Hand

The three men drove to the warehouse, where no one was allowed entry. But David pleaded with the man there, explaining some of his situation. The kind man graciously let him come in and get the restroom divider walls that he needed. They took a load of materials back to the restaurant and David got the men working on installing them. David and Paco went toward Nashville a third time to get more things out of the restaurant the Owner was closing there. Seeing they could not finish the required disassembly that night, the Owner got them a motel room.

Shuk

Yom Shishi (Sixth Day)

The young men who took Armando to the synagogue had told Emily about the *shuk* a few blocks away that was open on preparation day. They said things were very inexpensive there, especially around 3 PM, when they were shutting down for *Shabbat*. Emily remembered the place from when they had stopped at the edge of Kiryat Yam, just before Eti had called them about finding the apartment. That, too, was a preparation day, she remembered. Since they were still there, and now planning to be there for longer, she decided this would be the day to go.

The children found a stroller at the dumpster and excitedly brought it home. They convinced Mama she could push Natanyah in it to the *shuk*. Emily was all for the children getting plenty of exercise and preferred Natanyah walk, but did not want to disappoint them, and saw no harm in it. They happily got Natanyah situated, proud that they had found such a treasure. More than half of what they now owned had come from the dumpster, the children's treasure trove.

They walked east for a few small blocks, then turned north. After passing a grocery, not knowing there was one so close to their house, they walked past some big apartment complexes to the *shuk*, remembering when they had been there two weeks before. As they approached, a woman came out from one of the apartments across the street and began excitedly speaking Hebrew to the family. She asked the usual preliminary questions, as she quickly led Emily to the *shuk*, then told her, "Come with me. I'll get you good deals."

Emily followed, a little warily, but finding her newest friend to be quite an interesting person. She took her to selected stands, bargaining with the men selling produce until Natanyah was booted out of the stroller and it was filled to overflowing with fruits and vegetables that the vendors had been persuaded to give them. Emily was not accustomed to walking away with free things, and had tried to tell the woman she had money, but she would not allow her to pay for anything, saying, "It's almost *Shabbat*. They're going to throw them away, anyway."

Once out of the *shuk*, the woman commanded, "Wait!" as she ran across the street to the apartments, then returned with a large flour sack

233

completely full of bread that she had salvaged from a closing bakery just a few minutes earlier. She said blessings over Emily and the children and sent them on their way. Emily praised Yah again for His kindness to them through His people and for the stroller that was now so full of food that the suspension collapsed several times on their way back. Each time, they unloaded it, repaired it the best they could, and repacked.

Friday

David finally felt like he had things lined up and straightened out well enough to get tickets to fly back to Israel, but to be safe, he decided on ten days out, Monday the 15th, arriving in Israel Tuesday afternoon. This should give him time to get the jobs finished, get the Oklahoman settled at the farm, and tie up all loose ends before leaving.

He called Emily again as they were leaving Nashville so he could let her know of his plan. She was again surprised that he was in the Nashville area and still did not understand why he was away working there instead of finishing the jobs in Cookeville. He tried to explain to her that the Owner was not bringing him the things he needed, so he had to do it himself

She was glad to know he had her dad purchasing the tickets, but knew that the longer he waited, the less chance there would be for them to continue their bicycle travels, since she was growing closer to delivery. They had planned to get off the bicycles by *Yom Teruah*, the next new moon, which was coming in just a few weeks at the beginning of October, so his arrival on the 16th would give them less than two more weeks of riding once he got rested from his travels.

David knew she was really looking forward to getting back on the bicycles. She had always been very active and felt much better when she was pushing herself physically than when she was living a more sedentary lifestyle. She was quick to put on weight if she was not very active and because she felt so much better about herself in general when she was active, she really felt she needed that active time as she approached the birth. She also felt better about herself concerning food when they were on the bicycles. She did not eat as much and their diet consisted of mainly fresh fruits, vegetables, hummus and bread. While she was grateful for all of the kindness they had been shown, she lamented that once they got off of the bicycles and got in the house, eating the gifted food, they began eating things like couscous[165] and other more processed foods. She even began buying sodas, something she had not done in the US for years. She was just ready to get back with the plans they had made. Now she had to resign herself to knowing it would be nearly two more weeks. David heard the pain in her voice, the frustration with herself and with him. But he resolved within himself that he was doing the best he could to get back to them quickly

---

[165]Couscous - small bead-like wheat pasta, a staple in some parts of North Africa.

Chapter 25   *Abba*'s Hand

While they talked, Emily filled the bath tub with water and began filling the big refrigerator with food from the *shuk*, putting most of the bread in the freezer to keep it fresh. While the last of the children were bathing, Briana informed Mama that the Brothers, Sarah's sons, were at the gate. Emily walked out and the one who spoke English asked her, "Could Armando come for supper? Some of our cousins are here, about the same age as him."

"That would be fine," Emily replied. "When should he come?"

"Right now is good," he said.

Rabbi Questions Armando

Shabbat

Emily told Armando, who felt important at having been invited to a special dinner without the younger children; donned his *yarmulke*, which he wore most of the time now; and headed out the door. Once at the house on the other side of Elena's, Armando visited with the other boys his age. The main rabbi from the synagogue was also there for supper, and began questioning him.

Rabbi: So they tell me you're not Jewish.

Armando: No.

Rabbi: But you wear tassels. Why?

Armando: Because *torah* says to.

Rabbi, smiling with approval and intrigue: And why do your tassels have a blue thread?

Armando: Because *torah* says to have one.

Rabbi, chuckling: Ah, yes, it does. What does the blue represent?

Armando: Messiah.

Rabbi: And who is the Messiah?

Armando: Y'shua.

Rabbi, thoughtfully: But they say he was against *torah*.

Armando: It's not true. He lived *torah* perfectly and told us to follow his example. He never taught against it.

Rabbi: Interesting. What about circumcision. Are you circumcised?

235

Armando: Yes.

Rabbi: It is good to have you in synagogue. Would you like to open the ark[166] on *Shabbat?*

Armando: Yes.

Rabbi: Ok, then. We will see.

The Rabbi resumed his conversation with the other men there. Armando was glad the questioning was over. He could continue enjoying his meal and play with the other boys his age.

Emily and the six others enjoyed their supper without both of their men. It was a little lonely, but they felt honored that Armando had been invited to the special home two doors down. Not long after they cleaned up from supper, he came home reporting about his experience. Emily was particularly excited about the topics they had discussed with him and glad that they were willing to continue to accept him at the synagogue, even after the Rabbi learned that the family followed Y'shua.

~ ~ ~

After getting the rest of the equipment, the men drove back to Cookeville. David made sure the subs were busy and on track at the restaurant and then went to check on the spec house. He paid all of his helpers before sundown, including the driveway crew who had finished their job.

The animals at the farm had water, but because it came from a spring, sometimes a pipe would get knocked off the tank and the stock tanks would run dry. He was afraid to leave them alone for more than a couple of days, so went there to spend the night. On the way, he stopped and got juice to take as his contribution to the next day's *Shabbat* meal at the home where he would meet with the others.

Sabbath

When he got home, he took the mail from the box, which included a package which he recognized to be containing a circumcision shield Emily had ordered for their Former Amish friends. Apparently, she had mistakenly shipped it to their address, instead of to their friends'. David did not know when their baby was due, and was too tired to think about it, so tossed the package with the other mail into the passenger seat of his pick-up, cared for all the animals, and then went to bed, exhausted and glad for *Shabbat.*

---

[166]Ark - cabinet in the synagogue where the *torah* scroll is kept.

Chapter 25   *Abba*'s Hand

Shabbat at the House

After their special *Shabbat* breakfast of sweet bread and milk to go along
with their normal daily fruit and yogurt, the family readied themselves to
go to synagogue. The young men came by first to take Armando. Sarah
came later for the rest of the family. When it was time for the reading of
the *torah*, Emily was overjoyed as she watched Armando open the ark,
wishing David would have been there so see it. It was truly an honor for
them to be able to participate. As she and the children watched from the
balcony with the other women and children, they felt like part of the family.

On the way home, Emily asked Sarah if she would mind coming over and
reading the Psalms to the family. They sounded so beautiful in native
Hebrew. Sarah was visibly delighted, so came over just after lunch. Emily
had the children set up the roll away bed in the front room as a couch for
Sarah to sit on while she read to them. She arrived, and with Emily sitting
beside her and the children all around, began reading. Emily had not
realized when she asked her to read that the Psalms were prayers that
were commonly read in Judaism, being taught to the youngsters in school
so that they were most often read rhythmically and very speedily with the
reader rocking back and forth. It was interesting to hear and see, but Emily
had great difficulty following along. Soon Natanyah and Moshe were
asleep for nap time on the 'couch' behind the ladies. Sarah continued
reading for an hour before tiring. She and Emily were both blessed for the
experience, but some of the children were certainly glad when their hour
on the couch was finished and they were dismissed to play. Emily invited
her back for the next *Shabbat* and she gladly consented.

The honored look on her face pleased Emily. This precious lady, having
been widowed for under three weeks was finding comfort in doing what
Emily had asked of her. Emily had not considered that when she first made
the request, but praised Yah that he always works on behalf of everyone
involved who loves him.

After Sarah left, Emily rested for a few minutes, the four younger ones
already well into their nap. When they got up a short time later, they had
another pomegranate party. Afterward Emily tried phoning the house, but
got no answer. Knowing David was exhausted from the long hours and
stress he had been under, she correctly guessed he was still sleeping
soundly. With the milk cow at the Horse and Buggy community, he had no
reason to have to get up early. The rest of the animals were not as time
sensitive. Lonely, but not even considering the lasting loneliness of the
three widows just south of her, she fed the children supper as she watched
the sun sink behind the houses across the back alley.

Driving Angels

After sleeping late, eating some fruit, turning the goats out into the
appropriate pasture, then taking another nap, David awoke and prepared

to go to one of his helpers' houses for worship, fellowship, and study, which would last for the rest of the day. Since he was going by himself, the only thing he took for the meal was the grape juice for the blessing of the bread and wine. It had been waiting in his pick-up since he had purchased it the day before.

He drove out of the driveway, closed the gate behind him, and then zoned out thinking about all the events that had transpired in the past month. Nearly an hour later, he came back to his senses, not knowing where he was. The area looked familiar, but he could not figure out how to get to the man's house from here. Suddenly, a landmark caught his eye and he realized he was in Kentucky, about the same distance from his own house that his helper lived, but in the exact opposite direction, and now in a different state. He recognized the surrounding hills as the area where their Former Amish friends lived. He turned on the next road and drove straight to their house, immediately remembering that he had their circumcision shield in his truck and marveled at how Yah worked things out for him to get it to them.

The friends were very excited to see him driving up their driveway. The whole family came out of the big, partially finished Amish-style house carrying their baby boy, born just a few days before. They had wondered what had happened to the shield Emily had ordered for them and, since their baby was a boy, had surely hoped to receive it. When David pulled it out of his pick-up, they were delighted and praised Yah. They all went into the house and listened to the reports David brought concerning the cycling in Israel and what had happened in the U.S. to bring him back. They listened with interest, then had a Bible study and meal.

The Varelas had met this family when another former Amish family had asked if they could drive to Canada to bring them to Kentucky. In getting to know the first family, they realized what a sacrifice they had made to follow Yah's instructions, according to the scriptures. The Varelas had faced some rudeness and shunning from people when beginning to keep the Sabbath and then the feasts and other instructions, but nothing like what had happened to their Amish friends. These families had grown up in a culture of community, where everyone lives basically the same, the rules are known and followed, and people basically submit to one another on a level that makes things work.

When these families began to celebrate the seventh-day Sabbath, though, they were shunned from their communities, called 'contentious,' and, though continuing to live among the Amish for a while, were left to eat at a table by themselves during weddings, funerals, and other occasions, and snubbed and shunned in other ways by some. Finally, when it was established that things would only continue to worsen for them, they left the Amish to live alone. For a typical American, that would have been a challenge, leaving one way of life and merging into another, but for the Amish, who held to most of their former lifestyle, there was no merging into American life. They continued to use horses instead of cars, refused

Chapter 25   *Abba*'s Hand

electricity and indoor plumbing, and basically lived their lives as before, only keeping the Sabbath set-apart, instead of Sunday.

There were numerous challenges to that lifestyle, once alone. Now it would be miles in a buggy to ride to a store that would have their needed supplies, since most English stores did not carry them. And even if they had, it would still be miles for them to get to a town. Then there was the question of who their children would marry. One thing the Varelas really appreciated about both families was their willingness to give up all of their security and even their culture in order to follow Yah. And the family that David was currently visiting was further ostracized when they continued in their studies and began keeping Yah's feasts and calling upon his name, as instructed in scripture. When spending time with them, the Varelas were always reminded that what they suffered for the cause was not nearly as much as what their Former Amish friends suffered.

26 - *Arnav*[167]

Voice on the Line

Week 5   *Yom Rishon* (First Day)   9/6-7

Emily bedded down the children and just wanted to be asleep herself; to sleep for a week, and then to wake up with the whole family riding their bicycles north.

She tried again to call David, but still could not reach him. She was distraught with the whole situation and really needed someone to talk to. She went through the list of names in her U.S. cell phone and came to their friends in Missouri, who had spent some time in Israel and had really encouraged them in their trip before they left. Before returning home from her family's triennial family reunion earlier in the summer, they had traveled several hours to meet the family face to face and spent *Shabbat* in their home. Emily called the number and her friend answered.

Just to hear her caring voice on the phone caused Emily to break down weeping. Her friend, who recognized her from the caller ID, was then immediately concerned for her. Emily calmed down and began to share what was happening with the family in Israel. Her friend stopped her for long enough to get her husband on the line, so he could hear the conversation, as well.

The things Emily shared with them were hard for them to imagine - how they had stopped the bicycle riding because of David's problems back home in the business, how he was to return to Israel in 3 days, how his trip had been extended more than once, and how it now looked like he would be there even longer, while Emily was in a rented house in a beach town in Israel, eight months pregnant wondering if he would ever return. After hearing Emily's desperation and her heart, the friends prayed for her for several minutes, then ended the call after assuring her that they would continue praying. Emily felt better and was able to rest.

~ ~ ~

After returning from the Former Amish Friends' house, David brought the goats into the barn with feed, then went to bed, refreshed at having spent time in the company of dear friends and having seen Yah work another miracle in all of their lives.

---

[167]*Arnav* – Hebrew for 'rabbit.'

Chapter 26   *Arnav*

Scruffy

Learning of the grocery store so close to their house, Emily decided to take a walk when they finished lunch to see what kinds of items were sold there. Armando and Briana agreed to stay at the house and babysit sleeping Natanyah, while Emily went on the walk with the middle four. Just before reaching the store, three youths (two girls and a boy) came out of a house across the street, one of them carrying a cage housing a young, very scraggly looking bunny. One of the girls asked in Hebrew, "Would you like a rabbit?"

Emily replied, "I'm sorry. We can't take it. We're traveling by bicycle," but she was beginning to wonder if that were true anymore.

The children instantly fell in love with the wretched-looking thing and began their pleas, one by one.

Victor: Daddy's not back, yet. We might be here *forever*!

Rebeka: I could carry it on *my* bike!

Isabel: We can give it to someone else when we leave!

Moshe: Can we please have it, Mama?

The children were all excited, and Emily, being an animal lover since infancy, decided it would not hurt anything. Much to the children's delight, she told the youths, "Ok, we're on our way to the store. We can pick it up on the way back."

One of the girls happily replied, "We'll be waiting for you."

Now the children's excitement concerning what might be in the grocery store was diminished by the fact that they were going to have their first rabbit. The grocery held their interest for as long as Emily wanted to be there, anyway, now having an idea of the various items they sold. Though a much smaller store, it looked to be as complete as the grocery farther away in Kiryat Motzkin. This would become their new grocery.

As they walked out of the store, the youths rushed out of the house across the street with the rabbit in its cage. Emily asked them, "*Ma ze?*"168

They looked at each other comically. Then as if a light bulb had turned on in one of the girls, she said, "*Arnav.*"

Emily responded, "Rabbit."

168*Ma ze?* - Hebrew for 'What is it?'

Pedaling Home   Part 2 – The Scattering

They repeated, "Rabbit."

Emily asked, "What does it eat?"

"Lettuce," came the reply.

Emily seriously doubted that was all the poor looking creature needed. At any rate, they now had a pet. They thanked the youths, who were glad to get it off their hands, and walked toward home with their new pet, Emily hoping that it did not have a contagious disease or was about to die. It seemed they were often the beneficiaries of creatures in need of love and attention. This one would be named what he was, *Arnav*, so that the family could remember how to say 'rabbit' in Hebrew.

~ ~ ~

Natanyah awoke shortly after the others left, so Armando and Briana loaded her in the new stroller and pushed her to the dumpster. After boosting Briana up so she could get inside, Armando posted himself watchman on the outside with Natanyah. Briana called to him, "Is the coast clear?"

"Yeah."

Briana announced, "I don't see anything we want. I'm coming out."

As she stuck her head out, she looked around once, just to be sure all was clear, just as Emily and the children came around the corner from the store, several blocks away. "Hey, Mama's coming back! What's that they're carrying?"

Briana jumped out and they made their way toward the others. As soon as the other children saw them, Victor took off running up the sidewalk, screaming, "We got a rabbit!" The two groups hurried toward each other, all sharing in the excitement together, then continued the short walk home. Once there, Emily showed them how to fill up and place his water bottle, and they took turns giving him lettuce.

David called and shared with Emily the events of *Shabbat*, while the children bounced around trying to be quiet as they waited their turn to talk. It seemed like an eternity before Mama finally gave them the phone so they could tell Daddy about *Arnav*. He gladly shared in their excitement, happy they had a new special critter in their lives.

After the call, Armando suggested they go to the pet store and get some rabbit food. Emily agreed. *Arnav* definitely looked like he needed some nutrients he had not been getting. Besides, he certainly needed good bedding. His little feet were raw as if he had been kept in a dirty cage. After making sure he was cared for and safe from feral cats, the family walked the other direction to the pet store. Emily inquired about food for

242

Chapter 26   *Arnav*

an unhealthy rabbit and was given a special rabbit food and a salt lick, then bought some shavings for bedding. By the time they got home, most of the afternoon was gone. They took *Arnav* out of his cage and played with him for a few minutes before washing up for supper.

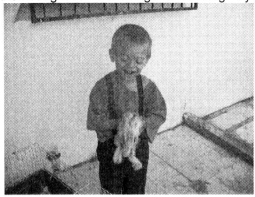
Moshe

Worries
Sunday

David turned the goats out to pasture, checked the cattle, chickens, geese, and guineas, and then drove to Cookeville to get people started on the jobs. Work at the restaurant was still waiting on the hood, so he got the painters started at the spec house and put the other subs to work on the porch rails while he ran to and fro buying supplies from various suppliers to keep things running smoothly.

David was surprised to get a call from Emily mid-afternoon. She should have been long asleep by them. "What's wrong?" he asked.

Emily: I can't sleep.

David: I'm sorry. Why not?

Emily: I just need you here. I'm tired. The baby's growing. What if our dates are off like they were with Moshe? What if she's a month early and you're not here?

David: Hey, don't worry. Everything will work out fine. Just calm down.

Emily: Are you even *planning* to come back?

David, now getting angry: Of course! I can't believe you would ask me that! I've been working till midnight most nights trying to get things done here so that when I leave it will all be finished. You can ask your dad. Ask any of the people here!

Emily: Ok, you don't have to get mad. It just looks really bad, and other people are wondering, too. I wonder what all these people around here think. We told them you'd just be gone for a few days. I keep saying you're coming and then we keep changing it.

David: Well, there's nothing I can do about it. I'm doing the best I can, and you can ask anyone if you don't believe me.
Emily: I'm sorry. I just had to ask. I couldn't sleep.

243

David: Of course I'm planning to come. I love you. You have my children. You have my baby!

Emily sighed and David told her, "Try to get some sleep."

They hung up and David went back to work, trying to focus on his job while attempting to see things from his wife's perspective. He knew she had a lot of responsibility there with the children in an unfamiliar place. And he understood her wanting him to return, wondering about the baby coming without him, dealing with pregnancy hormones and the stress of it all. He had not really considered all of that until she asked the crazy question. He desperately needed to get things done and get back. But he was waiting on others and trying to do what he thought was best for the family by having everything completed before he returned. He prayed for his wife and children and for progress on the job as he continued with the projects at hand.

Yom Sheni (Second Day)

Not having slept much, Emily woke up late and tired, missing her usual quiet time before the children awoke. Not getting enough exercise, her back was beginning to ache and her feet swell. After breakfast, she took the children to the markets, just to get them out of the house and get herself moving. They walked past the first shop where the man had ice pops for sale in a little cooler on the sidewalk. Though it was only mid-morning, it was getting hot already. Emily knew the children wanted one, but they had been trained not to beg. Once she told them 'no' they accepted it and followed her down the street, as she held Moshe and Natanyah's hands. It was easier to resist ice pops than rabbits.

They visited for a few minutes with various shop owners, then crossed to the other side of the street to the little grocery by the Post Office. Emily wanted to get some baking soda with which to make toothpaste. Inside the store, she was not able to find what she wanted, so they left and walked west past the clothing shops. As they strolled, Armando spotted the elderly man who had given them his lunch two weeks before. He was pulling a cart behind him partially full of aluminum cans. Armando pointed him out to Mama, who told the older two, "Go buy him something to eat. Get something in cans so it will keep if he doesn't want it right away."

They gladly left on a new assignment quickly walked to the busy street, waited for a break in cars, taxis, and buses, then crossed and went to the Floridians store, where they bought a can of corn and one of tuna. While they were in the open-front shop, the man disappeared down the street, and when they came out, they had lost him. They quickly ran in the direction they had last seen him, looking down each alley. When they spotted him again, Armando waited at the main street and Briana slowed to a quick walk, caught up to him, and gave him the cans of food. It was not much, just a token to thank him for giving them his lunch that day, but

Chapter 26   *Arnav*

he was touched and very grateful. He instantly put the cans in his cart, placed both hands on Briana's head and spoke blessings over her in Hebrew. It was not important that she had not understood all his words. She came away knowing she had been blessed.

She quickly returned to Armando and as they made their way up the sidewalk to join the others, they heard a woman calling from behind them, "*Yeladim! Yeladim!*"

They turned to see a middle-aged blonde woman. Not seeing any other children around and realizing she was calling them, they stopped and turned to face her. She handed each of them a white palm-sized booklet of the Psalms in Hebrew, and said in Hebrew, "Read this every day and get wise."

The children thanked her and assured her they would read them, then walked quickly to meet Mama as she crossed the busy street nearer their home. They walked home together as the older children told the story of what had just happened. When they arrived, they got back into their customary activities of lunch and then made soaps while others colored and the little ones lay down with Mama. When she awoke, she presented an idea that had come to her at the ice pop cooler. "Who wants to rub Mama's feet?"

The children looked at her as if they had not understood what she had just asked. She expounded, "I'll pay two shekels for ten minutes of foot massage. One ice pop costs two shekels."

All at once she had seven volunteers. "One at a time," she instructed. "Armando, you and Briana can take first shift, one on each foot."

They each diligently worked for the ten minutes and Mama's feet were greatly relieved. Briana stopped and turned her side over to Victor, while Armando continued, wanting to earn more money. Each child got their turn and was able to work for as long as they wanted, most tiring out at the end of their ten minutes, but each earning at least enough to buy one ice pop. Emily then sent the older four to the nearby shop to get a whole package, storing the extra ones in the freezer as payment for future foot massages. Emily loved to see the children excited and happy, and wished she knew how to get the same response out of them by giving them better quality things. She reasoned they were just too wealthy, too well off. They normally ate like kings, the best of the best - fruits, vegetables, nuts, seeds, clean meat, and dairy. All of those things were so common to them that they were often taken for granted. She praised Yah for the life of plenty to which He had allowed them to live thus far and prayed that the children would see how blessed they truly were.

Late in the afternoon, when businesses opened in Tennessee, Emily called the phone company to remove the long distance package they had put on for the New Yorkers and to make it more economical for David to call Israel

245

Pedaling Home   Part 2 – The Scattering

for the next few days that he would be staying at the house. The children played with *Arnav*, sharing him with their friends until time for supper.

Monday

David went to Cookeville, bought groceries and gas, then to the spec house to check on things. The deck man was finished and the painters were still working. The plumber was already at the restaurant working on the final restroom plumbing and some gas lines. And the Oklahoman called to say she was getting ready to leave.

Yom Shlishi (Third Day)

Emily and the children busied themselves with their usual activities, then delivered pretty soaps to friends and went the beach since it was day two of wearing their clothes. When they returned in the afternoon, Elena surprised them with a loaf of hot, freshly-baked Russian fruit-filled bread. Armando and Briana ran to the store to buy milk to go with their special treat, and they gave thanks for it and for Elena and their other new friends in Israel.

The ladies visited for a good part of the afternoon. Emily enjoyed talking with Elena. She was kind and funny, and very helpful with Emily's Hebrew. When she spoke, if Emily did not understand something, she sometimes went to great lengths using hand motions and funny facial expressions in order to convey the message of the word or phrase that had been unfamiliar to Emily. And when Emily misspoke, she corrected her, which was of great help in improving her Hebrew.

Emily's Story

During their conversations, Elena told of how she was born again and what brought her, her late husband, and young Olga to Israel several years before. Afterward, she began questioning Emily about her salvation experience and why the family kept what Elena had referred to as 'the Jews' *Shabbat.*'

Emily explained, "When I was seven years old, my parents gave me a whole Bible. Up until then, I had only had a little New Testament. My dad was my pastor and my parents served as home missionaries, planting Southern Baptist Churches in Wisconsin, Minnesota, and Iowa. Excited about my new Bible, I began reading it from the first page, like I did all the other books. At the start of chapter two, I read that God rested on the seventh day, blessed it and made it holy. I went to my dad and asked him why we rested on the first day when God rested on the seventh. He told me it was because Jesus rose on the first day. I didn't really understand how that answer went with that question, but he was my dad and the pastor, so I accepted it, and went on.

Chapter 26   *Arnav*

"But as I continued reading my Bible, I kept coming across this 'sabbath' on the seventh day and never saw how or why it changed. I continued asking questions, but after a time it became obvious that my questions were becoming an irritation. So I began asking my Sunday School teachers and others I thought also knew the Bible well. Upon moving to a bigger church in Tennessee when I was ten, I got a new pastor, so asked him my questions. I kept getting the same answers, but they just didn't make sense with what the Bible was saying. So I tried to ignore the questions and just do what I was taught, even though I didn't understand. I read the entire Bible, but never saw anything change concerning the Sabbath.

"To make a long story short, I went on with my life, straying from my Father in heaven, repenting and coming back to him, wondering about the Sabbath, among other things, burying my questions, straying again, and the cycle continued. The world and most of the church would have considered me a good person, but I was into things that I ought not to have been. I lived my life for myself, the way most Americans are taught to do, and became very successful in the field I entered, accomplishing the goals I had set out for myself by the time I was 30 years old. I went to church, read my Bible, and prayed regularly, which was easy working on the ranches, most of the time alone on the back of a horse. I had a relationship with my Father through the one I knew as Jesus at the time, but I was basically running my own life, not really considering what He would want me to do.

"I began to make bad choices and He allowed me to wreck my life. I wasn't really giving Him the credit he deserved, anyway. I knew He had given me talents and abilities, but I just wasn't really living for Him. I was living for me. When I wrecked my life, I was in the pit of despair. I cried out to Yah (who I knew as 'God'), 'Father, I've made a mess of my life. I don't want to live for me anymore. I see what I can do. I want to live for you alone.' That was about the time David and I married, and we were both at the bottom looking up.

"Our relationship had been built on study of the scriptures, and we continued in that, wanting to do whatever the Bible said, knowing that it was His words to us. After Briana was born, the Sabbath question really started bothering me again. I cried out to Father and said, 'I'm tired of this question. I have to have *your* answer. I'm going to read this book from cover to cover, and by the time I'm done, I want your answer. I don't care what anyone else says. I'm going to do what *you* say.'

"I began reading three chapters in the Old Testament and three in the New every day. Some days I couldn't get that much done, with two babies, but I did as much as I could. Within a few weeks, I had the answer, but didn't want to stop reading, in case it got changed somewhere. It took me about a year to completely finish reading, but once I did, I had the answer. The seventh day is still His Sabbath.

247

"I was sharing what I was reading with David, but he ridiculed me, saying I was just rebelling against my dad. Once I finished reading the scriptures and was convinced that the Sabbath was still the seventh day, I had to find out how it got changed. I began researching history and found that in the fourth century AD, Emperor Constantine officially changed the Sabbath to Sunday, threatening persecution to all who remained true to the Biblical Sabbath. I knew that no man had the authority to change the Father's commands, so I continued refraining from work on that day, as I had begun when I saw from the scriptures that it never changed.

"In the meantime, David said he was going to study it out to prove me wrong. We were attending, and very active in a Baptist church at the time, so he first went to talk to the pastor, then another pastor, then others that he thought were knowledgeable. Before he'd leave, I'd ask what he was going to ask them and he'd tell me. I'd tell him what they would say, and what the scriptures said, and he'd walk out the door. When he'd come back, I'd ask him what they told him and he'd admit that they said exactly what I'd said they would, and that it didn't match up with what the scriptures taught. After six months, he came to me and said, 'I've proved myself wrong.'

"At that time we were moving and soon found a seventh day church. But as we continued studying, *Abba* showed us that His feasts were not strictly Jewish feasts, as we had been taught. They were meant for all of His people. The New Testament was clear that when we turn to Him, we become His people, part of Israel, so we knew the feasts were for us. We also learned about the names at that time, and began changing more and more things in our lives. We had to stop celebrating Christmas and Easter because they're not Biblical feasts, and when we found out they were actually pagan festivals that had been 'converted' to Christianity, and by the very Constantine who 'changed' the Sabbath, we had to get away from them, too. So that's basically how we got where we are today. We now see that the New Testament message never contradicts the Old. It establishes it. Paul even said that."[169]

The conversation continued until Emily was mentally exhausted from using her new language and Elena needed to go home to prepare supper. Emily reminded the children to thank her again for the delicious bread before she left.

She was glad for Elena's visit. She was always rejuvenated to share with others what Yah had done in her life, and always prayed it would help them. And the conversations helped keep her mind off of her life's turn of events that she was still not accepting joyfully, not realizing that they were being set before her by her loving heavenly Father for the purpose of training her to more fully trust in Him and be grateful for all of the good

---

[169]Rom. 3:31 Do we then make void the law through faith? God forbid: yea, we establish the law.

Chapter 26   *Arnav*

things that He has and does for her. Just as she wanted her children to trust her and be grateful for the things she gave them, knowing that what she gave them was better than what they wanted themselves, her Father wanted her to trust Him and realize that the way He was working things out in her life was for her own good. He had shown her His Sabbaths, His feasts, His names, and other aspects of His instructions. Now He was showing her how to more fully trust in Him. In time, she would learn, but not until she released her own desires and submitted to His will like a well-trained horse readily bends to the slightest touch of its knowing master.

Tuesday

David cared for the animals, then went to town. The spec house was coming along nicely, and the Hood Man finally showed up at the restaurant, but David was getting frustrated about his slow pace in getting the hood installed. The plumber continued to work on the gas and plumbing, installed the hot water heater and got far enough along that David could start building the wall to make a storage room separate from the kitchen. When he finished at the restaurant, David sent him to the spec house to work on the final plumbing there. Both places were almost ready for inspections. His faithful people continued to work late in order to help him get the jobs finished, knowing that he now had to drive almost an hour home in the evenings to care for the animals at the farm.

David, too, was in the midst of spiritual training and growth, and not recognizing that there was a higher reason for the things occurring around him, he never stopped to realize the frustration being caused him by so many was being used by his heavenly Father to gently draw him closer, to show him what was really important in life. He had not yet learned that when someone's irresponsible behavior caused him strife, it was *Abba*'s way of trying to get him to see his own areas of failing to be responsible; that when someone's laziness caused him trouble, it was *Abba*'s way of showing him his own areas of laziness; that when someone's dishonesty made him angry, it was *Abba*'s way of showing him his own areas of dishonesty; that when things did not go his way, he needed to check to be sure that his way was lined up with the perfect way of his Creator. In time, he would learn the lessons, but just as his propane torch had to heat the copper pipe to the right temperature before it would submit and bend, he needed to be heated through circumstances to the point of bending in submission to the will of his Creator.

27 - Chatul[170]

Yom Revi'i (Fourth Day)

After breakfast, Armando, Briana, Victor and Isabel went to the dumpster with a bag of trash and took the opportunity to snoop around for treasures. As they looked over the things people no longer wanted and had set out, Briana peeked in the dumpster, "Hey, Armando, help me up. There's a broomstick in there."

He gave her a leg up, and she climbed in, pulled out the broomstick, handed it to him, and then grabbed a wooden chair that she passed to him, as well, while Isabel served as look-out. She got out, took the broomstick from Armando, and they turned to go around the dumpster to begin their short walk home, when Isabel heard a faint noise and said, "Listen! What's that?"

"What?" asked Briana.

"The noise. Listen!" she exclaimed as she stopped.

The other three stopped and listened, then heard the faint cry of a young kitten. They all four listened carefully to hear the faint cry and figure out from where it came. Armando and Briana got on their hands and knees on opposite sides of the dumpster to look underneath. "There it is!" said Armando. Give me the stick!"

The children all knew if they did not rescue the kitten, it would be crushed to death when the truck came. It was nestled in the tracks that the prongs of the truck stuck into in order to lift and dump the large, construction sized bin. Victor took the broomstick from Briana and quickly handed it to Armando, who carefully slid it inside the small rectangular track, as the kitten continued to cry. He gently pushed it with the rounded end of the broomstick until the entire broomstick was inside the track. "Get me something else! This stick's not long enough," he said.

Briana spotted a small stick of wood lying under the dumpster and passed it to Victor, who passed it on to Armando. He used it to push the broomstick until the kitten was close enough to Briana that she could squeeze her little hand into the hole and grasp one of its tiny paws between her first and second finger. She pulled the scared and lonely creature out

---

[170]*Chatul* – Hebrew for 'cat.'

Chapter 27   *Chatul*

and cuddled it in her hand, inspecting it. Its eyes were more closed than open, and it was too young to stand on its little legs.

Armando picked up the broomstick, but in their excitement, they forgot about the chair. Victor and Isabel were in the lead as they raced home and ran through the back yard, Victor's shrill voice screaming, "We got a cat!"

Just before they arrived, Elena had popped up over the fence at the front porch and was visiting with Emily. The children came rushing through the house, now trailed by the three younger ones, all full of excitement at their new find.

Emily and Elena both turned to see what all the commotion was about as the seven children came bustling out the front door, Briana gently holding the kitten. Emily's "Aww" was sharply interrupted by Elena's, "*Ma ze?*"

"A baby kitten," replied Emily.

"AHHH!" screeched Elena, then continued in Hebrew, "It's no good! Get rid of it!"

Emily asked what they should do with it, to which Elena replied, "Kill it! It's a cat! There are hundreds of cats here!"

Emily laughed, taking the kitten from Briana to inspect it. She estimated its age at under two weeks. Elena could not believe that her neighbors were going to try to save a cat. Knowing her advice was not to be heeded, and seeing that Emily had been distracted from their friendly chat, she waved, "Shalom", then popped down out of sight as she went to her house.

Emily took the kitten inside, followed by seven little people, and had Briana get the milk that was left over from *Shabbat* from the refrigerator. She poured a little in a dish, and stuck a finger into it, putting a drop on the kitten's mouth. He licked it enthusiastically, giving everyone hope that he would be all right. Emily told them, "We need to take it to the pet store to get some special milk and a bottle. He's very young and I don't remember the recipe to make special milk for little kittens."

They put him in the cage with *Arnav*, thinking it would be good to let the people at the pet store see him in case they could recommend something that would help his scraggly condition. They walked out of the house, Emily carrying the cage with *Arnav*, and their new pet, *Chatul*.

Down the street and past the pylons they walked, crossing Weisman and continuing in the direction of the pet shop. One of the Russian girls, a little older than Briana, from a few streets over that sometimes visited the family met them on the sidewalk, and Emily happily showed her their new pet. With a horrified look on her face and in a stern voice, she said in Hebrew, "Oh, *no!* A cat with a *rabbit!* It's not good! The cat will *eat* the rabbit!"

251

Emily smiled and told her, "They'll be fine. He's just a tiny baby. They need each other right now. We're going to get some milk for it."

Her face still showed questions when the family told her, "Shalom" and started walking again in the direction of the pet store toward the other side of town. They arrived a few minutes later and entered the little shop with the distinctive smell. The owner recognized the family as the ones who had been in to buy things for their new rabbit and was glad to help them find some milk replacer, a small bottle, and two kinds of food for the kitten, one dry and one moist in a can. Emily asked him, "What about Arnav? Does he need something more than the feed and salt?"

Orphans

The shop owner recommended mineral drops and assured Emily that he would be fine. Emily thought he already looked better, but was glad for the confirmation from the pet store owner. They purchased the items, then walked home, poured the special milk in the bottle and heated it in a pan of hot water before feeding the hungry kitten. His eagerness to nurse left everyone encouraged about his condition, as well. After the feeding, Natanyah took him and lay down on her mat, soon asleep, the need for ears satisfied by the soft little kitten.

The whole family was looking forward to David's return in a few days. Emily made a list on the calendar of little things she hoped he could bring back with them, including baking soda to make toothpaste. She had been unable to find any soda in Israel, not knowing what it was called there or how to describe it. She also wanted him to bring some colorful bandanas, since several of the young girls around really liked the ones their girls wore, and some small jugs of sorghum molasses from their Mennonite friends to share with some of their new special friends in the Land.

Wednesday

David left the farm and went to get pipe for the plumber to finish at the spec house. Later in the day, he passed the Mechanical Inspection at the restaurant. All that was left were a few details before he would be ready for the Final Inspection. He went to work on those with some of the subs while the others continued to ready the spec house for sale.

Chapter 27   *Chatul*

Yom Chamishi (Fifth day)

Emily was thankful that they had become an animal shelter. It gave another avenue for the children to expend their energies as they cared for their two orphaned critters. Between that and making soaps to give to their friends at the various shops, they seemed to be very content. Isabel, Rebeka, and Moshe particularly enjoyed the animals, and *Chatul* took up with Natanyah right away. After lunch was over, Emily sat on the front porch talking to Armando, Briana, and Victor as they told about their play times with their new friends. When she stepped inside to lie down with Natanyah, she was surprised to see her already asleep. *Chatul* was curled up in the blonde locks beside her face, Natanyah's fingers caressing the kitten as if it were Mama's ears. Emily was glad to see her finding something else for comfort. With the birth of the new baby, Natanyah's times with Mama would be more limited. Emily, heavy with baby and needing rest, lay down beside them anyway.

The older children kept themselves quietly busy coloring and reading. After nap time, Emily went to the refrigerator to get food out for supper. As she stepped back through the kitchen door with her hands full of vegetables, she felt a crunch beneath her foot. Stepping aside, she saw the biggest roach she had ever seen, over three inches long! She called to the children who came running. Setting the food down on the counter, she turned and joined the children squatted in a circle marveling at the fatally wounded giant. As her attention span came to its end, knowing work needed to be done, she stood to continue with her duties, deciding not to ask for help since a biology lesson was taking place amongst the young students. Just as she took a step toward the counter she saw a movement and turned to see a parade of ants marching toward the carcass. She announced it to the children who parted their circle to watch what was going on with the ants.

To everyone's amazement, hundreds of ants appeared one by one in rapid succession from a small hole in the tile just in front of the standing cabinet. They marched directly to the giant roach, made a circle around it, and then in perfect unison, picket it up, marching it back to the tiny hole as if they were its pall bearers. As they reached the hole, which was visibly too small for the giant roach to fit through, the family was even more amazed to watch as the army of pall bearers and assistants somehow, without dismembering their deceased, worked and wiggled the carcass until it did indeed go down.

Everyone was silent, a rare event in a family with so many young children, as they stared at the last of the army descending to the underworld, still wondering how it had been possible to accomplish such a feat. Once the last ant was out of sight, the questions and responses came flying one after another. They had witnessed a marvelous act of their Creator. Not only was He awesome, mighty, and powerful, they concluded that He must have delighted in putting on a custom show for their benefit, and Emily led them in thanking him for it.

253

Some girls from across the dumpster street came and invited Briana and the others to a birthday party. The Varela girls quickly gathered some of the soaps and pretty gifts they had made and the family walked the short block to the house with the little shaded pond full of large goldfish. They were served ice cream and other treats as Emily visited with the ladies of the house. The mother of the birthday girl was due to have twins any day.

Thursday

After his normal morning time in the scriptures and prayer and then caring for the animals on the farm, David began his day calling the painters and framers to line up the jobs. He called Emily, and she shared some of her recent conversations with him. David encouraged her and gave her additional scriptures supporting what she had told the ladies. He encouraged her in the work she was doing there with the children and with sharing the truth of the gospel with friends and neighbors as the opportunity arose. David then phoned the Oklahoman for a progress check and called Emily back to say that confirm that the woman was still on schedule to leave.

On the way into town, he stopped at the siding place, and then the supply store to get more paint, downspouts for the gutters, grass seed and straw for the lawn, as well as other supplies he needed to finish up the remaining details at both jobs. He paid the framer, and then helped the subs at the restaurant.

B'hai Gardens

Yom Shishi (Sixth Day)

The day had arrived to finally accompany Nikolay to B'hai Gardens. Emily did not like the idea of going without David, but did not know when he would ever return and was tired of postponing Nikolay. Besides, she knew she really did need to get out more and get her mind off of her situation. So she and the children stopped and got some milk and sweet breads since they would be easy to eat on the go, then caught the appropriate buses, riding into the big city on the hill of Haifa, overlooking the Mediterranean. Once off the last bus, they ate their breakfast before walking up the street to where they were to meet Nikolay.

As usual, he was happy to see them, and led them into the entrance of the gardens. They waited until the tour guide determined the appropriate number of people was there. One young lady wearing shorts and a small top was kindly asked to cover herself according to the rules of the gardens. Not wanting to adhere to the policy, she left with her party, and the rest of those waiting for the tour walked out of the shaded area, following the guide as he described the beautiful gardens, told stories, and provided information about the B'hai religion. Until that time, the family had not known of the religion of B'hai.

They saw the tomb of the prophet, but the spectacular part of the place was the absolutely beautiful and orderly gardens that were terraced down the side of a great, steep hill, facing the Sea. The children enjoyed the tour, as well, and when it was over, Nikolay gave them the special treat of riding the underground train. They did not need to go anywhere, but he knew riding the train would be fun for them, so had to share the experience.

Emily asked him if he knew of a place she could get sandals. She had looked in Kiryat Yam, but could not find any to suit her. Her favorite ones had been worn so much that there were holes in the bottoms of both of them. They only looked like sandals from the top. He knew of some shops, so the family followed him up and down stairs and hills through the steep city of Haifa, Emily doing her best to keep up with the young, fit cyclist, as she waddled along holding the hands of Natanyah and Moshe.

They checked in a couple of shops, but all they could find were dress sandals. She needed something useful, walking sandals, but she wanted her toes covered because she found that type to be more durable for different types of activities, particularly in her current situation, riding bicycles. Finally, they entered a Russian shop and Nikolay explained what Emily wanted. She liked one pair of leather sandals they brought her, except for the slight heel, having gone nearly barefoot for quite some time. But they were the closest thing she had seen to what she wanted, so after Nikolay negotiated the best price, she bought them, then put her old, favorite ones in the bag to take home. They stopped at a couple of other stores before Nikolay showed them how to get back to a different bus stop than the one at which they had arrived, and told them what bus number to take. He was always so helpful.

They returned home, having been busied in one of the most beautiful places they had ever seen, and tired out from the additional shopping.

Friday

The deck man called David first thing in the morning to update him on the spec house. David then called to check on Emily, and found her at B'hai Gardens. He decided to wait and call back around noon his time, so as to not distract her from the tour. He went to the restaurant and was annoyed to see the hood work had not progressed sufficiently. When he called Emily again, she and the children were lying on the back porch under the stars, some already asleep. He let her know that since no one was at the farm, and the stalling of the restaurant job was out of his control, he was going to have to postpone his trip back again. Though she had seen it coming, it was hard for her to accept. They decided that after *Shabbat*, she would change the tickets again to have him depart Sunday the 21st, arriving in Israel on *Yom Sheni* (Second Day). By then, there would be less than a week for them to be back on the bicycles. Her hopes and dreams of their time together in Israel was fading.

The workers reseeded the skimpy patches of grass at the spec house; the plumber finished hooking up the sinks; and other laborers helped out with miscellaneous jobs at both places.

Psalms with Sarah

The family awoke to another beautiful *Shabbat*, the third one they had been separated from their leader, and continued with the activities that had become the norm for them. After synagogue, Emily asked Sarah if she would mind coming over and reading the Psalms to them after lunch. She showed her the little white prayer books that the lady had given Armando and Briana a few days before. She seemed delighted and honored again at the invitation. The day was relaxing and the family enjoyed their new pets.

Sabbath

David woke up late at the farm, after getting a good night's sleep, again thankful for being commanded a day of rest. He was so thankful *Shabbat* began at evening. Otherwise, he would have worked late again the night before.

He left around noon with his grape juice and drove east toward the home of some of his helpers for fellowship, study and worship. He had a peaceful day there, mostly dozing on the couch out of exhaustion as the study and music lulled him to sleep.

After *Shabbat*, David left the town of Livingston and drove south toward the spec house in Cookeville, coordinating on the phone with the others to meet him there. Several joined and helped with various projects – painting, laying tile, touch-ups, and clean-up - until late into the night again. David was thankful for the help and support of the others, and on his way back to the farm that night prayed for them and their families who were also making a sacrifice to help his family.

28 – Mexican Surprise

Week 6   *Yom Rishon* (First Day)   9/14-15

Emily, not able to sleep anyway, counted the hours until she knew *Shabbat* would be over in Tennessee. She admired the moonlit faces of her seven sleeping blessings as she felt the kicking of the one growing in her womb. Remembering Moshe's birth, she wondered if she might have the baby before David returned.

~ ~ ~

It was early in 2004, when they learned they were pregnant with their sixth child. They had planned to go to Mexico to visit David's family in October, but moved their trip up a month to be sure they would be home in time to deliver there with the midwife. When they got the *aviv* barley[171] report from the land of Israel, they realized they had planned to be in Mexico during Sukkot. The year before was the first time they had celebrated, camping in the hay of their pole barn for the week. David had continued to work on the days that work was not prohibited. After guarding that feast the best they knew how from the scriptures and seeing the blessings that were being poured out on their family because of walking in obedience to their Father's instructions, they wanted to share the beauty of it with others. They decided to go into the Sierra Madre desert mountains where some of David's family lived among the Tarahumara Indians, travel to a village they knew, buy a cow from a local rancher, slaughter it and invite all the locals for miles around to the great feast, where they would teach them the scriptures. David had family and friends in the area who he thought would be open to the idea and, as time went by, they got more specific with their plans.

The midwife was planning her wedding and was not as attentive to Emily as she had been in the past. It did not bother Emily, who was busy with five children under eight years old, trying to home school, taking care of a farm, and doing accounting and office work for the construction business. She was not worried about having problems with the pregnancy. Everything had been normal on the two previous visits, so neither seemed concerned with prioritizing regular appointments. However, Emily was feeling extremely tired and heavy. She knew her life was too busy, David

---

[171]*Aviv* barley - The beginning of the scriptural new year is dependent upon the barley in the Land having reached the stage of *aviv* (about two weeks from ripe). Once that stage is reported, the following new moon begins the new year.

working five long days per week and just one day on the farm, so attributed the tiredness to that, but wondered at the heaviness. With reason to think she may be further along, she had the midwife return once more before their departure, but measurements showed her to be on schedule.

They drove three days to David's parents' house in Mexico, went through the fast of the Day of Atonement, and then began preparing for their trip to the mountains. The night before they planned to buy all the food they would take with them, David drove across his home city to visit two of his brothers. Emily went to bed with the children in the little brick room on top of his parents' house that had been built for their stay. The floors were unfinished concrete and there was no glass in the windows, making it cool that time of year. A little over an hour after she went to sleep with the children, she woke up wet, rolled out of bed, and realized her water had broken. This had never happened to her before. In her previous five deliveries, the water had not broken until she was pushing the baby out, though she had heard of many women whose water broke hours earlier. Knowing that for her, water breaking had always meant that the baby came within seconds, she instantly wanted David there with her. He had been there for all the previous births and she needed him now, especially since she had no midwife here.

She carefully walked down the uneven concrete steps and to the metal bedroom door of David's parents, cracked it open, and as quietly as she could while still being heard called, "Maggie, Maggie!"

The sleepy voice of David's mother came back, "*Que?*"[172]

Emily continued in Spanish, "I need Davie. My water broke."

She heard her mother-in-law get out of bed and stepped away from the door so she could come out of the room, "What's wrong, my daughter?" she asked.

"I'm having the baby. I need Davie."

"It's OK. He'll be back in a little while."

That was not comforting Emily at all. She knew that when he went to his brother's houses, he often stayed till two or three in the morning, talking about old times and current events in their respective lives. Emily told her again, "I'm having the baby. I need him now. Can someone go get him?"

"Hmm, I'll get his dad."

Emily heard her quietly wake up David's dad and tell him the situation. She heard his response, "He'll be back soon."

---

[172]*Que?* - Spanish for 'What?'

Chapter 28   Mexican Surprise

Again, that was no comfort to Emily. Maggie returned and told her, and Emily, desperate for her husband right then responded, "I'm going to the neighbors to see if they can go get him."

The neighbors that Emily spoke of lived across the dirt street and had a little store in one corner of their house. They were very friendly with Emily, and she did not know of property disputes that had stifled relations with David's family. Maggie went back to her husband, "She says she's going to get the neighbors to get him."

Emily heard the tired voice of her elderly father-in-law as he got out of bed, "I'll see if I can get the truck started and the tires aired up."

That was it! Emily needed her husband *now!* Visions of the elderly man doing mechanic work in the middle of the night flashed through her head. She was not ungrateful, just desperate. She walked back to the door and said, "It's OK. I'm going to the neighbors."

She stepped into the cold night in her wet clothes and barefoot, walked through the gate in the stone fence and across the dirt street to the neighbor's house. It was just after 10 PM and the store was already closed, so she knocked on the window of the lit room. An irritated-looking man peered out the window, then seeing it was the American woman, called his wife, who came out the door of the store. "What's happening?" she asked in Spanish.

Emily explained and asked if she could have someone get David from his brother's house. The neighbor replied matter-of-factly, "Well, gas costs money."

Emily replied, "I'm *paying* for the gas. Can you do it?"

David's mother stepped out of her yard gate and a conversation between the two women ensued. The neighbor agreed that she would give Maggie a ride, then stepped inside to go around back and get the car out of the yard. Maggie sent Emily home to lie down with her babies, Rebeka the youngest, being only 14 months old. By the time Emily got back up the stairs, she heard a familiar diesel car engine and looked out the glassless window to see Maggie opening the driveway gate for David. After pulling the car in and getting out, he asked his mother, "What's wrong? Why are you out here?"

"I was about to go get you. The neighbor was going to take me. Emily thinks she's having the baby. Her water broke."

David was shocked. Neither of them expected the baby to come for another month. Was something wrong? He had just arrived at his brother's house, gotten out of the car and greeted them when he got the

259

impression that he needed to go back. He said, "*Nos vemos,*"[173] to his brothers and came right home, arriving before the neighbor even had her car out of their yard. He looked up to the window, saw Emily standing there and called, "What's the matter?"

Emily: My water broke. The baby's coming.

David: What do you want me to do?

Emily: I don't know. Stay with me.

Maggie: What are you going to do?

David: I don't know.

Maggie: Do you want to go to Juanita's?

Juanita was the midwife who had delivered David and all of his brothers and lived just across the river that was the boundary for the family's yard.

David called to Emily: Do you want to go to Juanita, the midwife?

Emily: I don't know.

David: Well, what do you want to do? Stay or go?

Confused by the whole series of events and the possibilities that crossed her mind, and not wanting to leave the other children, all she could say was, "I don't know."

Maggie told David, "It would be good to go to Juanita's, where you can have the help of someone who knows."

David ran up the steps, saw Emily's wet clothes and said, "Let's go to Juanita's."

Emily asked, "What about the babies?"

"My dad will be here for them. They'll be fine," he assured her.

Emily got a change of clothes and David helped her down the stairs and to the car. Maggie got in the back seat and they drove out the gate, slowly dodging the potholes in the dirt street, then across the bridge over the river to Juanita's house. David knocked on the metal door, but heard nothing. After knocking again he heard a stirring, and a woman came to the door. David said, "I need Juanita. My wife's having a baby."

---

[173]*Nos vemos* - Spanish for 'See you.'

Chapter 28   Mexican Surprise

The kind woman replied, "She's not here. She's in the United States."

David thanked her, got back in the car, gave his wife and mother the news, and asked again, "What do you want to do? Go to the hospital?"

"No!" was the quick reply. She had never had a baby in a hospital and did not want to start now. "I think we should call the midwife. It's early for the baby. We need to find out what to do, find out if it's OK or not."

David drove the opposite direction he had gone the hour before, to the nicer house of another brother, one with indoor plumbing and a telephone. As they drove, Emily began having contractions. She begged him to hurry, afraid she would deliver in the car. He did hurry on the main paved street, but once turning off, had to carefully dodge the huge potholes and rocks on the smaller *barrio*[174] roads. When they arrived, he knocked on the metal door and his sister-in-law, Luli, came to the door, as Maggie and Emily got out of the car. "What's the matter?" she asked.

"Emily's having the baby and it may be too early. Can we use your phone?"

"Of course!" she replied, picking up a phone card and directing David to the phone.

David dialed the codes necessary, then the phone number that Emily handed him, and gave the phone to her. Waking from sleep, the midwife answered, "Hello?"

"It's Emily Varela," she announced, wanting to make sure the midwife was awake enough to know who she was speaking with.

Midwife: Yes, is everything OK?

Emily: We're in Mexico and my water broke. We don't know what to do.

Midwife: According to the records, you're at 36 weeks. That's a little early.

Emily: What does that mean? What can go wrong?

Midwife: The baby could need oxygen. How far are you from the nearest hospital?

Emily relayed the question to David in Spanish, the language she naturally spoke in Mexico. He looked at Luli, who said, "About ten minutes."

Emily told the midwife, who replied, "That's too far."

Emily, swallowing hard: Is there a chance the dates could be off?

---

[174]*Barrio* -Spanish for 'neighborhood.'

261

Midwife: Well, your measurements are consistent with the dates we have...

Emily heard a click: Hello? Hello!

Luli: The phone card probably ran out. It uses a lot of minutes to call the U.S.

David: Where can we get another one?

Luli: I don't know. It's late. All the stores around here are already closed.

David again asked Emily, "Do you want to go to the hospital?"

Emily replied, "No, but I don't want to do something stupid, either. What if it needs oxygen?" She stood and said, "I need to go to the bathroom."

Luli, a very diplomatic, down to business woman said, "I'm going to call a friend who can help."

David took Emily down the hall to the large tile bathroom, the floor stepping down a few inches into the shower beside the sink. She said, "We should just stay here. That way the mess will be easy to clean up."

David admired the way his wife always thought ahead and was considerate of others. She complemented him in that, as his calm, laid back ways complemented hers. He comforted her through the contractions as they discussed whether or not to go to the hospital. After making her call, Luli and Maggie joined the conversation at appropriate times from outside the bathroom door. Luli told David, "The hospital will not let you go in with her."

Emily was adamant that she did *not* want to go, especially under those conditions. He had been her support in the birth of all of the babies. Spanish was not her first language. What if they misunderstood something she said? She had already seen that when she tried to tell Maggie about her water breaking, since the phrase in Spanish does not tranclate literally from English. And she had never delivered in a hospital. What if they tried to make her take drugs? No, she just could not do it. But what if the baby needed oxygen? It was such a difficult choice. Where did faith end and stupidity begin? How does one even know the answer to that?

As they discussed those questions and wondered what to do, they heard activity in the hall, Luli rushing to the front door. Her friend had arrived, and the couple quickly learned she had called the ambulance. She opened the door as the paramedic asked, "Where's the woman in labor?"

Luli led him down the hall as she said, "Back here, in the bathroom."

Chapter 28   Mexican Surprise

Emily and David looked each other in the eye, each searching the other to see what they were thinking.

Luli: She doesn't want to go to the hospital. She's had all her babies at home.

EMT: What is she? Mennonite?

There were nearly 200 German Mennonite camps surrounding the city, and the locals were familiar with many of their customs, including home births still being quite common.

Luli: No, she's American.

Driver: I came to take her to the hospital. If she doesn't want to go, I can't help.

David and Emily continued looking at each other. David said, "Let's pray."

As Luli used her diplomatic skills on the paramedic in the hallway, David and Emily quietly cried out to their Father in heaven, asking for His guidance. They only wanted to live for Him. They wanted His will in their lives. They had trusted Him in all the births of their babies and were trusting Him with this one, but was He trying to tell them they needed professional help this time? How could they know? David asked, "Please, Father, give us a sign. Let us know for sure if we are to stay here or go to the hospital. In Y'shua's name, *Amein*."

Emily agreed, "*Amein*."

As they ended the prayer, they heard Luli, still questioning the EMT, "What will they have to do before they can leave the hospital?"

The driver answered, "The baby will have to be vaccinated for Hepatitis B..."

Emily's eyes instantly met David's again. "That's our answer!" she said.

"Yep," confirmed David.

Vaccine Lesson

Three years before, when Isabel was a baby, they still followed the advice of the medical community and took her to be vaccinated. They were naturalists about most everything else, but because of Emily's history in the commercial cattle business, and the fact that she had given hundreds of thousands of vaccines to cattle, the thought that vaccinating children possibly not being in their best interest had never crossed her mind. So off they went for the scheduled vaccines for their fourth newborn. A happy

263

baby going in, Isabel began screaming uncontrollably almost immediately after she received one of the shots. As soon as they were finished, Emily put her to the breast to nurse, but she would not stop screaming. Emily became worried because she had never had a baby refuse the breast before. The nurse told her not to worry about it, that she would be fine in a few minutes.

They drove home, Isabel screaming the entire way. Her screaming continued off and on for the next two days, as if she were in excruciating pain. It finally subsided, but not before it caused both parents to seriously reconsider vaccinations. Emily had recently joined MOMYS online, and over the next two months some discussions ensued concerning vaccines and their dangers. Emily had never heard of such things before and was not about to dismiss them after what had happened with Isabel. The more she became aware of the dangers and the lack of real evidence that they were even effective, the more she questioned giving them to her children. She was pressured by family and the medical community to vaccinate, but the more she became educated about the issue, the more concerned she got about ever having one vaccinated again.

As the next vaccination appointment rolled around, Emily got more nervous. She and David began praying for direction, but were not getting an answer. The morning they were scheduled to get the vaccinations, she opened her Bible to read after breakfast, as was their daily custom, and the place they were scheduled to read for that day began with Psalms 91. The first nine verses talked about how those who dwell under the shadow of YHWH's wings, obeying Him, would be protected by Him. The promises continued in verse 10, "There shall no evil befall you; neither shall any plague come near your dwelling."

The timing of that scripture reading gave them their vaccine answer then. They praised Him for answering their prayer and immediately called to cancel the appointment scheduled for later that day. And they never allowed another vaccine to be injected into any of their children after that. In the three years that had transpired, they had learned many more things about the evils and ineffectiveness of vaccines, as well as the outright sinister motives behind many who supported and tried to enforce vaccinating humans. Yah had answered their prayer three years ago by promising His protection on their home. And their decision to trust Him and accept His answer then gave them the answer to the prayer they had just voiced. They would not be going to a hospital that would require their newborn to be vaccinated, much less for a vaccine that was designed to protect from a disease that typically comes from unrighteous behavior.

Ambulance Parking

After the couple confirmed their decision to stay in the bathroom, Luli walked down the hall with the somewhat annoyed and perplexed EMT, as he made his way back to the ambulance. In her diplomatic way, she

Chapter 28   Mexican Surprise

explained more about the situation and asked if he could wait outside until he was needed somewhere else. He consented to her request, called dispatch and got the OK, then told her, "I'll wait outside, but if I get a call, I'll have to leave."

He went to the back, then gave her a packet of birthing supplies, including a clamp, scalpel, and disinfectant. Relieved, she carried it inside and continued to check on the couple as she and Maggie discussed the situation.

Thankful that oxygen was waiting outside the door, but knowing it could leave at any moment, Emily hoped labor would progress quickly, just in case. Within a few minutes, she was ready to push, so David helped her move the few steps to the shower area, where she squatted and delivered. David called to the ladies waiting outside the door to let them know the baby had come, and Luli rushed outside to notify the EMT. He grabbed his bag and entered the house behind her, rushing to the bathroom at the end of the hall. David had thoughtfully unlocked the door just before the delivery, and the man came right in, seeing the couple in the shower, Emily in her Tarahumara skirt that another sister-in-law had made her, and David behind and to her left, holding the little baby, with cord still attached. The EMT set his bag on the tiny sink and, hands shaking, opened the packet he had left them before. David, noticing his trembling hands, said, "I can cut the cord."

He then carefully reached the baby up for the man to take. When the baby boy changed hands, the man lifted him up to keep himself from having to bend over. The abrupt movement painfully jerked Emily, who was still attached to the cord. David cut the cord as the EMT checked the infant and reported that all was well. He appeared to be full term and did not need oxygen. He then had the ladies fill a bowl with warm water and bathed him, something the couple would remember never to do in the future. After seeing all was well, the paramedic departed and the family was left to care for Mama and baby. Emily went to the master bed that had been prepared for them. David brought the baby and laid him on her chest, but he was very cold. They realized the bath had been a big mistake because in the cold fall mountain temperatures he had become chilled from being put into the water. For an hour, the ladies warmed towels in the microwave and laid them on the naked infant who lay on its Mama's skin, trying to get warm enough to want to nurse. By the time he did, he was already named.

Moshe Rafael

The parents had chosen Moshe Rafael as their boy's name before he was born, and had never gotten around to choosing a girl's name. 'Moshe' meant 'drawn out of the water', which now proved to be even more

Pedaling Home   Part 2 – The Scattering

appropriate. And 'Rafael' meant 'El[175] (God) heals.' They had gotten the
names from their understanding of where they were in the eternal scheme
of things. 'Waters' in scripture represented 'peoples, languages, nations,
and tongues.' They had been drawn out of the waters and saved to walk
in the pure ways of the Creator of the universe. And Rafael came from a
verse in scripture that was prophetic concerning what YHWH would do to
His scattered people, Israel, in the last days.[176]

The birth of baby Moshe Rafael came at a time in their lives when they
were intensely aware of their prophetic calling. But when they chose that
particular boy's name, they had no idea he would be born in his Tio[177]
Rafael's house. And later that day, they were questioned by neighbors,
thinking that the reason Rafael was part of his name was because that day
in Catholic tradition was the day of the arch angels, Rafael, being one of
the three. It gave them many chances to explain the spiritual significance
of his names.

The Varela's had planned to leave Mexico in just over a week, celebrating
the final days of the feast of Sukkot with various people whose contact
information they had come across on the Internet and who were on their
path back home. David got to work trying to get the necessary paperwork,
which was no small task since the baby was born at a house with no forms
filled out or signatures of official witnesses.

Besides that, they had driven to Mexico in a seven passenger minivan,
and all five of their children still required car seats when traveling in the
U.S. David found a junk yard that had a bench seat he could use instead
of the two middle bucket seats, then found a booster seat for Armando and
moved all of the children up one car seat, leaving fourteen month old
Rebeka's baby seat for the new baby Moshe.

After visiting several offices trying to get a birth certificate, David was told
by a worker, "Your wife is an American. Just get one when you get back
to Tennessee. It will take at least two weeks for us to get you one here,
since he was not born in the hospital."

The Varelas had left their farm in the care of another family and had to be
back in less than two weeks to pay bills and to release the other family for
obligations they had of their own. David trusted the woman knew what
she was saying, and determined they would get a Tennessee birth
certificate. When he told Emily, she could not see how that made any
sense, but did not know at the time that children of one Mexican parent
born in another country, still received a Mexican birth certificate when they
applied for Mexican citizenship. When she learned this, she concluded

---

[175]El - Hebrew for 'God', abbreviated form of 'Elohim.'
[176]Hos. 6:1 Come, and let us return unto YHWH: for he hath torn, and he will
    heal us; he hath smitten, and he will bind us up.
[177]Tio - Spanish for 'uncle.'

266

that maybe the woman did know what she was talking about, so they decided to wait until they got home the next week.

Little Man Without a Country

When they crossed into the US border, the agent there asked for the passports. Emily was driving at the time and handed them the seven that they had.

"Are these all your children?" the female agent asked.

"Yes," Emily replied, expecting another question as to why one passport was missing. But the officer handed her the passports and waved the family through. They drove home, arriving three days later, then began the process of trying to get a Tennessee birth certificate, being thoroughly scoffed at and told that only people born in Tennessee could get one. When she asked what they were to do, the woman on the phone told her to go back to Mexico where he was born.

Having been warned that they needed to do it right away because the passage of time makes it more difficult, especially in the case of a home birth, the family found someone else to stay in their home for a couple of weeks so they could return on to Mexico, the drive being three days each way. By the time they had made arrangements, over two months had passed and the winter holidays were approaching. When the couple saw a Russell Stover Chocolate Store just off the interstate at the right time for a travel break, they were reminded of the one in Cookeville that sold very inexpensive, good quality chocolates. The family stopped for a break and to buy some small tokens of appreciation to give to kind people they would encounter on their trip.

Two days later, they crossed the Mexican border again, this time in a dangerous situation. Traveling across the border with an undocumented baby was grounds for having him taken by the authorities or professional kidnappers. They had not known that when they crossed into the U.S., but were in even more danger this time, going into Mexico.

Emily was driving when they crossed the border. A few weeks before, she had renewed the license tags on the van and had the paperwork in her glove box, but had forgotten to remove the sticker and put it on her license plate. The border crossing agent checked her tags and said they were expired. Knowing they were not, Emily opened her glove box and pulled out the documentation, handing it to him.

Not amused, in Spanish he declared, "This is no good! This is for last year!"

Emily took it back, surprised to see that she failed to put the sticker on the year before, as well. She looked through the glove box again and found the current paperwork with the stickers to go on the plates, but by this time, the agent was totally frustrated with her and the situation. She got out, cleaned the corners of the plates, preparing to put the stickers on, when he barked, "Move the vehicle over there, out of the way!"

She got in, stickers in hand, and moved the van to the parking area, where she promptly got out and adhered the stickers to their lawful place. Over two months before, when they had come through the first time, they were required to buy a vehicle permit, which they had understood to be for six months. Normally, the border agents check for windshield stickers when a vehicle crosses the border, but in his aggravation, he overlooked it.

Emily waited in the van with the children as well as their tiny 'man without a country' while David did the necessary border crossing paperwork inside. They were very thankful for the sticker they had bought on the previous trip, making it easier to get through this time. At the time of permit sticker purchase, all non-Mexicans coming into the country are required to register and buy permits. Since that had been done previously, no one had to know about undocumented baby Moshe this time, averting the horrible possible scenarios.

They got past border security, and stopped again at the 21 kilometer checkpoint, as required. Night had fallen and David was driving when the kind officer approached his window, saying, "*Buenas noches!*"[178]

"*Buenas noches*," David returned.

The officer continued in Spanish, "Where are you going?"

David: Cuauhtemoc.

Officer: What for?

David, knowing the less he said, the better: To visit family.

Officer: Your vehicle sticker is expired.

David looked at the date and realized it was only a one month sticker. He and Emily both thought they had purchased a six month sticker before. David told the man and said, "What do I need to do?"

The officer kindly replied, "You'll have to turn around and go back to the border to get one."

Emily was horrified, knowing that meant they would have to register everyone in the vehicle again. What would happen when they saw Moshe with no paperwork?

---

[178]*Buenas noches* - Spanish for 'Good night,' used as a salutation after dark.

Chapter 28   Mexican Surprise

Sweet Solutions

The man was very kind, and she knew there was nothing they could do about the situation. As David gently tried to get out of having to go back, Emily told Armando to reach into the back and get a tiny box of chocolates to give to the kind officer. He obeyed, handed one to Mama, who gave it to David, who passed it out the window to the kind man. Upon receiving it, the officer said, "Well, I guess I could just let you go on through."

As David was thanking him, Emily was so excited that she told Armando to get another box. The man was doing them a great favor at his own potential expense. David passed another box out the window and the officer said, "But you'd better hurry. There's an army checkpoint up ahead and they set up about this time of evening."

David thanked him for the additional information and they drove off, praising Yah for His favor in their situation. As they reached the military check point, the soldiers were already setting up. They motioned for the minivan to stop and two young men carrying military rifles nearly as big as they were stepped in front of the van, then began looking in the windows. After asking a few questions, they told David to open the back so the van could be searched.

Underneath the family's bedding was a used computer they were transporting to David's niece. While perfectly legal to import such things into Mexico, the authorities working for their own personal agendas, often confiscated the items and sold them. Computers, even used ones, were very expensive in Mexico and would bring a hefty price. David walked the men to the back of the van, opened the hatch, and just as one of them was about to lift the blanket covering the computer, grabbed a box of chocolate in each hand and stuck them out to the two soldiers, saying, "Do you like chocolate?"

Caught a little off guard, one responded that his wife did, while David stepped back and closed the hatch, telling them, "...something special for your wives."

Once again, the family drove away praising Yah. Upon arriving at David's home the next day, they went to work following the trail of red tape necessary to get the birth certificate. They found the paramedic who signed a form saying he was a witness to the birth, got a statement from a doctor friend, took those statements to the *Registro Civil*,[179] along with official documentation on both of the parents, and were finally given the birth certificate. Once back across the U.S. Border, they stopped and presented the birth certificate and the documentation to U.S. Agents and were given a 'Report of Birth Abroad', the official document necessary for

---

[179]*Registro Civil*-Spanish for Civil Register, office where birth certificates are processed.

someone not born in the U.S. to use in place of a U.S. birth certificate. With that, they were able to secure his U.S. passport.

Because of Moshe's birth experience and the ensuing events, Emily already knew what all would be necessary to get documentation for a child born in another country. Armed with this, she had checked online for more information from Israel, concerning having a baby there whose parents were not Israeli citizens. It was for that reason Emily always carried the number one backpack when they were traveling, since it contained all of the valuable documents. And David carried the number two, which contained copies of all of them, in case something happened to Emily's. Because of their experience with Moshe's accidental birth abroad and all of the ensuing events that occurred in a land border situation, the family was completely prepared for the documentation that would occur at an overseas out of hospital birth.

29 - Turmoil

Emily reflected on more of the amazing stories Yah had allowed to occur in the family's lives, as she frequently felt the kicking of the baby and looked at the moonlit faces of the others. At around 2 AM, she knew it would be nightfall in Tennessee and *Shabbat* would be over there, too. She phoned Byron and had him reschedule David to return in eight days, the first day of the following week. She had to pay an exchange fee, but was thankful that it was cheaper than having to start all over.

The children, having had a full night's sleep, began waking before Mama. Emily slowly got up to begin preparing their breakfast. Isabel, helpful as usual, got out her prized kitchen knife and began cutting fruit. The children were always hungry, it seemed. And Emily felt like she was always tired. David was supposed to leave the next day to return to them the following, but again, he would not. She had lost count of how many times his arrival had been postponed. She was beginning to think he had left them there permanently and wondered what it was that caused him to be so much in love with his job and to have so little interest in his family. The phone call from the week before was forgotten history as one negative thought took hold, then was pushed out of the way with a worse one until she was completely depressed. Finally, around 10:30 AM, knowing David would be asleep, she called anyway.

Sunday

David was startled awake at 2:30 AM by his phone. Emily was always respectful of his sleep time, so he knew something must be wrong. He answered to hear the sobbing of his distressed wife and tried to console her. She seemed inconsolable and began sharing with him the thoughts that were going through her mind. Did he even *plan* to return to them? Was she to have the baby by herself with the help of her children? Did he even love them? Why was his job so important to him? Didn't he care what she was going through a world away from him?

Not being able to answer her questions to her satisfaction, he became angry. Didn't he have enough to worry about with these jobs? He needed his wife *supporting* him, not blubbering about what a hard time she was having! Why couldn't she understand he was working day and night trying to get back to them? How could she possibly accuse him of not loving them? Didn't he just answer all these questions a week ago?

All the stress on both sides of the issue was mounting to the point that they forgot who their enemy was and began attacking each other. David finally ended the call and went back to sleep. Emily went in the bathroom and cried bitterly out of sight and hearing of the children. She knew she would have to do something to get her mind off of the situation, so decided to take them across town when they finished lunch. The walk would do her good.

They made their way to the pet store to get food and a mineral wheel for *Arnav*. On the way back they stopped at the dry goods store and bought two packages of diapers to give to the mother of Briana's friend across the block who had just delivered twins. After stopping at the house, the children all tasted *Arnav's* salty mineral lick wheel and Emily tied it in the cage; then they walked to the friend's house and delivered the diapers to the grateful family. Emily felt better afterward and was glad she had given the children another variation in their lives.

~ ~ ~

Having his deep sleep interrupted during the night caused David to awaken later than he had wanted to. He knew Emily must still be upset, since she hadn't called. He felt badly for not being more sensitive to his pregnant wife, so called and had a good talk with her, just as she was lying down for the night. They both felt better after the conversation.

The animals cared for, he drove to Cookeville, making calls to numerous people one after another, getting things lined up for the day's work. He got more bad news from the Restaurant Owner, who told him that the Hood Man had damaged the drop ceiling, something else David would have to repair. He got to the restaurant where the tile man was working and jumped in to help, as he taught one of his painters some tile tricks. Then he went to work repairing the drop ceiling.

A framer was at the spec house working on the back porch. Things were coming along well there and the house was almost ready to put up for sale. David again worked until after midnight, took Paco home, and then went to the farm for the night.

Playground Questions

Yom Sheni (Second Day)

Today's main activity was going to the library. When they walked in the door one of the librarians, recognizing the family and knowing that Emily always used the Internet while there, told her their Internet was down. So the family all went to the children's section just to the side of the main desk and she read books to the little ones, while the older ones read to themselves. After an hour, they walked back by way of the beach, strolling in the sand and picking up shells, then stopped at the playground for another hour before going home.

Chapter 29   Turmoil

While Emily sat on the bench watching the children speed down the three story slide on smashed two liter soda bottles, a trick they had learned from other Israeli children, a Russian woman approached with her young grandson. She sat next to Emily and began admiring the seven children. She spoke in Hebrew about what a blessing her children were. As they talked, a group of youths came with a hookah pipe and set up camp under the play set in the enclosed place beneath. The grandmother began scolding them about their language and the fact that they were smoking right there in the playground where children were playing. They paid her no heed as they turned their backs and continued smoking.

After telling Emily what bad children those were, she began inquiring of the family, asking the typical questions. As Emily answered them, she asked more, leading to Emily sharing the prophecies of the reunification of the two houses of Israel as described in Jeremiah, Ezekiel, and many other places in the scriptures.

The woman spoke, "You are very knowledgeable of the prophets. And you follow the *torah*. But you're not Jewish?"

Emily replied, "No. I grew up in a Christian home and was taught that Y'shua loves me, that he saved me from my sins, and that he was the Messiah. When I met my husband, because of differences in the two denominations' materials we were using, we agreed to set them aside and study the Bible alone, with only *Abba* to guide us. Soon afterward, He began showing us things that the religions were not teaching according to scripture -- things that were actually contradicting the scriptures.

"We saw that throughout the Bible, the Sabbath was never changed. So we researched and found out that it was the early Roman Catholic Church that actually changed the Sabbath to Sunday. Many people that we knew said that the Sabbath was 'done away with' or that 'Jesus was our Sabbath,' but as we studied the scriptures and let them interpret themselves, we saw that those things were not true. We wanted to live our lives according to the word of Elohim, like I was taught as a child. So we had to leave behind the errors that were being taught and cling to Him and His word.

"After we began to guard His *Shabbat*, He showed us how important His name and the name of His son were. Our Bibles have replaced His name with a title, even though thousands of times, it is written there in the Hebrew and He tells us in His own words that we are to 'call upon His name,' not to call upon a title that replaced His name. He also showed us His feasts and how they are for all of His people, not only the Jews, the House of Judah, but for everyone who chooses Him as their Elohim and chooses to serve Him. He showed us that if we do not obey His commandments, including guarding His *Shabbat* and His feasts, that we don't really love Him. That's why we're here."

273

Pedaling Home   Part 2 – The Scattering

The woman asked, "But you believe in *Yeshu*?"[180]

Emily answered, "No, not *Yeshu*. *Yeshu* is a bad name that the religious leaders gave him. His name is Y'shua, Yehovah's salvation. That's why the religious leaders don't like it. In fact, I think that's why Christianity uses a false name, also. Most Christians don't know they're using a name that he was never called when he walked the earth, but his true name is so significant that the adversary used religion to change it to something of lesser value.

"But, yes, we believe that Y'shua is the Messiah. We see him all over the *TaNaK*. According to the prophets, including Hosea, the house of Israel, the ten northern tribes, was scattered to the winds, but a redeemer would come and gather them together again, bringing in a renewal of Yehovah's covenant which would be written on the hearts of Israel. In other words, once we are redeemed, His instructions will be written on our hearts. We will want to follow them. We will no longer live in rebellion.

"So Y'shua came, lived a sinless life, was persecuted by the Jewish religious leaders because he went against their additions and changes to the written *torah*, then allowed himself to be tortured on a tree, to die the shameful death of one who is cursed,[181] before being raised to live three days and three nights later, like Jonah was in the belly of the fish. There were witnesses to this, more than the two or three required. But religion does not want to accept Yehovah according to His instructions, so they hide the truth. I'm not talking about people. I'm talking about religious spirits that keep us from seeing His truth.

"Scripture is clear that we must obey Him, His instructions of the *torah*. And Y'shua was clear about it as well. So Y'shua himself was persecuted by the Jewish religious leaders, but the message that he taught is being persecuted by Christian religious leaders as they tell their followers that he came to 'do away with' his Father's instructions, that they are 'free' from obeying the *torah*. If a person understands that choosing to obey the *torah* is choosing life, like scripture says, isn't it foolish to 'do away' with it or to desire to be 'free' of it? But that's what most Christian churches are teaching today. So instead of following the example of their Savior, the one who died to redeem Israel, they are eating ham on Easter Sunday and saying they are doing it unto Him.

---

[180] *Yeshu* - Hebrew acronym for '*Yimah Schimo Wezikhro*' meaning 'May his name and memory be stricken out,' used to refer to Y'shua (meaning 'YHWH is salvation') by those in the Jewish religious establishment who are against the idea that Y'shua is the living son of Elohim and the Messiah.

[181] Deut. 21:22-23 And if a man have committed a sin worthy of death, and he be to be put to death, and thou hang him on a tree: His body shall not remain all night upon the tree, but thou shalt in any wise bury him that day; (for he that is hanged *is* accursed of Elohim;) that thy land be not defiled, which YHWH thy Elohim giveth thee *for* an inheritance.

Chapter 29   Turmoil

"The problem is that religion has twisted the teachings of scripture. Christian teachings have twisted the meanings of their own New Testament because centuries ago they hated the Jews and distanced themselves from them in order to prevent being persecuted along with them. Only a remnant continued to follow the teachings of Y'shua, and most of them were killed, martyred. And the name of His son, Yehovah is Salvation (Y'shua) was adulterated through transliteration into Greek, then Latin, then English, changing it to a name that we were never told to call upon, and means nothing, in and of itself. Y'shua came to redeem the adulterous house of Israel that was divorced by Yehovah, as described in Jeremiah.[182] Of course he never transgressed the *torah* or did anything to negate it! He was sent to make a way for those who had!"

The woman declared, "You have inspired me. When I get home, I am going to begin to read the prophets!"

Emily was delighted that she was able to share truths from the scriptures with someone else. And it got her mind off of the fact that today was the day David was scheduled to have begun his trip back. She was often amazed that she could have such wisdom and knowledge in the scriptures, to the extent that sometimes well-studied people would recognize it, yet be so weak emotionally when it came to her marriage. She longed for the day that she would be free from the crippling effects on her emotions that his absences caused. She still had not realized that her loving *Abba* was trying to teach her to depend on Him and long for *His* company, the way she did for that of her husband.

Farm Help

Monday

David called Emily first thing in the morning to let her know that the Oklahoman was due to arrive later in the day to take care of the farm, and things were progressing for him to be able to return the next week. Emily had just left the playground, and shared with him the encounter she had with the Russian woman. They both rejoiced and prayed that her eyes would be open as she studied the prophets.

David took care of the animals, then left the farm and the hilly, wooded areas where there was no cell service, and began calling subs along the way. He went to the restaurant and helped with the paneling and gas line. He called the realtor to make arrangements for listing the spec house. And then he got the call from the Oklahoman, saying she had made it to the farm. He was relieved at that, knowing it would enable him to get a couple extra hours of work done per day instead of doing so much driving.

---

[182]Jer. 3:8   And I saw, when for all the causes whereby backsliding Israel committed adultery I had put her away, and given her a bill of divorce; yet her treacherous sister Judah feared not, but went and played the harlot also.

275

After a productive day on the jobs, David and Paco returned to the farm to show the Oklahoman around and to get additional tools and supplies they would need for the next few days, eliminating any need to return. They picked up the chainsaw so they could cut some unnecessary trees at the spec house, along with various other tools. David met her and the four children she had brought with her in person and expressed gratitude that they had been willing to come on the spur of the moment. He gave her instructions concerning the animals and farm, then he and Paco went back to Cookeville, where David went to sleep in the spec house.

Salt Water Tears

Yom Shlishi (Third Day)

Emily took the children to the library again then back to the beach. She sat on the damp sand and watched the older ones play in the water while the younger ones built sand castles, wondering how they could be so happy while she was so down. In a few minutes, a man appearing to be in his early 30's walked from the sand dunes behind her smiling at no one in particular. He laid his towel on the sand a few meters from Emily on the other side of where the younger children were building a sand castle. She watched him out of the corner of her eye, wondering why he chose that particular place instead of somewhere farther away.

He took off his T-shirt, laid it on his towel and ran, bounding into the water just like a child, the odd smile never leaving his face. He was too close to the older children in the water for Emily's comfort. She had never seen an adult act that way before and it finally occurred to her that he was either high on something, possessed by demons, or both. When she could, she got the attention of the children in the water and signaled them to stay farther away from him. He was not doing anything to threaten them, but Emily knew that could change at any moment.

She sat, watching him play in the water like a little child, smiling and laughing to himself at whatever he found so comical. She thought it ironic that she, a daughter of the King of kings, could sit so miserably, while someone who appeared to be possessed with demons could have such a good time. She could not tell if he were under the influence of drugs or not, but began to feel more and more depressed at the sight of him and the sadness in her own heart. She sat on the hot Mediterranean beach, the salt water licking at her feet, and the sea breeze rolling over her as silent salty tears streamed down her cheeks. She was glad everyone was having too much fun to notice.

When the children began to get tired, she called them together, had them gather their things and they walked to the playground to play until they were dry. The sand would then fall off on the way home, keeping the house cleaner.

Chapter 29   Turmoil

Armando, Briana, and Isabel were invited to a birthday party for the twins of the Family of Ten, who were turning 10 years old. Mama let them go ahead down the back street to their house, where they enjoyed eating cake and playing with toy cars. She brought the younger ones a little while later and visited with the mother when she was not busy with the party out back. Emily stayed on the front patio with the younger children where they entertained themselves with someone else's riding toys. She was glad the community had accepted them as one of their own.

Tuesday

David continued his work, keeping the subs busy and materials on hand for them. As he was paying his framer, the realtor called. "Hey, David, I've got some cabinets in an old house that are messed up and was wondering if you could fix them."

David replied, "I'm sorry, man. I won't have time to do something like that until I get back from Israel in November."

Just after David hung up, the framer, who had overheard the conversation, asked, "Is that something I can do?"

David answered, "Actually, yes. Do you have time?"

"Sure, I'm almost done here."

David immediately called the realtor back and told him, "I've got one of my guys who can do your cabinet job."

They agreed on a price, and the work began that afternoon, making everyone happy. The realtor would get his cabinets done right away. The framer would have more work. And David would make a little on the side since he would be responsible for the job.

30 - Akko

Yom Revi'i (Forth Day)

Nikolay seemed to detect Emily's sadness at not having her husband with her and continued to encourage her to get out and see the many things Israel had to offer. Emily knew their budget did not include money for 'touristing,' but after much insistence, and knowing it would probably be good for them, she decided to take the children to Akko, only five miles north of Kiryat Yam. After breakfast, they fed *Arnav* and *Chatul* and left them in their cage in the back room. Isabel and Rebeka proudly shouldered their purses from the Dead Lady, quite large for little girls of six and five years old, and filled with snacks and water bottles. Armando donned his *yarmulke* and took the backpack containing birth supplies (just in case) and more snacks and essentials. They all walked to the main bus stop in front of the produce market and caught a bus to Kiryat Motzkin.

The bus ride was second only to the wild taxi ride. Armando noticed when paying for the tickets that the driver sat in front of the front tires. When going around sharp curves or a round-about, he effortlessly spun the wheel with a little knob attached. When the bus turned, it leaned, Rebeka, Moshe, and Natanyah afraid at first that it would surely fall, the front corner extended over the sidewalk. Victor laughed with delight as the bus swayed and bounced along and rocked from side to side.

From Kiryat Motzkin, they caught the bus to Akko, having the driver drop them off near the historic section of town. Once at their destination, they stepped off the bus right in front of a falafel shop, and Emily decided they should eat there, not knowing anything about what they would be getting into once they got to their attraction. After enjoying falafel, they cleaned their outdoor table and walked toward the entrance to Old Akko. On the way, they came to a fork in the road with a house in the center of the fork. On the porch sat several young Arab men smoking hookah pipes and loudly laughing with one another. Emily was leading her crew with Armando at the back, as usual, since David was not with them.

As she approached the fork in the road, she noticed the young men looking at them in a threatening way, and turned a little toward the wall to her right so as not to be looking at them. Just as she turned, she saw one of the men get up and turn toward the door of the house. As she went around the corner, she almost crashed into another Arab youth leading a donkey. As she moved closer to the wall to avoid being run over, Armando was reaching the corner, but with his eyes on the men on the porch. The man

Chapter 30 Akko

Emily had seen turn toward the house turned back around with his pants down and did a half nude dance toward Armando, emphasizing his private area. After Armando got around the corner and they came to a wide place in the road, he called Mama, so she stopped and regrouped everyone. Armando told her what had happened and she advised him to be sure and stay even closer to them, making sure the children were safe.

None of the family was familiar with Akko, otherwise known as Acre, one of the oldest continually inhabited cities in the world. The towns they had already experienced in Israel had a mostly Jewish population other than the friendly Druze Osifia. She was amazed at the difference in feel to this Arab part of Akko, not friendly at all. On the contrary, it felt very hostile and she realized that their hostility was directed right at her and the children, though she did not immediately know why. As they entered the courtyard where they could purchase tickets for the tour, they found themselves among a grove of centuries old olive trees. They purchased tickets and the woman gave Emily two radio-like hand-held tour guides, which she programmed into English for her. Since they were eight people, Armando and Briana offered to pay extra, so that they could also carry a guide. Emily, Armando, and Briana, each placed one over their neck with the strap provided and watched the posted numbered signs which told them what direction to go and what number to key into the remote in order to hear the recorded guide message. The children all wanted to use one, so it was agreed that the younger ones would take turns wearing and using the fourth one. Isabel took the first turn and they began their walk, learning the history of the ancient city.

After several hours of walking along, listening to their private hand-held guides, and stopping to eat the food they brought, they began to walk around the outside of the city, going up the steps to the high part of the wall. Natanyah, barely two years old, stayed close to Mama, feeling like she would fall off the wall if she got too close to the edge. The older children ran and explored the upper area where cannons stood facing the Mediterranean to ward off enemies coming from the sea. They imagined being the warriors fighting a battle over the water. Emily stayed where she could see all of the children, but still allow them to run off energy and have a good time, knowing there was no one to bother and nothing that could be damaged. She walked to and fro, viewing from her high vantage point, the remainder of the old city with its ancient mosques and the newer part of the city in the distance. She was unaware that a quarter of the city's population were Muslim Arabs. They were beginning to understand

Israel's demographics, but it was a long process that would take years for them to fully comprehend.

The heat was sweltering and many of their faces and clothes were wet from perspiration. They took a few photos, then descended back to ground level and finished the tour in the cool stone buildings. The path led up stairs and through a door into a souvenir shop where various artisans displayed their beautiful works. Emily had brought along money from a friend who wanted her to bring something back from Israel. When they entered the silversmith's part of the store and saw the beautiful work there, she knew that was what she should get. The kind Arab man was beating out a sliver tray and the family stopped to watch. They were intrigued with his craftsmanship and picked out a small silver and brass tray to take to their friend back home. Emily gave the man the money, knowing she had not brought enough along that day for such a purchase, but sure they could make it home on what they would have left. Armando looked through a box of shofars to use for the next new moon, which would be the feast of trumpets, but found they were very small and were more for looks than for actually sounding. He left them as Mama called the children out the door into the markets outside. His attention was shortly drawn to a display of knives in another shop and between his desire to use his gift money to buy one and the vendor's pressuring, Emily gave him enough money to purchase it at a 70% discount from the price they were asking. She was thankful she did not have much money with her and was being honest when she told them she could only give them the meager amount. And while they seemed aggravated to sell it to the family at such a cheap price, Emily knew the fact that they sold it was proof enough that they had come out all right on the sale. She did not like haggling with people in the markets and felt a desperate need to get out of there, as vendors seemed to rush at her from every direction, trying to push their wares on both herself and her unsuspecting children.

As they left the markets on the way back to the court yard, Emily leading the way, she noticed two young Arab men, appearing to be in their late teens, approaching quickly walking with long strides toward the family. They passed Emily and the younger children, then as they reached Armando, the nearest one stretched out his left hand and grabbed Armando by the lobe of his left ear, pulling it violently, as he walked by. The young men laughed as they continued on their way. As soon as Emily got to a place free of people, Armando called to her, caught up with her, and then told her what had happened. As in the incident earlier that day, she had seen the threat, but never the actual offense.

Once back to the safety of the olive treed courtyard, they turned in their hand held guides and walked into the food markets to get something else to eat before going home, since their snacks were gone. They had seen Kiryat Yam from where the cannons were and Emily felt like it would be a nice, peaceful, though rather long walk home along the sea. They walked along the water edge of the city and climbed the steps to the top of the several foot thick stone wall, hoping to follow the sea home. As they walked, they saw a young man running across the wall toward them in the distance, then where the high wall turned, he jumped off into the sea. The family, looking below them to see huge rocks beneath the wall, was horrified. They continued walking that direction, though picking up speed in order to see what had happened to the young man, when another one came running at them and jumped off just like the first. They began to suspect they were missing part of the picture from their vantage point, and those thoughts were confirmed when a young lady followed the previous two examples. Shortly after she jumped, the family got close enough to see that there was a place at the bottom of the wall that did not have the huge rocks directly underneath. They looked down to see several wet and happy young people playing in the water a good twenty feet below. Emily was extremely relieved to see the new sight until Armando asked, "Can I jump in, Mama?"

She gave him a stern, "No!", as they continued toward the port.

Staying as close to the sea as possible, so as not to get lost in the confusion of the city, they walked across a plank bridge which was a dead end path to a nice restaurant. As they did, Emily continued to observe in the distance and noticed there was not a clear path down the beach from Akko to Kiryat Yam. A large area was fenced off, which would force them to have to walk more of the route they had come on the bus. At that, as tired as she, Natanyah, and Moshe were becoming, she decided it would be better to ride the bus home. They reached the end of the walk, which forced them to either turn around or enter the restaurant. They decided since they were already there, they may as well see what was inside, so opened the door and went in. It was an elegant little place, and a little embarrassed that they had entered such a fancy eating establishment in their sweaty condition, Emily hurriedly turned them around and headed back across the plank walk, then down toward the port. As they passed close by the colorful ships. An Arab man called out to them, offering them a ride on his boat. Emily asked his price and he called out 100 shekels. She told him she did not have enough and continued walking. The children began to ask if they could ride the boat, so she recounted her money and realized that they did have enough to go, but might be forced to walk home if they did. She did not like to get that low on money, but decided this was probably a once in a lifetime experience, told the children the possible consequences, and turned back toward the large wooden boat, its rails wrapped with red and white streamers.

The man welcomed them aboard his 35 foot vessel with long padded benches on the sides and another small area to sit in the bow. Above them was a canopy nearly the full length of the boat and just tall enough for him to walk comfortably beneath. In the center towards the stern was the captain's wheel and chair behind a white pulpit-looking enclosure with a blue dove painted on it and three types of Arabic writing around it. There was also a five digit identification number clearly displayed at the front of the boat, 72337. The man started the engine and steered the boat away from the dock, away from the port and into the Mediterranean. The children had mixed reactions as the boat bumped up and down with the waves. Armando, Briana, and Rebeka thought it was great. Victor was not too sure at first, but soon began to really enjoy the experience. Isabel, Moshe, and Natanyah were varied in degrees from slightly scared to terrified, Isabel immediately beginning to feel nauseous. Emily had them all get in the bow of the boat where they could sit together as a tight group, so she could be near all of the nervous ones at the same time. Once away from the city, the captain took them out beyond where the walls jut out into the sea. One of the reasons Akko was such an important city in ancient times was because of the fact that it was on the edge of the harbor, jutting out into the sea with water on two sides. It was a beautiful sight to see from this angle. Emily was very glad she had spent the money for them to have this rare experience, even though some of the children were still nervous. The smell of the sea was all they breathed in from here, no sand, no food, no exhaust fumes from cars and buses and, surprisingly no fumes from the boat's motor. Emily pointed out the apartments by the beach at Kiryat Yam just short blocks from where their house was and the massive city of Haifa with its ship port in the distance.

After getting them to the turnaround destination where they could see the North wall of the city, the captain asked Armando. "Would you like to sail the boat?"

Armando immediately looked at Mama, saw the approval, then quickly agreed and sat behind the wheel for a few minutes before the captain asked Briana. Armando turned it over to her and she gladly assumed the captain's position. She stayed there to help Rebeka when it was her turn, until she had the confidence to do it alone. After her, three year old Moshe, who was loving the experience by then, took the helm. Looking like a real (though tiny) captain, Moshe sailed the vessel beautifully until he turned too sharply towards Akko and the boat quickly tipped, heading toward a big rock. The captain quickly took two steps back to the wheel to get control of his boat, while Emily comforted those who had been panicked by the upset. Armando and Briana loved the whole adventure. After the captain had them heading in the right direction he turned it back over to Moshe, telling the family that he was a natural, never wincing when the boat quickly rocked. He let him sound the horn, which was actually seven horns mounted on top and sounded like a train whistle. Isabel and Victor, who was sympathetic to her discomfort, chose not to take advantage of the opportunity to be captain for a moment. Natanyah just wanted to be by Mama.

Chapter 30   Akko

As they approached the port, the captain again took over and brought the boat in to dock. Emily paid him his hundred shekels and a tip, exchanged thanks with him, then exited the boat with her little crew. The ride had given them a chance to rest their legs and cool off some before the trip home. Shadows were getting long by that time and some were getting hungry. Emily took them back through the markets to get some flat bread, but was intimidated by the rudeness of the Arab vendors in that part of the market. She wanted to get out of there as quickly as possible, remembering the two events that had happened earlier in the day and wanting to be away from the city before dark. The children, not knowing Mama's sense of urgency to get out of there, enjoyed looking at all the interesting and beautiful foods, and took in the smells of spices, fruit, breads, and meat as they walked by various vendors who were beginning to close down for the evening. As they exited the main part of the markets, Emily saw a fruit bar and stopped to get a bottle of freshly squeezed pomegranate juice. She soon realized she did not have enough money left for that much and to still pay for a ride home, so just bought one cup to share with everyone. It was not much, but at this point, was better than having a whole bottle and walking five miles.

The children ate some pitas and bananas as they walked toward the falafel shop where they had gotten off the bus. Seeing the sunset, Emily began to get more nervous about how they would get home. She found herself being aggravated with Armando for spending all his money on the knife. She was the banker, so even though he had money of his own for the trip, she had not brought it and instead, had let him use some of what she had budgeted for the day's events.

"I wish I hadn't let you buy that knife," she said to him. "I don't know if we'll have enough money to get home."

As soon as she said it, she felt horrible. Armando had spent a little, but she had spent a lot of the friend's money for her gift, and it had not been budgeted for that day either. How awful to blame a child, when she was the one ultimately responsible! She hated it when people blamed someone else for their own faults, and here she had done it to her child! She sometimes found herself giving in to them, especially Armando, it seemed, then getting upset with the end result. She told him, "Armando, I was wrong to say that. Do you choose to forgive me? If we don't have enough money, it's my fault, not yours."

Armando replied, "Yes, Mama, I choose to forgive you."

She felt better, but still hated that she had said that. They soon came to a bus stop that had 'Kiryat Motzkin' on the sign above it. They stopped there and in a few minutes a large *sherut* stopped, the driver asking, "Where do you want to go?"

"Kiryat Yam."

The Arab driver said, "I'll be glad to take you!"

"How much will it cost?"

The price he quoted was a few shekels less than the rest of the money she had with her. She breathed a prayer of thanks, then had everyone climb aboard. She was glad to be getting a direct ride in the *sherut* rather than having to ride the bus, not knowing what part of Kiryat Yam might be its destination.

On the way, the driver was very inquisitive and Emily began to feel uncomfortable at the line of questioning when he asked where her husband was. She answered all of his questions concerning what they were doing in Israel and what was going on with David back home, but quickly decided to be dropped off somewhere besides their house. "Where do you live?" he asked.

Emily answered, "By the apartments. You can just drop us off at the playground."

The driver, insistent, "No, I can take you all the way to your house."

She firmly maintained that the corner by the beach playground was as far as she needed to go. He reluctantly pulled over, accepted his pay and the tip she gave him, patiently waited for them to all get out of the van, and then zoomed off for his next client. Emily breathed a sigh of relief at being out of his car and back in their home neighborhood where she felt safe. She praised Yah for their successful day out, then led her little brood through the apartments before some began to run ahead toward the house.

Once home, the little family was exhausted. As Emily put the key in the front door lock, a wild stray cat jumped out through the kitchen window, something they had grown accustomed to by now. They were glad to find *Arnav* safe in his cage. They warmed milk and gave *Chatul* his bottle, then put their mats out and flopped down without eating supper, their tummies full enough of bread and bananas.

Wednesday

David continued work at the restaurant, helping with and overseeing the paint, water and gas plumbing, and hanging some doors. When not needed there, he drove to the spec house and answered questions about final touch-ups.

Roll Call

Yom Chamishi (Fifth Day)

The little family again went to the library, this time coming back by way of a small park instead of the beach. The children played on the various equipment while Emily watched them, feeling the little one move in her belly. After the children had their fill of play, they walked the rest of the way home.

When school let out, the Family of Ten children came over bringing several small packages of chips and animal crackers to share. They played for the rest of the afternoon in the back yard and played ball in the alley behind the house. Emily was back and forth from the house to the yard watching them and doing various meal preparation and housekeeping duties. Usually she had the children help her, but she was just glad they had friends to play with, so did the jobs herself. When she finished, she sat down to practice conjugating the verbs Elena had assigned her. She kept her mind busy practicing her Hebrew conjugations when there were not other things more pressing to do. After a bit of study, she looked out the back and took a mental roll call of the children beginning with Armando, as she always did...Briana...Victor...Isabel...Rebeka...Moshe...Natanyah...

Where was Natanyah? She looked again but did not see her with the others. She called to Briana who alerted the other children, but no one knew where she was. A panicky feeling came over Emily and she quickly prayed. Armando took Briana to the house behind them on the north side, having noticed someone outside a few minutes before. When he knocked, the IDF soldier who lived there came to the door holding Natanyah and invited him in. Emily was uncomfortable with the situation, but felt like she had already stirred up trouble with them once over the incident with the young man, the soldier's younger brother the first night they were there. She felt confident that Armando and Briana could handle whatever situation they encountered in the house, so waited patiently by the back door for them to return. When they did, they brought Natanyah and a bag full of cookies and candy that the family had been feeding her from inside.

Emily waved at the soldier, then when the sun set and all the neighborhood children went home, she got all the children together and warned them about going into people's homes, and about taking food from strangers. Armando gave the report from earlier stating that the woman of the house had seen Natanyah playing outside and determined it was too hot to be playing out there, so lured her into the house with cookies, which she gladly followed. They all impressed on Natanyah the need to stay with older siblings and everyone agreed they would keep a closer eye on one another.

Thursday

The electrician finished his work at both places and David oversaw the installation of shelves at the restaurant, as well as touch ups and final details. Things were finally coming together and he was ready to leave as soon as they did. The Oklahoman was at the farm, and once he got the Final Inspection, there would be nothing holding him back.

Fish Boy

Yom Shishi (Sixth Day)

Having learned that on preparation day the stores got very crowded mid-afternoon, Emily took the children early in the day to get their milk, sweet breads, and pomegranate juice. They stopped at the dry goods store and got some small plastic cups to drink their milk from, since they had only brought water bottles from home and Emily did not like to use the easily smashed disposable cups. At home, each child had a color of cup, plate, bowl, toothbrush, pillowcase, and marks on socks so that everyone knew whose things were whose. They hoped to find cups for each one but found that those at the little market only came in three colors, and most were lime green. They took the purple one for Mama, the orange one for Isabel, since her color at home was yellow, and got green ones for everyone else. After getting home, Emily took one of the markers that Eti had given them and wrote initials on all the green cups.

While getting the house cleaned and baths going, a Russian boy a little older than Armando showed up at the front gate with his younger brother, around Moshe's age, sporting three newly caught fish, each between four and five inches long. Briana recognized them as brothers of one of the friends of a Russian girl that she sometimes played with. The family went out to the gate and introductions were made in Hebrew. Fish Boy said, "I brought these for you." As Emily accepted the kind gift, he asked, "What will you do with them?"

Emily, having already noted that they had fins and scales[183] said, "We'll eat them!"

Fish Boy, making a sour face replied, "Good, because *I* don't want to eat them."

Emily thanked him and took the fish inside to the refrigerator to cook on first day. The boys left and the family went back to their *Shabbat* preparations. A little while later, Sarah came to the door bearing a beautiful loaf of challah[184] bread. Emily praised Yah for the many blessings He continued to send them. They had never experienced this kind of abundant blessing before and wondered if this was the treatment that all visitors to the Land got or if it was just special love notes from their Father to them. Emily felt ashamed that she had complained about David not being with them and asked Yah to forgive her. The horse's neck was beginning to bend.

---

[183]Deut. 14:9-10 These ye shall eat of all that *are* in the waters: all that have fins and scales shall ye eat: And whatsoever hath not fins and scales ye may not eat; it *is* unclean unto you.

[184]*Challah* - a special loaf of bread to be given to the priest, but in modern Jewish tradition referring to a braided loaf of sweeter bread eaten on Shabbat.

Chapter 30   Akko

Friday

David got up off the spec house floor, prayed, read his scriptures, and then got started with his regular work. He finished repairing the Hood Man's mess, but still had not been able to reach him to get the job moving. Since the man had an independent contract with the Owner, David had no control over the hood job and was stuck. The restaurant had to be completed before he returned to Israel so the contract deadline would be met.

Byron called and invited David for supper and to spend the night at their house. David gladly accepted, appreciating the comfortable bed they had there as opposed to the carpeted floor of the spec house.

Bird Man

Shabbat

After synagogue and lunch which included another pomegranate party, one of the members, a small Indian man invited Armando to go to his house a couple of blocks away to see his birds. After getting Mama's permission, Armando left with his new friend. He was enjoying being taken in by the men of the synagogue and they were enjoying adopting the currently fatherless boy. They walked down the street, crossed Weizman and went to his apartment. As soon as the door was opened, they were greeted with the voices of numerous birds. The apartment was neat and clean and smelled like the bedding in the birds' cages. There were five birds of various colors.

The man gave Armando a pretzel and crackers to feed them as he introduced the individual birds and told what was special about them. One of the colorful birds repeated whatever was said to it, in any language. The man instructed Armando to greet him.

Armando said, "Shalom!"

The bird replied, "Shalom!"

The man said, "Greet him in English."

Armando complied and said to the bird, "Hi!"

The bird in his squeaky voice returned, "Hi!"

Armando decided to get creative and told him goodbye in Spanish, "Adios!"

The clever bird repeated, "Adios!" and politely took his cracker. Armando spoke to him in Hebrew, English, and Spanish and he talked back each time mimicking his new friend for a cracker.

287

The man gave Armando peanuts to feed the others. He carefully reached out his hand toward the first bird who gently took the peanut in his claw, then pinched it open with his beak, dropping the shell to the floor of his cage. He fed all of the birds there, green, red, yellow, white, and just stared at the owl with big eyes who sat there on its perch staring back at him.

After introducing Armando to his 19 year old son, the man grabbed a handful of crackers and peanuts and motioned for Armando to follow him. They ate the snacks as the kind man walked Armando to his house before returning home.

Shortly after, Sarah came over to read the Psalms again. The children sat on the little 'couch' like they did the week before, the little ones falling asleep faster this time, knowing more of what to expect. After their hour of reading, Emily thanked her and she went home, glad to have done a *mitzvot*[185] for the family again.

When the little ones woke up, Emily took them to the beach to walk along the edge of the water and pick up shells. They stayed until *Shabbat* was almost over, then returned to their home. Shortly after, the phone rang and Emily answered to the voice of the friend from Colorado whose family had come to Israel the same day they had.

Friend: I just wanted to let you know that we had our baby.

Emily: Thank you! Congratulations! So everything went well?

Friend: Yes, and I wanted to let you know about a doctor who signed paperwork for us, so we can get a birth certificate.

Emily: Thank you, yes, we'll need someone to sign, since we don't plan to go to a hospital.

The friend gave her the information and Emily shared the news about David being gone. She was sympathetic and prayed with Emily. Emily thanked her for her friendship and for the information about the doctor, congratulated her again on the birth of her ninth baby, and wished their family well.

Sabbath

David woke up late and slowly to the sounds of his in-laws in the kitchen. He mozied in and they offered him eggs for breakfast, but he chose to eat cereal, not wanting someone to be cooking for him on *Shabbat*.[186] After

---

[185]*Mitzvot* - plural of *mitzvah*, Hebrew for 'commandment,' commonly referring to acts of kindness.

[186]Exo. 20:10 But the seventh day *is* the sabbath of YHWH thy Elohim: *in it* thou shalt not do any work, thou, nor thy son, nor thy daughter, thy manservant, nor

visiting with them for the remainder of the morning, he took the juice he had bought the day before and headed to the home of his painters for that week's assembly.

During the meeting, he again fell asleep sitting up on the couch. After it was over, he got ready to leave and go back to work. The energetic young woman again suggested they go help him finish up so he could get back to his family. The other workers that were there agreed, so off they all went to Cookeville, an hour's drive. They worked till after midnight before returning home, and David spent the night in the spec house.

---

thy maidservant, nor thy cattle, nor thy stranger that is within thy gates:

31 - Fishing

Fishing Buddies
Week 7   *Yom Rishon* (First Day)   9/20-21

This night was quite cool, the coolest they had experienced since being in Israel, an instant change. Emily realized that autumn officially began at midnight and thought it incredible that the weather had changed that very night. The cool air felt good, though the family was thankful they had been given a couple of blankets from Eti and the Dead Lady. Emily cooked the little fish that Elisa had brought on preparation day and they ate that for lunch along with their hummus and vegetables. It was very good and they gave thanks for Fish Boy, who had brought it to them. They gave a fish head to *Chatul*, and he got excited about it, tearing little bites off with his tiny sharp teeth. They concluded that dumpster cats must learn to eat very young. They stuck the other two heads in the refrigerator to give him on following days.

After fish for lunch, Armando and Briana were eager to try their hand at fishing. They now had a pole, two broomsticks Briana had brought back from the dumpster, and had found some bobbers, and sinkers near the stone pier at the beach. The family kept a roll of fishing line in their emergency supplies, but they had found enough line tangled in the rocks to use for their poles, so did not need the new line. Mama consented to them going during nap time, telling them to stay near the other fishermen at the pier, but not close enough to bother them. They agreed and were glad to be freed from the house and off on an adventure. They grabbed their pole and fishing things and quickly left before Mama could change her mind.

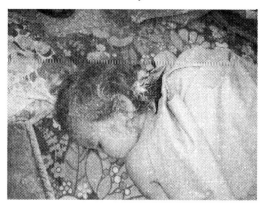
Natanyah

Victor, Isabel and Rebeka played and colored quietly in the kitchen while Mama took Moshe and Natanyah in the south room for their nap. *Chatul*, whose little tummy was now full of fish, was the first to fall asleep, nestled in the soft locks of Natanyah's hair. Emily thought of the irony of their situation, leaving a farm with many animals in the US, only to end up

Chapter 31   Fishing

taking in strays in Israel. But animals had always been a special part of her life, so she was glad to allow her children these experiences with them.

Armando and Briana walked purposefully to the beach past the playground and over the sand dunes to the pier where several fishermen were set up at the end, as usual. Nearer the beach, in the large boulders could be found tangled lines, hooks, and other fishing paraphernalia, so they stopped there to get their needed supplies. Armando climbed down onto a boulder near where he saw some tangled line. He pulled it in and, using the multi-tool he carried on his belt, cut the line off of the hooks, and then melted it with his lighter so they could be reused on his good line.

As he was preparing hooks, a group of five Russian youths, looking to be in their late teens, approached. Armando set his multi-tool down on the rock ledge of the pier so he could melt old line off of some hooks he was preparing on the rocks below. One of the young men bent down to get it and Armando quickly picked it up. The youth said in Hebrew, "Give me the knife."

Armando refused and the youth bent down, one knee on the rock and grabbed him by the throat with both hands, choking and shaking him. Briana, standing above, quickly raised her broomstick and yelled, "STOP!"

Her loud yell got the attention of everyone around: the youths, the fishermen at the end of the pier, swimmers, sun-bathers, and beach walkers. The youth choking Armando looked up to see a broomstick posed to come down on his head. A middle aged man walking on the beach quickened his pace towards the pier, yelling to three fishermen at its very end who had turned their attention in that direction. The youth let go of Armando's neck, pushing him away as he turned. Armando stumbled backward but caught himself before falling into the sharp rocks and strong current below. The fishermen yelled and took three steps toward them before the youths ran off the pier and north towards Akko, several people yelling at them, some in Russian, and some in Hebrew.

An English-speaking Israeli fisherman approached, and after confirming they were all right, told them to let him know if they had any more trouble. The children thanked him and they all went back to fishing. Armando finished tying hooks on the lines, baited them with a dough they had made from mixing water with flour as Fish Boy had taught them, and waited for fish to bite. Within two hours, they had caught five little slick brownish-gray fish that looked like sharks, the same type they had seen in the pet store. They threw back the smallest ones and kept the big one, about five inches long, for *Chatul*, since they had no scales and the family would not be eating them. They returned home with their cat food to find Emily studying her Hebrew verbs on the back porch while the children played ball in the little alley behind the house.

As *Chatul* enjoyed his fresh fish, Armando and Briana related the story of the attempted robbery to her, keeping it toned down so as not to ruin their

291

chances of going fishing again. Emily asked lots of questions to try to determine if it were safe to let them continue going. She hated to take the privilege away from them because she knew how much they enjoyed it, but could not risk letting them go if it was too dangerous. She felt overwhelmed by her situation and did not want the added stress of having to disappoint them. David was scheduled to leave again in a few hours, but she had lost hope that it would actually happen this time, either. Later in the afternoon, he called to inform her that her suspicions were correct. He would not be leaving today, as scheduled.

Her flock together again, Emily got the rent money and had them to go with her two short blocks behind to pay for the next month's rent. She and David had decided it would be good to have the house for the remainder of the time they were in Israel so they would have a home base. It would be cheaper to ride buses to the few places they had planned to go than it would be to rent motels for very many nights. They could keep the house for a month for the cost of four nights in a motel.

They knocked on Tzipporah's door and the kind woman invited them inside. Emily told her, "I brought the rent money for next month, since David's not back yet and I don't know when he's coming."

Tzipporah replied, "Oh, don't worry. It's not due for two days. Wait until then to pay."

Emily thanked her, then took the children back by way of the Family of Ten's house, so the children could play with them for a few minutes before supper. She visited with the mother who loved to practice English. They left in time to get supper finished before dark.

Endless Work

Sunday

David got up running again, trying to get ready for his flight that evening, but knowing deep down there was no way he could get things finished up in time. He dreaded talking to Emily, who he knew was losing hope that he would ever return. He was doing the best he knew to resolve the issues and working as hard as he could, but things just kept getting in the way. On top of it all, he did not have the support of his wife because she was having such difficulty being on the constant emotional roller coaster of being pregnant and raising the children in the circumstances where she was. He needed her support to get through what was going on with him, but knew she had nothing left to give him.

He called her and they made arrangements to change the tickets to Wednesday, arriving in Israel Thursday afternoon, at the end of *Yom Chamishi*. Emily then called and made arrangements with Byron again to buy the tickets. Afterward, Byron called David and invited him to Sunday lunch at their home.

Chapter 31   Fishing

When David got to a stopping place, he drove to their house for a home-cooked meal, glad to have their support. They had seen over the past few weeks how hard he was working and had tried to encourage him to slow down. They knew how badly he wanted to get back to his family and did not seem to understand Emily's impatience.

After the encouraging lunch, David went back to the job sites. The plumber was preparing for the final plumbing inspection. Things were wrapping up, but were not close enough for him to be able to leave with full assurance that there would not be more trouble.

Yom Sheni (Second Day)

In spite of the previous day's events at the pier, Emily let Armando and Briana go fishing again, but told them to stay closer to the fishermen. They agreed and left at nap time, which was earlier than usual, late morning, instead of early afternoon. Emily was down again, knowing that David would not be returning tonight as planned. She lay down with Moshe and Natanyah before lunch, too tired to go on. Victor, Isabel, and Rebeka busied themselves with writing and coloring.

When Armando and Briana returned, Emily had lunch with the hungry older children while the little ones finished their nap with *Chatul*. When finished, Aaron, the boy from the next block that often *played* with the Family of Ten's boys, rode over on his bicycle and asked if Armando and Briana wanted to go with him to the pet store to get food for his fish. They gladly accepted the invitation and walked and trotted alongside him while he rode. They enjoyed the sunshine and each other's company.

Monday

The job was down to the final details. The tile man had worked late the night before and finished his part. Most of the other subs were finished and had been paid. David called Emily to update her and give her hope that he would actually return as scheduled this time, Yah willing.[187] All was going well until the soda pop people showed up.

"Where do ya want this machine?" the big man asked the Owner.

"Over here," he said with his Spanish accent, leading him toward the kitchen.

"There ain't no lines here," replied the man.

The Owner brought David over to talk to him about the situation. David looked at the blueprints and saw there were no lines or drains showing.

---

[187]Jas. 4:15 For that ye *ought* to say, If the Lord will, we shall live, and do this, or that.

His plumbers had followed the prints exactly. The Owner and soda man insisted the restaurant had to have a soda machine. David knew that, even though it was not his oversight, he would have to make up for it. With no time to waste, he rushed to the store, bought a hammer drill and some other specialty tools he had been wanting anyway and hurried back to the restaurant to do the job himself. It would be faster than trying to find one of his subs available to do it on such short notice.

Yom Shlishi (Third Day)

Emily, tired and still down, had everyone go to bed even earlier than usual, wondering why things had turned out like this. She saw lots of positives about being where they were and was grateful for the opportunities they were having; she was thankful for the people whose lives were benefitting along with their own, but could not seem to get over the disappointment of the separation during this special together time. She drifted off to sleep, waking off and on to the light of the waning half-moon.

David and a laborer cut the concrete where the lines would need to run and put in the supply lines and drains. Then he realized they needed a connection that also was not on the blueprints. He had to improvise something that would work and pass inspection. He was thankful he had worked on lots of old buildings and in difficult situations in the past, giving him the experience necessary to solve problems like this one. Once finished, they continued the final touch ups, a few hours behind because of the soda machine, and worked into the night again.

Comfort Food

The family had been saving the last few pomegranates on the tree to share with Daddy when he came, but he kept not coming, so they gave up and picked and ate them without him. They gave thanks for the luxury of having the special tree in their yard. Later, they went back to Tzipporah's house and paid the rent for the next month. She asked, "What about your husband? When will he return?"

Emily, trying to convince herself, answered, "He's about got things finished there. He should be here soon," then asked, "Could I get a receipt for payment?"

Tzipporah, with a quizzical look on her face, replied, "Sure, I'll write you one."

Because she paid in cash, Emily felt she needed proof of the dates for which they had the place rented. She had learned years before from doing various forms of business that it was always better to have things in writing. And while she was beginning to trust most of the Jewish people, she did not want to do something foolish that would be detrimental to her family.

Chapter 31	Fishing

After getting home, she took Rebeka, Moshe, and Natanyah to the grocery store while the older children played with their friends. She bought pomegranate juice, soda, deli cheese, and some other treats to help ease the disappointment they were all experiencing.

When they returned, Eti came bearing lasagna for supper. Emily was again blessed beyond words. Why were these people being so kind? So many people had gone so far out of their way to do nice things for them. She had never experienced such love as these people were showing. How could they ever repay them?

Mere minutes after she left, Elena showed up at the door with another loaf of her fruit-filled bread. Emily sent Armando and Briana to the little store down the road to get milk for their traditional downing of Elena's delicious loaf while it was still hot.

Tuesday

David went into town and ordered appliances to have delivered to the spec house later in the day. He continued overseeing both jobs, while keeping Emily updated about his status there. He knew she was distressed about his not being there and was excited to give her the good news that he should be back soon.

The appliances arrived as David was rushing to get the bathroom mirror installed. The delivery man noticed his hurry and asked him, "Are you stressed, man?"

"Yeah, I need to get out of here. My wife is over eight months pregnant in Israel with our seven children. I had to come back to fix some things on a job and need to get things done so I can fly out tomorrow."

He replied, "Wow! I can see why. I'm supposed to go to another job, but let me call the boss and see if it's all right for me to give you a hand here with these installations."

David silently thanked Yah for the man's kindness and was relieved to hear the one sided phone conversation. When the man got off the call, he informed David, "I'll be glad to help you out. My boss has given me the OK to install all three, the microwave, stove, and refrigerator."

David replied, "Thank you, man. I'll remember you guys when I need more appliances."

David's phone rang and the Oklahoman asked some questions about rotating the animals to different pastures. David explained things, then told her, "I'm scheduled to fly out tomorrow. If there are any problems, be sure and let me know right away so I can get them taken care of before I leave."

The Oklahoman replied, "Everything's fine. Things here are simple enough. I don't expect any problems. Have a good trip and don't worry about anything here."

He was extremely relieved to hear that. He got some laborers working with a wheelbarrow and concrete pouring the sidewalk to get the house ready to list with the realtor the next day. They worked until eleven to the light of the nearly full moon that almost made the use of floodlights unnecessary.

Praying Mantis

Yom Revi'i (Fourth Day)

Emily canceled, for the second time, the family trip to a museum in Haifa that Nikolay had recommended, since David was still not back. She got up, praying things would finally go well enough for him to leave later in the day. It was hard to keep her mind on anything but what she imagined he was doing on the jobs to get ready to return.

The children busied themselves with their usual activities, including playing with their pets. *Arnav* was allowed to hop around the back yard as long as someone was there watching and protecting him from the feral cats that sometimes appeared out of nowhere. *Chatul* was still young enough that he spent most of his time sleeping, but was beginning to walk around and notice things like bugs and leaves that blew in the wind.

While enjoying the animals and playing in the back yard, Rebeka found a praying mantis, just as Emily heard Elena's *shalom* come from the open front door. She invited her in and sat on the 'couch' with her, where she had been writing Hebrew word conjugations. Her friend was glad to see her progress and was asking about David, when Rebeka came in to show the ladies the five inch long insect. Elena shrieked when she saw. "Kill it! Kill it!" she cried in Hebrew. "They are bad!"

Emily told her, "It's OK. We find them often in Tennessee, though not usually that big. Once Isabel brought in a ball of something and we didn't know what it was, so set it on the nature center on top of the piano where we had other neat things the children had found-feathers, rocks, antlers, beautiful leaves. A few weeks later, we noticed the house was full of baby praying mantises. They followed a trail of them to the ball on top of the piano, which was full of holes, and more insects coming out."

Elena was not happy to see a live praying mantis, but calmed down when the children took it out the front door and turned it loose somewhere in the yard, watching to see what it would do.

Emily told Elena, "David plans to leave tomorrow."

Elena replied, "I am glad for you. I know you've been missing him."

Chapter 31   Fishing

Then she began sharing about her life in Russia during the Chernobyl nuclear disaster. Emily listened with interest as she told about the members of her church praying for safety as those around them dropped dead. "No one in the village that worked in the plant lived, except those who were in the church. Most of those are still alive today."

After their chat, Elena returned home, about the time the neighborhood children came home from school. Various friends came over, giving the children fun things to do. Emily was thankful for this chance for them, since at home, all the fellowship they had was each other and the animals at the farm. They had no neighbors or other school age children nearby, so normally the only day they saw friends was on *Shabbat* or New Moon, and on those special days, activities were limited to what would be appropriate for the day.

Wall Between Us

Wednesday

David got up hoping everything would go as planned and that he would finally be heading back to Israel this afternoon, as scheduled. He made final payments to the remaining subs and suppliers, made sure the cleaning crew was at work finishing the spec house, returned a few things that were not needed on the jobs, then called Emily around noon, 8 PM and bedtime in Israel, to get his flight information. Emily was relieved that he was finally about to return and prayed nothing would get in the way this time. After speaking with her, he went to the restaurant to get the final payment from the Owners. The Final Inspection had been passed and everything was finished, including touch-ups. When he got there for the final payment, one of the Owners told him, "We're not going to pay."

David: Why not?

Owner: We don't owe you anything.

David: Of course you do! We have a contract. You owe me several thousand dollars. You owe me for everything on that contract.

Owner: Like what?

David, pointing to the wall he was standing beside: This wall, for one thing.

Owner: You didn't build that wall.

David: Of course, I did!

Owner: Nope, the Hood Man's son built that wall, probably. He put it up one night, and you're trying to get me to pay you for it.

297

David countered, "No, *I* built the wall." He reached into his pocket, rifled through his wad of receipts, and finding the appropriate one, said, "Here's the receipt for the materials."

The Owner, refusing to look at them, said, "I'm not paying anything else. You didn't build that wall."

David replied, "Call the guy. Ask him who built the wall."

The Owner called the Hood Man's son, who had joked that he had built the wall, but once confronted, clarified that David had built it. After getting off the phone, he said, "I'm not paying you, anyway."

David replied, "If you're not paying me, then this is still my wall, and I'll take it back." David had had enough. The Owner proved to be true to his reputation, so David calmly walked out to his pick-up, got his chainsaw that was still there among his other tools, and walked back into the building with it.

The Owner watched in surprise, then horror, as he saw David coming back. He quickly dialed 911 from his cell phone and told the dispatcher that there was a contractor there trying to destroy the restaurant. The dispatcher sent someone immediately from just down the block.

"The police are on their way!" The Owner told David in his native Spanish tongue.

David replied, "It's OK. I'm just taking my wall. You don't want to pay me for all the material and labor I put into this thing."

Once inside, David primed, then began to start the chainsaw. He had left his family thousands of miles away and worked long and unreasonable hours for a month to make sure this job got finished properly and on time, and now was being refused payment. His actions were completely justified in his frustrated and exhausted mind. The saw would not start right away, but that just gave him more time to justify his current actions, and he became more determined to take his wall back out of the building.

Just as he got the saw started, two local police officers rushed through the service entrance door of the restaurant just behind and to the right of him, pulled their guns and pointed them at him as one ordered, "Put down the chainsaw!"

David could not hear them over the roar of the motor, but could tell by their stance and pointed guns what they wanted. After he reluctantly turned the saw off, one of the officers demanded, "What are you doing?"

"I'm taking my wall home. I built this wall and now he doesn't want to pay me for it, or the rest of the last payment of the contract, so I'm just taking it home."

298

Chapter 31   Fishing

He heard a snicker from the older officer just before the younger ordered, "Put the chainsaw down."

David was not sure how to respond to two officers pointing guns at him. He bent, his back to them, to put the chainsaw down, then remembering his home in Mexico, where police were prone to be members of drug cartels and could not be trusted, jerked up and turned around, not wanting to have his back to them.

They backed up a step and the younger demanded, "Put the chainsaw down!"

David, in his usual calm manner, replied, "I'll put it down if you stop pointing your guns at me."

The officers lowered their guns and David set down the chainsaw, then stood and faced them. Once he was unarmed, they holstered their guns, then the younger walked to the Owner as the older told David, "Let's step outside."

Outside, David explained his side of the story to his officer, while the Owner was explaining his side to the officer inside. David's officer warned him, "If you take the wall down, they can charge you with vandalism and sue you for damages on top of not paying you for the job. You're better off to calmly leave and take them to court to present your case before a judge."

David was not happy about his solution, but decided he was probably right. Besides, he did not really have time to take the wall home that day before trying to catch his flight.

His officer went inside and joined the other conversation. They encouraged the Owner to pay David something to prevent his tearing down the wall, reminding him that he would not be able to open the restaurant if the wall was torn out. The Owner consented and paid David a little over half of what he owed. David put his chainsaw back in the pick-up and immediately took the check to the Owner's bank and cashed it to make sure he got his money. He then drove to his bank, put the cash in his account, went to Byron's, took a quick shower, left his pick-up there, and rode with Byron to the airport in Nashville.

Finally

Yom Chamishi (Fifth Day)

Knowing that David should already be at the airport for his flight in just over an hour and a half, Emily called to check his progress, reaching him just after he made it through security. Even though it was 1:30 AM in Israel, she could not sleep, wondering if she were facing yet another let down. She was relieved to learn he was at the airport. He tried to explain to her the incident that had happened at the restaurant, but she was so tired and just relieved that he was finally about to be on his way back, the story did not register. In fact, he seemed so distant to her by then that most of his explanations over the past couple of weeks had made no sense. She had scarcely heard anything he had said, being consumed with her own responsibilities there of guarding and training up the children, while growing an almost due baby.

Thursday

After getting off the phone with Emily, David called the farm to leave final instructions and make sure the Oklahoman understood everything and how to reach them if she needed to. He visited with Byron on the way to Nashville, thanking him for all of the support and help he had been. Byron dropped him off and he walked quickly to board his flight, glad to finally be leaving. He fell asleep almost immediately after sitting down, then woke up when they taxied into Atlanta, as the morning star was rising over Israel.

By the time the flight to Tel Aviv departed, morning was breaking and Emily was awake praying for his safe return and for the adjustment of the family being together again to be a smooth one, particularly that she would be understanding and forgiving of what she still saw as misplaced priorities on his part. David fell asleep again on the long flight, only waking up to eat. He was exhausted, majorly stressed, a condition that was not normal for him, and just ready to be with his family, looking forward to a warm welcome and a chance to get some much-needed rest.

Part 3

The Regathering

...then YHWH thy Elohim will turn thy captivity, and have compassion upon thee, and will return and gather thee from all the nations, whither YHWH thy Elohim hath scattered thee.

Deuteronomy 30:3

32 - *Echad*[188]

Throughout the day, Emily and the children talked about where Daddy was over the Atlantic, then over Europe. They did extra cleaning on the house to try to make it as nice as possible for his return. Mid-afternoon, they got cleaned up and headed out to Kiryat Motzkin to meet him at the train station. On the way, they stopped by their favorite shops to tell the owners that they were on their way to finally meet him. The market people's responses varied from shared excitement to looks of doubt as to whether it was really going to happen this time. Upon his arrival at Tel Aviv, he phoned Emily to let her know he had made it.

The lady at the bulk spice and bean shop suggested they take a bus or cab, but Emily assured her again that they all needed the good walk. They took their usual route, never having taken the long walk this late in the day, so it was a new experience for them and a refreshing one for Emily. She was exhausted from having the children for a month by herself in a place other than their home where they were free to safely roam and run out their energy during the day. As they walked past the huge apartment buildings, the peaceful parks, past the penguin fountain toward the train station, she looked forward to having the support of her mate to help with the day to day physical, spiritual, and emotional needs of the children, and was looking forward to getting some rest.

They went to the mall to get falafel and tell the man there that David was finally coming back. They bought four falafel for the eight of them to share, and after eating, walked south. The sun was almost down as they reached the big park on the left. Emily sat down on a bench to watch the children play on the various colorful playground equipment with other children. After a few minutes, a heavy, tired-looking young lady pushing a stroller with twins approached. She sat down on the bench next to Emily and they began to talk. She was surprised to learn that Emily was about to have her eighth, and Emily shared with her how things got much easier after she began to have more children, the first being the most difficult. The woman was encouraged by the time she left with her twins.

A few minutes later, a kind, older Russian lady sat down with her while her grandson played on the play sets near the Varela children. She was enamored with the children and asked Emily all the usual questions. The children came over now and then, and as they did, Emily introduced them to her. She had brought a snack for her grandson and wanted to share. So as they came, each one got some crackers.

---

[188]*Echad* – Hebrew for 'one,' as in 'united.'

Chapter 32   *Echad*

When they went back to play, the woman pulled out a sandwich and asked Emily, "Would you like this? It's an extra one. I don't need it."

Emily, opening it to see what was inside, said "Thank you. What kind of meat is it?"

The woman quickly began to apologize, "I'm so sorry. It is pork. I should have known, from all you've told me, that you don't eat pork. I'm really sorry."

Emily handed the sandwich back to her and said, "Don't worry. It's true we don't eat pork, but it was kind of you to offer your food to me."

The woman seemed surprised as she replied, "Some people often get very angry about such mistakes. I'm glad you're not upset."

Emily assured her, "There's nothing to get upset about. You didn't know."

The sun began to set and Emily knew it was time to take the children nearer to the station, not wanting to have them in the park after dark. She said shalom to her new friend and led her little crew south to meet her husband for the first time in a month. They stopped at a pizza place near the station and had a meal on the sidewalk outside, saving a couple of pieces for David before continuing.

Yom Shishi (Sixth Day)

Darkness settled on the palm-lined street as they made their final way to the train station and waited among several others who were there to board or to wait for those exiting the train. Just after 8:00, they finally saw the light coming down the tracks and they all got excited to see who could be the first to see Daddy. They watched and watched, but never saw him get off. Then, when they were just about to give up hope, he walked out of the little area for boarding. No one ever figured out how they had missed him exiting the train, as the children rushed to him, jumping up and down to tell him all about the things that had transpired while he had been gone, and excitedly giving him his pizza. Emily got her place near him and they embraced for a moment before beginning the trek home. Emily had brought the sling and gave it to David, knowing it would be past bedtime before they got back. David picked up Natanyah and put her in where she comfortably fell asleep shortly after they started the long walk.

On the way back they shared with Daddy all of the things that they had done at the various landmarks that they walked past, the dump where they had found the beautiful rugs and kittens, the parks, the stores, and the houses where various new acquaintances lived. At times he could not hear anything for the many voices all talking at once in their excitement to share their lives with him.

303

They got back to their little abode late and the children dropped off to sleep on their mats outside. David and Emily lay down on theirs as they shared a few things that had passed over the weeks they had been separated. It was late when they finally went to sleep.

The late night turned into a later morning than usual for the little family. Emily, not able to sleep late, got up and busied herself with her usual routine of prayer, reading, and preparing breakfast. The children got up one by one and snuggled up to Daddy trying to share more about their recent lives that he had missed, but he dosed in and out, trying to hear what they had to say, but too tired to stay awake. After an hour, they persuaded him to get up and eat their normal breakfast of fruit and yogurt. There were no pomegranates from the tree this morning, but there were lots of other fruits.

The day went on as they caught up on what they had missed of one another and talked about upcoming plans. Everyone knew it was too late in their stay to get back on the bicycles, but *Yom Teruah* was approaching and plans needed to be made as to how and where they would celebrate. Since they did not know many people who kept the feast according to the sighted or *Karaite* calendar, they decided to go to the Tiberius area, where they knew a few people who would be celebrating at the same time.

Discord

The morning went by quickly since they had slept late and gotten around slowly. The children were glad to be able to get on their bicycles again. They had been off limits while Daddy was gone. They rode around the streets in the front and back and Briana taught some of the neighborhood girls how to ride. They had never ridden bicycles big enough for their feet to be off the ground.

Emily tired as nap time approached. She had asked David earlier if he would take the other children to the beach at nap time and he had agreed. But just after lunch, he decided he was tired and needed a nap, as well. Emily knew the best way to overcome jet lag was to stay up during the daytime and sleep at night. She knew it was best for David to stay awake and could not think of a better way to do that than taking the children to the beach to play in the water. She tried to encourage that, knowing she would get much more rest without the other children there. While she had them trained well, nap time was never completely quiet with them there and she felt like she had been a month without a real nap. Not only that, she felt like after all that time raising the children alone, she deserved one. She was now over eight months pregnant and feeling very heavy, having gained extra weight since getting off the bicycles a month earlier.

David, too, felt like he deserved a nap. He had been away working frantically for a month and was jet lagged from his trip back. So, he decided to stay there and nap with Emily, letting the children play. He

Chapter 32   *Echad*

always slept hard and their noises did not bother him. But she needed complete silence in order to rest during the day, and she knew his snoring would not enable her to rest.

As Emily hung out a load of clothes on the line, the conversation about nap time escalated into an ugly confrontation, both of them feeling overworked and that they deserved what they desired. Emily was so tired and upset that she screamed at David, "I wish you had never come back, if this is the way you're going to treat me."

He reminded her in a smug way "You're not glorifying Yah by screaming at me."

Nothing more could be said and Emily, exhausted and too upset to rest, went about her work as David took a peaceful nap.

The children woke him up a couple of hours later and he then offered to take them to the beach so Emily could rest, but she knew that at the late afternoon hour, it would be useless and counterproductive to try. So, she went along to the beach with them licking her wounds and praying that Yah would give her rest that night.

Around 3:00 they left for the *shuk* to buy some fruit for breakfast. Upon arriving, Emily saw the woman who had first given them the huge bag of bread. Emily introduced her to David, on the verge of tears the whole time, as things had not gone well between them since nap time. The woman took them around the *shuk* again encouraging the different sellers to give them the things they were about to throw away as evening approached, while the children excitedly showed Daddy the different vendors and wares at the *shuk*. Emily was thankful for the woman's kindness, but did not feel like talking to anyone and was so distraught that she was even having trouble speaking Hebrew when necessary.

She went to sit down on the curb by the road in the sand while David and Armando bought some fish. The woman came over, noticed the tears about to flow, took Emily by the chin and cooed over her, asking why she was crying. Emily tried her best to explain that things were not going well, and the woman tried to cheer her up by telling her, "There's a place nearby where abused women can go. I can get you an apartment."

Emily explained, "It's not that bad. He doesn't beat me. I just want our family together and happy."

The woman spoke more kind words as David and the children approached. After seeing that Emily was determined to go home with her family, she hugged her, told her, "Shalom," and turned to go back to her apartment across the street.

Emily was alone, tired, and crushed in her spirit as they walked back to their little house, the children excitedly telling Daddy about all the

305

experiences they had had on this side of town. They stopped at the grocery store, where Emily picked out grape and pomegranate juice for *Shabbat* and the children continued showing their dad around.

Leaving the store, they headed south then west toward their little abode, Emily still in great pain, but glad that her children were enjoying David. She wondered if their marriage would ever reach the point that they could function as one, each caring for the other in a mature way.

Synagogue

After getting home, putting the food away, and taking baths, Armando took David across the street to the synagogue to share in the experience he had been having for the past four Sabbaths. They walked in, got their prayer books, and everyone shook David's hand, telling him they were glad he was back. Many of them could speak some English, so they were able to communicate well. The two brothers told him about bringing Armando to synagogue and explained the order of service, which began with the reading of the prayers. David was struck by what reverence the men had to the *torah* and YHWH, whose name they would not speak. He felt they were missing something, but respected the devotion and commitment they had to the fences that had been placed to keep His name from being abused. He saw great love among the men for one another as they gave affectionate man hugs.

The service continued with singing that could be heard down the street and into the houses all around. Emily and the others sat at home and quietly listened, being uplifted by the dedicated men's voices as they traveled outward and upward to the heavens. After the singing, the books were put back in their places and wine, juice, and bread were eaten after blessing YHWH, whom they called *Adonai*.[189]

David felt good being there in the Promised Land with his brother Judah, knowing that his presence was in fulfillment of scriptural prophecy that preceded the coming of the Messiah. Judah was also looking for Messiah to come, but many of them were unaware of what the prophets said about Ephraim returning. David was just glad they were allowing him and Armando to worship with them and that they had taken Armando in as their own in his absence. He was particularly grateful for the two brothers, sons of Sarah, and for the kindness their family had shown to his.

Next Door Questions

They came back around sundown, and ate the supper that Eti had brought and the girls had set out. Elena arrived just in time with another loaf of her

---

[189] *Adonai* - Hebrew for 'lord.'

Chapter 32   *Echad*

wonderful fruit-filled bread, and the children told David all about it before Emily sliced and served a piece to everyone. They began to share with Elena their plans for the next few weeks, including *Yom Teruah.*

"But *Rosh Hashanah* is a Jewish feast," she reminded them.

Emily lit up, still not feeling peace between her and David, but having a fire now lit inside her. She loved to share about the scriptural feasts and the pagan holidays because finding those truths had so changed the lives of her family. And she was getting fluent enough in Hebrew that she could explain things accurately. Besides, she knew Elena well enough by now that she would be corrected and learn Hebrew better if she misspoke. "Yes, *Rosh Hashanah* is a traditional Jewish feast, but the corresponding scriptural feast is *Yom Teruah.* Look here at Leviticus 23" as she handed her PDA to Elena. On her last trip to the library, she had downloaded e-sword in Russian for her benefit.

Elena was excited to read the Bible in Russian from the little device. Emily pointed out, "Yah is speaking in this passage and says they are 'my' feasts, not the feasts of the Jews. They were never abolished, and were always intended for all of Yah's people, not just the House of Judah."

Elena: But Christians don't celebrate those. We celebrate Christmas and Easter.

Emily: Yes, but that is tradition. It is not in the Bible. When we study the scriptures, we find that neither Y'shua, nor his disciples, nor the early believers, Jew nor Gentile, celebrated them. They were pagan feasts that were celebrated by pagan sun worshipers and called by different names. They were brought into Christianity in the fourth century by Roman Emperor Constantine. And they have nothing to do with our Savior. In fact, the observance of them is condemned in scripture.

Elena: But we celebrate the birth of Jesus because he came to save us from our sins.

Emily: What does that have to do with his birthday? Where does it say to celebrate it?

Elena: The wise men and shepherds celebrated it. That's why we do it.

Emily: The wise men and shepherds celebrated the day of his birth, not his birthday.[190] There's a difference. They celebrated the fact that a king

---

[190]While the wise men saw the star in the east and began their journey, they did not arrive with the three types of gifts until months later when the family was living in a house.

307

was born, but they did not continue celebrating the day year after year. That was a pagan tradition.

Elena: So you believe it is wrong to celebrate Christmas?

Emily: Yes, scripture tells us it is. It is a tradition that came from paganism. In fact, the very date that Christmas is celebrated on was celebrated for thousands of years as the birth of the sun god. Besides that, we know from scripture that Y'shua wasn't born that time of year. When we research history, it's very easy to see where Christmas and all of its traditions come from. The same with Easter.

Elena asked lots of questions, and after the conversation was over, Emily was exhausted. She had spoken well, but the events of earlier in the day combined with the effort it took to say all of that in Hebrew had her worn out.

Harmony
Shabbat

Elena went home and Emily flopped down on her mat outside, where several of the children were already sleeping. David apologized for being insensitive to her and reminded her that the enemy was probably trying to thwart the message she was giving Elena that night, by breaking her down during the day. Emily apologized, as well, and they drifted off to sleep, a peaceful family once again.

This morning was much better, with good fellowship restored in the marriage and both parents being more rested. They ate their fruit, sweet breads and milk, got dressed in their *Shabbat* clothes made by Grandmother, and David and Armando went to the early prayer service with the two brothers. This was David's first time in the synagogue for morning service, so Armando showed him what to do when. This was the week of the new moon of the seventh month, *Yom Teruah* or what the Jews now called *Rosh Hashanah*, so the special prayers were said. Later Sarah, affectionately known within the little family as *Torah* Lady stopped by to get the rest of the family. Victor met up with Daddy and Armando, but little Moshe went up to the balcony with Mama and the other women and children. Emily was getting better at following along in the *torah* and prayer book, but was glad to be able to get help from Sarah, as needed. She was thankful for her new friend. The children got restless before the service was over, but were used to sitting for long periods of time, so sat as quietly as they could and were not a distraction.

Matt. 2:11 And when they were come into the house, they saw the young child with Mary his mother, and fell down, and worshipped him: and when they had opened their treasures, they presented unto him gifts; gold, and frankincense, and myrrh.

Chapter 32   *Echad*

After services, the family returned home for a lunch of what was left of the things Eti had brought as well as the soup Emily had prepared. Then they walked several blocks east to a small *yeshiva* that some of the neighbors had been telling them about. Emily had waited until David was back before taking them, not knowing what to expect. They got there and were welcomed by a kind young rabbi who had enough patience to instruct the several youths that arrived. Most of them did not seem to take the experience seriously and seemed to be testing his patience. After the prayers, there was a snack time when sugary treats were served. Emily wanted to tell them how detrimental they were and counterproductive to what he was trying to do, but knew he very likely served them in an attempt to attract young people, just like many churches do. She kept quiet and she and David oversaw that their children got a minimal amount.

There was another class afterward where the language switched back and forth from Hebrew to English. The Varelas had learned that many Israelis enjoyed practicing their English and the family's presence was the perfect opportunity. Armando and Briana were able to answer several questions, and the rabbi seemed impressed. After the students were dismissed, he began to ask the family the usual questions. As David and Emily explained what the prophets said about Ephraim returning, he listened with great interest and was motivated to begin studying them. He was not familiar with many of the prophecies that they told him regarding the two houses of Israel being reunited before the return of Messiah.

The family strolled toward home, past the synagogue and their little street and on to the beach to spend the remainder of time before the sun went down, basking in their Creator's beauty and glad for another opportunity to share scripture with someone who was truly interested.. They walked in the damp sand and picked up the prettiest shells they found so far.

33 - The Galilee

Week 8   *Yom Rishon* (First Day)   9/28

After the whole family slept under the starlit sky, the children woke up excited about introducing Daddy to all their friends at the markets. David felt a little shy about being such a spectacle, but agreed to go along with their wishes. They went to shop after shop introducing him and hearing people tell him what a nice family he had. Once home, they washed clothes and hung them out so they would be dry by evening and ready to pack for their trip the next day.

Afterward, they went to introduce Daddy to the neighbors behind and the Family of Ten. The woman of the house invited the Varelas to celebrate *Rosh Hashanah* with them, but Emily told them they would be in the north at that time. The mother had learned that Moshe's birthday would be that night and she loved to throw birthday parties. She impressed on them the need for the two families to get together, since David was back. The families agreed that after Sukkot would be the best time. The mother insisted they would have two cakes at that time, one for Moshe and one for Isabel, who would be turning a year older then.

They were talking about who to have care for *Arnav* and *Chatul* when Olga stepped out of her house next door. They asked her, knowing her mom hated cats, but she said she planned to be gone over the next few days. They talked to a couple of the neighborhood youngsters and Aaron offered to come over and take care of them. He had a dog about to have puppies and several fish that he cared for, so the Varela family thought he was probably responsible enough. It seemed ironic that even on a temporary stay somewhere, they had become animal owners and were now looking for a pet sitter. She took the two oldest to his house to get the permission of his parents, who gladly agreed, but were not interested in their son accepting payment for the *mitzvot*. They offered for her to come back and use their Internet whenever she wanted, for which she was grateful because they were much closer than the library.

She had already agreed to ride to the library with Briana that day. They both enjoyed having the Israeli wind on their faces again after such a long break from the bicycles. Emily checked the emails and took care of some business, while Briana read a non-fiction book about a man on the SEAL team who had been tortured.

David gladly stayed home enjoying the children. They continued telling him stories of their previous adventures and sharing their pets with him.

Chapter 33   The Galilee

Once the girls were back, and supper was over, they took the clothes off the lines and got everything that they could ready for the next day's journey.

Afula

Yom Sheni (Second Day)

As they were laying their mats out on the back porch, they heard a man's voice call from the front and everyone went to see who it was. They were greeted by a fisherman with a pole. Armando immediately recognized the man as one of his friends from the pier who had chased off the attackers the week before. The fisherman had observed Armando and Briana scavenging the rocks for lost fishing equipment which they attached to their dumpster broom handles for fishing poles. He had noticed that the only fish Armando was able to catch were the tiny ones that swam around the crags in the rocks, so brought him a good quality pole that extended to a length sufficient for catching bigger fish farther out. The family thanked him for his kindness. He went on his way, and they bedded down talking about the showering of kindness they continued to experience in the special land.

The family rose a little more quickly this morning, like people with a purpose. They packed all of their necessary items (everything they had brought with them except the bicycle equipment and their *Shabbat* clothes) – two sets of clothes, bed mats, sheets, emergency supplies, stove, water, and tent – into three of the red panniers which converted into backpacks and a little pink backpack that Eti had brought with the toys the first day they were in the house. Emily put on her old sandals, not knowing how far they would be walking and afraid the new ones with their slight heal would make things difficult. She made a harness out of rope to tie on the stack of folded bed mats, making them easy for the children to carry as a backpack. David carried the tent, Emily, Armando, and Briana carried the packs, Isabel carried the pink backpack, and Victor started off as the mat carrier, and Moshe as the emergency bucket man.

After a quick breakfast, clean-up, and scripture time, they said shalom to *Arnav* and *Chatul*, who was now weaned from his bottle, and left them in the cage under the plywood-bucket-leg table, where Aaron would find them after school, and walked toward the bus stop in front of the markets. They caught the bus to the Haifa station and another from there to Afula to meet with the friends from Colorado who had arrived in Israel the same day as the Varelas, had their ninth baby there a few weeks before, and had referred them to the doctor that had helped them with their paperwork. Emily had been in contact with him and he had agreed to do their paperwork, as well. They made plans to see him while they were nearer his home in the north on their trip to Tiberius. They hoped it would work out for their friends to spend *Yom Teruah* with them, since their practices and family sizes were similar and they had a lot in common.

311

At Afula, Armando and Emily quickly ran to the market near the station and got food for the rest of that day and the next, as well as a package of diapers as a small gift for their friend's new baby, while David stayed at the station with the other children. They ran back in time for the family to catch the appropriate bus to get to the house where their friends were staying. They rode up the hill to a beautiful neighborhood overlooking the Jezreel Valley, got off at the bus stop and walked a few hundred feet downhill to the temporary home. Rebeka and Moshe took turns carrying the bag of diapers. The couple and their children welcomed the family and stayed in the front yard chatting with them for a few minutes, allowing them to come inside the spacious, immaculate home in two groups to use the restroom. After taking girls, then boys, the families again gathered together outside for a few minutes. David asked, "Would you like to celebrate *Yom Teruah* together?"

The Coloradan replied, "I don't know. I'm not sure what kind of plans we have."

David offered, "We'll, I guess we'll go to Tiberius and camp out at the Sea of Galilee. If you'd like to celebrate with us, we'd love to have you."

The Coloradan reminded him, "The last bus for the day leaves soon. *Rosh Hashanah* begins at sundown and the buses stop early today."

The Varelas thanked them for the information, gave them the diapers and another small gift, said 'goodbyes,' put their packs on and started up the hill toward the bus stop, with a couple of the Coloradan's older children. They were disappointed that the friends did not show much interest in being with them that day or for *Yom Teruah*, but knew that Yah was in control and would work out the best for all involved.

The bus arrived and they put their packs and other big things underneath. The only pack they carried on board was the number one pack, usually carried by Emily, which had all the important documents, as well as emergency supplies and other things the family might need wherever they happened to be at the moment. On board, Armando's attention was drawn to the back of the bus, where several IDF soldiers sat. He passed the groups of empty seats, leaving them for his parents and younger siblings, and took a seat amongst the uniformed men on the back row. The female soldier sat in the row in front of them and the young men began joking with Armando about dating the girl. He took their jokes in stride then just quietly listened to the conversations going on between them.

Tiberius

The bus left the residential area, then turned down the steep hill as the passengers' eyes were drawn to the beautiful Jezreel valley to their left, the site of the famous battle thousands of years before that had been won by Israel when David killed the Philistine giant Goliath. The closer they

Chapter 33   The Galilee

got to the Afula station, the more soldiers boarded the bus. The family, and especially Armando, were soon surrounded by the modern day fighting forces of Israel. It was ironic that the Philistines Israel had defeated on that valley so long ago still posed a daily threat to the peace of the people of Israel. The Philistines, now known as Palestinians, continued to violently attack Israeli people on a daily basis with stones, knives, guns, bombs, and missiles. The IDF was always on guard for the safety of its citizenry and those who came to visit their special land. Armando could tell they were nearing the station as more and more soldiers boarded at each stop. When they arrived, they had a few minutes' wait for the last bus out to Tiberius, earlier today than usual because their high day was approaching. Armando noticed a store with lots of military things and went inside, hoping to buy some handcuffs stronger than the toy ones that had broken a few weeks before. As he looked around, David called to let him know their bus was there and ready to board.

They loaded their packs underneath, boarded, and then enjoyed the ride north through beautiful country full of row after row of green fruit trees, grape vines, and vegetables. They marveled at what scripture described as a fruitful land and now understood why. They discussed pictures they had seen from the time Mark Twain had visited in 1867, the land looking like a vast desert with hardly a tree standing anywhere. What a difference had been made once the descendants of Jacob had begun to return to the land! They noticed the cleanliness of the Jewish farms and villages and the sharp contrast in the dirtier Muslim areas and discussed how Yah's land flourishes when His people are in it as opposed to when others occupy it. They talked about how they looked forward to the day when Ephraim would return and they would be part of the ones enjoying the fruit of the land.

They rode past Nazareth and saw Mount Tabor across the fruitful valley from them, past Taiwanese immigrants harvesting vegetables, an Arab man wearing a T-shirt and turban leading a donkey loaded with sacks of grain, tall stucco buildings and rocks of all sizes. While the rest of the family shared the new scenery with each other, Emily called the doctor whose number she had received from her Colorado Friend.

Emily, in Hebrew: Hello, I was given your number by my friend from the U.S. She said you did her paperwork and to call you. We're due to have a baby on the 21st and don't plan to go to a hospital.

Doctor: Ah, yes, I remember her. You can come to my house. I live in the Golan Heights.

Emily: Good, we're on a bus on the way to Tiberius now and plan to be camping at *Kinneret*.[191]

---

[191]*Kinneret* - Sea of Galilee, from the Hebrew word *kinor* meaning 'violin,' because of the shape of the lake.

313

Doctor: Oh, if you're on a bus, it would be better for me to come to you. I can meet you at the station in Tiberius.

Emily: Ok, that would be great!

Doctor: When do you plan to leave?

Emily: On *Yom Shishi*, early afternoon.

Doctor: Ok, I can meet you before you leave. Call me that day.

That was a great act of kindness. It would have been expensive for everyone to have had to go to where the Doctor lived. They made a mental note that they would need to leave their camp by noon in order to see the Doctor, then get home before *Shabbat*.

They enjoyed the ride north as they continued to see beautiful scenery. Briana was particularly grateful to be riding the bus and not carrying the heavy, flopping backpack, which would only adjust to the size just bigger than she was. They had put all their belongings besides Emily's bag below the bus and were enjoying being free of them. They also enjoyed the air conditioning and the driver's Israeli music.

The Singer

The sun was on its way down and the family did not know where they would be staying for the night, but trusted that Yah would, once again, take them where He wanted them to be. On the bus behind Emily was a thin woman with her black hair cut so short that her scalp showed through. She began asking the usual questions about the family and showed great interest in them and the answers she was getting.

The bus arrived at Tiberius with less than an hour before sundown. The family all used the restroom there, now knowing when their next chance would be, then put on their packs and headed down the stairs to the lower level from where they could head east toward the *Kinneret*. On the way down the stairs, they heard a booming opera voice echoing through the station, and turned to see it coming from their new shaven headed friend, her young daughter dressed in pink holding her hand. Just as they were about to cross the street near the station, she yelled at them, "Stop!"

They stopped at the bottom of the stairs and waited for her. On her way down, she asked, "Where are you going?"

Emily replied, "We're just going to camp on the beach. Do you know where we can camp for free?"

"Wait!" she said, then walked purposefully to the two taxis waiting on the lower level outside the station.

314

Chapter 33   The Galilee

The family waited patiently as they ate some oranges from their packs, thinking she was getting directions for them. In a few minutes she returned and said, "Wait here. The taxis are going to give you a ride."

Emily said, "Oh, no, really, we want to walk. We just don't know whether to go north or south from here."

The shaved woman said, "No, they want to do a *mitzvah*. They are going to take you to the free beach. You just need to wait because they have to give someone else a ride first."

Emily thanked her and the woman left smiling. David and Emily gave thanks to Yah once again for the kindness He was showing through unfamiliar people. Sundown was approaching and while more than happy to walk, they knew it was a blessing to be given a ride, especially since they had no idea where to find a suitable place to camp. The children continued to snack on fruit as the family waited for the taxis to return.

After waiting nearly half an hour, the family was beginning to wonder if they should start walking. It would be dark soon, and they did not even know where to go. But just as they were beginning to feel the urgency to leave, a taxi returned and the driver told them to wait for his partner. In a few minutes, as the sun was setting behind the steep hills to the west, the other taxi sped up the street, whipped onto the side road, and screeched to a stop in front of them. He jumped out and the two drivers began loading backpacks. David got in the front seat of one car with Briana, Victor and Isabel in the back, and Emily got in the front seat of the other with Armando, Rebeka, Moshe and Natanyah in the back. The children were excited, remembering their wild taxi ride the day they had arrived in Israel.

Emily's driver asked in Hebrew, "Where do you want to camp?"

Emily answered, "We don't know. Someone told us there was a place we could camp for free on the beach."

The Driver's eyes lit up as he said, "Ah, I know the best place," and he picked up his mouthpiece and told the other driver where to go.

They passed several camping resorts that the family later learned charged a fee, then passed a water park with a slide several stories high. About two miles south of the bus station, the first driver turned left into a large parking lot, then jumped out and began unloading backpacks, as his fellow driver followed suit. Once everyone was unloaded and the packs were all set out on the sidewalk, he reached into the trunk of his car, pulled out a two-liter bottle of water, two ice cold sodas, and a stack of disposable plastic cups, handed them to David, wishing them, "*Tov Rosh Hashanah!*"[192] in a way that clearly spoke, "You don't owe us anything."

---

[192] *Tov Rosh Hashanah!* - Hebrew for 'Good Head of the Year!"

315

Once again, all the Varelas could do was say, "*Todah rabah!*"[193] as enthusiastically as they knew how. They continued to be amazed at the generosity they were experiencing from the Jewish people. Was there a better way to express gratitude? Why were they the recipients of such generosity from so many different people? Briana was just thankful to have gotten out of two more miles of carrying that floppy backpack. They talked about the woman with the opera voice and shaved head and thanked Yah for her, asking His blessings upon her and their most recent taxi drivers.

Rosh Hashanah

Yom Shlishi (Third Day)   First Day of *Rosh Hashanah*

They waved as the drivers pulled away, and discussed how this blessing was exceptionally surprising, as it was now the Jews' high day of *Rosh Hashanah*, the first day of the seventh month on the rabbinic calendar. Normally, people who worked on the high days charged even more for their services, yet the Varelas had been given a free ride, without even soliciting a ride at all, besides the drinks!

Still in awe of their Creator and King and the provision with which He blesses His children, they gathered their packs and walked from the parking lot to the empty pebble beach down at the bottom of the concrete steps. It was a little eerie being the only campers after noticing many campers at the cleaner resort sites, but they enjoyed having the whole beach from which to choose their spot and knew they would enjoy the privacy. The water level in the Sea of Galilee was very low, usually coming up the cliff on the west side of the sea, but now it was down the cliff and about fifty feet from its edge, leaving the pebbles of the lake floor visible and dry. The ground was sloped, most of it quite steeply, and the family took a quick survey of where the best place to set up their tent would be. It looked like there was only one good place for a tent the size of theirs, so they cleaned the spot of trash and debris, noticing that there was significantly more here than any place they had seen in Israel other than the campsite at the top of Mt. Carmel, and laid out their bed mats, foregoing the tent since it was such a beautiful night.

As Emily was getting the food ready in the fading light, David watched the children investigate the beach and lake and pick up all kinds of treasures. Armando and Briana, always the ring leaders, became very excited to come upon a huge, beautiful rug. They dragged it up from the beach, beaming, to show it to Daddy and Mama. The parents agreed it was a great find, and one they could definitely use. They dusted off as much sand as they could, then laid it out as the marker of their campsite, while the little children picked up the plentiful tiny shells, much different than the

---

[193] *Todah rabbah* - Hebrew for 'Thank you very much."

Chapter 33   The Galilee

large ones they had found on the Mediterranean beaches. They quickly ate their hummus on bread, then bedded down under the stars and talked about Abraham, Y'shua, and others of the scriptures that this special place brought to mind.

Everyone was sleeping well, when Emily was awakened at around 4 AM by light rain drops. Not knowing how much rain might be on the way, she quickly woke David and they set up the tent as the morning star rose over the eastern side of the lake. After getting all of their little sleeping treasures in the tent, they enjoyed a couple more hours of sleep before waking to the sunlight and singing birds.

During breakfast the family talked about various events from scripture that had happened near where they were camped at the Sea of Galilee. They talked about Y'shua choosing his fishermen disciples there, giving the sermon on the mount at the north side of the Sea, walking on the water, the two miracles of loaves and fishes, Y'shua's rebuking the storm, having the apostles cast their nets on the other side of the boat to catch the fish, and cooking fish for his disciples after his resurrection.[194] They talked about Peter getting the tax from the fish's mouth,[195] and the children imagined that there must be treasure from wrecked ships on the bed of the sea. They looked across the beautiful lake and watched the fishing boats, many not looking much different than they would have 2,000 years before. They talked about the two possessed men who lived in the cemetery across the lake and the story of Y'shua casting their demons into the pigs who ran off the cliffs into the sea below.[196] The family looked at the steep cliffs across the lake and imagined the story taking place. Since their scripture readings over the past couple of weeks had been in the New Testament, many of the stories were fresh on their minds.

All the talk of stories of the sea, fish, and sunken treasure had the children raring to get to the lake. As soon as scripture time was over, David took them to the water's edge where they could swim, fish, and play. As the sun rose higher in the sky, people began arriving at the beach, both Arab and Jewish, and all were cordial toward them, the owners of the now very impressive big orange family tent on the top of the hill with the huge beautiful rug in front. As the day wore on, the beach filled with people. The Varelas were unaware that, besides being the first day of Jewish *Rosh Hashanah*, it was also the last day of Islamic Ramadan. As was their usual practice, the older children scoured the big boulders at the north end of the beach for abandoned fishing gear, left by frustrated or unknowing fishermen. They found several hooks, bobbers, and plenty of line to make themselves a way to fish.

---

[194]Matt. 4-8 and 14-15; Mark 4; John 21
[195]Matt. 17:27
[196]Matt. 8

317

Fishing Lessons

An Arab man, there with his family of young children, noticed them trying to fish with their little lines and called them over. It was not important that they spoke different languages. Verbal communication was not important for this friendship-building exercise. He took a two liter soda bottle, cut a three inch hole in one side of the middle, then put a handful of bread in the bottom of a plastic grocery bag, poked a few holes in the baggie, fed the handles of it through the hole he had made in the bottle, then back up through the neck, screwing the lid on over the baggie to secure it in place. He tied a piece of fishing line to the bottle, walked out waist deep, filled it with water and let it go. Immediately it was swarmed with a school of one to two inch fish, who entered the newly-cut hole in the bottle to eat the bread. He then picked up the bottle covering the hole with his hand and handed it to the children, who thanked him and ran excitedly to Daddy and Mama with their first catch of fish.

Emily watched how the other family was preparing their fish, and decided to try it herself. Another Arab family who had been cooking out and swimming on the other side of them, asked the children if they would like to have the new grill they had been using. It was a small lightweight apparatus the family had seen in various markets throughout Israel and had learned were considered disposable, the same type of grill the family had been served steaks from in the middle of the night at Kiryat Chaim on the Mediterranean. They thanked the family for the grill and Emily began preparing the fish like she had seen the woman do by cutting the heads at the gills, twisting them, and pulling out the innards before putting them on the grill. As she cooked, David helped the children enjoy the red air mattress the other Arab family had given them. Three to four at a time straddled it and happily rode through the water with Daddy pulling.

Once the fish were done, she called the family over to try their new cuisine, which she strategically named 'fish chips.' Chips were not something the family ate at home and they were a rare treat anytime. Just the 'chips' in the name was enough to have the children enjoy them until they were all gone and ready to head back to the water to catch more.

Emily took Natanyah and Moshe into the tent for a nap while the others fished and played in the water with David. She got up after her half-hour nap, and left them to sleep for longer so she could spend time with David watching the other children playing, discussing how blessed they were

Chapter 33   The Galilee

with their children and for the experiences they were having here in the promised land. Soon after Moshe and Natanyah woke up, the sound of music wafted down from the road above. The children noticed the familiar sound, cheerful metallic music which brought back memories of their visits to Mexico. Could it be, they questioned one another, the *ice cream truck*? Excitedly, they raced to and up the long flight of concrete stairs, Victor and the younger girls squealing with delight as they ran. When they reached the top, they were thrilled to see the ice cream van coming toward them and the driver was just as pleased to see the little mob of children dressed in wet orange shirts congregated in the entrance to the parking lot. The children waved Emily up the stairs, so she waddled quickly over with enough shekels to buy each of them an ice cream pop. Everyone, including the driver, went away very happy. The older children began eating theirs quickly to keep them from melting as they descended the steps toward the beach, where David and Natanyah waited for theirs. They all gave thanks for their special treat, then went back to their beach activities.

As the day wore on, more and more families arrived, mostly Arab, many with small tents that they set up on the tiny pebble beach. The Varelas, still unaware that it was the last day of Ramadan, were surprised to see their little lonely beach become so populated in such a short period of time. By late afternoon, most of those remaining on the beach were the couples and families who had set up tents.

319

34 - Celebrations

Yom Revi'i (Fourth Day)   Second Day of *Rosh Hashanah*

By nightfall, all of the Jewish families were gone and the beach began to get louder with music from various sites. A car parked above where the Varelas' tent was set up, and several young Arab men gathered, opening the doors and trunk so they could better enjoy their music while they stood outside and partied. The Varelas were glad they had set up the tent that morning, as they would have felt more vulnerable on their mats below whatever was going on around the car above.

The children fell off to sleep, in spite of the blasting music, but David and Emily were not able to rest well. Much of the music, if that was indeed what it was defined as, was in English with the crudest language they had ever heard in song, and both of them had been around some rough places in their past. The noise lasted until nearly 4 AM when the group packed up and left, and while David and Emily had drifted in and out of sleep a few times just from exhaustion, they were not well rested at all. So just before dawn, they fell into a deep sleep, glad their noisy neighbors had left.

The children awoke just after sun-up, but seeing their parents still sleeping, lay quietly, some falling asleep again. As the sun began to heat up the tent, they could be contained no longer. It was morning and they were at a lake. It was time to get up! David opened the tent door flap and was amazed at the sight. From his viewpoint in the doorway of the big tent on the hill at the top of the massive rug, he looked down toward the sea and to both sides to see that his little family was surrounded with small tents. He felt like a king in a castle surrounded by the dwellings of his subjects or, more appropriately, a sheik surrounded by his clan. His surprised reaction drew Emily to the tent door where she also marveled at the number of small tents that seemed to have shown up overnight. She wondered if their occupants had gotten any sleep with the music blasting.

Armando, Briana, and Isabel helped Mama get breakfast ready, while Daddy took Victor, Rebeka, Moshe, and Natanyah on a walk across the big boulders to the north. They admired the odd scene of their big tent perched on the hill with the majestic Arabic rug in front, and all the little tents in front of and beside it.

After breakfast and scripture time, they played in the water and tried their soda bottle fishing apparatus, catching over fifty small fish. The Guitar Couple now lived just up the shoreline in Tiberius, so came and met the

Chapter 34   Celebrations

family on the beach to visit for a little while, as they shared the fish chips the Varelas cooked on their new grill. After their visit, the children played more in the water, while Emily watched, perched atop her throne of stacked folded bed mats in the shade of the great tent.

When nap time had come and gone, the family walked the mile and a half north to the markets to buy food for the next day which would be the scriptural high day of *Yom Teruah*. Since it was a day set apart by Yah in the scriptures and not a day of business, they would have all their purchasing done before sundown. But when they got to town, they were surprised to learn the shops were closed. They were a little concerned because they did not have enough food to make it through the next day, but knew that Yah would provide what they needed and had learned over the years from keeping the fast of *Yom Kippur*,[197] that fasting for a few hours was not going to hurt anyone. They had water and fish. That was enough.

After returning, then walking back up to the public restrooms to empty their toilet bucket, the Oil Lady, who lived in a nearby village came for a short visit. Her friendly smile was always a welcome sight, and she brought along fruit and other snacks for the family. She informed them, "The Jews celebrate *Rosh Hashanah* for two days. That's why the shops are still closed."

They told her the story of how they had gotten to the beach, and she marveled, stating, "Wow, you all are truly blessed. I've never known of drivers to do something like that so near to the high day."

Once again, they felt the love of their Creator, knowing that He had been looking down on them, giving them blessings they could never even have dreamed of. And the family wondered again if the gift of the free ride and drinks came from the drivers or from the shaven woman with the opera voice.

Before the Oil Lady, David and Emily placed an order for small bottles of anointing oils to send to over ten dozen people who had been watching for their updates and praying for them. They had wanted to do something special for them and decided anointing oils made by their friend using olive and other essential oils from the Promised Land would be an appropriate thank you gift.

The children went back and forth between playing in the water, fishing, and climbing on the boulders. Natanyah, who had turned two years old just

---

[197]Lev. 23:32 It *shall be* unto you a sabbath of rest, and ye shall afflict your souls: in the ninth *day* of the month at even, from even unto even, shall ye celebrate your sabbath. - This verse references the fast of *Yom Kippur*, the Day of Atonement. Upon deeper study of scripture, it is a complete fast from all food and drink.

321

before the family left for Israel, thought she was just as big as the others and wanted to explore just like them. David and Emily did not let her play near the water without their supervision, but were not concerned about her climbing on the boulders with her older siblings. In Tennessee, their place had very steep, wooded hills, and one of the things the family often did together on the New Moons, since David was not working on those days, was to take hikes through the woods, sliding down one very long steep hill, climbing down a waterfall, following the path of the light streams of spring water down the rocks, then meeting another trickle, climbing up another water fall and then up the steep hill on the other side and back to the house. It was an adventurous climb, but the family was used to doing it together and sometimes took visiting friends along that were not accustomed to such extreme hiking. Natanyah, as well as the others, was used to climbing up and down, so David and Emily thought nothing of her climbing on the rocks with the others. However, Israeli onlookers that were unaware of the children's level of experience in rough climbing were not at all pleased with what they must have seen as irresponsible parents. First, David and Emily noticed a woman pointing, and when they did nothing but watch the children from a distance, a middle age Jewish woman angrily approached them, scolding them for allowing their little ones to do such dangerous activities. To calm her down, David climbed up the boulders where he could be closer to Natanyah and the other smaller children. Though that did not seem to completely pacify the woman, she did go back to her family of children and grandchildren.

Free Fish

After tiring of the boulders, the children came back, and the older four took their fishing lines and bottles and went across the boulders at the edge of the water north of the beach, hoping to catch some of the bigger fish they had seen swimming around them earlier. After several bites, but no fish, they returned to Mama telling her of all the fish the two Jewish men at the far end had caught. Emily decided it might be a good idea to buy the fish from them, since they did not have enough food to make it through the next day. With David's reluctant approval, she sent Armando and Briana to ask how much they would sell the fish for, instructed them how to ask in Hebrew, then watched as they approached the relaxed fishermen.

"How much do the fish cost?" questioned Armando.

Chapter 34   Celebrations

The men looked at each other, then back at Armando, shaking their heads and telling him, "They're not for sale."

Armando took the shekels Mama had given him out of his pocket and offered them to the men. The men looked at each other in surprise, discussed the situation, then mentioning something about *mitzvah*, they handed Armando the fish, stringer and all, and waved away the money saying, "Just take them."

The children thanked them, then ran, jumping from one boulder to another to tell their parents the great news. Free fish for breakfast tomorrow! David and Emily were astounded again and gave thanks to Yah, blessing the fishermen as they did. It had not occurred to them that the reason the fishermen would not take money may have been because it was *Rosh Hashanah.*

Armando took the fish to the water and secured them on the stringer between some rocks, so they would not get away. Sundown was approaching and they really wanted to see the New Moon of the seventh month, which would mark the beginning of *Yom Teruah* and finalize the dates for *Yom Kippur* and *Sukkot*, but the hill they would have to climb would have taken them at least a couple of hours, and they were not even sure if they would be allowed on the property, so they decided to be content knowing that the month was 30 days this time, since their American friend had informed them that the moon had not been sighted the night before.[198] The other campers, mostly Arabs celebrating after Ramadan, began to pack up and leave.

Yom Teruah

Yom Chamishi (Fifth Day)

By sundown, the beach was completely empty again except for the Varelas' great tent. They ate a light supper, bathed in the sea, put on their clean green shirt clothes, blew blasts on the short piece of hose they brought to use as a trumpet, then went to bed, the parents exhausted from lack of sleep the night before. Just as they lay down, a car pulled to the cliff above them, opened their doors and trunk, and the party that had begun the night before continued with even louder music. The exhausted family slept well, in spite of it.

---

[198]Biblical Hebrew months begin with the sighting of the first sliver of the New Moon just after sundown in the western sky. This begins day one of the month. The Biblical set-apart days of the seventh month, as explained in Lev. 23, occur on the 1st (*Yom Teruah*), 10th (*Yom Kippur*), 15th (Sukkot), and 22nd.(Eighth Day) and, cannot be established until the new moon is sighted and the first day of the month is determined.

The family awoke late again on this special feast day, but were glad for the good rest they got. Armando ran out to check on the fish he had procured the night before, only to find they had escaped, leaving the stringer behind. He was sad, but knew there was nothing that could be done about it, so brought the report back to Mama. She reassured him, telling him, "YHWH gives and YHWH takes away. Blessed be the name of YHWH."[199]

They ate the rest of the food they had for breakfast, the parents being careful not to eat more than necessary to help ration it throughout the day for the children. But everyone was satisfied. They used some of their bread to catch more fish with their soda bottle and Mama cooked them over the fire. As they prepared the fish, the Cell Phone Couple from Be'er Sheva called to tell them they were looking for the beach, so the seven children went up to the road where they could be seen easily. The mob of children was easy to spot in their green shirts and the couple recognized them, even though they had never met face to face.

Cell Phone Couple

The children led them down the stairs to the beach and proudly showed them their beautiful rug. The couples introduced themselves and the visitors presented the family with a bag full of tangerines, other snacks, and individual juices for the children. Emily told them what a blessing that was, and told the story of them not being able to purchase food the evening before and of the escaped fish. They were glad to have been used by Yah to provide another special treat for the family.

As they visited and got to know one another, the woman noticed Emily's tired appearance. Even though she was in her element living outside surrounded by her family, being over eight months pregnant and the stress of having to have gone through the last month without her husband had worn on her. The woman, a mother herself, knowing the self-sacrifice that goes with that position and the fact that mothers often neglect themselves for the sake of their families, instantly picked up on something kind she could do for Emily. Without saying anything, she reached into her purse, pulled out a pair of nail clippers and began to trim Emily's fingernails.

Emily was once again in awe of the kindness of the people that Yah had put them in contact with. She did not resist the gracious offer, knowing that her nails needed trimming and that the woman was performing an act of service after the likeness of Y'shua. After she finished the fingernails, she offered to do the toenails. Emily humbly consented, telling her that it would be a great blessing, since in her late stage of pregnancy, it was difficult to reach them herself. The woman served with gladness and Emily praised Yah for her and her kind ways. The man and David got acquainted with one another as they watched the children.

---

[199] Job 1:21

Chapter 34   Celebrations

The couple was enthusiastic about introducing the family to a friend of theirs that worked at the Galilee Experience in Tiberius. The Cell Phone Woman told David she was going to take his wife up the road into town, and before David and Emily could consult one another about it, she kindly took Emily's arm and whisked her away to the car. David and Emily were both shocked, but did not want to turn down the hospitality of this kind couple, so David went on with his conversation with the man, while she showed Emily around, driving her into town to become familiar with the area and the Galilee Experience. When they arrived, they were all surprised at the meeting because the friend of the Cell Phone Couple's that worked there was none other than the family's Host from Osifia at the top of Mount Carmel. He asked about the family and Emily explained how David had just returned after being gone for a full month. They both agreed that where they were was a better arrangement than his house would have been, since David had only planned to have been gone for a few days. The Host then invited, "We have a full-screen movie about the Galilee. We'd like to treat you to a showing of it. Why don't you bring the family in to see it?"

Emily replied, "Thank you! We plan to be walking back to the bus station tomorrow to go back to Kiryat Yam. Could we watch it then?"

The Host answered, "Sure, be here at 10 AM."

Emily agreed, looking forward to sharing the news with the family. They offered one another *shalom* and the woman took Emily back down the stairs and walked around on the pier and through some of the sites around that part of town.

While the ladies looked around in Tiberius, the ice cream truck reappeared at the beach. The Varela children knew they would not be getting ice cream today because it was a *'mo'ed,'*[200] an appointment with Yah, the feast of trumpets. The older children understood, but the little ones were disappointed to hear the bells and see other children buying, knowing they could not have any that day. And when they stood there watching, the ice cream vendor looked disappointed, too. David assured them there would be another time and that Yah would bless them for denying themselves on His special day.

After the Cell Phone Lady thought Emily had had enough of a break from responsibilities, she drove back to the pebble beach south of town where David and the Cell Phone Man continued to get to know one another as they celebrated the feast and the children played nearby.

---

[200]*Mo'ed* - Hebrew for appointed time, the word used in scripture to describe certain meetings with YHWH that are days of worship, and not for doing business.

It had been a peaceful day, full of the joy of being with other believers, and the family was once again blessed with kindness as well as having more than their needs provided. After sundown and the high day was over, the Cell Phone Woman told her husband, "It's time for supper. Why don't you take David in and get falafel for everyone."

"Ok," he replied, "How many?"

"Get one for each person, 11," she answered.

David, not wanting to take advantage of their generosity, reminded them, "The younger ones probably won't eat a whole one. We shouldn't need that many."

They all agreed and the two men got in the car and drove to Tiberius, while they talked about various things both from scripture and history that had happened in the area. After getting falafel, they returned to the beach, enjoyed their supper together, then the couple prayed with the family, then invited them to their home in Be'er Sheva before going back to the States.

"We'd love to," David and Emily agreed.

"Probably the best time would be after the baby is born, after Sukkot. We plan to rent a car at some point after that and can travel easier," said David.

The Cell Phone Woman was excited at the prospect of meeting the little one. The family stood on the curb and waved as the couple left for their long drive south to Be'er Sheva. They were thankful to have met such fine people.

The beach was nearly empty again. *Rosh Hashanah* was over the night before, Ramadan the night before that, so most people in Israel were back at their normal activities. The family walked to their tent, now void of all the little tents that had surrounded it the day before, admired the beautiful rug, and enjoyed watching the colors change on the cliffs and hills on the eastern side of the sea as the sun set in the west.

Galilee Experience
Yom Shishi (Sixth Day)

The family slept undisturbed and awoke at dawn, still catching up on rest various ones had lost over the past three nights, a little later than their normal time to wake, but getting up and about just after sunrise. This time, they tied up their bed mats, folded their sheets, and packed everything away. The children were sure to get the red air mattress completely deflated and packed in one of the backpacks, but they decided to leave the portable grill there for someone else, since they were already loaded. They packed and prepared to leave their latest home on the pebble beach. Everyone hated to leave the beautiful rug, but there was no way they could

Chapter 34   Celebrations

take it, and knew that it would be enjoyed by many others once they were gone.

They walked up the steps, turned north, stopping by the restrooms to empty and wash out the bucket, and then headed up the shore toward Tiberius. On the way, Emily called the doctor, who said he would meet them at the bus stop later in the morning. They stopped at the little shop on the west side of the road to get some cheese and fruit for breakfast and vegetables, hummus, and bread for lunch, then ate breakfast there on the sidewalk before going farther into town.

Once at the Galilee Experience, they watched the informative documentary, spent a little time talking to their Host from Osifia, then browsed the gift shop. Emily's parents had given each of the children a little money to spend while in the Land, so some of them chose to use it there. Moshe bought a tiny wooden chest engraved with a fish; Rebeka got one like it but engraved with 'Jerusalem;' Natanyah, a little sparkly metal box for storing small things; Isabel, a snow globe of Jerusalem to give to her grandparents and a refrigerator magnet of Jerusalem; and Briana bought a tiny *menorah* and saved the rest of her money to buy the Anne Frank book on the way back through Amsterdam. Victor decided to wait until later to get something, and Armando had already spent part of his on the knife and still planned to get the fishing equipment from the *shuk*. Isabel also still had money left over. Emily found a Hebrew song book, which included transliterations, what scriptures they came from, as well as piano notes, guitar chords, and a CD with some of the songs recorded. She thought it was horribly expensive at over 200 shekels (over $60), but most everything in Israel was expensive, so she used her gift money, adding a little extra of her own, knowing the book would greatly benefit them in their times of worship.

They left the gift shop and walked toward the bus station, as their appointment with the doctor approached. It was sad to once again be leaving a new home, but since they now had the more permanent place in Kiryat Yam, they looked forward to being there again. They crossed the busy street, walked up the hill to the bus station, then up the dingy concrete stairs to the bus level and sat down on benches to wait. Emily was a little nervous, wondering where exactly they were supposed to meet. They each spoke the other's language, but neither extremely well, so phone communication was difficult. Emily got up and paced back and forth between the buses and ticket windows with some of the children tagging along, to make sure she did not miss him. She certainly did not want to inconvenience him as he did them this great favor.

The Doctor

On one of her trips back toward the benches, she saw a tall, balding, friendly-looking man with a big smile walking toward her from the steps. Instantly, she knew it must be the Doctor she had spoken with on the

327

phone. He greeted the family and they introduced themselves. He asked, "How are you enjoying Israel?"

David, "It's great! We're having a good time here."

Emily had a little difficulty swallowing that one since he had just gotten there, but let it go, glad he was enjoying himself. He was not as much of a camper as she was and she was very glad he was being jovial about it. After a few more friendly questions, the Doctor informally got down to business scribbling the information he needed to help the family get the birth certificate after the baby was born. On his palm-sized notepad, he took down Emily's full name, age, date of birth, and a few personal facts dealing with the pregnancy. He explained the process and told her that after the birth, he would need to examine the baby to finish filling out the paper work. He would then give that form to them, they would take it to the *Misrad Hap'nim*,[201] and use it as proof of birth in order to receive the birth certificate.

The family had learned that the reason Israel required this paperwork for babies who were not born in a hospital or with a doctor is because of abuse of the welfare system by many non-Jews.   In the past, there had been repeated instances of a woman bringing a baby to the *Misrad Hap'nim*, getting a birth certificate, getting on benefits, then taking the baby and giving it to a friend, who brought it back, giving it a different name, in order to get benefits, then passing it down the line. To curb the problem, they began requiring any baby being born outside of a hospital or doctor setting to have documentation proving the woman was pregnant and then that the baby was born and alive before it could be given the birth certificate.

After finishing business, the doctor cordially invited the family, "You should come to my home to visit and meet my family. I can show you around the Golan Heights.[202] It's beautiful!"

Emily replied, "After the baby is born, we plan to rent a car. That would be a good time for us to come. We look forward to it!"

Besides being a particularly friendly individual, he was interested in families like the Varelas and the other large family from the U.S., who home birthed and had several children. He and his wife had five, and even though he was a doctor, had delivered some of his at home. He was an advocate in Israel for home birth and worked closely with midwives, and also did house calls and attended home births himself. He was the Varelas' kind of doctor, for sure.

After he left, they went to buy tickets to get back to Kiryat Yam. The man at the counter asked, "How many?"

---

[201] *Misrad Hap'nim* - Hebrew for 'Ministry of Interior.'
[202] *Golan* Heights - the northernmost part of Israel, bordering Syria and Lebanon.

Chapter 34   Celebrations

"Nine, seven are children," replied Emily.

"Where are you going?"

"Kiryat Yam," she answered.

"Kiryat Yam? Why not take a *sherut*? It will take you straight there. You won't have to change buses, and it will be cheaper."

Long Walk

Emily was delighted to hear that news and thanked the man for the advice. He showed them where to catch the *sherut* and she led the family in that direction. Once there, David, the negotiator, took over. The driver wanted twenty extra shekels to go to Kiryat Yam from where the highway turned off at Kiryat Chaim. David told him, "I'll pay you the twenty extra if you'll take us all the way to our home."

The driver agreed, so the family loaded their things in the back, except for the number one pack which Emily kept with her, and boarded the *sherut*. They enjoyed the peaceful ride west past forests, more agriculture, and towns of stucco covered houses.

The driver took them to the edge of Kiryat Chaim and said, "This is your stop."

David reminded, "You said you would take us to our home for twenty shekels more."

The driver rudely told him, "I don't have time to go to that section of town. This is where I am stopping."

He got out and unloaded the family's belongings. David paid him his fee, minus the twenty extra shekels that had been agreed upon to get them home. An argument ensued and the driver threw his hands up in the air and left.

It was a long walk from where he had let them off to their little home and *Shabbat* was quickly approaching. They stopped by the markets and bought bread, sweet breads, juice, fruit, hummus, milk, and cheese. They were fully loaded with their packs, tent, bed mats and now groceries, as they walked the final few blocks to their house. After unloading, Armando and Briana went to Aaron's house to get *Arnav* and *Chatul*, Emily started baths with the little ones, and David went to Tzipporah's house to pay the next month's rent. As she came to the door, he extended his hand with the money, but she refused it, saying, "It's too close to *Shabbat*. Come back next week."

329

David walked away, a bit puzzled, since it was not yet sundown. But he admired the way the Jewish people guarded *Shabbat* and knew he could learn from them how to do a better job, himself. He returned with the news about the rent and the big children returned with the pets. Everyone gave thanks for Tzipporah and Aaron and his family. After baths and supper, David and Armando went to synagogue.

Shabbat at Home

Emily stayed with the others and bedded the little ones down on the back porch. Shortly after the men returned, they heard guitar music coming from a nearby roof. Armando quickly discovered it was the Brothers. Emily remembered the new book she had just purchased, so sent it with Armando to see if any of the songs were familiar to them. He climbed up the bars at the big back window, onto the roof, then walked across Elena's roof and climbed the battlement[203] onto their roof.

Armando handed them the book, giving them the message from Mama. They flipped through it, noting that it had some good songs in it. But when they looked at the cover and saw that it said, 'Y'shua', the younger Brother said, "This is bad. We can't even have this in the house," as he handed it back to Armando. Armando promptly returned the way he had come, in order to bring Mama her new book back. She was saddened by the message he delivered, but knew what their religion taught about Y'shua, whom they derogatorily referred to as *Yeshu*.[204] She took it from him and he returned to let the Brothers show him some chords on the guitar.

The couple had some quiet time on the front porch, while Armando was gone. When he returned for the night, they went to sleep to the familiar sounds of their neighbors entertaining guests on the patio behind them.

The earlier risers woke up at dawn to the singing of the birds, but stayed in bed, enjoying the rest and quietness of *Shabbat*. After spending time praying, David and Emily got up and had a quiet snack, enjoying each other's company much more freely than they had the week before with the absence of jet lag and the stresses they had faced the previous month.

As the children got up, they put away their mats and sheets, dressed in their *Shabbat* clothes, then all sat down to eat together at the little bucket and plywood table on the front porch. After breakfast, they went to synagogue across the street, assuming their regular positions and enjoying the liturgy, songs, and reading of the *torah*. Emily and the

---

[203]Deut. 22:8 When thou buildest a new house, then thou shalt make a battlement for thy roof, that thou bring not blood upon thine house, if any man fall from thence.

[204]*Yeshu* - Hebrew acronym for '*Yimah Schimo Wezikhro*' meaning 'May his name and memory be stricken out.'

Chapter 34   Celebrations

children were becoming accustomed to and familiar with it, as David still adjusted to its newness.

After synagogue, they went home, ate lunch, and David took the children to the beach while Emily lay down for a nap with Natanyah. When they returned a couple of hours later, the family listened to some of the songs on their new CD, following in the book as they learned them and sang along. Moshe's favorite was the upbeat, middle-eastern *Ki Mi'tzi'on*,[205] and they all enjoyed singing it.

---

[205]*Ki Mi'tzi'on* – For from Zion, from Mic 4:2b ...for the law shall go forth of Zion, and the word of YHWH from Jerusalem.

35 - Ain[206] Arnav

Son of El

Week 9   *Yom Rishon* (First Day)   10/5

Her whole family together, having been soothed to sleep by the Mediterranean breeze caused Emily to awaken energetically. She got up ready to go to the market for breakfast food, since the family had returned from Tiberius too close to *Shabbat* to get it then. As soon as the store opened, she and Isabel quickly went and brought back fruit and yogurt for all, enjoying the brisk walk in the crisp autumn air. After morning routine, Emily and Briana rode their bicycles to the library so Emily could check emails and do some banking, while Briana read. It was good to have David back, to be on the bicycles again (even if for just short trips) feeling the wind on their faces.

David stayed home keeping the others busy cleaning, doing laundry, and mopping, a job that naturally accompanied laundry done by hand with several small children. By now, they knew the laundry system well, even though Elena and Olga had done most of it over the past few weeks. First the switch on the kitchen wall was flipped to start the water heating while the clothes soaked in the bathtub in cool water to get most of the grime out. Next, the clothes were moved to a laundry tub that Eti had given them while the bathtub was cleaned out and filled half full with hot water and soap and the clothes added back. Then the clothes were agitated with a stick, since the water was too hot to put hands into for long. Afterward, they were taken outside, where they were rinsed in buckets of cold water, which was then emptied onto the flowers. The clothes were wrung out well, then hung on the line. The little ones loved any job that involved water, so mopping was naturally next. The challenge was keeping their little wet feet out of the sand in the yard or at least keeping them out of the house afterward.

Armando, having outgrown laundry as a pastime, worked on the bicycles, doing minor repairs so they would be in good shape to give away. The family thought it would be better to bless people in Israel with them, than to go to the trouble of disassembling and boxing them to take home. Bicycles in Israel were very expensive, and would be a real treat for someone to receive.

Emily and Briana returned from the library and the rest of the day was spent visiting with the various neighbors. David met Aaron's grandfather,

---

[206] *Ain* – Hebrew for 'There isn't any.'

Chapter 35   *Ain* Arnav

Humberto, a Spanish speaker from Argentina who lived behind Elena's house. He was walking home when he saw David and called out, "*Buenas tardes!*"[207]

"*Buenas tardes!*" David returned.

The conversation continued in Spanish, the men introducing themselves. Humberto replied, "Varela, so you're Jewish!"

"Not that I know of."

"But Varela is a Jewish name," he said. "The reason it doesn't appear in the records is because the Varelas were the assassins. Varela comes from '*bar*' and '*ela*', meaning 'son of God' in Aramaic."

David had learned the year before during his Sukkot visit what 'Varela' meant and that it was recognized by those familiar with Jewish names, but this was news to him. He thought of the reputation his family had in Mexico for being good fighters who stood up for the underdog and those being mistreated; he saw the connection.

He visited with the neighbor at the stone fence in the back yard until just before sunset, when Humberto excused himself and walked the few steps on the brick road to his house across the narrow street.

Misrad Hap'nim
Yom Sheni (Second Day)

David rounded up the children for supper and they all bedded down under the stars, Natanyah relaxing herself by massaging Mama's ears. David and Emily discussed the next day's scheduled visit to the *Misrad Hapnim* and prayed for *Abba*'s will to be done.

In the morning as previously agreed, Emily took Briana out the back door to the neighbors' house behind at 10:00 AM, wearing their orange tops, long pin-striped denim skirts, and their usual head scarves, Briana's a bandana and Emily's a larger *tichel*,[208] tied with the long ends twisted and wrapped together over the top of her head in classic Yiddish manner. The neighbor was dressed in her usual fashion wearing skin tight shorts and a stylish tank top, loud but tastefully done make-up and very long fine fashion nails. They were an odd-looking threesome by American standards, but no one in Israel seemed to pay much notice. They briskly walked to Weizman then boarded the bus to the *Haifa Merkazit HaMifratz* station.

---

[207]*Buenas tardes* - Spanish for 'Good afternoon.'
[208]*Tichel*-Yiddish for head scarf.

Once on board, they sat facing a woman in her fifties who began chatting with the neighbor. The subject of *Rosh Hashanah* and *Yom Kippur* ensued. The bus soon neared the woman's stop and she got off. Emily asked the neighbor, "What do you do on *Yom Kippur*?"

"Oh, we fast from *everything*! - food, drink, cigarettes, computer, television, telephone, and we go to synagogue, the only time I go to synagogue."

Emily was surprised that secular Jews would go to such lengths of observance. She asked, "Why? Why do you fast on *Yom Kippur*?"

"Because the temple was destroyed," she replied nonchalantly.

Emily was a bit confused by her statement, but did not ask further questions. The woman was accustomed to hearing the book of Lamentations read the only day of the year she attended synagogue. The book of Lamentations was written by the prophet Jeremiah as he lamented the destruction of Jerusalem during his time because of the refusal of the House of Judah to turn back to the ways of YHWH. The House of Israel had been scattered almost 150 years before because of their refusal to follow YHWH's instructions. According to scripture, *Yom Kippur* was a time of affliction to be grieved by sin while atonement was being made by the high priest. For centuries, Jewish people had read Lamentations on that day as they fasted, since it was written by Jeremiah as he lamented the sins of Israel and Judah that brought about YHWH's punishment on them, including the destruction of the first temple.

The family had been observing the fast of *Yom Kippur* since 2004 and had always been surprised that there were not more people who completely fasted from food and drink on the special day. They fasted according to the command, and though fasting is not mentioned specifically in the instruction, they recognized from their study of scripture that the term 'afflict your soul' referred to fasting from food and drink, and was a time of deep introspection. As followers of Y'shua, they reasoned that obeying an instruction to fast for one day was the least they could do in response to what he had gone through for them. And now to learn that there were secular Jews who would go through so much suffering because of the destruction of the temple, a man-made building, really put things into perspective. It gave her even greater respect for the Jewish people and the dedication they had for their understanding of the things of YHWH.

Once in Haifa, they caught another bus to the *Misrad Hap'nim*. Inside the odd-shaped glass building, Emily removed her fanny pack, containing her money and knife, and handed it to the attendant as she passed through the metal detector. Briana unhooked her little gray coin purse, containing her knife, tweezers and two shekels, from her skirt and laid it in the bin as she walked through security.

They rode the elevator up to the office, took a number and waited their turn. Once they were called, the neighbor took Emily to the window, where

Chapter 35   *Ain* Arnav

a grouchy-looking official woman looked her over. The neighbor told her, "This is my friend. They are expecting their eighth child and want to get residency in Israel."

The woman looked at Emily and asked, "Are you Jewish?"

Emily replied, "I don't know. I don't think so."

"What right do you have to live in Israel if you're not Jewish?!?"

Emily already had her PDA out and opened up in Hebrew to Ezekiel 37, one of the scriptural prophecies that talk about Ephraim coming home. She started to explain by saying, "The scriptures say that in the last days, Ephraim will be joined with Judah and be brought back to the Land and the two will become one again."

The woman interrupted Emily by bursting out in hysterical laughter. Emily turned around to see the reaction of the thirty or more other people who were waiting in the room, but most had not seemed to notice. The woman stopped laughing only long enough to call out, "Next," without even excusing Emily.

The neighbor motioned for them to leave, and Emily and Briana hurried along behind her, Emily somewhat humiliated and wondering if the neighbor was, as well, though she did not show it.

After stepping back out to the elevators, she told Emily, "I can't believe she was so rude!"

Just then, a male officer stepped out of the private door behind them across the hall from the elevators. His eyes were quickly drawn to the appealing young woman and he asked, "Is there some type of problem?"

She explained the situation to which the man very amiably replied, "They would have much better success getting residency by visiting the Israeli Embassy in the U.S."

Emily had to guard herself from rolling her eyes at the manner in which the officer spoke to her friend. Just when she thought he was about to ask her for a date, the elevator bell rang, the door opened, and the ladies were rescued from the beauty-struck agent.

All Choked Up

Back at the house, David and the children did laundry. After it was hung out on the lines in the front yard, they went inside to get a snack and listen to their new CD, when they heard a rattling noise coming from *Arnav*'s cage out back. Armando led the pack of children outside to investigate and saw *Arnav* jumping from side to side as he crashed into the wires of the cage, while making choking noises like a cat about to vomit a hairball. *Chatul*, with a horrified look on his face, was dodging the crazed rabbit. Before anything could be done, *Arnav* fell over dead. In the ensuing investigation, Armando discovered that the ball in the water bottle had gotten stuck when *Arnav* got a drink, causing the water to come out too fast. *Arnav* had choked to death right there in front of them. They were all shocked and saddened at the loss of the once scraggly bunny who they were successfully restoring to good health with their prayers and loving care.

The three ladies caught buses back to Kiryat Yam and walked to their alley. Emily thanked the neighbor for trying to get them residency in Israel; then she and Briana went to tell David the news. As they came through the back door, the children rushed to meet them, Moshe, Rebeka, and Natanyah all crying. With everyone talking at the same time, Emily and Briana could not figure out what was wrong. When other voices quieted just a bit, Armando announced, unemotionally, "*Arnav*'s dead."

Emily was shocked, then saddened, as well, once she heard the breaking news story. Briana asked in disbelief, "What happened to him?!?"

Armando, having inherited his dad's propensity to take pleasure in causing others to react, sarcastically replied, "I killed him."

Briana was livid. "What did you do to *Arnav*?!?" she screamed at him.

Emily tried to shut down the ensuing argument as she comforted the crying little ones, as well as Briana, whose grief had erupted as blame. "It's OK. It's for the best. It sounds like he died very quickly and didn't suffer much. I know we'll miss him, but we'll be leaving in less than a month, anyway, and would have had to give him away. We got to take care of and love him for a few weeks. Maybe that's the only reason we had him, so that he could feel loved for a while."

Rebeka cried, "Why did he have to die?"

Emily replied, "I don't know, but Yah does. And he always does what's best for us. Let's just thank him for the time that he allowed us to have with *Arnav*, and for the time we have left with *Chatul*."

As Armando dug a grave under the pomegranate tree, Emily shared with David what had happened at the *Misrad Hap'nim*. David responded, "Well, I guess it wasn't meant to be. We don't want to be here if it's not the right time. And when it is, He'll make a way."

Emily agreed, as they walked to the funeral in the back yard. *Arnav* was wrapped in a small towel and laid in the shallow grave. Armando had the insight to put a board over him before covering the hole with sand, preventing the feral cats from digging him up again. The family stood around recalling special and comical events in the short time they had known *Arnav*.

Emily took Isabel to the market to get a few things to supplement what they had for supper. In the store, she began to get very tired, and by the time they returned, she was very weak, and went to bed early, the emotional stresses of the day having worn her down. David kept the children busy cleaning up the messes they made and playing with *Chatul*, who would also miss *Arnav*. Though he cuddled by Natanyah at nap time, ever since being adopted into the family, he had spent his nights snuggled with his the soft, fluffy companion.

The Science Museum

Yom Shlishi (Third Day)

At bedtime, they all lay on the back porch, *Chatul* going to sleep snuggled in Natanyah's wavy blond hair, so as not to be as lonely after the loss of his friend.

Nikolay continued to keep in touch with the family and encouraged them to see some sights while in Israel. They had recovered from their time being separated and then their trip to Tiberius, so were ready to go on another excursion. Their intentions in Israel had never been to be tourists, but to experience the land and the people, so they did not see the need to do much tourist activity. But at Nikolay's insistence, they boarded a bus to Haifa and went to the National Museum of Science, Technology, and Space. It was full of interactive exhibits which kept the children occupied. This season, there were hundreds of brontosauruses all over Haifa, colorfully painted by different artists, many of them at the museum. One of the main exhibits was that of early printing presses and included a copy of the Gutenberg Bible, the first major book printed in the west with movable type. There were also bicycle and driver safety exhibits, as well as lots of science exhibits. One room had a bed of nails, which Mama lay on to

Isabel

show the children that it really did not hurt. No one believed her enough to try it themselves. Then there was a room of various physics puzzles - things to keep little people busy for hours, and green energy exhibits. There was even a jet fighter outside that they could see close up and touch.

Pedaling Home   Part 3 – The Regathering

Late morning, Natanyah began to show her tiredness so Emily took her inside a white *sukkah*[209] that was set up outside near the jet. They lay down for a nap, as museum goers walked around outside it. David continued with the others through the museum, where there was something to keep everyone's interest.

They had not brought food, other than a few sunflower seeds and oranges, so decided to walk to the McDonald's across the yard from the museum. In the U.S., they did not eat out much, and when they did, tried to find the most nutritious restaurants they could afford. But after being gone for two months and not having had a hamburger, and very little of any other kind of meat, they decided to try it. They had heard the fast food meat in Israel was of better quality and hoped it was true. They all enjoyed their tasty hamburgers, sitting on the rock ledges in front of the museum. Moshe decided to take his to the dinosaurs in front of the museum. While petting one of the slick inanimate creatures, he dropped his burger on the ground. His little heart was broken, knowing a hamburger was a special treat. He started to cry, then picked it up, dusted it off and ate it before anyone could attempt to take it away from him.

After a long day, they caught the bus to *Merkazit HaMifratz*, the station on the north side of Haifa, past the *Misrad Hap'nim*, then got on the Kiryat Yam bus. The little family dressed alike always got the attention of others, which gave them the opportunity to meet many people and answer lots of questions about the way they lived, who they were, and the scriptures in general.

Shortly after arriving at their little abode, there was an unexpected knock at the door. David opened it to see two men from the synagogue carrying a huge box of non-perishable food, including couscous, beans, rice, seasoning packets, chocolate spread, crackers, and cookies. David thanked them, but did not understand why they were extending such kindness. The men smiled, waved at David, saying something he did not understand, then exited, closing the yard gate behind them, and marched purposefully back toward the synagogue. The family was puzzled, but excited to have the new food choices and dug in to figure out what to have for supper. Emily still had a chicken neck in the freezer, so she put that in the little pot on the hot plate for a soup to go with couscous.

Silly Girls

Yom Revi'i (Fourth Day)

As they ate the special supper, they asked blessings on the kind, generous men, then cleaned up and went to bed, to the sounds of their neighbors and friends enjoying each other's company late into the night.
With morning routines finished, Emily and Briana went to the library while

---

[209]*Sukkah* - Hebrew for tabernacle, booth, a temporary shelter.

Chapter 35   *Ain* Arnav

David and the children washed yesterday's clothes. Deep into the laundry process, Rebeka came in to tell David that Elena was there. He went to the door as she approached bearing another of her Russian, fruit-filled bread that the family always enjoyed. They were not able to communicate much, her first and second languages being Russian and Hebrew, and his being Spanish and English, so she scolded him as best she could for not bringing the laundry for her to wash, then left the bread, able to understand David's, "Thank you."

The children, always ready to eat, were excited, but knew they needed to wait until the others returned. When the two got back, Armando and Briana went to the store to buy milk. Upon their return, the family enjoyed the still warm bread with milk, as had become a regular tradition for them. When they finished, Isabel and Rebeka took Elena's tray back to her. They knocked on the door and Olga came, inviting them in. They stepped in, looking straight down the hallway, Rebeka giggling, as usual. Olga began laughing and Isabel asked her while using appropriate body language, "Where do you want the tray?"

Olga motioned toward the counter in the kitchen while giving instructions in Hebrew. The girls followed the hall to the end, where it turned right and went through the small dining room. There was a counter on the right side and the refrigerator stood in the corner beyond it. After setting the bread tray where they were instructed, the girls heard keys jingling and turned to see smiling Olga lock the door from the inside, then pull the keys out and playfully dangle them again.

Rebeka, still giggling, ran to grab the keys from her, but just as she reached for them, Olga picked her up, tossed her in a baby crib in the corner of the room beside the front door, and then dumped a bowl of hard, peppermint candies on top of her.

Isabel briefly sat down on the bed next to the crib, then jumped off and ran toward the front door, grabbing the keys off of the counter next to it to try and open the door. Olga quickly changed directions, grabbed Isabel, tickled her, then threw her on the bed, while Rebeka jumped out of the crib and ran for the door. The game continued with the girls alternating their plan of escape, all three of the ladies laughing, until Emily came to the door, wondering what had happened to her girls. She heard all the commotion through the wall of the house and had been afraid the girls were next door showing off as little girls are sometimes known to do. Olga told her, "We're just playing. It's fine if they want to stay for a while. Mother will be back soon."

Emily reminded them to be good and went back out the gate, through her own gate and into their house on the other side of the wall.

Eti called to say she was coming and to make sure the family would be there. A few minutes later she arrived, bearing homemade food in several of her usual plastic containers, but this time she got a surprise of her own.

339

Emily asked her, "Do you like to ride bicycles?"

"Oh, yes! But I don't have a bicycle," she replied.

"Well, you do now, if you want one. And we have one for your daughter, too," she said as Armando pulled out Isabel's bicycle.

"Oh, no! I could not take your bicycles!" she said.

"We can't take them with us. It's better for us to leave them here and we would like for you to have these if you could use them."

A big smile came over her face as she said, "OK, then. We will be glad to have them! Thank you very much!"

She was delighted. Since bicycles were so expensive there, it was a real treat for them, and Armando had them in tip top shape for their recipients. The family took them down their little street and put them into the trunk of her car parked on Weizman, feeling like it was the least they could do after all she had done for them since their first meeting seven weeks before. The sadness the family felt at knowing their cycling was over was overshadowed by the joy of seeing someone so happy to get the bicycles.

Since the time had changed earlier in the week, by the time Eti left, it was nap time for Natanyah. Emily did not like to start a nap too late in the afternoon because it would interfere with nighttime sleep. It was only 2 PM, but the daylight hours were the same, still just a few hours until sunset. Natanyah was getting very tired, and Emily herself could use the extra rest, so she lay down and let Natanyah cuddle *Chatul* in one hand and her ear in the other until she fell asleep.

David took the others to the beach, where the children planned to dig up their hidden surfboard and play in the water. As they walked past the play set, they met Aaron, who was chaining his bicycle so he could go swim. Armando asked Daddy, "Can Briana and I go with him and use the goggles that we got from Eti and the Family of Ten? We want to look for crabs and stuff on the rocks beside the pier."

They were both good swimmers and athletic, so he agreed and let them split off with Aaron, warning them, "Be careful."

Near Drowning

They all knew he would be close by watching them. Beside the rock pier that the fishermen used, there were dangerous undercurrents as the power of the waves hitting the pier forced the water beneath to rush back out to sea, sucking the sandy beach with it and creating deep sink holes. It was difficult to swim there, and the locals knew to stay a safe distance away for recreational swimming. The three youngsters enjoyed diving off

Chapter 35   *Ain* Arnav

of the rocks, then grabbing the rebar that stuck out of big pieces of concrete at the base of the pier to keep from getting sucked out by the waves. It took special skill to beat the undercurrents, but was a challenge for them that they enjoyed. To be successful, they had to time their dives just right and over the deep sinkhole. They waited until a wave got to the right place coming towards them, then dove far and fast, getting under the water before the wave hit the rocks and pulled out with an undertow. It was difficult to do, but they enjoyed the adrenaline rush that they did not get at the calmer sandy beach. It was dangerous, yet predictable enough to be safe for good swimmers.

David took the others on the path through the dunes that went more directly to the safer place to swim, ending up less than a hundred feet from the older children, but giving them some distance from supervision and younger siblings on the walk there. As they neared the water, they noticed a man looking to be in his sixties and another in his twenties taking off their shirts to prepare to go into the sea. They thought it looked like a father and mentally handicapped son, who appeared to be somewhat afraid of the water.

David led the younger children toward their safer swimming spot, then decided to take them up on the pier to watch Armando and Briana from above. As they walked by, the older man, wearing a *tallit katan*[210] with tassels began to push the younger one into the water, as if trying to encourage him to swim. Once the water was near waist high, the younger man began to scream and jump as the waves hit him. With each jump he got closer to the deep water by the pier. David and the children, now on top of the pier, stopped and watched, Armando and Briana having met up with him. The older man seemed to be trying to help the younger one get over being afraid of the water, but the younger was panicking and jumping in the wrong direction. A small wave came and the young man jumped and screamed, again getting another foot closer to the pier, when all at once, a big wave hit, sweeping him off his feet and into the deeper water. He went under and another big wave came. The older man tried to stay close to him, but the second big wave pulled him under, too. After the wave passed, the two came up, both screaming for help, then another wave crashed over them, taking them near the corner at the front of the pier where there was a strong whirlpool, water converging from both sides of the pier. As the older man tried to help the younger stay afloat, the younger flailed around and began pulling the older one under.

Armando, thinking quickly, told Briana and Aaron, "Follow me!" as he ran toward the buried surf board. They quickly dug with their hands, while he told them, "We can throw it to them so they don't drown!"

---

[210]*Tallit katan* - Hebrew for 'small tallit', a rectangular piece of fabric with *tzitziyot* on the four corners and a hole in the center big enough for the head to go through. It is often worn under other clothing to fulfill the command concerning wearing tassels.

Meanwhile, the fishermen above were rapidly reeling in their lines, knowing the men were in danger and trying to minimize the potential damage. The current was bringing the men, now clinging to one another, toward the big rocks at the front of the pier. The water there was a foamy, frothy, brownish-white from the violence of the waves crashing against the rocks, and in the oxygenated water it was even more difficult to stay afloat. The half dozen fishermen started yelling at one another, trying to decide what would be the best plan of action, as the men in trouble cried out in Hebrew every time they bobbed up out of the water, the younger one flailing, the older struggling to keep himself afloat while being dragged down by the younger.

By this time, all activity at the beach had stopped as everyone's eyes were on the two potential drowning victims. Swimmers, beach walkers, and fishermen were all yelling for someone to do something, but no one was in a good position to help. David, afraid the men were about to drown right in front of him, and having rescued people in the water before, let go of the hands of Rebeka and Moshe and told the children, "Sit down and don't move!" He quickly pulled his shirt off over his head, keeping it in his hand as he ran to the end of the pier. He stopped at the fishermen, looked below to see how far he would have to jump to clear the boulders, then caught his breath and backed up to get a running start. Just as he was about to take a running jump, he saw two swimmers coming from the north side of the pier. He could tell they were experienced and were about to reach the pair, so stayed in his place and watched, not wanting to get involved in the critical situation if he were not needed and might possibly be in the way.

The two swimmers reached the distressed pair just in time, each one of them getting one of the men. They obviously knew what they were doing as they pulled the victims toward the next incoming wave, using its force to push them toward the beach instead of back into the dangerous whirlpool near the end of the pier. The onlookers had stopped their screams and yells and were now cheering encouragement to the rescuers and victims. Now in the care of experienced swimmers, each incoming wave brought them closer to shore. Once they reached water shallow enough they could stand, more cheers went out from everyone around. Swimmers resumed swimming, walkers resumed walking, and fishermen resumed casting their lines into the water.

Armando and Aaron, carrying the surfboard, with Briana close behind, came running from the dunes just as the four men reached waist deep water. They looked to the pier and saw Daddy at the end with the fishermen patting him on the back. Seeing that the men were rescued, they took the board in and began riding it themselves, seeing who could stay on the longest.

As David put his shirt on, the fishermen thanked him for being willing to help. He and the younger children walked off the pier and joined Armando and Briana on the beach. They went past the newly rescued men who were still coughing and sputtering as the two very fit rescuers checked

Chapter 35   *Ain* Arnav

them over. Seeing all was well, and after the four thanked David for being willing to intervene, the family went about their play time. Rebeka and Moshe looked for pretty shells to take back to Tennessee for friends, as Mama had suggested. Since they were no longer traveling by bicycle, they could begin gathering souvenirs. Moshe spotted a rusty red object and dug in the wet sand to pull out a beautiful, bumpy five-inch shell, much larger and different than the kind they usually found.

~ ~ ~

After nap time, Emily went to thank Elena for the bread. While there, she told her about the mysterious visit of the men with the big box of food. Elena explained, "It's normal just before *Yom Kippur* for the Jewish people to show such acts of kindness. In their religion, one's good deeds, *mitzvot*, have to outweigh one's bad deeds. If the Day of Atonement arrives and the balance is the wrong way, they believe their name will be blotted out of the book of life."

Emily was intrigued with this new knowledge and went back to share it with her family who had just arrived from the beach. But as soon as they saw her, before she could say a word, they all started talking at once about the drowning incident, wanting to share the excitement of what she had missed. She listened to all their versions, as they prayed for the men who had been involved. Afterward, she shared what she had learned from Elena.

They began to wonder if the many acts of kindness they had been receiving all along were partly because of the teaching that was new knowledge to them, since they were sojourners in the land from the perspective of the Jewish people. The Israeli people certainly did seem to be generous, whatever their reasons. The family was in awe that their kindnesses were so in line with Y'shua's teachings, which were an extension of the *torah* itself - teaching people how to live according to the instructions of Yah given in the Old Testament. The Israeli people mostly walked according to the instructions of their Messiah, even though most did not know who he was. Their fruit showed that they were his, even though their eyes did not yet see it, just like the eyes of most in Christianity did not yet see that all his people are all to walk according to his instructions, as recorded in the Old Testament. Two groups of people, joined by one Elohim, each blinded to something vitally important involving His kingdom - the Varelas were becoming clearer concerning the reason they were spending this time in Israel.

As sundown approached, the synagogue across the street got busy. *Yom Kippur*, according to the Jewish rabbinic calendar would begin soon. Most Jews would completely fast from all food, drink, electronics, and cigarettes, and attend the prayers of repentance at synagogue, pleading that their names would not be blotted out.

36 - *Yom Kippur*

Rabbinic *Yom Kippur*

Yom Chamishi (Fifth Day)

The family watched out the window as people entered the synagogue, then listened to the prayers and singing as the sun set. They chose to remain indoors the entire 25 hours out of respect, not wanting to flaunt their food, drink, and energy in front of the fasting Jewish people. The day would be spent in prayer for brothers' eyes to be open: those in the synagogue to the identity of their Messiah, and those of Christian brethren to the beauty of Yah's instructions, including his feasts.

After a peaceful, quiet night with no activity from the neighbors, the family did all of their usual morning activities. But they ate inside instead of on the porch, so as not to be disrespectful of the fasting Jewish people who came and went at the synagogue across the street. They stayed indoors all day reading the scriptures, listening to their new music play softly, and learning songs. It was a beautiful day for them as they prayed often for the people they observed. Mid-afternoon they saw a young man, appearing to be *bar mitzvah* age on the first floor landing of the synagogue become sick with dry heaves from fasting. It brought tears to Emily's eyes to see him choosing to suffer in such a way as an act of obedience. The whole family gathered at the window and quietly prayed for him and the others who were there. Inside their house, they ate raw food, to keep from heating up anything that would cause wafting odors.

Yom Shishi (Sixth Day)

Having been inside all day, Armando was ready to get out as soon as the sun set. He went out the back door to find his friends, but only saw the twin girls from the Family of Ten and their older sister talking to some middle-age ladies in the street. He went back inside and asked if he could go to the synagogue. They had heard no singing for quite some time, but David gladly consented. Donning his *yarmulke*, he hurried out the front door, but not seeing signs of anyone there, walked toward the dumpsters and turned in the direction of the smaller synagogue from where he heard singing. When he got there, he saw the Brothers sitting inside, so stepped through the door to sit down with them. The Brothers saw him as he was greeted by two rabbis who promptly got in an argument about whether or not he needed to have a *tallit*.[211] One insisted he did, while the other

---

[211] *Tallit* - Jewish prayer shawl, having *tzitziyot* on the four corners.

Chapter 36   *Yom Kippur*

insisted he did not, since he had not yet reached *bar mitzvah* age. They conferred with another man who agreed the tallit was not necessary, and the young men welcomed Armando to sit between them. He followed along as best he could during the remaining prayers, singing, and readings, trying to keep up in the Hebrew books.

An hour after sundown, when three stars could be seen in the heavens, the whole atmosphere of the town changed. The singing got louder as they said their closing prayers, including the *Kiddush*[212]. As soon as it was over people could be seen laughing and playing as they ran down the streets to their homes to consume the first food and drink in over a day, besides the sample of bread and juice they had just had at synagogue.

The Brothers introduced Armando to some others there and then escorted him home, talking as they walked.

"How did you know where to find us?" one asked.

Armando replied, "I saw no one was at the big synagogue and heard the prayers coming from this one."

"Today, all the community gathered at the big synagogue in the morning, but at the smaller one for the evening service," he said.

They talked for a few minutes, walked together to the family's gate, then parted as the young men went beyond to their mother's house.

Just as they left, sirens could be heard starting in the south and going north. The family thought it was part of the celebration but later learned that just three miles north in the city of Akko, a major riot between Arabs and Jews had begun that would last for five days. Ignorant of the violence transpiring within walking distance of them, the family privately rejoiced with their Jewish friends at the end of their fast. The family would have their own type of post-fast celebration in two days. Soon after Armando returned, they all went to bed, giving thanks for full tummies and a secure place to sleep, while rioting continued in Akko, just up the coast.

After morning routine, the children went to the front yard to play; David, and Emily sat on the porch visiting, while supervising them. Sarah's younger son drove up, parked in his usual spot in front of their house and stopped to visit with the couple. Emily translated the events of the two nights before in Akko to David.

"At the beginning of *Yom Kippur*, an Arab who had been drinking, drove his car into a Jewish neighborhood, smoking and blasting loud music. The people asked him to leave, but he continued provoking them until some

---

[212]*Kiddush* - Hebrew for 'sanctification' or 'setting apart', used to denote the blessing over wine or grape juice to set apart special days.

345

men came out of the synagogue yelling at them. He then went back and a rumor ensued that the Jewish people had killed an Arab. The Arabs came back, burning cars and throwing rocks through windows. After the fast was over, the Jews came out in great numbers, rioting against the Arabs. Police and military were called in to stop the rioting, which is why you heard sirens last night."

David and Emily were thankful to have been in their safe little abode in the next town, an area of mostly Jewish people, during the fast. He then asked them, "Why were you not at synagogue, yesterday?"

Emily explained, "We go by the ancient Hebrew calendar. According to the ancient calendar, *Yom Kippur* will be on *Shabbat* this year. We will begin the fast this evening. We didn't want to go to synagogue having eaten, knowing the others had not. And we didn't want to fast twice," she said with a smile.

He was shocked and passionately declared, "It is *forbidden* to fast on *Shabbat!*"

Emily replied, "We have not seen that in the *TaNaK*. We just fast according to the instructions for that day, whichever day of the week it falls on."

He said, "A Jew always feasts on *Shabbat*. If *Yom Kippur* falls on *Shabbat*, it has to be moved to another day. *Shabbat* is for feasting! On *Shabbat* we always eat three big meals and have a nap!"

The couple was as intrigued with their young neighbor as he was with them. They wondered about the year of mourning he was observing and now the new information regarding Jewish *Shabbat* observance; he wondered about the strange family who lived by the written word alone and believed that Y'shua was the promised Messiah who would return, bringing the two houses of Israel together again. They smiled at one another as he departed to help his mother prepare for *Shabbat*.

The family had planned to be on the bicycles until just before *Yom Teruah*, stop wherever they were at that time, give away the bicycles and travel by bus, seeing some important sites on the way up to Jerusalem for Sukkot. Today they would have been at the Dead Sea. But because of the major shift in plans, they spent preparation day at home in Kiryat Yam, doing the usual food preparation, cleaning, going to the *shuk* just before 3 PM to get the best prices, then stopping at the grocery store on the way back to get pomegranate and grape juice. Armando and Briana went to the bread store and milk shop. They would have everything ready when it was time to break the fast the next evening. Shopping completed, it was time for baths, particularly important this day, as it was the ninth day of the month according to the ancient sighted calendar, making sundown the beginning of *Yom Kippur*. The family had a big meal and drank extra water before sunset, then went to sleep just afterward.

Chapter 36   *Yom Kippur*

Day of Atonement
Shabbat   *Yom Kippur*

They intentionally slept late, trying to save their energy for the remainder of the day. The family did not observe *Yom Kippur* just like the Jews because they followed only the written instructions of the scriptures, not the Jewish traditions. They 'afflicted themselves' by not eating or drinking and by being in prayer and confession of sin, thanking Yah for His Salvation (Y'shua) and the grace and mercy He extended to them by sending his son to redeem them from the slavery of sin and the curse of eternal death. They listened to the music on the CD and sang along, finding favorite songs in Hebrew and English. They read the story of Jonah and the repentance of Nineveh. They had a time of family repentance, asking each other for forgiveness, and studied the word on various subjects relating to the day, the fast, and repentance in general.

The day went by more slowly as it went along, as it had in the previous four years they had observed the fast. By midafternoon, the little ones were complaining of being hungry. Their parents assured them that they had made it through most of the fast and that when evening came, they could eat. They had blocked the kitchen with chairs so no one was tempted to enter, and had set a chair in front of the refrigerator as a reminder. They took a nap late morning and another midafternoon. As people got hungry, they would talk about those around the world who were hungry every day and how their family was blessed to have access to most any kind of food they wanted any other day of the year. And they reminded the children that Sukkot was coming, a special time of feasting and celebration. It was a lesson in patience, self-denial, and endurance

347

37 - Ain Chatul

Week 10   *Yom Rishon* (First Day)   10/11-12

After it was obvious the sun had set over the Mediterranean and there were no more rays to be seen, the family celebrated with bread and juice, then a delicious soup made with chicken neck and vegetables over couscous. They again thanked Yah for his Salvation, for food, for those who had blessed them with it, and for their time together in his special land. They went to bed with full tummies again.

Blue T-shirts

The family's clothes had become quite worn during the time they had been in Israel, the green and orange shirt outfits having been worn around 30 days each already. The orange ones had been made with the help of their Horse and Buggy friends just before leaving the U.S., but the green ones had already been worn over 50 times before embarking on the trip because they were first made as the family's *Shabbat* clothes the year before. David thought the family needed to look nicer and insisted they buy new clothes. Emily was opposed to the idea because she was experienced in trying to find clothes for the family, which is why she began making them in the first place. There were several qualifications that they had to meet, and the combination made clothing very difficult and very expensive to find. The Varelas carefully budgeted their money, and it horrified Emily to think of what might have to be spent to replace the clothes. Besides that, though the clothes were worn and beginning to fade from being in the intense Israeli sun, Emily kept them clean, though some had become a bit stained. She could not justify the expense to replace clothes that still, in her opinion, had a lot of wear left in them. But at David's insistence, they decided they could just get some T-shirts, something that would match the girls' green, blue, and white checkered skirts.

It was difficult enough to find clothing that matched for a family of their size, which included baby clothes all the way to adults, but it became trickier because of the other requirements the family had in clothing. They wore nothing but 100% natural fibers because of their understanding of scripture.[213]

---

[213]Deut. 22:11 Thou shalt not wear a garment of divers sorts, *as* of woollen and linen together.

Chapter 37   *Ain Chatul*

They had studied the Hebrew word '*sha'atnez*', and found that there was no known usage of the word except for the two examples in scripture and was understood to be 'linsey-woolsey', a mixture of linen and wool spun together. Since there was no proof of what the word actually meant, they chose to avoid a possible transgression by wearing garments where the fibers were a mixture of anything that would be considered different kinds. They knew their Creator knew and desired what was best for His people, and they wanted to follow His instructions to the best of their ability. They also knew that man-made fibers, like polyester, were unhealthy to wear, so stayed away from them and wore natural fiber as much as possible.

Besides the type of fabric, the style was important to them. They wanted to be sure they were following their Creator's desire that their bodies be covered properly. They knew from scripture that He considered the thighs to be 'nakedness', so they wanted to be sure theirs were covered.[214] There was no problem with the ladies' skirts and dresses, but in order to cover the thighs of a man completely, they needed longer shirts than what most of their culture wore. T-shirts would not reach long enough, unless they were oversized and then would look sloppy. They decided that this time they would have to compromise and go with the T-shirts, since that would be all they could probably find. The boys' pants were loose enough that it should not be an issue.

Emily went to the store with Armando, Briana, and Isabel, not really expecting to find anything that would work. She did not like to wear a T-shirt because they made her feel exposed, especially in her late stage of pregnancy. She much preferred the tunic, but was having to push away her preference and comfort to conform to the desires of her husband. She continued to learn her place as a wife, and though she often did not agree with the decisions being made, she recognized that in order for the marriage to work properly, she had to submit her will to his, at least half the time. As long as his will was not in direct violation of scripture, she was willing to do that. And she was thankful that his desire was, like hers, to walk in Yah's ways.

They walked past the produce shop and the bread shop before crossing the street to the little strip of stores by the Post Office. Just north of the grocery store, there was a small clothing shop with stacks and stacks of T-shirts on the shelves of each wall, barely enough room for two people to pass between. Emily did not know how to say 'cotton' in Hebrew and could not find it in her PDA's Hebrew dictionary. She tried to explain to the clerk what she was looking for, but to no avail. Finally, she picked up a shirt and read the Hebrew on the tag, hoping to be able to figure out what kind of fibers they were. She was relieved to discover that Hebrew for 'cotton' was 'cottonah', which made shopping easier.

---

[214]Exo. 28:42 And thou shalt make them linen breeches to cover their nakedness; from the loins even unto the thighs they shall reach:

She saw some 100% cotton T-shirts there in a light blue that would go with the skirts, but they were only in adult sizes. They went two shops down to the children's' store, just as cluttered with stacks and stacks of clothes though the walls were farther apart and racks of hanging clothes were in between. Still, there was barely room to move.

She was able to find seven little light blue T-shirts in 100% cotton which would fit the children, though Natanyah's would be big for her and the color was a shade lighter than the adult shirts. She bought those, then the four of them went back to the other store to buy the adult shirts. After completing their purchases, they walked the two blocks home and showed the new shirts and prayer books to the excited bunch there.

Briana reminded Mama that one of the little gowns they had made for the baby while still in the States was almost the same color as the T-shirts. Emily again blessed Yah for giving them not just their needs, but their desires, as well. Even after the baby came, the family would all match!

Gifting

After lunch, they took their last trip to the beach for a while. Tomorrow they would start up to Jerusalem for Sukkot. While at the sea, Armando tried out his new pole and David received a call back from their Host in Osifia who gladly accepted the offer of bicycles. He said he could use one for himself to ride along with his children; the smaller bicycles he could donate to the Sudanese at *Or HaCarmel*. After a good break at the beach, the family went home and met their former Host, who came with his wife, daughter, and mother-in-law. They had a joyful reunion and the adults talked, while the children showed the little girl around their home, and introduced her to *Chatul*. She instantly fell in love with the tiny creature and brought it to show her parents and grandmother.

David and the man loaded Emily's bicycle with Natanyah's seat on the back into their vehicle, then added the smaller bicycles belonging to Victor, Rebeka, and Moshe for the Sudanese children. Emily commented to the ladies about how much the little girl liked the kitten and that the family was going to have to find a good home for him before they went back to the U.S. The little girl's eyes lit up as she asked her mother, "Can we keep it?"

Her mother looked at the kitten as Emily told its history, then asked her husband, "What do you think?"

The man agreed it would be all right, as Rebeka looked on in disbelief. She asked Mama, "Do we have to give him away? Can't we take him home with us?"

Emily softly smiled, "No. I'm sorry."

"Why not?"

"Because we would have to get all sorts of papers for him. It would be a lot of trouble. It's better just to find a good home for him here. Since they're here now and want to give him a good home, it would be best to let them have him. Otherwise, we'll have to find someone to take care of him while we're gone to Jerusalem."

Sad and disappointed, Rebeka took *Chatul* from the little girl and gently caressed him until the group was ready to leave before giving him back. Once the friends drove away, Rebeka began to cry. "What's wrong?" David asked.

"I wanted to keep *Chatul*," she said through her tears.

Mama hugged her, "Rebeka, we couldn't take him home. It's better this way. He'll have a good home and we won't have to worry about him during Sukkot."

Briana spoke up, "I think we should have given it to the Family of Ten or Aaron. The girl's grandfather hates cats. He might kill him."

Emily replied, "I don't think they would have taken it just to have it killed. I'm sure he'll be fine."

None of the children were happy about the decision to give away *Chatul* that day, but it was done and there was nothing they could do. Natanyah went to sleep that night alone, massaging Daddy's ear, without the cuddly creature she had become accustomed to lying in the locks of hair by her neck as she slept. The parents were sad, as well, especially Emily who had also become attached to the kitten. But she had known all along, and had made it clear to the children from the first day, that there would come a time of separation and felt like today was the best time.

South by Bus

Yom Sheni (Second Day)

In the morning, the family once again packed their mats, sheets, tent, one bucket, other supplies, and clothes and walked to the bus stop. After the twenty minute ride to *Merkazit HaMifratz*, which included a stop at the military base, David bought tickets, while Emily took the girls across the bus entrance to the restroom. She paid the required shekel to the woman guarding the door, then took the girls inside and back out quickly, so as not to miss the next bus to Jerusalem.

The bus left the station and turned west at the major corner intersection the family had crossed in the dark on their longest day. It drove along the Mediterranean Sea, passing the *Misrad Hap'nim*, B'hai Gardens, and the port, where huge cargo ships were docked, and wound around curves and went up and down the steep hills of Haifa.

Emily and the children told David some of what they had learned on their tour of B'hai Gardens with Nikolay. The bus pulled into the other main station on the south side of Haifa, still near the Sea, waited for a few more passengers to board, then drove south with the beaches and expanse of the sea on the right and the beautiful, fruit-filled hills on the left, passing by stacked villages, towns, and cities on hills. They saw grapes, bananas, citrus, fig, pomegranate, and numerous other types of trees and orchards along the way. Israel indeed was a fruitful land. They looked forward to the day it would be cleaned up and living in peace, as foretold by the prophets.

The bus continued down Highway 4 then turned southeast on Highway 1, towards Jerusalem. About half an hour before their expected arrival in Mevaseret, where their warmshowers.org Contact lived, they felt an explosion as the bus jerked, then veered off the side of the road. Several passengers were very startled, being accustomed to living with terrorism and never knowing when the bus they are on will be targeted for attack. But someone quickly informed the other passengers that a tire on the bus had blown out. After waiting for a few minutes the driver announced another bus would be coming to pick them up. Groans came from various directions, as people's schedules were changed because of the flat tire. Some patiently dealt graciously with the situation, while about a quarter were very annoyed at being put late for whatever their next destination was. The Varelas were thrilled that they were able to experience another adventure. How many people get to be on a bus when a tire blows out? They felt blessed to be able to experience this and thanked Yah for keeping them and everyone aboard safe.

While waiting for the other bus, Emily called their Contact to inform him they would be later than expected. He had agreed to pick them up at another bus stop, so she wanted to be considerate and make sure he was warned about the change of schedule. Shortly after, the bus driver told his passengers to get out and gather their belongings from below the bus, since the other one was about to arrive. The family got out and Emily kept the children on the shoulder to protect them from the rushing traffic on the other side of the bus, while David and Armando got the packs and other belongings. They loaded the new bus and took off east again toward Jerusalem.

Chapter 37   *Ain Chatul*

Mevaseret Zion

Within half an hour, the bus pulled to the stop and the family got out with a few others. Emily called the Contact again, who told them to hike up the steep hill to the local stop at the top, about half a mile up. They followed his directions and on their way saw a man selling beautiful fresh flower arrangements. Armando thought it would be really nice to get some for the man, since he was hosting them at his place. The parents agreed and Armando and Mama went across the street to pick the prettiest one, then joined the others at the local bus stop. After a few minutes the Contact hurriedly arrived in his tiny station wagon, jumped out and opened the trunk. He authoritatively informed the family in English, "I'll take half of you to the house, then come back and get the other half."

David decided Emily should go first with the little ones and he could wait there with Armando, Briana, and Victor. They were both glad they each had a cell phone. Armando gave the Contact the carefully chosen flowers, which he tossed in the back of the car, and then began stuffing backpacks in. Emily noticed the expression on Armando's face and hoped he was not hurt by the seeming disregard for the gift he had chosen. She got in the front seat and had Isabel, Rebeka, Moshe, and Natanyah buckle up in the back. Then she got in and the Contact jumped in and took off in a hurry, making a quick U-turn to head back to his place. He asked, "What are your plans? You know the buses don't run tomorrow, right?"

Emily answered, "Yes, we plan to backpack to Jerusalem tomorrow and hope to stay in our tent on the roof of the Petra Hostel during Sukkot."

He pulled up to the curb in front of his tree shaded house, and they hurriedly got their things out and carried them up the stairs as he directed. The Contact said, "Wait here until I come back with the others," then rushed back to get them.

David, Armando, Briana, and Victor waited at the bus stop, watching people who walked or drove by them. A group of soldiers approached to wait for a bus, and talked to them. Since young childhood, Armando had been interested in all things military, so enjoyed talking to the soldiers and admiring their gear and weapons. When he asked if the holes in the wall of the concrete bus stop shelter were from bullets, they confirmed that they were.

A few minutes after the Contact left, they saw his car speeding toward them again, so readied themselves to load their things into the back. David got in the front seat and the children in the back and they hurried off. The man began to ask David more questions about the family's plans and let him know that the buses would stop running in an hour or so and not begin again until the next night because the high day of Sukkot was approaching at sundown. David was not aware of that, but was not concerned, as Emily had expressed interest in back-packing to Jerusalem, anyway. The man seemed annoyed, as if he were afraid the family might be with him for more

353

Pedaling Home   Part 3 – The Regathering

than one night, and also aggravated that they planned to sleep outside in Jerusalem. He was not impressed at all and told David, "I'm leaving to be with family in Haifa tonight, but as soon as I return tomorrow evening, I'm going to take you to the bus station and send you back to Kiryat Yam. It's not good for you to be in Jerusalem."

Misunderstanding the tone of the statement, David replied, "Thanks for the offer. But we're planning to stay in Jerusalem for the feast."

They pulled up to the shaded yard and dodged branches from the trees as they got their things unloaded from his car. They followed him up the stairs to join the rest of the family. He took them inside and showed them around his abode, telling them, "You're free to use the kitchen and here's a bedroom with a television. Help yourself."

David thanked him, "That's very generous, but we just need the yard."

He took the beautiful flowers, now a little smashed, put them in a vase and set them in the center of the table as he said, "They'll look nice on the table here."

In spite of his hastiness, the family was amazed at his hospitality to a group of total strangers. He told them where to leave the key if they went out and said, "I'm leaving, but my daughter and her family live upstairs and will be home if you need anything. She's actually the one who is on warmshowers.org."

The family thanked him again, surprised that he would be so hospitable to leave them alone in his home with all his belongings. His walls were lined with all sorts of books, both religious and secular. The home was filled with various neatly arranged articles, both useful and aesthetic, including beautiful vases, a mosaic, a hookah pipe and tobacco.

As he went out the front door, the family exited through the sliding glass door to the back yard. They decided the weather was nice enough and the yard private enough, having a fence and trees all the way around, they would just sleep on their mats instead of setting up the tent. As they unpacked their food and began to have supper, the man's daughter, a fit, attractive woman came from the upper house and introduced herself. After getting to know her a little and learning that she and her husband enjoyed cycling with their two young children in a trailer behind them, Emily asked, "What's the best way to hike to Jerusalem from here?"

She replied, "There's a path at the end of our street, where it dead-ends. It leads straight through the forest to Jerusalem."

Emily was excited to learn that, and the family saw, once again, that Yah was taking care of them and had put them in this particular place for this time. After a comfortable visit, the kind young woman said as she left for her home upstairs, "Be sure to let us know if you need anything."

354

38 - Up to Zion

Yom Shlishi (Third Day)   High Day   Day 1 of Rabbinic *Sukkot*

They laid out their beds and went to sleep under the stars again, the soon rising of the full moon serving as a reminder that it was almost *Sukkot*[215]

Emily awoke long before daylight, nervous and wanting to get out of there. She did not want to take a chance on the man returning and somehow keeping them from hiking up to Jerusalem. She was afraid he was very serious about telling them it was not good for them to go and meant what he said about taking them to the bus station. She woke David and the children and rushed them to get their sheets and mats folded and put away. They ate a quick breakfast, then put their packs on, left a thank you note on their picture postcard, and left, following the Contact's instructions concerning locking the door and hiding the key.

They backpacked down the hill towards the end of the little road, and once there, easily spotted the trail that went along the dry creek bed between the cedar covered hills on either side of them. Not long into their journey, Armando saw a cave, and he and Briana asked if they could cross the creek bed to check it out. Permission being granted, they took off their packs, leaving them with the rest of the family so they could travel unhindered. They ran through the bushes, bounded over the creek bed, and continued up through the trees to the shaded entrance of the dark, cool cave, where their attention was immediately drawn to piles of old books written in Hebrew. Briana, the reader of the family exclaimed, "Whoa! Look at all these books!"

Loving the smell of old books, she deeply inhaled as the familiar fragrance penetrated her being, causing her to want to sit and read for hours. The smell took her back to the library in the old building of their little town and to Granddaddy's book-filled basement. She remembered the leather-bound Young Ladies Journals from the 1800's the family had found when cleaning out a storage shed for an elderly lady. She wondered how long the books had been here. How old were they? What stories did they contain? Why were they here?

As they investigated, they found that the piles were actually stacks that had fallen. Behind the piles were more stacks that covered the entire

---

[215]Because the first day of the scriptural month begins with the sighting of the new moon and Sukkot starts on the 15th, the moon is always full at the beginning of Sukkot.

length of the cave, stacked several feet high and went back several yards. They had been bricked in with a wall, but it appeared vandals had broken it down, causing the books to fall out in piles. Many were falling apart.

Briana continued examining books, thumbing through one, then another. Being convinced they were discarded, she began stacking some to take with her. She could not yet read much Hebrew, but was now motivated to learn.

Armando, thinking there had to be something better in there than just books with no pictures in a language he could not yet read, began looking for clues to where the real treasure must be hidden. What if he found the Ark of the Covenant? Probably not, but maybe a gold coin? The sounds of his siblings playing outside near the trail mingled with the echoing sounds of pages being turned and books carefully bumping each other, as Briana looked through one book after another. He turned to see her amassing a stack of books and cried, "What are you doing?!?"

"Getting some books to take with me. How many do you think I can carry?" she asked excitedly.

"Well, I don't know. But you can't take more than two. We're backpacking!"

His statement brought her back from heaven into reality. She chose two that were in better condition, and they left the cave as they heard Daddy call them. Confidently, they walked, eager to share their great find with the rest of the family. Once across the dry creek and back to the trail, Briana showed off her treasures. They described the cave, wanting the whole family to come, but their parents told them they needed to continue the journey, not knowing what all they might face on their way up to Jerusalem.

David and Emily would love to have seen the sight, but not knowing the surroundings well, nor where they would be spending the night, felt like the priority was getting closer to their destination. Those who had taken off their burdens, including the children who had been running around playing, replaced them and the journey continued. A little farther down the trail and on the more forested side, Armando saw another hole in the side of the hill, so he stopped, stooping down to take a closer look. He moved leaves and a vine to find a deep hole carved into the side of the rock hill. He called, "Hey, guys, look at this!"

Everyone stopped again to see his new discovery. Inside was a rectangle carved out of the rock floor that had contained some type of box. Behind that was another arch that had been sealed. Armando wanted to break down the opening, but David said, "It's not yours to break into. It's likely an old tomb."

What they could see in the front opening contained a copper pipe, a broom, and other parts of tools as if an amateur had been excavating.

Chapter 38 — Up to Zion

Armando

What was behind the closed arch? Bones, treasure, the ark[216]...?

As badly as Armando wanted to find out, his parents were saying, "No." He knew they were telling him to do the right thing, and wondered why obedience so often had to be choosing to do the opposite of what was fun and exciting. He quietly submitted to their request to get moving again, but with images of what must be behind the wall going through his mind as he walked.

They hiked on and came to a huge cemetery carved into the rock on the north side of the creek. There were thousands of tombs of various social classes. Natanyah and Moshe were getting tired and hungry, so the family sat down on the dirt and rocks in front of a fenced area on their right. As Emily prepared the food, including crackers from the box the kind men from the synagogue had brought, Armando looked around and found hundreds of shells that he recognized to be from military rifles. As he investigated, he found that their current picnic spot was the entrance to an IDF training facility. He stuffed as many shells into his pockets as he could find before cleaning his hands with water from a bottle and wiping them with the hand towel Mama kept tied onto her pack. After eating, they continued their hike, now going more steeply up to Jerusalem. As they went, they sang together a song based on the prophecy in Isa. 2:3 and Micah 4:2:[217]

"Come let us go up to the mountain of YHWH to the house of the El of Jacob."

For the parents, it was a thrilling time. They knew the time of the fulfillment of the prophecies had not arrived, but that it was getting closer and that they were a part of it. To breathe the air and scent from the evergreen trees and sagebrush-like shrubs, to feel the sun and wind, as they walked on the dirt and rocks of the land of Israel, heading up to Jerusalem, as so many had done for thousands of years before them was exhilarating. For the children, it was another adventure in finding treasures and learning to

---

[216] Ark of the Covenant.
[217] Mic. 4:2 And many nations shall come, and say, Come, and let us go up to the mountain of YHWH, and to the house of the Elohim of Jacob; and he will teach us of his ways, and we will walk in his paths: for the law shall go forth of Zion, and the word of YHWH from Jerusalem.

push themselves past their natural limits. For the youngest ones, it was tiring and they would be glad to get to a place where they could do something they considered more interesting. But they were little troopers, and with encouragement, made it up the steep climb.

As they neared the top, they looked back over the valley they had walked through, seeing the huge cemetery below them, as well as Hwy 1, and the town of Mevaseret Zion in the distance. The trail got even steeper as they entered the cedar towards the top, and with one more push of energy, and another drink of water from the bottles they shared, they came to the pavement at the summit.

Jerusalem

They had backpacked to Jerusalem! Modern Jerusalem, that is. They had yet to reach the Mount Zion spoken of in the scriptures, but were not far away. They sat in the shade for a few minutes, admiring their accomplishment. From where they sat, they looked back down at the dirt road they had just come up. Lining it in various places were crashed and burned semi-trucks and buses carefully placed to prevent erosion and concrete culverts awaiting their permanent home. They decided to pack a little farther before eating lunch, so started again. The first building they came to was a fruit distributor, closed because of the holiday. As they walked by the fenced entrance, the security guard approached them, intrigued by the little backpacking family. He greeted them and offered them water.

Having learned about *mitzvot* and humbling themselves enough to be a blessing to others, they gladly accepted his offer. He walked to the building he was guarding and returned with two, two-liter bottles of frozen water that had begun melting in the Middle Eastern heat as soon as he removed them from the freezer. After presenting them to the family, he began with the regular questions. They visited with him for nearly half hour, until his curiosity had been satisfied, and left him with new things to think about. He, like most secular Jews they had met, was unaware of the prophecies of the scattered tribes of Ephraim coming home before Messiah returned. He was excited to learn and said he would go home and read his *TaNaK*. Moshe gave him one of the postcards with their picture and the scriptures on the back, to which he responded with a big friendly smile, "*Todah rabah!*"

They walked on, glad to have met yet another friendly person with whom they were able to share beneficial information that could be life changing. They crossed an empty street that would have been busy any other day and walked through a neighborhood, heading in the direction of the Old City. They soon realized it was a religious neighborhood, as they began to meet only Orthodox Jewish men, dressed in black, walking two and sometimes three together, coming from the other direction. They were

Chapter 38   Up to Zion

greeted with, "*Chag Sameach!*"[218] to which they answered back likewise. On one of their meetings, after greeting them, two men stopped the family and asked in Hebrew, "Would you like to come to our *sukkah*?"

Emily translated as David answered the men, "That's very nice of you. Where is it?"

They pointed to the hill in the direction from which the family had just come and said something that Emily did not understand. Though it may not have been far, the couple did not want to backtrack. "Thank you. We think we'd better keep going this way."

"Where are you going?

"To the Old City."

They nodded with knowing and approving smiles, as the parties went their separate ways, with another, "*Chag sameach!*"

They continued walking and entered a street that was blocked off to traffic. They later learned that often in religious neighborhoods, the streets would be blocked on Sabbath and high days to keep people from driving through and disrupting the peace, preventing occurrences like the one that was just simmering down in Akko. People from both sides of the street watched them from synagogues and apartments as they walked by, dirty from the hike, and packing their belongings on the Jewish high day. They stopped at a bus stop with benches in the shade to eat, since the buses would not be running until after sundown. They sat down, some on benches, some on packs, and removed the hummus, vegetables, and bread. Emily realized she had forgotten to bring something along to mix the food with, but found a piece of *lulav*[219] on the top of the stone covered trash receptacle, looked it over, wiping it until she deciding it was clean, then used the stiff end of it to stir the hummus. Armando cried, "Mama!"

Emily: What?

Armando: What are you doing?

Emily: Fixing lunch.

Armando: But why are you using that? It's part of their religious observance.

Emily: I don't think they'll mind. It was in the trash.

---

[218]*Chag sameach!* - Hebrew for 'Joyful pilgrimage feast!'
[219]*Lulav* - from the date palm tree, one of the four species commanded to be waved (Lev. 23:40) in rejoicing during the feast of Sukkot.

359

Armando had spent more time at synagogue, and was not sure the onlookers felt the same way. He felt the stares of many people looking in their direction.

She used her new utensil, with its two-foot long leaves to spread the hummus on the pitas and distributed it to David and all the children before eating what had stuck to the new tool. Armando tried hard to keep from rolling his eyes, hoping no one was watching his mother. She was a country girl, and her actions did not bother him at home, but here in front of people, he was greatly embarrassed.

Religious Rules

The bus stop was in front of a synagogue and across from apartments. Around fifty feet west of them, at the entrance of the apartments, stood a group of six Orthodox ladies, watching the family and talking amongst themselves. After the meal, several of the children needed to use the restroom. In the woods, finding a rest area was not a problem. They just relieved themselves, burying the waste according to scripture.[220] But here in town with many eyes on them and no restroom in sight, they had to figure out something else. Emily decided that since the women had been watching them for some time, she would ask them if the family could use the restroom in one of their apartments. She angled across the street toward the women, who became more curious. When she arrived, she greeted them with, "*Chag sameach!*" and they returned the greeting before she, using knowledge she had gained during their time in Israel, asked them the big question. "Do you have a restroom *bishvil hayeladim*?"

The ladies talked quietly amongst themselves, then the bravest one began asking questions in Hebrew:

"Where are you from?"
"America, Tennessee."

"What are you doing here?"

---

[220]Deut. 23:13 And thou shalt have a paddle upon thy weapon; and it shall be, when thou wilt ease thyself abroad, thou shalt dig therewith, and shalt turn back and cover that which cometh from thee:

Chapter 38 Up to Zion

"We came for Sukkot. We rode a bus to Mevaseret yesterday and backpacked up from there."

"Where are you going?"

"To the Old City. We have a spot reserved on the Petra Hostel to set up our tent tomorrow."

After a mildly approving look, she said, "You may use my restroom."

Emily waved the children across to her, and they all came but Armando, still in shock over the insensitivity he perceived by his mother to their treasured practices. David also declined, saying they could wait until later. The brave woman escorted them up the stairs to her second floor apartment on the right. They walked into the little space to see three small children and a man in the bedroom with a baby. The woman showed them the tiny restroom and Emily sent Victor, then Moshe, Rebeka, Isabel, and Briana in one at a time. She then went in herself with Natanyah, to make sure things were left neat and clean. There was barely room for Emily, in her nine month pregnant state, and Natanyah to both fit in the tiny room. Emily noticed the toilet did not flush, but dismissed it, knowing that a family with several small children probably had a reason for the water being turned off. She would let the hostess deal with it. Emily let Natanyah out, looking on the wall for the light switch. She was always conscious of conserving resources and careful to turn off lights when they were not necessary. Not seeing a switch on the wall, she stepped out of the tiny restroom, so small that the door had to open to the outside. She looked behind the door in the entry way and spotted the switch there, just behind her huddle of children. She reached to turn it off and just as her finger hit the switch, the woman excitedly shouted, "NO!"

Before the word was out of her mouth, the light went off, but Emily, realizing at the very split second what was happening, flipped it back on before realizing her second action was worse than the first! It was a high day on the Jewish calendar and, as on *Shabbat*, the Jewish people, according to rabbinic tradition, leave lights on all day to prevent transgressing the command in scripture concerning kindling a fire on *Shabbat*.[221] Even though she was aware of their custom and would have respected it in their home, she had forgotten that it also applied to the high days and that today was the high day they observed. She felt horrible, but there was nothing she could do now except apologize.

The woman's face turned red and Emily was not sure what would happen next. The woman then, as calmly as possible in a situation like this, asked in Hebrew, "Are you Jewish?"

---

[221] Exo. 35:3 Ye shall kindle no fire throughout your habitations upon the sabbath day.

361

It had not occurred to Emily that she may have thought the family was Jewish. Maybe it was David's beard, the boys' tassels (the girls tassels were discretely on the bottom of their pen-striped denim skirts), the *yarmulkes* Armando and Moshe wore that day from their elderly lady friend in Kiryat Yam, and the fact that David and Victor both had their heads covered with a cap and hat respectively. Or maybe it was assumed because they were in Jerusalem for the feast. Whatever the reason, the question came with the air that Emily surmised they would not have been given the hospitality had the woman known they were not Jewish. Emily quickly began to explain, "No. We are not Jewish that we know of. We believe we are from the House of Israel, the scattered tribes of Ephraim who were called back to *torah* and back to the land in the last days before the return of Messiah."

She pulled a postcard with the explanatory verses on the back out of the bicycle bag that she now wore on a strap around her neck to give the woman. She wanted to write a thank you note first, but did not see her pen in the bag. She asked the woman, "Do you have a pen?"

She gestured toward the kitchen, and then replied, "I have one, but I cannot pick it up today."

Emily then remembered that rabbinic oral tradition also kept the Jewish people from picking up a writing instrument on *Shabbat*, among numerous other prohibitions. Emily said, "Ok, I was just going to write you a note thanking you for your kindness. Thank you for letting us use the restroom. And I'm very sorry about the light."

She gave her the picture, and the woman glanced at it, then set it on her table as she replied, "*bevakasha*."[222] She then opened the door for Emily and the children. As they left, they all said, "*Shalom*," and Emily followed the children down the stairs, as they heard the bang of the closing door, then the husband's loud voice. Had the door been slammed? Was there trouble inside because their law had been broken? Or was the door just hard to close? Emily would wonder for years to come.

Downtown

As they walked by, she handed the other ladies at the bottom of the stairs each a postcard before crossing the street with her little brood. She then relayed the events to David as they all put on their packs and walked east toward the Old City. They packed down the hill and past the barricaded entrance at the other end of the community, turned south and walked toward the giant bridge being built to resemble the harp of King David. Soon after starting up the next hill, two women approached and began asking the family questions. They invited them to their Sukkah, but once

---

[222]*Bevakasha* - Hebrew for 'you're welcome.'

Chapter 38   Up to Zion

again, it was in the opposite direction from where the family was going. The parents discussed whether they should go, but decided they really should get closer to the Old City, since they were still nearly three miles away. Emily had really wanted to spend the night in someone's Sukkah, and hated to pass up the kind offers, but they wanted to get closer to Mount Zion in plenty of time to find a place to sleep. Packing with little ones, they had to budget their time and distance carefully.   But for years to come, they would wonder if they had passed up two different appointments arranged by *Abba* himself.

They turned east on Jaffa Street and walked up the hill past the Central Bus Station on the left. Everything on this Jewish high day was quiet on this normally very busy street except for an occasional car or taxi. The family packed up the hill, encouraging the little ones that it was not much farther to Independence Park, where they hoped to camp for the night. After reaching the top of the hill, they decided to look for a place to stop to have a snack and a short nap. Emily was beginning to feel contractions coming on, and since she was only a week away from her due date, knew she could deliver at any time. They had packed over three miles that day already, and she and the little ones were beginning to feel it. They spotted another bus stop and knew it was still several hours before the buses would run. Under the small roof, Emily lay down on the bench, David held Natanyah, and Armando and Briana peeled oranges and sectioned them for everyone.

After the sweet refreshment and the encouragement that they were near their destination, the family moved on, soon reaching the large Independence Park. Upon arriving there and seeing the playground, the formerly tired children came to life. They tried out all the various rocking toys, slides, swings, and other equipment, while David sat with his tired, heavy-with-child wife on the grass watching them. When the children had been given ample break time to play, the family loaded up again and packed across the park toward the Old City. On the way, they passed an elderly gentleman sitting on a bench surrounded by cats – cats on the bench, on the ground, on his lap – over 15 of the furry little creatures, despised by many Israelis, had found a friend in the old man on the bench.

Sukkah in the Park

Wondering where the best place to set up for the night would be, they turned toward the little building housing restrooms and saw a Sukkah bigger than their tent. It was the only one in the park and looked like the perfect place for them to stay. Emily was overwhelmed with joy, having said just hours before that she wanted to stay in a Sukkah. And here it was! They took their things inside, moved the two picnic tables to one end, and laid their mats on the floor. In a few minutes, an elderly lady stepped inside, startled to see the family. They greeted her with, "Chag *sameach!*", and welcomed her inside.

She responded in Hebrew, "*Chag sameach!* I was just coming here to pray."

Emily offered, "Come in! We're just laying things out for the night."

The woman said apologetically, "Thank you. I didn't want to bother you. I just saw the Sukkah here and thought it would be a good place to pray. I've been coming to this park every day for years, and this is the first time it's ever been here. Do you plan to sleep here?"

Emily answered, "Yes. We've come from the United Stated to celebrate Sukkot and have reservations on the roof of the Petra Hostel beginning tomorrow night, but were hoping to stay in a Sukkah somewhere tonight. We were planning to stay here in the park and then saw this. So we just moved in for the night."

She replied, eyes twinkling, "It must have been set up just for you, then."

David and Emily looked at one another and smiled, once again amazed at the love their Father was bestowing on them in His special land by giving them not only their needs, but also their desires

Yom Revi'i (Fourth Day)   Day 2 of Rabbinic *Sukkot*

The sun was setting as they prepared their supper of bread, hummus and vegetables. It was a beautiful night so they would sleep on their mats in the sukkah instead of setting up the tent outside, enjoying more of the fresh air. The sukkah's cloth walls provided a sense of security, and the stars could be seen through the scant roof of palm branches. They talked about other families in the past who had made the journey to Jerusalem by foot, carrying their necessary belongings, remembering the story of a man named Joseph and his very pregnant wife, who traveled to *Bet Lechem*,[223] only five miles south of where they were now, over 2,000 years ago. They talked about how it was probably around this time of year, since the shepherds were in the fields now,[224] but would soon be bringing their sheep in because of the weather change that happens just after Sukkot. And they discussed the trip for Passover that twelve year old Y'shua made with his parents, brothers, and other family and friends to Jerusalem from Nazareth farther north.[225]

Just after dark, after the children had fallen asleep, a man stepped inside the Sukkah. Emily watched him with eyes closed as much as possible, as

---

[223]*Bet Lechem* - Hebrew for 'House of Bread', Bethlehem.

[224]Luk. 2:8 And there were in the same country shepherds abiding in the field, keeping watch over their flock by night.

[225]Luk. 2:41 Now his parents went to Jerusalem every year at the feast of the passover.

364

Chapter 38   Up to Zion

he moved closer to examine the family. She was about to sit up and say something, when he decided to leave, but she did not have a good feeling about him. Over the course of the next hour, two other men separately looked into the Sukkah, then left. Emily's contractions continued to come, regularly enough that she began to time them – one about every seven minutes. She woke David and told him, asking if he would mind getting up with her. He agreed and they stepped outside, walked about twenty feet to a big boulder surrounded by green grass, and half sat, half leaned on it, David holding Emily, as her pains continued. The full moon was high in the sky, and there was a breeze blowing that hinted of rain. It was a beautiful place to be and a wonderful time to be there.

Suddenly, from around the corner of the Sukkah, came another man who stepped inside. Just as David was about ask him what he was looking for, he walked back out and left. By this time, the couple had figured out what was going on and began praying against the evil forces that were operating in the park. They prayed for protection on their children and that Yah would use them to help thwart the evil, even if just for that night. After sitting on the boulder for over an hour, Emily felt that labor was not progressing and that it would be better to get some sleep. As clouds began to move in, they talked about setting up the tent so they would be ahead if it started to rain. The time of Sukkot begins the rainy season in Israel, though it often does not rain until afterward. It is said that it is a good sign and a blessing if one's Sukkah gets rained on. Since the Varelas had experienced one blessing after another on this trip, they decided the odds were for rain. So, as tired as they were, they set up the tent

It took just a few minutes to put it perpendicular to the Sukkah, so it would be level in the right direction and easily accessible if they needed it. The couple returned to their mats in the Sukkah, still preferring it over the tent. About 2:00 AM, light rain began to fall. Emily woke David from his sound sleep and told him it might be better to go ahead and move the children in case the rain got heavy. One by one, he took the children, starting with Natanyah, while Emily woke Armando and Briana, who helped move the mats and sheets. Moving children in the night was never an event any of them looked forward to. The older ones worked together quickly to get beds out from under sleeping siblings before they woke up and began crying. The task was accomplished in record time, and in under three minutes they were all back in bed, this time in the tent. And the rain stopped.

Around 3 AM, Emily awoke with a start to water slamming against the sides of the tent. She quickly realized they were once again being bombarded with the local sprinkler system, as they had been when camped on the lush green grass at Or Akiva. She praised Yah for both the Sukkah and the tent as she fell back into a deep sleep, knowing they would be dry as they received the blessing of rain.

The family awoke in the morning to light rain, knowing the Jewish people were celebrating the blessing of rain on Sukkot. They ate in the tent, then when the rain stopped for a few minutes, packed everything, including their wet dwelling, loaded their possessions on their backs and set off on their one mile journey toward the Old City as the rain continued and increased in intensity.

Activity was in full force today and buses, taxis and other autos crowded the streets. Within a few minutes they could see the prominent wall of the Old City of Jerusalem with the Tower of David jutting up near the Jaffa Gate entrance. They were walking the path that millions of people over the course of history had walked, the Jaffa Road being a highly traveled route from the Jaffa port of the Mediterranean Sea for thousands of years. They walked under the huge stone gate, traveling on the brick road towards the entrance to the markets in front of them, passing by vendors of bread and fruit, with their carts covered to protect them from the light, but persistent rain.

Rooftop Sukkah

Just before entering the crowded market on David Street, they turned left at the money changer's booth and went up the stairs to the Petra Hostel. At the desk on the first floor, David paid for the family's stay for nine nights, which would take them to the morning after the Last Great Day celebration at the end of Sukkot.[226] They planned to leave on preparation day before *Shabbat*. After getting settled with the Arab man behind the counter, who recognized David from his two previous visits to Jerusalem one and three years prior, they climbed a flight and a half of tile stairs, then continued up the last half of rickety winding steps, with spaces between the railings way too big for toddlers' safety, in order to get to the roof. They opened the door to see their new temporary home, a black tar roof with white patched seems and several large humps to accommodate the domed ceilings in the rooms beneath. There was an apartment in the center of the roof where the Hostel Manager and his family lived. Around that was a space of about 20 feet on the north, west, and south sides with a much larger area on the east that was a few steps above the rest of the roof and had chairs set up for people to gather and enjoy the air and view. Because so much could be seen from there, many occupants from the hostel frequented the roof, and others who wanted to experience the sights were charged five shekels each just to come up and look off. The various humps on the three sides were up to three feet high, around ten feet in diameter, and took some getting used to as a walking surface.

The north side of the roof, where they entered, was empty, but the big humps made it a difficult place to set up a large tent. They went around the apartment, checking all sides. There were already several tents on

---

[226]Lev. 23:39 Also in the fifteenth day of the seventh month, when ye have gathered in the fruit of the land, ye shall keep a feast unto YHWH seven days: on the first day *shall be* a sabbath, and on the eighth day *shall be* a sabbath.

the more level south side of the roof and one on the west side. They soon learned that these campers were all followers of Y'shua who were in Jerusalem for the feast. Besides being a good vantage point for the Mount of Olives and the Temple Mount, looking down from the east side, the view was of Hezekiah's pool, now filled with debris and used as a grazing place for sheep and goats. As they looked for a good place to stay, they also had to dodge the hostel's laundry lines, so found the best place to set up the large tent was at an angle in the northwest corner, with the door facing southeast toward the apartment. This would keep them out of the way of the launderer and still give people room to walk around. Under them to the north was a Catholic School and to the west, the Imperial Hotel. David and Emily were both satisfied with the potential escape route, if one became necessary, by climbing down to the roof below, then getting out by the stairs that descended from there.

They quickly set up the tent, not wanting it to be packed long while wet. Then the children began exploring the roof with the other children that were there, enjoying running up and down the big humps and looking off at the traffic and pedestrians below. They met the two sons of the Hostel Manager, the age of the middle Varela children, and were quickly invited to use the riding cars and other toys they had on the roof. They, like the Varela children, did not have a lot of contact with other children, so the two families were glad for each other's company. The Varela children, having trouble remembering the significant Hebrew name of the oldest son, affectionately called him 'Noodle head' because of the long golden bushy Afro locks of hair that had grown past his shoulders and looked like noodles. His parents, like the Varelas, were serious about following the ways of the Most High, and had him living as a Nazarite.[227]

After getting their Sukkot dwelling in order and meeting several other people who were staying on the roof, the family went down the dangerous steps and into the market below to get food, since the high day according to the ancient scriptural calendar would begin at sundown. The Varelas would get their food purchased and make sure all work was done and bodies clean and in clean clothes before the sun set.

---

[227] Nazarite - one separated unto YHWH, having taken a vow as described in Numbers 6, mentioned also concerning Sampson in Judges 13.

Old City Markets

At the bottom of the steps, past the Arab money changer's booth, they turned left into the crowded markets of the Old City. They walked the stone street, going down the slick steps with ancient slick stone ramps beside for vendors' carts. The streets were particularly slippery today because of the rain, and though the first street was covered with canopies the water tracked in by people's shoes made the already slick stones almost treacherous. They passed by vendor after vendor, all Arab in this section of the city, many trying to convince the parents to come into their shop. David was accustomed to this, having been there before, but for the rest of the family, it was a new experience. Emily never liked to be rude to people, so was prone to get sucked into their schemes, but David just came along behind her and pulled her into the middle of the small alley, so tourists on either side of her would be the ones to be preyed upon. The children loved the slippery stone ramps, and since there were not as many people out today in the intermittent rain as there usually were, there were several opportunities for them to slide down them with their slick sandals, trying not to fall. Emily led, walking down the steps beside them, glad she was wearing her favorite old flat sandals with the worn hole in the bottom, which served as extra traction. David followed at the rear for security, Emily glancing back from time to time to know where to turn.

He signaled her to turn north toward the Damascus Gate to get out of tight quarters. Even though crowds were sparse that day, it was still chaotic for the family who was not accustomed to being around so many people. They stepped into a courtyard and regrouped, going over the list again of what they would buy-fresh fruits and vegetables, hummus, tuna, olives, bread, and sweet breads and milk, since the high day was coming. They walked on, glancing at the beautiful clothing, bags, crafts of various types, and other wares before turning west, then south again entering one of the numerous *shukim*[228]. Once again they were in a crowded place, barely enough room for two vendor carts to meet. They found a tiny grocery on the right and Emily went in to get the things they needed while David kept the children near the wall outside, watching the passersby. Among the tourists, they saw religious priests, Catholic, Armenian, Orthodox Christian, as well as lots of Arabs and a handful of Jews, all easily distinguishable by their apparel. Emily came out with what they needed, and David showed her the shop he had been eying across the tiny alley that sold various pastries. The children were getting restless, so David took all but Isabel up the alley while she and Emily shopped for treats for the high day.

The Arab vendor could tell they were not familiar with his pastries and asked, "What would you like?"

Emily, pointing at the baklava, asked, "What is this?"

---

[228]*Shukim*, plural of *shuk*, an open-air market.

"Baklava," he said, confidently, as he reached down with his tongs, picked up one of the one by three inch rolled pastries, and gave it to her to try, then gave one to Isabel. "I am fourth generation baklava maker; my father, his father, and his father before him."

It was an instant hit. She ordered twenty, two for each family member for the high day plus two just because twenty sounded better than eighteen, then got some of the sweet breads like they had traditionally gotten before every *Shabbat* since they had been in the Land. After paying, they met David and the children, and they all walked back up the slippery steps toward the entrance of the city and then up the wobbly stairs to their roof abode.

Outside Jaffa Gate

When they arrived, they met their newest neighbors, a woman and her adult son, Americans who now lived in Arad. They were from Kentucky, not far from where the Varelas lived and six of their 12 children still lived across the Atlantic. They, too, were followers of Y'shua, there to celebrate the feast. They were given mattresses and blankets by the hostel and settled in on the west side, not far from the family tent.

Those paying for the roof were given access to the showers below, so the family took their set of clean clothes down and men went into one shower room and ladies into the other, the parents keeping towels and clean clothes from getting wet, making sure bodies got clean and dressed, and seeing that all dirty clothing got bundled in towels to take back to the tent.

39 - Old Jerusalem

Yom Chamishi (Fifth Day)
Day 1 of *Sukkot*   High Day   Day 3 of Rabbinic *Sukkot*

After their usual supper and welcoming in the feast, they lay down in their tent on the roof. Just across from the hostel to the southwest was the looming Tower of David. Each night, there was a light show that played on the inside wall of the fortress and the sound and lights from the movie penetrated the family's tent. The younger children had no trouble sleeping through it, but the older ones became curious and went out to see what they could. The view outside was not much better than from inside the tent, just flashes of color on the parts of the fortress they could see from their perch. All they knew about the show was that there was something about war and fire because they could hear the battle cries and flames burning something. After their curiosity was satisfied, they went back to the tent with the rest of the family and all went to sleep, as the show played on and then played again before the night was over.

The family awoke at 5 AM to the blasting of the Muslim prayers coming from the speaker near the corner of the hostel roof. David, having been in Jerusalem before, was not shocked out of his deep sleep like Emily was. The experience would not have been quite as bad had the chanted prayer been coming from only one speaker, or even if it had been coming from multiple speakers at the same time. But one by one, new speakers began to sound with the same prayer being sung just a few seconds apart from one another. Feeling like she would go insane before it was over, she covered her ears with her clothes that she used for a pillow until it finally stopped several minutes later. The children went back to sleep easily, but she was awake for the remainder of the day. While being tormented by the prayer, she admired the devotion of the Muslim people who faithfully stopped whatever they were doing five times per day to get down on their mats and pray in the direction they had been taught pleased their Elohim. Emily felt sad that few of Yah's people seemed that devoted and resolved within herself to take a lesson from the Muslims in that regard.

The rest of the family slept a little later this high day, then awoke to a beautiful sunrise over the Old City of Jerusalem. They had put their milk in the refrigerator down in the kitchen, so David took Briana to get it and some coffee for himself while Emily got out the sweet breads, yogurt, and fruit. Father and daughter descended the two flights of stairs to the lobby, then turned away from the stairs that went to the markets to descend a maze of smaller staircases that mimicked the maze of Jerusalem streets and tunnels. When they returned from the kitchen, the family had a

Chapter 39   Old Jerusalem

peaceful breakfast, including the new baklava, overlooking the Temple Mount on the east side of the roof.

After clean-up, they walked down the three flights of stairs, straight past the Tower of David along the stone streets, past the Armenian Quarter[229] and into the Jewish Quarter on their way to the Temple Mount, Armando packing the backpack that had water and all the necessary birthing supplies in it, just in case the baby came while they were out. The bag contained sheets for privacy, chuck pads to prevent messes, cord clamp for the navel and a scalpel to cut it, nasal aspirator, cloths to clean the baby, essential anointing oil to be used on Emily if necessary and on the baby's navel to prevent infection, a little blue outfit for the baby that ended up matching the new T-shirts they had just bought, made at their Horse and Buggy friends' place back home, and a little baby hat. Isabel also had a pack containing more water and some fruit, in case they got hungry before returning.

The scriptures say that when the whole family comes for Sukkot in the seventh year, the year of release of slaves and of the land sabbath, they are to gather together and read the book of instructions, the Varelas understanding that to be the book of Deuteronomy.[230] Even though they had Bibles in their home and could read it any time they wanted, one of the main intentions of their trip was to read Deuteronomy during the feast. The family planned to begin to read that day on the Temple Mount, where the first two temples had stood. David knew that Bibles were not allowed on the Temple Mount, but Emily always carried the PDA that had her free e-sword program installed.

Temple Mount

The family approached the security entrance to the Temple Mount, walking in formation, Emily at the lead and David watching everyone from behind. As they waited in line to go through security, Emily strategically placed the children to the left of the entry way so that she would be presented first with the passports. David was able to move up beside her and behind two elderly American women, who were just at the entrance. Beside him was

---

[229]The Old City of Jerusalem is divided into four quarters: Northwest the Christian Quarter, Northeast the Muslim Quarter, Southeast the Jewish Quarter, and Southwest the Armenian Quarter.

[230]Deut. 31:10-12 And Moses commanded them, saying, At the end of every seven years, in the solemnity of the year of release, in the feast of tabernacles, When all Israel is come to appear before YHWH thy Elohim in the place which he shall choose, thou shalt read this law before all Israel in their hearing. Gather the people together, men, and women, and children, and thy stranger that is within thy gates, that they may hear, and that they may learn, and fear YHWH your Elohim, and observe to do all the words of this law:

a Jewish man who struck up a conversation. While they exchanged general information, the two women were told by the Arab security officers to put their Bibles on the little metal table with all of the other things from previous people that were awaiting the return of their owners. Muslims now controlled the Temple Mount, so no Bibles were allowed because they were said to be provocative. Religious Jews were only permitted at certain times, even though the site had much more historical significance for Jews than it did for Muslims. The ladies protested leaving their Bibles, but were given no choice. Bibles were not allowed. The guard informed them they would still be there when they returned. One woman turned to the other and said, "I hope no one steals them."

Emily and the children thought that was a funny statement. Would a thief steal a Bible? And if so, wouldn't he need it more than the women? She used the comical statement as a teaching opportunity while they waited. The man next to David was permitted entry with the two ladies and then let out the other side since he only had a water bottle with him. The family was next in line and stepped up on the steps ready to go with no visible Bibles and the passports having been moved from the carrier around Emily's neck to her hand. One Arab officer called for the backpack, which David placed on the conveyer. The children waited just behind him outside the entrance, as the little ones stepped up and down on the wooden steps held up by concrete blocks, trying to keep their minds off of the intense heat that rose off of the Jerusalem stone and surrounding pavement.

As the pack began its short voyage into the x-ray machine, the second officer looked at the passports and began questioning Emily in Arab-accented English. "Where are you from?"

"The United States," she said a little more quietly than she had intended, then quickly adding with a stronger voice, "Tennessee," trying to eliminate the next question that was most often asked.

Meanwhile, the x-ray machine beeped, and the first officer stopped it and began questioning David concerning its contents, "Do you have alcohol?" he asked.

David: No.

Officer 1: You are lying. There is alcohol.

David: No, there's a bottle of oil.

Officer 1: No! It's not oil! It's alcohol! You cannot bring alcohol! Open the bag!

David opened the bag, pulled out the small bottle of anointing oil made in Israel, that somewhat resembled an airline whiskey bottle. As he handed it to the officer, he saw a large group of Israeli guards approaching from the west side of the ramp. The man smelled the oil, just as David heard

Chapter 39   Old Jerusalem

Emily say, "Tennessee." Feeling compelled to help her with her officer and not having heard her say "United States" at first, he told her quietly, "Tell him the U.S."

The first officer, who had just been convinced that the substance in the bottle was indeed oil, overheard David and shouted, "You're lying! You're changing her story!"

The second officer, not finding Tennessee in his computer, was agreeing with him and said, "There's no such country."

David took a step closer to him, getting in a protective position in front of his wife and said, "Tennessee is in the United States. Look at the passports."

Just then the Israeli guards David had seen arrived at the private door to their left. The spiked metal gate opened and a tall Jewish man with a long beard, wearing a kippah, glasses, and a dressy suit coat and carrying two rolls resembling blueprints stepped out from the midst of armed security guards and in through the door. At that moment, the office door opened on the other side of the little cubicle and an Arab man came out to greet the tall Jewish man. The small security room was getting very crowded. As the two officers were accusing the couple of lying, the Jewish man turned to David and the guards and asked, "What's going on here?"

As the tall man eyed David from top to bottom, then Emily, and took notice of the children waiting just outside the doorway, noting the way they were dressed, including their tassels with the blue thread, the first Arab officer told him in Hebrew, "These people are lying!"

The tall man with the peaceful face directed his question to David, "Where are you from?"

"America, the United States."

"Are you Jewish?"

David answered, "I don't think so. We think we are from Ephraim."

His smile grew from just his natural demeanor to intentional, and his eyes sparkled with interest. He was one of the few they had met in Israel that appeared to be familiar with their position. He turned toward the boss of the Arab soldiers and said in Hebrew, "They're OK. Let them go up."

The first officer, looking past the tall man toward his own boss, pleaded, "They're lying! And they're Jewish! Look at them!"

The tall man, having some type of authority, repeated to the boss sternly, but with his natural smile, and waving his hand, "They're not Jewish. Let them go up."

The Arab boss who had come out to meet with the tall Jewish man ordered his subordinates in Arabic, "Let them go!"

The tall man turned back and smiled at David, as David wondered if they would make the family leave their pack there, and said, "Go up. And take your bag."

As David picked up the pack, he looked at the first officer who begrudgingly gave him the signal to proceed, while the tall, politically important man smiled broadly. And the family walked out with the pack which contained the birthing supplies. In all the confusion, the x-ray guard had never gotten past the bottle of oil to see the sharp scalpel!

The family had watched the heated exchange with amazement and saw the officers submit. As they exited the security booth, David and Emily discussed who the tall Jewish man must have been. Was he an important politician? Or an influential member of the Temple Institute?[231] If the latter, he would certainly be more understanding of the Varelas position because of his study and understanding of the scriptures, including the prophets. They were once again in awe of their Creator and Savior as they realized they would have been refused entry to the Temple Mount, had the man not shown up exactly on time.

They walked up the covered walkway that looked to be under construction over an archeological excavation site and the Western Wall with all of the praying people below. They stepped onto the Temple Mount where armed guards stood at their entrance and at another entrance that they later learned was for Arabs, to the north of where they were. David gave them a tour of the site, sharing information he had learned from various sources on his previous visits to Israel, as well as knowledge he had gained from his study of the scriptures. They walked past the beautiful Dome of the Rock, with its marble pillars and mosaic tile work, but did not enter.

He then led them to the little Dome of the Spirits, thought by many to be the former site of the ark of the covenant, and explained the theory of how the ark was able to avoid capture by the Romans around 70 AD through a brilliant Egyptian engineering design used during King Solomon's time by way of his marriage to Pharaoh's daughter. He showed them what appeared to be the keys used to lower the huge rock like an elevator so that the ark could be carried away in a tunnel beneath, ending up below the crucifixion site outside the city across from the Damascus Gate. A group of tourists approached as he was explaining things to his family and began asking questions, so he took a few minutes to answer them before leading his family back in the direction of the courtyard near the entrance.

---

[231]Temple Institute - the organization in Israel that works toward rebuilding the temple, studying scripture and other writings to make sure they are properly making the temple service instruments, priestly garments, and other items for the temple, as they wait for the time for it to be rebuilt.

Chapter 39   Old Jerusalem

Victor

The children had asked to use the camera and were taking turns taking pictures of various points of interest at the site of the former temples of first Israel, then of the Jews, the House of Judah who began returning from Babylonian captivity around 537 BC. Moshe was ready for his turn with the camera and saw an older Arab gentleman sweeping the courtyard. He asked if he could take his picture, but the man, not understanding English, nodded and reached out his hand to take Moshe's camera from him, thinking Moshe wanted the man to take *his* picture, as he had probably done many times before for tourists on the site. Emily told him in Hebrew, which he still did not seem to understand, that no, Moshe wanted to take *his* picture. Once he understood, he was surprised, but posed, smiling, as he leaned on his broom.

The children explored, running from place to place, discovering wells, beautiful stones, and talking about the different structures at the site, taking pictures of whatever interested the one with the camera at the time. After seeing most everything of interest, the family walked down the few steps they had come up and headed toward the entrance, where they knew there was some shade by a retaining wall where they could sit to read their scriptures. David and Emily sat on the ancient stone pavement, the younger children beside them and the others perching on the waist-high retaining wall just behind them. Emily got out her PDA and found Deuteronomy, reading the chapters one through four, while an Arab boy around Armando's age who sold postcards walked back and forth, trying to get close enough to see what they were doing

40 - Wedding

As Emily read from Deuteronomy under the shade of the tree, a smiling, large-framed American man approached them from the entrance. The children, recognizing him as having brought his family to their home in Tennessee, jumped up and down excitedly telling their parents who had arrived. It was a friend of theirs from Ohio.

Meeting the Ohioan

In 2005, David made his first trip to Jerusalem for Sukkot, having made arrangements to meet up with a friend from California. The friend got there a few days before David, and was turned back at the port of entry, unable to enter the country. David's tickets were already purchased, so he continued with his plans to go. When he got to New York, he noticed a young man wearing tassels with the blue string board the flight to Tel Aviv with his wife and baby. Once through customs at Tel Aviv, he wondered what to do next. He knew nothing about Israel or how to get anywhere, not even where Jerusalem was. If he could not find where he was going, he might need a place to sleep. He reasoned that a car would provide him both transportation and shelter, so was thinking of renting one when he turned to see the young family man with the blue string in his tassels.

While the man waited for his rental transaction to complete, he turned and upon noticing David's similar tassels, introduced himself as being from Ohio. David told him he lived in Tennessee, but was originally from Mexico, to which the man cheerfully greeted, "*Buenos dias!*"[232] and shook David's hand. They spoke in Spanish and English as the conversation continued, "What are you doing in Israel?"

"I'm here for Sukkot," David replied.

"Oh, really! So are we. Where are you staying?"

"The Scottish Inn, in Jerusalem."

"Really! We're staying just two blocks from there. Do you want to ride with us?"

David thought that was a great idea! The Ohioan had been there before and was somewhat familiar with things, so he gladly accepted the offer. As they rode toward Jerusalem, they learned they had much in common

---

[232]*Buenos dias* - Spanish for 'Good day,' most often used before noon.

Chapter 40   Wedding

concerning their beliefs and practices. Before arriving at the Scottish Inn to drop David off, they traded contact information and the man offered, "Hey, we're going to a friend's house for supper tomorrow night. Would you like for me to pick you up and take you with us? I'd love for you to meet some friends."

David, not having any plans other than to celebrate the feast said, "Sure."

The Ohioan said, "Great! You'll really enjoy meeting these people." And they agreed upon the time for him to return to pick him up.

David walked into the lobby, with its beautiful view of the Old City, and paid for his stay. Emily had reserved him a room, but the Inn was overbooked, so the manager offered to let him stay in the bomb shelter for a discount. David gladly accepted, just happy to have a place to sleep, and decided this one would be particularly safe. After checking out the room and leaving his bag there, David returned to the lobby to look around. A few minutes later, he met a man from Nevada in person that was also planning to meet the friend from California before he was denied entry, and whom he had brief Internet contact with before leaving the U.S. They visited for some that day and also the next. The jovial Nevadan invited, "Hey, I'm going to a friend's house tonight for supper. Why don't you join me?"

"I'd like to, but I've already made plans with someone else."

"Aw, that's too bad," said the Nevadan, adding, "I'd really like you to meet these guys."

"Thanks for inviting me," David replied. "Maybe I can meet them another time."

David rode with the Ohioan to dinner with his friends. On the way, the Ohioan shared a little about the people they would be meeting. Once inside the house, David was surprised to see the Nevadan he had turned down the dinner invite from. He was just as surprised, as was the Ohioan, the hosts and the other guests at dinner when they heard the story. So began the friendship of David and the already bonded Ohioan and Nevadan.

The Ohioan greeted, "*Buenas tardes, Amigo!*"[233] and the conversation continued in Spanish, "How've you been, my brother?"

"Fine, fine! How about you?"

Changing to English, he said, "Great, everything's good! It's good to see you and your beautiful family," nodding at Emily and the children.

---

[233]*Amigo* - Spanish for 'friend.'

After catching up for a few minutes, he asked David, "Have you heard from the Frenchman?" referring to a friend he had introduced David to in Jerusalem the year before.

David replied that he had not, and the Ohioan broke the news, "He's getting married in a couple of hours at a restaurant just inside the Jaffa Gate. You should come, my brother!"

The Prophecy

David's eyes lit up as he remembered the man, "Do you remember what I told him last year when we were leaving?" he asked.

The Ohioan looked blankly at him, "No."

"Remember when we went out to eat, and there were 12 of us, and we discovered that there were 12 nations represented there eating together after the last high day was over?"

Now, the Ohioan's eyes lit up as he remembered. The Israeli waitress had asked them if they were there on business and was surprised to learn that they were there for the feast, then shocked when she found out most of them were not Jewish. She said it was like the 12 tribes coming back together. Many of the men were then surprised to learn that the prophesied regathering of the 12 tribes of Israel was so well-known in Israel because in most of their home countries, few were aware of it, even though scripture refers to it in multiple places in both testaments.

The Frenchman was always ready to share the gospel and began witnessing to the waitress, who was very interested and paid as much attention as she could while working. As the meeting broke up and they prepared to leave, the Frenchman said he hoped to see the two men again, but learned that both of them were leaving that night. David's new friend reassured him with the popular statement of hope, "Next year in Jerusalem!" regarding where they would be keeping the festival.

David in the presence of the Ohioan and others, without even thinking about what he was saying, prophesied, "I think next time I see you, you'll be getting married."

It was not a secret that the Frenchman was concerned that he was over 30 years old and had still not been able to find a suitable wife. But David's words out of the blue, as bold as they were, came as a bit of a shock to him. All three men laughed, said shalom, and parted ways.

After hearing David retell the events of the year before, the Ohioan did indeed remember the occasion and the prophecy. "That's all the more reason you should come!"

Chapter 40   Wedding

David replied, "No, man, I'm here with the family this time. I just want to be with them."

Emily, realizing the significance of the whole episode told David, "We should all go! I'm sure, the way you describe him, he'd love to have us there at his wedding!"

"I don't think that would be nice. We're a bunch of people," he replied.

The Tour Group

Being encouraged by his wife and friend that it was the right thing to do, he agreed to pray about it. He told the Ohioan friend what they were in the middle of, so he stayed and listened as Emily resumed reading. The family huddled around her and the Arab boy began spying on them again. Just as she finished, a large tour group appeared through the entrance. David recognized the guide as the man whose house he had eaten dinner in when the Ohioan and Nevadan had reunited his first time in Israel three years before. Since then, David had grown a beard and was now surrounded by children. The man did not recognize David, but stopped at the family sitting there with the Ohioan standing beside them and turned motioning toward his group as he said to the family, "*Hinei,*[234] *Ephraim!*" Then, he turned, motioning toward the family and said to his group, "*Hinei, Yehudah!*"[235]

Emily, not taking time to explain to David what was going on, quickly said in Hebrew, "No, we too, are Ephraim!"

After finding out the family was from the U.S., the guide was shocked and switched to English, the first language of most of his group, telling them, "These are also brothers from Ephraim!" which caused rejoicing within the group. Then he turned toward the family and said, "I thought you all were visiting from Hebron or Judea-Samaria."

Emily took it as a great compliment that an Israeli resident would confuse them with people who were local to Israel. The girls' long skirts and head scarves and David's black beard and dark skin *could* confuse some people in that manner, which they would realize even more profoundly later. The guide then recognized David and began talking to him. Just then, an older woman from the group stepped forward and asked enthusiastically, "Are you the *cycling* family?" to which Emily responded affirmatively.

She excitedly turned toward the group and began telling them, "This is the family I was telling you about! I've been on their updates list, praying for them. They were traveling by bicycle through Israel and the husband had

---

[234]*Hinei* - Hebrew for 'Behold.'
[235]*Yehudah* - Hebrew for 'Judah.'

379

to return to the States, leaving the rest of them here. Here they are!" She then turned toward Emily and introduced herself.

Emily recognized her name as the woman from Oklahoma who was an instructor of Hebrew in a group there. Her introduction of the family caused several others in the group to approach to meet them and learn more, and some began to hand them money. David and Emily looked at each other in surprise and quickly told the people they did not need their money, but they insisted, handing them folded bills, some in dollars and some in shekels. The couple thanked them graciously, as the group quickly disappeared behind the guide, who needed to keep his tour on schedule. During all of the commotion, the Ohioan had greeted his friend, the guide, then excused himself, and rushed off to prepare for the wedding.

Prophecy Fulfilled

The Muslim call to prayer went out and everyone was ordered off the Temple Mount. The family exited and walked back through the Old City, taking routes that avoided markets as much as possible, since it was the high day. As they walked around the edge of the city, where it was much less crowded, they talked about the wedding. Emily convinced David that the Frenchman, whom she had never met, would love to have them. The biggest thing that concerned them was that it was at a restaurant where food was being catered, meaning they might be having servants on the high day serving them food. The second issue was that, since they were not personally invited, their numbers might place a burden on the wedding party. David had prayed about it, and they decided to go, making sure they had their own food with them. They stopped by the hostel, put more food in their pack, walked down the three flights of stairs to the street, turned right and then right again at the next street, just before the city wall. They walked up the hill, not able to remember the name of the restaurant the Ohioan had told them about. Deciding they had passed it, they turned around and met a family that also looked like they were looking for a special event. About that time, a man came out of the restaurant they were standing in front of and asked if they were there for the wedding. The families smiled at one another, then at the man, who opened the door wide for them and pointed them all toward the wedding party.

Once inside, they walked through the restaurant and out the back way under the huge tarp, hanging from the inside of the city wall, to where a large party was gathered. The Frenchman spotted David and immediately rushed over, hugging him and exclaiming in his French accent, "David, how are you, my brother? I am so glad to see you!"

David replied in his Spanish accent that he was doing well, and introduced his family and the Frenchman introduced his bride. He neglected his many other guests for a few minutes to catch up with David and to tell him that he remembered the prophecy, telling him how he and his wife had met just a short time later. He told the family to get as much food as they wanted,

380

Chapter 40   Wedding

that there was plenty. David told him they had not planned to eat, but the Frenchman assured them again that there was plenty.

About that time, a Mexican friend that David had met in Jerusalem the year before saw David and came to speak to him. And then Emily saw a friend from Tennessee they had met at a meeting in a little country church near Nashville, where the Intercessor was speaking a couple of years before. She sat with the family, sharing the nuts that she had brought. The Ohioan also came and sat with the family, sharing his snacks, as well. It was a feast (of snacks) within a feast (a wedding) within a feast (Sukkot).

Soon the wedding of the smiling Frenchman began. Throughout the ceremony he continued to glance at David, almost not able to contain his joy at the fulfillment of last year's prophecy. The couple stood under a *choopah*[236] held up with poles by four people, one at each corner. The French pastor had come from Las Vegas to perform the ceremony and spoke truths about the importance of the marriage relationship.

A group of conservatively dressed people resembling Mennonites sang several songs, joined by David's Mexican friend. It was a beautiful ceremony in the courtyard surrounded by palm trees and several different types of flowering bushes. After the wedding, the family said their goodbye's to the Frenchman and his new wife. The Mexican introduced them to the singers, a Christian group from a community in Zichron Yaakov. The name of the town rang a bell and the family realized they were the people that the locals had asked them if they were a part of when they cycled through their area two months before. The members of the community were often seen riding bicycles and the ladies wore conservative dresses, similar to what the Varela girls wore. The German young people were very interested in getting to know the family better and invited them to the community before their departure from Israel.

Physics Lesson

They left the restaurant and went back towards the hostel, saying goodbye to the Ohioan, as the lady Tennessean went with them to see where they were set up. On their short way back, they were approached by a young

---

[236]*Choopah* - Wedding canopy made with a *tallit* or sheet, held up at the four corners by poles or attendants.

man wearing a cowboy hat along with his sidekick, an American missionary who lived in Israel. He greeted David with, "You have a beautiful family."

David thanked him and asked where he was from. "Oklahoma," he replied. "What about you?"

And so began the customary line of questioning until David got to the part about the reason they were in Israel. When he told the men they were there for the feast of tabernacles, he detected aggravation in the voice of the Sidekick when he said, "What for? That stuff's been done away with."

David replied as they walked together, now a group of 12, "We don't see it that way at all. The instructions in the scriptures are for life. Following them is described by the Psalmist as wisdom."

As they walked below the Petra Hostel, the Cowboy said, "This is interesting. I've never heard this before. I'd love to talk with you more."

"Sure, we'd love that, too," David replied.

"Where are you staying?" he asked.

"Right here," David pointed up toward the roof, explaining that they had their tent set up there. "Would you all like to come up?"

"We're kind of busy right now. We've got an appointment with someone. But would it be OK for us to come back in the evening?"

"Sure. We'd love to have you."

As they turned to leave, the Sidekick piped up, "We'll be back later to prove you wrong."

David replied with a smile, "We'll be waiting."

As they talked, Emily and the children heard people excitedly discussing the Parade of Nations, put on by the International Christian Embassy in Jerusalem. Hearing that it was passing by the Old City just outside the Jaffa Gate, they changed directions and walked out the gate and down the steep hill to watch as thousands of people - organized by country and carrying their respective flags, some in beautiful traditional costumes - walked by. It was a great geography and sociology class for the children. After seeing the last part of the parade, they turned and went back to the hostel with the Tennessean. She followed them up the stairs, Isabel holding one hand and Rebeka the other. Once at the top, Emily broke out the pomegranates they had bought before for the festive day, while the children showed the Tennessean all around their new home on the roof. David and Emily began peeling and separating the pomegranates into sections to make them easier for the children to eat without wasting. The

Chapter 40   Wedding

children soon brought their Tennessee friend over to share a snack and they all enjoyed the sweet fruit and conversation.

When the older ones finished eating, they went back to the metal railing to watch the people below. Moshe, not wanting to miss anything, took a quarter of a pomegranate with him so he could enjoy the best of both worlds - eating and being with the bigger children. The parents had not noticed him walk off with a big piece of fruit and continued to section more for themselves since the children were finished. Moshe stood by his bigger counterparts, looking down at the crowds of tourists, locals, and celebrants passing below. He held the pomegranate quarter carefully and began to pry it open, trying not to lose any of the precious arils[237] before getting them to his mouth. As his just-turned-four-year-old hands worked with his mouth to accomplish the important and satisfying task, a loose aril began to roll away from the rest. Moshe quickly took the quarter from his mouth and tried to catch the aril. As he did, he lost his grip on the quarter, so quickly forgot about the single airl in an attempt to catch the rest of them. He recovered the quarter, but not without disturbing the other loose arils which fell from their source and passed through his hands towards the ground three stories below.

~ ~ ~

As the bald American tourist stood unsuspectingly on the streets of the Old City, taking in the sights, he felt a sharp pain on the top of his head. He instinctively looked up, and was hit in the face and glasses with numerous other unidentified falling objects, which burst upon impact, blinding him with red, sticky liquid. Jerking off his glasses, he saw a group of children standing on top of the hostel, and yelled, "Hey!" after which all of the children instantly vanished from sight.

~ ~ ~

The children, seeing the angry man below and being witnesses to what had just happened, ran away from the rails toward the tent where their parents and friend were still preparing their fruit and talking with one another. Moshe was horrified at first, then remembered the comical sight and began laughing with the older ones who had also found the event to be anything but serious. The parents looked up with questioning expressions at the hurried manner of their mysteriously laughing children coming their direction. Emily asked, "What's the matter?"

Armando replied, "Moshe dropped pomegranate on a man's head."

Emily cried, "Moshe!"

~ ~ ~

---

[237]Arils-small, juicy, edible parts of a pomegranate containing the seeds.

383

Armando intervened, "He didn't mean to. He just dropped it and it fell on the man."

It was time for school. Today's lesson was about physics, the laws of gravity, velocity of a falling object, and results of impact of objects raining down from the heavens on mankind. The parents made sure that everyone understood the seriousness of what had just happened and were assured that precautions would be taken to ensure nothing like that would happen again. They gave thanks that what was dropped was only pomegranate seeds and that the victim of the accident was wearing glasses. They prayed for him, told the children to make sure nothing was in their hands when they were by the rails and that nothing could fall off of the roof onto the people below.

The Cowboy and the Sidekick

David's phone rang and he answered to hear the Oklahoma drawl of the Cowboy on the other end, who was waiting with his missionary Sidekick in the lobby. The two of them had been wanting to look off the Petra roof anyway, so were excited to learn that they could go up for free as the family's guests. David went down to meet them and bring them up to the roof.

The Cowboy greeted him and the Sidekick said, "We're back to prove you wrong."

David chuckled and replied, "Well, let's go up."

Jaffa Gate from above

When they stepped through the upper door, they were impressed by the incredible view of both Old Jerusalem to the east and the new city to the west. The family walked with them, pointing out sites of interest before the children resumed playing with their friends and the parents sat to talk with the guests. Emily sat on her regular seat, a stack of the family's folded bed mats, and the Tennessean sat in a plastic chair. David offered the two men the best seats that were left, a five gallon bucket and a concrete block stood on end that he found near the roof apartment, and pulled another block up for himself. David then asked, "What are you doing in Jerusalem?"

Chapter 40   Wedding

The Cowboy pointed at the Sidekick and answered, "He's a missionary here. I'm here sharing the good news of Jesus and passing out New Testaments. I've made arrangements to procure a horse from the mounted police and plan to ride into the Old City later in the week to draw attention to the gospel."

They began to discuss scripture, being intrigued that the family guarded the commands, even though they were not Jewish and were followers of Y'shua. David and Emily were always glad to show people from the scriptures why they walked the way they did, showing them how Y'shua never transgressed the commands of His Father, how His Father's instructions were never nailed to the cross, and how all of the early believers continued to live by the Old Testament scriptures.

41 - Cowboy Questions

The Cowboy began to inquire about the family's presence in the 'Holy Land.' "So you said you're here for the feast of tabernacles?"

David: That's correct.

Cowboy: Why do you think we're still to celebrate those feasts of the Old Testament, even though Jesus died and had all those things nailed to the cross?

David: Did Y'shua keep the feasts?

Emily, interjecting: We use the Hebrew names for the Father and Son. Do you know why?

Cowboy: No, tell me.

Emily: Our Bible comes to us in English, the Old Testament translated from Hebrew and the New from Greek.

He nodded knowingly as she continued, "In the Old Testament, the name of the Father is written over 7,000 times, but because of a Jewish tradition which started in Babylon, the Jews quit saying the name, not wanting to 'take it in vain.' Actually, *not* using His name in appropriate situations falls into the category of 'taking it vain' or 'bringing it to nothing', which is a more thorough understanding of the Hebrew term used there. Continuing with the Jewish tradition of replacing YHWH with *Adonai,* meaning 'Lord', the first translators of the Bible into English translated the Hebrew letters of His name, 'yud,' 'hey,' 'vav,' 'hey' as 'the LORD' over 6,000 times. They translated it 'Jehovah' only four times.

"In Hebrew, every word, every letter, every name means something, so to speak someone's name, you're actually making a statement. For example, in English, if someone's name is Rose, I think of a rose when I speak to her. Every name is like that in Hebrew, unlike in English, where many people have their names just because the parents liked the sound of them. Do you remember the account of the angel Gabriel coming to Joseph when he learned that Mary was pregnant?"

Cowboy: Yes.

Chapter 41   Cowboy Questions

Emily: In English, it says, 'And you shall call his name Jesus because he shall save his people from their sins.'[238] I remember reading that as a young child and having a question. 'What does Jesus have to do with saving people from their sins?' It didn't make sense to me when I was a child, and I was always puzzled by the passage until I learned what it really says in Hebrew. The name Y'shua means 'YHWH is salvation' or 'YHWH saves.' So in Hebrew, the verse says, 'You shall call his name YHWH saves because he shall save his people from their sins.' Do you see how important the difference is?

Cowboy, nodding: Oh, yes!

Emily: Even though the New Testament comes to us from Greek, we know that his parents and all the people he was surrounded by spoke Hebrew and Aramaic (which is very close to Hebrew). So as he grew up, His name continued to be Y'shua. That's what his disciples and everyone else called him, and that's what he was called in the original writings that later became the New Testament. It wasn't until the New Testament writings, having been written by Hebrew speakers, were translated into Greek, years after his ascension that he began to be called anything different. As the translations were done, the Hebrew letters were transliterated to corresponding Greek letters, instead of the name being written using the Greek letters that most resembled their sound. Once that was done, an 's' was added to the end, making it more closely follow the traditions of the Greeks and their gods-for example, the pagan god Zeus. From the writings, his name, once full of meaning, began to be pronounced *Iesous*. When the Greek scriptures were translated into Latin, [239] it retained basically the same sound, which is why Jesus in Spanish and many other languages is pronounced, Hey-sus. But because the letter 'j' was added to the English language in the 1500s, his name began to be pronounced 'Jesus.' So, actually, the name Jesus has only been in use for around 500 years.[240]

"We prefer to refer to him by his Hebrew name, still full of meaning, and to the Father by His name instead of by a title that actually translates back into Hebrew as 'Ba'al.'

Emily added, "While I'm clarifying the names we use, I should go ahead and tell you that instead of 'God,' we use the Hebrew word it is translated from, 'Elohim.' It can mean any type of great one, like judges and such, but is most translated as God or gods. The reason we say 'Elohim' instead of 'God' is because there is a scripture that tells us not to even have the

---

[238]Matt. 1:21

[239]The final 's' was added in Latin, not Greek.

[240]Though the written 'j' came into English in the 1500's, the pronounced 'j' evolved later. The name 'Jesus,' with the 'j' sound did not come into being until sometime during the 1600's, making it less than 400 years old.

387

names of false gods on our lips.[241] Since we speak English, and that is the term used, it puts us in a difficult position because there was actually a false god, the god of fortune referred to in the Bible, whose name was pronounced 'God.' Because of the command, we believe it does not do Yah service for us to call Him by a name that was the name of a false God. So we prefer to use the term 'Elohim.' Some pagans did refer to their deities as 'elohim,' but since Yah describes Himself using that word, we feel it is a better choice than its English counterpart."

The Cowboy was soaking in the clarifying information that Emily spoke, as his Sidekick seemed impatient and annoyed, seemingly wondering what was so important about all of that.

David: She loves to share the name stuff with people. And it helps to make sure the people I'm talking to understand who we're talking about.

Cowboy: I agree. That *is* important information.

Sidekick: So you're saying that if we're saved in Jesus' name, we're not really saved.

David: No, we're not saying that at all. We're saying that we've been deceived concerning the importance of his name. Emily and I were both saved in the name 'Jesus,' like millions of others are because we serve a gracious Elohim, full of loving-kindness and mercy. We're saying that it's important to know his real name because it has very significant meaning. Words are powerful. The Heavenly Father created the heavens and earth by speaking them into existence and scripture is very clear that words are extremely important and powerful. So, understanding that, we want to make sure we're calling him by his real, given name, instead of an adulteration of it. And once we are saved in Jesus' name, we want to walk like he did and continue learning and growing in truth and righteousness. Once we learn his correct name, we'll want to use it, just like I'll call you by your name and not your name transliterated into Greek then transliterated again into some other language.

David continued with his original question, "Did Y'shua keep the feasts?"

Cowboy: Yes.

Sidekick: But he was Jewish.

David: But whose *feasts* are they?

Sidekick: The Jews'.

---

[241]Exo. 23:13 And in all *things* that I have said unto you be circumspect: and make no mention of the name of other gods, neither let it be heard out of thy mouth.

Chapter 41   Cowboy Questions

David: *Are* they the Jews feasts? Let's look at Leviticus 23.

Cowboy: I just have the New Testament.

David replied with a smile as he opened his scriptures, "Then you don't have the foundation. The foundation of the New Testament is the Old. If you don't have the foundation, you can't understand much of the meaning and context of the New. Here, use mine. Read right here," he said, mischievously pointing to the Spanish side of the page."

The Cowboy laughed and said in his Oklahoma drawl, "Well, I can't read *that*."

David laughed with him, pointed to the other side of the page and said, "I just like to have fun with people. Read this."

The Cowboy read verse one and two in the English NIV translation on the opposite side of the page, "The LORD said to Moses,   "Speak to the Israelites and say to them: 'These are my appointed feasts, the appointed feasts of the LORD, which you are to proclaim as sacred assemblies."

David: *Whose* feasts are they?

Cowboy: The feasts of the LORD.

David: And remember that 'the LORD' is not the actual translation, and it should say 'Yehovah' there. So they are the feasts of Yah, right?

Cowboy: Right. Yes, I see that.

David: And who are they for?

Sidekick: The Jews.

David: No, not the Jews. Look again.

The Cowboy looked at the passage again and answered with a perplexed look on his face, "The children of Israel. Isn't that the Jews?"

David directed his attention to Emily, knowing this was another of the areas about which she was passionate and knowledgeable, and she began to clarify, "The Jews are only three tribes of the children of Israel: Judah, Benjamin, and Levi. It begins in I Kings 11. Because Solomon took many wives and then began to worship their gods/elohim, Yah tore the kingdom of Israel away from him, only leaving two tribes for him to rule over because of his promise to his father, David.[242] The prophet Ahiyah was

---

[242]The tribe of Levi received no land inheritance because they were privileged to minister before YHWH, having all of their needs met by the tithes of the rest of

389

sent to Jeroboam, the supervisor of King Solomon's Israelite workforce, tore his own new cloak into 12 pieces, and gave ten of them to Jeroboam in a prophetic declaration that he would be ruler over the 10 tribes of Israel, but not until Solomon's death. The fulfillment of the prophecy happened a short time later, after Solomon's death and his son, Rehoboam, became king of Israel.

"When the ten tribes revolted because of labor issues, they made Jeroboam their king and the once great kingdom of Israel was divided into two kingdoms, known as the House of Israel and the House of Judah. The house of Israel made their headquarters in Samaria and became known as the Northern kingdom, and the house of Judah kept their headquarters in Jerusalem and became known as the Southern kingdom. The house of Israel or Northern Kingdom is also referred to in Scripture as Ephraim or the House of Ephraim, which I'll call them to avoid confusion, since sometimes scripture uses the term 'Israel' to refer to the entire House of Israel and sometimes only to the ten tribes of the House of Ephraim.

"Jeroboam then set up two golden calves, one at Dan in the north and one at Bet El, just north of Jerusalem and told Ephraim to worship there instead of going back to Jerusalem as instructed by Yah. He also changed YHWH's feast of the seventh month, tabernacles, to the eighth month and chose whoever he wanted to be priests, instead of using the Levites, as Yah had instructed. He earned himself the description of the most mentioned bad guy in scripture because of these three things, one of which, remember, was changing YHWH's feast date. Scripture mentions over and over that Jeroboam caused Israel to sin.

"Because of their sin and idolatry, Yah sent prophets to warn Ephraim to turn back to Him, but they refused until finally, as the book of Hosea so clearly prophesies, he scattered them to the winds, never to be heard from again until the last days, the times in which we now live. Then, about 150 years later, after sending more prophets to the House of Judah, but with them also continuing to wander from His ways, he promised that they would be exiled from their land, held captive in a foreign land, then restored to their own land 70 years later, after the land had received its Sabbaths that they had not given it.[243]

"While captive in Babylon, the House of Judah began to be referred to as what we now know as 'Jews.' So when we read in scripture of Jews, we're only reading of three tribes, along with a few from the Northern tribe that stuck with them because they loved Yah and wanted to worship according to His instructions. So, the Jews of today, are only a small percentage of

---

Israel. When the division occurred, they remained with the house of Judah in Jerusalem where the temple had been built.

[243]Lev. 26:34 Then shall the land enjoy her sabbaths, as long as it lieth desolate, and ye *be* in your enemies' land; *even* then shall the land rest, and enjoy her sabbaths.

Chapter 41   Cowboy Questions

the whole house of Israel, which scripture says will come back together in
the last days, with the coming of Messiah. We're all awaiting the same
Messiah - the Jews that have a lineage and the house of Ephraim that is
being restored as the *torah* becomes written on their hearts, as it says in
Jer. 31."[244]

David: Let's look at Hebrews 8:8-10,"[245] then turning to the passage Emily
had just referred to said, "Read this."

The Cowboy read the passage from his New Testament, "But God found
fault with the people and said: The time is coming, declares the Lord,
when I will make a new covenant with the house of Israel and with the
house of Judah. It will not be like the covenant I made with their forefathers
when I took them by the hand to lead them out of Egypt, because they did
not remain faithful to my covenant, and I turned away from them, declares
the Lord. This is the covenant I will make with the house of Israel after
that time, declares the Lord. I will put my laws in their minds and write
them on their hearts. I will be their God, and they will be my people."

David said, "That is a quote straight from Jeremiah 31. Look here,"
pointing to his own Bible.

He continued, "The new covenant is only for the House of Israel, not the
Gentiles. But Paul tells us that when we believe on Y'shua, we become
grafted into Israel,[246] even if we are not direct descendants of one of the
12 tribes. We are grafted in through belief. The Hebrew word 'belief' is an
action word. It means walking like you say you believe. So if we say we
believe in Y'shua, then we need to walk like He did, in obedience to his
Father's instructions."

---

[244]Jer. 31:31-33 Behold, the days come, saith YHWH, that I will make a new
covenant with the house of Israel, and with the house of Judah: Not according
to the covenant that I made with their fathers in the day *that* I took them by the
hand to bring them out of the land of Egypt; which my covenant they brake,
although I was an husband unto them, saith YHWH: But this *shall be* the
covenant that I will make with the house of Israel; After those days, saith
YHWH, I will put my law in their inward parts, and write it in their hearts; and
will be their Elohim, and they shall be my people.

[245]Heb. 8:8-10 For finding fault with them, he saith, Behold, the days come, saith
the Lord, when I will make a new covenant with the house of Israel and with
the house of Judah: Not according to the covenant that I made with their fathers
in the day when I took them by the hand to lead them out of the land of Egypt;
because they continued not in my covenant, and I regarded them not, saith the
Lord. For this *is* the covenant that I will make with the house of Israel after
those days, saith the Lord; I will put my laws into their mind, and write them in
their hearts: and I will be to them an Elohim, and they shall be to me a people:

[246]Rom. 11:17 And if some of the branches be broken off, and thou, being a wild
olive tree, wert graffed in among them, and with them partakest of the root and
fatness of the olive tree;

Pedaling Home   Part 3 – The Regathering

The Sidekick, misunderstanding Col. 2:14,[247] countered, "But he nailed all that to the cross."

David: What he nailed to the cross were ordinances that were *against* us. Yah's instructions were always *for* his people, not against them. Following them brought *life* not death.[248] It was the addition of man-made laws that contradicted His instructions that brought death, like Jeroboam's law to change the feast of tabernacles from the seventh month in Jerusalem to the eighth month somewhere else.[249]

Sidekick: Scripture says we are not under the law, but under grace.

David: What was nailed to the cross was the law of sin and death,[250] the law that works in our members and makes us want to sin. That is the law that was against us, not the instructions that Yah gave his people.

The Cowboy seemed to be beginning to understand.

David continued, "His dying on the cross doesn't give us a license to sin. The *torah*, actually better understood as 'instruction,' is what *defines* sin. If we throw away *torah*, we don't even have anything to define what sin is. If we throw away *torah*, there is no more sin, so we can do whatever suits us. We can kill whoever we choose and it's OK because our definition of sin has been nailed to the cross."

Sidekick: He changed *torah*. There are many proofs. You're deceived.

David: I don't see where he changed anything. I guess our understanding is different.

Sidekick: Like washing of hands. Now we don't have to wash hands to eat. That's done away with.

David: The washing of hands for the general population was never a law in the scriptures. That's a tradition added by the rabbis. In fact, the

---

[247]Col. 2:14 Blotting out the handwriting of ordinances that was against us, which was contrary to us, and took it out of the way, nailing it to his cross;

[248]Deut. 30:19 I call heaven and earth to record this day against you, *that* I have set before you life and death, blessing and cursing: therefore choose life, that both thou and thy seed may live:

[249]1Ki. 12:32 And Jeroboam ordained a feast in the eighth month, on the fifteenth day of the month, like unto the feast that *is* in Judah, and he offered upon the altar. So did he in Bethel, sacrificing unto the calves that he had made: and he placed in Bethel the priests of the high places which he had made.

[250]Rom. 8:2 For the law of the Spirit of life in Messiah Y'shua hath made me free from the law of sin and death.

passage makes it clear that it was a man-made tradition.[251]

~ ~ ~

The children were busy playing with the Hostel Manager's children and their riding toys on the roof. They all had great fun pushing them to the tops of the humps and racing back down. Their parents sat outside their front door overhearing the conversation going on between the Varela couple and the two men.

The children in front of King David's Citadel

The Tennessean who had been with the family when the men arrived, also knew and appreciated the Hostel Manager's family, so excused herself from the scriptural debate to visit with the other couple. They had all discussed scripture at length with David on his previous visits and respected the fact that he, like they, were serious about following Yah according to His word. By sundown, though, all the children were getting tired and hungry, so they got up and went inside to prepare their supper. Emily had Briana bring her the ingredients for their supper, as well, and she prepared things as the conversation continued, feeding the children as they came by on breaks from their playing.

As the couple talked with the men, the door to the roof opened and a backpacker walked through, then another and another. They continued coming through and the couple's eyes widened wondering where all of those people were going to sleep. After the stream stopped, they learned that they were a group of Christian backpackers from South Africa, almost forty of them, who planned to stay on the roof over the weekend. None of them set up tents, just their mats lined up one after another, mostly on the west side of the roof. The couple looked at each other, wondering if the birth would end up being a public event.

~ ~ ~

The Sidekick continued trying to prove that Y'shua went against the *torah*, "What about that we can eat anything we want to now? Everything is now clean."

Cowboy: Yeah, what about that?

---

[251] Matt. 15:2 Why do thy disciples transgress the tradition of the elders? for they wash not their hands when they eat bread.

Pedaling Home   Part 3 – The Regathering

David: OK. So when did it become clean? When he died? When he rose? When he ascended? And if everything became clean, why didn't Peter, one of Y'shua's three closest disciples, know anything about it years after Y'shua ascended when he saw the vision of the sheet?

Cowboy: Well, I don't know, but it said to kill and eat and not to call anything unclean.

David: The vision doesn't give us license to eat unclean animals. The chapter you're referring to, Acts 10, explains itself; and it's explained again in Acts 11. The vision was to get Peter's attention, to draw his attention to the fact that Yah had made the *Gentiles* clean. It has nothing to do with eating unclean meats. Notice how Peter is confused when he sees the vision, and even says, 'I've never eaten anything unclean!'

David continued: That was years after Y'shua ascended. And he's still not eating unclean meats. After he goes to Cornelius's house, he explains the meaning of the vision to them. Look at verse 28.[252] It's making a point about people, not meats. And again in chapter 11, verse 18.[253] The Jewish believers' reactions to Peter's vision was not going out and getting a pork chop. It was glorifying Elohim for what he was doing in the lives of the Gentiles.

The Cowboy seemed to be getting it.

Sidekick: I still believe it means everything's clean now.

David: If everything is clean, then why does Revelation 18 talk about unclean birds? That wasn't written until even decades later.

Cowboy: Where does it say that?

David: Revelation 18:2.[254] Read it for yourself.

After reading it aloud, the Cowboy said, "Hmm, I've never seen that before. I just studied Revelation a few months ago, but never noticed that. That gives me a lot to think about."

---

[252]Acts 10:28 And he said unto them, Ye know how that it is an unlawful thing for a man that is a Jew to keep company, or come unto one of another nation; but Elohim hath shewed me that I should not call any man common or unclean.

[253]Acts 11:18 When they heard these things, they held their peace, and glorified Elohim, saying, Then hath Elohim also to the Gentiles granted repentance unto life.

[254]Rev. 18:2 And he cried mightily with a strong voice, saying, Babylon the great is fallen, is fallen, and is become the habitation of devils, and the hold of every foul spirit, and a cage of every unclean and hateful bird.

Chapter 41   Cowboy Questions

>40 backpackers on the roof

The Cowboy seemed to notice the agitation of his Sidekick, and stood as he said, "This has been a good discussion. It really has me thinking. We'd better go so you all can get to bed."

As David stood up to shake hands, his tassels flopped forward. Pointing to them, the Sidekick said, mockingly, "You know, there's no place in scripture that says you have to wear those little strings. I've searched and it's just not there. You're even deceived about that."

David said with a smile, "Actually, it *is* there, in two different places, back in the foundation."

Sidekick: It's not there. I've looked.

Cowboy, looking at his Sidekick: Are you sure?

David, smiling: Let me show you in *my* Bible...since it has the foundation.

Sidekick: He's not gonna find it.

David turned to Numbers 15 and reached his Bible out to the Sidekick, who ignored it. So he gave it to the Cowboy to read, saying, "Read verses 38-40."[255]

The Cowboy read it aloud, then exclaimed, "Well, it *is* there! Oh, wow! I've never seen that before, either!"

The Cowboy seemed impressed, but not surprised by now, seeing that everything the couple said, they backed up with scripture. The missionary Sidekick did not look happy. He had tried to get the final jab in before leaving, but even that had backfired on him. David doubted he would be back.

---

[255]Num. 15:38-40 Speak unto the children of Israel, and bid them that they make them fringes in the borders of their garments throughout their generations, and that they put upon the fringe of the borders a ribband of blue: And it shall be unto you for a fringe, that ye may look upon it, and remember all the commandments of YHWH, and do them; and that ye seek not after your own heart and your own eyes, after which ye use to go a whoring: That ye may remember, and do all my commandments, and be holy unto your Elohim.

Pedaling Home   Part 3 – The Regathering

The Cowboy said, "We really do need to go. Maybe we'll catch you another time before you leave. I'll be riding through the Jaffa Gate carrying a Christian flag and passing out New Testaments in a couple of weeks."

David replied, "We'll be gone by then. But we'll be here until next preparation day. Maybe we'll see you again. We've really enjoyed the discussion. You all are welcome back anytime."

The Cowboy smiled and said, "We'll be back to meet the new baby after it arrives!"

The men left and the couple discussed how honored they were to be used of Yah to help people see the fullness of the gospel. They loved to show how the message of the New Testament was not at all contrary to that of the Old, with which the Jewish people were familiar. Once the misunderstandings were erased, the entire message flowed together smoothly, and when that message was presented to a Jewish person, there was nothing to stand in the way of their acceptance of it, besides religion, the same beast the Varelas came against in the Christian world.

42 - Shabbat Labor

Preparing for Shabbat

Yom Shishi (Sixth Day)
Day 2 of Sukkot   Day 4 of Rabbinic Sukkot

David remembered the money the people had given them earlier that day on the Temple Mount. Since the high day was over, they got it out and counted it. After they converted the dollars to shekels, they came up with 540 shekels, around $175! They praised Yah, blessed the people who gave it, and asked Him to show them how they were to spend it, then put their little ones to bed in the tent, to the sounds of the light show across the street and the reactions of the hoard of backpackers to them. The Hostel Manager approached and asked for David, who stepped outside the tent to talk to him. "I overheard a lot of your conversation with those guys," he said. "I've never seen anyone defend the Old Testament like that with a Christian."

David understood the man's position. He did not believe that Y'shua was the Messiah, and though he spent hundreds of hours studying, had come to the conclusion that the New Testament was not true. He was accustomed to David defending the New Testament against *his* attacks and those of anti-missionaries.[256] Now he was seeing David defend the Old Testament against the attacks of a Christian. "I just don't understand how you can believe and walk the way you do and still believe the New Testament."

David replied, "It's easy. It all goes together. When everything is taken in context, nothing disagrees. Y'shua told us that until heaven and earth pass away, not the tiniest mark of the *torah* would be changed and that whoever breaks or teaches others to break the commands of his Father would be called 'least in the kingdom.'[257] Many Christians use Paul's writings to say that the instructions in the Old Testament have been done away with. If Paul really taught us not to follow the instructions, to break the commands, Y'shua says he'll be called 'least in the kingdom.' I don't

---

[256] Anti-missionary, or counter-missionary – someone, usually associated with an organization in Israel, who actively and often aggressively works to prevent the proselytizing of Jews by other religions, primarily Christianity.

[257] Matt. 5:18-19 For verily I say unto you, Till heaven and earth pass, one jot or one tittle shall in no wise pass from the law, till all be fulfilled. Whosoever therefore shall break one of these least commandments, and shall teach men so, he shall be called the least in the kingdom of heaven: but whosoever shall do and teach *them,* the same shall be called great in the kingdom of heaven.

Pedaling Home   Part 3 – The Regathering

want to listen to someone who'll be called 'least in the kingdom.' But I don't think that's what Paul is saying. Peter warned his readers in the first century to be careful about Paul's writings, saying that those who are unlearned and unstable were already, at that time, twisting them to their own destruction, to the error of those without *torah*.[258] If they were already taking Paul's words out of context and saying he was telling them to disregard the written words of Yah, it only makes sense that that's what's happening today within Christianity, where people are taught that those Old Testament laws were for someone else a long time ago or for the Jews of today. No, scripture is clear Paul kept the *torah* diligently,[259] and that he followed Y'shua, who obeyed the commands of his Father perfectly.[260] So if I read something Paul wrote that sounds like he's making himself least in the kingdom, I have to check myself and realize that I must not understand something correctly. And the more I have learned *torah*, the more I understand the context in which Paul is speaking."

The Hostel Manager was amazed at David's words and told him he would study further, having never considered that perspective. David stepped back into the tent and lay down with his family as the Hostel Manager left for his night duties at the front desk below. David knew that in his lonely nighttime hours at the desk, he would be studying the scriptures, as usual.

The Muslim prayers blasted at five o'clock, startling everyone awake again to varying degrees. They all went back to sleep except Emily, who was peeping out the tent door to see the reaction of the backpackers, most of whom just buried their heads in their sleeping bags or the thick blankets provided by the hostel.

After breakfast, the family read Deuteronomy, Chapters five through nine, then began washing their orange shirt outfits so they could have them down and put away before *Shabbat*. The Hostel Manager's wife came out of her apartment and visited with Emily as their children played together on the roof. They hung the clothes on the lines over the tent and had just finished when the hostel Laundry man came with a load of sheets,

---

[258] 2 Pet. 3:15-17 And account *that* the longsuffering of our Lord *is* salvation; even as our beloved brother Paul also according to the wisdom given unto him hath written unto you; As also in all *his* epistles, speaking in them of these things; in which are some things hard to be understood, which they that are unlearned and unstable wrest, as *they do* also the other scriptures, unto their own destruction. Ye therefore, beloved, seeing ye know *these things* before, beware lest ye also, being led away with the error of the wicked, fall from your own stedfastness.

[259] Act 21:23-24 Do therefore this that we say to thee: We have four men which have a vow on them; Them take, and purify thyself with them, and be at charges with them, that they may shave *their* heads: and all may know that those things, whereof they were informed concerning thee, are nothing; but *that* thou thyself also walkest orderly, and keepest the law.

[260] John 15:10 If ye keep my commandments, ye shall abide in my love; even as I have kept my Father's commandments, and abide in his love.

Chapter 42   *Shabbat* ~~Labor~~

complaining about so many campers on the roof in the way of his lines. He was a comical sort of fellow, even in his grouchy state.

When laundry was hung, the family visited with several of the families in the hostel before lunch, then went out to get their food for *Shabbat*. They purchased their normal Israeli fare, including *Shabbat* goodies. And Emily went back to her new Baklava Friend at the pastry place, this time buying 40 pieces.

Karaite Clean and Unclean
Shabbat
Day 3 of *Sukkot*   Day 5 of Rabbinic *Sukkot*

They returned, got their showers, contributed to the community supper on the top floor of the hostel, and had food and fellowship until bedtime. Peaceful *Shabbat* morning was interrupted at 5 AM with the Muslim prayers. Emily covered her head and said her own prayers to Yah, Creator of heaven and earth, as the rest of the family momentarily woke up, then went back to sleep. After the prayers ended, Emily too was able to go back to sleep for an hour or so before waking and enjoying the beautiful sunrise and peacefulness of Old Jerusalem early on *Shabbat* morning.

After the others awoke, dressed, and ate their special breakfast, which they shared with the elderly American woman and her son from Arad, they read Deuteronomy, Chapters 10-13, then decided to go to the *Karaite* synagogue. The *Karaites* understood scripture basically the same way they did, celebrating the feasts according to the ancient calendar which is based on the ripening of barley and the sighting of the new moon from the land of Israel. They also used the name, YHWH, as commanded in scripture, and rejected the extra scriptural teachings of the rabbis. The main difference between them and the Varelas, as far as the family knew, was the fact that they rejected Y'shua. In spite of that, they wanted to attend the synagogue they had heard so much about, knowing there would be hidden believers there, as there were in many synagogues throughout Israel. As they got ready to go, they learned that their friends from Arad were also planning to worship Yah there that day. Since their friends had attended before, the family followed along, glad to be with someone who knew the way and the *Karaite* customs.

When they arrived at the synagogue, the woman led them through the sukkah set up in the patio area outside, then to the door which led to the stairs that went below to the synagogue. It was a narrow stone passage, only wide enough for two very thin people to meet passing and only if they turned sideways. At the bottom, there was a laver for hand and foot washing. Emily was in her usual position at the front of the bunch, and a man standing in the small opening at the bottom asked her in Hebrew if everyone was clean. She was not expecting the question and it did not

399

register at first, so in her silence he asked again. When she realized what he was saying, she quickly told him, "*Ken*."[261]

Karaite Synagogue – Isabel & Natanyah

The family and their friend sat in the back, preferring to be more isolated so as to prevent distractions by the children, and were given prayer books. The service was much like that in the Indian synagogue they had been attending in *Kiryat Yam*, except they used the name YHWH, instead of saying "*Hashem*"[262] or "*Adonai*" in its place. About half an hour into the service, the Tennessean and another woman appeared at the bottom of the steps. The man went and asked them if they were clean, which seemed to bother the other woman.

They did not know to wash their hands and when they started in, he stopped them and had them do so. Then he asked if they were friends of a particular *Karaite* Jew who had become popular in the Christian and Messianic communities because of some work he had done to help some of them better understand Hebrew, Hebrew culture, and the Hebrew scriptures. He was beginning to come under fire within the *Karaite* community because of his close ties to the Christian world, and when the women said they knew him, the man had them sit in the back with the Varelas, who had chosen to sit there.

The women appeared disenchanted by the whole ordeal and soon left. The family stayed for the remainder of the service, their children all sitting quietly in the chairs, while other children ran around and made loud noises in the kitchen area to the left of them. The Varela children had been trained to sit quietly, so were accustomed to doing so in places where it was proper. But when the service was over, they were ready to go eat. They walked up the narrow stone steps, then out of the Jewish Quarter to the hostel, where they had their traditional lunch, this time on the roof with the mother and son from Arad.

Messianic Birth Pangs, Wrath, and Salvation

After a nap, they decided to go to a Messianic worship service that another man on the roof had told them about at the Christ Church, just across from

---

[261]*Ken* - Hebrew for 'yes.'
[262]*Hashem* - Hebrew for 'the Name,' a substitution for YHWH.

Chapter 42   *Shabbat* ~~Labor~~

the Tower of David. Emily began having mild contractions, like the ones she had in the park three nights before, but they were not enough to prevent them from worship on Yah's set apart day. Unaware of the exact starting time of the service, they got to the upstairs room to find the door already shut and a sign posted saying that children were to be quiet and well attended to. They had never encountered a sign like that and wondered if they should even enter. As well behaved as their children were, one never knew when something would go wrong. They decided to risk it.

Carefully opening the door, they found themselves at the very front of the room, having to enter near where the speaker stood. They walked in as quietly and orderly as possible in formation past the speaker, then turned down the center aisle to walk to the only available group of seats...at the very back. It was a difficult task, trying to inconspicuously move nine people (very obviously almost ten) dressed alike right through the center of an attentive assembly, but they did their best. As they approached the rear of the room, people kindly moved in order to give the family an area where they could sit together. They recognized the elderly Intercessor lady friend, who smiled at them from near the back and the man who had invited them, but saw no other familiar faces. Every eye seemed to be on them.

The floor in the room was tile, as in most buildings in Israel, and the seats were wooden folding chairs, which made horrendous noises on the tile when moved. The service was being filmed, so every sound was making it on video. Emily, always sensitive and not wanting to bother people, was cringing until they all made it to their seats. David, on the other hand, gave no thought to all the noise he made getting his children situated. They ended up having to sit in two rows, Victor, Moshe, and Armando behind the rest of the family. The couple usually sat together with the children around them, but did not want to move to do that under the circumstances, so Emily sat near the aisle and David held Natanyah at the other end of the row near the wall.

The upper room had big windows on the north and east sides that overlooked an area of the Christian Quarter. The video recorder was in the center of the room, several feet in front of where the family sat. The program continued like a church service, with announcements being made, including advertising for their upcoming tours and mentioning that parents needed to keep their children quiet. All of the negative emphasis on children made the couple wonder if the leaders did not like children or if they had just had bad experiences with unruly ones. In any event, it made the atmosphere especially tense for Emily, who continued to have contractions, horrified at the thought of the service being interrupted for her to deliver. Just in front of David sat another man holding a baby. There were two more rows of people behind the boys, and almost all of the seats were full. Every time someone moved on their wooden chair, it screeched across the tile floor, and echoed through the room.

401

Emily's contractions grew more intense. She was not able to pay much attention to the speaker between being nervous about every move her children made and now the discomfort and sometimes pain. The service wore on and on, until several people were asleep and Emily hoped she would not go into actual labor before it was finally over. She was sure that would further ruin the people's opinion of children. She was amazed at the contrast in this service and the synagogues they had been attending. The music was livelier, for sure. The preaching was lighthearted instead of reverent. The prayers were impromptu instead of liturgical. And the children seemed to be abhorred, instead of embraced, at least by the leadership. She remembered the service that morning at the *Karaite* synagogue, with the rather disruptive children, seemingly not bothering anyone. She felt both were in error according to scripture, this one for their harsh, disapproving looks, the other for its tolerance of inappropriate behavior. Those and other thoughts occupied her mind, as she tried to focus on the message.

Another contraction, every four minutes now, but the service seemed to finally be winding down. Emily had not been able to tell David what was going on, but he knew by a couple of looks she had given him. Natanyah was getting squirmy, and nothing he did seemed to console her. The baby in front of him was beginning to fuss and cry. The speaker stopped his message and told David that if the baby was not going to be quiet, to take it out. David knew it was not his child making the noise, but took the opportunity to get up and walk the two steps to the tiny restroom on his left, taking Natanyah with him. He consoled her there and convinced her they were leaving soon, as the speaker continued to wrap up his message.

Victor had curled up in his chair and gone into a deep sleep, as was his custom in situations like these. As he changed positions without waking, his weight shifted to the front of the small wooden folding chair, and it began to tip forward. A daring, courageous American woman sitting directly behind him with her husband and child about his age saw the impending doom and acted quickly but silently. With lightning speed, she jumped forward, wrapped her arms around Victor, chair and all, and carefully set the seat back on all four legs, all in the split second before Victor and the chair could crash to the echoing tile floor, igniting the wrath of the speaker and his video crew. She then repositioned his body so that most of his weight was again at the back of the chair, Victor still sleeping peacefully.

Whew! Emily carefully let out the breath she had involuntarily sucked in when she saw what was about to unfold, too far away for her to do anything about it. She silently thanked Yah for the Savior Woman, and mouthed 'thank you' to her, as she returned a kind smile. Contractions were still coming four minutes apart, though the most recent event nearly sent her into labor right then. She breathed a sigh of relief, as did many others, it seemed, when the speaker finally finished his message and they were invited to stand. People woke up, wooden chairs scooted on the floor, and the masses came back to life, ready to stretch out and move around. As

Chapter 42   *Shabbat* ~~Labor~~

people exited, the speaker and his wife cordially greeted them, thanking them for coming. When the family approached, the speaker and wife both became busy with others, for which the family was glad, as it made their escape easier. But not so fast! Though they had been ignored by the speaker, two elders stepped up to David. "How'd you like the service?" asked one.

David looked at them, wondering how to put his words together in a nice way. The other one asked, "Well, what did you think? How did you like it?"

David replied, "I liked it fine. I just don't like it that he was advertising on *Shabbat* and the way he talked about children."

At that, both men turned to get the opinion of someone else, while the family walked out. On the way back to the hostel, they spoke with a couple of friends and Emily was confident enough of her labor that she mentioned it when asked how she was feeling. They walked the short distance back to the hostel, where the contractions stopped almost immediately. David met the man who had invited them to the meeting and his young adult daughter. From him, he learned more about the speaker and possibly why he had been so abrasive to him and had ignored the family on the way out. The man told him that this particular teacher taught against women wearing their heads covered, as well as teaching that it was wrong, even a sin, for women to wear tassels. Obviously, the family had made a bad impression walking in late wearing two of the things he taught against in front of a full audience, mostly comprised of his followers who had come to Israel to spend the feast with him. The family had been completely unaware of all of this when they innocently accepted the invitation from the man at the hostel. David got into a good discussion with him and showed him from the scriptures why their women wore heads covered and the tassels commanded for the children of Israel to wear. The man and David ended up becoming quite close and would spend more time together later in the week.

Young Woman Questions

Emily spoke with his daughter while the men conversed, and shared the same things with her. She asked about Emily's tassels as they overheard what the men were saying.

Emily told her, "His position is coming from the fact that 'children of Israel' in scripture comes from the Hebrew 'b'nai Israel', which literally translates 'sons of Israel.' The problem with applying the wearing of tassels to only the men is that all Israel, not just the men, were commanded to follow the instructions. The tassels are commanded to be worn so that we remember the commands and do them. Since women are also commanded to obey, our position is we should also wear the tassels."

403

"We think part of the problem with English speakers is that in English, we have sons, daughters, and children. In many other languages, including Hebrew and Spanish, there are only sons and daughters, and if the crowd is mixed, it is referred to as sons. Think about it. Who came out of Egypt?"

"The children of Israel," she replied.

"Exactly! So was it just the men? Or was it everyone?"

"It was everyone."

"Right, so by saying 'sons' it can be talking about only men or a mixed group. Since women are included in the covenant and are to keep the commands, we believe we need to wear the tassels, since the tassels are given to remember and do the commands."

"I see. Yes, I understand," she said thoughtfully.

"Once our family began wearing the tassels, David noticed something interesting. He often does not see his own tassels. How often is he looking down at himself? But he sees ours all around him, always reminding him who we serve."

"I never thought about that side of it," she acknowledged.

She was very open to what the scriptures taught, and said the words rang true in her spirit. She then asked Emily, "What about the head covering? Why do you wear it?"

Emily explained, "It is a personal choice based on scripture. It's not like the Sabbath, which is there in black and white. If you do not guard the Sabbath, scripture calls that 'sin,' but I cannot say that about not wearing a head covering. I can only tell you my story."

"I'm interested," she said.

"I remember, as a child, reading Paul's words about a woman covering her head, and I would always wonder why we didn't do that. I asked a few Sunday School teachers, and was mostly told that it used to be a cultural thing. I never really could see it that way from the writing, but accepted their explanation. I often thought, though, 'If I'm not supposed to and I do, it's no big deal. But if I'm supposed to and I don't...' That was a scenario I wasn't comfortable with. As I got older, I learned that even in the U.S., most women covered their heads until the 1900s, and in church until way later than that, many still donning Easter hats when I was young. I let the topic go and tried not to think about it much as I went on with my life.

"As an adult, I made some poor choices and got myself in a mess. My only way out of the pit was to cry out to my heavenly Father in repentance, turning my whole life over to Him. At that time, everything changed for me

Chapter 42   *Shabbat* ~~Labor~~

and I began reading His word with the intention of following all of His instructions the way He would want me to. After our first child was born, I was reading the scriptures and came across Paul's comments again.[263] I remember thinking, 'What would it hurt?' As a cowhand, I wore a hat for years. What would it hurt for me to put something on my head now? Paul's words told me that when I prayed or prophesied (meaning sharing Yah's words through reading His scriptures or sharing with others), I should be covered. So I resolved to cover my head during my morning prayer time.

"The next day, I was standing at the sink doing dishes and was praying, like I usually did. I realized, 'I'm praying without my head covered.' I had covered it that morning for prayer, but now I was praying at the sink uncovered. Then I remembered Paul's words, 'Pray without ceasing.'[264] I realized I just needed to wear it all the time. There were numerous times during the day that I prayed. It would be ridiculous to go find something to put on my head. Why not just wear something all the time? So I tied on a bandana and never looked back.

"That same week, I was reading in my scriptures and came across two different passages that confirmed to me I needed to keep my head covered. The first was in Numbers 5, where the woman whose husband suspects her of adultery brings her to the priest. The first thing the priest does is 'uncovers her head.'[265] It was a shameful position to be put in. And she had to have her head covered in the first place to have it uncovered. The second, a few days later was in Isaiah 47, where Yah is comparing Babylon to a woman. He tells her to uncover her locks, expose her thigh, and that her nakedness will be seen.[266] Again, another shameful instance, even equating being unveiled with nakedness. All this came after I was already covering my head, but the memories of how all that came about keep me covered. It doesn't hurt anything - keeps the sun off in the summer and keeps me warmer in the winter," she finished smiling.

The soft-spoken young lady absorbed everything Emily said, and continued to ask questions, as the men discussed various topics. As they talked, two different people came to the roof asking if Emily were having the baby. She wished she had never said anything. She should have known by number eight that they come when they are ready and talking about it does not make it happen any faster. It just causes people, mostly herself, to get impatient. She was glad, though, that it looked like they might not be having it on the roof with the large crowd that was now staying there, many very close to their tent. But she would not be able to walk

---

[263] I Cor. 11:5-6 But every woman that prayeth or prophesieth with *her* head uncovered dishonoureth her head: for that is even all one as if she were shaven. For if the woman be not covered, let her also be shorn: but if it be a shame for a woman to be shorn or shaven, let her be covered.

[264] I Thes. 5:17

[265] Numb. 5:18

[266] Isa. 47:1-3

down and through the hostel again without people asking when she was
going to have the baby.

As evening approached, the family ate supper on the roof and watched
below as group after group of Orthodox Jewish men came from the
direction of the *Kotel*,[267] many of them singing and dancing in worship to
the Almighty, carrying their four species[268] instructed to be used for
rejoicing before Him during Sukkot. Wives and children, many in strollers
accompanied several of them. The family admired the zeal and passion
they had in their celebration and longed for the day they would be reunited
with their brothers.

---

[267]*Kotel* - Western Wall, or Wailing Wall, what is commonly believed to be a
foundation wall, the only thing left of the temple which was destroyed in 70
AD.

[268]Four species - Jewish term for specimens from trees, as instructed in Lev 23:40
And ye shall take you on the first day the boughs of goodly trees, branches of
palm trees, and the boughs of thick trees, and willows of the brook; and ye shall
rejoice before YHWH your Elohim seven days.

43 - Wall Labor

Accounting Angels

Week 11	*Yom Rishon* (First Day)	10/19
Day 4 of *Sukkot*		Day 6 of Rabbinic *Sukkot*

Shortly after sunrise, the South African backpackers got up, packed their things, and left for the rest of their tour of Israel. Emily, now anxious to have the baby, was ready to get more exercise than she could on the roof. The family washed their *Shabbat* clothes and hung them out. Next to the west wall of the apartment, the American mother and son were packing their things. David asked, "Where are you going?"

The mother replied, "Back to Arad."

"Don't you want to stay for the rest of the feast?" he questioned.

"We'd love to, but we live on a very small income, and only had enough to be here through today."

Emily overheard as she was putting away the laundry supplies, and looked out the tent where her eyes met David's, as he turned to see if she had heard. They both instantly knew what they were to do. "So it's only because of the money. I mean, if you had the money, you'd stay?"

"Yes," she replied, "but we don't want money. Yah always provides what we need."

Emily visited with her, as David went down to the desk and asked how much it would cost to keep the two of them there for five more nights. That would get them through the last great day. The Arab attendant told him it would be 540 shekels - 540 shekels, the exact amount they had received on the Temple Mount from the tour group on the high day! He paid for their stay, then went back to the roof with a big smile on his face and gave the news to Emily. Emily told the woman, "Yah has provided for your stay for the rest of Sukkot."

Emily related the story of their experience on the Temple Mount three days before. "We didn't know what to do with the money. It was the high day and we didn't even want to take it, but knew it was from Yah for something. We just didn't know what. We prayed and asked Him to show us. And He just did."

She protested, "I don't want you all to pay for our stay. I wouldn't feel right about it. You'll need the money for something. You have children."

Emily reminded her, "It's not our money. Yah just entrusted us with it until the right time, so you could worship Him here during Sukkot. And it's too late, anyway. David's already paid."

The woman held back tears of joy and love as she realized how Yah had done things to enable the two of them to stay for the entire feast. They all blessed Yah, Emily and the woman embraced, and the woman and her son laid their beds back down on the roof. Afterward, they went to the east side and all read Deuteronomy, Chapters 14-18 together, rejoicing in what Yah had allowed them to be a part of that day.

Private Maternity Suite

Three of the small tents set up on the south side of the manager's apartment belonged to couples, including three nurses. They packed their things that day to leave, and one of them asked the family if they could use the extra tent, a large two person with almost enough room to stand inside. After talking it over, they decided it would come in handy after the birth of the baby, as a private place for Emily. They agreed to take it, thanked the donors, and then moved it to the north side of the roof just east of their big tent.

They spent the rest of the day visiting with the various people that came to the roof, while the children ran and played with the Hostel Managers' children. Emily had contractions off and on all day, but nothing of any significance. Before sundown, they took the dry *Shabbat* clothes down, folded them neatly, and packed them away for the next *Shabbat*. As they did, the children watched a man below playing two *shofrot*[269] at once and sounding out 'Amazing Grace.' They brought their parents to watch and listen to him, waving at him when he looked up. Between songs, he returned their waves. They soon learned the Shofar Guy was staying in a room below, so saw him often over the next few days.

Old City Tour

Yom Sheni (Second Day)
Day 5 of *Sukkot*   Day 7 of Rabbinic *Sukkot*

Another night came and went with no more signs of labor beginning. After breakfast and the reading of Deuteronomy, Chapters 19-23, they decided to take a free two-hour walking tour of the Old City. David questioned Emily about walking that much, but she was adamant about going. She

---

[269]*Shofrot* – plural of *shofar*, the horn of an animal, usually a ram or African kudu, blown like a trumpet for signaling, very rarely used to play tunes.

Chapter 43   Wall Labor

was in Jerusalem for the first time in her life and did not want to miss anything waiting on a baby that might not come for a week. Besides that, walking would keep her mind off of things and give the children something different and educational to do. They took the pack with the birthing supplies, and another small pack with water and fruit, and joined the group forming just inside the *Jaffa* Gate, a stone's throw from their roof abode.

Once with the group, a small, kind young woman approached and introduced herself. She was from France, a friend of the Frenchman and had seen them at his wedding. Various members of the family visited with her while walking through the Old City. When the guide stopped his large, inquisitive group, they listened to him inform of interesting sites and historic events that took place there. Lunch break was at the courtyard in the *Cardo*.[270] David recommended a good pizza place and the family ate with the French Lady, as other members of the tour group asked questions about the family's lifestyle and purpose for being in Israel.

After lunch, the tour continued, the guide advertising his friends along the way. "This guy has really good, fresh pressed juice. You should try it!" he said in front of the kiosk, where his friend pressed oranges, grapefruit, and pomegranates.

The little dark-skinned French Lady asked Emily, "What kind of juice do you like best?"

Emily replied, "Pomegranate is my favorite."

The French Lady bought a juice for herself and one for Emily. All of the children wanted to try it, and David knew if they did, there would be nothing left for Mama. So he had Emily buy another one for the children, and they all enjoyed the sweet, fresh juice as they stood sweating from the hot sun and its heat reflected off of the stone street. The younger children, careful as they were, could not drink pomegranate juice without displaying the evidence on their faces and clothes. Emily had grown accustomed to having dirty children, but it still bothered her when they were that way in public. She called Armando, poured some water on the corner of the rag that dangled from the backpack he wore, and washed their faces as best she could. Their little lips were bright red, and there were red spots on some of their little shirts, but they once again resembled clean children.

As the tour group resumed walking, a young couple approached Emily and began conversing with her about her pregnancy. "When is your baby due?" the woman asked.

"Tomorrow," Emily replied.

"Tomorrow?!?" she exclaimed. "And you're taking the *tour*?"

---

[270]*Cardo* - a well-known plaza in Old Jerusalem's Jewish Quarter.

409

"Yes. I don't like to be still when it's getting close. I do much better moving."

"I'm already tired, and I don't see how you can just keep going in your condition," she said.

Emily laughed and told her, "Maybe walking will help get it over with quicker."

Somehow, she did not think the woman, young and just married herself, could relate to that comment and her way of thinking. Maybe she would one day.

They continued talking as they walked up the *Via Dolorosa*[271] between the Damascus Gate and the Dome of the Rock. Contractions came and went, but not regularly. As they talked, the woman noticed the children's' red lips and told Emily, "You know, it's not good to drink too much pomegranate juice, right?"

Surprised, Emily replied, "No, why is that?"

"It has lots of iron. It's not good for pregnant women to drink too much."

Emily tucked that away in her mind for future reference, wondering when she would ever have the opportunity to drink too much pomegranate juice. It was horribly expensive and she had never even seen a pomegranate in a store in the U.S. before.

The tour continued, running late because of the larger and more inquisitive than usual group. The guide was impressed with the stamina of the pregnant woman and small children, as others in the group began to get very tired. After four hours, they finally reached the little park area outside the Jaffa Gate, where the tour ended. They tipped the guide, said 'shalom' to the French Lady and their new friends, and the tired little family went back to their nearby hostel.

As sundown approached, they again looked down from the roof to see numerous groups of Orthodox Jews descending on the Old City for the celebration of *Shemini Atzerit*. It was a joyous time, the last great day of festivities before life would return to ordinary again for several months. They enjoyed watching the families and the dedication shown to their Creator and Savior. The sights and sounds of groups of men singing as they walked were enhanced as a van drove by blaring music out of speakers while several young men danced atop. Their passion in rejoicing encouraged the joyful spirit in those who saw them.

---

[271] *Via Dolorosa* - Latin for 'Painful way,' referring to the route traditionally taught to be the path in which Y'shua carried the cross through Jerusalem before his crucifixion.

Chapter 43   Wall Labor

Scheduling Conflict

Yom Shlishi (Third Day)   Day 6 of Sukkot
Rabbinic *Shemini Atzeret* and *Simchat Torah*[272]

By now, all the Jewish shops were closed and the streets were full of
rejoicing which carried on throughout the night as the family slept above.
Emily awoke around 3 AM, long before the Muslim prayers, with a fairly
strong contraction. She looked at her watch and went back to sleep, but
was awakened again in ten minutes. Today was the due date, but she
knew that did not necessarily mean it was birth day. They had only had
one baby early, Natanyah by five days, and all the others had been up to
five days late. She went back to sleep, but was awakened again in another
ten minutes. She continued to drift off to sleep and be awakened by
contractions, the intervals in between going to nine minutes, then seven
by the time of the blasting prayers. By then, she was no longer able to go
back to sleep, so woke David to tell him she thought she might be in labor.

Ever since the day they packed into Jerusalem and contractions had
begun, Emily had been expecting the baby to come at any time. Once
they started, she was always ready to get it over with, but knew from
experience that labor was not especially predictable. Before Armando's
birth, the couple had learned of natural ways of speeding labor. Soon after
trying one, Emily felt her water had broken. Moshe's birth was the only
one of the seven where that had happened before the actual pushing
began, so she did not really know how much time she had. Besides, she
never seemed to remember *anything* from one labor to the next.

She looked at her watch which showed 6 AM and decided they would
surely have the baby by ten. At eight, David's cell phone rang and since
he was busy helping Natanyah with her sandal, Emily answered,
"Shalom."

It was the Ohioan, who was with the Nevadan whom David had met in
Jerusalem three years before. The Nevadan had corresponded with the
family a few times through email over the past months, hoping to see David
and meet the rest of the family during Sukkot. The Ohioan continued,
"He's flying back home tonight, so today's the last chance you guys will
have to meet up. When would you like for us to meet you?"

Emily replied, "Well, it looks like we're having a baby, so we'll be busy for
a little while."

"When do you think you'll be ready for us?" he asked.

Remembering Moshe's birth, Emily responded confidently, "In a couple of
hours, probably by 10:00."

---

[272]*Simchat Torah* – Rejoicing in the *Torah*; a Jewish celebration coinciding with
   Shemini Atzeret.

David looked up, a quizzical expression on his face. The Ohioan agreed to call them back, they exchanged, "Shalom," and the call was ended.

David asked, "What did he say?"

"He wanted to know when we can meet them."

David, shocked, asked, "And you told him 10:00?!? You told him we'd be done having the baby by 10:00?!?"

"Yes," she replied, wondering what the problem was.

Normally Emily's memory of past events was clearer than David's, particularly as it related to timing. But when it came to birth of the babies, his memory was much more intact. He remembered all the false labors they had had in the past and just shook his head in disbelief. He could see this day would have much work cut out for him in reminding his wife to be patient.

After breakfast and their family reading of Deuteronomy, Chapters 24-27, they got the laundry supplies out and began washing the pomegranate stained orange clothes they had worn the two previous days. While Emily sat on a five-gallon bucket washing, the Hostel Manager's wife came out and suggested she stand to do laundry, thinking it might bring on labor faster. She had delivered three babies herself there on the roof, and like Emily, preferred to move things along naturally. Emily agreed and stood for the next hour while she and David washed clothes. Since the children had friends to play with this week, unlike their usual life at home on the farm, the parents did the laundry alone and spent the time talking about various experiences they were having in the Land. Emily was particularly glad for the break from the children at that point, and by the end of hanging the laundry was irritated that she felt no closer to having a baby than when washing began. The only difference was that now her back ached from standing in one place for so long. She began to get impatient and more irritable. She knew there were guests somewhere in Jerusalem who were waiting for a baby to be born before coming to visit. It was way past ten o'clock and labor had come to a halt.

The Western Wall

The Ohioan called again and asked if they had the baby yet, to which David responded negatively. They were busy with something, so said they would call back later. From the roof, the family watched as groups of Jewish people celebrating came in and out of the Jaffa Gate. After a light lunch, the family went to the *Kotel* to join in with tens of thousands of people celebrating *Shemini Atzeret*.

At the *Kotel*, David took the boys to the men's side and Emily took the girls to the women's side to pray. As the ladies entered, women handed them

Chapter 43   Wall Labor

prayer books, and Emily kindly took one, not knowing how to use it, but grateful, none-the-less. They walked past the elderly women sitting at desks to pray and squeezed between the numerous other women, children, and strollers so they could reach the massive wall, built with huge stones. Emily was awed seeing women from so many different nations in different types of dress, though all appropriately covered, and praying to the Elohim of Abraham, Isaac, and Jacob. It was a beautiful sight. Some wailed; some rocked back and forth in rhythm; some prayed quietly, hands folded, hands raised, or hands on the stones - smooth and shiny from so many people touching them over the years. Many kissed the wall before leaving, something the Varelas could not bring themselves to do, though they did understand the meaning of praying at the wall. They had explained it to the children before coming:

> When Solomon built the first temple and dedicated it to Yah, he prayed that Yah would hear the prayers of His people and all the nations and answer them when they prayed at this place, or even when they faced this place from a distance, being scattered in faraway lands. He prayed and asked Yah to hear His people's prayers of repentance and forgive them and to hear the prayers of the nations when they chose to repent and pray, lifting their hands toward this place. For that reason, the Jews and other Bible believers face Jerusalem when they pray, having faith that their prayers will be answered, based on having faith that Solomon's were.[273]

Thousands of tiny papers stuck out of the crevices where the stones joined one another, and the floor near the wall was littered with many more that had fallen since the sweepers came by earlier. Natanyah curiously pulled one out of the wall. Emily carefully took it as she said, "These stay there. Someone wrote a prayer on it and has placed it here in the wall, trusting their prayer will be answered. We need to leave it here because it's not ours."

Briana found herself a place on the stair railing that led to a synagogue on the south end of the wall and sat, watching Mama and the crowd of other ladies. She kept her eyes mostly closed, not wanting people to see her looking around. She did not understand why people kissed the wall. Didn't they know about germs?

Rebeka, not old enough to care if people saw her looking at them, stood beside Mama with her eyes open and watched the ladies. She noticed that many were dressed in white.

At the north end, on the men's side of the partition, David prayed while Armando admired the ancient wall, noticing the huge stones and the massiveness of the wall itself. How would it have been to have built that?

---

[273]2 Chr. 6, especially verses 38-39.

He, Victor, and Moshe followed David out then waited for Mama and the girls. Then they all walked together back to the hostel, still not much sign of a baby coming.

Dinner Date

The Tennessean came to check on the family and to see if the baby had been born yet. She had offered earlier in the week to take the children so the couple could have some time alone or so Emily could just rest. But the couple was not accustomed to having someone else take care of the children; now they were thousands of miles from home in a big city, so had declined her sweet offer. But that day, they rethought things and began to feel more comfortable with the idea, so asked her if she would like to keep the children while they went out to eat a late lunch. She gladly accepted, and Armando suggested, "Why don't we go walk around the wall?" referring to fortress wall encircling the Old City.

None of them had been there, and everyone thought it sounded like a good idea. David took the backpack of birthing supplies and they all left - the couple to eat a meal together, and the others to get a different view of Jerusalem, both Old and New.

As they walked down the stairs together and turned toward the Jaffa Gate, David asked Emily, "Where do you want to eat?"

"It doesn't matter. What about you?"

David, having prior experience with his wife due to give birth, safely answered, "This is for you. You decide."

Emily suggested, "Maybe we should eat at the restaurant where the Frenchman had his wedding. It seemed like a nice place, and we didn't try their food the other day."

After a few more steps, David, carrying the backpack, and Emily, not having many contractions and feeling agitated, turned right up Latin Patriarchate toward the restaurant, while their friend took the children to the gate, then up the stairs to buy tickets for the walk around the wall. Just as the group split up, Emily's contractions started again.

The couple walked through the indoor part of the restaurant and out under the shade cloth to a cozy table against the wall of the city, sitting down near two cats sleeping under the big tree next to their table.

Youngsters in High Places

The Tennessean took the seven children up the steps near the Jaffa gate, paid everyone's admission for access to the wall, and then followed the

Chapter 43 — Wall Labor

eager children through the entrance. They met a few people coming and going as they began their sightseeing.

Old City Wall – Armando & Briana

Little Moshe looked all around, holding onto the widely-spaced metal rails that were on the inside of the wall and sticking his face through to get a better view. Others noticed the benches near the outside stone part of the wall, and they all enjoyed exploring the arrow slits, narrow, vertical openings in the wall built for archers to be able to safely defend the city. The friend walked over to see what they were looking at and screamed, "Ahhhh!" jumping backwards in shock over the distance below them on the outside of the wall, and even more terrified to realize that the hole they were looking out was big enough for them to fall through.

"I'm afraid of heights," she informed the children. "I'm afraid someone's going to fall. Let's get away from here. I can't watch everyone at the same time."

Briana, already convinced that this was one of the most historically significant places she had ever seen said, "Ok. I'll help you with the little ones."

As they walked, Briana holding the hands of Moshe and Natanyah and the friend holding the hands of Isabel and Rebeka, they reached the tarp covering the area where their parents were waiting to dine. "There's Mama!" Rebeka cried, and all the children excitedly ran to the place where they could view their parents under the tarp.

On the way, Natanyah slipped, sending shocks through the Tennessean's heart. She stood a few feet inside the paid entrance, looked down the outside of the massive rock wall to the new city, then turned back and looked over the metal railing that protected them from falling into the Old City. The vertical rails were far enough apart that a child could slip through; there was a good gap between the bottom rail and the walkway; the stones were well worn and slick; the walkway was slanted toward the inside; and she could tell that in some places, they would be walking quite high above the city. She looked at the well-behaved children as they ran toward their parents in the restaurant below and her stomach began to churn. Seven children from 11 to 2 years old, not her own and barely known by her, and she being afraid of heights was too much. She called the children back and told them, "We'll just walk around and see the city from below."

As the couple looked over the menu, they heard familiar voices and looked up to see their crew of children in the matching blue T-shirts coming towards them on the wall above. They briefly greeted each other through spaces between the tarps. Armando then turned and herded the others back to the Tennessean. The couple assumed the children had crossed over them on the wall and were on their way around it.

Contractor Manages Contractions

As they ate, drawing the attention of the formerly dozing cats, the contractions continued five minutes apart. The two tossed their chicken bones to the grateful creatures to keep them from jumping on the table to get them and discussed the upcoming birth, their children out there without them, and the planned visit with the two men who were waiting to see them. When they finished eating, David asked Emily, "Do you want to go back to the hostel?"

"No," she answered quickly and definitively remembering the previous *Shabbat*, "I don't want to get back there and it stop again. It's been hours since my water broke. It's getting to be too long. You only give a cow four hours and a heifer six before doing something to help. We've not had any prenatal care, and I just want to have the baby and know that it's fine. At this point, I'd rather have it in the street than to go back there and have labor stop."

David could not see her logic that returning to the hostel would somehow stop labor, but was not about to argue with her, "Where do you want to go?"

"I saw a camping store outside the gate and down the stairs, at the end of the mall. Maybe we can go there and get a camping chair for me to use after the baby is born."

David paid and they began their walk through the *Mamilla* Mall just outside the Jaffa Gate, the contractions continuing to be regular and having decreased to every 4 minutes. Their mind on having the baby, they had forgotten today was the Jews' high day until they saw the shops closed. They continued the walk anyway, just to keep Emily occupied and her mind off of the contractions as much as possible. Upon reaching the camping store and peering in the window, they began walking back toward the Old City, Emily now beginning to slow significantly when the contractions came. They walked up the steps coming out of the mall and were surprised to see a familiar group dressed in light blue T-shirts at the little park just outside the gate. David called to them and they hurried toward their parents, who were surprised they were already down from the wall.

When they met, the friend explained her reasons for not continuing their elevated walk after purchasing the tickets. Not wanting her to have wasted the money she had paid for the tickets, Emily suggested, "Why don't the two of us buy tickets and we can all go up together. Would you be OK up there if we're watching the children?"

The Tennessean was much more comfortable with that idea, only having to deal with her fear of heights and not the added responsibility of the children. By this time it was 4:30 PM and the ticket booth closed at 5:00, so they walked up and David bought the two additional tickets while Emily took the girls to the restroom near the booth.

On the Wall

The sun was going down and the wind getting a bit chilly as they began their walk around the ancient city. They met a group of three people coming from the other direction and about to exit the wall, the only people they would see on the wall for the rest of their trip. Emily was watching like a mama cow for a good place to give birth. It was much more private up there than in the city streets and she was thrilled to see little patios inside the battlement, originally made for the city's defenders to be able to gather out of the way of the walkway. She noticed how private the areas were, needing only to have one sheet held up in the corner to make one side of a triangle, the large stone walls making the other two. She began to think of how exciting it would be to give birth there on the wall and in a corner out of the wind, as the contractions got stronger and more frequent.

The couple was very sympathetic with the Tennessean's original decision to refrain from taking the children, when they saw how unsafe if was. Their family had been on numerous adventures, so they were not concerned that they could not safely make the walk, but the conditions were definitely not up to any U.S. codes. The children enjoyed the freedom within the boundaries, and Victor and Isabel made a game of running back and forth between the brick benches in the little patios, bouncing up and returning like little kid goats.

44 - Stones

Cow Sense in the City

Yom Revi'i (Fourth Day)   Day 7 of *Sukkot*

The group walked along the wall, Armando and Briana going ahead, noticing all the sights, sounds, and smells, and talking about various things that may have occurred at this place or that, as Emily's contractions increased to two minutes apart. As they walked north overlooking the Christian Quarter, one of the green Crocs that Briana had gotten out of the box from the Dead Lady slipped off her foot and fell off of the wall into the Old City. Briana watched in dismay as it landed in the courtyard of a domed building beneath them. As Armando and Briana were trying to devise a plan to retrieve it, their parents caught up with them, and Mama said, "Well, there's no way we can get it from here. Just toss the other one down beside it so when someone finds them, they'll have a pair. Maybe some unknown person needs a pair of shoes."

Briana continued barefoot, which was her preferred way of walking, anyway. Soon after, they came to the northwest corner, made the turn east and walked over the New Gate as darkness fell. They reached the Damascus Gate and crossed over it into the Muslim Quarter, stopping to look across the busy, lighted street outside the Old City at Golgotha, as Emily had another contraction. They were coming harder now and she was having to stop walking to breathe through them. It gave David plenty of chances to point out things from the wall that could only be seen from that vantage point. "You see the huge rock formation over there?" he questioned." The children nodded and he continued, "See how it looks like a skull? That's how it got the name 'Golgotha' or 'Place of the Skull.' The Romans had a crucifixion site on top of it, which is where Y'shua and many others were crucified. Now look to the left a little. Do you see the garden there?" They nodded. "That's where we think, based on the scriptural account, that Y'shua was put in Joseph of Arimathaea's tomb, carved in the rock. The reason we know it was there instead of inside the city, as traditionally taught, is because scripture says it was outside the city. Not only is this garden outside the city, but it is right next to Golgotha."

"So why do people think it was inside the city, in the Church of the Holy Sepulcher?" Armando asked.

David answered, "In the fourth century, Roman Emperor Constantine's mother named a bunch of places, crediting them as being sites of special events, but most of those sites are not backed up by scripture. She named Mt. Sinai in Egypt, and millions of tourists pay to go see it, when scripture

Chapter 44   Stones

tells us Mt. Sinai is in Arabia.[274] There's actually a mountain there, still charred by the fire of the presence of Yah. Lots of archeological finds have been seen there, but there's a fence around it and the government won't let anyone in. The only people who have seen it have risked their lives to get in and out, but some have made it with videos that prove what's there. If we go by scripture to get clues to where things are, the Bible comes to life over here. It's amazing."

As David was proving historical points from the scriptures, the Ohioan called back for the third time, trying to get a time that he and the Nevadan could meet with the family before the latter had to leave for the U.S. David told him, "We're at the Damascus Gate, walking around the wall. We should be back in a couple of hours."

The Ohioan said he would call back. Emily's contraction being over, David stopped his teaching and the older children ran ahead. Natanyah was tired of walking, so David called Armando back to give him the backpack. Armando went ahead to lead the others, and David put Natanyah in the sling where she quickly fell asleep massaging his ears as he walked behind Emily who held Moshe's hand.

The family continued, crossing over Herod's Gate as they approached bright lights that illuminated a basketball court inside the Muslim Quarter. Armando, Briana, Victor, Isabel, Rebeka, and the Tennessean continued walking, but Emily, knowing another contraction was coming soon, asked David to stop while they were still in the darkness, not wanting to expose her condition to the group of young men there playing basketball. As the contraction came on, Emily released Moshe's hand and held onto David, who had Natanyah in the baby sling, while she breathed through. As soon it was over, she took Moshe's left hand in her right, and walked briskly through the lights past the men, knowing that another contraction would soon come. David followed, Natanyah on his right hip towards the Old City, watching the men play. As soon as they were in the dark again, another contraction started.

The group of wall-walkers was quite strung out. Armando and Briana, the adventurers, were far ahead of anyone else. Their Mama had taught them since early childhood to function well in the dark without the aid of flashlights. As they reached a place in the wall where it was close to ground level, their well-trained eyes saw two boys dressed in dark clothing standing on the road inside, about six feet from the wall. The two Palestinian youths started walking closer to the wall, yelling something in Arabic. Briana asked Armando, "What are they saying?"
Armando replied, "I don't know. It just sounds like blah, blah, blah to me. But I think they're cursing us, from the sound of it."

---

[274]Gal. 4:25 For this Agar is mount Sinai in Arabia, and answereth to Jerusalem which now is, and is in bondage with her children.

At once, the two Arab youths pulled slingshots from their back pockets and began pelting Armando and Briana with small rocks, the size of large pieces of gravel. Being trapped between the large rock wall on the outside and the metal railing on the inside, the two turned to run back toward the others. As they began to run, one of the Arab youths stopped shooting rocks, put his hand to his mouth, and whistled loudly. The two ran back to the Tennessean who was with, Victor, Isabel, and Rebeka. Slightly panting, they announced together, "There are boys up there shooting rocks at us with slingshots. When we took off running, one of them whistled."

The Tennessean said, "Just stay closer to us then."

The two agreed, then resumed their natural birth order role as guardians. The group continued on more tightly, past the area where the attack had occurred, but this time no one was there. They continued until they came to a patio in the wall, where they could be together as they waited for their parents.

While the rest waited, Armando and Briana ran back to tell their parents, who had their two youngest siblings with them. Upon getting the word, Emily repeated the Tennessean's instruction, "Just stay closer to the others. Don't get ahead."

David asked him, "Where are they?"

"They were right up ahead, but they're not there anymore."

David instructed, "It's OK. If anything else happens come tell us. Otherwise, wait with the others."

The two obeyed, and David closely followed Emily through the dark, thinking about the report their older children had just brought back. Emily was about to dismiss it as children playing when a terrible thought came to her mind. If someone really wanted to do damage to them, all they would have to do would be to take out David. Here she was almost at the end of labor with seven children under 12 years old and another woman. Armando and Briana were very capable, but still children. Just as she was about to put that thought out of her mind, she and David heard a whizzing noise and then a crash just behind them on the rock wall. And then another. David turned to his right, as he flung Natanyah in her sling to his left side where she would be on the side toward the rock wall, protected by his body. He saw grown men hurling softball sized stones at them.

Emily turned toward the sound hitting the wall and looked over her left shoulder as David yelled and bent down, picking up large pieces of the stones that had broken apart after hitting the wall. Astonished, not only by the fact that she knew they were being stoned, but to see her husband arming himself to fight back instead of running ahead with the rest of the family, she flung Moshe to the inside, switching him to her left hand, then

420

Chapter 44   Stones

took off running as fast as he could run and she could waddle. She had seen cows run while in heavy labor, but had never experienced the effects of it herself. Fight-or-flight response kicked in and contractions stopped as she caught up with the others and told them what was happening. Her voice sounded calm to her, but adrenaline was pumping along with the hormones that were readying her body for delivery, and the children knew she was distressed. She told them, as quietly but urgently as possible, "They're trying to stone us. Stick together and keep going. Armando, get in the back until your dad catches up."

As she quietly instructed him, the younger children talked to the Tennessean about various experiences they had back on the farm. Occupied with them, she was unaware of what Emily had reported to Armando. They walked in a tight single file line, led by Emily, through the dark toward the Temple Mount, Armando and Briana the only ones aware of what was happening, watching for any move inside the wall to their right.

~ ~ ~

David's upbringing in Mexico, defending himself against the *cholos*,[275] was paying off at the moment. He knew the lives of his family members were at risk, the stones being hurled at them over half the size of Natanyah's head. As his body kicked into auto pilot, he grabbed large pieces of broken stones he had stashed in Natanyah's baby sling and flung them back at the assailants in order to put distance between them and his little family. Startled by the offensive reaction of their newest victim, the Palestinians slowed their fire, being careful to dodge the stones that were flying back at them. David reached in his sling, pulled out another large piece of a stone, what was left of a larger stone that had barely missed him and broken against the massive wall, reared back, holding Natanyah securely with his left arm over the sling, and fired with precision, hitting one of the Palestinians in the thigh. The man went down with a cry of intense pain, and David saw six others scatter in the night. After scoping for movement, he walked briskly toward his family.

Getting Away

Emily and the others continued moving, unaware of what was going on with David and the attackers behind them. They passed a set of metal stairs at the Lion's Gate going down into the Muslim Quarter, and she carefully watched for ambushers that might be in the trees growing next to the steps. She continued on, not wanting to put themselves in the path of more attackers. After passing, what turned out to be the last set of steps off of the wall, a man below shouted to them in Hebrew, "This is the end of the wall. You have to come down here. It does not continue. It is blocked off over there," pointing in the direction they were going.

---

[275]*Cholos* - In this context, Mexican gangs.

421

Emily, not knowing he was the Tourist Police, and thinking it may be a trap, wanted to see the dead end for herself. She waved at the man, told him they were just going to see, then led the others a short distance ahead to where the wall was, indeed blocked off, preventing travel over the Golden Gate. Knowing the man was still watching them, she, the Tennessean, and the children looked out over the Temple Mount area, noting things of interest before turning back toward the steps. She had another contraction there and was wishing David would hurry and catch up with them.

As they walked back, Emily was on high alert and watching for suspicious activity below. It was now just the two women and six children, making them even better prey. As they started down the stairs, Emily wondering if attackers would jump out of the bushes below, she heard voices and spotted a Muslim woman with two children walking down the road from the direction of the stoning. At that instant, she spotted David coming towards them. She decided the safest place to be was as close to that woman as possible, hoping they would not stone their own people. She gave quick and quiet instructions to her little crew, then they fell in uncomfortably close to the woman, who did not seem bothered at all by all the extra bodies around her. Just before turning right to go toward the Christian Quarter, David fell in behind them, his sling still full of stones, in case they were needed again. Emily was relieved to see him and Natanyah unharmed.

The Tennessean walked ahead, the children following, and their parents bringing up the rear as they followed the *Via Dolorosa* toward the Christian Quarter and their hostel. Emily asked David what had happened and he related the story, intermittently, as they met and passed Palestinians in the marketplace. He showed those nearest him his sling full of stones. The children were amazed and delighted at their new keepsakes, but Emily was horrified and yelled in a whisper, "You can be *arrested* for carrying rocks like that around here!"

"Don't worry. I'll get rid of them, as soon as I know I don't need them, anymore," he said with his usual calm smile.

They both began praising Yah for His protection and salvation. Emily, calming down enough to laugh by then said, "This whole thing reminds me of the scripture that says if you walk in His ways, one of you would put ten of your enemies to flight," not realizing she was slightly misquoting the passage.

David laughed and said, "Sorry Honey, there were only seven."

The adrenaline was calming down in David, but Emily was still in labor. Now that the excitement seemed to be over, her body got back to the work of having a baby. But now, it was becoming even more difficult for her to walk. The contractions had become less painful, but were almost debilitating and she felt her body was nearly shutting down as each one came. She had to stop walking, no longer because of the pain, but because her body would just not go anymore once a contraction began.

She also desperately needed to use the restroom, as her bladder was full and the baby was pushing down on it, but there was none in sight. As they continued to walk west toward the Christian Quarter and Jaffa Gate, she now hoped they would make it back in time to have the baby there. The last place she wanted to deliver and have a tiny newborn was among the hostile Palestinians they had just encountered.

The group finally entered the Christian Quarter and the areas with which they were more familiar. Emily was relieved when they had completed the ¾ mile walk up the *Via Dolorosa* and had gotten to the steps going up to the Petra Hostel, knowing it was just one flight up to the bathroom. The Tennessean left them, going back to her hotel in the new city. The children ran up ahead, but were instructed to wait on the first floor. Once Emily and David made it up, she took the girls with her and he took the boys, since there was no restroom on the roof.

They reunited in the lobby and walked the additional flights of stairs to the top, passing a party of their friends on the second floor, including the Colorado Family that was staying in Afula. Many of their friends celebrated the feasts by the Jewish calendar and were in the middle of a celebration, as the last day had ended at sundown three hours earlier. They asked the family to join them, tempting the children with getting to stay up late and eat cake and cookies. Then Coloradan Lady, a young mother of nine herself, knowingly observed the look on Emily's face about the same time someone else said, "You're sweating! And panting! Are you OK?"

Emily replied as she continued walking up the steps, "Yes, they tried to stone us, and we're about to have a baby."

Someone asked David, who was coming up right behind her, "Is she serious?!"

David opened Natanyah's sling, still full of stones and replied, "Yes, look at what's left of some of the stones."

Meeting Goes On

They continued up the steps, followed by the children who had started up first but had stopped to talk to their friends. Once on the roof, Emily immediately lay down in their new smaller tent as Armando and Briana got the exhausted younger ones down in the family tent. David squatted outside the small tent near his wife, making sure she was all right before he went to help the older children get the younger ones settled. Within seconds after lying down and beginning to wonder if the contractions had stopped, Emily had a horrendous pain, accompanied by three almost simultaneous pops in her pelvic area. It felt like bones popping, and she wondered if her pelvic bones were being pulled apart. Immediately after that, she had a major contraction and knew it was almost time. It was 8 PM. Just then, David's phone rang.

Pedaling Home   Part 3 – The Regathering

David: Shalom.

Ohioan: Shalom, Brother! We're here in the lobby to see you before our brother takes off in a little while!

David covered the phone and told Emily, "They're in the lobby. What do you want to do?"

Emily: Please don't leave me. Can you just go get them and bring them here? You guys can go to the front corner of the roof and Armando or Briana can get you when it's time. Then we can all meet your friend.

David: Are you sure you want them up here?

Emily: I'd rather have them up here than you down there. We'll be hidden behind the apartment. They won't even know where we are. It won't hurt anything. And they've been waiting on us all day.

That sounded like a win-win situation for everyone, so David told the Ohioan, "I'll be right down to bring you up."

He checked on the children, then told Emily, "The little ones are sleeping already. I'm taking my phone. Call if you need me before I get back." Then to the two older children, "Take care of your Mama and do whatever she tells you."

Armando had taken off the backpack and began to unload the birthing supplies, putting them in the main tent as instructed. Emily stood up before the next contraction came, dreading another pain like the one she had just had and wanting to be able to move with it instead of being trapped in a lying position. Once the supplies were in order, Armando came and asked, "Now can we go to the party? The others are sleeping already."

"Not now," she replied. "Wait for your dad to get back. I'll need you to help me. The baby's coming."

Disappointed, but knowing that the birth was about to happen, the two older children stood ready to help. Emily exited the small tent, Armando and Briana at her side as she paced back and forth on the north side of the roof next to the apartment. They stood by her for support as she held onto the wall through another contraction, just as intense as the first.

~ ~ ~

David hurried down the stairs and was met with cheerful greetings as he reached the party below. Someone asked, "We heard you got stoned."

"Yes, we did, but I'll have to tell you about it later," he called back. "We've got people waiting on us downstairs and my wife's about to have the baby."

Chapter 44   Stones

It had been less than 15 minutes since they had arrived, and the news of the stoning and eminent delivery had spread throughout all floors of the hostel, even reaching the family's guests waiting in the lobby. When David got to the bottom, he saw his two friends talking to a man from the Netherlands who had already heard about the stoning from people at the party upstairs. "Shalom, shalom!" they all greeted one another, as they shook hands and bear hugged, each expressing gladness at seeing one another again this year in Jerusalem.

The Ohioan said, "We're just coming to see you before our brother here takes off tonight. We heard you got stoned," he stated in a tone that requested more information.

"Yes, we did," David replied, "I can tell you in a little bit. But can we go up because my wife's about to have a baby?"

The jubilant Nevadan laughed out loud and said, "You're kidding, right? You're going to have it on the roof?"

David: Yes.

Nevadan: You mean, you're not going to a hospital or somewhere?

David, smiling: No, my wife's afraid of hospitals.

Nevadan: Are you some kind of doctor or something?

David: No, I'm a carpenter.

All three men laughed again as they started up the stairs.

The amazed Nevadan continued, "I can't believe you're about to have a baby up there."

David led his friends up the stairs, past the party, then up the last flight, onto the roof and to the southeast corner, opposite where his family was. As they went by, Emily signaled him that everything was all right but the unsuspecting friends never saw them in the dark. Upon arriving at the corner overlooking the lights of the city, David reminded them, "If she calls me to have the baby, I'll have to go."

The Nevadan, still not believing asked again, "Are you kidding?"

"No, I'm not kidding," David answered, and the topic changed to catching up with each other over the past year.

45 - Birth

Warning: The following material contains graphic birth details which may not be appreciated by those unaccustomed to natural birthing events.

~ ~ ~

After two more serious contractions, Emily told Armando, "It's time. Go get your dad."

Briana stayed by Mama's side and Armando ran to David on the other side of the apartment. David watched as he approached, and seeing the excited nervousness on his face, quietly asked, "What's the matter?"

Softly, he replied, "Mama needs you. The baby's about to come."

David turned toward the men and said, "I'll be back. I'm going to deliver the baby. Pray for me, that everything turns out well."

As he walked away with Armando, the men immediately turned toward the Temple Mount and began praying.

When he got to Emily, she was going into the small tent. She had planned to deliver in the big tent, but when she got to the door, saw five children laid in various positions, taking up the entire entrance. Not wanting to disturb them, she moved back to the small tent, telling Armando and Briana to bring the birthing supplies. Just as they had them gathered and reached the tent, she had another contraction. Miserable because she had to bend over instead of being able to stand, she moved back to the bigger tent as David moved all the children closer to their usual sleeping places and out of the way of the door. Armando and Briana, learning the ways of a woman in labor, gathered and moved the birthing supplies again.

Once inside, Emily had another powerful contraction and knew it would be time to push with the next one, so removed clothing that would be in the way, leaving her outer clothing on. She wanted to hold onto David, but he had to be available to catch the baby. In the tent, there was nothing else for her to grasp, so she braced herself by placing her hands on her thighs and squatting just a little. She pulled her skirt up high enough that David could help from his squatting position, surprised at how stable she felt like that. As the contraction told her it was time to push, she bore down and was startled as her water broke. She was comforted by the fact that it had not actually broken that morning, as she had thought, but did not have much time to think about it before the baby's head descended. David saw

Chapter 45   Birth

the gush of water mixed with blood hit the chuck pad she was standing on and was startled, not remembering that part of previous deliveries.

Armando and Briana stood just outside the door ready to help, Briana shining the flashlight for David. Just as the water broke, the flashlight died. David ordered, "Run downstairs and see if someone there has one we can use!"

Briana ran through the roof doorway, and down the rickety stairs, the sound alerting the people below. The mother of nine asked, "What's the matter?"

Briana replied, "Mama's having a baby, and the flashlight went out! Do you have one we can borrow?"

One of her older children ran into their room, came out with a light, and handed it to Briana, who thanked her as she ran back up the stairs. The mother of nine called after her, "Let us know when it's born!"

~ ~ ~

David was squatted at Emily's right side, ready to do whatever was necessary to help. She clenched her teeth, kept her voice low and pushed with everything she had in her. As the head began to exit, the stretching of her tissues burned and she felt like she was delivering a bowling ball. Her low voice got higher as the burning increased, but was drowned by the sounds of the light show at David's Citadel across the street. Feeling like she did not know if she could push out such a big head, she cried, "Help me!"

David reached out his hands, on which Armando had just poured oil, and immediately, the head popped out. All he could see in the dark was the head dangling from between her legs under her skirt. Startled to see a little person in such a predicament, he cried, "Push!"

Emily had not even finished taking a breath from the first push, but thought there must be some emergency, so braced and pushed again. The baby's shoulders fully cooperated and it slithered out quickly into David's hands. Emily's moaning turned into whimpering, as the intense burning lingered. It was 8:30 PM. Her voice altered by the pain, Emily asked, "Is everything all right?!?"

David, feeling the breaths of his eighth baby exclaimed, "Yes, *halleluYAH!*"

The baby cried.

Emily: Is it a boy or girl?

David: I don't know! I cannot see it, Honey!

Emily: Well, can't you tell by feeling!?

427

David: It's too slippery! I can barely hold onto it!

Briana returned with the flashlight and turned it on before getting to the tent door. She shined it on the dark-haired baby in Daddy's hands, and he exclaimed, "It's a girl!"

Armando went with Briana and the light into the small tent to gather some of the supplies that had been forgotten in all the confusion of moving from the big tent to the small, then back again in the dark. They gave Daddy the items he asked for beginning with the towel for cleaning the baby. As she cried her newborn cries, Armando called quietly to wake up the other children, but most were sound asleep.

Introductions

Just behind Emily was Natanyah who awoke from all the commotion. She groaned and sat up to hear Briana say, "Natanyah, you have a baby *sister!*"

Natanyah groaned again and said, more asleep than awake, "I wanna go to sleep," then lay back down.

Briana again said, "Natanyah, you have a baby sister!"

Natanyah sat up and replied, still crying, "I don't care!" then lay down again.

Once more, Briana said, "Natanyah, look! You have a baby sister!"

Sitting up again, and using both hands for emphasis, little two-year-old Natanyah, who had missed her nap that day, cried out, "*I just want a naaap!*"

Rebeka, on the other side of the tent with Victor, Isabel, and Moshe, woke from all Natanyah's dramatics and sat up. Briana said, "Rebeka, we have a new baby!"

Rebeka, rubbing her eyes, asked, "Is it a boy or girl?"

Briana said, "It's a girl!"

Rebeka replied in a smiley, pleasant tone, "Good!" then lay back down and went to sleep.

Victor and Isabel slept through the whole ordeal. Moshe woke up and watched Daddy clean the baby with a towel and wrap it, handing it to Armando. The short cord was white by then and had stopped pulsing, so David called to his assistant, Briana, who handed him the clamp then the scalpel. He clamped and cut the cord and Emily delivered the placenta as David wrapped an extra towel around his new daughter.

Chapter 45   Birth

Briana went to tell the men waiting on the other side of the roof. As she rounded the corner of the apartment, the Nevadan called to her in a nervous voice, "Is the little lamb born?"

"Yes," she called back, then returned to the tent to help with clean-up.

The men on the roof approached the tent, and the Nevadan quietly called, "Hey, brother, I'm gonna go. It sounds like you're busy in there, and I've gotta catch a flight."

Emily felt badly that he had been waiting all day to meet them. She told David quietly, "We're almost done here. We can go out and meet him. He can be the first to meet the baby."

David told him, "If you can wait just a minute, we're almost done cleaning up and will be coming out, anyway. We're going to move her and the baby to the other tent."

"OK, sure, I can wait," he replied.

They finished picking up and stuffing the used chuck pads in a trash bag, then exited the tent, David holding his new baby girl. Emily greeted the two men, and David introduced her, Armando, and Briana to the Nevadan. He commended and congratulated them all on the birth of their new baby, then left with the Ohioan to catch his flight. Emily and Briana went to the smaller tent, and David gave her the baby for the night. Briana sat with her until the baby began nursing.

After checking that all was well with the younger children, David went to Emily and asked, "Do you want to take a shower? The Hostel Manager's wife said you could use their personal shower after the birth so you don't have to use the public one downstairs."

Emily, snuggled in the cozy tent with her newborn replied, "I cleaned up well enough in the big tent. It's awfully cool outside and I don't really want to go to bed wet. Besides, I don't want to take a chance on waking their family. I don't see any lights on there. I'd rather wait till early morning."

David, knowing she was exhausted from all she had been through in the past few hours, left her to rest. Knowing the little ones were out for the night and safely in the tent next to Emily's, he went downstairs with Armando and Briana to take the borrowed flashlight back to the party, where they could share the news. They reported the events of the past few hours to their friends, while enjoying the food and fellowship. The children talked and laughed with all their new friends while they ate cake and cookies on this special occasion, which now had another reason to be festive. Everyone rejoiced over the escape of the family from the stoning and for the birth of their new healthy baby girl. The Colorado Mother told them to keep the flashlight for the night, in case they needed something.

429

~ ~ ~

Emily called to give her parents the good news. They were thankful and relieved that all had gone well. The baby finished nursing and Emily lay next to her, not able to see her face in the dark, giving thanks to Yah for the beauty of this birth experience and to have another healthy baby, this one born in the Promised Land in their sukkah during His feast. She could have asked for nothing better. She drifted into a postpartum sleep, the kind that women who birth naturally have that keeps them constantly aware of their baby and its needs.

~ ~ ~

Festivities continued into the night until, one by one, people began to retire or leave for flights back to their country of origin. The three tired but happy Varelas said their goodbyes and shaloms, then went back to the roof. David checked on Emily again, then went to bed with Armando and the younger ones, as Briana took her nursemaid's place on the mat next to Mama.

Emily slept well, but lightly, nursing the baby at intervals during the night, Briana by their side. At the blasting of the Muslim prayers before daybreak, she got up, went to the larger family tent and asked David if he would go with her to shower. He agreed that now was a good time, while all the children were still sleeping, so they quietly snuck into the apartment and David held the baby while Emily showered and changed into clean clothes. She then cleaned the baby, now that she could see it, and dressed her in a little light blue gown she had made for her at their Horse and Buggy Friends' place, not knowing that it would match the clothes they would be wearing when she was born.

They took turns admiring the beautiful dark-haired, dark-eyed baby with the cutest round head and face they had ever seen. They had always been blessed with beautiful babies, but they marveled at the beauty of this one, not remembering that the others had also been this precious. They watched as the sun rose over the ancient city and the light reflected off of the golden topped mosque that had been the landmark of the Old City for the past few hundred years. They praised Yah for allowing this new child into their home and family and for allowing this awesome experience at the time of her birth.

Briana got up and prepared their usual breakfast, as David took care of the needs of the other children. The Hostel Manager and his wife came out of their apartment, and approached the couple with their new baby.

"We didn't know you had the baby," the woman said, "until we saw the towel in the shower had been used. Is it a boy or girl?"

Emily: A girl.

Chapter 45   Birth

Woman: When was she born?

Emily: Last night, at 8:30. I'm glad you didn't know. I was afraid we would wake you up. We didn't come in to shower until early this morning.

Woman: You were quiet. I never heard you.

Hostel Manager: What is her name?

Emily: We don't know yet. Because she was born just after the end of the Jews' *Sukkot* and towards the end of *Sukkot* on the calendar we observe, we wanted her name to say something about rejoicing in Yah, but have not come up with a first name that is suitable. Her middle name will be *Batzion*[276] because she was born in the Old City.

Hostel Manager: We'll study and see if we can help you with it.

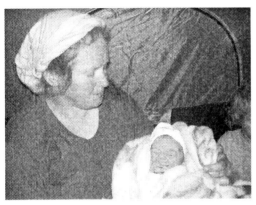

The new parents thanked them as the resident couple returned to their apartment. After they left, Emily took the baby down the stairs through the hostel, out past the money changers and to the Arab market next door that she knew had a produce scale. Seeing the owner behind the cash register, she asked in Hebrew, "Could you weigh my baby? She was born last night and we'd like to have her weight for the records."

He looked confused for a moment, Arabic being his first language, and not accustomed to people wanting to weigh babies on his produce scale. But once the question and statement registered with him, he smiled, nodding his head enthusiastically as he said, "*Na'am!*"[277] and quickly balanced his scale. Emily undressed the baby, leaving her wearing only a diaper. After carefully weighing her, they weighed a new diaper, so they could subtract, getting an accurate weight for the baby. After calculating, the result was 3.6 kilos or 7 pounds, 14 ounces, the biggest baby the Varelas had ever had. She thanked the shop keeper, who seemed proud that he could assist her in the project. She then asked him if he would have his picture made with the two of them by the scale. He flashed a big smile as his helper snapped the photo. Emily thanked him again and took the baby back up the three flights of stairs to their roof home.

---

[276]*Batzion* - Hebrew for 'Daughter of Zion.'
[277]*Na'am* – Arabac for 'yes.'

Living Words

The city began to come to life, more slowly than it had for the previous days during the Jewish celebrations. After breakfast and clean-up, the family went to the east landing and sat facing the Temple Mount, except for Emily who faced them to read from Deuteronomy, where they had left off the morning before. She began reading at the beginning of chapter 28, "And it shall come to pass, if thou shalt hearken diligently unto the voice of YHWH your Elohim, to observe and to do all his commandments which I command thee this day, that YHWH your Elohim will set thee on high above all nations of the earth: And all these blessings shall come on thee, and overtake thee, if thou shalt hearken unto the voice of YHWH your Elohim..."

She paused reading to comment, "OK guys, listen to the blessings He gives us when we obey him, when we follow the instructions that He had Moshe[278] give the people that day, the ones we've been reading about all week."

"Blessed *shalt* thou *be* in the city, and blessed *shalt* thou *be* in the field."

She asked, "How are we blessed in the city?"

Rebeka answered, "We got a baby and a neat place to set up our tent!"

"Good. How are we blessed in the field?" she asked.

Several of them answered, naming various animals they had at home and the beautiful gardens they had grown for the previous six years.

She continued reading, "Blessed *shall be* the fruit of thy body..."

She stopped and they all marveled that this passage was scheduled to be read by them this morning, just hours after the birth of their newest family member. Yes, He had blessed the fruit of her body!

David spoke up, "You know, we planned to come here for Sukkot in obedience to His instructions. We didn't know how it would happen, and when we planned it, we didn't know we would be having another baby. I believe having her here is His reward to us for striving to walk according to His instructions."

Emily agreed and continued reading, "...and the fruit of thy ground, and the fruit of thy cattle, the increase of thy kine, and the flocks of thy sheep. Blessed *shall be* thy basket and thy store. Blessed *shalt* thou *be* when thou comest in, and blessed *shalt* thou *be* when thou goest out. YHWH shall cause thine enemies that rise up against thee to be smitten before

---

[278]*Moshe* - Hebrew for 'Moses.'

Chapter 45   Birth

thy face: they shall come out against thee one way, and flee before thee seven ways."

She stopped, stunned, as chills came over her arms and tears filled her eyes. David was awestruck. She had misquoted the scripture the night before after they had escaped their attackers. The scripture said that their enemies would come from one direction and flee in *seven*! That's exactly what had happened! They were, once again amazed, at how Yah works in the lives of His people. They continued on, reading the next three chapters, before closing their *torah* reading for the day. But the effect of those verses, particularly the ones about the fruit of the womb and their enemies, would forever be with them because of all they had been through in the past 15 hours.

The children were dismissed to play with their friends on the roof. David kept an eye on them, while his wife called the Doctor to let him know they had delivered a healthy baby girl. He said he would not be coming to Jerusalem, but that he had a doctor friend there who would sign the papers for the birth certificate and gave her his number. She called and he said he would gladly do it for 2,000 shekels. Emily was horrified at the price, which was much higher than the price the other doctor had quoted to sign *both* sets of papers. Her kind doctor had already done the first set. She told David what she had learned, and they decided to try to have it done at a local hospital, where the Hostel Manager said it would be free. She called the second doctor back and let him know they would not be needing his services, but thanked him for his willingness to help them out.

Word spread around friends in Jerusalem that the baby had been born on the roof, and throughout the day, the family had several visitors. The Shofar Guy came up, called the whole family together inside the big tent, then spoke blessings over the baby and the rest of them. The Colorado Mother of nine and her oldest daughter came up from the floor below, the new friend from France they had met on the tour brought a little onesie for the baby, two couples from the Zichron Ya'achov community they had met at the wedding brought a bag of goodies made at their community, and the Cowboy came, all at different times of the day to offer their 'mazel tov'[279] and to see the precious new life that graced the sukkah in Old Jerusalem.

The Launderer came in with a friend of his to see the new baby. As they spoke with David, the friend gave him directions to a Messianic Synagogue in Kiryat Yam that he visited whenever he was in Haifa over *Shabbat*. Emily was surprised they had never heard of it, having been there a month and both Jews and Christians there knowing they followed Y'shua. The couple told him they would look it up and make a point to visit there before going back to Tennessee.

---

[279]*Mazel tov* - Hebrew 'Good constellation,' but in modern usage, 'Congratulations!'

While the parents visited with one guest after another, Armando and Briana went to the markets to buy food for the high day which would begin at sundown. They bought pomegranates, persimmons, and milk, then went to Mama's Baklava Friend to buy treats. Recognizing them, he asked, "Where's your Mama? You have a baby now?"

They answered that they did and he gave them extra treats for the new mother. They thanked him and walked through the Old City markets, to the hostel, then up the stairs. On the way, one of the second floor guests, the mother of some little boys that were often on the roof playing with the younger children, gave Briana a book she had finished reading, *Miracle among the Muslims*. Briana thanked her, always glad to have new reading material.

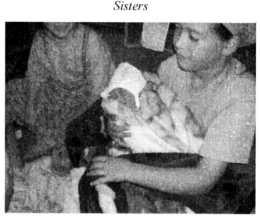

Sisters

Tennessean meets Launderer

The Tennessean checked out of her hotel in the New City and came to the roof so she could help Emily after having the new baby. She needed a blanket for the hostel mattress that she laid on the roof, so the Manager told her to get one from the Launderer. As she was going up the stairs, she met him coming down with an armload of blankets to wash. She told him what she needed and he pulled one off of his pile and gave it to her. She said, "This one's dirty."

He replied, "If you don't want a dirty one, you can't have one."

Heated, she came up to the roof and told the family what had just happened. Armando, who felt like he had a good relationship with the Launderer, and Briana went back down with her to the laundry area. From the lobby, they went through the door that opened to a fork; one side, a small bridge that went to a rooftop outside, the other shorter one, going down steps to the kitchen. They passed the kitchen and continued the descent on another set of stairs winding with landings. They found him there amidst mounds of blankets and sheets piled high on the floor and asked for a clean blanket.

Overwhelmed with the amount of bedding he was still washing since the backpackers left three days ago, he said, gesturing toward mountains of blankets waiting to be washed, "You can't have a clean one. I don't have clean ones. I have thousands of dirty ones."

Chapter 45   Birth

The Tennessean disgustedly turned to leave. As she stormed out, he grabbed a ragged blanket and threw it into her arms. Then he looked at the children and said, "Come on. Get out of here. You're not supposed to be in here."

Armando and Briana followed the Tennessean out, where she left the dirty blanket on another pile outside the doorway. The three walked up the stairs, the Launderer following. As they turned and walked through the lobby to ascend up the two remaining flights to the roof, the children noticed him turn to go down the outside stairs to the street. They stopped and watched him descend the exit stairs as the Tennessean continued up. She noticed them not behind her, stopped and said, "What are you doing?"

Armando: Where are you going?

Tennessean: Back to the roof.

Armando: Why not go back and get clean blankets. He left.

Tennessean: I don't really want to go back. He's upset.

Armando: Briana and I will get one for you. Don't worry.

Tennessean: Are you sure?

Armando: Yeah, no problem!

She walked back down and sat in the lobby, waiting for them. The two opened the door and descended, walking through the mountains of dirty sheets and blankets to the small stacks of neatly folded ones. They got a nice blanket and a set of clean sheets, then started back up the steps, when they heard the door at the top of the stairs open and close.

They looked at each other, eyes wide, as they heard a throat clear. They could tell it was a smoker by the way he panted as he descended. Armando quickly surveyed the surroundings, then jumped up on an old washing machine and had Briana pass him the covers. She then jumped up as he climbed on top of the adjacent refrigerator. She again passed him the covers before climbing up herself. Armando climbed up the nearby railing and jumped over the short wall to the bridge on the other side and had her pass him the things once more, then pulled her up by her arms.

Briana was scurrying up the railing as the Launderer came around the corner. He saw her above the refrigerator, trying with all her might to get over the wall. She resembled a giant mouse, and he was instantly angry. Armando helped her over, as the Launderer began running around his work area to get to the stairs, then up to meet them from the other side. The Tennessean heard the commotion, got up, started up the stairs and seeing the children come over the bridge railing said, "Let's get upstairs as fast as we can!"

435

They heard the lower door slam as they went through the door to the roof. The three reached David's side safely, and had a few seconds of rest before the Launderer appeared panting through the door, panting angrily. He saw the Tennessean standing with her clean, neatly folded blanket and sheets and said, "I'm taking those away from you!"

David stepped in and told him, "No, you're not. Calm down. She needs clean stuff just like everyone else."

The Launderer, having taken a liking to David, grumbled something under his breath, then walked back down all the stairs to his piles of laundry. The Tennessean laid her bed down around the corner from the family, and Isabel and Rebeka promptly moved their mats out, one on either side of her bed, and took their blankets from the tent that the Launderer had given the family earlier in the week.

The Tennessean took Isabel and Rebeka shopping while the parents continued to entertain visitors on the roof. She held a little girl's hand in each of hers and began walking through the markets looking at the beautiful clothing, jewelry, and gifts. Isabel saw a small backpack that she liked, made out of beautiful fabric, hand woven in a Middle Eastern pattern. She decided that is what she wanted to use the rest of her gift money from the grandparents for. She would tell Mama when they got back, since she did not carry money to the market with her.

An English speaking couple began talking to the Tennessean, asking if they were her girls. They certainly looked like they could have been, all three of them being slender with long dark hair. They all three enjoyed the thought that others thought they were family, as they continued through the markets. The Tennessean stopped to purchase something and released the girls' hands as she got her money. The girls turned to watch the people behind them, and the unknowing Tennessean began walking again. When the girls finished staring at the first large family they had seen since being in Jerusalem, they turned to see their friend gone. They both got lumps in their throats, wondering how they would ever find her in the great crowds. They did not wonder for long, as missing her two little hands, the Tennessean quickly returned to find her girls standing in the same spot. Reunited, they strolled through the markets, looking at things they found interesting. Rebeka found a stuffed camel, and when she picked it up, it said, "I love you."

She laughed and said, "I bet Moshe would love that."

The Tennessean bought it and gave it to her to take to her little brother, then finished their shopping and returned to the hostel. She gave Moshe his camel and he was delighted. He pressed the button over and over to hear it tell him, "I love you." When he finally got tired, Natanyah took over, and then it was passed along to all the other children who came to play on the roof.

Chapter 45   Birth

The Hostel Manager came back and told them they could take the baby to one of the Muslim hospitals to get the papers signed, but that Emily would need to be careful and wear her scarf in a more traditionally Arab way, as opposed to the more Hebraic way she usually wore it. She and David agreed to go ahead with that plan, since there was no way they could go to the doctor's place before the last high day began in less than an hour. After the high day, the 48 hours would have passed, potentially making the paperwork void and causing them much more difficulty getting the birth certificate. So he walked her to the taxis parked just inside the Jaffa Gate and sent her on her way with a blessing before going back to the children. Emily was getting nervous, as sundown was approaching quickly. She sat in the rear of the taxi holding the precious baby in the sling, and watched the sun getting closer to the horizon, while the taxi sat still, stuck in traffic. She was not willing to break the sanctity of the high day by doing business in a hospital, a place she had intentionally kept herself and her babies out of for years. She told the driver, "Just turn around and go back to the Old City as soon as you can. It's too late."

He followed her request, whipped the car out of the traffic at the first street, and got her back in time that she could pay his fee before sundown. She was relieved at that, but then wondered how they would possibly get the documents within the required time limit. She trusted that Yah would bless her for not transgressing His set-apart day, and carrying the baby in the sling, climbed the steps to reunite with her family.

437

Part 4

The Last Days

Hear the word of YHWH, O ye nations, and declare it in the isles afar off, and say, He that scattered Israel will gather him, and keep him, as a shepherd doth his flock.

Jeremiah 31:10

46 - 8th Baby, 8th Day

Yom Chamishi (Fifth Day)   *Hayom Hashemini* (The Eighth Day)

From their vantage point at the hostel, they watched the activities below. Following the ancient scriptural calendar often made things more difficult for them. On the Eighth Day of the modern Jewish calendar, there was great rejoicing and men dancing in the streets. This evening, it was much quieter, with more of the usual Jerusalem atmosphere below. A few *Karaite* Jews could be seen walking toward the wall, but it was much quieter than it had been the night before. There were still several believers in the hostel who celebrated by the ancient calendar though, so the family had plenty of people with which to gather. After praying and welcoming in the high day on the roof, David took Armando and Briana to a meeting below, and Emily stayed with the little children until they went to sleep, then took the baby into her smaller private tent.

The family woke up later on the high day, as usual, then had their special breakfast, which now included treats from their new Baklava Friend in the market. They met with different people during the day; walked to the Wall; studied together with the Hostel Manager, his wife, the American lady from Arad, and others; and prayed. They wound down the last day of the feast fellowshipping with friends, new and old, from various parts of the world.

The Hospital

Yom Shishi (Sixth Day)

After sunset, they said *shalom* to those who were leaving, then the whole family, the Mexican friend who had been at the wedding, and a friend of his walked west into the new city to a Jewish hospital someone had told them about. They had less than an hour to get the paperwork done before the 48 hours deadline had passed. Emily phoned as they walked, and it was confirmed that the service she was seeking was free. They left the hostel, the baby in Emily's sling and Natanyah in David's arms. Each parent, as well as Armando and Briana held a hand of Victor, Isabel, Rebeka, or Moshe. For the sake of fairness, they rotated every few minutes so that each one could have a chance to walk with Mama and Daddy.

Everyone was doing fine on the brisk walk in the dark, though every muscle in Emily's body ached from the events that had surrounded her labor. She was nervous about meeting the 48 hour deadline, and then learned that the friend who was leading them had taken a wrong turn. Her adrenaline was rushing and she wanted to run to the front of the group and at least lead *faster*, even though she was no more familiar with the area than the one leading. But she quietly controlled herself and continued the not-brisk-enough-for-her pace, until they finally reached the hospital.

At the Hospital

They were stopped by a guard outside who searched them before they entered the gate. Leaving the new friend outside in the yard with the older children and the backpack containing water, David and Emily took the two babies and entered with the Mexican friend. At the desk, an angry-looking woman glared at them and asked why they had come. David explained the situation and was told to wait in the waiting area. Time ticked away as they were exposed to whatever illnesses the other people in the room had brought along. Finally, they were instructed to come to the back office, where they were met by an angrier-looking young woman, who they were sure was not happy to see them. She informed them that it would cost 700 shekels to get the paperwork done, contrary to the 'no charge' that Emily had been told over the phone less than an hour before.

David and his friend used their Mexican negotiating skills to try to get the price lowered to something reasonable, while Emily waited outside in the cold with the others, not wanting to spend any more time in the contaminated waiting room exposing the babies to who-knew-what. She tried to remain calm, but missing deadlines always caused her to feel stressed. She watched the children playing in the hospital yard in the dark, always finding a way to have fun, wherever they found themselves.

The men having been unsuccessful, they finally left, Emily not knowing what to do and knowing they had only minutes left to get all the paperwork done before the family was scheduled to leave in less than two weeks. No one else seemed to be concerned about it. She called the doctor again and told him what had happened. He told her not to worry about it and that he would take care of everything if they could come to his place next *Yom Rishon*. She was relieved, but still not completely calm, knowing the time limit would be past and wondering if that would cause them problems later. But, knowing there was nothing anyone could do about it now, she put it out of her mind and followed the leaders to a pizza place on the way back to the Old City.

The family and friends enjoyed their pizza and their last night together as they told stories from their respective countries, their upbringings, and how they had ended up in Jerusalem for the feast. After supper, they parted ways, the family going back to their tents on the roof. They fell asleep in their respective tents as the now familiar sounds of the Citadel light show filled the air.

It was sad to wake up to the Muslim prayers this morning. Even though the recordings were loud and out of sync with each other, the family knew that to refrain from hearing them again meant they were leaving the special city. They would be missed, along with all the other one-of-a-kind features, both good and bad.

Giliyah Batzion

The Hostel Manager finished his night shift and came onto the roof as the family ate breakfast, announcing, "I've found an alternate word for *simcha* that might work for the baby's name."

"Great!" David said. "What is it?"

He answered, "*Gilah*, Hebrew for joy, can be made into the phrase, 'Yehovah is my exceeding joy,' or 'Yehovah is my delight,' by combining the Hebrew letters to pronounce *Giliyah*."

The name rang well with the couple, so they quickly looked up all of the scriptures on their e-sword program that contained the word, '*gil*.' After reading them all, they decided it was just right and thanked the Hostel Manager for helping them. Their baby girl now had a name, 'Giliyah Batzion Varela,'"Yah is my delight, daughter of Zion, child of El."

The Shofar Guy came and offered to take Armando and Briana shopping for good shofars. The parents consented, knowing the older ones had a lot of responsibility and needed to be rewarded sometimes. The three took off to the Shofar Guy's favorite markets, blowing all the horns that looked good to see which sounded the best. When they had each picked out one, he insisted on purchasing them, even though the children were prepared to pay for their own. Once back at the hostel, he asked the parents if he could take Briana's picture wearing a necklace that was a reproduction of the priests' breastplate, having 12 different stones, each representing a different tribe of Israel. After permission was granted, Mama helped her put on the necklace, he snapped a picture, showing only the neck area, then told her she could keep the necklace. The family thanked their new friend for his sweet, generous spirit.

Emily began packing things as soon as she could, while the others got breakfast ready and the newly named Giliyah slept. They had planned to go to Ezuz in the Sinai desert and spend *Shabbat* with a family they had met online through friends. Emily contacted the woman of the house, who was surprised they would try to make the trip with such a young baby. The family fully intended to go, but as the day wore on, and it seemed like it was taking forever to get their few belongings packed, they decided it would be too difficult. Emily was the family organizer, and her time was now being spent caring for the baby.

Throughout her child rearing years, she had learned to be thankful that babies need to nurse so often. It had bothered her greatly when Armando was a baby. She related everything back to the cows she was so accustomed to caring for and living with. When they had a calf, they went straight back to their regular work. Emily expected to be able to do the same. Never having been around pregnant people or babies, she was anxious to get that big baby out of her tummy so she could get to gardening and other projects more effectively. After his birth, she was shocked and dismayed at the amount of time she would spend just nursing him. The thought finally hit her that all a cow's job is after calving is to eat and sleep- no gardening, no projects. So she had to accept that fact for herself, as well, but it took time.

It was not until after Briana was born that she was able to finally resolve that her job was now to take care of babies. And even then, it went against her natural, physically hard-working ways, to accept. Now with number eight, she was getting better at it, but it still pained her to sit and try to instruct the others as to how to neatly pack everything for the trip, feeling like it would be much more satisfying to do it herself. But being older now, she was learning to appreciate the rest time that holding and nursing the baby gave her. She knew if the baby did not need to be held so much, she would likely set it aside, to the detriment of them both. She praised Yah for designing everything perfectly.

Sukkah to Home

The big tent had served them well and was showing the signs of being well-used by the young family. They would no longer need it on this trip, since they would be going back to the house at Kiryat Yam until leaving in two weeks. They asked the Hostel Manager if he had any use for it and he gladly had them leave it set up as a playhouse for his children. The family was happy that their most recent birthing place would be put to good use until it was completely worn out.

Before leaving the Old City, they made another trip to their new Baklava Friend, to buy treats for *Shabbat*. He seemed honored to meet the new baby. They went back to the roof, picked up all their belongings, their new small tent, laundry bucket, backpacks, and bed mats, and went down the stairs, saying 'shalom' to the few remaining friends. It was mid-afternoon, and the family had forgotten how busy things got on preparation day until they got to the taxis below. They had to wait a few minutes before they got two taxis to take them to the bus station. Once there it was a madhouse. Emily guarded tiny Giliyah, with her hand in front of the baby's head, while she struggled through the crowds, baby in the sling in front, backpack in rear. David tried to keep everyone together behind her as she

443

got the tickets and tried to find the bus to Haifa. When they got to the correct terminal, they realized the bus about to leave was the last one out that day. Emily got a confirming nod from David, then rushed to the bus, knowing the children were not right behind her, hoping to secure a place for the family in the line that was quickly forming. David, seeing she had made it aboard and was getting approval from the driver, quickly loaded their belongings into the crowded luggage bin under the bus, trying to keep everything together, while Armando and Briana kept the younger children in a pack.

Emily handed the driver the tickets for the 10 of them, then waved for them to come on. The scene was chaotic, very busy, and Emily felt it was unsafe for such a tiny babe. She was glad to sit down to escape the rush, but would not relax till all the family was on the bus. Shortly after being seated, a very angry Israeli woman boarded, glared her in the eye, and scolded her loudly for what she saw as cutting line. Emily had not broken into the line, but had given the driver the tickets for the rest of the family. She began to feel very badly that the woman thought she had done wrong. She sat alone with her baby, tears running down her face at the thought that maybe she *had* done wrong and had not been a good example to others. Their desire in coming to Israel was that they would bless the people there, not offend them. The ride north, David behind her, and the children scattered throughout the bus, was a trying one for her. And it got worse when she realized she had underestimated the time it would take to get to Haifa, meaning they would be getting back to Kiryat Yam after *Shabbat* had begun. She was beginning to feel like a real failure.

Shabbat

When they got to the HaCarmel Station most everyone got off. The driver was surprised to see the family staying put and asked where they were going. They told him Kiryat Yam, which was past the HaMifratz station on the north side of Haifa. They had planned to get off there and catch a cab to Kiryat Yam, since it would be too late for the buses. There were a few others who knew the route and stayed on the bus, getting off at various places in Haifa. Most of Haifa was shut down, as it was already dark on *Shabbat*, but the Russian communities were going full force.

After dropping everyone else off, the driver began speaking with Emily, who was now sitting on the front seat so she could answer his questions. He was interested in the fact that they were not Jewish, yet tried to keep *torah*. Emily was upset that they were riding public transportation on the day of rest, and he seemed to be sympathetic. He told her, "I live in Akko. When we get to HaMifratz, stay on the bus. I'll take you to Kiryat Yam on my way home and drop you off at Highway 4."

Wow! What a blessing. What were the chances of them catching a ride with a driver in Jerusalem who lived just beyond where they did and to have him offer to drop them off on his way home? She told David what was happening and they thanked their Creator again, who was so merciful

Chapter 46   8th Baby, 8th Day

to them when they had erred in the guarding of His *Shabbat*. The driver pulled down the ramp at Kiryat Yam and let them off, wishing them, "*Shabbat* shalom."

They returned the salutation, praised Yah for the kind man, and wondered how long it would take them to find a cab big enough for the whole family. As soon as the bus pulled away, a *sherut* pulled up behind them. David and Emily looked at each other in amazement at Yah's provision and wondered if the bus driver had ordered it for them when they had seen him using his phone from Haifa. In any case, he was a very nice man, as was the driver of the *sherut*. He asked where they needed to go, then asked friendly questions with interest about the family as he drove them home.

Once on Weizman near their little street, Emily asked the price, expecting it to be very high, since it was *Shabbat*. But the man charged them much less than the regular fare. She gave him the amount he quoted and a good tip, still feeling badly that all this was taking place on Yah's set-apart day. She and David prayed and asked Yah to forgive them and to cause them to do better, as the little family tiredly walked to their home, exhausted and ready for the peacefulness of *Shabbat*. Once inside, they untied their mats, dropped to the floor and fell asleep.

The first *Shabbat* with their newest member visible began later than usual for the family. As they awoke, the children took turns holding and admiring the beautiful baby. After breakfast, David took all but Emily and Giliyah to the synagogue across the street, leaving them home to rest. According to scripture, a woman would be in her time of separation for 80 days after having a baby girl,[280] so they assumed women with new babies would not be welcomed at the synagogue, anyway. David took the boys to the men's section on the main floor, Armando and Moshe wearing their *yarmulkes*, and David and Victor their caps. Briana followed Sarah to the women's section above. Before the service was over, Moshe began missing Mama. David kept him as comfortable as possible, as Briana kept the girls quiet in the balcony. Once it was over and time for bread and wine, the children enjoyed the cookies and soda that the ladies offered them. Mama was not there to object, so they partook at the insistence of the cheerful ladies.

Their friends were glad to see them and to hear of the birth of Giliyah. After services, they invited the family to the basement of the synagogue, where they were having a celebration, since it was the beginning of the *torah* cycle, the week of the year that they start over at the beginning of the Bible. The children rushed home to tell Mama, who had a hard time believing that they were all invited. Sarah came right behind them and reiterated that Emily and Giliyah were welcomed and invited. So she went, wondering where she would sit.

---

[280]Lev. 12:5 But if she bear a maid child, then she shall be unclean two weeks, as in her separation: and she shall continue in the blood of her purifying threescore and six days.

Pedaling Home   Part 4 – The Last Days

It was the first time any of them had ever been in the basement. After descending the steps into a foyer area, they turned left into a larger room crowded with rectangular tables set along the walls, leaving an open space in the middle. The room was full of cheerful, celebratory people and lots of specially prepared finger foods. The family took a seat at the far end of the nearest table after being directed by some of the ladies. Armando went around the closest corner and sat between the brothers who had taken him in. Ladies brought the special delicacies and gave one to each person, while other food was passed down the tables. The couple was amazed and honored that their family would get such special treatment. They had contributed nothing, yet were welcomed and treated like royalty. There were only a handful of children there, besides theirs, and the older people seemed to really enjoy their presence.

Throughout the celebration, there was singing, and tears came to Emily's eyes when they sang, *Hava Nagila* and *Roni Roni Bat Zion*, both songs that contained her baby's names, *Giliyah*, and *Batzion*, respectively. At one point, an older gentleman took sleeping Giliyah, kissed her and spoke blessings over her, then passed her around the crowd for others to kiss and bless. It was a very special occasion for the family in many ways. After each song the men took a drink and by the time the program was nearing its end, some of them were quite happy with liquor. An old man there was celebrating his ninetieth birthday and when he stood up to make his speech he fell backwards, crashed onto and beyond the chair behind him, then was helped up by the other men, as they all laughed jovially and continued celebrating. It was quite an experience for the little family.

Afterward, they went home and spent the remainder of *Shabbat* resting and talking about Giliyah and the events surrounding her birth, as well as discussing plans for the next day, when they would go to see the Doctor to get the papers signed. While sitting outside in the front yard, the younger brother came from the synagogue on his way home and stopped to see the baby, asking what her name was.

"Giliyah," Emily replied.

"Galiyah?" he questioned, knowing it to mean 'YHWH is my redeemer.'

"No, Giliyah," she repeated. Emily thought the name he spoke was interesting, and true, but not what they were after at the time of her naming. He made over the little one, blessed her, and then went to his mother's house.

Elena came to see the new baby and visited for a good part of the afternoon.

47 - Documents

Golan Heights

Week 12   *Yom Rishon* (First Day)   10/25-26

After sundown, *Shabbat* being over, David took Armando on the bus to *Merkazit HaMifratz* and walked to the rental car place next door. There was one vehicle available that the whole family could fit into. David began filling out papers, then tried to pay with his credit card, only to find that it would not work for a charge of that size. The bank in the US had protective measures on the cards to prevent fraud, but this time it had created a problem. He called Emily, who suggested he just reserve the car and go back in the morning with a card she had from another bank. He agreed to that plan, and the two came home to join the rest of the family for another peaceful night. They laid out their mats inside this time, since the weather had gotten chilly at night with the passing of Sukkot, and they only had a few blankets. They remembered the nice one they had left at Chabad and blessed and prayed for all those that came to mind with that memory.

David hurried through breakfast, then rode and walked back to the car rental place. Once there, he was told that he could not rent the car because the credit card was in Emily's name. She would have to rent the car herself. Emily, having just nursed Giliyah and being sure she would sleep for a while left the children with instructions to stay in the house, and took a bus. David got on a bus right away and headed back toward the children waiting there without him. Once Emily began the paperwork, she learned that she would have to be the driver, since the card was in her name. They could not add David on as an additional driver without his signature, but he was already back to Kiryat Yam, and the family would be driving the opposite direction when they left.

When learning of their proposed route, the workers told her there was another rental place they would be passing, where they could add him as a driver. She was relieved at that, preferring for him to drive and her to navigate.

David walked to Tzipporah's house in the block behind theirs to pay the rent for the next two weeks. Tzipporah cheerfully answered the door, as usual, her kind eyes sparkling. David reminded her that the family would be flying out in two weeks, and asked if they needed to pay for a full month's rent. She told him that it would not be necessary to pay for time they would not be staying there. He had the money to pay rent for the two weeks, but she refused it and told him to wait until they were ready to leave. He was rather perplexed, never having met a landlord who postponed payment, let alone more than once, but thanked her, then walked back home and reported to Emily, who had just arrived, what had happened. They were both unsure of why she would want to put it off, but shifted their attention to making sure they were ready to leave.

They packed everything they had brought with them besides the tent, not knowing how many days they would be gone or exactly where they would be sleeping. They traveled north on Highway 4 for around ten miles to *Nahariya*, then east on Highway 89 toward *Tz'fat*. They soon found the rental place, got David's name added to the contract, and switched drivers, each being more comfortable in their customary roles. They likened their marriage to their position as driver and navigator, as well. David made the final decisions as driver and head of the house, but was learning Emily's importance in the relationship as navigator to help keep him going the right direction. Since beginning to see marriage from more of a scriptural perspective than they had for many of their years, they had begun to work together much more harmoniously, and things continued to get better, in spite of their rough beginnings, as they learned to function each one in his gifting.

Doctor's Hospitality

As they traveled, they enjoyed the beautiful scenery of hills and trees in northern Israel and continued to be astounded at how small the country was, how quickly they came to one town after another. They passed *Tz'fat*, where they had hoped to spend a night while on the bicycles before their plans had been changed, then turned north on Highway 90. They drove a short distance before reaching the Burger King the Doctor had mentioned. They stopped there to use the restroom and got hamburgers for everyone, not wanting to arrive at his house hungry. They called to tell him they were there, and he drove to meet them, then led them the few miles to his house in a community near the Jordan River. They were impressed by his warm manner, as he welcomed them into his home, treating them like family. He offered them drinks and citrus fruits that had been picked from their trees. With the children occupied with their snacks and new surroundings, he got more information from David and Emily, then printed out the paperwork and gave it to them. They paid him his fee, which they had come to realize was very reasonable, then were prepared to leave. But he was not in such a hurry. He asked, "Would you like to tour the area?"

They glanced at one another and decided that this would be too good to pass up. He first took them on a walking tour of his community, past orchards of lemon, orange, grapefruit, pomegranate and other fruit trees. As they walked by a pomegranate orchard, the children picked up pomegranates off the ground to eat, already understanding that the laws in Israel made that an acceptable practice. The doctor lightly scolded, "No, no. Pick them off the *trees*."

Chapter 47   Documents

They hated to see the ones on the ground go to waste, but their host wanted them to have the best, so they allowed the children to pick a pomegranate each from the trees, while keeping the cracked ones they had found on the ground. They walked to a small petting zoo owned by European immigrants, where they were given a private tour and saw various animals including a donkey, ducks, geese, and a fuzzy, stinky billy goat, and were allowed to pet a llama and a small camel. The parents visited with the Doctor and owner of the private zoo, and then were met by another friend of the Doctor who shared more about the kind community. On the way back to his home, he showed them some old houses that were for sale, just waiting for someone to restore and move into them. He invited the family to come live in their little community, and they were quite attracted to the idea of living among such kind, generous people of various cultures and religious practices, but all getting along as a community working together. It was so different to the situations they were familiar with in the States.

Upon arrival at his home, they crowded into his car, Emily holding Giliyah in the front, David, Armando, and Briana in the rear seat, and the other 5 children in the back of the closed jeep-type vehicle. He drove east to the Jordan River, then turned north, pointing out notable sites along the way. The fact that the east side of the highway was lined with tall trees, did not draw the attention of the visiting family, accustomed to living around lots of trees, until the Doctor pointed to them and asked, "Do you know why the trees are there?"

As soon as he asked, they noticed the oddity of trees lining only one side of the highway, "No, why?" David asked.

Pointing to the grassy hills half a mile to their right, he answered with his kind smile, "Years ago before the Six Day War, Syrian snipers sat on the hills over there and shot at civilians traveling this road. So we planted trees to protect the citizens on their way to work and school."

They were struck with the nonchalant way he said it. There was no indication of irritation or bitterness in his voice, just matter-of-factness. They were learning first hand that being preyed upon was a fact of life for Israelis. They were glad to be in the Land, even with all odds against them. They knew YHWH, the Creator of the universe and Savior of their souls watched over them in His land. And they accepted that when it was their time, he would take them, and not before. They observed the amazing faith of another Israeli as they rode through the beautiful green area of the Golan Heights, watered by the Jordan River, only a couple of miles from the now retreated Syrian border.

Yom Sheni (Second Day)

Just as the sun set, displaying beautiful colors over northern Israel, they arrived at a nature reserve where the Doctor pointed out thousands of migrating birds stopped at the water on their way to Africa for the winter.

449

Pedaling Home   Part 4 – The Last Days

They watched them circle the marsh, land, and settle for the night as darkness descended.

After returning to his house, he introduced them to his wife and the children that were there. He had told them he had five of his own that he had delivered himself, some at home, which explained why he was such an advocate of home-birthing and probably why his price for the paperwork was so reasonable. After exchanging 'shalom' and thanking him for his kindness in showing them around, the family got in their rental car and drove south to Tiberius, where they could turn in the paperwork at the *Misrad Hap'nim*. Although there was one in Haifa, they thought it would be better to go to the one closer to the doctor, where he was well-known and close by in case there was any trouble. Their Colorado Friends who had delivered in Israel just weeks before had run into trouble with the paperwork process. Since the Varelas' flight left in just over a week, they needed everything to work smoothly and quickly.

Misrad Hap'nim, Tiberius

On the way south, they called the Guitar Couple, who were glad to be informed of the birth of Giliyah. The family spent the night at a motel in Tiberius they had passed when they had camped in the area for *Yom Teruah*. The room was simple but comfortable, and they all got a good night's sleep.

After their typical breakfast, this time in their room, the family checked out and drove a few blocks northwest to the *Misrad Hap'nim*, went through security, and walked into the waiting area, where the children sat quietly. The couple, with Emily carrying Giliyah in the sling, approached the desk with all the necessary paperwork when they were called. The serious woman behind the desk asked several questions and began typing Emily's responses into her computer. When learning the name of the baby, she typed it in as if it were a common name, never questioning it. Emily was glad to know that it was so understandable to a Hebrew speaker. After a few minutes, the woman handed her the birth certificate. It was blue and white and written in Hebrew, making it something even more special to the family. It was beautiful to see their daughter's name written in the language of scripture, knowing that each letter had a special meaning and that the meaning of her name, 'Yah is my delight' would be uttered every time her name was spoken.

The next step was to get her U.S. passport, which had to be done at the U.S. consulate. There were a few choices: Jerusalem; Tel Aviv, much closer to the airport; and Haifa, much closer to their home base. David asked Emily, "Where do you think we should get it?"

Instantly, she replied, "Jerusalem," without even thinking. She continued, "I know it doesn't make sense. The only reason I can come up with is that if the passport doesn't get back in time, I would rather be in the Old City of

450

Jerusalem to wait for it than in Tel Aviv or Haifa. I know Haifa is so close, and we already have the house rented...I just can't explain it."

David replied, "There's just something about Jerusalem, isn't there? I understand. Jerusalem it is," he declared as he turned east out of the parking lot toward Highway 90, which followed the *Kinneret*, then continued south along the Jordan River. They drove past where they had the free taxi ride and had backpacked back to Tiberius, then past their previous camping place. At the south end of the lake, they met their friend that mixed the anointing oils and picked up the things they had ordered from her. She cooed over Giliyah and gave her a sweet little outfit. They spoke for a few minutes before each hurried to their own responsibilities.

The family continued along the Jordan River, at one point being just yards from the Jordanian border, and continued driving with the river to their left, noting the frequent guard towers on either side of the border between Israel and Jordan, just across the river from them. David wanted to take the family to the Dead Sea on the way to Jerusalem, but could not remember where the free beach was, having only been there once before. Where they stopped was quite expensive to enter, so they decided to eat their snacks beside their vehicle, then travel on. He drove farther south and pointed out Masada, Sodom and Gomorrah, and Qumran telling them interesting things along the way. As his crew began to get hot and tired of the sun reflecting off the desert sand, he turned the car around and drove back up the sea to Highway 1, heading towards Jerusalem. On the way, they saw Bedouin camps, shepherds with their flocks, some riding camels, and other camels stationed outside their owners' tents. Once in Jerusalem, they parked near the west side of the Old City wall and checked into a dorm at the Petra Hostel. The room was situated on the front side of the building with a porch overlooking Jaffa Street, and they were the only occupants.

They walked through the Old City, buying food at the markets before getting to bed early. The experience of staying in a room was much different than staying in their tent on the roof. Some preferred the roof, but all were happy to have a comfortable place to rest for the night.

United States Consulate

Yom Shlishi (Third Day)

The Muslim prayers were much less obnoxious from inside the thick stone walls of the hostel. In fact, the sound of them was quite pleasant from there, compared to how it had been on the roof. The family got up, had breakfast, walked a few blocks north to the U.S. embassy, and waited in line outside with around 20 other people seeking services. An elderly Jewish lady walking down the street saw Giliyah and quickly approached, bending down toward Emily's belly to kiss Giliyah's head. She then spoke blessings over the baby, and others began to ask about her.

"How old is she?" someone asked.

Emily replied, "One week today."

"She's so beautiful!" said another.

"She's so tiny!" said a third.

"So since she was born here, she's an Israeli, right?" asked an American.

Emily responded, "No, she has an Israeli birth certificate, but is not an Israeli citizen. The government does not let foreigners claim citizenship for their babies. There have been abuses to the system and allowing that could cause them in two generations to lose control of their land to those who want to destroy them."

Other conversations took place, some asking the typical questions to which the family had grown accustomed. Finally, they were allowed through security, then waited again in the waiting area. David and Emily were soon called to the window to present their paperwork. The Israelis working behind the window asked for the birth certificates, parents' passports, marriage certificate, and numerous other documentation. Emily had studied carefully before leaving the US to know exactly what all they would need to secure the proper paperwork. But had it not been for Moshe's accidental birth in Mexico four years earlier, she would still probably have forgotten something

Emily pulled each document out of her folder one by one as they asked for it. After the main documents were presented, and she continued to present one after another, they began to look at each with odd expressions. The couple noticed that people at the windows on both sides of them were being turned away for lacking required documentation. Finally, after Emily presented the last document, one attendant said to the other in amazement, "They have *everything!*", and Emily once again gave thanks to Yah for preparing them well for this experience.

The young man finished processing everything, gave Emily a receipt and said, "We're putting a rush on it, since you're scheduled to fly out next week. It is doubtful it will arrive in time, but not impossible. We'll call you when it arrives. Remember the only time to pick up passports is between 2:30 and 3:30 in the afternoon."

The parents thanked them, exchanged shalom and walked outside with the children, glad to be successfully out of the government office. They walked the few blocks south and entered the Old City through the Damascus Gate, stopping by to see their Baklava Friend and get goodies for the upcoming *Shabbat*. Since their time at the consulate had not taken as long as expected, they took their time walking through the *shuk*. Moshe bought a shiny little metal box and Isabel got a magnet showing the Old City with their remaining gift money from the grandparents.

452

Chapter 47   Documents

They continued to their room at the Petra Hostel where they repacked their loads. Armando opened the French doors to their little balcony and saw the Shofar Guy below at his regular spot on the corner. The family enjoyed the small balcony and were surprised a short time later to see the cowboy come riding through the Jaffa gate carrying a Christian flag. He stopped just under them and began passing out New Testaments to soldiers as they passed by. Later in the afternoon, the family was able to visit with both the Shofar Guy and the Cowboy as they admired little Giliyah.

Comfort ~~Inn~~ in Be'er Sheva

After the short visit, they walked to the rental car and began the drive south to Be'er Sheva to see the Cell Phone Couple. David drove through the sandy hills of the Negev Desert and they saw Bedouins[281] with their camels, sheep, and goats, women walking across the hot sand in their long black *burkhas*,[282] and camel crossing signs that amused everyone. They arrived at a checkpoint and were thoroughly investigated, while other cars passed through easily.

A soldier asked David, "Where are you going?"

David: *Be'er Sheva*

Soldier: What are you planning to do there?

David: Visit friends.

Soldier: Who are all these people with you?

David: My family, my wife and children.

Soldier, as if in disbelief: They're *all* your children?

David: Yes.

Soldier: Do you have documents to prove this?

David: Yes, we have passports.

Soldier: Step inside, please.

Another soldier searched the vehicle as the family went into the checkpoint where their passports were checked. They were immediately released back to their vehicle, then south toward Hebron. They decided to go

---

[281]Bedouins - clans of predominantly dessert dwelling-Arabs.

[282]*Burkha* - garment that fully covers the body, and in this case, the face, worn by some Islamic women.

around the city and stay with the more scenic view, not realizing taking the more direct route could have been very dangerous for people of their appearance. They later learned that families like them were often the targets of (sometimes deadly) rock throwing attacks by Palestinians. They continued to Be'er Sheva, everyone getting tired of riding in the car. Emily remembered the times on the bicycles and was so thankful David had agreed for them to travel that way at the beginning of their stay in Israel. It was a special memory that she would cherish for the rest of her life. Riding in cars and buses was not something she particularly enjoyed, and with children, it was even less appealing.

They arrived at the couple's house and were warmly welcomed. The woman had supper cooking in the kitchen and a special treat for the new mom. She had Briana and the other girls take care of Giliyah, then led Emily to the candlelit bathroom, where she had a tub filled with warm water. Emily remembered back to the time the kind woman had cut her fingernails at the *Kinneret* beach and sent up prayers of blessing for this precious, serving woman.

As Emily enjoyed the luxurious candlelit bath, the Cell Phone Couple made over their other guests, expressing how happy they were to have them in their home. The atmosphere made it obvious the guests had been well prepared for. Appropriate children's books were set in strategic places, supper was cooking on the stove, and the woman took time to read to the children in between visiting with them. The man and David got to know each other a little more as the children busied themselves with new books.

Yom Revi'i (Fourth Day)

Emily enjoyed the bath for as long as she could without feeling guilty, then joined the rest of the family in the living room. They sat down at the table for a supper of spaghetti, the hostess apologizing for accidentally putting jalapenos instead of bell peppers in the sauce, especially since she loved bell peppers and had put a generous amount before realizing that was not what they were. Most of the younger ones did not eat as much as they might have, but David and Emily thoroughly enjoyed it. The Cell Phone Couple excitedly told them of a special place they wanted to take them the next day, and the parents agreed they would have time to go. After supper, they went to sleep in thoughtfully prepared beds.

The family arose after a comfortable night's rest, and the Cell Phone Couple took them to Arad to see what they described as "the best thing you'll see in Israel." The attraction was kept a secret, so when they stepped inside the door, they were totally unprepared for what they would see. Inside the open air theater was a convex block and stone wall with seven sculptures protruding from the wall depicting Y'shua at the crucifixion. In front of each station was a life-size bronze sculpture depicting an individual during the Holocaust. There was also a bronze sculpture of Y'shua in agony from his prayer time in the garden, and another bronze sculpture of an oven containing a burning little boy,

Chapter 47   Documents

representing the suffering of the Jews during World War II. The display was amazing, and showed that great thought, skill, and countless hours of time had gone into the work.

Upon stepping through the door, Emily got a horrible feeling in her stomach, which remained the whole time they were there. She and David did not talk much while inside, trying to appear normal as they spoke with the artist and his wife, who had done this amazing feat. Both parents had the same initial reaction which overshadowed the entire moving experience that thousands of tourists had experienced in the past. They were appalled at the sight of graven images representing Y'shua. Horrified, yet trying to relate to the talented artists who had done the work for such passionate reasons, they were unable to speak. While most would have been focused on the message that would relate the suffering of Y'shua on the cross to the suffering of his Jewish brothers during the Holocaust, the parents were speechless at seeing the Jewish Messiah portrayed in graven image form, directly transgressing his Father's third command. They were even more horror struck to learn that many kneel at the images and pray, a form of worship.[283]

They were awed by the incredible talent displayed and did not want to disappoint their gracious friends nor the wonderful artist, but were not quite sure how to react. The sight was both amazing and troubling. They thanked the artist for the private presentation they got and hoped they had seemed grateful enough, but left feeling like something was horribly wrong. It was another instance of how hard it was to live life in a pagan society while trying to obey the commands of YHWH. It was impossible for most people to understand them, and they often felt alone in their walk with Him. They wished they knew words to express their thoughts and to call people back to His ways without upsetting or offending them. They left wondering how they could ever tell their friends the truth about how they felt in a way that would honor them as the kind, generous people they had found them to be.

They left the scene with appreciation for both the artists and their friends, but knowing they had missed much of the intended meaning because of the way the graven images had affected them. They were just glad the place was one that most often drew solemnity from its viewers. Maybe their reaction had not been so obvious. They wished they knew how to put their thoughts into appropriate words that would help people. They thanked their friends for the hospitality, then drove northeast on Highway 40 across the desert toward Tel Aviv.

---

[283]Exo. 20:4 Thou shalt not make unto thee any graven image, or any likeness *of any thing* that *is* in heaven above, or that *is* in the earth beneath, or that *is* in the water under the earth:

455

Kibbutz Bet-El

The hot noonday sun reflected off the sand as they passed by Bedouins with their camels and herds of sheep and goats. In less than an hour, they approached the huge city of Tel Aviv and intentionally drove past it on Highway 4, as they continued north. Everyone was ready to be home, but they had one more stop to make on the way. The conservatively dressed friends they had met at the Frenchman's wedding and who had brought gifts after Giliyah was born had invited them to their community. Mid-afternoon, they arrived at the factory where whole grain breads and crackers were made. They were welcomed by their friends and introduced to more of the community, then given a special tour of some of the facilities, which included areas that produced some high tech medical equipment used in various parts of Israel and the world and contamination suits to use in emergency situations. After the tour, the family was taken to the kitchen, where they were fed wonderful, wholesome whole grain crackers and jellies, all made there in the community.

The cordial people then took the family to see a school and day care facility where members of the community left their little ones as they worked in the factories. The family enjoyed the visit and meeting all of the kind people. At the day care, an elderly lady approached them, commenting in German about how beautiful and tiny Giliyah was. She then motioned to Emily to follow her into the nursery area. Emily quietly followed, Giliyah in the baby sling, as the woman walked to a crib and pointed at the biggest baby Emily had ever seen. The woman told her he was three months old, yet he was at least four times the size of Giliyah! The rest of the family came in, as well as some of the other workers, as they all marveled at the giant baby. Before leaving, the elderly lady presented Emily with a bag of knitted clothing for Giliyah - caps, booties, sweaters, and pants. They also presented the family with a package of diapers and more snacks for the little ones. Once again, the family was awed by the generosity and kindness they were being shown and thanked Yah for His blessings through all of the wonderful people they had been privileged to meet.

48 - Foiled Robbery

German Dinner

Yom Chamishi (Fifth Day)

They were invited for supper to the home of one of the community elders and humbly accepted, feeling a little awkward at the ten of them eating at someone's house without bringing anything to contribute. Once inside the beautiful home, along with some of the younger people they had met in Jerusalem, they began getting to know their host. After learning more about the family, the man offered, "We have a good community here. We need more people working for us, people who work hard and have good values."

David and Emily looked at each other, not knowing if he were actually offering them a job. They would love to move to Israel, but did not know about putting their children in day care so that Emily could work, even if she were to work in the day care herself. They seemed like a great group of people, but the couple did not know if the lifestyle changes they would have to make would work for them.

"What are you doing in Israel?" he asked.

David looked at Emily, then replied, "I'll let my wife explain. She tells it better."

Emily smiled and began, "We came for Sukkot, but did not want to spend the money it would take to get here for just a week. So we figured out a way we could come for three months and get our money's worth. We started out traveling by bicycle and camping in free places. We even rode through the edge of Zichron Ya'achov, and people asked us if we were part of your community."

Man: Why do you celebrate Sukkot? You're not Jewish.

David: Scripture says that Yah's people are to do it forever, throughout their generations.

Knowing they were German Christians, he added, "Y'shua celebrated it. We're just following his example."

Man: But all that was done away with at his death.

Pedaling Home   Part 4 – The Last Days

David: We don't see it that way. We see that he never transgressed his Father's commands and told us to follow him as he followed his Father.

The look on the man's face changed and so did the topic of conversation. David and Emily both recognized what had happened, though they sensed that some of the younger people in the room related to what they were saying. When the meal was over, the host family loaded up their guests with a large box of bread, crackers, and jelly, telling them to come back and visit the next time they were in Israel. The Varelas thanked them for their kindness, hospitality, and generosity, left them their family post card thank you note, and drove the remaining half hour to their little home in Kiryat Yam. It was late and they were glad to get back on their mats on the back porch, in the cool of the autumn night.

The Chase

In the morning, David returned the rental car to Haifa and rode the bus back. While he was gone Emily did laundry with the younger children and sent Armando and Briana to the pet store to donate *Arnav*'s cage. They were always glad to go on missions without the others. On the way back, they planned to stop at the Post Office to buy minutes for the cell phones. The family wanted them to be as fully charged as possible before giving them back to the generous Cell Phone Couple. As they returned through the park, staying on paths between the dry sandy areas where it was difficult to walk, they saw coming toward them on bicycles Fish Boy, his little brother riding with training wheels, another boy around Armando's age and an older Sudanese boy. When they met, Fish Boy greeted them, but had a strange look on his face they had not seen before and was staring at the coin purse that Briana wore attached to the top of her skirt. He pointed and asked, "What's that thing?"

Before she could answer, he tried to grab it, but she backed up quickly out of his reach, he straddling his bicycle. He tried again, but Armando said, "Run!" so she bolted and ran in the direction of home, staying on the paths where she could run faster. The boys, facing in the wrong direction of the park's concrete walkway that was laid out in a circle with paths going out like spokes of a wheel, took off on their bicycles, going around the circle, where they could meet up with Briana again and Armando, who was at her heals. As they neared Briana, Armando told her, "Run into the sand!"

Next to the outside of the circle was a dumpster, beside which lay a large pile of palm branches that people had discarded after having used them as roofing for their tabernacles during Sukkot. As the two ran into the sand, the two older boys on bicycles tried to cut across toward them, but their bicycles were bogged down and they fell over. As Fish Boy continued his pursuit, Armando noted the branches and slowed, allowing Briana to get farther ahead. The two older boys quickly remounted their bicycles and got back on the pavement, heading toward Armando from two different

458

Chapter 48   Foiled Robbery

directions. As Fish Boy quickly approached with an angry look on his face, Armando said under his breath, "Watch out."

He picked up a long palm branch and swung just as Fish Boy reached him. The impact knocked Fish Boy down, crashing his bicycle in the sand, his face and arms scratched from the sharp palm fronds. His little brother began crying that he wanted to go home, and the older two, unable to pursue in the sand, left their bicycles and began chasing Briana, who was nearing the edge of the park.

Fish Boy sat stunned for a few seconds, giving Armando the opportunity to make his escape, running as fast as he could toward home. The two boys chased Briana until she turned up an alley street, where the Sudanese boy stopped and waited, knowing it was a dead end. Briana continued running, passing a group of elderly ladies having tea on a porch. She yelled for help in Hebrew, but they just smiled and waved. The boy continued chasing and throwing rocks at her until she realized she had to turn around. Dodging him, she ran back toward the bigger street, passing the smiling ladies again.

Armando neared the bus stop on the main road just beyond the dead end. He looked back and saw Fish Boy catching up to him, so he stopped, looked past him and yelled, "Your bike!"

Fish Boy stopped and turned to see what Armando was talking about, and turned back around into Armando's fist, knocking him down, and Armando took off again.

As Briana ran, still having rocks thrown at her, she saw Armando up ahead. He stopped to catch his breath and saw two people in front of him, not realizing who they were until he saw rocks rolling on the ground near him that had just been thrown by Briana's pursuer. The Sudanese boy stepped out and began throwing rocks at Armando, and Fish Boy, having fallen, got up and was coming fast again. As Briana ran towards them, she saw Armando throw a rock and hit the Sudanese in the leg. As he shook it off, limping away, Fish Boy approached with a rock in each hand. As the siblings converged, Armando threw a rock at Fish Boy, then told Briana, "Get across the road as soon as you can!"

Briana turned the corner and ran into the Sudanese boy. He picked up a palm branch and swung it at her as she protected her face with her arm. She punched him in the face, kicked him in the shin, then tried to run across the street, but two buses were coming. While the Sudanese was holding his leg, Armando grabbed Briana and ran across the street behind the buses, but ahead of a box truck carrying potato chips coming from the other direction. Fish Boy crossed the first two lanes right behind them, but could not beat the chip truck across the next set. He was stuck in the median holding a palm branch in one hand and a stone in the other. He threw it at them, missed, then picked up another and threw it, hitting a parked semi.

459

Armando and Briana, close to the Floridians' store, yelled after he threw the rock at them, then continued running inside the store. Fish Boy picked up the rock that had bounced off the truck and came around as one of the Floridians stepped out. The man yelled at him in Hebrew and he ran off. The children told him what was going on and that they had needed to buy minutes. He told them he would watch out for them.

After the Floridian watched them safely cross the street again and enter the Post Office where they purchased minutes for the phones, they walked home and told their parents what had happened. Briana showed the scratches on the arm she had used to protect her face. Emily was glad they had made it through the month David was gone without incident. Everyone had enjoyed the freedom that the children had been able to have going out in the neighborhood and to the shops. Had something like this occurred earlier, Emily would have had them stay closer to home.

That evening, David took Armando and Briana to Fish Boy's house across Weizman and several blocks down. They walked under the shady grapevine canopy, opened the gate, walked in, and knocked on the door. A kind Russian woman came to the door and asked in Hebrew, "What do you want?"

David replied, "Are you [Fish Boy]'s mother?"

"Yes."

The children, who had learned to speak a fair amount of Hebrew, translated for David, "He and some friends were throwing rocks at my children."

He pointed to Briana's left arm and face where she had been cut by the palm branch.

The woman sadly said, "He has been in trouble all of his life. He was kicked out of school. He really needed his father. He runs wild on the streets. When he gets put back in school, he runs away from school. I am sorry. There is nothing I can do."

David replied, "I understand."

As they spoke, Fish Boy walked through the gate, and his mother had him apologize. That would be the last time the family saw him, but feeling badly for him, he would be in their prayers for years to come.

Morning came and it was sad to realize this was their last preparation day in Israel, but they prayed that it would be the last for *all* of them, knowing there was a good chance that Emily and Giliyah might have to stay behind if the passport did not get back in time. They went to the markets to say goodbye to all of their friends, giving them another look at Giliyah. In the afternoon, they visited the *shuk* to buy a few more vegetables and fruits

460

for the coming days and Armando bought three very big fishing weights to give to his uncle Bob, who liked to fish.

Israeli Farewell Dinner

Eti came by again bringing them a hot meal for *Shabbat*. When she left, they went to the home of the family of ten that lived on the street behind them. The Family of Ten had wanted to give Moshe a birthday dinner, but his birthday on the Gregorian calendar fell at the time they were in Tiberius for *Yom Teruah*. The Family of Ten decided to give him a supper the same time they gave one to Isabel. So besides sundown marking the beginning of *Shabbat* and the beginning of the eighth month, this evening would be a special occasion to say farewell as they gave thanks for the completion of Moshe's fourth and Isabel's seventh years.

The children merged with their family, as usual. The Varelas had not been to their home much, but some of the Family of Ten children had spent quite a bit of time with the Varela children while David was gone. They would all miss each other when the Varelas went back to Tennessee, but their play did not seem to be affected by the fact that they may never see each other again. The children played in the back yard with riding cars and sparklers. They enjoyed the tiny puppies born just days before to their little white dog.

Shabbat   *Rosh Chodesh* (New Moon) 8

The meal was wonderful and the families had good fellowship at the *Shabbat* table, then visited for some time afterward. When little ones began showing signs of being tired, they said shalom and walked to their house to sleep under the stars for their final *Shabbat* on their little back porch.

Their last *Shabbat* in Israel, the family enjoyed the baklava from Jerusalem for breakfast, along with sweet breads they had gotten from their favorite bread market. They also had their customary yogurt and fruit.

Meeting Neighbors

They opted to look for the Messianic synagogue they had learned of while in Jerusalem. They walked the beautiful palm-lined street and continued to an inconspicuous building where they saw multiple cars parked and a small sign on the door. Inside and up the stairs, they were greeted by friendly people, and then stepped into a large open, but crowded, room. An elder approached them and greeted, "Shalom! Where are you from?"

"The United States," David answered, then seeing the question in the man's eyes, continued, "Tennessee."

Pedaling Home   Part 4 – The Last Days

"Oh, so you're part of the group!"

David was puzzled. "No."

Man: You came by yourself?

David: Yes, just myself and my family.

Man: Oh, OK. It's nice to have you. It's just that there's someone here from Tennessee to speak today, a man and his family.

David and Emily instantly knew who he must be talking about. It was a family with 11 children who lived a couple of hours southwest of them in middle Tennessee and had a ministry in Israel helping with grape harvest. Several times over the years, they had been asked if they knew the family, but had only briefly met them once. Both families had attended a worship service near Nashville years before when the Varelas were new to following both testaments of the scriptures. At the time, they only had five children and Armando was seven years old. The Grape Father, along with some other men had prayed over four-year-old Victor because of the Varela family's concern that he still could not talk. His speech began improving, and the Varelas always remembered that brief contact with the Grape Family, who since that time had become quite well-known for their ministry of volunteering for farmers in Israel.

The Varelas had tried to make contact to see about working with them, but even though they had numerous mutual friends, the attempts were not successful. They finally concluded that Yah had other plans for them in Israel besides helping with what the Grape Family was doing. After being questioned numerous times, they finally had a fun story with people.

~ ~ ~

Some friends of the Grape Family invited them over for supper one evening. After preparing a meal large enough for the family of 13, along with their own family of five, the Grape Family called and said their vehicle had broken down and they would not be able to make it.

Not knowing how they could possibly eat all that food, the friends thought of the Varelas and called, asking if they could bring them supper. Always enjoying eating food prepared by others, they family gladly accepted and a little over an hour later were happily eating the supper specially prepared for the Grape Family. Since then, whenever anyone asked if they knew the family, they could say, "No, but we ate their supper once."

~ ~ ~

Finally, they would meet the people who had missed the great healthy meal. The whole family was excited, but the music was already beginning, and the man at the sound booth adjusting the volume. Another man gave

Chapter 48   Foiled Robbery

David a headset which translated the Hebrew service to Spanish and one to Emily which translated it to English. They enjoyed the music, then the presentation describing the Grape Family's work there in the Land, and the speaker's message. As the service was ending, Natanyah needed to go to the restroom. Glad to be sitting in the back, Emily took her, Rebeka, and Isabel, knowing they would also need to go soon. When she stepped inside, she saw the Grape Lady, who instantly recognized and greeted her.

Emily was surprised that the famous woman knew her, never having met before. As they briefly conversed, Emily learned that their family had been following the Varela's adventure through mutual friends. It was interesting to learn that the Grape Family was also sometimes asked if they knew the Varelas. As the ladies returned to the service to hear the ending announcements, the Grape Lady said they would like to talk to the Varelas afterward. Emily was glad she had said that because the Varelas typically stayed out of the way of people who they thought of as busy or famous. It was not that they did not find them interesting or want to get to know them better. They just figured people like that had plenty of friends and fans and probably needed to be left alone more often than they actually were.

Once down the stairs and out the door, they saw some of the Grape Family standing against the wall. The Varelas walked to them and the children began speaking with each other while Emily and David spoke with their mother. After a while, the father also approached and they had a short visit before the busy family was whisked away to another appointment.

The little family dressed in their soft blue *Shabbat* shirts walked the several blocks home, glad to have finally officially met the people whose supper they so enjoyed several months before. They also thought it odd, that although they lived only about two hours apart in Tennessee, they had their first official meeting at a hidden synagogue that they were both visiting for the first time in a little city in Israel. As they walked, they discussed their meeting and prayed blessings upon the family and the big little hidden synagogue.

Rebeka

They ate lunch, then walked to the beach and picked up a few more shells to take home. They enjoyed each other's company and treasured these last moments together in their special place, not knowing if Mama and Giliyah would be separated from the rest of them in a few days.

463

49 - Moving

Packing

Final Days   Yom Rishon (First Day)   11/2

With their regular morning activities finished, the family began cleaning and packing. They had to make decisions about which of the gifts from others to leave and which to take with them. They lined up all their backpacks along one wall of the extra room and put the things they knew they would keep in sorted piles. They had removed the pannier racks from the bicycles they had given away and kept the panniers, all their camping supplies besides the big tent they had left with the Hostel Manager, and Natanyah's helmet. They gave the other helmets to the people they had given the bicycles to. Their clothes did not take up much space, but there were numerous things they had received from special people that some of them wanted to take home.

Emily packed her backpack with her clothes and Giliyah's, a few emergency supplies, diapers, and their documents, in case they were delayed and not able to go home with the rest of the family. Then they packed the rest of the supplies in the other packs. David went to the markets and got some boxes for the panniers and bicycle supplies, as well as the special things they had acquired on their trip: art and soap molding supplies from Eti; linen garments, a coat, boots, and slippers from the Dead Lady, a red pillow from the Family of Ten, baby dolls from the Host Family in Osifia, gifts they had purchased, shells from the beaches, and a few more special things from various places. They set the boxes in front of the sorted stacks on the floor. Emily made sure the essentials were packed, then left the rest for the family to finish the next day, just before leaving for the airport.

Fish Boy's sisters came to visit and held Giliyah for a little while. When they left, the family made one last trip to visit and say 'shalom' to other friends, including the Bird Man, Elena and Olga, Sarah, the Family of Ten, the two other Russian families, Briana's friend, the ladies behind, and Aaron. Then they went to the falafel place, where David had made a new friend since returning, to celebrate their last night in their Israeli home.

Yom Sheni (Second Day)

After a good supper at a discount from David's friend, they went home, put their mats down on the back porch for the last time, and went to sleep under the stars. The warm breeze from the salty Mediterranean peacefully blew, as they voiced gratefulness for all they had experienced in the Land.

After breakfast, they tied the bed mats, packed the sheets and sleeping clothes, and finished cleaning the house, returning all of the buckets, tables, chairs and other things they had scavenged back to their dumpster. They left the refrigerator, roll-away bed, and cot that the Interpreter had brought, to be picked up the next day. David went to Tzipporah's to pay the final rent. She met him at the door again wearing her usual kind smile. David handed her the rent for the previous two weeks, "Here's the rent we owe you. We'll be leaving this evening."

In her calm, pleasant tone she replied, "Keep it. You can use it for the baby."

David was speechless. He thanked her, offered shalom, and then walked home praising Yah for His loving people. He reported the story to Emily and the children, and they praised Yah together.

Separated Again

Just before noon, Emily put Giliyah in the sling, David carried her backpack and the family walked together to the bus stop. Emily hugged David and all the children, telling them to be good and help their dad, then said *shalom*, not knowing when she would see them again, or whether it would be at Ben Gurion Airport in a few hours, or in Tennessee days or weeks from now. David handed her pack to her, and she got on the bus, Giliyah sleeping in her sling like a kangaroo joey. The family watched the bus drive away, then began the short walk to the house, everyone thinking about what life might bring them over the next few hours, days, and weeks. Armando spoke up first, "What if the bus gets blown up?"

Briana replied, "Or the hostel?"

David detoured their thought process, "Yah will protect them. They're going to be fine."

They ate the leftovers and food in open packages they would not be able to give away, then did the final packing and cleaning. David had the children take the readied packs and boxes to the front door, while he finished sweeping the rooms. Isabel, always prepared, packed her own pink backpack, making sure to include her favorite kitchen knife, the large one with the wooden handle that had come from the Dead Lady. She also packed nuts, fruit, and other snacks, as well as water for the trip. Having made sure the essentials were in, she added some colored pencils and coloring books to keep herself and the others occupied on the long flights.

Briana cleaned out the kitchen cabinets while Armando wiped the counters, then helped Victor clean the bathroom. Rebeka watered the flowers in the front yard. Once finished with their jobs, Armando and Briana rode their bicycles to say a final 'shalom' to their personal friends. Armando left his bicycle and helmet with Aaron, who had been riding an older bicycle, and Briana left hers with the daughter of the Family of Ten that was just older than she.

It was a time of mixed feelings for everyone. The excitement of packing to leave and getting ready to ride a *sherut*, then train, then plane, and getting back to the farm and animals they all missed was in the air. Briana looked forward to catching salamanders at the edge of the pond and in the spring. Isabel remembered the beautiful green colors of the grass and trees at home. Rebeka wondered what kind of movies would be showing on the plane.

Briana, Mama's right hand girl, wondered what it would be like flying home without little Giliyah, with whom she had already bonded since her birth two weeks before. How long would they be separated? And would Giliyah's birth in Israel enable the family to stay longer next time they came? Question after question went through her mind as she went about the duties she knew needed to be done.

But in all the excitement, there was a sadness. Even though David had not been in their little home for long, he hated to leave the community atmosphere of the town that had taken care of his wife and children while he was gone. He was ready to go home, but would miss this special place. He knew they could not have had a better base from which to operate while in Israel and gave thanks again to Yah for providing it.

And besides sadness, there was apprehension because of another possible separation. David wondered if the passport would arrive, knowing it would have to be a miracle. But he believed in miracles, even passport miracles, and had faith that it would.

Jerusalem Bound

Emily changed buses at *Merkazit HaMifratz* in north Haifa and then at *Merkazit HaCarmel* in south Haifa. She remembered the hectic time of traveling with Giliyah when she was two days old. Things were much calmer now in the middle of the week and she felt more secure since her little one was almost two weeks old now. She was not secure, though, thinking about David flying home alone with all the children. He was not used to managing them by himself, a job she knew well, and one that could be very demanding. She hoped and prayed that the passport would be there waiting when she arrived. On the bus to Jerusalem she sat next to a heavy middle aged woman. She was kind and encouraging, but seemed lonely herself. She seemed to enjoy hearing Emily tell stories about her family, and commented about how blessed she was.

Chapter 49   Moving

Around 2 PM, when they were just outside of Jerusalem, Emily's phone rang. She answered, thinking it was David.

Man: Hello, Emily?

Emily: Yes?

Man: I'm calling from the U.S. consulate to let you know that Giliyah's passport has arrived.

Emily: Great! I'm on a bus about 15 minutes away. I'll come right there.

She praised Yah, shared the great news with the lady sitting beside here, and they both rejoiced. She would be able to go home with her family, after all. Off the bus in Jerusalem, she got the first taxi to the embassy, was let right in and given Giliyah's passport. The Israeli who gave it to her told her, "You must be blessed. It is not often that a passport comes back that fast."

Emily agreed. She was indeed blessed!

Rejoicing and hardly able to keep an obvious smile off her face, she left the embassy and walked to the Damascus Gate and into the Old City. She called David and told him the great news and that she was going to pick up a few things in Jerusalem. He said they were nearly ready to go and would be leaving Kiryat Yam in a *sherut* at 6 PM. He told the children and she heard the joyful excitement coming through the phone. They ended the call and she left, bouncing through the market areas of the Old City, smiling at all the people she met, even the grouchy ones who glared at her. She went to the Baklava Man, bought a few kilos to take to the U.S., and told him and his family her happy story of how they would all get to return together.

Nikolay Returns

Nikolay, knowing the family's situation with Giliyah's passport and that Emily had left for Jerusalem, made arrangements for a *sherut* to pick up the others. To their surprise, he met them at the little house to help load the *sherut*. His eyes widened in amazement when he saw all the boxes they were taking back. He knew they had decided to leave their bicycles in Israel and never imagined they would be taking back nearly as much as they had brought. He helped David and the little ones get all of the bags and boxes to the dumpster street, and the *sherut* arrived promptly at 6 PM. The younger children were excited about their mode of transportation and could hardly wait to get in. Nikolay helped them load their things, then decided he should go with them to the train station to help there, as well. Before leaving, David left the house keys by the plant, as instructed by Tzipporah, glad for the help and company of another adult.

467

On the way, Nikolay gave David instructions to make things easier on the train. David gave him money to buy the train tickets, knowing he would get the job done much easier. Once at the station, the two men and seven children got out of the *sherut* and each got their appropriate loads, taking them to the train's loading area. Nikolay spoke to a guard, then went to the ticket counter returned with an extra ticket telling David, "I'm going with you. You have too much stuff. You cannot get the things on the train and off in the amount of time they have the doors open. And you have to watch the children."

David, knowing the sacrifice he was making and having seen him go out of his way so many times for the family asked, "Are you sure?"

"Yes," he replied. "It's not a problem."

"Thank you," was again, all David could say.

Nikolay replied with his usual, "You are very welcome," and David knew he genuinely meant it.

After getting in the train, David was especially glad for Nikolay's assistance. He had not realized how much help Emily had been to him on the way there until now that he was without her. He was learning to really appreciate her organizational skills, the way she handled the children, and her ability to think quickly and move things along. They went to the lower level, and found seats, David next to Natanyah and positioning himself so he could see all of the children, across from Nikolay and Moshe and the older ones in a booth across the aisle. The sun set and darkness settled as the train made its way south. As David and Nikolay talked, the older children watched Israel pass by outside their window and observed others on the train. Nikolay got a call from the *sherut* driver who said that he had found a fishing pole in his vehicle. In all the rush, they had left Armando's new pole from his fisherman friend. Nikolay said he would retrieve it later and keep it until David returned to Israel for another feast.

Natanyah fell asleep getting David's ears, and Victor, Rebeka, and Moshe fell asleep on their own. Isabel was tired, but stayed mostly awake, not wanting to miss anything. David tried to express the family's gratitude for the treatment they had received from Nikolay. He mostly dismissed it and shared that he was glad to have gotten to know the interesting family, and that he hoped they would all come back and he could see them again.

Bad Taste

As she was walking through the markets on her way toward the Jaffa Gate to exit the Old City, she saw a young Arab man playing a handmade flute. She bought one for Victor, since he had not spent his gift money yet, then saw a beautiful red purse that converted to a backpack, like the gray one Isabel had wanted. She bought it for her, then continued at a good pace

Chapter 49   Moving

up the hill through the markets. As she walked determinedly, an older Arab man stepped in front of her and motioned her to look at the beautiful skirts in his shop. She did not need a skirt, but was not in a particular hurry, since David would not be at the airport for a while.

"Which skirt do you like best?" the man asked with a smile.

"They're all beautiful," she replied, "but I don't need one today. Thank you," as she tried to walk past him.

He stepped in front of her again and said, "You must look inside. There are more in the back. Don't be in such a hurry."

She did not like the man, but did not want to be rude. She had never been good at getting away from sales people, and was really missing David at the moment. He would have given him the look, and the man would have stepped aside. She wondered why she could not do that herself. Not knowing a polite way to escape, she walked into the narrow shop, the walls lined with hundreds of beautiful tiered skirts. The man picked up one, then another to show her. Beginning to get nervous, she said, "They are very beautiful. But I don't need one."

"Let me ask you a questions?" he said. "What kind of person are you? Are you Jewish? Are you Christian?"

The line of questioning had begun, and she did not want to avoid an opportunity to share something with him that could potentially change his life. She reluctantly took a seat on the stool he offered her and began answering his questions, but they quickly changed from the usual ones posed by Jews, Christians, or even the Arab Druze people she had met. When answering his questions, she shared that the family believed and lived by the whole Bible, and that the New Testament did not contradict the Old. Answering one of his questions, she explained that the scriptures teach not to eat things like pork.

"The Koran also teaches this," he replied.

"Yes, there are many things we have in common," she confirmed, thinking he was actually interested in the answers she was giving him.

He asked, "So how long after the baby is born until you sleep with your husband again?"

She did not think the question was appropriate coming from a male who was a total stranger, but in the context of the conversation, she thought it safe to answer with the scriptures, "After a boy, it is 40 days; after a girl, 80 days."[284]

----

[284]Lev. 12:2-5

He replied, "That is good." Then with a laugh that made her stomach churn, he said, "The Koran says to wait, but most Muslim men don't wait."

That was enough for her. "I've got to go."

He blocked her way, holding up a skirt in each hand, "Which one do you want?"

Emily insisted, "I don't need a skirt. I told you that before."

The man ordered, "But you must take one. I give you good price."

Just wanting to get out of there, she asked, "How much are they?"

"I let you have one 150 shekels," he announced, as if he were giving her a good deal.

She pulled out a hundred shekel bill and gave it to him. "I'll take the blue one."

He quickly hung both the skirts he was holding and gave her a red one. She did not care; she did not need a skirt; she did not want a skirt. She just wanted out of there, and fast. She took the red one and quickly walked out of the shop, her heart racing. She did not realize until she got onto the next street that he had gotten exactly what he wanted. She had played right into his game. She felt violated and robbed. She wished David had been there to keep her out of trouble. She was confident alone in the country, where the only dangers were the elements and creatures of nature. In town around people, she felt uncomfortable, vulnerable, and unsafe. For the first time on their three month trip, she longed to return to the peaceful place they had left in Tennessee. She walked on, disgusted with the man and with herself. She knew he had tricked her into getting what he wanted, and that she had gotten a beautiful red skirt that she would never be able to wear without feeling like a harlot. Once outside the markets, she folded the skirt and put it in her pack, getting it out of her way and out of her memory.

50 - Home in Exile

Reunion

Yom Shlishi (Third Day)

As the sun set, Emily walked out of the Old City at the Jaffa Gate, then up Jaffa Street toward the bus station. She wandered in and out of shops on the way whenever she saw something of interest, feeling safer among the Jewish people. She reached the bus station in under an hour and was waved through by the guard without having to remove her pack or run the bag of baklava through the scanner as he smiled at her and Giliyah. Once inside, she went to buy a ticket to the airport. The kind woman at the counter said it would be better to take a *sherut*. The woman called and made arrangements for her, then told her what hotel to go and what time the *sherut* would be there to pick her up. She stepped outside and got a taxi to take her to the hotel. When she arrived and stepped out of the taxi, her pack caught on something and one of the straps broke loose. That made things significantly more difficult. She now had to have the pack in one hand and the bag of baklava in the other, while trying to guard Giliyah in the sling in front of her.

She stepped inside the beautiful lobby of the hotel to sit and wait. She watched people coming in and out, and realized it was the first time in years she had done that. She was usually busy with the other children. Now it was just herself and baby Giliyah who slept most of the time, so her world was completely different. She continued to relax as a kind young lady sitting next to her began asking the usual questions. The sincerity in her voice helped to make up for the ugliness of the Arab man, which had sucked the energy out of Emily's spirit. She began to come to life again as she answered the kind, interested woman with information about their family and what they were doing in the Land.

As it got close to time for the *sherut* to arrive, she took her pack in one hand, the bag in the other and walked outside into the crisp night air, Giliyah doubled up sitting snugly in the sling. Just then, a kind woman from Australia stepped up and asked if she could take a picture of the baby. She was impressed with how cute Giliyah was, sitting like a joey in her pouch. Emily told her it would be fine and she snapped a few pictures. She then reviewed the photos on her screen and with a big smile showed one to Emily. Emily now knew why the woman wanted to take the pictures. Little two-week old Giliyah had the most beautiful, alert smile on her face!

She never thought to ask the woman if she could send her a copy of the picture, but later wished she had.

The *sherut* arrived shortly, and Emily boarded with several others on their way to the airport. She was more alert than usual to her surroundings, knowing this may be the last time she would see any of this for seven years when the family planned to return again during the next sabbatical year for Sukkot. She thought of all she would miss and all she would be glad to miss once they left. She gave thanks for the experiences they had there, including the incredible birth of little Giliyah. And she gave thanks for their peaceful place on the little farm back home. She gave thanks for being able to reunite with her family now, instead of having to be separated by thousands of miles for an unknown amount of time. Within an hour, the *sherut* pulled up to the airport and she got out with her broken backpack in one hand, half-way slung over her shoulder, and the baklava in the other, Giliyah asleep in the sling.

She walked to the train stop inside the airport, then called to let David know she was there. They arrived shortly and Nikolay helped David get the children and luggage past security. Emily met them there and they all went to the waiting area in the airport. Nikolay stayed for a few minutes before returning on the train to his family in Haifa. He had proven to be more than they could have ever imagined and had earned himself ten friends for life.

After he left, the parents sat on the seats with their children and encouraged them to go to sleep. David untied the bed mats and had Emily and some of the children lie on them on the floor. Others lay across the seats, trying to get some sleep before midnight, when they would go through security. David watched over his sleeping family, while keeping an eye on the late night airport activity.

Security

He woke them up when it was time to go and they retied the bed mats and got in the long security line. Some people around them seemed to enjoy seeing a large family traveling together, while others seemed annoyed that they had to be in the line behind them. They placed the luggage to be checked on the conveyers one at a time and all but two boxes made it through without having to be searched. Emily went with those, hoping they would not disturb and break things or make the boxes unable to be repacked as they searched them.

A few things were briefly questioned, but Emily's answers seemed to satisfy them. They advanced to the area to check-in. When they had bought the round trip tickets, there were only nine of them. It never occurred to them that they would have to purchase a ticket for Giliyah on the way home because she was an infant who would be traveling in Emily's lap. They knew from previous flights that most airlines did not charge for children under two years old unless they would have their own seat. The woman at the counter seemed extremely aggravated that they had not purchased a ticket for the baby and sent Emily around the corner to the special ticket purchase place, hidden in a back hallway. Once there, she learned that, although the ticket was free, Giliyah was still charged airport taxes, which amounted to several hundred dollars. That was an expense the family had not planned for and their money was running short. Emily paid the fees, just thankful they were still able to travel together.

While she was gone, David kept the sleepy children occupied by pointing out paintings on the ceiling and other features of the beautiful airport, as well as interesting looking people who walked by, some with angry faces, some with friendly ones. Emily came back to the counter and presented the ticket to the grouchy clerk and felt the irritated looks of several customers, as well as a few much appreciated kind ones from others. Once they had their boarding passes, they began walking toward the terminals when all at once, they were surprised by several people running straight towards them, followed by security officers, yelling in Hebrew, "Go back! Get out!"

The family quickly changed directions and ran out with the others, not knowing what was going on at the gates beyond. After a few minutes, they were released to proceed to the gates and learned there had been suspicion of a bomb in someone's luggage as it went through the x-ray machine. The security team and bomb experts were called in to make sure everything was safe before other passengers were allowed to go through the area.

Once at the security check-point with the officers still on edge from the previous scare, the family laid their carry-on baggage on the conveyer belt. Emily was focused on trying to get her sandals off without dumping Giliyah out of the sling where she slept. Suddenly, her focus was interrupted by a familiar beep and the conveyer stopped. She wondered what could be in one of their carry-on pieces that would cause problems. She had carefully packed all the backpacks herself before leaving Kiryat Yam. She then realized it was Isabel's bag they were looking at. The female guard asked, "Whose bag is this?"

Isabel, innocently smiling, volunteered, "It's mine."

Emily looked questioningly at barely-seven-year-old Isabel who maintained her cheerful smile. Everyone looked at the security officer and watched as she slowly unzipped the little pink backpack, then reached in and just as slowly pulled out a very large kitchen knife.

Emily, having already been reminded by the beep and stopping of the conveyer of a time in her distant past when she spent a short time in jail for accidentally having a gun in her luggage, was horrified and cried, "Isabel! Where did you get that?"

Isabel responded in her sweet, innocent tone, "From the Dead Lady."

David could not help chuckling, which did nothing to ease Emily's horror as she quickly but intently studied the expression of the guard, at the same instant wondering what Israeli jails were like and which family members would be taken. Simultaneously, she began her defense of Isabel, explaining who the Dead Lady was and how the knife got in the backpack without the parents' consent. The officer seemed immune to emotion, as she asked Isabel a couple of questions and was satisfied with her answers. She then discarded the knife, much to Isabel's disappointment, as she told her and the others that knives could not be carried on the plane.

Emily's adrenaline was rushing as they finished the security process and headed towards the gate. She calmed down by the time they got there and passed through passport security before sitting again until it was time to board the plane to Amsterdam. David was his usual calm self and together they kept the children quiet and content for another half hour until the announcement was made to board the 3:30 AM flight.

They were blessed to be able to sit together this time, something for which the parents were particularly grateful. Most were able to get a little sleep on the four hour flight, some of which was still in the dark of the early morning. The flight attendants were quite impressed with little Giliyah, and before landing gave her a special gift to commemorate the first flight of her life, a little collectable numbered ceramic row house, the type common to the canal streets in Amsterdam. On the bottom was stamped the name of the manufacturer, the piece's production number, and the name of the airline. Emily tucked it away for safekeeping among the soft clothes in the backpack, which she had repaired while waiting to board.

There was only enough time in Amsterdam on the return trip to comfortably get from one terminal to another and have a snack. The family soon boarded the flight to Memphis and once again was blessed to be able to sit together. Giliyah did not do as well on this flight and cried a good part of the way. Emily tried nursing her, but could not keep her contented. David, who had always been good with the babies, also tried to quiet her, but was only partially successful. Emily was uncomfortable, knowing that some around her were not happy about hearing the baby cry. The good news, she thought, was that such a young baby did not cry nearly as loud as an older one. She comforted herself, knowing they were doing the best they could, and felt sorry for the tiny baby, who must have been in terrible pain from the air pressure. By the end of the flight, Mama was exhausted.

The family gathered their things, exited the plane, and proceeded to customs. The flight attendants had kept them well fed, so the two beautiful pomegranates they had brought along to eat on the way were still in the bag. Once the customs agents spotted them, they were confiscated. Emily tried to convince them that the ten family members could gobble them up quickly right then and there, but they were not persuaded. The family members were all sad to see them thrown in the trash.

474

Chapter 50   Home in Exile

The next flight plane landed in Memphis and the family boarded a small jet to Nashville for a short flight. Once they retrieved their luggage, they carried it outside and were met by Emily's parents driving the family's 14 passenger van. They quickly rushed through the customary greetings and while the grandparents cooed over their new grandchild, David and the older children loaded their things in the van. They had a good reunion on the way back to Cookeville, Granddaddy driving. On the way, he stopped to feed them supper at his favorite restaurant, then invited the tired family to stay overnight at their home, so they could be good and rested before going back to the farm. Since the Oklahoman and her children were there, that sounded like a plan that would work for everyone.

Back to the Farm

Wednesday

After sleeping later than usual, the nearly 80 year old grandparents prepared a big breakfast of waffles and eggs for the family. They listened to the family share about their trip and caught them up on what they had missed in the U.S. while they had been gone. Afterward, the family got in their van and drove the 45 minutes to the farm, everyone now ready to get back to their home and animals.

They drove the reverse route they had taken on the bicycles as they trained for their trip. The drive reminded them of their time on the bicycles as they passed by the familiar stores in town and then the sights in the country. As they neared the river, they slowly wound down the steep, narrow, curvy highway, now covered in fallen autumn leaves of every color. The smell of fresh air surrounded them and made them forget the smells of exhaust, bus diesel, and urine in solitary corners that they had become accustomed to in the cities of the Promised Land. They wondered why the Promised Land was that one and not this one, with its bountiful rivers and food growing wild on every hill. They resolved that only Yah knows why He does things, and while grateful they lived here in such a beautiful place, knew it was not really home for them - that one day, according to many scriptures, they would be gathered together in that land, and that it would once again be a paradise. They lived by faith, not by sight.[285] For now they would be content in the beautiful, peaceful place where Yah had so graciously planted them seven years before.

After crossing the river, they drove up the steep, curvy, narrow back road on the other side, then made the two turns to get onto their little road. They drove onto their property, then went through the long gate at the entrance, past the old barn where the goats spent most of their nights, and saw the goats, goat dogs and cattle, before being welcomed home by the little, scraggly dog, Bingo, who was extremely happy to see them. They had

---

[285]2Cor. 5:7 (For we walk by faith, not by sight:)

picked her up on the side of the road a couple of years before and she had immediately become part of the family.

David was glad to have his family safely back to their property. The Oklahoman came out of the house and all but David met her in person for the first time, though Emily felt like they had been friends for a while. She introduced the children she had with her, then finished packing and left for their long trip home. They had done a wonderful service by rescuing the family in time of need and were given a refreshing experience in return.

The days and weeks following had the family traveling to their Horse and Buggy friends to pick up the milk cows and horse they had left there, cleaning, doing repairs, and getting back into life on the farm with the addition of the new family member. They soon replaced the bicycles they had given away and took a few rides together before winter arrived. The time they had spent in Israel had changed their lives forever. They were grateful for so many things, while missing so many others. They were glad to be back at their peaceful place in the country, but all looked forward to the next seventh year, 2015, when they planned to return home to the Promised Land.

Say unto them, Thus saith the Lord YHWH; Behold, I will take the stick of Joseph, which is in the hand of Ephraim, and the tribes of Israel his fellows, and will put them with him, even with the stick of Judah, and make them one stick, and they shall be one in mine hand.

Ezekiel 37:19

Afterword

Seven years later, the family remains on their Tennessee homestead working the construction business with the love of Abba, His land, and His people at the forefront of their lives. David continues to travel to Israel for the yearly pilgrimage feasts, taking at least one family member with him each time. Airline tickets are purchased and plans underway for the whole family's 2015 Sukkot pilgrimage.

The family has not grown in number, but the children are seven years older; even little Giliyah is big enough to carry her own pack. Armando, Briana, Victor and Isabel no longer look *up* into Mama's eyes; Rebeka, Moshe, and Natanyah are not far behind them.

The Varelas continue to see miracles in their lives regularly as Abba watches over them, orchestrating things for their growth and ultimate good. As time progresses, they watch the prophecies unfold more quickly and stronger, like birth pangs, as Ephraim and Judah move closer to unification in the hand of YHWH. They see more of their Christian brothers waking to the importance of a life of obedience, following the example of their Jewish Messiah and more of their Jewish brothers recognizing that Messiah ben Yoseph (the Suffering Servant) will return as Messiah ben David (the Conquering King). As the world becomes more wicked and violent, they pray for the day that all religion with its lies and divisions will vanish and peace will reign with the coming of Messiah.

Only a few of the miracles the Varelas saw prior to their 2008 adventure were written in Pedaling Home. The events that took place on the trip filled a book much larger than they ever intended to write. YHWH willing, a sequel will come from their 2015 journey, containing more amazing stories from the past as well as those they have lived since 2008.

From Mama Emily

When we began trip planning 2006 and David announced we should write a book about what happens, sharing what the Father has shown us, I thought it was a great idea. Throughout my life I had been encouraged to write, so I knew the time had come. However, I had no idea what I was getting into.

Soon after returning from Israel, I began writing for an hour per day in the very early morning, finishing Parts 1, 3, and 4. Part 2 required researching phone records, receipts, and bills in order to piece together the day by day events in their proper order. We were very concerned that the book be accurate. During lunch, I would read to the family so they could critique and correct any errors. This went on through three readings as I corrected, read aloud, and corrected again.

Not only was Part 2 difficult to write because of the logistics, it was emotionally taxing as we struggled with growth in the same areas in our daily lives that we had in Israel. Finally, writing came to a halt with our busy schedule of home school, business, and farm. And because all that was left of the writing was the difficult process of combining the daily lives of Part 2, the idea of starting back was overwhelming.

Finally, in 2012, breakthroughs occurred in our lives, healing of past hurts began, and David worked with me by providing suggestions on how and where I could continue writing. The difficult parts could not be done in a busy household full of responsibilities that constantly called me. In late 2013, I began what I thought were the final stages. After all, the book was basically finished. Since that time, I have gone on several writing retreats with one or two of the children. The book was in a constant stage of 'almost finished' for over a year as I honestly thought one more week would be enough. I will never *ever* pick up a book and look at it the same way again. I never imagined the time authors and publishers invest.

The book could not have been completed without the strong support and encouragement of David, whose vision it was, and the help and cooperation of Armando, Briana, Victor, Isabel, Rebeka, Moshe, Natanyah, and Giliyah, who took on my household and business responsibilities for months so I could focus on writing. I pray the book will be a blessing to them and their descendants, and that the time I have been away will produce more good fruit than what was sacrificed by being gone.

Glossary

Abba	Heb. - Father or Daddy; often used to refer YHWH.
Adonai	Heb. - Lord
Amein	Heb. - so be it; commonly anglicized as 'Amen.'
Arnav	Heb. - Rabbit
Bar mitzvah	Heb. - Son of the commandment; a rite of passage for young men, usually at 13 years of age.
Bat Tzion	Heb. – Daughter of Zion
Bedouin(s)	Arab(s) from clans primarily dwelling in the dessert, many still in tents.
Bevakasha	Heb. - You're welcome; please
Bishvil hayeladim	Heb. - For the children
Brit Chadashah	Heb. - Covenant New, as in the sense of renewed like the new moon is a renewed moon each month. The Hebrew word for 'month' or 'new moon' is '*chodesh*' and is directly related to the word '*chadashah*.' The *Brit Chadashah* is what Christianity refers to as the New Testament
Calendar	YHWH's calendar is described in the scriptures and is based on the movement of the heavenly bodies (Gen. 1:14), except for Shabbat which has occurred every seventh day since creation. Both the Gregorian (used worldwide) and the Jewish calendars are fixed and determined by calculation.
Cama ze oleh?	Heb. - How much does it cost?
Chag haMatzot	Heb. - Pilgrimage (or Feast) of Unleavened Bread.
Chag sameach!	Heb. - Joyful pilgrimage feast!; greeting during the festivals.
Chatul	Heb. - Cat
Circumcision	The act of circumcising; a first century group of Jewish followers of Y'shua.
Druz	An Arab people who are not Muslim, but whose religion broke from Islam in the eleventh century. Most are considered friendly by the nation of Israel and faithfully serve in the Israeli Defense Forces (IDF). They have the reputation of being a very friendly, hospital people.

Ephraim	Heb. – Double fruit; name of Joseph's younger son; tribe of Israel; alternate name of the House of Israel, as opposed to the House of Judah; scattered in 722 BC by the Assyrian Empire; prophesied to be reborn and joined to the House of Judah in the last days coinciding with the coming of Messiah; see Appendix B.

Ephraim   Heb. – Double fruit; name of Joseph's younger son; tribe of Israel; alternate name of the House of Israel, as opposed to the House of Judah; scattered in 722 BC by the Assyrian Empire; prophesied to be reborn and joined to the House of Judah in the last days coinciding with the coming of Messiah; see Appendix B.

E-sword   E-sword – free downloadable Bibles in numerous translations, as well as other study tools, maps, concordances, etc. from www.e-sword.net.

Halleluyah   Heb. - praise be to Yah (YHWH).

Hava Nagila   Heb. – Let us rejoice; a well-known song.

Hayeladim   Heb. – The children.

Israel   Heb. – He who overcomes with *El*; name given to Jacob, name of the descendants of Jacob; a land in the middle east; see Appendix B.

Judah   Heb. - Praise; name of Jacob's fourth son; tribe of Israel, one of the two Houses of Israel; taken into Babylonian captivity in the sixth century BC; prophesied to be joined to the House of Israel (Ephraim) in the last days coinciding with the coming of Messiah; part of the Promised Land; see Appendix B.

Karaite   From the Hebrew word Karaim; *B'nei Mikra* or followers of scripture; a sect of Judaism that follows only the TaNaK (as opposed to the oral torah).

Ken   Heb. – Yes.

Kibbutz, pl. *kibbutzim*   Heb. - Gathering or clustering; a collective community traditionally based on agriculture.

Kinneret   Sea of Galilee, from the Hebrew word *kinor* meaning 'violin,' because of the shape of the lake.

Kippah, pl. *kippot*   Heb. – dome; small disc-like head covering worn by many Jewish men.

Kol hakavod   Heb. – literally, 'all the respect,' modernly used as Great job!

Kotel   Western Wall or Wailing Wall, commonly believed to be a foundation wall, the only thing left of the temple which was destroyed in 70 AD.

Ma ze?   Heb. - What is it?

Menorah   Heb – Seven-branch candlestick; represents Messiah. A large one was used in the tabernacle and temple.

Misrad Hap'nim   Israeli Ministry of Interior; office which deals with birth certificates and immigration issues, among others.

Mitzvah, pl. *mitzvot*   Heb. - command, commonly referring to acts of kindness.

Mo'ed   Heb. - appointed time, the word used in scripture to describe certain meetings with YHWH that are days of worship.

MOMYS	Mothers of Many Young Siblings; an internet support group for Mothers who have had at least four children under the age of nine at any point in their lives.
New Testament	Writings of the Bible from the first century AD.
Old Testament	Writings in the Bible prior to the first century AD.
Oral *torah*	Body of regulations followed by Rabbinic Jews and included in the Talmud, a book containing writings from the third to sixth centuries A.D. It is said to have been passed down by Moshe (Moses), however, many of the rulings and traditions contained therein are opinions of rabbis from thousands of years later, some of which contradict the written scriptures.
Orthodox	Branch of rabbinic Judaism practicing strict religious observance.
PDA	Personal Digital Assistant; small hand-held device that functions much like a basic computer.
Pesach	Heb. – pass over; Passover, scriptural feast held on the 14th day of the first month.
Pimsleur	Audio language program found at www.pimsleur.com.
Rosh Chodesh	Heb. – Head of the month; new moon.
Rosh haShanah	Heb. - Head of the Year; Jewish celebration on the first day of the seventh month.
S'dot Yam	Heb. - Sea Fields; a Kibbutz south of Haifa on the Mediterranean Sea.
Shabbat	Seventh day of the week, Sabbath; from the Hebrew word 'to rest' or 'to cease'; occurs from sundown Friday to sundown Saturday.
Shalom	Heb. – peace, but with a fuller meaning; common salutation used for hello and good bye.
Shaul	Heb. – Asked of *El*; Hebrew name of the famous apostle Paul, author of 13 books of the New Testament.
Shavuot	Weeks; often referring to the scriptural Feast of Weeks (Greek *Pentecost*), held just over seven weeks after *Pesach* (Passover).
Sherut	Heb. – service; short for *monit sherut*, share taxi; usually minivans that can carry 12-15 passengers which run along bus routes, but not on bus schedules, and can somewhat customize the route for the passenger.
Shemini Atzeret	Heb. - Eighth Day of Assembly; a scriptural celebration held on the 22nd day of the seventh month.
Shofar, pl. *shofrot*	Heb. - horn of a ram or kudu, blown like a trumpet as a signal.
Shuk, pl. *shukim*	Heb. - open air market
Simchat Torah	Heb. - Rejoicing in *Torah*; a Jewish celebration

	coinciding with *Shemini Atzeret.*
Sub	Subcontractor; an independent worker who hires himself out to other individuals and contractors.
Sukkot	Heb. - Tabernacles, booths, or temporary dwellings; Feast of Tabernacles, held from the 15th to the 21st of the seventh month.
TaNaK	Acronym for *Torah* (instructions), *Nevi'im* (prophets), *Ketuvim* (writings); Hebrew Bible; Christianity's Old Testament.
Tefillin	*Tefillin* – a set of small boxes tied to the arm and head by many Jews during prayer, the rabbinic interpretation of Deut. 11:18 – Therefore shall ye lay up these my words in your heart and in your soul, and bind them for a sign upon your hand, that they may be as frontlets between your eyes.
Tichel	Yiddish for head scarf.
Todah	Heb. - thank you
Torah, pl. torot	Heb. – instruction; refers to the first five books of the Bible; often translated 'law.'
Tzitzit, pl. tzitziyot	Heb. - tassels or fringes worn on the four corners of the garment, as instructed in Numbers 15:38-40 and Deut. 22:12.
Via Dolorosa	Latin for Painful Way; referring to the route traditionally taught to be the path in which Y'shua carried the cross through Jerusalem before his crucifixion.
Yah	Abbreviated form of the name, Yehovah, Creator of the universe; appears at least 49 times in the Bible and is translated 'the LORD' in most English versions, except in Ps. 68:4, here it is rendered Jah.
Yah's Salvation	Meaning of the name *Y'shua.*
Yarmulke	Yiddish - a type of head covering worn by many Jewish men, resembling a brimless cap.
Yeladim	Heb. - Children
Yeshiva	Heb. - Religious school.
Yeshu	Hebrew acronym for *Yimah Schimo Wezikhro* (May his name and memory be stricken out); used to refer to Y'shua (YHWH is salvation) by those in the Jewish religious establishment who are opposed to the idea that Y'shua is the living son of Elohim and the Messiah.
Yom Chamishi	Heb. – Day Fifth; from sundown Wed. until sundown Thurs.
Yom haBikkurim	Heb. – Day of First fruits; wave sheaf offering of barley made on the first day of the week during the feast of *Chag haMatzot.*
Yom haKippurim, *Yom Kippur*	Heb. - Day of Atonement; scriptural feast held on the 10th day of the seventh month.

483

Yom haShemini	Heb. – The Eighth Day; scriptural feast held on the 22nd day of the seventh month.
Yom Revi'i	Heb. – Day Fourth; from sundown Tues. until sundown Wed.
Yom Rishon	Heb. – Day First; from sundown Sat. until sundown Sun.
Yom Sheni	Heb. – Day Second; from sundown Sun. until sundown Mon.
Yom Shishi	Heb. – Day Sixth; from sundown Thurs. until sundown Fri.
Yom Shlishi	Heb. – Day Third; from sundown Mon. until sundown Tues.
Yom Teruah	Heb. - Day of noise (or blasts); scriptural Feast of Trumpets, held on the first day of the seventh month.
Y'shua	Heb. - YHWH's salvation or salvation of YHWH; the original name of 'Jesus.' (In this book, to prevent pronunciation debates, we use the contracted form of the name.)

Appendix A

Special Hebrew Names and Titles

Elohim, Eloah, El

Elohim - Translated to English as 'God', 'god', 'gods;' can also be translated 'mighty ones;' plural form of the word '*eloah*' translated 'God' and 'god.' In scripture, the Creator often refers to Himself using this term.

Eloah – God, or god; singular form of *Elohim*.

El - God, abbreviated form of *Elohim*.

YHWH, YHVH, Yehovah, Yah

YHWH or *YHVH* – transliterated name the Creator most often uses for Himself in scripture, the Hebrew letters being '*yud*'-'*hey*'-'*vav*' (or '*waw*')-'*hey*,' and pronounced most often (as best understood by this author) as 'Yehovah.'

Yehovah – The pronunciation of the name of the Creator which this author typically uses in place of the English substitute, 'the LORD' or the Hebrew substitutes, '*Adonai*' (Lord), or *Hashem* (The name).

Yah – abbreviated form of the name, *YHWH*; appears at least 49 times in the Bible and is rendered 'the LORD' in most English versions, except in Ps. 68:4, where it is rendered, 'Jah.'

Y'shua, Yah's Salvation

Y'shua - Hebrew for '*YHWH*'s salvation' or 'salvation of YHWH;' the original name of 'Jesus.' (In this book, to prevent pronunciation debates, we use the contracted form of the name.)

Yah's Salvation – meaning of the Hebrew name, Y'shua.

Appendix B

Names of Israel

Israel
1-Father of the 12 tribes of Israel whose name was changed from Jacob;
2-Collective name of all of Israel's (Jacob's) descendants – whole House of Israel, headquartered in Jerusalem;
3-Collective name for the Northern Kingdom, the 10 tribes that split away from Judah after King Solomon's death – House of Israel, headquartered in Samaria;
4-the land promised by YHWH to the descendants of Abraham, Isaac, and Jacob (Israel);
5-a modern nation situated on part of the land given to Abraham, Isaac, and Jacob;
6-a modern land, boundaries having been established in the past century;
7-the people who are citizens of the current nation of Israel.

Judah
1-Fourth son of Jacob (Israel);
2-name of a tribe of Israel, descendants of Judah;
3-name of the Southern Kingdom, one of the two houses of Israel after the split, comprised primarily of the tribes of Judah, Benjamin, and Levi, headquartered in Jerusalem, never divorced by YHWH; referred to in scripture as 'Judah,' 'the house of Judah,' or 'the Jews.'
4-land belonging to the tribe of Judah.
5-land belonging to the house of Judah, which includes Benjamin's land.

Ephraim
1-Younger of the two sons of Joseph, blessed by Jacob (Israel) as his own, receiving first-born status;
2-name of a tribe of Israel, descendants of Ehpraim;
3-name of the Northern Kingdom, one of the two houses of Israel after the split, comprised of ten tribes (Ephraim, Menassah, Reuben, Simeon, Gad, Asher, Dan, Naphtali, Zebulun, and Issachar), headquartered in Samaria, divorced by YHWH (Jer. 3:8); referred to in Old Testament scripture as 'Ephraim,' the 'House of Ephraim,' or often as 'Israel' or 'the house of Israel,' and in the New Testaments as 'strangers,' 'Gentiles,' and 'nations' because they abandoned the covenant of YHWH.

486

Appendix C

Yearly Appointments of YHWH
Lev. 23 & Deut. 16

1st month

(Determined by the barley in the land being at the aviv (green ears) stage (about two weeks from ripe).

14th day	*Pesach*	Passover
15th - 21st	*Chag haMatzot*	*Pilgrimage of Unleavened Bread*
First day of the week during *Chag haMatzot*	*Yom haBikkurim*	Day of First Fruits

3rd month

49 days after Yom haBikkurim	*Shavuot*	Feast of Weeks (Gk. Pentecost)

7th month

1st	*Yom Teruah*	Day of Blasting (Feast of Trumpets)
10th	*Yom haKippurim*	Day of Atonements
15th – 21st	*Sukkot*	Tabernacles (Feast of Tabernacles)
22nd	*Yom haShemini*	The Eighth Day

Maps

Flight from Tennessee to Israel by way of Amsterdam

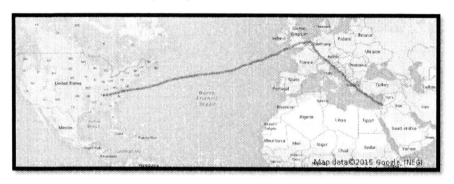

Varela family Bicycle Route

11-*Kiryat Yam*
10-*Kiryat Chaim*
9-*Haifa*
8-*Osifia (Isifia)*
7-*Daliat El Carmel*
6-*Elyakim*
5-*Bat Shlomo*
4-*Zichron Ya'achov*
3-*Benyamina*
2-*Or Akiva*
1-*Kibbutz S'dot Yam*

Kiryat Yam, Israel
(Areas *Gimel* and *Dalet*)

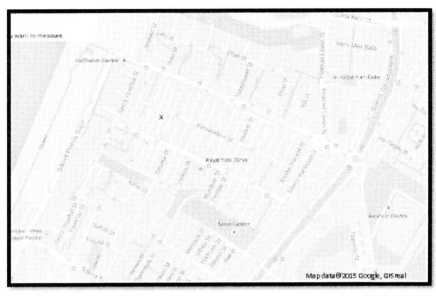

Varela home marked with 'X'

Jerusalem Old City
Varela tent at top of 'X'

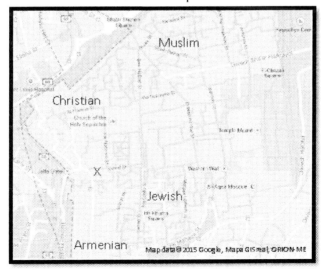

Size Comparison

Israel

Tennessee

Index

Afula	311-13, 423
Akko (Acre)	105, 118, 153-5, 158, 189, 278-84, 291, 345, 359, 444
Arad	369, 399-400, 407, 440, 454
Bat Shlomo	80, 82, 84-5, 488
Be'er Sheva	25, 324, 326, 453-4
Bedouin(s)	451, 453, 456, 480
Benyamina	46-8, 58, 74-6, 488
Brit Chadashah/ New Testament	41-2, 63, 111, 169, 220, 222-4, 248, 275, 317, 385, 387, 389, 391, 396-7, 453, 469, 480, 482, 486
Calendar	114, 117, 222-4, 252, 304, 316, 343, 346, 361, 367, 399, 423, 431, 441, 461, 480
Caesarea	46, 49-50, 58-60, 62, 68
Chabad	139-40, 143, 145, 154, 159, 447
Chag haMatzot (Unleavened Bread, Feast of)	223, 480, 487
Circumcision	
The act of	118-12, 114, 235-6, 238, 480
The group	112, 480
Daliat El Carmel	87, 91-2, 98, 488
Dead Sea	346, 451
Druz	87, 92-8, 100-102, 108, 114, 279, 469, 480
El/Elohim/God explained	386-88, 485
Elyakim	80-1, 488
Ephraim, house of	40, 133-4, 141, 162-4, 232, 306, 309, 313, 335, 358, 362, 373, 379, 390-1, 477-8, 481, 486
E-sword	31, 66, 307, 371, 442, 481
Feasts, Biblical	See *Pesach* (Passover), *Chag haMatzot* (Feast of Unleavened Bread), *Yom haBikkurim* (Day of First Fruits), *Shavuot* (Feast of Weeks, Pentecost), *Yom Kippur* (Feast of Trumpets), *Yom haKippurim/Yom Kippur* (Day of Atonement), *Sukkot* (Tabernacles/ Booths), *Yom haShemini* (The Eighth Day)

Feasts, Jewish	See *Pesach* (Passover), *Chag haMatzot* (Feast of Unleavened Bread), *Shavuot* (Feast of Weeks), *Yom haKippurim/Yom Kippur* (Day of Atonement), *Sukkot* (Feast of Tabernacles), *Shemini Atzeret, Simchat Torah, Rosh Hashanah*
God	See *Elohim*
Haifa	50, 58, 105, 117-8, 123-5, 127-8, 158, 167, 189, 232, 254-5, 282, 296, 311, 333-4, 337-8, 352, 354, 433, 450-1, 444-5, 458, 466, 472, 482, 488
Hava Nagila	93, 446, 481
Hebron	379, 453
IDF/Israeli Defense Force	128, 144, 207, 285, 312, 357, 480
Jehovah	See *Yah*
Jesus	41, 246-7, 273, 307, 385-8, 484-5
Judah	
The house	40, 75, 80-4, 141, 162-4, 232, 273, 275-7, 334-5, 390-1, 477-8, 481, 486
The land	392, 486
The tribe	40, 375, 379, 481, 486
Karaite	*57, 223, 304, 399-400, 402, 440, 4818, 225, 306, 401-2, 404, 441, 481*
Kibbutz Bet-El	456
Kibbutz S'dot Yam	See S'dot Yam
Kibbutz, plural *kibbutzim*	25, 42, 46-7, 49-51, 54-5, 59, 61-2, 65, 82, 456, 481-2, 487
Kinneret/Sea of Galilee	25, 312-4, 316-7, 451, 454, 481
Kippah, pl. *kippot*	66, 149, 373, 481
Kiryat Chaim	124, 138-45, 153-4, 158, 161, 196, 206, 318, 329, 487
Kiryat Motzkin	176, 183-4, 187, 194, 207-8, 225, 230-1, 241, 278, 283, 302
Kiryat Tivon	167
Kiryat Yam	154-5, 158, 191, 205, 208, 233, 255, 279-84, 325, 327-9, 336, 338, 346, 354, 362, 100, 433, 443-5, 447, 458, 467, 473, 488-9
Kotel/Western Wall/Wailing Wall	374, 406, 412-4, 481
LORD, the	See *Yah*
Misrad Hap'nim	214, 328, 333-4, 336, 338, 352, 450, 481
Mitzvah, pl. *mitzvot*	48, 84, 288, 310, 315, 323, 343-5, 358, 480-1
Mo'ed/Appointed Times	325, 481
MOMYS	4, 25, 31, 264, 482

Netanyah	47
New Moon	See *Rosh Chodesh*
New Testament	See *Brit Chadasha*
Old Testament	See *TaNaK*
Or Akiva	50, 58, 65-6, 72, 79, 88, 365, 487
Or HaCarmel	92-3, 95, 98, 104-6, 123, 350
Oral *torah*	57, 150-1, 213, 223-4, 481-2
Orthodox	67, 86, 122, 139, 146-7, 358, 360, 368, 406, 410, 482
Osifia (Isifia)	92, 97, 102, 104, 106, 108, 117, 279, 325, 327, 350, 464, 488
Passover	See *Pesach*
PDA	30-1, 66, 207, 220-1, 307, 335, 349, 371, 375, 379, 482
Pentecost	See *Shavuot*
Pesach/Passover	110, 223, 364, 482, 487
Petra Hostel	353, 361, 364, 366, 382, 384, 423, 451, 453
Pimsleur	4, 482
Rosh Chodesh/ New Moon	41, 217, 219, 220-9, 230-1, 234, 257, 280, 297, 308, 322-3, 355, 399, 401, 461, 480, 482
Rosh haShanah	223, 307-12, 315-7, 320-3, 326, 328, 334, 482, 382
S'dot Yam	25, 46, 49-50, 54, 58, 64, 68-9, 82, 99, 482, 489,1, 55, 59, 69-70, 83, 101, 482, 489
Shalom – defined	8, 482
Shaul/Paul	63-4, 109, 111-13, 169, 220, 222, 248, 391, 397-8, 404-5, 482
Shavuot/Weeks, Feast of Weeks/ Pentecost	223, 482, 487
Shemini Atzeret	223, 410-2, 441, 482, 487
Sherut	67, 184, 186, 283-4, 329, 445, 466-8, 471-2, 482
Shofar, pl. shofrot	219-22, 280, 408, 442, 433, 453, 482
Shuk	154-5, 233, 235, 305, 327, 346, 368, 452, 460, 482
Simchat Torah	411, 482
Sukkot	15, 17, 25, 42, 44, 86, 140, 154, 223, 257, 266, 310, 323, 326, 333, 346-7, 350-1, 353, 355, 359, 361, 364-7, 370-1, 376, 381, 397, 399, 406, 407-8, 411, 418, 431-2, 447, 457-8, 472, 478, 483, 487
TaNaK/Old Testament	23, 27, 41, 54, 63-4, 66, 90, 108, 217, 220, 247, 274, 343, 346, 358, 385-6, 397-8, 481-3, 486
Tefillin	146, 483
Tiberius	25, 304, 311-4, 320, 325-7, 332, 337, 450-1, 461

Tzitzit, pl. *tzitziyot*/tassels	39, 56-7, 67, 69-70, 88, 108, 140, 149, 162, 169, 213, 235, 341, 344, 362, 373, 377, 395, 403-4, 483
Unleavened Bread, Feast of	See *Chag haMatzot*
Wall, Wailing/ Western	See *Kotel*
Weeks, Feast of	See *Shavuot*
Via Dolorosa	410, 422-3, 483
Yah/YHWH/ Jehovah/the LORD - *explained*	386-88, 485
Yah's Salvation	41, 63, 112, 274-5, 347-8, 387, 398, 423, 483, 485
Yarmulke	194-6, 235, 278, 344, 362, 445, 483
Yeshiva	122-3, 309, 483
Yeshu	274, 330, 483
YHWH	See *Yah*
Y'shua- explained	386-88, 485
Yom haBikkurim/ Day of First Fruits	223, 483, 487
*Yom Kippur/Yom haKippurim/*Day of Atonement	223, 258, 321, 323, 334, 343-7, 483, 487
Yom Teruah/ Feast of Trumpets	56, 219, 222-3, 234, 280, 304, 307-8, 311-12, 321, 323, 325, 346, 450, 461, 484, 487
Zichron Ya'achov	72, 74, 76, 79-80, 97, 381, 433, 458, 488